The Routledge Handbook of Vegan Studies

This wide-ranging volume explores the tension between the dietary practice of veganism and the manifestation, construction, and representation of a vegan identity in today's society.

Emerging in the early 21st century, vegan studies is distinct from more familiar conceptions of "animal studies," an umbrella term for a three-pronged field that gained prominence in the late 1990s and early 2000s, consisting of critical animal studies, human–animal studies, and posthumanism. While veganism is a consideration of these modes of inquiry, it is a decidedly different entity, an ethical delineator that for many scholars marks a complicated boundary between theoretical pursuit and lived experience. *The Routledge Handbook of Vegan Studies* is the must-have reference for the important topics, problems, and key debates in the subject area and is the first of its kind. Comprising over 30 chapters by a team of international contributors, this handbook is divided into five parts:

- History of vegan studies
- Vegan studies in the disciplines
- Theoretical intersections
- Contemporary media entanglements
- Veganism around the world

These sections contextualize veganism beyond its status as a dietary choice, situating veganism within broader social, ethical, legal, theoretical, and artistic discourses. This book will be essential reading for students and researchers of vegan studies, animal studies, and environmental ethics.

Laura Wright is a professor in the Department of English at Western Carolina University, USA.

The Routledge Handbook of Vegan Studies

Edited By
Laura Wright

First published 2021
by Routledge
2 Park Square, Milton Park, Abingdon, Oxon OX14 4RN

and by Routledge
52 Vanderbilt Avenue, New York, NY 10017

Routledge is an imprint of the Taylor & Francis Group, an informa business

© 2021 selection and editorial matter, Laura Wright; individual chapters, the contributors

The right of Laura Wright to be identified as the author of the editorial material, and of the authors for their individual chapters, has been asserted in accordance with sections 77 and 78 of the Copyright, Designs and Patents Act 1988.

All rights reserved. No part of this book may be reprinted or reproduced or utilised in any form or by any electronic, mechanical, or other means, now known or hereafter invented, including photocopying and recording, or in any information storage or retrieval system, without permission in writing from the publishers.

Trademark notice: Product or corporate names may be trademarks or registered trademarks, and are used only for identification and explanation without intent to infringe.

British Library Cataloguing-in-Publication Data
A catalogue record for this book is available from the British Library

Library of Congress Cataloging-in-Publication Data
Names: Wright, Laura, 1970- editor.
Title: The Routledge handbook of vegan studies / edited by Laura Wright.
Description: Abingdon, Oxon ; New York, NY : Routledge, 2021. | Includes
bibliographical references and index
Identifiers: LCCN 2020044915 (print) | LCCN 2020044916 (ebook)
Subjects: LCSH: Veganism.
Classification: LCC TX392 .R75 2021 (print) | LCC TX392 (ebook) | DDC
613.2/622–dc23
LC record available at https://lccn.loc.gov/2020044915
LC ebook record available at https://lccn.loc.gov/2020044916

ISBN: 978-0-367-89746-8 (hbk)
ISBN: 978-0-367-74230-0 (pbk)
ISBN: 978-1-003-02087-5 (ebk)

Typeset in Bembo
by SPi Global, India

Printed in the United Kingdom
by Henry Ling Limited

Contents

List of illustrations ix
List of contributors xi

PART 1
History and foundational texts   1

1 Framing vegan studies: vegetarianism, veganism, animal studies, ecofeminism   3
 Laura Wright

2 Pythagoras, Plutarch, Porphyry, and the ancient defense of the vegetarian choice   15
 Joanna Komorowska

3 Vegetarian and vegan histories   27
 Tom Hertweck

4 The analytic philosophers: Peter Singer's *Animal Liberation* and Tom Regan's *The Case for Animal Rights*   39
 Josh Milburn

5 The "posthumanists": Cary Wolfe and Donna Haraway   50
 Eva Giraud

PART 2
Vegan studies in the disciplines: humanities   63

6 Vegan literature for children: epistemic resistance, agency, and the Anthropocene   65
 Marzena Kubisz

7 Veganism, ecoethics, and climate change in Margaret Atwood's "MaddAddam" trilogy   76
 Tatiana Prorokova-Konrad

Contents

8 Vegan Cervantes: meat consumption and social degradation in *Dialogue of the Dogs* 89
José Manuel Marrero Henríquez

9 A quiet riot: veganism as anti-capitalism and ecofeminist revolt in Han Kang's *The Vegetarian* 101
Liz Mayo

10 Causal impotence and veganism: recent developments and possible ways forward 111
David Killoren

11 By any means of persuasion necessary: the rhetoric of veganism 122
Christopher Garland

12 Veganism and the U.S. legal system 134
Tim Phillips

13 Vegan studies in sociology 150
Elizabeth Cherry

14 Psychology and vegan studies 161
Adam Feltz and Silke Feltz

15 Vegan studies and food studies 172
Jessica Holmes

PART 3
Vegan studies in the disciplines: religion 181

16 Veganism and Christianity 183
Allison Covey

17 Yes, but is it Kosher? Varying religio-cultural perspectives on Judaism and veganism 194
Barry L. Stiefel

18 Veganism, Hinduism, and Jainism in India: a geo-cultural inquiry 205
Saurav Kumar

19 The interface between "identity" and "aspiration": reading the Buddhist teachings through a vegan lens 215
Joyjit Ghosh and Krishanu Maiti

20 Veganism and Islam 226
Magfirah Dahlan

PART 4
Theoretical engagements — 235

21 A vegan ecofeminist queer ecological view of ecocriticism: a Costa Rican natureculture walk in literary/environmental studyland — 237
    Adriana Jiménez Rodríguez

22 Veganism in Critical Animal Studies: humanist and post-humanist perspectives — 250
    Jonathan Sparks-Franklin

23 Vegan studies and queer theory — 261
    Emelia Quinn

24 "You would betray your own mother for meat": a postcolonial vegan reading of Tsitsi Dangarembga's *Nervous Conditions* — 272
    Sarah Rhu and Laura Wright

25 Radical recipe: veganism as anti-racism — 282
    Marilisa C. Navarro

26 Vegan studies and gender studies — 295
    Alex Lockwood

PART 5
Veganism in the media — 307

27 Screening veganism: the production, rhetoric, and reception of vegan advocacy films — 309
    Alexa Weik von Mossner

28 (Mis)representing veganism in film and television — 319
    Matthew Cole and Kate Stewart

29 Merchandizing veganism — 333
    Simon C. Estok

30 "Friends don't let friends eat tofu": a rhetorical analysis of fast food corporation "anti-vegan-options," advertisements — 343
    Erin Trauth

31 The vegan myth: the rhetoric of online anti-veganism — 354
    Carmen Aguilera-Carnerero and Margarita Carretero-González

PART 6
Vegan geographies — 367

32 Vegan food tourism: experiences and implications — 369
    Francesc Fusté-Forné

Contents

33 Toward a new humanity: animal cruelty in China in light of COVID-19 381
    Ruth Y. Y. Hung

34 Vegan geographies in Ireland 394
    Corey Wrenn

    Index   407

Illustrations

Figures

14.1	Framework for skilled decision making	168
17.1	The Village Green	199
17.2	The Jewish scribe Shlomo Washadi and Abram Ajwar	200
29.1	Google trends Vegan	335
31.1	Caricature of Joseph Ritson by James Sayers (1803)	355

Tables

28.1	A typology of vegan representational theses and their antitheses	321
32.1	Profile of the participants	372

Contributors

Carmen Aguilera-Carnerero got her degree and PhD at the Department of English and German Philology at the University of Granada (Spain), where she currently teaches. She is also a Senior Research Fellow at the Centre for the Analysis of the Radical Right (CARR). Her post-doctoral research has focused on the study of extreme speech online, especially on CyberIslamophobia, the online discourse of the post-war ethnic conflict in Sri Lanka, the discourse of the far-right, the visual side of terrorism, and the expression of minorities through graffiti.

Margarita Carretero-González is a tenured senior lecturer in English Literature at the University of Granada (Spain) and a Fellow of the Oxford Centre for Animal Ethics (U.K.). Most of her research concerns the critical exploration of cultural representations of other-than-human nature, and she has published extensively on ecocriticism, ecofeminism, critical animal studies, and vegan studies. She is a consultant editor of the *Journal of Animal Ethics* and her most recent publication is the edition of *Spanish Thinking about Animals* (Michigan State University Press, 2020).

Elizabeth Cherry is an associate professor of sociology at Manhattanville College in Purchase, New York, where she teaches and researches on issues relating to animals, the environment, culture, and social movements. She is the author of *For the Birds: Protecting Wildlife through the Naturalist Gaze* (2019) and *Culture and Activism: Animal Rights in France and the United States* (2016).

Matthew Cole is lecturer in Criminology at The Open University in the U.K. His current interests focus on the sociology of veganism and anti-veganism and the expansion of a zemiological framework to include attention to social harms inflicted on nonhuman animals. His first book, *Our Children and Other Animals: The Cultural Construction of Human–Animal Relations in Childhood*, co-written with Kate Stewart, explores how children are socialized into accepting and reproducing human domination of other animals.

Allison Covey, PhD, is an assistant teaching professor in the Ethics Program at Villanova University. She teaches moral philosophy and Christian moral theology, specializing in animal and environmental ethics. Her current research places ethology, evolutionary biology, and paleoanthropology in conversation with Christian theology to explore the relationships between humans, other animals, and the environment. Covey's other research interests include the construction of religious identity, the religious/secular boundary, and religion and human rights law, particularly as it applies to veganism.

Magfirah Dahlan, PhD, is an instructor in philosophy, religion, and political science at Craven Community College. She has published works on religious ethics, animal ethics, Islamic food justice, identity politics, and multiculturalism. She is the author of *Sacred Rituals and Humane Death: Religion in the Ethics and Politics of Modern Meat* (2019).

Contributors

Simon C. Estok is a full professor and Senior Research Fellow at Sungkyunkwan University (South Korea's first and oldest university). He teaches literary theory, ecocriticism, and Shakespearean literature. His award-winning book *Ecocriticism and Shakespeare: Reading Ecophobia* appeared in 2011 (reprinted 2014), and he is co-editor of four books: *Anthropocene Ecologies of Food: Implications and Perspectives from the Global South* (Routledge, 2021), *Landscape, Seascape, and the Eco-Spatial Imagination* (Routledge, 2016), *International Perspectives in Feminist Ecocriticism* (Routledge, 2013), and *East Asian Ecocriticisms* (2013). His much anticipated *The Ecophobia Hypothesis* was published in 2018 by Routledge and reprinted (with errata) as a paperback in July 2020. Estok has published extensively on ecocriticism and Shakespeare in such journals as *PMLA*, *Mosaic*, *Configurations*, *English Studies in Canada*, and others.

Adam Feltz is an associate professor of psychology and member of the Center for Applied Social Research at the University of Oklahoma. He is an award-winning expert in decision making related to informed decisions, values, and knowledge. He has authored more than 50 peer-reviewed articles in psychology, philosophy, ethics, and cognitive science focused on diversity and informed decision making. He is on the Board of Directors for the Riskliteracy.org project.

Silke Feltz is an assistant teaching professor in the English Department at the University of Oklahoma. She is an expert in the rhetoric of veganism/vegetarianism and associated educational practices. She has published in leading interdisciplinary journals concerning human–animal interactions including *Food Ethics* and *Human–Animal Interaction Bulletin*. She is an award-winning teacher and is the founder and director of AnimalIQ.org.

Francesc Fusté-Forné is professor and researcher in the Department of Business, Faculty of Tourism, Universitat de Girona. He is also Instructor at the Universitat Oberta de Catalunya. His research is focused on food and gastronomy. Particularly, he has studied the food tourism phenomenon by bringing connections between authenticity, food heritages, landscapes and landscapers, regional development, rural activities, and tourist experiences.

Christopher Garland is an assistant professor in the Department of Writing and Linguistics at Georgia Southern University. He has also taught at the University of Southern Mississippi and the University of Florida. His writing has appeared in the *Journal of Social and Economic Studies*, *Contemporary French and Francophone Studies*, *Writing Visual Culture*, and *Mediascape*, as well as in the edited collections *Hollywood's Africa after 1994*, *Haiti and the Americas*, and *The Opioid Epidemic and U.S. Culture*.

Joyjit Ghosh is professor of English, Vidyasagar University, Midnapore, West Bengal, India. He did his M. Phil on the novels of D. H. Lawrence and his doctoral thesis was on Lawrence's letters. His works include a fair number of articles on D. H. Lawrence, Langston Hughes, Rabindranath Tagore, and other great minds, published in journals of national/international repute. His book *Imaging D. H. Lawrence: His Mind and Art in Letters* was published in 2012. Dr. Ghosh has his research interests also in Indian Writing in English, Diaspora Studies, Ecocriticism, and Translation Studies.

Eva Giraud is a senior lecturer in Media at Keele University, U.K. Her research explores frictions between activist practice, particular social and political values, and the media technologies activists use to communicate their aims: with a focus on environmental, anti-racist, and animal activism. She is also interested in tensions between "non-anthropocentric" theories and activist practice and has published on these themes in journals including *Theory, Culture & Society*, *Social Studies of Science*, and *New Media & Society*. Her monograph *What Comes After Entanglement? Activism, Anthropocentrism and an Ethics of Exclusion* was published in 2019.

José Manuel Marrero Henríquez is a key figure in Hispanic and European ecocriticism. Poet, writer, essayist, and tenured professor of Comparative Literature and Literary Theory at the Universidad de Las Palmas de Gran Canaria, Spain, he has published extensively on landscape and animal representation in literature and on a variety of topics and authors of the Spanish and Latin American literary traditions.

Tom Hertweck is a lecturer in the department of English and Communication at the University of Massachusetts Dartmouth. A teacher and scholar of 20th- and 21st-century American literature and culture, he is the editor of *Food on Film: Bringing Something New to the Table* (2014) and (with Iker Arranz) editor of the book series "Cultural Ecologies of Food" for the University of Nevada Press. He is currently working on a book about the development of food commodity paratext and the contemporary landscape of food consumption.

Jessica Holmes is a PhD candidate in English Language and Literature at the University of Washington in Seattle, where she teaches in the English department. Her research areas include environmental humanities, contemporary poetry, and animal studies. She was a 2019 Mellon Fellow for New Public Projects in the Humanities, served as the Assistant Director for the University of Washington in the High School program and co-founded the Teaching Workshop on Environment at the University of Washington. She holds a Master of Fine Arts in poetry from the University of Washington. In her spare time, she participates in environmental and animal rights activism.

Ruth Y.Y. Hung is Associate Professor of Comparative Literature at Hong Kong Baptist University and Advisory Editor of boundary 2: an international journal of literature and culture. Author of Hu Feng: A Marxist Intellectual in a Communist State, 1930-1955 (NY: SUNY, 2020), Hung has lectured and published widely on modern and contemporary literatures and cultures. Her latest essay, published in 2020 in boundary 2, is on the prize-winning novel Wolf Totem. It defends the wolves against the violence of allegoresis as a critical device within the totalization of non-teleological academic Marxism.

David Killoren is a Research Fellow in moral philosophy in the Dianoia Institute at Australian Catholic University in Melbourne, Australia. He has interests in metaethics, normative ethics, and animal ethics.

Joanna Komorowska is an author of numerous publications on ancient Greek astrology, imperial astrological literature, imperial philosophy, and Classical tragedy. She also translated (into Polish) several philosophical works, including Alexander of Aphrodisias *De fato* and *De anima*, Plutarch's exegetical works, and considerable fragments of Ps.Simplikios' commentary on Aristotle's *On the Soul*. In her spare time she teaches Greek and Latin literature at the Cardinal Stefan Wyszyński University in Warsaw.

Marzena Kubisz si an associate professor in the Institute of Literary Studies, University of Silesia, Poland. Her academic interests are in cultural theory, resistance studies, animal studies, and vegan studies. She has been researching everyday resistance in terms of its corporeal dimensions (*Strategies*

Contributors

of Resistance. Body, Identity and Representation in Western Culture, 2003) and of cultural acceleration (*Resistance in the Deceleration Lane. Velocentrism, Slow Culture and Everyday Practice*, 2014). She is an associate editor of the Polish academic journal *Er(r)go. Theory-Literature-Culture*. She is presently working on the monograph about continuity and change in vegan narratives for children.

Saurav Kumar is UGC Junior Research Fellow in the Department of English, Banaras Hindu University, Varanasi, India. He is working on his PhD dissertation titled "Fiction as Gerontological Resource: A Critical Study of Select Novels." His research areas are literary and cultural gerontology, post-structuralism, and vegan studies. He has contributed a chapter on envisioning literary gerontology in South Asia to the forthcoming *Routledge Handbook on Transcultural Humanities in South Asia* (eds. Anwar and Yousaf). Currently, he is working on a chapter outlining the representation of older women in Hindi short films for *The Springer International Handbook of Abuse, Disability and Welfare of Older Adults*.

Alex Lockwood, PhD, is a senior lecturer in Creative and Professional Writing at the University of Sunderland. His research explores vegan life practices in relation to cultural narrative, creativity, political theory, the climate and ecological emergencies, activism, and gender, especially the construction of masculinities. He is the author of *The Pig in Thin Air* and other titles.

Liz Mayo has published in a variety of genres including literary analysis of writer Carson McCullers, for which she won an award from the Carson McCullers Society, and in creative nonfiction published in *The Chronicle of Higher Education* and in *Inside Higher Ed*. She holds a PhD in English from the University of Memphis and is Professor of English at Jackson State Community College. She lives in rural Tennessee where she works to educate the community on veganism.

Krishanu Maiti teaches English at the Department of English, Panskura Banamali College, West Bengal, India. His doctoral thesis was on the representation of animals in the poems of D. H. Lawrence and Ted Hughes. His areas of interest include literary animal studies, posthumanism, and environmental humanities. His co-edited book, *Global Perspectives on Eco-Aesthetics and Eco-Ethics: A Green Critique* was published by Lexington Books, USA in 2020.

Josh Milburn is a moral and political philosopher who is presently a British Academy Postdoctoral Fellow in the Department of Politics and International Relations at the University of Sheffield. He has previously worked at the University of York (U.K.) and Queen's University (Canada). Much of his research concerns animal ethics and food ethics; it has been published in a variety of philosophy, politics, and animal studies journals. He is a section editor of the journal *Politics and Animals*, and presently working on books on the ethics of feeding animals and the politics of near-vegan food systems.

Marilisa C. Navarro, PhD, is an assistant professor of African American Studies at Thomas Jefferson University. She teaches African American Studies and American Studies. Her areas of research focus on critical race theory, cultural studies, food studies, and critical gender studies. She earned her PhD in Ethnic Studies from the University of California, San Diego.

Tim Phillips is an attorney practicing in the areas of civil rights litigation and criminal defense. He has been vegan since 2000 and has represented many vegans in lawsuits and criminal cases. He lives in Minneapolis and is licensed to practice law in both Minnesota and California.

Tatiana Prorokova-Konrad is a postdoctoral researcher at the Department of English and American Studies, University of Vienna, Austria. She holds a PhD in American Studies from the University of Marburg, Germany. She is the author of *Docu-Fictions of War: U.S. Interventionism in Film and Literature* (University of Nebraska Press) (2019), the editor of *Transportation and the Culture of Climate Change: Accelerating Ride to Global Crisis* (West Virginia University Press, 2020), *Cold War II: Hollywood's Renewed Obsession with Russia* (University Press of Mississippi, 2020), and a co-editor of *Cultures of War in Graphic Novels: Violence, Trauma, and Memory* (Rutgers University Press) (2018).

Emelia Quinn is a lecturer in English Literature at the University of Amsterdam. Prior to this post she completed her DPhil in English at the University of Oxford. Her work is situated at the intersections of vegan theory and queer theory and she is co-editor of *Thinking Veganism in Literature and Culture: Towards a Vegan Theory* (Palgrave Macmillan, 2018). Her most recent work on vegan aesthetics, "Notes on Vegan Camp," is published in *PMLA*.

Sarah Rhu is an English MA student with a concentration in Literature at Western Carolina University, where she teaches in the Writing, Rhetoric, and Critical Studies program. She earned her BA in Women's and Gender Studies from the University of South Carolina. Her research interests include vegan studies, animal studies, postcolonial literature, feminist theory, and queer theory.

Adriana Jiménez Rodríguez has been a professor of English Literature at the University of Costa Rica for over fifteen years. Her original field of expertise, feminism, has evolved through the years into what she now terms queer vegan ecofeminism. Her work includes articles that range from women's writing, madness, and sexuality to afrofuturism and veganism. She is deeply interested in queer ecofeminist research that highlights the multidimensional interconnections between all types of patriarchal oppressions. As a queer mother of two, she centers her work in making the invisible visible, in hopes that one day academia will become less asphyxiatingly masculinist. As such, her writing and teaching practices strive to create thinking exercises that erase the manmade division between the professional and the personal, between the cerebral and the physical, and between the human and the nonhuman.

Jonathan Sparks-Franklin is an Adjunct Professor of Theology at Xavier University. He has his PhD in Religious Studies from Indiana University where he focused on religion and animal studies. Working at the intersection of critical animal studies, post-humanist theory, and postmodern theology, his research works to theorize postmodern theology as animal and explore its constructive implications for animal ethics. His dissertation, "Rituals of Response: Religion, Critical Animal Studies, and Dispossessed Subjectivity," aims to further advance the concrete praxis of Jacques Derrida's approach to animal ethics by exploring the religious dimensions of it through a post-humanist engagement with recent developments in radical and death of god theologies.

Kate Stewart is Principal Lecturer in Sociology at Nottingham Trent University in the U.K. Her research focuses on how our uses of other animals are represented in mainstream and popular culture, and how these representations reinforce practices that perpetuate marginalization and harm. Her work explores how these representations also contribute to maintaining intersecting oppressions and stereotypes relating to gender, sexuality, ethnicity, and age.

Barry L. Stiefel, PhD, is an associate professor in the Historic Preservation and Community Planning program at the College of Charleston. He is interested in how local preservation

Contributors

efforts affect regional, national, and multi-national policies within the field of cultural resource management and natural heritage conservation. Dr. Stiefel has published numerous books and articles, including several on Jewish Studies and Sustainability Studies.

Erin Trauth is an assistant professor of English (professional and technical writing) at High Point University. She serves as an assistant editor for *Rhetoric of Health and Medicine*. Her work has appeared in *Community Literacy Journal*, the *American Medical Writer's Association Journal*, and the *International Journal of Sociotechnology and Knowledge Development*. Erin has work forthcoming on the rhetoric of vegan and vegetarianism in the *Rhetoric of Health and Medicine* and *The Rhetorical Construction of Veganism and Vegetarianism*.

Alexa Weik von Mossner is associate professor of American Studies at the University of Klagenfurt. Her research explores the intersections of cognitive narratology, ecocriticism, and empirical studies of environmental literature and film. She is the author of *Cosmopolitan Minds: Literature, Emotion, and the Transnational Imagination* (2014) and *Affective Ecologies: Empathy, Emotion, and Environmental Narrative* (2017).

Corey Wrenn is lecturer of sociology with the School of Social Policy, Sociology and Social Research (SSPSSR) and Co-Director of the Centre for the Study of Social and Political Movements at the University of Kent. She served as council member with the American Sociological Association's Animals and Society section (2013–2016), was elected Chair in 2018, and co-founded the International Association of Vegan Sociologists in 2020. She serves as Book Review Editor to *Society & Animals*, is a member of The Vegan Society's Research Advisory Committee, and hosts *Sociology & Animals Podcast*. In July 2013, she founded the Vegan Feminist Network, an academic-activist project engaging intersectional social justice praxis. She is the author of *A Rational Approach to Animal Rights: Extensions in Abolitionist Theory* (Palgrave MacMillan, 2016), *Piecemeal Protest: Animal Rights in the Age of Nonprofits* (University of Michigan Press, 2019), and *Animals in Irish Society* (SUNY Press, 2021).

Laura Wright is the founder of the field of vegan studies. She is professor of English at Western Carolina University, where she specializes in postcolonial literatures and theory, ecocriticism, and animal studies. Her monographs include *Writing Out of All the Camps: J. M. Coetzee's Narratives of Displacement* (Routledge, 2006 and 2009), *Wilderness into Civilized Shapes: Reading the Postcolonial Environment* (2010), and *The Vegan Studies Project: Food, Animals, and Gender in the Age of Terror* (2015). Her edited collection *Through a Vegan Studies Lens: Textual Ethics and Lived Activism* was published in 2019.

Part 1
History and foundational texts

1
Framing vegan studies
Vegetarianism, veganism, animal studies, ecofeminism

Laura Wright

(Excerpted from *The Vegan Studies Project: Food, Animals, and Gender in the Age of Terror*, 2015. Prior to the publication of *The Vegan Studies Project*, there was no cultural studies monograph that examined the social and cultural discourses that imagine the vegan body and vegan identity. This work is considered the foundational text in the field of Vegan Studies. Omitted material is indicated by "★★★".)

[…] To be vegan, according to a memorandum of association of the Vegan Society, is to ascribe to a

> philosophy and way of living which seeks to exclude—as far as is possible and practicable—all forms of exploitation of, and cruelty to, animals for food, clothing or any other purpose; and by extension, promotes the development and use of animal-free alternatives for the benefit of humans, animals and the environment. In dietary terms it denotes the practice of dispensing with all products derived wholly or partly from animals.

But this definition simplifies the concept of veganism in that it assumes that all vegans choose to be vegan for ethical reasons, which may be the case for the majority, but there are other reasons, including health and religious mandates, for why people choose to be vegan. Veganism exists as a dietary and lifestyle choice with regard to what one consumes, but making this choice also constitutes participation in the identity category of "vegan." The tension between the dietary practice of veganism and the manifestation, construction, and representation of vegan identity is of primary importance to this study, particularly as vegan identity is both created by vegans and interpreted and, therefore, reconstituted by and within contemporary (non-vegan) media. In order to better understand this tension, it is necessary to examine the history of veganism as both practice and identity and then to read beyond that history into a changed politics of vegan representation that is not reflected in that history.

The history of a paradox

Tristam Stuart's *The Bloodless Revolution* charts the history of vegetarianism in the West from 1600 to the present as an entity that was named in England in the 1840s and fully codified by the founding of the Vegetarian Society in 1847, the creation of which made "'vegetarianism' a fixed identity—indelibly associated with crankiness" (423), which, in turn, allowed for vegetarianism to be easily "pigeonholed and ignored" (xvii). This codification and naming classified "vegetarian" as a homogeneous entity emptied of intellectual nuance and, therefore, made vegetarianism both easily quantified and dismissed. Such authors as Stuart, Colin Spencer, and Karen and Michael Iacobbo have written various histories of vegetarianism as a dietary sociopolitical discourse with ancient origins, so I do not need to provide an extensive rehashing of those histories here. What I do wish to do, however, is look briefly at the ways these studies posit vegetarianism as a paradoxical ideology and the ways these studies treat veganism within the larger context of vegetarian history.

Stuart's study situates vegetarianism as a philosophy rooted in the ancient past, with the West's "'discovery' of Indian vegetarianism" in the seventeenth century having a basis well before Alexander the Great reached India in 327 BC (40); furthermore, he finds it an "extraordinary coincidence that roughly contemporaneous seminal and Greek philosophers, the Buddha and Pythagoras both taught … that it was wrong for people to eat animals" (41). In his exhaustive and meticulously researched work, however, while he utilizes the terms "vegan" and "veganism" throughout, Stuart never examines veganism as a separate identity that may be dependent on factors distinct from those that have influenced the cultural, religious, and social histories of vegetarianism.

What Stuart's work does do, however, is present ethical vegetarianism as a paradox, at once interested in the preservation of life, even as the vegetarian is implicated, like any other living creature, in the cycle of life and death. As a perfect example, he cites Henry Brougham's attack on Joseph Ritson's *An Essay on Abstinence from Animal Food, as a Moral Duty* (1802) as an indictment of Ritson and those who agreed with his philosophy that animals have a natural right to their existence (362). Brougham claims that Ritson, despite being vegetarian, was nonetheless guilty "of starving calves by drinking milk, aborting chickens by eating eggs, and murdering whole ecologies of microscopic organisms every time he washed his armpits. Even while Ritson was in the act of writing his vegetarian arguments, he was using a quill plucked from a goose, ink made from crushed insects all while lighting his desk with a 'whale-tallow candle'" (368). Brougham, like Darwin, makes explicit the ways that being caught up in the "great chain of life also meant submitting to the great chain of death" (368), noting that preventing killing was not only unnatural and antithetical to the very act of existence but also impossible. In *Vegetarianism: A History*, Colin Spencer likewise points to the tension inherent in the pursuit of a vegetarian ethic: "We do not adequately realize today how deep within our psyche is the reverence for the consumption of meat or how ancient in our history is the ideological abstention from the slaughter of animals for food" (331).

At its core, ethical vegetarianism does embody this paradox, the desire to preserve life even as one's very existence implicates one as caught in the inevitable cycle of life and death; essentially, one cannot live without causing death, and death is the inevitable outcome of being alive. Further, Stuart notes that "Western society has fostered a culture of caring for animals" even as "it has maintained humanity's right to kill and eat them" (xvii), based in large part on the biblical narrative of Genesis, in which God grants human beings "dominion" over the animals. In the service of this paradox, however, the Bible's various dictates have allowed omnivores and vegetarians alike to fashion it into a treatise in support of either tenet; in seventeenth-century England, for example, Thomas Tyron and Roger Crab were both able to twist "the Bible into a vegetarian manifesto" (61). Furthermore, in 1817 a group that called themselves the Bible Christian Church traveled from Britain to the New World to freely practice their faith, which they based on the Bible, "one bit especially: Genesis chapter one, verses 29—30, which commands that humans eat only herbs and vegetables—a wholly vegetarian diet. This, they maintained, was God's original will" (Linzey ix).

★★★

For Spencer, as for many vegans, veganism is an attempt—an "ideal"—to balance the needs of the body with the cultivation of the spirit, but in its pursuit of this ideal, veganism also embodies vegetarianism's paradox in even more profound ways, a truth exemplified in the fourth episode of the twelfth season of the animated sitcom *The Simpsons* called "Lisa the Vegetarian." The episode features eight-year-old Lisa Simpson, one of the first vegetarian characters to be featured regularly on prime-time television, as she attempts to save Springfield's oldest tree from being cut down.[1] She falls in love with an environmentalist named Jesse Grass and, in an attempt to impress him, tells him that she is vegetarian. Grass scoffs and responds that vegetarianism is a nice start: "I'm a level five vegan. I won't eat anything that casts a shadow." In what constitutes *The Simpsons*' typically astute ability to satirize the social zeitgeist, Grass's dismissal of Lisa's vegetarianism elevates his veganism as more pure and more aligned with an environmental ethic; in this light, veganism is an arrogant confrontation and a one-upping of a presumed less rigorous (and therefore less serious) vegetarian ideology. But Grass's assertion that he eats nothing that casts a shadow also reveals the infinite regression that characterizes the paradoxical nature of a vegan position as vegans seek to remove themselves from the machinations of social processes and dictates with which they disagree. How far should—and how far can—one go to avoid all supposedly unethical consumption? In order not to eat any- thing that casts a shadow, one would be unable to eat anything; one would die instead. To be such a vegan is to be disembodied, because if one *is* a body, there is no way to opt out of the cycle of life and death, however much one might try. And if there is no way to avoid implication in the cycle of life and death (which there is not), then vegans, in their quest for the ideal that veganism purports to offer, are perhaps the most paradoxical consumers of all.

Identity and practice

As I noted earlier, veganism constitutes both an identity category—like those that constitute race, sexual orientation, national origin, and religion, for example—and a practice dependent upon the eschewing of all animal products from numerous aspects of one's life. Given the nature of its paradoxical status and the fringe position that vegans occupy, what causes some people to become vegan? Consider that veganism has been around for thousands of years and present in vastly different cultures, but veganism has never been the dominant ethical and dietary position in any culture at any time. So what causes people, over vast amounts of time and in decidedly different cultures, to be vegan, particularly given the minority status that such an option has always mandated? Being vegan, no matter where and when, has always constituted a nonnormative position, one that has often inspired persecution. While there has been precious little research about what makes people decide to become vegan, there has been some research that considers that decision either as motivated by an animal-advocacy ethic that is *inherently* manifest in certain people or as a dietary preference influenced by external factors. Barbara McDonald's "'Once You Know Something, You Can't Not Know It': An Empirical Look at Becoming Vegan" examines the experiences of a group of "successful and committed vegans" (19) in order to ascertain why they became vegan. She notes that "becoming vegan represents a major lifestyle change, one that demands the rejection of the normative ideology of speciesism" (3). McDonald's study looks at ethical veganism based on an animal-rights position and identifies a process involving catalytic experiences—such as being exposed to images or literature about the suffering of animals—that lead individuals to seek education about the plight of animals, which then leads to the decision to become vegan. She situates veganism as an activist position in that vegans "reject institutional power by choosing cruelty-free products and by engaging in protests and other activism" (17). What makes McDonald's study provocative are two points that she raises: first, that "most of the participants claimed to have been 'animal people' *all their lives*" (6, my emphasis), and second, that for the participants in this study, the decision to become vegan felt "inevitable," "comfortable," and "final" (15).

In this sense, McDonald reads ethical veganism as a kind of *orientation*—a preexisting condition, if you will—one that is there prior to the potential vegan's ability to act on it through catalytic experiences, education, and information. It is, in this reading, innate. But we tend to consider veganism as a lifestyle *preference* based generally on deeply held beliefs that consuming animals and animal products is wrong. As a result of this belief, one *chooses* not to consume those things, opting instead for a diet and lifestyle that are devoid of such items. In this context, veganism is no more an "orientation" than is purchasing a Honda instead of a Toyota. Again, the terms are paradoxical, positing veganism as orientation even as veganism is a choice made for various reasons. But I want to trouble the notion of what constitutes an "orientation." The third definition of "orientation" that is found in the *Oxford English Dictionary* is the one that pertains to our thinking about sexual orientation (remember that we used to refer to sexual *orientation* as sexual *preference*): "a person's basic attitude, beliefs, or feelings; a person's emotional or intellectual position in respect of a particular topic, circumstance." And "basic" in this sense means "fundamental," or "essential." For one to be "oriented" toward something implies, at least in the case of sexual orientation, an *essential* or *fundamental* position; an orientation, therefore, is something much more deeply rooted than a mere preference. The idea that there is some essential quality in certain people that makes them vegan may seem hokey, and although we should be wary of essentialism, considering veganism as an orientation allows for an understanding of that minority position as a delicate mixture of something both primal and social, a category—like sexual orientation or left- or right-handedness—that constitutes for some people, just perhaps, something somewhat beyond one's choosing. Such a reading, however, is dependent upon a very selective group of people, all of whom became vegan because of their feelings about animals.

A. Breeze Harper, whose blog, *Sistah Vegan Project*, and whose book, *Sistah Vegan: Black Female Vegans Speak on Food, Identity, Health, and Society*, chronicle the experiences of black female vegans, troubles the notion of orientation by positing that "the culture of veganism is not a monolith and is composed of many different subcultures and philosophies throughout the world" ("Going Beyond" 158). Furthermore, she acknowledges that people become vegan for a variety of reasons other than some sort of orientation in that direction: the spectrum ranges from "punk strict vegans for animal rights, to people who are dietary vegans for personal health reasons, to people who practice veganism for religious and spiritual reasons" (158). Harper discusses the reasons that constitute differences in the ways that veganism is manifest within white and black communities, as well as the ways that race, class, and space are linked, noting that

> collectively low-income urban black Americans in the USA *know* that a holistic plant-based diet is most often nearly impossible to achieve; simultaneously, the collectivity of white middle-class urban people *know* that a holistic plant-based diet is generally easy to achieve. (155)

From her work on and with black female vegans, Harper asserts that black women are more likely to choose a plant-based diet in order to combat "racial health disparities" (157)—like diabetes and fibroids—and as a way of "decolonizing their bodies from the legacy of racialized colonialism" (157) than for reasons related to an animal activist position.

Harper's work undermines the notion that there is a singular reason for veganism and that there is a singular, representative vegan body, and she even wrests veganism away from its presumed necessary linkage to animal advocacy, noting that collectively black people are still dealing with "*human rights* to health and food security" ("Going Beyond" 163, my emphasis), a point that supports ecofeminism's view that "the many systems of oppression are mutually reinforcing" (Gaard, "Toward" 114), even as it turns the ecofeminist approach upside down, requiring that human rights must be acquired *before* one can consider the liberation of animals and of "nature" more broadly. Furthermore, Harper questions the omission from the mainstream vegan media of such foundational African American figures as social activist and raw foodist Dick Gregory and holistic healer Queen Afua, both of whom have been instrumental in promoting veganism within the African American community. If, as Andrew Linzey asserts in his foreword to Karen Iacobbo and Michael Iacobbo's *Vegetarian America: A History*, "the omnivores who have written history have largely written vegetarians out of it[; indeed,] the vegetarian voice is almost absent from all human studies" (x), then the vegan voice is more deeply in shadow, and the voices of nonwhite vegans, as Harper's work makes clear, are the most rigorously marginalized of all.

★★★

The three-pronged field of animal studies

If I am to posit a field of vegan studies, it is necessary for me to situate it as at once informed by and divergent from the field of animal studies, which is in itself multifaceted, consisting of critical animal studies, human–animal studies, and posthumanism. In her overview, *Critical Animal Studies: An Introduction*, Dawne McCance traces the origins of critical animal studies to the seventeenth century and the emergence of our modern conception of individualism as "a single, detached, and soon autonomous entity, itself divisible into lower and higher parts, animal body and animating mind" (1). Such a conception of the mind and body dualism contributed to our contemporary treatment of animals as "inert objects" (3) in the service of human intellectual advancement. She posits that "critical," in the case of critical animal studies, has three simultaneous and connected meanings. First, to be critical of something is to question it; second, if something is critical, it is grave—as, she argues, is the nature of our treatment of animals; third, the critical moment is the turning point, the opportunity for change to take place. As a field, critical animal studies became codified with and after the publication of Peter Singer's *Animal Liberation* in 1975 as a "specialization within analytic philosophy, one that sets out to expose, and to offer ethical responses to, today's unprecedented subjection and exploitation of animals" (4). As such, critical animal studies theorists grapple with issues of—and distinctions between—liberation, rights, and advocacy for animals. The utilitarianism that underscores Singer's argument, for example, is countered by Tom Regan in his 1983 "The Case for Animal Rights," in which Regan asserts that determining who or what is deserving of rights should not be dependent on the consequences—or utility—of a given action: "A good end does not justify an evil means. Any adequate moral theory will have to explain why this is so. Utilitarianism fails in this respect and so cannot be the theory we seek" (580). Yet both, as McCance notes, make their cases for the ethical treatment of animals based on how like human beings animals are.

Such a stance, even as such theorists as Singer and Regan are involved in a project of critique with regard to the Cartesian dualisms that perpetuate animal subjugation, continues to reinforce a duality in its insistence that "animals" and "humans" are of different orders and that the rights humans might grant to animals are dependent upon the ability of animals to demonstrate their likeness to us. In the service of this comparison, Singer initiates his argument against speciesism via an analogy to racism and sexism, noting that

> many philosophers and other writers have proposed the principle of equal consideration of interests, in some form or other, as a basic moral principle; but not many of them have recognized that this principle applies to members of other species. (6)

More recently, critical animal studies scholars have begun to challenge advocacy based on likeness and have worked to call into question the stability and constancy of the very categories of "human" and "animal." For example, Paola Cavalieri's 2001 *The Animal Question: Why Nonhuman Animals Deserve Human Rights* calls for an expanded theory of rights that would require all intentional beings be given moral status: "What does it mean to say of a being … that it has intrinsic value? Basically, it means to affirm that the value of a being is not bestowed from outside but is an integral part of the being itself" (36). In *The Animal That Therefore I Am (More to Follow)*, a series of lectures given in 1997 and published posthumously in 2008, Jacques Derrida critiques our very conception of rights as Cartesian in nature, and he notes that human arguments for animal rights actually enforce human conceptions of domination over animals (insofar as humans are capable of speaking for the needs of animals, in this case, the need for rights). According to Derrida in the first of the lectures that constitute *The Animal That There-fore I Am*, the very term "animal" constitutes the animal (an abstraction) as "other": "The animal, what a word! The animal is a word, it is an appellation that men have instituted, a name they have given themselves the right and the authority to give to another living creature" (392).

If critical animal studies is primarily interested in theorizing the nature of rights and arguing in terms of ethical responsibility with regard to the animal, even going so far as to challenge the category of animal as reinforcing Cartesian dualisms that will always privilege humanness over animalness, then human–animal studies constitutes an "interdisciplinary field that explores," according to Margo DeMello, "the spaces that animals occupy in human social and cultural worlds and the intersections humans have with them" (4).[2] In this sense, human–animal studies, which emerged as a field in the 1990s, is not invested in overtly challenging the human/animal binary but in examining how humans and animals negotiate relationships across the species boundary. Human animal studies scholars work in a diversity of fields in the social sciences, humanities, and natural sciences, and the field arose out of interest in animal imbrication in human society; therefore, even though human–animal studies may have real-world policy implications and, in fact, gave rise to the animal protection movement, it is not a means of advocating for animals (17). Human–animal studies recognizes that human existence is intimately connected to the lives of nonhuman animals and does work to "take seriously and place prominently the relationships between human and nonhuman animals, whether real or virtual" (7).

In *Animals and Society: An Introduction to Human–Animal Studies*, DeMello provides a list of definitions aimed at distinguishing between this field and others related to it. These include animal rights, "a as a social movement that advocates for providing nonhuman animals with moral status and, thereby, basic rights"; critical animal studies, "an academic field dedicated to the abolition of animal exploitation, oppression, and domination"; and human–animal studies, "the study of the interactions and relationships between human and nonhuman animals" (5). She notes that animal studies, a term generally used in the natural sciences "to refer to the scientific study of, or medical use of nonhuman animals," is, in the humanities, "the preferred term for what the social sciences call HAS [human–animal studies]" (5). In other words, not only are there theoretical and practical differences between the different branches of animal studies broadly defined, but the terminology for what constitutes a specific branch may differ depending on the scholarly field. As evidence of this complex diversity, the Animals and Society Institute, a nonprofit organization that promotes the study of human–animal relationships, has published a series with such titles as Nik Taylor's *Animals at Work*, Ryan Hediger's *Animals and War*, John Knight's *Herding Monkeys to Paradise: How Macaque Troops Are Managed for Tourism in Japan*, and Sandra Swart and Lance van Sittert's edited collection *Canis Africanis: A Dog History of South Africa*. Of critical importance to the work of human–animal studies is an examination of the constitution and construction of interspecies relationships, the reasons for those relationships and interactions, and the political and social implications of such relationships.

Cary Wolfe asserts that what began in the mid-1990s as "a smattering of work in various fields on human–animal relations and their representations in various endeavors—literary scientific—has … galvanized into a vibrant emergent field of interdisciplinary inquiry called animal studies or sometimes human–animal studies" (99), but he notes that both terms remain problematic. Posthumanism—a position that comes both before and after humanism, according to Wolfe (xv)—constitutes the most recent theoretical foray into the field of animal studies, and it takes into account both critical animal studies and human–animal studies in its impetus to situate our understanding of species in a space that challenges our conceptions of what it means to be human. In fact, the first section of Donna Haraway's *When Species Meet* is entitled "We Have Never Been Human." To support this assertion, Haraway notes that the human genome is found in only about 10 percent of all the cells that make up the human body:

> The other 90 percent are filled with genomes of bacteria, fungi, protists, and such, some of which play in a symphony necessary to my being alive at all, and some of which are hitching a ride and doing the rest of me, of us, no harm. … To be one is always to *become with* many. (3–4)

Haraway considers that species exist in a knot of interactions that coshape one another "in layers of reciprocating complexity all the way down. Response and respect are possible only in these knots, with animals and people looking back at each other, sticky with all their muddled histories" (42).

For Haraway and for other posthumanist theorists, species may be distinct from one another, but they are always enmeshed with one another as well from the level of their DNA to the level of the body. Such a notion compromises the concept of individualism on which much of critical animal studies has hung its hat. If Cartesian dualism is the framework that has allowed human mistreatment of animals, it is also, as I have noted above, the operating principle behind a rights-based position with regard to animals. Haraway offers a series of historical incidents, suggested by Freud, as "wounds to the primary narcissism of the self-centered human subject, who tries to hold panic at bay by the fantasy of human exceptionalism" (12). These incidents include Copernicus's realization that the earth is not the center of the universe, Darwin's theory of evolution (that animals are evolving in relation to one another, and "man" is not the culmination of evolution), and Freud's theory of the unconscious. Haraway adds the figure of the cyborg—an entity that "enfolds organic and technological flesh and so melds the Great Divide as well" (13) as a fourth "wound." For Cary Wolfe, posthumanism "names the embodiment and embeddedness of the human being in not just its biological but also its technological world, the coevolution of the human animal with the technicity of tools and external archival mechanisms (such as language and culture)" even as it also names a historical moment "in which the decentering of the human by its imbrication in technical, medical, informatics, and economic networks is increasingly impossible to ignore" (xv). The appeal of the posthumanist position is its situation as a counter to the humanism and anthropocentrism of critical animal studies and human–animal studies.

Feminism, ecofeminism, and vegan studies

While the project of vegan studies owes much to all of the animal studies approaches above, it is decidedly different in that it is focused on what it means to be vegan, a singular identity category that may or may not be linked to an ethical imperative with regard to one's feelings about and advocacy for animals. For Haraway, ethical veganism

> enacts a necessary truth, as well as bears witness to the extremity of the brutality in our 'normal' relations with other animals. However, I am also convinced that multispecies coflourishing requires simultaneous, contradictory truths if we take seriously *not* the command that grounds human exceptionalism, 'Thou shalt not kill,' but rather the command that makes us face nurturing and killing as an inescapable part of mortal companion species entanglements, namely, 'Thou shalt not make killable'. (105–6)

The fact that veganism remains such a fraught position within the realm of animal studies is telling if not particularly surprising. A special 2012 issue of the journal *Hypatia* titled "Animal Others," edited by Lori Gruen and Kari Weil, contains essays that engage with the intersections of race, class, gender, and species, and Gruen and Weil invited six feminist scholars to weigh in on how these intersections impact animal studies. One of those feminists, Traci Warkentin, notes in "Must Every Animal Studies Scholar Be Vegan?" that there has been an increasing tendency for animal studies conferences to be vegan affairs, but she feels unease with regard to that prospect, as participants often feel the need to declare whether or not they are vegan:

> I … want to be cautious … about the emergence of a reversed dualism— vegan versus carnivore—arising in animal studies that oversimplifies the choices people make as all-or-nothing, and may force us to have to proclaim allegiance to one side or the other, potentially generating a troubling mentality of you're either with us or against us. (501)

Warkentin also finds troubling a "problematically uncritical promotion of veganism and a seeming lack of presence of environmental/eco/feminist praxis in animal studies generally" (499) in proclamations from animal studies scholars that other such scholars have a moral imperative to become vegan.[3] She carefully unpacks a broader set of considerations with regard to the supposed morality of veganism, in particular the fact that in the United States, Monsanto monopolizes soybean production—and soy foods are marketed as an ethical alternative to meat, even as Monsanto's soybean seeds are genetically modified and are, therefore, potentially dangerous. According to Warkentin, they are "genetically modified organisms, designed to be grown according to unsustainable, monocrop practices, which are chemical- and fossil-fuel-energy-intensive and environmentally destructive" (502).

Warkentin asks that animal studies scholars look critically at veganism and that in weighing the ethics of veganism, one's perspective be influenced by ecofeminist theory in order to fully realize and recognize that oppressions are linked, intersectional, and codependently reinforcing. Similarly, philosopher Deane Curtin offers the concept of "contextual moral vegetarianism" (and veganism) to trouble an uncritical reading of universal veganism as an ethical imperative. He notes that he

> *can* ... imagine saying to a dominant white culture, which has perfected the global food market and excelled at industrial farming, that we have an obligation to be vegetarian. In fact, the vastness of food choices available to white people ... results in a particularly strong argument for the conclusion that the 'winners' in the colonial struggle for power are morally compelled to be vegetarian. (Environmental Ethics 143)

But even as he recognizes the reasons why members of such a society should be compelled to eschew eating animals, Curtin also recognizes that context is a significant factor in considering whether or not one should—or even *could*—be vegetarian. Curtin argues that even though he is a "committed moral vegetarian," he feels that there are circumstances that would compel him to eat meat: "Would I not kill an animal to provide food for my son if he were starving?" ("Toward an Ecological" 70). He offers further geographical and cultural considerations that make vegetarianism difficult, dangerous, and often impossible. He does note, however, the ecofeminist position that veganism constitutes an antipatriarchal form of activism in that, since "the consumption of eggs and milk have in common that they exploit the reproductive capacities of the female ... , to *choose one's diet* in a patriarchal culture ... marks a daily bodily commitment to resist ideological pressures" (71).

I want to take up Warkentin's charge and work to address the academic omission of the foundational tenets of ecofeminism—by such scholars as Carol J. Adams—as theoretical perspective and lived ethic in the field of animal studies, which perpetuates the myth that its history is male authored. As I have previously detailed, this history seemingly began with utilitarian philosopher Peter Singer, was bolstered by Tom Regan's argument for intrinsic value, and gained rarefied scholarly status when Jacques Derrida took on the question of the animal in the aforementioned *The Animal That Therefore I Am (More to Follow)*. Since Derrida, the works of other, predominantly male authors—like Cary Wolfe (author of *Animal Rites* in 2003), for example—have been credited with keeping the field vibrant. The absence of the ecofeminist perspective that has as long a history as animal studies indicates a troubling dismissal of such a position's tenets and that, in terms of Adams's absent referent, repackaging and renaming can constitute a dangerous erasure that removes from view that which is of primary importance: as Adams notes, "meat" renders "animals" absent. I would argue that "animal studies" does the same thing to "ecofeminism."

Warkentin claims that "ecofeminism ... has been operating 'under cover' with many aliases ... including ecological feminism, feminist environmentalism, environmental feminism, material feminism, gender and environment, and queer ecologies," and in considering what a "vegan studies" project might look like, I am not attempting again to reconstitute via a different name an already extant field of engagement, as I am incredibly aware of how such a move serves to erase the history of previous linked modes of scholarly inquiry. But I am convinced that, given the ways that veganism's rhetorical treatment both in the academy and in mainstream U.S. culture and the ways that veganism intersects as a social movement with race, gender, sexual orientation, and species-based struggles, it is worth pulling veganism as a supposedly ethical *action* out of its enmeshment with its *philosophical* linkages to animal studies and instead situating it as an activist, theoretical mode of scholarly and lived experience that, in the ways that it operates in scholarly discourse, owes much to ecofeminism.

... The primary tenet held by ecofeminists is that various forms of oppression are the result of a devaluing of those things that are designated inferior (and as feminine) in a binary construction of the world. In this conception, animals, women, and nature (as well as children and colonized "others") are placed on the same side of the binary divide as oppositional to humans, men, and culture. In "Living Interconnections with Animals and Nature," Greta Gaard defines ecofeminism as follows:

> Drawing on the insights of ecology, feminism, and socialism, ecofeminism's basic premise is that the ideology that authorizes oppressions such as those based on race, class, gender, sexuality, physical abilities, and species is the same ideology that sanctions the oppression of nature. Ecofeminism calls for an end of all oppressions, arguing that no attempt to liberate women (or any other oppressed group) without an equal attempt to liberate nature. (1)

The ecofeminist view holds oppressions as rhetorically linked, for example, by the treatment of women as "pieces of meat," or of colonized peoples as subhuman, as "brutes," and argues that such rhetorical linkages work to establish the psychological justification of actual—not rhetorical—oppressions.[4] Furthermore, the ecofeminist position offers that as all oppressions are linked and codependent, there can be no freedom from one form of oppression unless there is freedom from all of them.

What ecofeminism does *not* do is hold that these divisions are in any way essential or natural, despite many theorists' dismissal of ecofeminism based on such inaccurate readings.[5] Ecofeminists recognize the duality that privileges all things coded as male and rational and devalues all things coded as female and emotional as socially constructed, as ecofeminism is a form of material feminism, seeking to expose the cultural conditions that contribute to a devaluation of those categories relegated to the subordinate side of the binary. And in the realm of animal studies and ecocriticism, there has been some attempt to address the way that the recognized "legitimate" scholarly discourse has essentially written certain foundational female ecofeminist theoreticians right out of existence, as male scholars, one after another, appear to invent, as if for the first time, the field of animal studies.

For example, in the first edition of *Ecocriticism: The New Critical Idiom*, Greg Garrard failed to include Adams's concept of the absent referent in his chapter on animals—an error he corrected in the book's second edition in 2011, but only after he had been challenged for this oversight.[6] Adams herself discussed this with him via email in 2009.[7] Greta Gaard takes up the omission of female writers like Adams in a 2010 article in *ISLE* in which she advocates for a more feminist ecocriticism, one that addresses the ecocritical revisionism—by such writers as Garrard and Lawrence Buell—that has rendered a feminist perspective largely absent. She notes that omissions of foundational ecofeminist texts in

> ecocritical scholarship are not merely a bibliographic matter of failing to cite feminist scholarship, but signify a more profound conceptual failure to grapple with the issues being raised by that scholarship as feminist, a failure made more egregious when the same ideas are later celebrated when presented via nonfeminist sources. ("New Directions" 3)

And in a 2012 essay in *Critical Inquiry*, Susan Fraiman tracks gender in animal studies, noting that

> in 1975, Peter Singer galvanized the modern animal-rights movement with *Animal Liberation*, a work that would be heralded as one of its founding texts. That same year, *The Lesbian Reader* included an article by Carol Adams entitled 'The Sexual Politics of Meat,' inspiration for a book eventually published in 1990. Her scholarship contributed to a

growing body of ecofeminist work, emergent in the early 1980s, on women, animals, and the environment. (89)

Unlike Adams (and other ecofeminists as well), who has written consistently over a period of nearly five decades on the subject of animals, Derrida, on the other hand, produced only the aforementioned singular sustained commentary *The Animal That Therefore I Am (More to Follow)* (despite, I should add, having felt that he was moving in the direction of animal studies for much of his career).

Fraiman's work is concerned with the revisionist history that places Derrida at the fore as the father of *legitimate* animal studies and erases from that discourse the voices of pioneering women—like Adams, Lori Gruen, Marti Kheel, and Greta Gaard. What Derrida did was to remove the gendered component from the analysis, to take animal studies away from various lineages at the point at which it had maintained established linkages with *women's studies*. What I want to do is not necessarily argue that veganism and vegan studies be dependent upon ecofeminism per se, as the reasons for why people become vegan (and the discourse generated with regard to that decision) are complex. But I want to restore ecofeminism to the conversation and to put forth that an ecofeminist approach to veganism allows for what I feel is the most inclusive politics with regard to that position, and such theoretical grounding provides a scaffolding onto which I can build my concept of vegan studies. And finally, I want to posit that veganism, as a field of study and as lived practice, owes much to ecofeminism's argument in favor of it.

★★★

Notes

1 Lisa became vegetarian in 1995, during the show's seventh season.
2 McCance also includes in her introduction to critical animal studies a section on cultural studies, art, architecture, and literature in which she notes that such media constitute the opening of the field of critical animal studies to broader multidisciplinary analysis.
3 Warkentin is speaking specifically about Gary Steiner, who made this proclamation at the 2011 New York University Animal Studies Initiative.
4 Consider Joseph Conrad's Kurtz, who, after having succumbed to the "heart of darkness" in the Congo, writes that he wants to "exterminate all the brutes!"
5 For how this assertion has played out, see Carlassare; Gaard, "Ecofeminism Revisited."
6 See Estok 71 for a discussion of this omission.
7 Adams and I discussed this issue via email on May 18, 2013.

Works cited

Adams, Carol J. *The Sexual Politics of Meat: A Feminist-Vegetarian Critical Theory*. New York: Continuum, 1990.
Carlassare, Elizabeth. "Essentialism in Ecofeminist Discourse." *Ecology: Key Concepts in Critical Theory*, edited by Carolyn Merchant. Humanity Books, 1999, pp. 220–234.
Cavalieri, Paola. *The Animal Question: Why Nonhuman Animals Deserve Human Rights*. Oxford University Press, 2001.
Cherry, Elizabeth. "Veganism as a Cultural Movement: A Relational Approach." *Social Movement Studies*, vol. 5, no. 2, 2006, pp. 155–170.
Curtin, Deane. *Environmental Ethics for a Postcolonial World*. Rowman & Littlefield, 2005.
"Definition of Veganism." *The Vegan Society*, n.d. https://www.vegansociety.com/go-vegan/definition-veganism.
DeMello, Margo. *Animals and Society: An Introduction to Human–Animal Studies*. Columbia University Press, 2012.

Derrida, Jacques. "The Animal That I Am (More to Follow)." *Critical Inquiry*, vol. 28, no. 2, 2002, pp. 369–418.

Estok, Simon C. "From the Fringes: Animals, Ecocriticism, and Shakespeare." *Mosaic*, vol. 40, no. 1, 2007, pp. 61–78.

Fraiman, Susan. "Pussy Panic versus Liking Animals: Tracking Gender in Animal Studies." *Critical Inquiry*, vol. 39, no. 1, 2012, pp. 89–115.

Gaard, Greta. "Ecofeminism Revisited: Rejecting Essentialism and Replacing Species in a Material Feminist Environmentalism." *Feminist Formations*, vol. 23, no. 2, 2011, pp. 26–53.

———. "Living Interconnections with Animals and Nature." *Ecofeminism: Women, Animals, Nature*, edited by Greta Gaard, Temple University Press, 2010a, pp. 1–12.

———. "New Directions for Ecofeminism: Toward a More Feminist Ecocriticism." *ISLE* vol. 17, no. 4, 2010b, pp. 643–665.

Garrard, Greg. *Ecocriticism: The New Critical Idiom*. Routledge, 2004.

Haraway, Donna. *When Species Meet*. University of Minnesota Press, 2008.

Harper, A. Breeze. "Going Beyond the Normative White 'Post-racial' Vegan Epistemology." *Taking Food Public: Redefining Foodways in a Changing World*, edited by Psyche Williams Forson and Carole Counihan, Routledge, 2011, pp. 155–174.

———, editor. *Sistah Vegan: Black Female Vegans Speak on Food, Identity, Health, and Society*. Lantern, 2010.

Iacobbo, Karen, and Michael Iacobbo. *Vegetarian America: A History*. Praeger, 2004.

"Lisa the Vegetarian." *The Simpsons*, Season seven, episode five. Writ. David X. Cohen, 1995.

Linzey, Andrew. "Foreword: Veggie Pilgrim Fathers." *Vegetarian America: A History*, edited by Karen Iacobbo and Michael Iacobbo, Praeger, 2004, pp. ix–xi.

McCance, Dawne. *Critical Animal Studies: An Introduction*. Suny Press, 2013.

McDonald, Barbara. "'Once You Know Something, You Can't Not Know It': An Empirical Look at Becoming Vegan." *Society and Animals*, vol. 8, no. 1, 2000, pp. 1–23.

Regan, Tom. "The Case for Animal Rights." *Earthcare: An Anthology of Environmental Ethics*, edited by David Clowney and Patricia Mosto, Rowman & Littlefield, 2009, pp. 574–583.

Singer, Peter. *Animal Liberation*. Harper Collins, 1975.

Spencer, Colin. *Vegetarianism: A History*. Four Walls Eight Windows, 2000.

Stuart, Tristam. *The Bloodless Revolution: A Cultural History of Vegetarianism from 1600 to Modern Times*. Norton, 2006.

Warkentin, Traci. "Must Every Animal Studies Scholar Be Vegan?" *Hypatia* vol. 27 no. 3, 2012, pp. 499–504.

Wolfe, Cary. *What is Posthumanism?* University of Minnesota Press, 2010.

Wright, Laura. *The Vegan Studies Project: Food, Animals, and Gender in the Age of Terror*. University of Georgia Press, 2015.

2
Pythagoras, Plutarch, Porphyry, and the ancient defense of the vegetarian choice

Joanna Komorowska

To fish and beasts and winged birds allowed
Licence to eat each other, for no right
Exists among them; right he gave to men

(Hesiod, *Works and days*, v. 277–279)

Nothing that flies or swims or moves on land escapes your so-called civilized and hospitable tables

(Plutarch, *Gryllus* 991d)

Nature disavows our eating of flesh

(Plutarch, *On the eating of flesh* 995a)

There can be little doubt that of the three names mentioned in the title, that of Pythagoras is the most recognizable and, incidentally, most frequently mentioned in the context of history of vegetarianism and treatment of animals. The sage of Crotona is famous for his assertions concerning the practical dimensions of metempsychosis, transmigration of souls, known to pass from human to animal form and back. Even more importantly, he is also famous for formulating a number of dietary prohibitions, the most famous of which is most likely the strict (and largely incomprehensible) ban on consumption of broad beans. Yet he is hardly unique in his choice of diet: of those known to the readers, one may mention the Latin poet Ovid and the philosopher Seneca. Also Plato is known to have shown notable appreciation of plant-based diet throughout his dialogues,[1] similar preference being displayed in everyday life by the immediate successor of Aristotle, Theophrastus, and by the founder of Neoplatonist school, Plotinus.[2] In fact, the surviving testimonies paint a fascinating portrayal of ancient defense of vegetarian diet, a defense which in its various stages involved (and possibly challenged) the established notions of humankind, cult, and even civilization. Yet, one may ask, whence comes the need for defense? At this point it is important to remember that dietary preferences may, in some instances, translate into exclusion from basic communal activities. Among Greeks and Romans these activities included sacrifices; the accepted mode of these latter, in turn, relied on a ritual spilling of animal blood and on shared consumption of sacrificial meat.[3] Given this particular, vegetarians would be necessarily excluded from the rite seen as standing at the heart of communal experience. It is thus unsurprising that the most famous of ancient vegetarians are portrayed as unique, atypical figures, standing, in many ways, above societal limitations: the case of the Orphics or Pythagoras and his followers, who effectively formed a society on their own, remains illustrative of this tendency. This non-conformity of the vegetarian choice, its association with outstanding wisdom (and above average virtue) is confirmed and emphasized by all major studies on the subject.[4] Still one immediately notices that vegetarian attitude is nevertheless portrayed as a correlate rather than as a primary factor of this divergence from norm: a sage, a theurge, or even a loner may be a vegetarian, but vegetarianism is not in itself sufficient to qualify someone as an outstanding individual.

The sources

Despite Pythagoras's elevated standing as the animal-friendly sage, it is philosophers of the imperial era who remain our principal witnesses for the existence of what one may term "the vegetarian argument." The most exhaustive discussion of the vegetarian issue is Porphyry's *On Abstinence*, a four volume treatise addressed to a fellow student of Plotinian school (and a former, or "lapsed," vegetarian), Firmus Castricius. Written between AD 263 and 271,[5] the treatise comprises an overview of all possible reasons to turn or remain vegetarian.[6] In this, it constitutes a definite account of vegetarianism, from its philosophical relevance, through ritual challenges and issues related to the status of animals, to the discussion of various foreign dietary preferences. It is, one should remember, a response to various attacks on vegetarian choice: as a result, its comprehensiveness provides a valuable testimony to the existence of a wider debate: to put it simply, the issue may have been discussed more widely than one could infer from the principal sources.[7]

An earlier group of testimonies comes from the Middle-Platonist philosopher and biographer Plutarch of Cheronea (AD ca 50-ca 125). Of particular importance for the present discussion are his *On Animal Cleverness (De Sollertia Animalium)*, *Gryllus (Bruta Animalia Ratione Uti)*, and *On the Eating of Flesh (De Esu Cranium)*. It is important to note their differing styles: *De Sollertia* and *Gryllus* are both philosophizing dialogues (with *Gryllus* being considerably lighter in tone), while the *De Esu Cranium* is a highly rhetoricized polemical display piece.[8] Still, due to their focus on animal status, all the three are of paramount importance for the discussion of vegetarianism, the highly charged tone of *De Esu Carnium* attesting to the emotional investment of the author.

Scala Naturae

Problems involving animal sentiency and, more pertinently, rationality provide a good starting point for a discussion of the vegetarian argument. After all, one of the main premises of *sarkophagia* (consumption of meat) depends on the assumed superiority of humankind, i.e., on the assumption that human rationality results in human dominance over all the non-rational creatures in the world. Given this basic premise, any argument in favor of animal rationality can reflect on the diet-issue. Should we consider reason as something distinctively and exclusively human? If so, animals, like children, need to be seen as distinctly non-rational, enjoying no benefits of *to logikon* or *logike psyche*.[9] This traditional ex scala naturae argument can be encountered even today, particularly in certain anti-ecological discourses.[10] In its most basic form it claims that animals can be slaughtered for human use because of their non-rationality. This, one needs to remember, is quite different from stating that animals have no soul—indeed, animals are usually recognized as possessing the *pathetikon*, i.e., sensory ability. Strikingly, the strongest support for the argument was provided by Stoics, otherwise champions of human equality—according to their views humans are different from other living beings precisely because of their capacity for rational behavior.[11] In introducing this clear divide between human and animal nature and identifying the differentiating element as rationality, Chrysippus and his followers provided (unintentionally) support for the "supremacy" claim. Conversely, a defense of vegetarianism can gain support from collapsing the alleged divide. This collapse, in turn, is facilitated by observation and experience, our chief sources being Plutarch in his *On Animal Cleverness* and Porphyry in Book III of his *On Abstinence*.

Still, related to the sentiency argument is another, stemming from the doctrine of transmigration of souls (*metempsychosis*): in this case, however, the ban on meat consumption is linked to the assumption that a rational (i.e., human) soul can get embodied in an animal form. This belief reflects on the assumptions concerning the status of animals and may—as in the case of the famous anecdote on Pythagoras—translate itself into varied assumptions concerning animal sentiency. When Pythagoras is said to have recognized a deceased acquaintance in a mistreated donkey, the fact both underlines the Samian's uniqueness and, at the same time, reemphasizes the complexities of ensoulment. How can we know that an animal soul is non-sentient if it could have belonged—at some point of its existence—to a human? Still, in order to duly appreciate the nuances entailed in the debate on animal sentiency, it may be useful to look at some other issues beforehand.

Lost innocence

Among the grounds for rejecting consumption of flesh, the golden age or natural affinity argument emerges as the most lucid. The rationale emphasizes either the primary nature of vegetarian diet as one reflecting the choice of our ancestors, or the natural affinity of the plant-based diet with the human body. Its highly rhetorical echo can be found in the opening of Plutarch's *On the Eating of Flesh*[12]:

> For my part I rather wonder both by what accident and in what state of soul or mind the first man who did so, touched his mouth to gore and brought his lips to the flesh of a dead creature, he who set forth tables of dead, stale bodies and ventured to call food and nourishment the parts that had little before bellowed and cried, moved and lived. (993b)

Clearly, the decision to consume dead flesh lies with humans—or, at the very least, with a human. This decision is portrayed in particularly ominous way, as the Cheronean immediately moves his discussion onto a highly ethical ground, painting a horrifying image of beast-like feast of gore and cruelty, of consumption of cadavers. Further, his original meat-eater had desired to consume flesh of animals as they were still breathing, thus relegating living beings to the position of a "walking meal"[13]:

> that sort of dinner is really portentous—when *a man craves the meat that is still bellowing*, giving instructions which tell us on what animals we are to feed while they are still alive uttering their cries, and *organizing various methods of seasoning and roasting and serving*. (993c)

Two points are made here: first, consumption of meat translates into general disregard of animal life; next, it facilitates further spread of vice—it encourages men to indulge their tastes rather than satisfy hunger. Indeed, for some thinkers it was precisely the lack of "natural" nourishment that justified the original turn to consumption of flesh.[14] Further, the claim that men were driven to this dietary choice by hunger highlights the unnaturalness of *sarkophagia*. As emphasized in *On the Eating of Flesh*, our ancestors turned to animal slaughter only in the direst of times:

> What wonder, if, contrary to nature, we made use of the flesh of beasts when even mud was eaten and the bark of trees devoured, and to light on sprouting grass or the root of a rush was a piece of luck? (993e-f)

Further, the dearth of nourishment in the past era is put in contrast with the present abundance of "natural" food: hence, the "hunger" justification results self-defeating. Even worse, continued consumption of flesh can be seen as blasphemous when gods bless us with slaughter free nourishment. Clearly, once the threat of starvation is removed, it is at best imprudent, at worst impious to cling to the unnatural meat diet. In addition, such a diet carries yet another burden: while stressing the respective innocence of the primitive diet, ancient philosophers often emphasize the connection between consumption of meat and slaughter of humans. The link is highlighted by Porphyry when discussing the account of early human history provided by Dicaearchus[15]:

> That is what Dicaearchus says in his account of the ancient history of the Greeks and his exposition of the blessed life of the most ancient people; and abstinence from animate creatures was a major contribution to it. For that reason there was no war, because injustice had been expelled: *war and aggression toward each other, came in later, at the same time as injustice toward animals*. So I am astonished at those who say that abstinence from animals is a mother of injustice, when *research and experience tell us that luxury, war and injustice came in together with the slaughter of animals*. (*On Abstinence* 4. 2. p. 231, emphasis mine)

Consumption of meat is thus expressly associated with the emergence of war and privilege—hence, with injustice. The slaughter of animals anticipates the corresponding disregard for human life as disappearance of golden age abundance pushes humans to seek different ways to sustain their own lives. Meat, originally consumed as a "last resort" of hungry people, becomes a staple element of diet, while savagery takes the place of innocence. As scarcity of corn forces humans into animal-slaughter, they become inured to bloodshed, which results in internecine feuds. In slaying animals, humans train themselves for kin slaughter, the shift in diet being seen as corresponding to a shift in moral attitude: consumption of meat precedes a collapse of wider taboo on bloodshed.[16] This association in question is also recognized by Plutarch—in his *On Animal Cleverness* the Cheronean notes, "thus the brute and the natural lust to kill in a man were fortified and rendered inflexible to pity, while gentleness was, for the most part, deadened" (959e).

The association of animal and human killings has profound ethical connotations for defenders of plant-based diets who emerge as seekers of primeval innocence. In their rejection of slaughter, they seek to emulate their long gone, better ancestors, to return to a lost time of abundance and natural leisure. In Plutarch, this nostalgia motivates Pythagorean prohibitions on flesh consumption:

It was in this way, on the contrary, that Pythagoreans, *to inculcate humanity and compassion*, made a practice of kindness to animals; for habituation has a strange power to lead men onward by a gradual familiarization of the feelings. (On Animal Cleverness 959f, emphasis mine)

The quote manifests the problem at heart of flesh-based diet: the implicit dulling of compassion leads humankind away from the unisverse-oriented mindset and weakens moral sense, thus facilitating a vision of hunting as "fun" activity.[17] Indeed, as noted by Plutarch, the long tradition of sarcophagy had deadened humans' moral sense to the extent where their yearning for living food collapses the gap separating man from beast. In his *On the Eating of Flesh*, he compares human cruelty to the behavior of wild beasts: "their slaughter is for their living, yours is a mere appetizer" (994b). Clearly, the starvation motivated choice has led humans far from the innate innocence of their ancestors: unsatisfied by gifts of Demeter and Dionysus, we persist in killing animals not in order to find sustenance, but to amuse ourselves.

Reciprocal relationship

The moral degeneration of humankind reflected in the emergence of wars is not the only consequence of the fatal choice: there is an even more insidious result. Incidentally, this latter has to do with another type of pro-meat (or, at least originally, pro-hunt) argument, i.e., the notion that humans have to protect their life against the threats posed by animal life. Yet animals chosen for consumption present at best little threat to humans: in fact, many of them are renowned for their meekness and obedience to humans; in addition, some provide express benefits to humankind—for instance, wool and milk come from sheep, labor from bovines.[18] In slaughtering these animals humans prove themselves not only cruel, but also ungrateful.

Originating in the venerable concept of reciprocity, the idea that consumption of meat entails a denial of *kharis* appears particularly striking, for it makes sarcophagy contrary to justice (and hence, to ethical advancement). The issue figures prominently in the discussion of Plutarch, once he makes his argument in favor of animal sentiency and (at least partial) rationality. In answer to the objections raised by Soclarus (and derived from the writings of both Stoics and Peripatetics, as paraphrased in 963f–964c), Autoboulus asserts that human life remains livable even should one refrain from consumption of meat. His point is made succinctly in *On Animal Cleverness*:

> there is an alternative, an inoffensive formula which does not, on the one hand, deprive beasts of reason, yet does, on the other, preserve the justice of those who make fit use of them. When the wise men of old had introduced this, gluttony joined luxury to cancel and annul it; *Pythagoras however, reintroduced it, teaching us how to profit without injustice*. There is no injustice, surely, in punishing and slaying animals that are anti-social and injurious, while taming those that are gentle and friendly to man and making them our allies in the tasks for which they are severally fitted by nature. (964ef, emphasis mine)

The purpose of Pythagorean teaching on animals emerges here as reintroduction of the essential justice within man–animal interaction. The same idea underlies what Porphyry subsumes under "living well" in the already mentioned *On Abstinence* 3.18. 207: in using animals according to their natural predisposition, humans can avoid basic injustice of unnecessary and unlawful slaughter. Effectively, Plutarch portrays Pythagoras as a firm believer in animal rationality but also as a supporter of reciprocal relationship connecting humans with animals, maintaining that benefits derived from an animal should be repaid, not disregarded. What he envisions is two-sided relationship, with the animal viewed as an active contributor to human welfare.

There is more: driven by gluttony, humans disregard the balance of world arrangement, relegating animals to non-rational status and viewing them as food or work force. Thus, rationality (and sentiency) of animals becomes a casualty of meat consumption: by demoting animals to non-rational status, humans facilitate their objectification into fodder, while liberating themselves from any justice-based obligations. This false liberation is accompanied by the rise of luxury and further dulling of compassion and empathy, a tendency resulting in the emergence of culinary art (or, to be specific, *mageiria*) and gourmande tastes which, as illustrated by Seneca, tend to explicitly abuse the natural riches of the universe.[19] Significantly, a similar process is noted by Plutarch and Porphyry.[20]

In addition, several ancient sources emphasize the particularities of man's physical build—unlike the truly predatory species, humans are not physically suited for a carnivorous diet: indeed they need to process meat in order to consume it. In learning to process the originally inedible food or to regard act of the nourishment as something to be enjoyed, they further dull the their sense of right and wrong, distorting an originally simple act of nourishment: the consequences are once again highlighted by Plutarch: "driven on by luxurious desires and satiety with merely essential nourishment, he pursues illicit food, made unclean by the slaughter of beasts; and he does it in much more cruel way than the most savage beasts of prey" (*On the Eating of Flesh* 994cd). Clearly, humans are portrayed as striving for something contrary to their original nature and twisting the custom in order to accommodate their unnatural urges. The emergence of these latter, however, stems from the original contrariety between human nature and meat consumption. By nature, humans are not suited for meat consumption, as manifested even by their physical build with its absence of claws or modest dimension of incisors as compared to those of animal predators.[21]

Unhealthiness and unsuitability

Still more can be said on the general unsuitability of meat-based diet. Indeed, in his *On the Eating of flesh* Plutarch emphasizes its harmful effects by saying: "Note that the eating of flesh is not only physically against nature, but it also makes us spiritually coarse and gross by reason of satiety and surfeit" (995d-e), and later, as he emphasizes the dulling effect that consumption of meat has on the psychic functions (995f). This point is particularly important given that a properly human life relies primarily on the intellect: with such an approach certain restraint with regard to meat consumption appears only natural for any true human. The effectiveness of this argument can be improved through references to the soul being embodied as punishment for some transgression, the possibilities being murder, cannibalism, and consumption of flesh, which not only emphasizes the already highlighted connection between flesh consumption and acts of extreme violence, but also serves to denounce flesh consumption as a perpetuation of the original transgressive behavior. It is in this context that Plutarch invokes the Orphic myth of Dionysus being slaughtered and consumed by Titans (*On the eating of flesh* 996c), thus relating sarcophagy to the most important event of Orphic anthropogeny and the true cause of mankind's proclivity to evil. In consuming the flesh of a living being (or in slaughtering a living being for food) we recreate the original crime of the Titans, thus hindering the chances of our soul being purified and ultimately liberated from the body. This particular effect of sarcophagy is particularly manifest in the concluding part of Porphyry's *On Abstinence* One, as the Thyrian remarks on the importance of purity and purificatory rites, while stressing the opposition between these and flesh consumption (57).

Let us briefly consider the rationale given by Porphyry for this particular ban on meat consumption. A philosopher (i.e., a perfect human) refrains from flesh consumption because of meat's harmful effects on intellectual capacities. In fact, sarcophagy does not differ from overindulgence in bodily pleasures, a point elaborated throughout *On Abstinence* Book One[22]:

> That is why abstinence, both from meat and from contact with bodily pleasures and actions, is more appropriate for moral people, because when someone is in contact with bodily things, he must descend from appropriate behaviour to undertake the tutelage of the unreasoning in us. (On Abstinence 1.45.120)

As the principal aim of philosophy is "assimilation to god," which entasils the curtailing of bodily yearnings, the end of life is often understood in terms of soul's liberation from the limitations imposed by the body.[23] Clearly, in nutritional terms such distancing from the body manifests through abstinence from any "heavy" nourishment.[24] Understood as in terms of repression of bodily demands a rejection of *sarkophagia* becomes an emblem and a choice of a truly philosophical mind. It is because of this that abstention from meat may be seen as the philosophical choice in the sense of a choice advisable for a philosopher, a point emphasized in *On Abstinence* 2.3.133: "Abstinence from animate creatures … is not advised for everyone without exception, but for philosophers, and among philosophers chiefly for those who make their happiness depend on God and the imitation of God." Manifestly, as far as it concerns those who do not aim at intellectual excellence, consumption of flesh appears acceptable: after all, a professional athlete would consume an above-average amount of meat in order to maintain his strength and stamina.[25] In general terms an outright claim that meat as such exercises adverse influence on human health understood in medical terms could be at the very least disputed: thus, an argument for preferability of the vegetarian choice relies on prior (and major) premises stipulating that *cura animae* should remain the primary and the natural choice of the human being.

Animal sentiency, animal rationality

As noted above our sources repeatedly suggest that consumption of flesh, particularly that of domesticated animals, should be considered unjust. This injustice is linked to the perceived two-sidedness of the human–animal relationship: given the reciprocal benefits, slaughter of an animal can be viewed as violation of reciprocity principle. Yet there is a further dimension to the issue. The two-sidedness, as emphasized throughout Plutarch's *On Animal Cleverness* and *On the Eating of Flesh* and also in Book Three of Porphyry's *On Abstinence*, relies—to a considerable extent—on the acceptance of some form of animal rationality. Both the authors are firm in their assertions that animals are—to some extent at least—rational. To argue for this rationality, both Plutarch and Porphyry quote the opinion of the Peripatetic Strato (like the Stoics, Peripatetic philosophers were typically exponents of animal non-rationality, in accordance with the principles laid out by Aristotle himself in his *On the Soul* or *Eudemean Ethics*[26]): "there is, in fact, a work of Strato, the natural philosopher, which proves it is impossible to have sensation at all without some action of intelligence" (*On Animal Cleverness* 961a).[27] In being able to learn, to act on experience, to recognize danger, animals consistently prove themselves capable of some basic form of understanding—both Plutarch and Porphyry provide a number of examples of animal forethought, cleverness, and generally understood rationality.[28] Also animals' ability to recognize remembered and imminent threats appears similar to what is usually assumed about imperfect humans (as per Stoic teachings, most men, with the sole exclusion of sage, act—at least in some instances—on impulses stemming directly from perception). In emphasizing this point, both philosophers insist on blurring the allegedly clear-cut difference between humans and animals: in explicit contravention of their vaunted rationality, large number of humans can be shown to rely mostly on sensory cognition.[29]

In blurring the difference between humans and animals the philosophers appear to rely on the common experience which points to some kind of cleverness as being present in animals and, should one look for a more elevated rationale, look back to Pythagoras with his metempsychosis doctrine.[30] The result, however, is that both Plutarch and Porphyry further their own agenda of portraying animals as worthy of our respect and sympathy. In the words of the Thyrian (*On Abstinence* 3.19. 209): "It is in nature of animals to have perceptions, to feel distress, to be afraid, to be hurt, and therefore to be injured." In Stoic philosophy, those emotions are viewed as primary motivating forces of majority of human decisions—after all, only a select few reach the stage where their life is governed by intellect.[31] It is also widely recognized fact that animals love and protect their offspring, a point particularly important in debates against the followers of Chrysippus, otherwise firm believers in the theory of *oikeiosis*, which starts, after all, with a natural feeling of protectiveness toward offspring.[32] The alleged differences separating humans and animals are thus blurred, complicating the issue of flesh consumption. If this were not enough to argue for the basic injustice of flesh consumption as source of harm to other rational creatures, there is also the issue of the soul, a point for particular importance for Porphyry, who emphasizes the basic similarity of emotions that link humans to their animal kin (for kin indeed they are). In *On Abstinence* 3.25. 221:

> Thus also we posit that human beings are kin to one another, and moreover to all the animals, for the principles of their bodies are naturally the same. [...] *We posit this more strongly because the souls of animals are no different, I mean in appetite and anger, and also in reasoning and above all in perception.* (emphasis mine)

Clearly, the souls of animals are kin to those of humans: after all, humans grow into rationality, children being often regarded as *aloga* (having no *logos*). In addition, as attested by everyday experience, animals do communicate, even if humans remain mostly incapable of understanding animal communication (much in the manner of foreign language), which entails some form of rationality.[33] Further, a majority of humans remain non-rational throughout their life span, which brings into question the basic premises of *sarkophagia*, i.e., the alleged inferior status of animal life. Acceptance of soul kinship alone is enough to question the rationale motivating the consumption of flesh, but it is further strengthened by the argument aptly termed (by Dombrowski[34]) as "from marginal causes": the fact that some humans can be shown to base their actions solely in sensory experience is enough to collapse the divide between animal and human. And with the collapse of this divide one cannot insist either on inferiority of animal life or on permissibility of flesh consumption.

The sacrifice

Let us conclude with the communal aspect of the vegetarian controversy, i.e., the issue of sacrifice. As many rites (particularly those of public nature) involve bloody animal sacrifices culminating in sacrificial feast abstention from meat borders on withdrawal from public ceremonies and communal experience. In addition, it is rejected by supporters of tradition because of claim of divine approval upon customary forms of sacrifice (as sanctioned by historical custom). This complicates apologetic efforts: after all, reliance on recognized tradition and custom is paramount to ancient concept of the communal. Thus, Porphyry opts to portray feasts as tangential to actual sacrifice: the fact that an animal is sacrificed needs not lead to consumption of its flesh.[35] Also, both Plutarch and Porphyry appear to consider the entire custom of blood sacrifice to be essentially mistaken. For the Thyrian (as it was for Theophrastus) the animal sacrifice is recent development from much simpler and more natural form of sacrifice which involved burning of crops (as manifested by terms *thusia*, *aromata*, etc.).[36] Indeed, some testimonies of this original harmony survive into the imperial era, as the Altar of the Pious, a holy location on the island of Delos, where no bloody sacrifice was ever allowed.[37] The loss of innocence in the face of starvation caused humankind to forgo these natural rites in favor of either complete neglect of the divine (absence of sacrifice) or unlawful slaughter of living beings (originally humans). Animals, he argues, are offered in place of human sacrifice and the bloody rite is usually rooted in some misfortune: "The sacrifice of animals, then, is later than the other forms, indeed the most recent, and its cause is not a benefit, as for the sacrifice of crops, but a problem arising from famine or some other misfortune" (*On Abstinence* 2.9.139).[38] Thus, except for some cases of misconception, blood sacrifice appears as a late invention stemming from the original fall of humans:

> Originally, then, sacrifices to the gods were made with crops. In time we came to neglect holiness, and when crops were lacking and through the dearth of lawful food people took to eating each other's flesh, then, imploring the divine with many prayers, they first offered the gods sacrifice from among themselves, not only consecrating to the gods whatever was finest among them, but taking in addition others of the race who were not among the best [...] Thereafter they moved on to substitute the bodies of other animals for their own bodies in sacrifice. Conversely, it was through satiety of lawful food that they moved towards forgetfulness of piety, and as they reached insatiability they left nothing untasted or uneaten. (On Abstinence 2.27.156)

The sacrificial flesh consumption is thus regarded as resulting from (a) an act of desperation and hunger, (b) an effect of moral degeneration facilitated by excess of food. In both cases the consequences are harmful, which leads Porphyry to advocate abstention even in sacrificial context (cf. *On Abstinence* Book One). Accordingly, he portrays the Pythagoreans as reluctant to participate in the custom: the correct for of worship is described as being wholly removed from the sensory world (the divine is after all, devoid of senses, which should lead a true philosopher to contemplate its perfection in the way removed from the world of sense). The assumption that the divine rejoices in bloody sacrifice, for all its entrenchment in human culture, appears at best mistaken. In assuming that slaughter of helpful and meek beast satisfies some divine desire humans project onto the divine their own guilty beliefs, seeking excuse for their own greed and gluttony.

Conclusions

The above is hardly a comprehensive portrayal of the ancient defense of vegetarian choice. Still, even this necessarily brief outline provides us with some insight on the relevant discussion. Throughout our sources, the vegetarian choice emerges as a correlate of *cura animae*, a way to both reestablish the prior innocence and further one's own perfection as a human. Coextensively, the original choice to consume animal flesh is seen as an act of desperation, perpetuated through intellectual error, and reflected in grave misfortunes that befell human race: cruelty, war, and feud follow the decision due to the dulling of kinder sentiments necessary for slaughter of animals. Yet despite the frequent emphasis on diverse dangers stemming from flesh consumption the arguments also rely, quite heavily at that, on the interrelated notions of reciprocity and justice, on the recognition of animal sentiency, rationality and kinship with men. Even should we disregard the concept of metempsychosis, souls of human beings remain much similar to those of animals, principal emotions and principal urges being much similar across the officially recognized "discursive rationality" divide. In recognizing this basic soul kinship, Dombrowski rightly stresses, Porphyry, albeit starting from Platonic theory of ensoulment, comes close to anticipating number of modern notions concerning animal agency and animal rights.[39] The majestic figure of Pythagoras, the celebrated mathematician and forefather of philosophy as love of wisdom shines as an example not only of ultimate sagesse but also as kindness toward our animal kin, a true believer in the natural innocence of man, a harmony effectively lost with the first, unnatural, bite of flesh.

Notes

1 See Dombrowski (1984b).
2 For a list and relevant discussion, see Dombrowski (1984). One may also note that Theophrastus is also renowned for having written a comprehensive treatise in defense of vegetarianism—though the work is lost, it was used by Porphyry throughout the composition of his *On Abstinence* Book Two.
3 Ancient sacrificial rite was studied in number of important works (see, e.g., Burkert 1984, Détienne and Vernant 1998), the most recent contribution to the field being the collection edited by Ian Rutherford and Sarah Hitch (Rutherford and Hitch 2017).
4 See Bouffartige and Patillon (2003: lxi–lxviii), Dombrowski (1987, 1983); the groundwork for all later studies on ancient vegetarianism was provided in the exhaustive monograph of Haussleitner (1935).
5 For the dating see Bouffartige and Patillon (2003, XVIII–XIX).
6 As pointed out by Dombrowski (1987), the part of argument most relevant to the modern understanding of the vegetarianism comes in Book Three, which in a broad outline deals with animal sentiency and rationality.
7 On the nature of Porphyry's treatise and its lost adversary, see the comprehensive study of Ribero Martins (2018).
8 On the genre and form of Plutarch's *Moralia*, cf. Gallo (1996).
9 The notion emerges clearly in Aristotle's discussions of agency throughout the *Eudemean Ethics* Book Two and the *Nicomachean Ethics* Book Three. In addition, animal soul is considered lacking in rational part throughout the *On the soul* Book Two. For Aristotle's position on children, cf. most recently Monteils-Laeng (2017).
10 To provide an example: in contemporary Polish public debate, Catholic church hierarchs are renowned for invoking the celebrated passage of *Genesis* 1.28 when opposing what they perceive as an ecologist ideological offensive.
11 Stoics were famous for claiming that the majority of humankind went against their human nature by ignoring the call of reason, and thus reducing themselves to nonhuman status (cf., e.g., Graver 2007: 128–132, Brennan 2005: 95 sq).
12 All quotations from Plutarch follow the Loeb Classical Library translation (authored by William C. Helmbold) as published in Plutarch, *Moralia* vol. XII, Cambridge Ma. 1957.
13 The passage quoted contained a clear reference to the feast of Odysseus' hapless companions in *Odyssey* XII: the sailors sacrilegiously consumed the sacred cattle of the Sun-god Helios. And thus: *The hides crawled, the flesh, both roast and raw, bellowed upon the spits, and there was a lowing as of kine*; *Od.* XII 395–396, A.T. Murray).
14 For this, cf. Plutarch *On the eating of flesh* 993d-f.
15 For a discussion of Dicaearchus' anthropology, see Saunders (2001). All quotes from *De abstinentia* appear in Gillian Clark's translation as published in the *Ancient Commentators on Aristotle* series (*Porphyry: On Abstinence from Killing Animals*, London, 2000).
16 To that one may add the additional element of animal *logos*: in some accounts of golden age, humans and animals can communicate (capacity of speech, i.e., *logos*, being usually identified with rationality)— on the issue, see Gera (2003: 57–67).
17 Cf. Plutarch *On Animal Cleverness* 965b.
18 The argument figures, for example, in Plutarch *de esu carnium* 994b, while being frequently linked to the sentiency issue.
19 Condemnations of this particular art as a bastard *tekhne* have a long tradition in ancient literary sources, the cook being frequently portrayed as an immoral flatterer by comic drama (on the subject, see the comprehensive study of Wilkins 2000: 369–414).

For the critique of degenerate Roman gourmands, cf. Seneca *Quaestiones naturales* 3.17-18 (culminating in *oculis quoque gulosi sunt*; 3.18.7).
20 For Plutarch, see *On Animal Cleverness* 965a "living is not abolished nor life terminated when a man has no more platters of fish or pâté de foie gras or mincemeat of beef or kids' flesh for his banquets." Cf. Porphyry *On Abstinence* III 18. 207: "Abstinence for these has not disadvantaged us either for living or for living well."
21 See *On The Eating Of Flesh* 994f-995ab.
22 Cf. *On Abstinence* 1.51. 125: "Thus flesh-eating does not remove any trouble of our nature, or any want, which, if not satisfied, leads to pain. The gratification it provides is violent, and quickly mixed with its opposite. For it contributes not to the maintenance of life but to the variation of pleasures: it resembles sex or drinking imported wines, and our nature can survive without these."
23 Assimilation to god is often seen as the definiens of philosophy itself, cf., for example, Ammonius' commentary on Porphyry's *Isagoge (In Isag.)* 2.22-9.6 B.
24 The point is made, for example, in *On Abstinence* 1.38.114-115.
25 In his *On the eating of flesh* 995e Plutarch quotes the words of medical writer Androcydes: *For wine and indulgence in meat make the body strong and vigorous, but the soul weak.* Cf. the slightly more cautious attitude of Porphyry in *On Abstinence* 1. 51-52.125-126).
26 Still, it is worth remembering that as Clark rightly points out (2000: 162, n. 381), Aristotle did acknowledge that animals could be endowed with both *phronesis* and *pronoia*, thus allowing them practical sense and forethought (most prominently in *Metaph.* 980b19-28).
27 Mirrored by Pophyry in *On Abstinence* 3.21.213: *There is, indeed, an argument of the scientist Strato which demonstrates that perception itself cannot occur at all without thinking.*
28 Plutarch throughout the *On Animal Cleverness*, Porphyry chiefly in *On Abstinence* Book Three.
29 On this, one may compare *On Abstinence* 3.18. 209: "We see that many people live only by perception, having no intellect or logos, and that many surpass the most terrifying beasts in savagery and anger and aggression."
30 On Porphyry's complex attitude toward the transmigration doctrine, see Smith 1984.
31 On the rarity of Stoic sage, see Brouwer (2014: 97–112); cf. also Graver (2007: 109–132).
32 For a brief yet illuminating overview of *oikeiosis* (Lat. *conciliatio*) theory, see Pembroke (1971). For an extensive study of the concept, cf. the study of Engberg-Pedersen (1990).
33 See, for example, Plutarch *On the eating of flesh* 994e: *... we go on to assume that when they utter cries and squeaks their speech is inarticulate, that they do not, begging for mercy, entreating, seeking justice each one of them say* etc. See also Porphyry *On Abstinence* 3.5-7. 192–196, perhaps most clearly in 5. 192: *How then can it not be ignorant to call only human language logos, because we understand it and dismiss the language of other animals? It is as if ravens claimed that theirs was the only language, and we lack logos, because we say things which are not meaningful to them,* etc. The issue of animal rationality as linked to the communicative abilities and, hence, rationality, was studied in detail by Sorabji (1995).
34 Cf. Dombrowski 1984, see also *idem*, 1987: 774. It is to be remembered, however, that an interesting possibility that Porphyry's argument is a purely dialectical device developed in order to counter the Stoic assumption of animal non-rationality was raised by Edwards (2016). In this latter interpretation, the argument fails to reflect personal beliefs or philosophical position of Porphyry, instead constituting a proof of his mastery of philosophical discourse.
35 On this, see *On Abstinence* 2.2-4.86-89, where the Thyrian argues, for example, that some sacrificial animals are in fact considered inedible.
36 On this, cf. *On Abstinence* 2. 5sq.
37 On this, see *On Abstinence* 2.28.157-158.
38 One may also compare *On Abstinence* 2.12.142: *First, people sacrificed animals because of major necessity (...) had us in its grip: famine and war were to blame, and also imposed the necessity of eating animals.*
39 Cf. Dombrowski (1987) 774–777.

Works cited

Bouffartige, Jean. *Plutarque: Oeuvres morales, traité 63: L'Intelligence des animaux*, Paris: Les Belles Lettres, 2019.
———. *Porphyre: De l'Abstinence*, vols I–III, Paris: Les Belles Lettres, 2003.
Brouwer, René. *The Stoic Sage: The Early Stoics on Wisdom, Sagehood and Socrates*, Cambridge University Press, 2014.

Burkert, Waler. *Homo necans: Anthropology of Greek Sacrificial Ritual and Myth*, translated by Peter Bing, University of California Press, 1984.

Clark, Gillian. *Porphyry: On Abstinence from Killing Animals*, Geral Duckworth & Co., 2000.

Détienne, Marcel and Jean-Pierre Vernant. *The Cuisine of Sacrifice among the Greeks*, tr. by Paula Vissing, University of Chicago Press, 2nd ed., 1998.

Dombrowski, Daniel A. "Vegetarianism and the Argument from Marginal Cases in Porphyry." *Journal of History of Ideas*, vol. 45, 1984a, pp. 141–143.

Dombrowski, Daniel A. "Was Plato a Vegetarian?" *Apeiron*, vol. 18, 1984b, pp. 1–9.

Edwards, G. Fay. "The Purpose of Porphyry's Rational Animals: A Dialectical Attack on the Stoics in On Abstinence from Animal Food." *Aristotle Re-Interpreted: New Findings on Seven Hundred Years of the Ancient Commentators*, edited by Richard Sorabji, Bloomsbury, 2016, pp. 263–289.

Engberg-Pedersen, Troels. *The Stoic Theory of Oikeiosis: Moral Development and Social Interaction in Early Stoic Philosophy*, Studies in Hellenistic Civilization II, Aarhus University Press, 1990.

Gallo, Italo. "Strutture letterarie dei *Moralia* di Plutarco: aspetti e problemi." *Estudios sobre Plutarco; aspectos formales. Actas del IV simposio español sobre Plutarco, Salamanca 26-28 de Mayo de 1994*, edited by J.A. Fernández-Delgado, F. Pordomingo-Pardo, Salamanca, 1996, pp. 3–16.

Gera, Deborah Levine. *Ancient Greek Ideas on Speech, Language, and Civilization*, Oxford University Press, 2003.

Graver, Margaret. *Stoicism and Emotion*, University of Chicago Press, 2007.

Haussleitner, Johannes. *Der Vegetarismus in der Antike*, Religionsgeschichtliche Versuche und Vorarbeiten 24, Berlin: Töpelmann, 1935.

Komorowska, Joanna. "Quid est praecipuum: status and function of physics in the Naturales Quaestiones of Seneca the Younger." *Symbolae Philologorum Posnaniensium*, vol. 22, 2012, pp. 33–48.

Monteils-Laeng, Laetitia. "Le valeur d'infance chez Aristote." *Archives de philosophie*, vol. 80, 2017, 654–676.

Pembroke, Steven G. "Oikeiôsis." *Stoic Studies*, edited by A.A. Long, London, 1971, pp. 114–149.

Ribero Martins, Pedro. *Der Vegetarismus in der Antike im Streitgespräch: Porphyrios' Auseinandersetzung mit der Schrift 'Gegen der Vegetarier'*, Beiträge zur Altertumskunde Bd. 360, Walter de Gruyter, 2017.

Rutherford, Ian and Sarah Hitch, editors. *Animal Sacrifice in the Ancient Greek World*, Cambridge University Press, 2017.

Saunders, Trevor J. "Dicaearchus' historical anthropology." *Dicaearchus of Messina* (Rutgers University Studies in Classical Humanities, vol. X), edited by W. Fortenbaugh, E. Schütrumpf, 2001, pp. 237–254.

Smith, A. "Did Porphyry reject the transmigration of soul into animals?" *Rheinisches Museum*, vol. 127, 1984, pp. 277–284.

Sorabji, Richard. *Animal Minds and Human Morals*. Cornell University Press, 1995.

Striker, Gisela. "The role of *oikeiôsis* in Stoic ethics." *Oxford Studies in Ancient Philosophy*, vol. 1, 1983, pp. 145–167.

Vidal-Naquet, Pierre. "Plato's Myth of the *Statesman,* the Ambiguities of the Golden Age and of History." *Journal of Hellenic Studies*, vol. 98, 1978: pp. 132–141.

Wilkins, John. *The Boastful Chef: The Discourse of Food in Ancient Greek Comedy*. Oxford University Press, 2000.

Williams, G. "Interactions: physics, morality and narrative in Seneca's *Natural Questions* I." *Classical Philology*, vol. 100, 2005, pp. 142–165.

3
Vegetarian and vegan histories

Tom Hertweck

Any field of intellectual inquiry requires the production of a usable past in order to explain itself and do its work. No problem—from class-based struggle to self-determination in the face of gender-policing hegemony—has much of a chance without the richness of context that tells practitioners from whence they come and how these contexts continue to exert a force on the present. In the case of vegan studies as a new and still-developing field, two reasons to work historically present themselves. On the one hand, for the interested, the history of veganism is an essential point of scholarly reference: to think through a vegan studies lens requires understanding that the movement toward abolishing the use of animals in the name of human nutrition, so-called well-being, and vanity necessarily delves into the extant work of those who have puzzled the current arrangement out. For those seeking to begin their own critical trajectory, there are many matters to take seriously and which have already received attention. At the same time, on the other hand, while there are several comprehensive works available, an expansive and fully engaged vegan studies will also benefit from continued historiography. Many gaps in the record exist, and in the name of intellectual honesty as well as an invitation for others to join in on the work, there is an urgent need for a fully internationalized and inclusive depiction of vegan stories and practices. I therefore situate the ongoing development of the field by examining the major arguments in vegan studies in and among the established works of vegan (and vegetarian) history, and look to the future of vegan studies by signaling where important work might yet expand. By no means exhaustive, my hope is that the following will provide a more-than-representative wealth of resources about the discussions already underway. Because vegan studies commits itself to a project of social change, the primary focus is on cultural history—i.e., history inflected by social movements and the events that mark the ways groups have differentially imagined human–nonhuman animal relationships.

The trouble when talking about veganism and its fellow-traveler vegetarianism is that neither is merely an arbitrary restrictive dietary choice, but rather an ethical system, a religious imposition, a complex semiosis, a spiritual attachment, a mode of social reform, an agricultural imperative, a way of viewing social relations *among* humans and *between* humans and nonhuman animals, an ecological necessity, a material expression of value, a response to economic conditions, and more—and sometimes all at once. To speak of the historiography of veganism (what we might out of convenience call *veg-history*) is therefore to attempt to capture not the entirety of a movement or its motivations—a wholesale impossibility, though some have tried with more and

Tom Hertweck

less success—but instead to crystalize moments in the past to better understand our current challenges. Though some might wonder if as a result it is an imperial scholarly project meant to subsume other disciplines in its service, vegan studies as a field of academic inquiry nonetheless encompasses myriad disciplinary positions in its project of disrupting the representational apparatuses, power dynamics, and ideological constructs that support the consumption of animals in day-to-day life, both materially and metaphorically.

In that sense, vegan studies' use of veg-history emerges out of academe's connection of critical theory and popular movements, and is therefore precisely the sort of work that cultural historian Stuart Hall goes on to elucidate in his generative work "Notes on Deconstructing 'the Popular'" (1981). Here Hall defines popular culture not as the mere phenomena of the masses, but as a relational terrain of struggle:

> In our times, [struggle] goes on continuously, in the complex lines of resistance and acceptance, refusal and capitulation, which make the field of culture a sort of constant battlefield. A battlefield where no once-and-for-all victories are obtained but where there are always strategic positions to be won and lost. (235)

Just as classic works like Peter Singer's activist-philosophical treatise *Animal Liberation* (1975) opens by pointing out the historical absurdity of depriving women of fundamental human rights in the 18th and 19th centuries, Hall points to the way that all struggle is socially and historically situated, conditioned by the attitudes particular to that moment and out of which thoughtful intellectual and activist responses emerge. That in our time the consumption of animals is normalized to the point of invisibility may seem to be accepted as absolute or unchangeable—but is in fact neither. Veg-history is always a form of social protest, constellated among various efforts to unmoor hegemonic speciesism from its at-best-shaky foundations. It is, in other words, cultural studies in the best sense of the term, and one might persuasively argue the dominant mode of inquiry within vegan studies. Likewise, one might also provocatively mark this as an essential distinction between vegan studies and its near-relative animal studies. Whereas animal studies can be (but certainly is not always) undertaken as a wholly conceptual endeavor and without regard to anything resembling the advancement of nonhuman animal interests, vegan studies takes as a foundational premise the troubling ways in which human consumption of animals is to be undone through activism. To write veg-history is therefore to unsettle.

Locating the usable past

Properly vegan history is paradoxically very easy but also difficult to find. On the one hand, it is easy to find in the sense that personal veg-history, usually in the form of a kind of conversion narrative, pervades vegan cookbooks, such as Tanya Barnard and Sarah Kramer's *How It All Vegan!* (1999) and Isa Chandra Moskowitz's *Vegan with a Vengeance* (2005), as well as in vegan lifestyle books, such as Alicia Silverstone's *The Kind Diet* (2011). Usefully, in many cases, such personal histories include a gloss of veg-history so as to contextualize the recipes as both innovative—which would be necessary for a cookbook's entrance into the marketplace—as well as partaking in a much longer tradition of animal abstention. Among those that take this conception of history more seriously, Bryant Terry's exceptional *Vegan Soul Kitchen: Fresh, Healthy, and Creative African-American Cuisine* (2009) serves as an object lesson in the ways a cookbook can approach and undertake veg-history as a project of wholesale social chance. While Terry produces his own conversion narrative to explain why vegan food was part of a personal reorientation to improve his health and ethical relationships with the world, he acknowledges the ways in which health and well-being for all African Americans had been corrupted by 20th-century food practices, reminding the reader that "before the widespread industrialization of food in this country—African Americans living in the south included lots of fresh, nutrient-dense leafy greens, tubers, and fruits in their everyday diets" (xxi). In his vision, acts of eating are laden with political and social import just as much as they provide a way to keep the body well. While his is no treatise on vegan food history as such, the book nonetheless appends to the recipes an immense collection of non-food sources, from songs to documentaries and works of art, that contextualize the act of eating as (especially in the context of African American self-actualization) an act of personal development and social struggle. For example, a recipe for the beverage "Pure Strawberry Pop" suggests listening to Lead Belly's "Green Corn" and vegan Wu-Tang member GZA's "Labels" as well as watching the 2007 documentary *King Corn* as a way to think about corn syrup's replacing sugar as a sweetener in soda (31). As such, for many interested in veganism, a first encounter with veg-history—as a motor for enacting social justice for all beings—happens within the space of cookery, and an important part of that encounter is bringing the newly initiated into the mindset of personal and social change that dietary shifts can be a part of.

On the other hand, more formal, direct accounts of veganism's history are harder to come by. As the exception that proves the rule, perhaps the only focused discussion of any length, *A Vegan History: 1944–2010* (2011) by Vegan.com publisher Erik Marcus, provides a (very) brief yet useful overview of (mostly American) points of reference for veganism's emergence onto the world stage. Other semi-formal sources are reasonably disaggregated, as with the many blog entries on vegan and vegetarian history made available online by the International Vegetarian Union (Davis), Vegetarian Resource Group, and Vegan Society. In each, those interested in vegan studies can find an origin story. These usually begin with its discursive entrance into culture in 1944 by Donald Watson who, by eliminating all but the beginning and ending of the word *vegetarian*, coined the term *vegan* to signify abstention from animal products to an even greater degree and founded the Vegan Society in Leicester, United Kingdom—marking *veganism* as a term and set of legible cultural practices a distinctly Western phenomenon despite (as others mention in passing in their accounts) a nonetheless extant fellow-traveler where vegetarianism was practiced on the global stage. While living through the Blitz, Watson, a carpenter, teacher, and hiking guide, transformed his intuitive ethical vegetarian beliefs established as a teenager by rationally expanding his moral circle to include all the ways animals are implicated in human life. As veg-historian Colin Spencer explains, "To many then and now veganism seems the logical outcome of vegetarianism, for in refusing all animal products, including eggs and dairy products…they are making a stand against modern farming and all animal exploitation" (293). For these early vegans as with today's devotees, the recognition that the use of any animal product, including those consumed economically as well as bodily, aids and abets the systematic exploitation of nonhuman animals' lives, and so is worthy of avoidance. Spencer goes on to describe how the need for a separate vegan society came about because the well-established Vegetarian Society in Britain (founded in 1847) flatly refused to promote this version of vegetarianism because it viewed it as "anti-social," impractical, and simply too extreme, complaints that linger today in some sectors (293-94). Even so, Watson relished the ways that critics insisted one could not survive on an entirely non-animal diet, and died (60 years after he began adhering to the practice) at the age of 95 in 2005, having expanded the word of veganism globally, and making the Vegan Society a premier organizer of vegan ideas as well as the purveyor of a leading commodity certification program whose trademark appears on food and consumer goods the world over as a sign that a given product contains no animal ingredients and did not exploit animals in its production.

The 20th-century emergence of veganism goes some way toward explaining why little sustained work in singularly vegan history exists. At the same time, as suggested above, veganism did not emerge out of nothing, but rather from existing debates about animal abstention. In this way, the veg-historian is well served by looking into the several vegetarian histories available.[1] As with any historical endeavor, the extant histories of vegetarianism are as limited as their defined projects allow. Even so, scholars will benefit from looking at the two attempts at comprehensive histories of vegetarianism: Janet Barkas's *The Vegetable Passion* (1975) and Colin Spencer's *Vegetarianism: A History* (1993, originally published as *The Heretic's Feast*). Written for a popular audience, *The Vegetable Passion* is an enjoyably readable first crack at tracking vegetarianism, though it makes no pretense of being either rigid scholarship nor exhaustive in its scope. Rather, Barkas's approach is a combination of great moments in veg-history combined with character sketches of specific figures. Of the former, Barkas details, for example, the roots of religious vegetarianism in India, focusing on Jainism's and Hinduism's various approaches to non-violence toward other humans and species, a common theme that many rehearse. Of the latter, Barkas produces biographical details and lively anecdotes surrounding the lives of notable vegetarians in the modern era situated in national contexts, such as Upton Sinclair in the United States, George Bernard Shaw in the United Kingdom, and Leo Tolstoy in Russia. Notably, Barkas is one of the few veg-historians to have more than a paragraph or two in service to indigenous peoples, though her placing them into a chapter that puts them in the same conversation as precursors to *Homo sapiens* and nonhuman apes is unfortunate if reasonably forgivable. Taken as a whole, *The Vegetable Passion* is a worthy first contemporary effort to catalog such a wide-ranging topic and which is just as useful to future vegan studies for its sources as it is for its conclusions. Colin Spencer's more recent history produces more in the way of scholarly apparatus and detail than Barkas's, and usefully treads, much of the same ground but in a more systematic way. Ranging from plant-eating in species evolution through key moments in humanity's social development, *Vegetarianism* engages more with the intellectual histories of vegetarianism's various forms and its spread along ideological lines. (For a more recent, narrower book that focuses exclusively on the history and debates of only the ethical dimensions of vegetarian thought, one may consult Rod Preece's *Sins of the Flesh*.) Though some might quibble with a few of the things he elects to include given their relative unimportance to the center of the vegetarian narrative—the promulgation of Mortimer Wheeler's generally discredited "Aryan Invasion" theory as part of the spread of Indian vegetarianism, for example—it is nonetheless the case that the vegan studies scholar will be grateful for the level of detail he provides as a baseline for scholarly discussion as it is an essential reading.

Other veg-histories, then, are more limited in their intellectual topography, constraining their projects to national contexts or phenomena in a specific time period. Among the most important of these is Tristram Stuart's *The Bloodless Revolution: A Cultural History of Vegetarianism from 1600 to Modern Times*—though it is more clearly understood by its original U.K. subtitle, *Radical Vegetarians and the Discovery of India* (2006). An exhaustive account of vegetarianism's entrance into Western thought through the conduits of exploration and empire, Stuart looks at Western European, and especially British, vegetarians through the middle of the 19th century (with glances in an epilogue at moments beyond this). Key among the many debates about social organization and moral obligation that these radical vegetarians found themselves attempting to sort out is Stuart's focus in the end on Rousseauian sympathy for others pitted against Hobbesean self-interest. He paints a nuanced and thoroughgoing analysis of the various ways that vegetarianism was pulled into service on such problems as Malthusian population growth, ecological balance, moral righteousness, the golden age of early modern philosophy and science, and the era of violent revolutions his book covers. In each case, Indian-inflected vegetarianism serves as a more-than-coincident specter haunting Europe throughout the time period, given the ways that thinkers then found kinship in Indian thought for Christian and Jewish ideals of care and refracted those moral deliberations back onto the consumption of food. Within this more expansive vision of a moral world, Stuart argues, Indian vegetarianism took on a particularly Western character that we would do well to recover in the name of intellectual accuracy.

Much more attention has been given to the 19th century as an age of important and expansive vegetarian development in several contexts, owing in large part to the formalizing of social movements and the insertion of rationalism (no matter how faulty it has proven to be over time—see Haubrich) into dietary discourse. Generally speaking, attention to the century has focused on British and American contexts. On the British side, given that vegetarianism has existed in an orderly fashion since the middle of that century and there exists a strong emphasis in British academic circles on social movement history, much of the focus has been on the ways vegetarian groups effected social change. For example, 19th-century animal rights activist Charles Walter Forward's *Fifty Years of Food Reform* (1898) provides a robust account of vegetarianism's history in England from within the movement, while 20th-century scholars like Julia Twigg focus on the ideological aspects of vegetarianism in the public sphere and move from the 19th century into the contemporary moment it was completed in 1981; similarly, Ian Miller looks at the particular evangelical bent of the early vegetarian organizers. Across the pond, as both Margaret Puskar-Pasewicz and Adam Shprintzen persuasively argue, despite the engagement with philosophical rationality that pervaded a substantial portion of European thought before the early 1800s, America's vegetarian heritage is decidedly that of a moral reform movement founded in Christian belief, which emanated from the healthful body. From the Philadelphia Bible Christians (who had moved from Britain to expand their church) to the Seventh Day Adventists, from professionalized organizations like their counterparts in the United Kingdom to scientific dietary reformers, social reform began with bodily reform, and bodily reform began with abstention from meat. For these reformers, much more so than those in England, upright morals in diet were distinctly connected with the body politic, and so meshed neatly with major social issues in circulation in the United States at the time, such as the abolition of slavery. More than anything, however, the 19th century provided a moment of crucibilic change for vegetarian thought, where it transitioned from the outlier ideology Stuart writes about in the earlier era and becomes a viable way of life. As Shprintzen summarizes,

> The arc of the movement's history from the early 19th century through the early 20th century allowed vegetarianism to occupy a unique space in American food culture and reform—neither pure subculture nor mainstream ideology. And yet movement vegetarians…were able to question American dietary practices and the effects of these food choices.
>
> *(9)*

For a moral argument of this kind to take hold in either the United States or Britain, visibility and cultural legibility were essential. The histories of the 19th century detail this important work.

One particular point of reference from the close of the 19th century deserves special attention. British humanitarian Howard Williams's *The Ethics of Diet: A Catena of Authorities Deprecatory of the Practice of Flesh-Eating* (1883, rev. 1896) chronicles hundreds of figures and texts throughout human history to his own moment and presents them to the reader as a first attempt at a comprehensive account of the usable past for the late 19th century's interest in vegetarian diets. Tracking back as far as antiquity, Williams leverages the words of figures as various as Seneca, Thomas More, and Arthur Schopenhauer to provide a sustained, reasoned basis for vegetarianism as an antidote to a world that seemed to be decaying morally as well as materially before his eyes. In his hands, vegetarianism—what he refers to generally as "Dietary Reform"—becomes something close to a panacea for social ills, describing it as resting on:

> the teaching of (1) Comparative Anatomy and Physiology; (2) Humaneness, in the two-fold meaning of Refinement of Living, and of what is commonly called "Humanity;" (3) National Economy; (4) Social Reform; (5) Domestic and Individual Economy; [and] (6) Hygienic Philosophy, all of which are amply displayed in the following pages... The *accumulated* weight of all, for those who are able to form a calm and impartial judgment, cannot but cause the subject to appear one which demands and requires the most serious attention.
>
> *(xxvii, emphasis original)*

Williams's project is nothing short of the total reorganization of social life by the reevaluation of diet. Moreover, and in juxtaposition to many of his forebearers earlier in the century who focused solely or in large part on the spiritual aspects of flesh eating, the total response in *The Ethics of Diet* is one that begins and ends with a rational process of responding to the evidence of more than a millennium of human thought. His editor, acclaimed feminist veg-historian Carol J. Adams is right to point out that his is an immensely masculine work of a bygone era in its being blinkered to the contributions of women. At the same time, Adams's assessment of his position as an embodied thinker rather than someone who attempts to erase himself from the text so as to appear objective is an apt one: "He destabilizes the gender politics associated with the appearance of a class of [all-male] professional historians by assuming this authorial position: he refuses to be invisible and he refuses to be calm" (xix). While this in no way diminishes his focus on male thinkers, Williams nonetheless opens up a space in historiography that would not develop for decades, and which replicates the rhetorical and intellectual position of contemporary cookbook authors and activist veg-historians. As a result, and despite its blindspots, Williams remains an essential touchstone of veg-history in its own right for his animation and commitment as much as for the value of the sources he produces.

Williams's ways of thinking about vegetarianism in relation to the entire social body makes him more than a chronologically convenient figure with which to transition into the 20th century. Indeed, after the turn of the century, vegetarianism throughout the world became a way to change the body, spirit, and community, and brought the full force of rationality to bear on its claims. What had been for reformers like the Bible Christians or Sylvester Graham a dietary way to discipline an unruly and immoral body, vegetarianism benefited from an era of rational, scientific progress across all ways of thinking. With the rise of the capitalist practices entailed by widespread Taylorism and Fordism at this time, it also became possible to see vegetarianism as a kind of efficiency and sign of success, as Shprintzen discusses at the end of his history. At the same time, despite vegetarian lifestyles being practiced by many across the globe, it was during this time—and as a result of the United States's (and to a degree, Britain's) hyperrationalized and capitalist ways of life—that vegetarianism and especially veganism as a political movement became most deeply ingrained as a Western mode of social thought. As Stuart points out, despite drawing inspiration from India, "[t]he raw food diet and other innovations such as abstinence from milk, were clearly fads which had roots in the Western vegetarian tradition, and numerous observers at the time pointed to Gandhi's debt to the West," noting that Gandhi had met Williams and read his book while in England (427). India may have provided a blueprint for vegetarian lifestyles in a dietary sense, but its circulation into and transformation by the West through moral and rationalist arguments provided a political edge. And so, for Gandhi as with others, vegetarian (especially raw) diets were a tool toward greater liberation to the degree that they freed people from the drudgery of food preparation while also cleansing them of moral taint—an argument for modern efficiency as much as ethics, making the two strands of thought richly entwined. Vegetarianism and veganism had a radical effect on many social reformers during this time—with Gandhi being perhaps the most effective example—and such themes become only more common as the century progressed, being reproduced by movements as disparate as the Nation of Islam, to the American hippie counterculture, to punk and straight-edge as ways of embodying the change they wished to see.

In this context of bodily and political efficiency, veg-historians have cataloged the ways that the more recent developments in vegetarian history are themselves part of debates in what might be best understood as political economy, again largely in the United States and British contexts. Karen Iacobbo and Michael Iocobbo's *Vegetarian America* (2004) covers much of the same terrain as the earlier works. However, some of their best work is in their discussion of 20th-century policy debates, especially in the ways that public pronouncements about vegetarian and vegan healthfulness have been met less with the public ridicule (as outright absurdity) of earlier eras, but rather condemnation by capitalist special interest groups, as in their discussion of the meat and dairy industries' quashing revisions to the FDA's "food pyramid" that would have diminished their place in the diagram (209–16). Most compellingly, Corey Wrenn's account of "movement professionalization"—the process by which amateur adherents take public and make social causes visible—of the Vegan Society is essential reading for anyone interested in activism at an institutional level. In some ways, this is the predominant shift of more recent struggles within vegetarian and vegan ways of life: now that veganism and especially vegetarianism have reached mainstream legitimacy, the battles are less about being able to practice such a lifestyle, and more about the ways in which various political and economic forces seek to diminish their shares of the literal and ideological marketplaces. If anything, more recent veg-history narrativizes a story of success—i.e., the struggle to maintain a place at the table and to resist forces (like the dairy industry, whose sales have decreased dramatically each year for nearly a decade) that are plainly under duress and so have to resort to strong-arm tactics in the market and on the ballot rather than relying on vegetarianism's and veganism's curiosity as a diversionary tactic. As we move deeper into the 21st century, then—and without diminishing the fact that animals are *still* killed and otherwise exploited by the billions and billions in the name of human nutrition, vanity, convenience, and entertainment—vegetarian and vegan histories are well established and this is an excellent body of work that the veg-historian can stand firmly upon with an eye to what one hopes is a future of further success.

Veg-historical vistas: the future of vegetarianism and veganism's past

The above characterization of vegan and vegetarian history, while coming from a robust collection of documents and sources, is in no way a complete picture of vegan studies but, for those interested in extending our understanding of veg-history, is sufficient as a point of departure for further inquiry. Indeed, since Laura Wright's instantiation of a coherent field in 2015, scholars have responded to the call for a more coherent, organized approach to animal consumption in academic discourse. And yet, one suspects that the account of veg-history as it stands now also includes some glaring omissions, overlooked topics, and understudied aspects: missing voices, perspectives, and ways of thinking. Furthermore, if we're to return to the form of cultural studies I delineate for veg-history in the opening of this essay, then it seems urgent, in the hopes that better understanding leads to a more just treatment of animals and one another, that one propose a list of areas of investigation. Though these may be merely as idiosyncratic and particular as their author's field of vision, they should be expansive enough to allow the new vegan studies scholar to enter into the fray.

Recovery

Long a hallmark of traditional historical research, recovery of little-known sources will be essential for providing a more complete picture of veganism/vegetarianism on its own, for the disciplinary self-correction of errors in the extant histories, and in service to opening up any subsequent vegan studies. And while there remains no way to schematize such work—archival work being as much luck and dogged persistence as it is a systematic process—such a practice would include many trajectories: returning to well-known archives (like those of the Vegetarian Society or the British Archives, say) for new leads, following up on figures or texts mentioned in passing that have yet received no direct attention, and simply keeping a weather eye out for chance encounters with lost texts and new archives. Similarly, because some of the best of recovery work happens in the numerous academic disciplines vegan studies touches, one ought not limit their discoveries to historically oriented journals. Placing a hitherto unknown literary text from veg-history in *PMLA*'s recurring section "Little-Known Documents" will, for example, not only have the effect of establishing a new text but also expand the reach of vegan studies into the center of a discipline. For an exemplary way of handling recovery, readers should consult Carol J. Adam's article on Robert Morris's nearly lost treatise *A Reasonable Plea for the Animal Creation* from 1746, which until Adams's discovery had simply been unknown to scholars. For more traditionally historical work that antedates vegan studies' beginnings but might still be counted as veg-history, see Allen and Myers's work on the Harmonial Vegetarian Society in Arkansas.

Vegans and vegetarians of color

To even the most casual reader, the above picture of veg-history suffers from a radical absence of people of color as a part of the narrative. Even when vegans and vegetarians of color do intersect with the discussion in a central way—as with the case of Indian vegetarianism that appears at least as a footnote in most—it is often to instrumentalize the culture and history of others in service to the moral and dietetic development of Western, primarily white people. Unsurprisingly, this has resulted in a useful correction to the veg-historical record at the level of personal and community-driven testimony. As A. Breeze Harper (in her 2010 collection *Sistah Vegan: Black Female Vegans Speak on Food, Identity, Health, and Society*) and Julia Feliz Brueck (in her 2017 collection *Veganism in an Oppressive World: A Vegans of Color Community Project*) detail, even though vegans are united by dietary practices, the reasons for doing so and the expressions through which each adheres to them differ according to struggles based out of identity, as foodways are always conditioned by actually existing contexts. Likewise, as Harper rightly points out, mainstream veganism has a unity problem, such that "it has been the *tone and delivery* of the message—via the white, class-privileged perspective—that has been offensive to a majority of people of color and working-class people in America" (20, emphasis original). At this juncture, I would even go so far as to suggest that finding ways to include non-white voices is the single widest avenue for future scholarship in vegan studies in terms of its ability to scale-up and maximize its efficacy and reach. Given the lessons learned from both the civil rights and feminist movements, social change often happens at the expense of peoples already at the margins (women in the former case, women of color in the latter). To avoid the same pitfalls, vegan studies requires both welcoming scholars of color to the field as well as attending to and including the particular histories of struggle that all the world's peoples have faced *in the particular ways they have faced them* into honest accounts of veganism. Such an expansive vision is not merely more just but also quite insistent in the name of accuracy.

Internationalization and translation

As with the situation regarding people of color described above, veg-history is a relatively Western, but especially American and British, enterprise. While some of this owes to the organic ways that vegetarian and vegan diets became modes of social reform in these regions, a serious look at veg-history in the service of changing minds across the globe will require internationalized histories. Some recent examples seek to remedy this situation, such as Edgar Crook's *Abstainers! A Vegetarian and Vegan History of Australia* (2018), though even this follows much of the same plotline as those I described here given Australia's relationship to Britain. At the same time, the problem of internationalization necessarily begets the intimately related problem of translation. For example, Peter Brang's study *Ein Unbekanntes Russland* (2002) provides a thorough historical account of Russian vegetarian movements, focusing especially on the various organizations that attempted to unify traditional Russian food practices with the imperial, communist, and democratic movements that swept the nation. Available at this moment only in the original German and a Russian translation, Brang's would provide insight for those seeking to understand state–organization relations—if only one had the relevant language literacy. I acknowledge that a limitation of this essay is itself a function of my own blindness to languages that I simply cannot access using my own language skills (meager at best) and the scholarly tools at my disposal. To what degree are there authoritative histories, or responses to the many described above that by dearth of scholarly translation remain outside of the conversation? For example, Guillaume Rozenberg's essay on vegetarianism in Buddhist historical texts is cataloged in English databases under an English title, but not available at this moment in translation. What texts are not even indexed? To be sure, the problem of translation is one that afflicts every academic discipline. Even so, intellectual honesty demands we account for it ourselves as well. With that in mind, for the neophyte vegan studies scholar who may not yet feel as if they have an argument of their own to forward, the act of translation presents itself as a profoundly helpful place in which to do too-often-undervalued work.

Micro- and macro-scale cultural studies

The final direction I offer that vegan studies might take is to keep doing what it has been doing since Wright opened up the territory: historically and culturally contextualizing case studies of struggle such that a clearer sense of animal exploitation and its effects present themselves. As I began, this mode of cultural studies which takes seriously the everydayness of life and the normalcy of animal consumption within it makes *any* moment of analysis through a vegan studies lens a site of popular struggle. Anything, one might reasonably say, is fair game, so dig right in. To wit, the past few years have seen criticism attend to the vicissitudes of culture writ large, and that work places vegan studies in league with the other scholarly endeavors it intersects with—critical race theory, gender and sexuality, consumerism, class-based struggle, new media, and so on—that have an expansiveness of vision to see the entire world as complicit in its object of study. For example, our more recent moment in which celebrity has emerged as part of our cultural ecology allows another vantage from which to assess consumption in situ, as in Julie Doyle's analysis of the popping up of vegan celebrity lifestyling across traditional and emerging media. Harkening to a more historical angle, Michael Owen Jones's study of Percy Shelley as "the first vegan celebrity" trains our attention on a need for more critical vegetarian and vegan biographies. These would differ from biographies that happen to be about people who were incidentally vegetarian and vegan, and focus their attention on the subject's eating and living against animal exploitation in a central way. One close contender in this vein is Brian C. Wilson's biography of dietary reformer and cereal magnate John Harvey Kellogg (2014), though scholars should look beyond those immediately implicated in the movement as such. Where is, in other words and only half in jest, the scholarly, vegan-cognate version of *Profiles in Courage*? Joshua Specht's *Red Meat Republic* (2019), a commodity history of beef in the United States, also suggests a need to follow distinct commodities and strands of thought against which veganism stands in order to better comprehend the terrain upon which we fight. Finally, the wide range of disciplines that Josh Berson's impressive *The Meat Question: Animals, Humans, and the Deep History of Food* (2019) entangles itself suggests the myriad ways in which rich interdisciplinarity can be marshaled into service for vegan studies: here Berson merges evolutionary science, archaeology, ecology, economic history, nutrition science, the legacies of racism, infrastructuralism, and more into an evidence-based narrative that unmoors meat consumption from its seemingly naturalized foundations.

Vegan studies engages in veg-histories as struggle precisely because it is geared to the abolition of animal exploitation as a part of human life—to say nothing of the equally important possibilities for human liberation that divesting ourselves of animal exploitation will also entail. In short, we as vegan studies scholars have as much to learn from each other as from our pasts because, at whatever scale, the lived experiences of each vegetarian and vegan's past informs the story of how we might widen our circle of concern to those who—as it stands now—have no say in their own futures. The task of the vegan studies scholar is to collect these, honor their contribution, and stand witness to their truth for those that follow.

Note

1 Here one laments the vegetarian histories that might have been, such as Bible Christian minister and president of the Vegetarian Society of America Henry S. Clubb's attempt that he began when he was 80 years old, which Shprintzen describes as "so detailed and ambitious that when it concluded at Chapter 13, he had only covered through the years of early Christianity" (203–204).

Works cited

Adams, Carol J. "Robert Morris and a Lost 18th-Century Vegetarian Book: An Introduction to Morris's *A Reasonable Plea for the Animal Creation.*" *Organization & Environment*, vol. 18, no. 4, 2005, pp. 458–466.
Barkas, Janet. *The Vegetable Passion*. Scriber, 1975.
Barnard, Tanya, and Sarah Kramer. *How It All Vegan! Irresistible Recipes for an Animal-Free Diet*. Arsenal Pulp, 1999.
Berson, Josh. *The Meat Question: Animals, Humans, and the Deep History of Food*. MIT Press, 2019.
Brang, Peter. *Ein Unbekanntes Russland: Kulturgeschichte Vegetarischer Lebensweisen von den Anfängen bis zur Gegenwart* [*A Hidden Russia: A Cultural History of Vegetarian Ways of Life from the Beginnings to the Present Day*]. Böhlau, 2002.
Brueck, Julia Feliz. *Veganism in an Oppressive World: A Vegans of Color Community Project*. Sanctuary, 2017.
Crook, Edgard. *Abstainers! A Vegetarian and Vegan History of Australia*.
Davis, John. "Vegetarian History." *IVU.org*. International Vegetarian Union, 2020. Web.

———. *World Veganism: Past, Present, and Future. IVU.org.* International Vegetarian Union, 2010–2012. Web.
Doyle, Julie. "Celebrity Vegans and the Lifestyling of Ethical Consumption." *Environmental Communication*, vol. 10, no. 6, 2016, pp. 777–790.
Foer, Jonathan Safran. *Eating Animals.* Little, Brown, 2009.
Forward, Charles Walter. *Fifty Years of Food Reform: A History of the Vegetarian Movement in England.* Ideal Publishing Union, 1898. Print. *Internet Archive.* Archive.org, 2016.
Hall, Stuart. "Notes on Deconstructing 'the Popular.'" *People's History and Socialist Theory*, edited by Raphael Samuel. *Routledge*, 1981, pp. 227–240.
Harper, A. Breeze, ed. *Sistah Vegan: Black Female Vegans Speak on Food, Identity, Health, and Society.* Lantern, 2010.
Haubrich, William S. "Sylvester Graham: Partly Right, Mostly for the Wrong Reasons." *Journal of Medical Biography*, vol. 6, 1998, pp. 24–43.
Iacobbo, Karen, and Michael Iacobbo. *Vegetarian America: A History.* Praeger, 2004.
International Vegetarian Union. "History of the International Vegetarian Union." *IVU.org.* International Vegetarian Union, 2020.
Jones, Michael Owen. "In Pursuit of Percy Shelley, 'The First Vegan Celebrity': An Essay on Meat, Sex, and Broccoli." *Journal of Folklore Research*, vol. 53, no. 2, 2016, pp. 1–30.
Leitzmann, Claus. "Vegetarian Nutrition: Past, Present, and Future." *American Journal of Clinical Nutrition*, vol. 100, 2014, pp. 496S–502S. https://doi.org/10.3945/ajcn.113.071365.
Lestel, Dominique. *Eat This Book: A Carnivore's Manifesto*, translated by Gary Steiner, Columbia University Press, 2016.
Marcus, Erik. *A Vegan History: 1944–2010.* Amazon, 2011. E-book.
Miller, Ian. "Evangelicism and the Early Vegetarian Movement in Britain c. 1847–1860." *Journal of Religious History*, vol. 35, no. 2, 2011, pp. 199–210.
Moskowitz, Isa Chandra. *Vegan with a Vengeance: Over 150 Delicious, Cheap, Animal-Free Recipes that Rock.* Marlowe, 2005.
Preece, Rod. *Sins of the Flesh: A History of Ethical Vegetarian Thought.* University of British Columbia Press, 2008.
Puskar-Pasewicz, Margaret, editor. *Cultural Encyclopedia of Vegetarianism.* Greenwood, 2010.
Puskar-Pasewicz, Margaret. *"For the Good of the Whole": Vegetarianism in 19th-Century America.* Diss. Indiana U, 2003. University of Michigan Press, 2004.
Rozenberg, Guillaume. "Végétarisme et Sainteté dans le Bouddhisme du Theravāda: Pour une Relecture des Sources Anciennes à la Lumière de la Réalité Contemporaine" [Vegetarianism and Holiness in Theravada Buddhism: Rereading Ancient Sources in the Light of Contemporary Reality]. *Archives de Sciences Sociales des Religions*, vol. 120, 2002, pp. 5–31.
Scott, Kim Allen and Robert Myers. "The Extinct 'Grass Eaters' of Benton County: A Reconstructed History of the Harmonial Vegetarian Society." *Arkansas Historical Association*, vol. 502, 1991, pp. 140–157.
Shprintzen, Adam. *The Vegetarian Crusade: The Rise of an American Reform Movement, 1817–1921.* University of North Carolina Press, 2013.
Silverstone, Alicia. *The Kind Diet.* Rodale, 2011.
Specht, Joshua. *Red Meat Republic: A Hoof-to-Table History of How Beef Changed America.* Princeton University Press, 2019.
Spencer, Colin. *Vegetarianism: A History.* London: Grub Street, 2000. Rpt. of *The Heretic's Feast*, 1993.
Stuart, Tristram. *The Bloodless Revolution: A Cultural History of Vegetarianism from 1600 to Modern Times.* New York: Norton, 2007. Print. Rpt. of *The Bloodless Revolution: Radical Vegetarians and the Discovery of India.* Harper, 2006.
Terry, Bryant. *Soul Vegan Kitchen: Fresh, Healthy, and Creative African American Cuisine.* Da Capo, 2009.
Twigg, Julia. "The Vegetarian Movement in England, 1847–1981: with Particular Reference to its Ideology." Diss. London School of Economics. 1981. Print.
Vegan Society. "History." *The Vegan Society.* https://www.vegansociety.com/about-us/history. 1944–2020.
Vegetarian Resource Group. "Vegetarian/Vegan History." *VRG.org.* The Vegetarian Resource Group. 1996–2020.
Whorton, J. C. "Historical Development of Vegetarianism." *American Journal of Clinical Nutrition*, vol. 59, 1994, pp. 1103S–1109S.

Williams, Howard. *The Ethics of Diet: A Catena of Authorities Deprecatory of the Practice of Flesh-Eating.* 1883. Introd. by Carol J. Adams. University of Illinois Press, 2003.

Wilson, Brian C. *Dr. John Harvey Kellogg and the Religion of Biologic Living.* Indiana University Press, 2014.

Wrenn, Corey Lee. "The Vegan Society and Social Movement Professionalization, 1944–2017." *Food and Foodways,* vol. 27, no. 3, 2019, pp. 190–210.

Wright, Laura, editor. *Through a Vegan Studies Lens: Textual Ethics and Lived Activism.* University of Nevada Press, 2019.

———. *The Vegan Studies Project: Food, Animals, and Gender in the Age of Terror.* University of Georgia Press, 2015.

4
The analytic philosophers
Peter Singer's *Animal Liberation* and Tom Regan's *The Case for Animal Rights*

Josh Milburn

Many of the questions central to vegan studies (VS) have a recognizably philosophical dimension. Conceptual questions about what veganism is (e.g., Quinn and Westwood) and different kinds of veganism (e.g., Jones) are ubiquitous; ethical questions, often reflecting the personal dilemmas faced by scholars (e.g., Salih) are frequent; and political questions underlie the desire to do VS at all (Wright, *The Vegan Studies Project* passim). Indeed, the link between veganism/VS and philosophy/ethics is "overt" (Quinn and Westwood 16), while VS scholars are themselves vegan for explicitly ethical reasons (Wright, "Vegans in the Interregnum" 31). Unsurprisingly, then, VS scholars do look to philosophers. Often, these are *continental* philosophers, reflecting VS's origins in literary and cultural studies. For example, VS scholars look to Jacques Derrida (Schuster) and Judith Butler (McKay), who are not the best authors for those seeking determinate answers to philosophical puzzles. It would be a stretch to call Derrida or Butler *animal ethicists*, anyway; neither spends much time writing about the eating of animals, animals' rights or worth, or the moral dilemmas encountered in the lives of vegans. The animal ethicist most engaged with by VS scholars is probably the South African novelist J.M. Coetzee's protagonist Elizabeth Costello—a fictional character.

Despite this relative exclusion of animal ethics, it is acknowledged that animal ethicists make up an important part of the prehistory of VS (Wright, *The Vegan Studies Project* 11), and that discussions of animal rights and animal liberation form one of the field's building blocks (Wright, "Doing Vegan Studies" xv). Scholars of VS should thus be aware of historical and contemporary discussions about the moral status of animals and the ethics of eating animal products. Not only will it help them to situate their work in a wider conversation, but it could prove useful in addressing the philosophical questions they face. Even if, ultimately, VS scholars are not satisfied with the answers emerging from animal ethics, familiarity with the field will be valuable. They do not need to start from nothing; there is an academic community that has been doing this work for decades.

To that end, this chapter offers an introduction to philosophical animal ethics for the VS scholar. *Animal ethics* is the normative study of human/animal relationships, the study of how humans *should* interact with animals. *Philosophical* animal ethics, meanwhile, is animal ethics using the tools of philosophy. Here, my focus is on *analytic* philosophy, which arose in the United

Kingdom at the start of the 20th century. Analytic philosophers take their lead from the sciences, valuing rigor, precision, and logic.

This introduction is focused around the two most influential figures of 20th-century animal ethics—those acknowledged as part of VS's prehistory—and what they say about eating. These figures are Peter Singer, a "welfarist" who belongs to the philosophical tradition of utilitarianism, and Tom Regan, a "rightist" who belongs to the philosophical tradition of deontology. Constraints of space mean that this chapter cannot introduce other strands of 20th-century animal ethics. Animal-sympathetic approaches in care ethics (Donovan and Adams), for example, have had currency in ecofeminist approaches to animals. These are explored elsewhere in the current volume, and are a central influence on VS. Wittgensteinian approaches to animal ethics, typified by the work of Cora Diamond, are occasionally referred to in VS work (e.g., McKay 259–63). And Mary Midgley's communitarian approach to animals has been influential among philosophers, though, admittedly, less so among VS scholars. Care-based, Wittgensteinian, and communitarian animal ethicists, however, typically situate themselves in opposition to Singer/Regan. Thus, even if we ultimately want to end up with a position like (say) Diamond's, it makes sense to look first to Singer.

Though there are strands of 20th-century animal ethics that cannot be explored here, the chapter will not be limited to introducing Singer and Regan. Instead, it will look to some 21st-century debates in animal ethics that can be seen as an intellectual legacy of their work. In these debates, scholars of VS will, if they scratch the surface, find a great deal of value for their own work. It is the contention of this chapter that analytic philosophy and animal ethics should be more than a stepping-off point on the way to VS. Indeed, animal ethics may be able to provide the kind of *vegan theory* that VS scholars seek (Quinn and Westwood)—or, at least, the normative dimension of such a theory. Thus, though VS and animal ethics are different disciplines, they can be closely allied.

Peter Singer and *Animal Liberation*

Animal ethics is part of the mainstream of analytic philosophy, and the Australian philosopher Peter Singer is (largely) to thank for this. Additionally, he has had a major impact on animal activism worldwide. His work—especially his *Animal Liberation*—is widely read, often rousing people from (to borrow a term with philosophical pedigree) their "dogmatic slumber," helping them to see the wrong in the exploitation of animals. Singer was awoken from his own dogmatic slumber while a student at Oxford. The "Oxford Vegetarians" played an important part in his intellectual development. *Animal Liberation*, for example, ultimately arose from a review he wrote of the now little-read *Animals, Men, and Morals*, edited by Oxford's Stanley Godlovitch, Ros Godlovitch, and John Harris. For more on the Oxford Vegetarians, see Garner and Okuleye.

Singer situates animal liberation as a natural extension of women's liberation, Black liberation, and so on. He asks us to consider the basis of moral equality between humans, as held dear in these movements. The moral equality of (say) men and women does not rest upon the fact that there are no differences between men and women. There are differences—or there might be. Instead, moral equality rests upon the fact that both men and women have important *interests* that should be protected. *Interest* is a primary moral concept and thus hard to define in non-circular way. In short, all beings with a welfare—a life that can go better or worse for them—have interests. They have interests in things that make their life go better or stop it getting worse (Zuolo 173–4). In some cases, the interests of men and women will be the same—for example, both men and women have an interest in being able to vote. In other cases, they will not be. Singer's own (old-fashioned) example is that men do not have an interest in having access to abortion services. But animals, too, have interests. At least, *sentient* animals, or animals able to experience pleasure/pain, have interests. Crucially, any animal able to experience pain has an interest in not being in pain—their life will be worse if they are in pain.

It is sexist to exclude the interests of women from equal consideration simply because those interests do not belong to men, and, according to Singer, it is *speciesist* to exclude the interests of animals from equal consideration simply because they do not belong to humans—and the two *isms* are equally confused. The word *speciesism* now gets used in all kinds of ways, but Singer's own definition is hard to beat: speciesism "is a prejudice or attitude of bias in favor of the interests of members of one's own species and against those of members of other species" (*Animal Liberation* 6), though we should add that speciesism need not be about favoring members of one's *own* species. The way many favor dogs over pigs looks like speciesism.

What interests do animals have? Singer focuses on their interest in not suffering. The suffering of animals is just as bad, from the "point of view of the universe," as the suffering of humans. And their interest in avoiding suffering is just as strong as ours. In order to avoid the charge of speciesism, then, we have to afford equal consideration to the suffering of animals and the suffering of humans. And this gets us a long way toward veganism. After all—and as Singer goes to great lengths to show—animal agriculture and fishing lead to horrendous levels of animal suffering. (Readers can be spared the grisly details.)

However, Singer's arguments do not get us *all* the way to veganism, and, over the next few paragraphs, we will explore some of the reasons that Singer's position is not wholly vegan. The first is that it focuses, as explained, on the possession of interests. It is surely plausible that some animals do *not* possess interests. Certain bivalves may be a case in point. In the first edition of *Animal Liberation*, Singer explicitly allowed that these animals were probably not sentient. Initially, therefore, he continued to eat them. He later went back on this position (*Animal Liberation* 174), though his stance is a little ambiguous, as he seems to recommend their consumption sometimes (Singer and Mason 133). Whatever Singer's personal practice, we can say that *if* oysters (or mussels, or…) are not sentient, *then* Singer's position permits their consumption—or, minimally, does not forbid it for their own sake.

In principle, too, it might be permissible on Singer's account to eat *sentient* animals. Singer allows that we can eat animals who are already dead. No additional suffering is created by my eating a lamb who has been killed on the road ("Utilitarianism and vegetarianism" 237–8). Singer also explicitly argues that animals can be killed and eaten in times of dire need (*Practical Ethics* 122). However, these examples are hardly unique to his position. It would be tricky to find an animal-ethical framework that did not permit genuine subsistence hunting. Meanwhile, there is something of a consensus (though not universal agreement) among animal ethicists that some or all "freegan" practices are permissible. *Freeganism*, which relates to veganism in ways yet under-explored by scholars of VS, refers to lifestyles (often tied up with anti-establishment/anti-capitalist views) in which individuals seek out and utilize food (and other goods), including animal-based products, that would otherwise go to waste. The paradigm freegan activity is "dumpster diving" (see Singer and Mason 260–9).

A puzzle that is much more distinct to Singer's position—and one that has sparked a large and complex literature—is the "replaceability argument." This will be explained shortly; however, to understand the argument, we first need to think a little about Singer's view of killing animals, and his utilitarianism.

First, killing. That sentient animals have an interest in not suffering does not necessarily mean that they have an interest in not being killed. In principle, someone—let us call them Crofter—could accept Singer's claim that humans and animals have an interest in not suffering, but argue that painlessly killing animals is unproblematic. Singer's response is the "argument from marginal cases" (Dombrowski), better named the "argument from species overlap" (Horta, "The scope"). It is true, Singer says, that many animals have a lower interest in continued life than the person reading this chapter. This is because of their more limited psychological capacities. (There is an easy response accusing Singer of tying worth to being like him. However, Singer holds that there are *good reasons* to believe that animals who cannot conceive of themselves existing over time have a lower interest in continued life. A more compelling challenge to Singer would engage with these reasons, and offer counter-reasons. We do not have the space to do this here.) But there are also some *humans* who have these more limited capacities: young children, for example. To avoid inconsistency, Crofter would have to accept that it is permissible to kill these *humans*, too—but that, Singer thinks, is implausible.

Importantly, Singer does *not* argue that all animals and all humans have an equal interest in continued life. Instead, he proposes that *some* humans and *some* animals have less of an interest in continued life than the reader of this chapter. Some might have none at all. This depends upon the level of *personhood* that these beings possess; the extent to which these animals are "rational and self-conscious beings, aware of themselves as distinct entities with a past and a future" (Singer, *Practical Ethics* 94). A *person* is any being with some level of personhood; the term is not, for animal ethicists, synonymous with *human*. (Singer's bar, here, is relatively low; other philosophers might reserve the term *person* to refer to anyone with a *sufficiently high* level of personhood.)

Second, utilitarianism. Utilitarianism, which Singer endorses, is an ethical theory concerned with maximizing good consequences, and minimizing bad consequences. Utilitarians say that the right thing to do in any situation is the thing that will lead to the greatest balance of good over bad. For *preference utilitarians*, the good is preferences being realized, and the bad is preferences being frustrated. For *hedonistic utilitarians*, the good is pleasure, and the bad, pain. Confusingly, Singer changes teams; having spent most of his career a preference utilitarian, he now endorses hedonistic utilitarianism (Singer, "Afterword"). More confusingly still, *Animal Liberation* itself is not a work of utilitarian philosophy; instead, it relies upon what is called "common-sense morality" (DeGrazia). The replaceability argument, however, rests upon utilitarianism.

So what is the replaceability argument? Persons generally have an interest in not being killed, as they generally have preferences about ongoing projects or simply about going on living. On the other hand, for Singer, any badness from killing merely conscious animals—i.e., animals that are sentient, but not persons—comes from the fact that, with the happiness of these animals out of the picture, there is less happiness in the world. If the author has a group of happy tetras (imagining that these fish are "merely conscious") living in a tank, and he painlessly kills them, the universe is a slightly less happy place—there is a bit less (tetra) happiness. (There may be third-party effects, too—the author's tetra-loving partner might be unhappy—but let us leave these aside.) But if the author *replaced* these tetras with other equally happy tetras, who would not otherwise exist, it seems like there is no less happiness in the universe, making the initial killing morally unproblematic (from Singer's perspective).

Why does this matter? It opens the door to farming:

> Suppose we could be confident that chickens, for example, are not aware of themselves as existing over time (and as we have seen, this assumption is questionable). Assume also that the birds can be killed painlessly, and the survivors do not appear to be affected by the death of one of their numbers. Assume, finally, that for economic reasons we could

not rear the birds if we did not eat them. Then the replaceability argument appears to justify killing the birds, because depriving them of the pleasures of their existence can be offset against the pleasures of chickens who not yet exist and will exist only if existing chickens are killed. (Singer, *Practical Ethics* 120)

Singer has spent a great deal of intellectual energy explaining why this replaceability argument does not extend to persons, thus opening the door to farming any animal (as long as it is done *very* "humanely"). However, it is not clear that he has been successful. What is more, as noted above, Singer has now embraced hedonistic utilitarianism, while his previous discussions of replaceability were explicitly preference utilitarian. If his comments about hedonistic utilitarianism in these discussions are to be believed (*Practical Ethics* 111), he is now committed to the claim that *all* animals are, in principle, "replaceable." This means that all animals, *in principle*, could be farmed.

Where does this leave us? Vegans could still embrace Singer's case for animal liberation. Perhaps discussions of replaceability are a distraction; while the sort of puzzle that excites philosophers, it is only (perhaps) a minor part of Singer's thought, with (perhaps) little practical import. Singer's case will be particularly attractive to those "welfarist" vegans who are concerned about animal *suffering*, but not about animal *death*. Such vegans might well be open to a form of highly humane pastoral farming *in principle*, and might be willing to sign on with Singer when he is at his most conciliatory. This conciliatory attitude, which has vexed VS scholars (Kirkpatrick 8), is concerned first and foremost with reducing animal suffering rather than with abolishing the institutions that exploit animals. It should not be surprising, given his utilitarianism.

But however influential Singer has been in converting people into activists, and however compelling his approach may be to many vegans, the approach is not a vegan theory. We should not exaggerate Singer's non-veganism. He is most certainly not a critic of veganism, unlike, say, Donna Haraway and many other posthumanists—as discussed in the present volume by Eva Giraud. But his theoretical approach does reluctantly take him to some non-vegan places. When we scratch beneath the surface, Singer's philosophy does not sound like a compelling one to undergird a *vegan* society, a *vegan* movement, a *vegan* theory, or a *vegan* studies.

Tom Regan and *The Case for Animal Rights*

Though the name is often applied to Singer, Tom Regan is probably the real "[philosophical] father of animal rights." For a start, unlike Singer, he actually defends animal *rights*, and not just better treatment for animals. His *Case for Animal Rights* is not as widely read as *Animal Liberation*, to which it responds. This is partly because it is a tougher read. Regan is writing primarily for academic philosophers, and his ideas rest upon some tricky philosophical ideas. Nonetheless, the book is a masterpiece, essential reading for those interested in the moral status of animals, and worth the effort. Helpfully, Regan wrote some widely reproduced summaries. These are useful places to start.

Regan seeks to explore the basis of the "inherent value" that we perceive in ourselves and other humans. *Inherent value* is value that we have in and of ourselves, independently of any value we have to others, and of any value our experiences (e.g., pleasure) have. Note, already, the very different starting point to Singer, for whom value rests in the satisfaction of preferences, or pleasure.

Regan concludes that we have inherent value because we are *subjects-of-a-life*, and all subjects-of-a-life have inherent value equally. Someone is a subject-of-a-life

> if they have beliefs and desires; perception, memory, and a sense of the future, including their own future; an emotional life together with feelings of pleasure and pain; preference- and welfare-interests; the ability to initiate action in pursuit of their desires and goals; a psychophysical identity over time; and an individual welfare in the sense that their experiential life fares well or ill for them, logically independently of their utility for others and logically independently of their being the object of anyone else's interests. (Regan 243)

Regan thus seems to set a higher bar than Singer, given the latter's reliance on sentience. (We will return to this.) In *The Case*, Regan uses the example of mammals of at least one year of age as subjects-of-a-life, but these are not the only subjects-of-a-life.

What is the significance of having inherent value? Beings with inherent value are owed *respect*. And they are owed this respect as a matter of *justice*—it would not merely be good, or nice of us to respect animals. We, morally speaking, *must* respect them. Most importantly, we *fail* to treat them with respect when we treat them as if any value they have is dependent on the value they have to others or on the value of their experiences, as if they are just receptacles for valuable things—like pleasure—rather than valuable themselves (Regan 248–9). This position, of course, sharply contrasts with Singer's view. Regan has no time for the replaceability argument.

Regan reaches his ultimate position—the rights view—by arguing that the duty to respect subjects-of-a-life means that subjects-of-a-life have a *right* to respectful treatment. All kinds of things that we do to animals violate their rights. As such, the consequences of the rights view are radical. Crucially, vegetarianism (read: veganism) is obligatory; institutions of farming, hunting, trapping, and fishing must be abolished; animals may no longer be considered property; and more.

Readers now have an idea of the outline of Regan's theory. Naturally enough, there is room for puzzles at the edges. For example, there is a question-mark over the place of genuine subsistence hunting in Regan's theory (Nobis). And there is room for asking whether he would be open to genuinely harm-free forms of non-veganism—though recall that he is not concerned with whether animals are used in ways that are painful, but whether they are used at all (or, at least, used disrespectfully). Could the rights view permit freeganism, as Singer's welfarism does (Abbate, "Veganism" and "Save the meat for cats")? How might the rights view deal with backyard chickens (Fischer and Milburn)?

There are also fundamental philosophical questions to ask. While we cannot get into them all here, one concerns the mysteriousness of the notions underlying the rights view. Consider inherent value. What *is* this? Where does it come from? Why do we need this idea (Rowlands 86–97)? VS scholars might well be reluctant to rest their theories on such mysterious foundations. Then again, they might value the mystery; some VS scholars celebrate uncertainty (Quinn), and others draw comparisons between veganism and religion (Covey).

In any case, Regan's rights view seems like a much more viable basis for a genuinely *vegan* approach (to scholarship, politics, life…) than Singer's welfarism. However, let us not leave the matter there. To get to the bottom of this debate, it is worth fast-forwarding to the 2020s, and pointing toward some of the live debates in animal ethics that can be seen as taking place in Singer and Regan's shadows. This will help shine a light on the value of Singer and Regan's frameworks—and frameworks they inform.

Singer's legacy: harm reduction

The influence of Singer's focus on harm reduction can be seen in a range of contemporary debates in animal ethics that will be of interest to VS scholars, either because they address veganism, or because they will show what a vegan life could be. For a flavor, consider two.

First are questions about the causal impact of our dietary choices. Singer, recall, is interested in actually making a difference in the lives of animals. He thus takes very seriously the fact that a refusal to buy a burger from McDonald's likely has no impact upon the lives of any animals. Naturally enough, the animal in question is already dead—but refusing to buy a burger will not have any impact on any *future* animal, either, because the decisions of McDonald's to buy more burgers are not sensitive to one person's refusal. Now, they *are* sensitive to the decision of *lots of people* to *repeatedly* refuse. But that we *collectively* have a responsibility to do something does not straightforwardly translate to the claim that we *individually* have a responsibility to do that same thing—especially if our *individual* action (unlike the collective action) will have no impact. Similarly, the fact that it is wrong to harm animals on farms when we could all thrive as vegans does not straightforwardly translate to a claim that it is wrong to eat the products of animals harmed on farms—especially, again, when said refusal will have no impact. Trying to get to the bottom of a justification for veganism given consumers' causal impotence is something that concerns a lot of contemporary animal ethicists working in Singer's shadow—for example, it was a real theme of a recent handbook of food ethics (e.g., McPherson; Nefsky). So seriously do philosophers take this problem that at least one vegan philosopher has concluded that, despite the wrong of raising and killing animals for food, it is not impermissible to purchase and eat the products of animal agriculture (Fischer). VS scholars who worry about the causal impotence of veganism (e.g., von Mossner 34–5) may be able to find much of value in these debates, and could do little better than starting with the works just cited.

Second are questions of impactful *activism*. Singer himself has written a considerable amount on this; for example, he has provided the philosophical underpinning for the effective-altruism movement (*The Most Good You Can Do*). Effective altruism is about doing the most good that we can, given our finite resources. Better to donate to a charity that will make effective use of my money than one that will not; better to save more lives than fewer. In the animal case, this has some unsurprising results. Given the numbers involved, their comparative neglect by philanthropists, and that we have relatively clear routes to measurable impact, animal activists and animal philanthropists would do better to focus on farmed animals and diet than on (say) companion animals. We can see these trends reflected in the charities recommended by Animal Charity Evaluators. At the time of writing, their "top" charities are the Albert Schweitzer Foundation, Anima International, The Humane League, and The Good Food Institute. But it might also have some results that are uncomfortable. For example, effective animal altruists face criticism (the fairness of which is disputed) for focusing on welfare reform at the expense of system change—in part because the former is more measurable, and we have clearer ideas about how it is achieved. Some of these will not sit easily even with those who reluctantly support welfare reform, such as encouraging people to change from eating chicken and fish to eating beef: Chickens and fishes are smaller than cows, which means more death and more suffering per meal (Cooney chap. 1). It also may have results that sound, for those unfamiliar with animal ethics, bizarre. For example, effective animal altruists might well focus on wild-animal suffering. Though there is a literature on wild-animal suffering in animal ethics (e.g., Horta, "Debunking"), and though a utilitarian should not distinguish between wild and domesticated animals, talk of interfering in predator–prey relations can be met with incredulous stares.

These debates serve as examples of the questions that contemporary Singer-influenced animal ethicists address. Both are relevant to VS scholars, who reflect upon the impact of their choices (von Mossner 34–5); the underlying tensions of their vegan position (Quinn); and what it means to live a vegan life beyond diet (Quinn and Westwood). No doubt, then, there is much of interest to VS scholars in these conversations, whether or not they are ultimately drawn to Singer's utilitarianism.

Regan's legacy: abolitionism and the political turn in animal ethics

Animal rights neither begin nor end with Regan. Contemporary strands of animal-rights theory, however, clearly display the influence of his position. Earlier, we saw the strength of Regan's rights view as a vegan theory; it is worth briefly comparing this to major 21st-century approaches to animal rights to ask whether they could provide viable ethical underpinnings to VS.

The abolitionist approach to animal rights—championed by Gary Francione and Anna Charlton—foregrounds the rights view's rejection of the property status of animals and its abolitionist (in contrast to welfarist, reductionist, or reformist) conclusions (Francione and Charlton). Though explicitly building upon the rights view, it requires sentience (not the subject-of-a-life criterion) for individuals to be counted as full and equal members of society. Most importantly for current purposes, however, is abolitionism's focus on veganism. For abolitionists, veganism is a "moral baseline"; it is what is required of us, with no ifs or buts. Thus, abolitionists have no interest in many of the arguments, puzzles, and exceptions surveyed above. And animal activism, for abolitionists, should consist primarily in vegan education: leafleting, cooking demonstrations, conversations with colleagues, and so on. Abolitionism provides a powerful and undeniably *vegan* ethical system—indeed, more vegan than even Regan's rights view.

Before rushing to embrace abolitionism, however, scholars of VS should be aware that it comes with baggage. The objection to the consumption of *any* animal products is consistently grounded on an out-and-out rejection of animal *use*. This means not only that animals cannot be used for food production, or as experimental test subjects, but that they cannot be "used" as animal companions. Abolitionism is an "extinctionist" philosophy. It calls on us to make this generation of domesticated animals the last. Abolitionism means the end of dogs, cats, chickens, cows, pigs, horses, goldfish, and the rest. For VS scholars, this envisioned separation of humans and animals might sound like a dystopia (Wright, *The Vegan Studies Project* chap. 3), rather than a future of respectful human/animal relations. Abolitionism also takes a hard line on the kind of activism to be favored. Abolitionists are not interested in welfare reforms; indeed, they are, as a rule, suspicious of activist organizations generally. They not even keen on vegan education when it is framed incorrectly. Veganuary, for example—which sees people going vegan for the month of January—would not be well-received by abolitionists, as it focuses on only one month.

There is another branch of animal rights that may be attractive to those worried about abolitionism's implications. Indeed, it is established explicitly *in opposition* to abolitionism. These are the normative frameworks emerging from the "political turn in animal ethics." Proponents of the political turn foreground the rights view's focus on justice and begin to ask constructive questions about how we could reorder and reimagine our societies and relationships with animals:

> the crucial unifying and distinctive feature of these contributions—and what can properly be said to mark them out as a 'political turn'—is the way in which they imagine how political institutions, structures and processes might be *transformed* so as to secure justice for both

human and non-human animals. Put simply, the essential feature of the political turn is this *constructive* focus on justice. (Cochrane, Garner, and O'Sullivan 263–4)

The best-known work in this subfield comes from Sue Donaldson and Will Kymlicka. In their *Zoopolis*, they agree with the abolitionist focus on sentience, and on the rejection of the property status of animals. However, they explicitly set themselves against extinctionism. Instead, they offer exactly the kind of a constructive, justice-based vision mentioned in the quote above. They imagine a future society in which domestic animals are conceived as our co-*citizens*, afforded membership-related rights (and responsibilities!). Donaldson and Kymlicka detail (at a range of scales, from the household to the international arena) a host of ways that we could live with animals *differently*. For example, they point to the practices of sanctuaries for formerly farmed animals ("Farmed animal sanctuaries"), and envision urban spaces in which animals can negotiate the terms of co-living (*Zoopolis* chap. 5). Other theorists drawing upon Donaldson and Kymlicka's approach look at other kinds of co-relations. For example, Eva Meijer—in her *When Animals Speak*—explores human/animal encounters from her very personal negotiation with her dog, to the participation of "problem" geese in conversations about goose–human conflict, to the relationship between worms and the humans who research them.

The place of food in these systems, meanwhile, is up for grabs. While Donaldson and Kymlicka *do* talk approvingly of widespread shifts to vegan diets (*Zoopolis* 202), they also raise questions about whether respectful co-living with animals could be consistent with eating animal products. Zoopolitical rights certainly preclude killing, confining, or torturing animals for food—but they may not preclude eating the eggs of chickens with whom we live as equals (*Zoopolis* 138). And Donaldson and Kymlicka puzzle over the feeding of carnivorous non-human members of mixed societies. If cats cannot be safely fed a plant-based diet, where does this leave the prospect of living with them (*Zoopolis* 152)? The visions of the proponents of the political turn *could* be wholly vegan, but need not be. If VS scholars seek a theory focusing on constructing novel ideas about close and respectful co-relations with animals, however, they could do much worse than start with Donaldson and Kymlicka's zoopolitics.

Conclusion: animal ethics and vegan studies

This chapter has reviewed Singer's welfarism and Regan's rights view, with a focus on what use they may have for VS scholars. It has argued that Singer's vision is far from a vegan theory. Nonetheless, an intellectual legacy of Singer's—a focus on the reduction of harm—means that there is much contemporary scholarship on many of the practical questions with which VS grapples. Regan's rights view, meanwhile, is a contender for the ethical underpinning of a VS perspective. As a legacy of Regan's rights view, we have two sets of normative frameworks that may be even more attractive to the VS scholar than Regan's rights view. Abolitionists stress the veganism of Regan's theory, but the natural conclusion of this is a human/animal separation. The "political turn in animal ethics"—epitomized by Donaldson and Kymlicka's zoopolitics—stresses Regan's focus on justice, constructing visions of respectful future co-relations with animals. This comes at the expense, however, of abolitionism's firm line on veganism. Abolitionst or zoopolitical approaches could form the underpinnings for VS scholarship, and for a vegan perspective on the world.

In this chapter, the case has been made that attention to animal ethics will be valuable for VS scholars. In future work, it is worth flipping this question. What is the value of engaging with work in VS for animal ethicists? Consider just one example: perhaps VS can help to develop a society in which failures of imagination are corrected, allowing us collectively to imagine utopias in which humans and animals live in harmony (Cooke). If so, VS will be of considerable value to animal ethicists who—according to Steve Cooke—should be in the business of not only imagining such utopias, but identifying those failures of imagination that hinder respect for animals. Crucially, work in this area could take its lead (and benefit) from literature and the arts—and who is better placed to aid with this than VS scholars? But this is just an example of what VS could add to animal ethics. More work needs to be done.

While we should keep VS and animal ethics separate, there is every reason that they could and should be close cousins—or even siblings.

Acknowledgments

This chapter was written while I was a British Academy Postdoctoral Fellow at the University of Sheffield (grant number PF19\100101). I thank the British Academy for their support, and thank Laura Wright for some valuable comments.

Works cited

Abbate, Cheryl. "Save the meat for cats: Why it's wrong to eat roadkill." *Journal of Agricultural and Environmental Ethics*, vol. 32, no. 1, 2019a, pp. 165–182.
———. "Veganism, (almost) harm-free animal flesh, and nonmaleficence: Navigating dietary ethics in an unjust world." *Routledge Handbook of Animal Ethics*, edited by Bob Fischer, Routledge, 2019b, pp. 555–568.
Charlton, Anna, and Gary Francione. *Animal Rights*, Exempla Press, 2015.
Cochrane, Alasdair, Robert Garner, and Siobhan O'Sullivan. "Animal ethics and the political." *Critical Review of International Social and Political Philosophy*, vol. 21, no. 2, 2018, pp. 261–277.
Cooke, Steve. "Imagined utopias: Animal rights and the moral imagination." *Journal of Political Philosophy*, vol. 25, no. 4, 2017, e1–e18.
Cooney, Nick. *Veganomics*. Lantern Books, 2014.
Covey, Allison. "Ethical veganism as protected identity: Constructing a creed under human rights law." *Thinking Veganism in Literature and Culture*, edited by Quinn and Benjamin Westwood, Palgrave Macmillan, 2018, pp. 225–248.
DeGrazia, David. "Review of Singer: *Animal Liberation* (Second Edition)." *Between the Species*, vol. 8, no. 1, 1992, pp. 44–51.
Diamond, Cora. "Eating meat and eating people." *Philosophy*, vol. 53, no. 206, 1978, pp. 465–479.
Dombrowski, Daniel A. *Babies and Beasts*. University of Illinois Press, 1997.
Donaldson, Sue, and Will Kymlicka. *Zoopolis*. Oxford UP, 2011.
———. "Farmed animal sanctuaries: The heart of the movement?" *Politics and Animals*, vol. 1, 2015, pp. 50–74.
Donovan, Josephine, and Carol Adams, editors. *The Feminist Care Tradition in Animal Ethics*. Columbia UP, 2007.
Fischer, Bob. *The Ethics of Eating Animals*. Routledge, 2019.
Fischer, Bob and Josh Milburn. "In Defense of Backyard Chickens." *Journal of Applied Philosophy*, vol. 36, no. 1, 2019, pp. 108–123.
Garner, Robert, and Yewande Okuleye. *The Oxford Group and the Emergence of Animal Rights*, Oxford UP, forthcoming.
Godlovitch, Stanley, Ros Godlovitch, and John Harris, editors. *Animals, Men, and Morals*. Victor Gollancz, 1971.
Horta, Oscar. "The Scope of the Argument from Species Overlap." *Journal of Applied Philosophy*, vol. 31, no. 2, 2014, pp. 142–154.
Horta, Oscar. "Debunking the Idyllic View of Natural Processes: Population Dynamics and Suffering in the Wild." *Télos*, vol. 17, no. 1, pp. 73–88.
Jones, Robert. "Veganisms." *Critical Perspectives on Veganism*, edited by Jodey Castricano and Rasmus R. Simonsen, Palgrave Macmillan, 2016, pp. 15–39.

Quinn, Emelia. "Monstrous Vegan Narratives: Margaret Atwood's Hideous Progeny." *Thinking Veganism in Literature and Culture*, edited by Emelia Quinn and Benjamin Westwood, Palgrave Macmillan, 2018, pp. 149–174.

———. "Thinking through Veganism." *Thinking Veganism in Literature and Culture*, edited by Emelia Quinn and Benjamin Westwood, Palgrave Macmillan, 2018, pp. 1–24.

Kirkpatrick, Kathryn. "Vegans in Locavore Literature." *Through a Vegan Studies Lens*, edited by Laura Wright, University of Nevada Press, 2019, pp. 3–16.

McKay, Bob. "A Vegan form of Life." *Thinking Veganism in Literature and Culture*, edited by Emelia Quinn and Benjamin Westwood, Palgrave Macmillan, 2018, pp. 249–272.

McPherson, Tristram. "The Ethical Basis for Veganism." *The Oxford Handbook of Food Ethics*, edited by Anne Barnhill, Mark Budolfson, and Tyler Doggett, Oxford UP, 2018, pp. 209–240.

Meijer, Eva. *When Animals Speak*. NYU Press, 2019.

Midgley, Mary. *Animals and Why They Matter*. University of Georgia Press, 1983.

Nefsky, Julia. "Consumer choice and Collective Impact." *The Oxford Handbook of Food Ethics*, edited by Anne Barnhill, Mark Budolfson, and Tyler Doggett, Oxford UP, 2018, pp. 267–286.

Nobis, Nathan. "Xenotransplantation, Subsistence Hunting and Pursuit of Health: Lessons for Animal Rights-based Vegan Advocacy." *Between the Species*, vol. 21, no. 1, 2018, pp. 197–215.

Regan, Tom. *The Case for Animal Rights* (Updated version). University of California Press, 2004.

Rowlands, Mark. *Animal Rights*. 2nd ed. Palgrave Macmillan, 2009.

Salih, Sara. "Remnants: The Witness and the Animal." *Thinking Veganism in Literature and Culture*, edited by Emelia Quinn and Benjamin Westwood, Palgrave Macmillan, 2018, pp. 57–77.

Schuster, Joshua. "The Vegan and the Sovereign." *Critical Perspectives on Veganism*, edited by Jodey Castricano and Rasmus R. Simonsen, Palgrave Macmillan, 2016, pp. 203–223.

Singer, Peter. "Afterword." *The Ethics of Killing Animals*, edited by Tatjana Višak and Robert Garner, Oxford UP, 2016, pp. 229–236.

———. *Animal Liberation*. 2nd ed., Pimlico, 1995.

———. *The Most Good You Can Do*. Yale University Press, 2015.

———. *Practical Ethics*. 3rd ed., Cambridge UP, 2011.

———. "Utilitarianism and Vegetarianism." *Philosophy & Public Affairs*, vol. 9, no. 4, 1980, pp. 325–337.

Singer, Peter, and Jim Mason. *The Way We Eat*. Rodale, 2006.

von Mossner, Alexa Weik. "How we Feel about (not) Eating Animals: Vegan Studies and Cognitive Ecocriticism." *Through a Vegan Studies Lens*, edited by Laura Wright, University of Nevada Press, 2019, pp. 28–47.

Wright, Laura. "Doing vegan studies: An introduction." *Through a Vegan Studies Lens*, edited by Laura Wright, University of Nevada Press, 2019, pp. vii–xxiv.

———. "Vegans in the Interregnum: The Cultural Moment of an Enmeshed Theory." *Thinking Veganism in Literature and Culture*, edited by Emelia Quinn and Benjamin Westwood, Palgrave Macmillan, 2018, pp. 27–54.

———. *The Vegan Studies Project*, University of Georgia Press, 2015.

Zuolo, Federico. "Equality, its basis and moral status: Challenging the principle of equal consideration of interests." *International Journal of Philosophical Studies*, 25, 2, 2017, pp. 170–188.

5
The "posthumanists"
Cary Wolfe and Donna Haraway

Eva Giraud

The aim of this chapter is to understand points of commonality between vegan praxis and scholarship, on the one hand, and posthumanism, on the other, while also elucidating tensions that have historically undermined these potentials. After offering a brief sketch of key affinities and frictions, I discuss two figures whose work crystallizes these—always complex and sometimes fraught—relationships between vegan studies and posthumanism: Donna Haraway and Cary Wolfe. Both thinkers' work has promised less anthropocentric ways of conceiving of and acting in the world, which has been taken up widely in the interdisciplinary academic field of animal studies. However, as I go on to elucidate, even though posthumanism has offered a rich set of conceptual tools that some scholars have put to work in support of critical-liberationary research, other aspects of this body of theory have lain at odds with vegan ethics. Building on research within vegan studies that has engaged with these tensions, I conclude by exploring how criticisms leveled at veganism from key posthumanist thinkers can be read back against this body of work, with the aim of creating space for more productive dialogue.

Defining posthumanism and understanding key tensions

As with other theoretical terms that have *post-* as a prefix, posthumanism is a slippery concept to define. To begin with, thinkers who are frequently labeled posthumanist themselves reject the label, as with Donna Haraway (16–17). Others—particularly working in fields such as geography, science and technology studies (STS), and the environmental humanities—deliberately use alternative terms such as "more-than-human" (as with Sarah Whatmore's more-than-human geographies, Thom van Dooren's framing of extinction as a more-than-human phenomena, or Maria Puig de la Bellacasa's exploration of a more-than-human ethics of care). Prominent essays that have traced the genealogies of posthumanism's influence upon animal studies throw up further complications. Susan Fraiman, for instance, situates the origins of animal studies' theoretical turn in the early 2000s with the uptake of earlier forms of poststructuralism, arguing that Jacques Derrida in particular has been positioned as "forefather of a dramatically renovated version of animal studies, extending across the disciplines and linked to the theoretical project of 'posthumanism'" (91). This expanded category of posthumanism, as pointed to by Fraiman (that also encompasses certain strands of poststructuralism and other allied bodies of thought such as the new materialisms), tends to be what is referred to as "posthumanist animal studies" in vegan studies contexts (Wright, *The Vegan Studies Project* 11).

The purpose of this chapter, however, is not to map posthumanism(s) (though see Castree et al. "Mapping Posthumanism" or Braidotti, *The Posthuman* for informative overviews), but to probe its messy relationship with vegan studies. For now, therefore, while recognizing complications surrounding the label, broadly speaking, I use posthumanism as a placeholder in reference to a range of work that has emerged over the past three decades, which has troubled not just what it means to be human but the very category of the human itself.

It is possible to group a number of heterogeneous texts together as posthumanist because, for all of their tensions and differences, these strands of theoretical work share certain aims. Firstly, these texts trouble the stability of the human by elucidating its dependency upon and entanglement with other nonhuman beings: From co-evolutionary relationships with companion species such as dogs (e.g., Haraway's *Companion Species Manifesto* and *When Species Meet*), to agricultural processes and food-webs that tie humans together in complex configurations with plants, microbes, and other animals (Puig de la Bellacasa, *Matters of Care*). Recognizing these material, ontological entanglements also has epistemological implications for how the world is conceived, troubling the categories, classifications, and conceptual frameworks that have conventionally been used to separate human from nonhuman (as interrogated by Wolfe's body of work). Perhaps the most significant intervention made by posthumanism, which resonates most strongly with vegan praxis, however, is the set of ethical questions that it opens up. As Stacy Alaimo puts it in the opening passages of *Exposed*: "What forms of ethics and politics arise from the sense of being embedded in, exposed to, and even composed of the very stuff of a rapidly transforming material world?" (1). Over the past ten years some of the key assumptions of this body of theory have been problematized, particularly its neglect of the relationship between species and race, and its corresponding tendency to assume that "the human" is a universal category that is always privileged above "the animal" (see Jackson, *Becoming Human*).

Alongside these wider critiques, the question that a growing body of academic work in vegan studies has been exploring is whether a vegan ethic might offer a response to the line of questioning that Alaimo (and allied theorists) have put forward. Does veganism, in other words, offer a framework, or series of practices, that might dislodge an anthropocentric humanism that has historically placed the needs of particular groups of people above those of nonhuman animals? While a number of thinkers in vegan studies itself, as well as strands of Critical Animal Studies (CAS), have answered this question with a resounding yes (see for instance Twine 12; Stephens Griffin 9), this sentiment is far from universal. Indeed, veganism has historically been criticized by non-anthropocentric thinkers who have depicted it as an overly naïve, dogmatic approach that fails to grasp the complexity of food systems (for explorations of this stance, see Haraway, *When Species Meet* 80 and 297; Probyn, *Eating the Ocean* 3; Shotwell, *Against Purity* 120).

Posthumanism has, in turn, been criticized for removing stable coordinates from which to contest animal exploitation (see Weisberg, "Broken Promises of Monsters"). While unpacking distinctions between human and nonhuman might be important in challenging anthropocentrism, the flattening of such distinctions can make it difficult to identify any responsibilities that humans might have in ameliorating anthropogenic problems that already exist. Helena Pedersen, for instance, reads posthumanist theory against CAS to argue that a theoretical emphasis on entanglements with other species often manifests itself as "a form of metonymic desire; a (human) desire to be part of an expanded context and community of lifeforms" (72). In failing to grapple with questions about the specific privilege and power of certain humans in fostering relations that are dangerous or violent toward the other species they are entangled with, Pedersen continues, this posthumanist desire: "much like anthropocentrism, operates in the opposite direction: Rather than disturbing species boundaries, it does a colonial work of reinscribing them" (73).

Tensions do not just exist between vegan praxis and posthumanism but also between this body of theory and vegan *studies*. Vegan scholarship has criticized posthumanism not only for failing to offer a firm grounding for ethical action but also for overshadowing work—such as ecofeminism—that has similar conceptual aspirations but *does* offer this grounding (Wright, *Vegan Studies Project* 14). Indeed, Laura Wright suggests that these political and scholastic issues are connected: it is the erasure of ecofeminism by posthumanism, she argues, which has meant the former's ethical grounding in vegan praxis has also been displaced. As I explore in more depth below, this set of academic moves on the part of certain brands of posthumanist animal studies is what has resulted in veganism being seen as at odds with posthumanism's conception of the world as irreducibly complex and entangled. While I conclude this chapter by reframing vegan praxis as something that, instead, offers a possible response for navigating this complexity, to set the stage for this argument it is important to develop a clearer understanding of how tensions between posthumanism and vegan studies arose in the first place. I now turn to Wolfe and Haraway as two thinkers who are useful for drawing out these debates.

Beyond "the human"? Cary Wolfe and Donna Haraway

Although both Haraway and Wolfe have been hailed as central figures in posthumanist animal studies, the specific disciplinary fields in which their work has gained purchase are slightly different. Haraway has perhaps held more universal appeal and continues to be engaged with in science and technology studies (her disciplinary home), but her work has also gained a considerable following in the social sciences and in social and cultural geography, in addition to cultural and literary theory more broadly. Wolfe has been similarly influential in the theoretical humanities, but less so in the context of fields that have a more social-scientific grounding. In light of the heterogeneous body of work that is beginning to coalesce around the label of vegan studies—which spans from literary and cultural studies-focused scholarship (e.g., Wright *Through a Vegan Studies Lens*, "Vegan Studies and Ecocriticism"); to more sociologically oriented research (e.g., Castricano and Simonsen, *Critical Perspectives on Veganism*)—both theorists thus have ongoing resonance to the emerging field.

Wolfe's *Animal Rites* and *What is Posthumanism?*

Wolfe's much-cited definition of posthumanism describes this body of thought as: "a historical moment in which the decentring of the human by its imbrication in technical, medical, informatics, and economic networks is increasingly impossible to ignore, a historical development that points to the necessity of new theoretical paradigms" (Wolfe, *What is Posthumanism?* xv–xvi). Wolfe finds the resources to develop these paradigms in continental philosophy and literary theory, drawing on Derrida in particular to ground his interrogation of how the human is predicated on the exclusion of the animal. In earlier works such as *Animal Rites*, for instance, Wolfe marshals a number of complex texts—from psychoanalytic theory to Deleuzian materialism as well as deconstruction—in order to trace various process of subjectification that have constituted the category "human" in Anglo-European thought systems by distinguishing it from the animal. These distinctions, he argues, are what make it "institutionally taken for granted that it is alright to systematically exploit and kill nonhuman animals simply because of their species" (*Animal Rites* 8).

Notably, although Wolfe's work has been seen as erasing ecofeminism, *Animal Rites* does situate its critique in the wake of thinkers such as Carol Adams. In the book's introduction, for instance, Wolfe anticipates potential criticism of his attempts to dismantle the human:

> It is understandable, of course, that traditionally marginalized peoples would be sceptical about calls by academic intellectuals to surrender the humanist model of subjectivity, with all its privileges, at just the historical moment when they are poised to "graduate" into it. (7)

To ameliorate these concerns, he argues it is precisely this understanding of the human subject, as predicated on the distinctiveness of the human as "species," which reinforces other forms of discrimination. In Wolfe's terms: as long as "the humanist discourse of species" exists it "will always be available for use against other humans as well" who can be Othered due to socially constructed notions of difference (8). In support of this argument, he holds up Adams's *Sexual Politics of Meat* as an instance where these connections between different oppressions have already been firmly articulated. As Fraiman (2012) points out, however, Wolfe's theoretical emphasis, as well as his subsequent influence, is rooted in other lineages of continental philosophy. In particular, Wolfe's explication of Derrida's concept of "carnophallogocentrism" (97–121)—or examination of how species discourse is reproduced via exclusions that render other beings legitimately consumable or exploitable for human benefit—has played an important role in shaping the contours of animal studies.

At the same time, and in part because of, the uptake of Wolfe and other posthumanist thinkers within animal studies in the early 2000s, the field as a whole began to fracture. CAS, for instance, was founded explicitly to redress the allegedly apolitical tendencies of mainstream animal studies. These tendencies, it was argued, were fueled by the theoretical obscurantism of posthumanism distracting from the relationship between animal studies and concrete political change (e.g., Best, "Rise of Critical Animal Studies"). These debates set the stage for subsequent tensions between posthumanism and vegan studies, for while vegan ethics has consistently been held up as central to CAS (e.g., Taylor and Twine 12) such a stance is difficult to reconcile with posthumanism's critique of normative rights and advocacy frameworks (for an overview of key frictions see Giraud, "Beasts of Burden" and "Veganism as Affirmative Biopolitics"). In part these tensions have been fueled by the reductive way veganism has been portrayed by certain posthumanist texts (as discussed in more depth below), which often fail to recognize the complexities of embodied vegan praxis (cf. Hamilton, "Sex, Work, Meat") or engage with more recent work that is less hostile toward theory and has sought to refine and complicate how veganism is understood. For instance, despite scholarship that has been hugely influential in CAS—such as A. Breeze Harper's early call for a vegan studies that centers intersecting oppressions and recognizes that single-issue veganism itself is not enough to address the complexity of food systems—two-dimensional stereotypes about veganism still often persist when it is evoked in posthumanist animal studies.

Wolfe's later *What is Posthumanism?* perhaps most fully delineates, and indeed concretizes, how and why points of tension between posthumanism and CAS's vegan ethics emerged. As a whole the book offers a complex overview of a theoretical work that has challenged both the notion of discreet species (i.e., the human/animal boundary) and any sense of boundary between organism and environment (drawing on systems and cybernetic theory that has shown how organisms are constituted by and through feedback from their environs; see Hayles, *How we became Posthuman*). But while Wolfe's book focuses on "posthumanizing" knowledge production that has conventionally been grounded on notions of the knowing human subject, aspects of the text further his earlier critique of conventional frameworks used in animal activism.

What is Posthumanism? builds directly on criticisms raised in *Animal Rites*, notably Wolfe's previous argument that the approach adopted by animal advocacy groups "takes for granted and reproduces a rather traditional version of … the discourse of species—a discourse that in turn reproduces the institution of *speciesism*" (2). He subsequently builds on these concerns, dedicating a chapter in *What is Posthumanism?* to fleshing out different perspectives within animal studies, which culminates in a diagram setting out different conceptual standpoints (125). Animal rights and liberation perspectives appear in the bottom right corner of this schema, described as a form of "humanist posthumanism." At the far left, in contrast, are thinkers such as Donna Haraway, whose work is positioned as a "posthumanist posthumanism." Humanist posthumanism, Wolfe suggests, attempts to extend ethical value beyond the human but undercuts its own aims by using humanist frameworks—and notions of social justice—to do so (see Milburn, this book, for a more complicated narrative about such approaches). The inference in *What is Posthumanism?*, then, is that conventional animal rights and/or liberation praxis contradicts itself by shoring up value systems that are rooted in anthropocentric norms. Also inferred is that Haraway—and others categorized in this way—offers a more radical approach that not only unsettles the human but also the humanism that sustains human exceptionalism, in refusing existing knowledge systems and advocacy frameworks. While "humanist posthumanism" reinscribes notions of species and preserves space for speciesism, "posthumanist posthumanism" works to dismantle these constructs.

Wolfe's schematic has significant implications, in that it effectively positions conventional frameworks used in activism as a retrograde approach in comparison with more radical posthumanist approaches. This stance, moreover, is not unique to Wolfe. Other otherwise nuanced and thoughtful overviews of developments in animal studies have also framed "critical" approaches and vegan ethics as clinging onto the vestiges of humanism, inferring that these approaches both undercut their own aims and lag behind more conceptually radical work (e.g., Lorimer, "multinatural geographies"; Buller, "animal geographies III"). The danger of this line of argument is that it obscures other, far less radical implications that posthumanism itself might have (as identified by Pedersen in the opening discussion). As Pedersen points out, even though this body of theory might unsettle certain speciesist discourses, the capacity of posthumanism to offer a more fundamental disruption of species hierarchies is undermined by its refusal to fundamentally question the material practices that sustain these discourses. This is a slightly complex argument, so to fully grasp it, it is useful to turn to another thinker who lies at the heart of these debates: Donna Haraway.

Haraway: from ethical responsibility to response-ability

Although Wolfe cites Haraway's work as offering some of the foundations for posthumanism, she herself disavows the term, arguing that it still centralizes humans by positioning a generalized concept of "the human" as the primary entity that needs to be transgressed (*When Species Meet* 16–17). This concern has been strengthened by her more recent work, with texts such as *Staying with the Trouble* (2016) pointing out the danger of using labels such as "Anthropocene," because such terminology centers a homogenized version of "the human" (as something opposed to and damaging "nature") at the very moment when less anthropocentric ways of conceiving of and acting in the world need to be crafted.

As an alternative framework to posthumanism, Haraway instead offers the more "rambunctious" concept of companion species, with this term referring not just to human–animal relations but underlining that all nonhumans are "lively" entities in their own right (see Bennett *Vibrant Matter*), which have "agency" to shape the world in particular ways (see Latour, *Reassembling the Social*). One of the other ways Haraway's "companion species" exceed Wolfe's account of posthumanism is in insisting that human exceptionalism has *always* been illusory. Building on Bruno Latour's *We Have Never Been Modern* (1993), which sees the nature/culture dichotomy as a modern phenomenon that hides hybrid relations between species that blur this boundary, Haraway entitles the first section of *When Species Meet* "We Have Never Been Human." Haraway, in other words, sees the destabilization of the human not as something that has emerged suddenly with the advent of digital media technologies or the product of new-found vulnerability in the midst of environmental catastrophe. Instead, she emphasizes that humans have always been dependent on and profoundly shaped by their relationships with animals.

To underline the illusory nature of human exceptionalism, Haraway's work charts entanglements between humans and animals that have mutually transformed both partners. This argument is scaffolded by the work of thinkers such as Karen Barad, notably Barad's concept of intra-action, a term that is deliberately set in opposition to inter-action: or the idea of two distinct entities—say, a human and a dog—engaging with one another. Instead, the concept of intra-action suggests that what it means to *be* either human or canine has only emerged through these encounters. These mutually transformative intra-actions occur on different scales and temporalities: From long processes of co-evolution that have shaped the living patterns and even the physical attributes of each partner, to microbial exchanges between companion species and humans sharing households on an everyday level. For Haraway, in other words, the relation is the foundational unit for understanding the world, as nothing exists outside of its relations with other beings. Any ethics, correspondingly, has to use the relation (rather than the notion of separation, protection or distance) as its starting point.

For many in animal studies more broadly, Haraway's emphasis on the co-shaping encounters between humans and animals has been ethically important in redistributing agency so that certain humans are no longer held up as having sole dominion over the so-called "natural world." Yet while this line of argument has proven valuable in departing from anthropocentrism in one sense, it has given rise to other tensions. Unlike other thinkers who have eroded distinctions between humans and nonhumans (e.g., those working within object-oriented ontology; see Bogost, 2009), Haraway recognizes that the distribution of agency is not symmetrical, as humans have the disproportionate power over the lives (and deaths) of animals. While this recognition is important, her emphasis on relational ethics makes it difficult to critique, let alone intervene in, relationships that might harm or exploit nonhuman animals: and it is this difficulty that has both put her at odds with CAS and the wider project of vegan studies.

Haraway, like Wolfe, is directly suspicious of animal advocacy frameworks, accusing them of inadvertent anthropomorphism and anthropocentrism: "we do not get very far with the categories generally used by animal rights discourses, in which animals end up as permanent dependents ('lesser humans'), utterly natural ('nonhuman'), or exactly the same ('humans in fur suits')" (*When Species Meet* 67). Although these concerns were reiterated in the wake of *When Species Meet*, in both Haraway's own work (see Haraway, "Species Matters, Humane Advocacy") and beyond, her arguments build on far longer concerns regarding the paternalistic dynamics of advocacy. In "The Promises of Monsters," published in the early 90s, for instance, Haraway is already concerned about the way the nature/culture dichotomy is not just inscribed by those seeking to justify domination over the more-than-human world, but reproduced by advocacy groups that wish to contest this domination. Such approaches, she argues, perpetuate hierarchical relationships between particular humans and the rest of the world, by positioning activists as being in a privileged position to speak for a passive nature. More, for Haraway, advocacy frameworks often shut down or deny the irreducible complexity of the world by trying to create distance and separation between species when their prior intra-actions mean this is impossible.

Instead of the responsibilities fostered through conventional rights and advocacy frameworks, Haraway draws on other thinkers, such as Vinciane Despret and Isabelle Stengers, to argue for situated forms of *response-ability* that emerge from relations with animals. What Haraway means by this concept of response-ability is that rather than imposing ready-made, defined-in-advance frameworks (such as rights, social justice, or vegan ethics) instead it is necessary to respond in situated ways to our existing, irreducibly entangled, relations with animals. One of the key ways of doing this, she suggests, is through creating space for being affected by animals in ways that attune us to their requirements. Through spending time with animals and paying attention to how they express themselves, Haraway argues that it becomes possible to learn how they signify their needs and be responsive to these needs in ways that move beyond anthropomorphism (i.e., beyond the "humans in fur coats" logic she attributes to animal advocacy).

Although Haraway herself is wary of veganism, this line of argument *has* been (critically) taken up in certain contexts to support a vegan ethics. In *Entangled Empathy* (2015), for example, Lori Gruen has used the recognition that humans are entangled with nonhumans as a framework for thinking about how more ethical relations can emerge. For Gruen, an entangled empathy that emerges from existing relations with animals can exceed the limitations of rights and liberation approaches—which she argues are not as effective in practice as they are on paper—by illustrating the social and political change that can be brought about through being open to animals affecting us emotionally. In subsequent work, Gruen has argued, moreover:

> That we are already, necessarily, in these relations should move us toward more conscientious ethical reflection and engagement … Relationships of exploitation or complete instrumentalization, which is how we might characterize the bulk of our relationships with other animals at the moment, are precisely the sorts of relationships that should change. ("What Motivates Us to Change What We Eat?" 2)

However, arguments in favor of relational ethics have also been used to support more welfarist approaches in contexts that map onto the very sites of exploitation and instrumentalization Gruen is criticizing. Despret, for example, draws on Temple Grandin's work in slaughterhouses to argue that the act of fostering felt understanding and attentiveness toward animal needs can be used to refine the slaughter process. Although such an approach might improve animal welfare, it is far from the sustained critique of human–animal relations offered by ecofeminism. Indeed, the fact that relational ethics can be applied at all to such contexts is why Adams sought to critique Haraway's initial *Companion Species Manifesto*. For Adams, Haraway's relational ethics is dangerous not just because it offers "an impatient … dismissal of 'animal rights'" ("An Animal Manifesto" 125), or because it involves "the categorical disparagement of animal rights that, with a broad sweep includes even those animal advocates who challenge 'rights language', a large majority of whom are women" (125). Instead, Adams suggests that there is something intrinsically worrying about grounding an ethics in recognition of entanglement and relationality between species, if this means that even categories such as "livestock" can be rendered an "untouchable natureculture intersection" (126).

These tensions are compounded by the explicit criticisms that Haraway and others have leveled at veganism. Throughout *When Species Meet*, for instance, veganism is evoked as a totalizing ethical approach that offers false moral solace by failing to recognize that no way of eating avoids violence (80). These arguments are underlined by Haraway's final chapter, "Parting Bites," which discusses tensions arising from a departmental event when vegan faculty clashed with another staff member who wanted to serve meat from a hog he had hunted. Haraway's conclusion, that the problem is dogmatism rather than a particular practice in and of itself, has resulted in concern that—taken to its extreme—posthumanism can become a form of relativism that defers scope for making any form of clear ethical decision at all. To revisit Adams's critique: "Perhaps an academic finds ambivalences more acceptable than the activist, who desires something more tangible: non-ambivalent action. And perhaps it is an 'easy out'—sweeping away difficult questions because it appears the answer, i.e. 'rights language', is wrong" (126). These arguments resonate with my own research, where I elucidate how an overly hasty embrace of pluralism has long been seen as problematic in activist contexts, because advocating a diversity of consumption practices often means that normative eating patterns are allowed to continue as normal, in ways that shut down reflection on what alternatives to the status quo might look like (*What Comes After Entanglement?* 88).

Since *When Species Meet*, Haraway's stance on activism has shifted, in part due to interventions by Adams (who she describes as being in "allied friction" with; Haraway, "Staying with the Manifesto" 56) and dialogues with scholars such as Annie Potts (whose work has made important critical interventions into meat cultures in its own right). In an interview with Sarah Franklin, Haraway reflects on these tensions stating that she "hadn't paid adequate attention to the conditions of labor for animals and human beings in industrial-animal factories" and values the way that "vegan feminists called me to account" ("Staying with the Manifesto" 55–6). Now, she continues, she has "a profound respect for veganism as a kind of witness, as a kind of No, a kind of loud No! as well as an affirmative politics" (56). While such discussions are generative, they nonetheless perpetuate tensions as even here vegan ethics remains framed as a politics of refusal. What this framing misses out, I suggest, is scholarship that has explored the *new* relationalities with food systems that could be opened up through vegan praxis (as explored in early initiatives by the Vegan Society and persist today in attempts to craft veganic agriculture; see Cole, "The Greatest Cause on Earth"), a point I revisit in the conclusion.

Before moving to these concluding thoughts, however, I wish to shift the focus slightly; to use Haraway's turn of phrase the relationship between posthumanism and scholarship committed to vegan praxis has often been one of "allied friction" and—though my focus here has been on this friction—more productive exchanges also exist that are worth dwelling on in more depth.

Future potentials

Although tensions have often made for fraught dialogue between vegan praxis and posthumanism, there have been increasing attempts to navigate these tensions and reframe critical approaches more generally and vegan praxis specifically not as relics of humanism but approaches that contribute to dislodging anthropocentrism (for divergent responses to this task see the work of Matthew Calarco, Tom Tyler, or Patricia MaCormack, or the valuable research gathered together in Seán McCorry and John Miller's *Literature and Meat Since 1900* for instance).

In the context of literary and cultural theory Emilia Quinn and Benjamin Westwood's edited collection *Thinking Veganism in Literature and Culture: Towards a Vegan Theory* contains a number of essays that explore the theoretical provocations veganism offers. Robert McKay's essay "A Vegan Form of Life," for instance, combines queer theory with Derridean notions of carnophallogocentrism to explore how certain conceptions of "the human" are distinguished from the "animal" through everyday practices of animal product consumption, in order to position veganism as something that disrupts such processes of demarcation. Tom Tyler's "Trojan Horses," in contrast, reframes the frictions between posthumanism and veganism as themselves productive, tracing how criticisms by thinkers such as Haraway have created opportunities for other scholarship not only to counter stereotypes but offer affirmative arguments in favor of vegan praxis.

Although it has taken more time for critical engagements with posthumanism to make inroads into conventionally humanistic disciplines such as Sociology, here too dialogue has begun to emerge. In part these inroads are due to the longstanding efforts of thinkers at the borders of CAS and posthumanism, such as Erika Cudworth, who has offered persuasive illustrations of the need to expand the boundaries of the social to nonhuman animals (e.g., as in her excellent monograph *Social Lives with Other Animals*). What is notable about Cudworth is that her work utilizes posthumanism at the same time as engaging with rather than erasing the legacies of ecofeminism.

Unlike other posthumanist texts, for Cudworth, the recognition that "social and natural systems are co-constituted" is not a reason to celebrate relationality, but a jumping off point for understanding the specific institutional arrangements that make some of these relationships exploitative, with the aim of creating possibilities for change. To understand "farmed animal agriculture," she argues, it is vital to position it as "an integral element of a social system of species relations in which domesticate nonhuman animals are oppressed" and that "is also constituted by relations of capital, colonialism and patriarchy and shaped in important ways by intra-human difference" ("Intersectionality, Species and Social Domination" 101). Disrupting these relationships, Cudworth suggests in a different essay, demands "analysis of the processes of historical change, in its attention to both the power of ideas and beliefs and the analysis of concrete social practices" ("Beyond Speciesism" 32). Her work traces how ecofeminism can play an important role in grasping the dynamics of aspects of these processes, such as the specific violences faced by female animals in particular contexts. At the same time, Cudworth is wary of using one set of oppressive relations as an explanatory lens for grasping all others, hence her preference for posthumanist-inflected notions of webs of relations as a means of articulating this complexity.

What Cudworth points toward in drawing different theoretical perspectives together is potential not just for more productive conversations between posthumanism and vegan studies, therefore, but the way that social-scientific work—with its focus on situated social practices and institutional arrangements—could play an important role in using its disciplinary tools to further such dialogue. The focus on specific institutions offered by Cudworth, in other words, could help further the aims of vegan studies, by showing how particular practices, which unfold in particular settings, undermine posthumanism's conceptual attempts to unsettle species discourse. This approach, in other words, elucidates why—though a useful analytical framework for moving beyond anthropocentrism—a posthumanist recognition of entanglement and complexity is not enough in itself to tackle the type of questions being pushed for in vegan studies about how to realize alternative relationships between human and nonhuman animals.

Conclusion

In summary, just as the relationship between vegan studies and the other "prongs" (to use Wright's phrasing) of animal studies are complex, so is the field's relation with posthumanism. Firstly, posthumanism itself is a messy category, which goes beyond texts that are strictly defined in this way to encompass both those who actively reject the label (Haraway) and poststructuralist theories preceding the term (Derrida), in addition to work that actively uses the label (Wolfe). Secondly, the ethical commitments and practices articulated by posthumanism and vegan studies, respectively, often lie in conflict. In part, these conflicts relate to veganism's association with other forms of animal rights praxis (as articulated by CAS), which are often framed as part of an anthropocentric humanist project that clashes with the more radically non-anthropocentric aims of posthumanism. As ongoing debates between vegan-feminist scholarship and Haraway show, despite dialogue slowly becoming more productive, vegan praxis remains framed as a politics of refusal and disengagement rather than an opening for reflecting on how food systems could be organized differently.

What I have hoped to elucidate here is that—despite and perhaps because of its "allied frictions" with vegan praxis—posthumanism could still hold value moving forward. In particular, the specificity with which posthumanism approaches questions about the relationship between anthropocentric practice and species discourse and its resistance to universalizing ethical frameworks offers a degree of analytical nuance. That said, posthumanism itself has been accused of universalism in its homogenization of "the human" that needs to be moved beyond (e.g., as pointed out in powerful critiques by Zakiyyah Iman Jackson, Juanita Sundberg, and Kim TallBear). In my own work I have built on these criticisms to make a slightly different point. One of the problems with posthumanism is that in some contexts what is important is less finding ethical value in entanglement and more the task fostering distance and detachment from animals in ethically responsible ways (cf. Latimer, "Being Alongside"; Ginn, "Sticky Lives"). At present posthumanism offers little in the way of coordinates for approaching this task. Future dialogue with vegan praxis could, I suggest, offer a means of honing in on these questions by elucidating how the situated response-ability emphasized by Haraway should not come at the expense of more sustained questions about the ethical *responsibilities* of certain humans, in specific institutional and cultural contexts, for shoring up structural oppressions.

Works cited

Adams, Carol J. "An Animal Manifesto Gender, Identity, and Vegan-Feminism in the Twenty-First Century." Interview by Tom Tyler. *Parallax*, vol. 12, no. 1, 2006, pp. 120–128.

———. *The Sexual Politics of Meat: A Feminist Vegetarian Critical Theory*, 2nd edition. Continuum, 2000.

Alaimo, Stacy. *Exposed: Environmental Politics and Pleasures in Posthuman Times*. University of Minnesota Press, 2016.

Barad, Karen. *Meeting the Universe Halfway*. Duke University Press, 2007.

Bennett, Jane. *Vibrant Matter: A Political Ecology of Things*. Duke University Press, 2010.

Best, Steve. "The rise of Critical Animal Studies." *Journal for Critical Animal Studies*, vol. 7, no. 1, 2009, pp. 9–52.

Bogost, Ian. *Alien Phenomenology*. University of Minnesota Press, 2009.

Braidotti, Rosi. *The Posthuman*. Polity, 2013.

Buller, Henry. "Animal Geographies III: Ethics." *Progress in Human Geography*, vol. 40, no. 3, 2016, pp. 422–430.

Calarco, Matthew. *Zoographies: The Question of the Animal from Heidegger to Derrida*. Columbia University Press, 2008.

Castricano, Jodey, and Rasmus R. Simonsen, eds. *Critical Perspectives on Veganism*. Palgrave Macmillan, 2016.

Castree, Noel, et al. "Mapping Posthumanism: An Exchange." *Environment and Planning A*, vol. 36, no.8, 2004, pp. 1341–1363.

Cole, Matthew. "'The Greatest Cause on Earth': The Historical Formation of Veganism as an Ethical Practice." *The Rise of Critical Animal Studies, from the Margins to the Center*, edited by Nik Taylor and Richard Twine, Routledge, 2014, pp. 203–224.

Cudworth, Erika. "Beyond Speciesism: Intersectionality, Critical Sociology and the Human Domination of Other Animals." *The Rise of Critical Animal Studies, from the Margins to the Center*, edited by Nik Taylor and Richard Twine, Routledge, 2014, pp. 19–35.

Cudworth, Erika. "Intersectionality, Species and Social Domination." *Anarchism and Animal Liberation*, edited by Anthony J. Nocella II, Richard White and Erika Cudworth, McFarland, 2015, pp. 93–107.

———. *Social Lives with Other Animals: Tales of Sex, Death and Love*. Palgrave MacMillan, 2011.

Despret, Vinciane. "Responding Bodies and Partial Affinities in Human—Animal Worlds." *Theory, Culture & Society*, vol. 30, no.7–8, 2013, pp. 51–76.

Fraiman, Susan. "Pussy Panic Versus Liking Animals: Tracking Gender in Animal Studies." *Critical Inquiry*, vol. 39, no.1, 2012, pp. 89–115.

Ginn, Franklin. "Sticky Lives: Slugs, Detachment and More-than-Human Ethics in the Garden." *Transactions of the Institute of British Geographers*, vol. 39, no. 4, 2014, pp. 532–544.

Giraud, Eva. "Beasts of Burden: Productive Tensions between Haraway and Radical Animal Rights Activism." *Culture, Theory and Critique*, vol. 54, no. 1, 2013a, pp. 102–120.

———. "Veganism as Affirmative Biopolitics." *PhaenEx*, vol. 8, no. 2, 2013b, pp. 47–79.

———. *What Comes After entanglement? Activism, Anthropocentrism and an Ethics of Exclusion*. Duke University Press, 2019.

Gruen, Lori. *Entangled Empathy: An Alternative Ethic for our Relationships with Animals*. Lantern Books, 2015.

———. "What Motivates Us to Change What We Eat?" *The Philosopher*, vol. 108, no. 1, 2020, pp. 39–43.

Hamilton, Carrie. "Sex, Work, Meat: The Feminist Politics of Veganism." *Feminist Review*, vol. 114, no. 1, pp. 112–129.

Haraway, Donna. *The Companion Species Manifesto: Dogs, People, and Significant Otherness*. Prickly Paradigm Press, 2003.

———. "The Promises of Monsters." *Cultural Studies*, edited by Lawrence Grossberg, Cary Nelson, and Paula Treichler, New York: Routledge, 1992, pp. 295–337.

———. "Species Matters, Humane Advocacy." *Species Matters: Humane Advocacy and Cultural Theory*, edited by Marianne DeKoven and Michael Lundblad, Columbia University Press, 2011, pp. 17–23.

———. "Staying with the Manifesto: An Interview with Donna Haraway." Interview by Sarah Franklin, *Theory, Culture & Society*, vol. 34, no. 4, 2017, pp. 49–63.

———. *Staying with the Trouble*. Duke University Press, 2016.

———. *When Species Meet*. University of Minnesota Press, 2008.

Harper, A. Breeze. "Race as a 'feeble matter' in Veganism." *Journal for Critical Animal Studies*, vol. 8, no. 3, 2010, pp. 5–27.

Hayles, N. Katherine. *How We Became Posthuman*. University of Chicago Press, 1999.

Jackson, Zakiyyah Iman. *Becoming Human: Matter and Meaning in an Antiblack World*. New York University Press, 2020.

Latimer, Joanna. "Being Alongside: Rethinking Relations Amongst Different Kinds." *Theory, Culture & Society*, vol. 30, no. 7–8, 2013, pp. 77–104.

Latour, Bruno. *Reassembling the Social*. Oxford University Press, 2005.

———. *We Have Never Been Modern*. Harvard University Press, 1993.

Lorimer, Jamie. "Multinatural Geographies for the Anthropocene." *Progress in Human Geography*, vol. 36, no. 5, 2012, pp. 593–612.

Lorimer, Jamie. *Wildlife in the Anthropocene: Conservation after Nature*. University of Minnesota Press, 2015.

MacCormack, Patricia. *The Ahuman Manifesto: Activism for the End of the Anthropocene*. London: Bloomsbury, 2020.

McCorry, Seán, and John Miller. *Literature and Meat Since 1900*. Palgrave Macmillan, 2019.

McKay, Robert. "A Vegan Form of Life." *Thinking Veganism in Literature and Culture*, edited by Emilia Quinn and Benjamin Westwood, Palgrave MacMillan, 2018, pp. 249–272.

Pedersen, Helena. "Release the Moths: Critical Animal Studies and the Posthumanist Impulse." *Culture, Theory and Critique*, vol. 52, no. 1, 2011, pp. 65–81.

Potts, Annie, editor. *Meat Culture*. Brill, 2016.

———. "Kiwi Chicken Advocate talks with Californian Dog Companion." *Feminism & Psychology*, vol. 20, no. 3, 2010, pp. 318–336.

Probyn, Elspeth. *Eating the Ocean*. Duke University Press, 2016.

Puig de la Bellacasa, Maria. *Matters of Care: Speculative Ethics in More-than-Human Worlds*. University of Minnesota Press, 2016.

———. "Matters of Care in technoscience: Assembling Neglected Things." *Social Studies of Science*, vol. 41, no .1, 2011, pp. 85–106.

Quinn, Emelia, and Benjamin Westwood, editors. *Thinking Veganism in Literature and Culture: Towards a Vegan Theory*. Palgrave Macmillan, 2018.

Rose, Deborah Bird, Thom van Dooren, and Matthew Chrulew. *Extinction Studies: Stories of Time, Death and Generations*. Columbia University Press, 2017.

Shotwell, Alexis. *Against Purity*. University of Minnesota Press, 2017.

Stephens Griffin, Nathan. *Understanding Veganism: Biography and Identity*. Routledge, 2017.
Sundberg, Juanita. "Decolonizing Posthumanist Geographies." *Cultural Geographies*, vol. 21, no. 1, 2014, pp. 33–47.
TallBear, Kim. "Beyond the Life/Not Life Binary: A Feminist-Indigenous Reading of Cryopreservation, Interspecies Thinking and the New Materialisms." *Cryopolitics: Frozen Life in a Melting World*, edited by Joanna Radin and Emma Kowal, MIT Press, 2017, pp. 179–200.
Twine, Richard. *Animals as Biotechnology: Ethics, Sustainability and Critical Animal Studies*. Earthscan/Routledge, 2010.
Tyler, Tom. *Ciferae: A Bestiary in Five Fingers*. University of Minnesota Press, 2012.
———. "Trojan horses." *Thinking Veganism in Literature and Culture*, edited by Emilia Quinn and Benjamin Westwood, Palgrave MacMillan, pp. 107–124.
Van Dooren, Thom. *Flight Ways: Life and Loss at the Edge of Extinction*. Columbia University Press, 2014.
Weisberg, Zipporah. "The Broken Promises of Monsters: Haraway, Animals and the Humanist Legacy." *Journal for Critical Animal Studies*, vol. 7, no. 2, 2009, pp. 22–62.
Whatmore, Sarah. "Materialist Returns: Practising Cultural Geography in and for a More-than-Human world." *Cultural Geographies*, vol. 13, no. 4, 2006, pp. 600–609.
Wolfe, Cary. *Animal Rites: American Culture, the Discourse of Species, and Posthumanist Theory*. University of Chicago Press, 2003.
———. *Before the Law: Humans and Other Animals in a Biopolitical Frame*. University of Chicago Press, 2012.
———. *What is Posthumanism?* Minneapolis: University of Minnesota Press, 2010.
Wright, Laura, editor. *Through a Vegan Studies Lens: Textual Ethics and Lived Activism*. University of Nevada Press, 2019.
———, editor. "Vegan Studies and Ecocriticism." Special cluster *ISLE: Interdisciplinary Studies in Literature and Environment*, vol. 24, no. 4, 2018, pp. 737–802.
———. *The Vegan Studies Project: Food, Animals, and Gender in the Age of Terror*, University of Georgia Press, 2015.

Part 2
Vegan studies in the disciplines
Humanities

6
Vegan literature for children
Epistemic resistance, agency, and the Anthropocene

Marzena Kubisz

Visitors at the exhibition "Marvellous and Mischievous: Literatures' Young Rebels," hosted by the British Library from November 2019 to March 2020, may leave the exhibition rooms with a conviction that literature for children is vibrant, responsive to contemporary challenges, and ready to engage young readers in the issues many adults find difficult to handle. Next to such well-known characters as Mary Lennox (*The Secret Garden* by Frances Hodgson Burnett), Pippi Longstocking (*Pippi Longstocking* by Astrid Lindgren), and Max (*Where the Wild Things Are* by Maurice Sendak), there appears a colorful gang of modern protagonists who, as the organizers explain, "break rules and defy conventions to make the world a better place for others": Julian (*Julian is a Mermaid* by Jessica Love) wants to be a mermaid and his adventures support transgender children in their own identity quest, Ahmed (*The Boy at the Back of the Class* by Onjali Q. Raúf) is a refugee from Syria whose dramatic experiences mobilize his school colleagues to help, and Clarise Bean (*What Planet Are You From, Clarise Bean?* by Lauren Child) stands up to protect an old tree.

The timing of the exhibition is not accidental. Organized at the time when children of the world, inspired by Greta Thunberg, demonstrate their determination to fight for a future already jeopardized by the greed and environmental myopia of the adults, the exhibition highlights children's creativity, empathy, sensitivity, and sensibility. It also shows that contemporary children's books are taking up the most demanding and complex social, political, and emotional issues. The wide choice of books whose protagonists are confronted by "adult problems," such as a refugee crisis, sexual identity, or environmental emergency, is emblematic of the fact that literature for children is facing new challenges. As Katherine Rundell, the author of *Rooftoppers* and *The Good Thieves*, observes:

> [a]s the world transforms so swiftly, children's fiction needs new, ever-more-various stories, from all across this kaleidoscopic planet on which we stand—already it has begun, but we need more; new ideas, new mediums, from places and voices we've hitherto failed to listen to: new jokes, new riches. (58)

This newness is exactly what the exhibition shows: "new jokes, new riches." But it also shows one more thing: that there is a "niche inside of a niche" (Roth) which is occupied by vegan literature. Ever more popular among readers and authors committed to raising our awareness of animal suffering, vegan diet, sustainable living, and ecological alertness, vegan literature for children enjoys what one may term "invisible visibility." While veganism is not only becoming more common as a lifestyle and philosophy, it is also gradually changing its legal status: in January 2020 an employment tribunal judge in Norwich, England, ruled that veganism classifies as a philosophical belief (Drewett). And yet the omission of vegan rebels in the British Library exhibition's coverage of children's books demonstrates the reading world's failure to acknowledge the rise of vegan literature and to grant it the recognition it deserves. Hopefully, it is only a matter of time before vegan literature for children, as well as other forms of children's involvement with vegan cultures, will find its place in the general history of children's literature, cultural history of vegetarianism and veganism, and in vegan studies. Matthew Cole and Kate Stewart's analysis of the representations of human–animal relations in vegan children's literature in *Our Children and Other Animals* and Marjorie Koljonen's article "Thinking and Caring Boys Go Vegan: Two European Books That Introduce Vegan Identity to Children," two of the main academic examinations of the topic to have appeared so far, provide vital points of departure for vegan critical readings of the literature in question.

If we approach vegan literature for children as a sub-genre of children's literature which familiarizes young readers with the questions of both vegetarianism and veganism (the term veganism was introduced in 1944; before that time veganism did not exist as named and separate form of dietary regime and did not have its own identity as a social movement), we realize that it is and, at the same time, is not a new literary–cultural phenomenon. On the one hand, it is true to say that the 21st century has witnessed an unprecedented explosion of vegan books for children, thus prompting us to think that the type of children's literature which addresses the relevance of ethical food choices is indeed the product of the "vegan turn" (Wright, "Vegans in" 35–38). On the other hand, however, it is also true to say that the popularization of a vegetarian diet among children in the form of stories written for young readers was a distinctive feature of Victorian and Edwardian vegetarian cultures, in which "[c]hildren became an important target audience" (Gregory 148). As the last decades of the 19th century and the beginning of the 20th century produced a variety of vegetarian narratives aimed at children, they can be seen as an early stage in the history of vegan literature for children, allowing us to place it in the wider context of the cultural history of vegetarianism and veganism. Viewed in this light, the term "vegan literature for children" is inclusive and embraces both *vegetarian* literature for children (mainly vegetarian magazines and short stories) created in the late 19th and early 20th centuries, and contemporary *vegan* books (fiction, non-fiction, poetry, cook-books) published in the 20th and 21st centuries.[1]

To establish a sense of continuity and change in the development of vegan children-oriented narratives in Western culture, it is worth looking at the Victorian vegetarian societies that played a significant role in the promotion and popularization of vegetarian diet among children. The Vegetarian Society had a children's section known as *The Daisy Society* which published a 16-page long magazine for children called *The Daisy Basket* (1893–1894), one of the first vegetarian magazines for children. Another English vegetarian society, The London Vegetarian Society, published a vegetarian magazine for children called *The Children's Garden. Magazine of the Juvenile Vegetarian Movement* (1900) whose editor-in-chief was Frances L. Boult. After her death the Society began publishing a new magazine: in 1906 the first issue of *The Children's Realm* came out.

Frances Boult was a dedicated promoter of children's vegetarianism, and in September 1897 she delivered a speech about "Organization of our Work Among Children" at the Vegetarian

International Congress in London. This was one of many instances of her commitment to the promotion of a meat-free diet among young Victorians, an issue situated high on the agenda of the vegetarian movement. According to Arnold Frank Hills, the author of the foreword in the first issue of *The Children's Realm*, Boult deeply believed that children's innocence may become a source of "redemptive energy" (Hills 1). Her mission was to "[g]ather in the children; teach them the wonders of Vegetarian truth; and make them be heralds of the coming Golden Age" (1). Boult was of the opinion that children should be instructed and educated by adults "for the triumphs of mercy and gentleness and kindness" (1). She also believed in the need to create Children's Branches, which would, as Hills put it, "serve as a nursery for the preparation of the little soldiers for the battle of good against wrong" (1).

While Boult was an editor and a campaigner, George Bedborough was one of the authors who wrote for the young vegetarians. His stories, which originally appeared in *The Children's Realm* and were later published by the Vegetarian Federal Union as *Stories from the Children's Realm* (1914), provide a principal source of knowledge about how and by what means literature for children was familiarizing them with the idea of meat-free diet. Didactic and openly moralizing—"the author has left his readers in no doubt as to the end he has in view" (Cole 3)—the volume, in a manner most typical of children's literature of the period, is dedicated to teaching young readers how to be "kind to each other and animals" (3). The book sees a vegetarian diet as a manifestation of human kindness to animals and an important element of human moral development.

After the period of lively growth for early vegan literature, the end of which may be placed symbolically in 1914 when the last issue of *The Children's Realm* was published, there follows a certain standstill in the development of vegan literature for children. Although the 20th century saw dynamic growth of animal rights movements, popularization of veganism and the rise of animal studies as well as environmentalism, ecocriticism, and environmental vegetarianism, vegan literature for children was not very common and did not form a literary phenomenon with its own distinctive literary and cultural identity. *The Shadow Castle* (1945) by Marian Cockrell and its vegetarian dragon, *Charlotte's Web* (1952) by E.B. White, which opens with the description of the girl saving a pig from being slaughtered, and *The BFG* (1982) by Roald Dahl, whose Big Friendly Giant, unlike his carnivorous relatives, is a strict vegetarian, are rare examples which demonstrate how vegetarianism (rather than veganism) was slowly reaching young readers.

The early years of the 21st century have witnessed a veritable explosion of vegan (rather than vegetarian) literature for children. Framed by the increasing popularity and viability of veganism (Joy and Tuider vi), and more and more frequent debates about the challenges of contemporary childhood, vegan literature for children started its (in)visible growth. While it is generally agreed that the first vegan book for children in this century was published in 2009 (*That is Why We Don't Eat Animals* by Ruby Roth), contemporary vegan literature for children has a forerunner. In 1994, British poet and performer Benjamin Zephaniah published a children's poetry collection entitled *Talking Turkeys*, the first of his series of other vegan volumes to be published in later years, which showed veganism as one of the strategies of building a better world for people and for animals, and which opened children's literature for ethical veganism. The year 1994 may thus be seen as the turning point in the history of vegan literature for children, initiating what may be called the Vegan Renaissance.

To adopt the term "the Vegan Renaissance" allows us to underline a sense of continuity in the development of children's vegan literature and to highlight the fact that what is often seen as the product of the present-day visibility of veganism is, in fact, the extension of a tradition which goes back to the 19th century when children were perceived as important participants in the creation of alternative social and cultural reality. The Vegan Renaissance is marked not only by an unprecedented proliferation of vegan literature for children in English but also by the influence that this literature has started to exercise internationally, inspiring literary representations of veganism in non-English speaking countries such as Germany, Spain, France, Finland (Koljonen 13), and Poland and Russia. Placed in the broader context of the history of vegetarianism and veganism and its exchanges with children's culture, the contemporary explosion of vegan publications for children appears to be the next stage in the not-so-short-as-you-may-think history of the pro-animal and children-oriented Western vegan narratives for young and very young readers. The latest vegan literature for children embraces a rich body of texts that vary in terms of mediums (websites and paperbacks), genres (nursery rhymes, poems, adventure books, fairy-tales, cook-books, and informative–educational publications) and narrative styles, which are determined by the age of readers and their reading levels.

If we agree with Katherine Rundell, who says that children's literature "stands alongside children" (6), then we will see that vegan literature for children stands alongside vegan children (and parents), and may accompany them in the process of vegan education in all stages of their cognitive, social, and emotional development. Teaching children what veganism is, explaining to them how a meat-free diet is connected to ecological concerns, helping young vegans to overcome the sense of alienation and frustration caused by a feeling that they can do little to alleviate animal suffering, and empowering them with a sense of vegan pride—these are the dimensions of vegan growth that can be assisted by literature which, like any good literature for children, has the power to "arm them for the life ahead with everything we can find that is true" (Rundell 4).

In vegan literary education the first contact with abstention from animal products is mediated by nursery rhymes, "little stories for little people" (Celia Lottridge qtd. in Mullen 47), designed to amuse children while supporting the development of their literacy skills. Among the sources which provide a wide range of vegan literature for children, the website *Vegan Children's Stories* by Violet Plum is one of the richest. In 2015, two years after starting the website, Plum published *Why are you a Vegan? and Other Wacky Verse for Kids*, which is a paper version of the stories and poems available at the website, including nursery rhymes. The same year saw the publication of another collection of poems for the youngest vegans, entitled simply *Vegan Nursery Rhymes*, soon followed by *More Vegan Nursery Rhymes*. Interestingly, the author Kate Foster, like Violet Plum, found traditional English nursery rhymes a great inspiration. Embedded in the long history of short songs and verses for children, which goes back to the 18th century when the first major written work containing traditional rhymes (*Tommy Thumb's Song Book*) was published, nursery rhymes have demonstrated their vitality and ability to adapt to new cultural conditions. Such well-known poems for children as "Baa Baa Black Sheep," "Old MacDonald had a farm," and "Higgledy Piggledy" have attracted the attention of both authors, who replaced the motifs of animal exploitation (wool taken from a sheep, eggs taken from hens) with images inspired by respect for animal life.

In the "Introduction" to the 2019 edition of her collection, Foster uncompromisingly refers to traditional nursery rhymes as "one of the earliest forms of indoctrination" (ii). Since one of the features of nursery rhymes is that they are passed from one generation to the next, they continue to reinforce what in the anthropocentric environment is believed to be a set of "sustaining truths to which we can return," to borrow a phrase from Rundell (5), at the heart of which operates the oppressive model of the human–animal relationship. Foster's intention is to break the tradition of learning rhymes which reinforce and support anthroparchy, and to provide vegan parents with an educational alternative, hoping that "one day *these* rhymes will become old fashioned, a part of history in a world that no longer tolerates the use and abuse of animals" (Foster iii). Vegan nursery rhymes offer the first lesson in anti-speciesist education and by challenging the representation of veganism as "a threat to a fundamental aspect of the hegemonic socialization process in the contemporary West"(Cole and Stewart, 2014, 151) build the foundations for further vegan pedagogy.

Nursery rhymes are not the only literary texts available to parents who want to familiarize their children with veganism at an early stage of their development. *Libby Finds Vegan Sanctuary* by Julia Feliz Brueck (2016) and *That's Not My Momma's Milk* (2017) by Julia Barcalow, board books published by Vegan Publishers, teach very young children compassion toward animals (Brueck) and provide an important lesson about things human and animal mothers have in common (Barcalow). The similarity between human and nonhuman animals is also the main theme of *We All Love. A Book for Compassionate Little Vegans and Vegetarians* (2017) by Julie Hausen, in which having a family, playing, feeling pain or happiness, and being hungry are not restricted to people only but are represented as characteristic features of the social and emotional lives of all sentient beings, thus stressing the inseparability of humans and animals "in their shared earthly rootedness" (Oppermann and Iovino 5).

While very young children learn about things they share with animals because this is an issue they can easily understand, older children are faced with a broader and more demanding range of themes which are related to the oppression of animals. Educational books for vegan children are rich in facts about animal farming and its impact on the environment, about where the food that children eat comes from, and about the responsibilities that compassionate and caring people must take in order to make a difference. Some of the first informative–educational vegan books for children were written by Ruby Roth, an American artist, writer and activist, whose decision to start writing for vegan children was motivated by her failure to find a book she could use to explain to her elementary school pupils her own vegan dietary habits (Roth, "Interview"). Her first book, *That is Why We Don't Eat Animals*, the first vegan non-fiction book in children's literature to focus on such "non-children" topics as animal suffering and factory farming, was published in 2009. It was followed in 2012 by another educational book, *Vegan is Love: Having Heart and Taking Action*, which conveys the most comprehensive understanding of veganism. No longer reduced to a diet—being vegan means being aware of the ways in which the principles of anthroparchy shape the clothing industry, medical laboratories, and the world of entertainment—but also embracing an awareness of the interconnectedness of various forms of animal and human oppression, the veganism Roth talks about falls into the category of revisionary political veganism, which Robert C. Jones explains as including

> a moral and political commitment to active resistance against institutional and systemic violence, exploitation, domination, objectification, and commodification directed against all sentient beings—human and non-human—as well as the natural environment that supports and sustains them. (29)

Roth confronts children with a veganism that is intersectional in the way it addresses the consequences of the animal industry for the world's agriculture and establishes a connection between veganism, world hunger, and malnutrition. "The world grows enough grain to feed everybody… but not everybody eats. Why?" asks Roth (*V is for Vegan* 30). Such a representation of food-related issues arms children with the cognitive tools necessary to position veganism in the frame of interrelated forms of oppression and encourages them to consider their own potential to perform acts of "active resistance."

Another important aspect of vegan literary pedagogy is that apart from teaching children the facts about human–animal relations, it also invites them to enter the world of the creative imagination and to learn through the experience of literary encounters and discoveries. Vegan adventure books and fairy-tales build alternative realities where dinosaurs do not eat meat (*T. VEG* by Smriti Prasadam-Halls and *Linus the Vegetarian T. Rex* by Robert Neubecker), vegan superheroes display their super powers (*The Amazing Adventures of Wonderpig* by Phil Tutton and the series of books about the adventures of Veggie Vero by Veronica Green), and where even reindeer-oppressing Santa Claus undergoes a metamorphosis and realizes that "sentient beings must be respected" (Ravin, *Santa's First Vegan Christmas* 25). Following narrative patterns typical of diverse genres, vegan fiction creates a gallery of archetypal characters: talking animals, human and animal superheroes, and human (never animal) super-villains. Entertaining as they are, they also help young vegans to come to terms with their own otherness and make identification with other like-minded children possible.

Vegan literature for children—regardless of whether we talk about nursery rhymes, board books for those who are not old enough to receive formal education, or fairy tales and poems for older children—is about understanding connections and bringing about a change for animals, people, and the environment. "All change begins with knowledge," says Veggie Vero in *Veggie Vero & The Sandwich Imposter* (Green 1). The education of children about the "secret" life of animals, which they are forced to sacrifice for our dietary habits to continue, remains a central theme in many vegan books. Acquiring knowledge about the connection between animals and the food children eat is important in two ways. When it takes place on the level of individual experience, it often starts with what may be called the vegan "epiphany," a painful realization of the hidden truth about the sources of food which a child has to learn to admit and confront. When approached from the social perspective, vegan knowledge reveals the power of those cultural mechanisms that condition us to live in "an environment, in which the practice of eating animals is omnipresent and virtually always uncontested" (Joy and Tuider vii). The environment remains uncontested because, until recently, its principles have been rigorously protected from being exposed.

Gene Baur, the president and co-founder of Farm Sanctuary, an organization which protects farm animals, writes in the Foreword to Stephanie Dreyer's *Not a Nugget*:

> Most children have a natural connection with animals, but few make the connection between their love for animals and the habit of eating them. Engaging children early in the discussion about the origins of our food, and the impact on ourselves, animals and environment is critical. (7)

Listening to stories told not only by children but also by grown-ups, remembering those often traumatic moments when they realized the truth behind food practices, reveals a clear need to guarantee adult-assisted access to knowledge about human abuse of animals and the ways to resist it in everyday life. It also forcefully encourages one to pose questions concerning *the right* of a child to know and to make their own choices. A few examples of vegan autobiographical accounts provide a valid insight into what turned out to be for many future vegans life-turning moments. This is how Petra Sindelarova, a Czech activist and a vegan, refers to the day when she learnt the truth about animal farming:

when I was 13 years old, I accidentally saw a TV programme about factory farming and slaughtering animals for food. I was horrified. I just could not believe what I saw. […] Why had no one ever told me about it? Was it a taboo? (Katz 29)

In his autobiography Benjamin Zephaniah remembers the day when, at the age of eleven, he suddenly saw a connection between his dinner and an animal which had to be killed:

I asked her where she'd got the meat from and she said from the butcher. So I asked where the butcher had got it from, and she said the farmer. So I asked where the farmer got it from, and she said he got it from the cow. I thought, what a clever cow, and then asked, 'What is the cow doing with meat?'
She said, 'You silly boy, this is the cow!'
I was horrified. I had never connected the meat on the plate with the cow in the field. (75)

Vegan stories for children make invisible visible, and by doing so provide their readers with the tools of epistemic resistance. Carnistic strategies which render eating meat as "normal, natural and necessary" (Joy and Tuider viii), coupled with the ways in which an animal is turned into an "absent referent"—when it is killed, when its body is fragmented to become bacon and hamburgers, and when it is turned into a metaphor to talk about humans (Adams 40–42)—successfully separate our daily culinary and dietary experiences from the truth about animals' role in the production of food. For children, to realize what happens before the food they eat lands on their plates is twice as hard because they "enjoy" double protection. Seen as emotionally fragile and inexperienced, they are supposed *not to know* about the animal industry which many adults also either refuse to acknowledge or do not notice. This double wall of "protection" guarantees a continuity of epistemic blindness, efficiently produced by carnistic defensive strategies.

The inheritance of epistemic blindness is challenged when children are supported in their epistemic resistance and this is where literature has an important role to play. Zephaniah remembers the time, after his food epiphany, when he was educating himself in food history: "I worked it up for myself that mothers produced milk for their children, and not for the children of others, especially others of another species […]. I hadn't read any vegan magazines—there weren't any" (76). Today, the readers of *Steven the Vegan* by Dan Bodenstein are taken on a trip to a farm sanctuary where they establish a connection between the cows they fondly pat and hamburgers, the chickens they admire and nuggets, and the playful piglets and bacon, while in Ruby Roth's *V is for Vegan: The ABC for Being Kind* they learn the letters of the vegan alphabet in which "E is for eggs—from a chicken's butt?! Wow" (7) and "H is for honey? That's food for bees!" (11). The information about what happens to animals is filtered to match readers' cognitive levels. From very simple sentences and colorful images of animals in their natural environment to more demanding and informative texts for older readers, vegan literature accompanies children in the process of transition into knowing subjects.

The connections established by vegan literature for children embrace not only the relations between the food we eat and animal suffering but also those between animal industry and the environment, the identification of which allows young readers to see "the enmeshed oppressions—of the land, the animals, and the people—as necessarily inherently linked and mutually reinforcing" (Wright xiv). In an epoch which has already earned the name of the Anthropocene, the epoch of man, the impact of animal farms on the environment is more and more frequently placed within the broader context of an environmental emergency. In his latest book, *We Are the Weather. Saving the Planet Begins at Breakfast*, Jonathan Safran Foer, the author of *Eating Animals*, announces loudly and clearly what most of us do not want to acknowledge: that "we cannot save the planet unless we significantly reduce our consumption of animal products" (64).

Read from the perspective of Robert Macfarlane's claim that in the Anthropocene "a need has grown for fresh vocabularies and narratives that might account for the kinds of relation and responsibility in which we find ourselves entangled" (2016), vegan literature for children presents itself as a form of "fresh" narrative through which children can understand the issues of animal well-being and the connection between the food we eat and sustainable, ecological living. Situated next to such books as *Bee and Me* by Alison Jay, which teaches children about the importance of bees, *The Great Kapok Tree* by Lynn Cherry, which illustrates the significance of trees, *Kenya's Art* by Linda Trice educating children about the need to recycle, and Michael Foreman's *One World*, which emphasizes the danger of pollution, vegan books for children show that caring for the planet may also embrace the choice of the food we eat and the products we use in our everyday life. Vegan books offer an exercise in ecopedagogy which, in the words of Greta Gaard, "asks for personal and socio-political changes for the health of the earth as well as its inhabitants" (21). In *Lena of Vegitopia and the Mystery of the Missing Animals* by Sybil Severin the issue of environmental awareness is woven into the plot and speaks imaginatively through the setting: Lena, the vegan protagonist, visits the castle of the carnivore Carnista (an archetypal female villain who has stolen baby animals), a gloomy place shrouded by the smog so thick that "the sunlight could barely get through the dark and dirty clouds above" (16). The happy ending of the fairy tale brings about a reunion of the baby animals and their parents, and the transformation of Carnista and her castle: "The smog above the castle lifted, and the foul stench went away because she no longer cooked animals for dinner" (38). While Severin introduces elements of ecological awareness by using the convention of fairy-tale, Katie Clark in *I'm a Supervegan*, an illustrated conversation between a young girl called Elizabeth and her mom, openly places veganism next to other environment-friendly practices, such as reusing bags, and teaches children that "[v]egans protect the rainforests they belong in" (17). Ruby Roth in *Vegan is Love* is equally straightforward and informative when she says about meat consumption: "This way of eating has been a mistake" and explains how the animal industry contributes to polluting the earth (27).

Teaching children about the connections between what they eat and the condition of the planet they inhabit may be seen as an element of ecological literacy which, according to David Orr, "begins in childhood" (86). For Orr, being ecologically literate means to be able to "think broadly, to know something of what is hitched to what" (87). This is precisely what vegan literary ecopedagogy does when it reveals veganism's potential to address a variety of new issues, some of which have been brought to the spotlight as a result of "the consequences of human degradation of the landscape at a planetary level" (Malone 2) experienced by children and adults alike. Unsurprisingly, in various discourses of the Anthropocene the scale of the problem is often addressed in terms of human agency as these question individuals' potential to react to the environmental emergency.

By revealing "what is hitched to what," vegan literature for children invests the "new eating identities" (Foer 65) with new responsibilities which children are encouraged to take. Interpreted from the perspective of the challenges that children meet in the Anthropocene, children's vegan literature turns out to be deeply committed to empowering children by providing them with vegan role models and by showing them that they do not have to feel helpless when confronted by the scale of the problem. Vegan ecopedagogy brings an answer to the question many adults cannot easily answer: What can *I* do in this time of the environmental emergency? In Roth's *V is for Vegan*, the letter Y "is for you because your choices matter" (30). Rather than being paralyzed by the scale of the problem, young vegan protagonists do not suffer from what Clare Mann called "vystopia," a sense of "an existential crisis experienced by vegans, arising out of an awareness of the trance-like collusion with a dystopian world" (6), and are instead ready to engage in whatever it takes to save animals and the planet. "A big change starts small, with everyday choices" (Clark 1) seems to be the motto of many vegan protagonists who help children understand the inseparability of human and other-than-human lives. A similar sense of agency and empowerment permeates a little essay by Greta Thunberg entitled "No one is too small to make a difference," in her 2019 book of the same title.

It is certainly too early to look at recent vegan literature for children from a perspective which would allow us to see how it has been changing since the beginning of the 21st century. Yet even though it is one of "vegan children's cultural artefacts" and as such "operate[s] at a miniscule scale" (Cole and Stewart 152), it is the most thriving field of vegan literary representations today. Its future developments arouse scholarly and reading curiosity as veganism itself is evolving: it is likely that veganism's recent cultural associations, such as status, race, and class, will find their reflections in children's vegan literature yet to be written.

So far, vegan literature for children has remained on the margins of vegan studies' concerns. The focus of vegan scholars on social, cultural, psychological, historical, or literary dimensions of stories for children which familiarize them with animal-friendly lifestyles opens up a new space of inquiry for vegan studies. It also extends the cultural history of veganism by including the voice of those whose experience and participation in veganism, until recently, has been largely ignored. Reading children's literature through a vegan lens also allows one to see how vegan studies and childhood studies can inform each other while "[a]sking questions about the relational encounters and the emerging entanglements of children with the world at large" (Spyrou 433). By initiating a debate about a child's right to know the truth behind our food practices and to make their own conscious choices, the vegan studies perspective can make a valid contribution to the rethinking of the categories of "childhood" and "child" recently postulated by scholars of childhood studies (433).

"Vegan is love," says Ruby Roth. Does that sound idealistic? Surely it does. "[A]ll living things have a right to be free," writes Carlos Patiño (32). Utopian? Without a doubt. It is true that vegan literature for children is generally idealistic, utopian, didactic, instructive and moralizing. And while it is openly and unashamedly so, it is also creative, playful, and inspiring. It is on a mission of educating children about the significance—ethical and environmental—of their own choices, allowing them to see those choices in the broader contexts of interrelated oppressive practices which affect people, animals, and the planet, providing them with "critical-ethical argumentation" (Horsthemke 219) to support their views. Committed to raising critical awareness, it is adapted to the age of the readers and their cognitive skills, and it assists children at various stages of their development empowering them to be responsible and, just like Supervegan Elizabeth, "brave, caring and smart" (Clark 5). The utopian character of children's vegan literature is not about the impossibility of an all-vegan environment. Instead, it seems to follow a Fredric Jameson-inspired understanding of utopia as a method consisting not so much in the presentation of radical alternatives which can replace faulty, malfunctioning social or political orders and structures, but rather in the warrant to envision such alternatives: "a contribution to the reawakening of the imagination of possible and alternate futures" (42). Vegan literature for children helps us all realize that as long as we keep imagining that other options are possible, the change that we so desperately need is still achievable.

Note

1 I am currently working on a monograph entitled *"I am not dinner!": Continuity and Change in Children's Vegan Literature* in which I read vegan literature for children—its historical development and its present growth—from the perspective of vegan critical theory and the cultural history of veganism.

Works cited

Adams, Carol J. *The Sexual Politics of Meat: A Feminist-Vegetarian Critical Theory*. Polity Press, 1990.
Baur, Gene. Foreword. *Not a Nugget*, by Stephanie Dreyer, VeegMama, 2015, p. 7.
Bedborough, George. *Stories from the Children's Realm: A Book for Those Who Love Children and Animals*. Vegetarian Federal Union, 1914.
Clark, Katie. *I'm a Supervegan: A Confidence-Building Children's Book for Our Littlest Vegans*. Longview Ink, 2019.
Cole, A. M. Preface. *Stories from the Children's Realm: A Book for Those who Love Children and Animals*, by George Bedborough, Vegetarian Federal Union, 1914, p. 3.
Cole, Matthew and Kate Stewart. *Our Children and Other Animals: The Cultural Construction of Human–Animal Relations in Childhood*. Routledge, 2014.
Drewett, Zoe. "Ethical Veganism' Is a Philosophical Belief, British Court Rules." *Metro*, www.metro.co.uk/2020/01/03/ethical-veganism-philosophical-belief-court-rules-11995724/. Accessed 27 January 2020.
Foer, Jonathan Safran. *We are the Weather. Saving the Planet Begins at Breakfast*. Farrar, Straus and Giroux, 2019.
Foster, Kate. *Vegan Nursery Rhymes*. CreateSpace Independent Publishing Platform, 2019.
Gaard, Greta. "Toward an Ecopedagogy of Children's Environmental Literature." *Green Theory & Praxis: The Journal of Ecopedagogy*, vol. 4, no. 2, 2008, pp. 11–24.
Green, Veronica. *Veggie Vero & The Sandwich Imposter*, Veronica Green, 2017.
Gregory, James. *Of Victorians and Vegetarians: The Vegetarian Movement in Nineteenth-century Britain*. I.B. Tauris, 2007.
Hills, Arnold Frank. Foreword. *The Children's Realm*, no.1,1900, pp. 1–2.
Jones, Robert C. "Veganisms." *Critical Perspectives on Veganism*, edited by Jodey Castricano and Rasmus R. Simonsen, Palgrave Macmillan, 2016, pp. 15–39.
Horsthemke, Kai. *Animal Rights Education*. Palgrave Macmillan, 2018.
Jameson, Fredric. "Utopia as Method, or the Uses of the Future." *Utopia/Dystopia: Conditions of Historical Possibility*, edited by Michael D. Gordin, Helen Tilley, Gyan Prakash, Princeton University Press, 2010, pp. 21–44.
Joy, Melanie and Jens Tuider. Foreword. *Critical Perspectives on Veganism*, edited by Jodey Castricano and Rasmus R. Simonsen, Palgrave Macmillan, 2016, pp. v–xv.
Katz, Butterflies, editor. *Why I Will Always Be Vegan: 125 Essays from Around the World*. CreateSpace Independent Publishing Platform, 2015.
Koljonen, Marianna. "Thinking and Caring Boys Go Vegan: Two European Books That Introduce Vegan Identity to Children." *Bookbird: A Journal of International Children's Literature*, vol. 57, no. 3, 2019, pp. 13–23.
Macfarlane, Robert. "Generation Anthropocene: How humans have altered the planet for ever." *The Guardian*, 2016, www.theguardian.com/books/2016/apr/01/generation-anthropocene-altered-planet-for-ever. Accessed January 27 2020.
Mann, Clare. *Vystopia: The Anguish of Being Vegan in a Non-Vegan World*. Communicate31 Pty Ltd, 2018.
Mullen, Ginger. "More Than Words: Using Nursery Rhymes and Songs to Support Domains of Child Development." *Journal of Childhood Studies*, vol. 42, no. 2, 2017, pp. 42–53.
Oppermann, Serpil and Serenella Iovino. Introduction: The Environmental Humanities and the Challenges of the Anthropocen. *Environmental Humanities: Voices from the Anthropocene*, edited by Oppermann and Iovino. Rowman & Littlefield International, 2017, pp. 1–22.
Orr, David W. *Ecological Literacy: Education and the Transition to a Postmodern World*. State University of New York Press, 1992.
Patiño, Carlos. *Dave Loves Chickens*. Vegan Publishers, 2013.
Plum, Violet. *Why Are You a Vegan? And Other Wacky Verse for Kids*. CreateSpace Independent Publishing Platform, 2015.
Roth, Ruby. *That is Why We Don't Eat Animals*. North Atlantic Books, 2009.
———. *V is Love: Having Heart and Taking Action*. North Atlantic Books, 2012.

———. *V is for Vegan: The ABC for Being Kind*. North Atlantic Books, 2013.
———. An Interview with Ruby Roth. Interviewed by Annika Lundkvist. *Vegan for All Seasons*, 2016, www.veganforallseasons.com/2016/07/10/vegan-mama-ruby/. Accessed February 7 2020.
Rundell, Katherine. *Why You Should Read Children's Books, Even Though You Are So Old and Wise*. Bloomsbury Publishing, 2019.
Severin, Sybil. *Lena of Vegitopia and the Mystery of the Missing Animals*. Vegan Publishers, 2014.
Spyrou, Spyros. "Time to decenter childhood?" *Childhood*, vol. 24, no. 4, 2017, pp. 433–437.
Thunberg, Greta. *No One is Too Small to Make a Difference*. Penguin Books, 2019.
Wright, Laura, editor. *Through a Vegan Studies Len: Textual Ethics and Lived Activism*. University of Nevada Press, 2019.
Wright, Laura. "Vegans in the Interregnum: The Cultural Moment of an Enmeshed Theory." *Thinking Veganism in Literature and Culture: Towards a Vegan Theory*, edited by Emelia Quinn and Benjamin Westwood, Palgrave Macmillan, 2018, pp. 27–54.
Zephaniah, Benjamin. *The Life and Rhymes of Benjamin Zephaniah: The Autobiography*. Simon & Schuster, 2018.

7
Veganism, ecoethics, and climate change in Margaret Atwood's "MaddAddam" trilogy

Tatiana Prorokova-Konrad

Veganism is perceived rather controversially in most parts of the globe. It has been associated with a number of issues, including health, ethics, and even religion, and remains unwelcome in the majority of Western countries. In what follows, via an analysis of Canadian writer Margaret Atwood's "MaddAddam" Trilogy, I examine veganism through the prism of the current environmental crisis and argue that veganism can be viewed as a pro-environmental strategy. Industrialization and the capitalist ideology have led to current environmental degradation, making the West (or the Global North) responsible for this destruction. And while we continue to debate the ways through which climate change can be minimized, foregrounding cheap energy as the most crucial issue in this environmental debacle, we seem to fail to understand that our primary aim today must be "to invent new ways of being, belonging, and behaving" (Szeman 46). This aim, however, should not be reduced to energy only (although doubtless this is a significant problem for us to address), but instead should consider numerous other aspects related to the transformation of our cultural and ethical consciousness. Veganism, as I will argue throughout this chapter, brings the question of ethics to the fore, questioning what it means to be human in general and in the era of climate change in particular. While I do not want to reduce veganism to its ethical imperative only, I reveal how important the issue of ecoethics is today and demonstrate that veganism is perhaps the most illustrative tool through which to understand the acute necesity of such ethics.

This chapter focuses on Canadian novelist Margaret Atwood's "MaddAddam" trilogy—*Oryx and Crake* (2003), *The Year of the Flood* (2009), and *MaddAddam* (2013)—to discuss veganism as a powerful ideology in ecologically precarious times. The trilogy envisions a post-apocalyptic world that is the result of humanity's careless treatment of the environment. Veganism becomes a tool through which Atwood's novels provide a harsh critique of capitalism and its major aspects—abundant production and conspicuous consumption. In doing so, the trilogy indicts humanity's avaricious attitudes to the environment that is taken for granted, exploited, and abused. Revealing the naked truth about our current reality, that even in the times of climate change remains focused on the comforts of civilization and financial benefits, Atwood's novels display consumption of meat as a cultural product of the Anthropocene, the era of humanity's colonization and rapid destruction of nature. In the trilogy, veganism censures our current food habits and traditions, criticizes the modes of consumption and production as the key triggers in our culture, promotes animal rights, and reinforces the nature of the current environmental collapse as explicitly human-made.

Veganism in the era of climate change

When in 2013 *Forbes* included vegan food in the Top Ten food trends, scholars started to talk about "a shift in media representations of vegan food from dull to desirable" (Doyle 777). To what extent this idea of "desirability" promoted by the media is successfully conveyed to and received by audiences worldwide remains suspect. Certainly there are more vegan restaurants available now in bigger cities; increasingly more people share their personal stories of being or choosing to become vegans, yet veganism remains a phenomenon that is misinterpreted, criticized, and ridiculed by many.

Veganism is defined as "a diet based upon the non-consumption of meat, dairy, eggs and honey; the nonuse of animal (by)products (such as leather and wool) for clothing and other goods; and the avoidance of animal tested products" (Doyle 779). The Association of the Vegan Society provides a more detailed explanation, suggesting that to be vegan is to follow a

> philosophy and way of living which seeks to exclude—as far as is possible and practicable—all forms of exploitation of, and cruelty to, animals for food, clothing or any other purpose; and by extension, promotes the development and use of animal-free alternatives for the benefit of humans, animals and the environment. In dietary terms it denotes the practice of dispensing with all products derived wholly or partly from animals. (qtd. in Wright, "Introducing" 727)

Veganism is thus not only about refusing to consume animals—in any form—but also about preserving the environment. Veganism and environmentalism go hand in hand, considering that "meat and dairy production/consumption" is "one of the single largest contributors to global greenhouse gas emissions and climate change" (Doyle 777–78). Veganism can hence be viewed as one of the ways to fight the environmental degradation and reduce the consequences of climate change.

Yet even in such environmentally precarious times in which we are living, veganism is questioned by many. Most importantly, its *availability* is doubted. Through the notion of "vegan privilege" in particular, veganism is imagined as a lifestyle affordable for selected individuals only, and it remains unclear "whether veganism requires affluence, whether it assumes whiteness, first world privilege, and cultural insensitivity, and whether it encourages self-righteousness and condescension towards non-vegans" (Greenebaum 356). Vegan studies scholar Laura Wright explains the division of society into vegans and nonvegans through the prism of various political, social, economic, and cultural factors combined together and concludes: "Veganism continues to be a largely white, upper-middle class identity; it is often depicted as an elitist endeavor, and it is gendered as a female undertaking and, therefore, often dismissed as naively emotionally motivated—or characterized as disordered consumption" ("Introducing" 728). Despite veganism's rather peculiar sociocultural position, it should be understood as an effective tool to fight the current capitalist reality that has caused this environmental havoc. Although the number of vegans throughout the world is dramatically low, Wright sees pro-environmental potential in veganism as an ideology, lifestyle, and culture, and argues that veganism is

> marked by conscious individual actions that nonetheless stand in stark opposition to the consumer mandate of capitalism, and for this reason, the actions of individual vegans pose

a substantial—if symbolic—threat to such a paradigm. Whether one is vegan for ethical reasons, for health benefits, or because of religious mandates, adopting a vegan diet constitutes environmental activism, whether or not the vegan intends such activism. ("Introducing" 728)

If veganism is one of the ways to deal with the problem of climate change (among other environmental issues), why does humanity not switch to the vegan diet? Many of the reasons are deeply cultural. For example, Karen S. Emmerman points out that

> Many familial and cultural traditions rely on animals for their fulfillment—think of Christmas ham, Rosh Hashannah chicken soup, Fourth of July barbeques, and so forth. Though philosophers writing in animal ethics often dismiss interests in certain foods as trivial, these food-based traditions pose a significant moral problem for those who take animals' lives and interests seriously. One must either turn one's back on one's community or on the animals. (77)

Veganism can thus be interpreted as a dangerous choice that can be perceived with suspicion and even anger by the nonvegan majority. And this is exactly what happened in some Western countries after the terrorist attacks on September 11, 2001, in New York. As Wright outlines in her book *The Vegan Studies Project: Food, Animals, and Gender in the Age of Terror*, shortly after the attacks the vegan diet was profoundly misinterpreted to strengthen the nationalistic, xenophobic thinking and fuel the process of *Othering* of certain individuals and even nations (30). September 11, 2001, and the ideology of the war on terror turned the practice of eating meat into a criterion by which American goodness could be largely defined. Being vegan in the post-9/11 era, according to Wright, signified "the choice … to step outside of the confines of what constituted an agreed-upon 'American' identity" (31). Essentially, such an attitude to veganism helped further shape the discourse of *Otherness*:

> We were American, and they were "Al-Qaeda." We were good, and they were evil. We were Christian, and they were Muslim. We ate like Americans, and they ate according to the dictates of Islam, which expressly forbids the ingestion of pork and requires strict adherence to halal standards of animal slaughter. We are humans. They are animals. (35)

It is particularly important to note that Atwood was writing the first book in the trilogy, *Oryx and Crake*, in the wake of 9/11. She later discussed how uncomfortable it was to try to imagine catastrophes and then find out about the terrorist attacks on September 11, 2001:

> I stopped writing for a number of weeks. It's deeply unsettling when you're writing about a fictional catastrophe and then a real one happens. I thought maybe I should turn to gardening books—something more cheerful. But then I started writing again, because what use would gardening books be in a world without gardens, and without books? And that was the vision that was preoccupying me. (Atwood, "Writing *Oryx and Crake*" 285)

The novel's images of veganism were thus shaped by the reality of 9/11 that brought to the fore the feeling of unsafety and the end of the world as we had known it before the attacks.

The resistance to veganism can be also explained by the very misinterpretation of veganism and massive spread of such information. For example, veganism is frequently described as unhealthy, specifically so with the reference to B12 deficiency, despite scholars' vehement attempts to prove the opposite: "There's little risk of B12 deficiency in a vegan diet ... But the myth continues" (Tristam Stuart qtd. in Wright, *The Vegan Studies Project* 31). In addition to this misinformation, media portrayals of veganism accentuate the fact that in order to be vegan one should *stop* consuming certain products, thus promoting a distorted perception of veganism as a practice of depriving oneself of food: "a veganism-as-deviance model that fosters academic misunderstanding and misrepresentation of the meaning of veganism for vegans" (Matthew Cole and Karen Morgan qtd. in Wright, *The Vegan Studies Project* 32).

Another reason for a rather cautious attitude toward veganism combines both cultural and medical aspects and results from misinterpretation, too. Historically, meat-eating was largely coded as a male practice. Elaine Schowalter gives an illustrative example:

> Meat, the "roast beef of old England," was not only the traditional food of warriors and aggressors but also believed to be the fuel of anger and lust. Disgust with meat was a common phenomenon among Victorian girls; a carnivorous diet was associated with sexual precocity, especially with an abundant menstrual flow, and even with nymphomania. (qtd. in Adams 149)

Being formulated as a product for men, meat has become largely associated with the male body and male masculinity in general. This association has dramatically influenced the cultural image of the vegan body, turning it into a "feminized" body and thus discriminating against male vegans (Wright, *The Vegan Studies Project* 31). Additionally, the idea that "caring for animals" is "a sign of weakness and femininity" further undermines veganism as an option for men (Greenebaum and Dexter 638). The misinterpretation of veganism through gender-related debates is further reinforced by false contentions regarding the influence of the vegan diet on male health, including Jim Rutz's stance on soy as food that "is feminizing, and commonly leads to a decrease in the size of the penis, sexual confusion and homosexuality" (qtd. in Wright, *The Vegan Studies Project* 31). This assumption that a vegan diet is emasculating can perhaps explain why veganism is persistently viewed as a female practice.

Despite various misinterpretations and instances of misuse of the term, veganism has a number of advantages, including its pro-environmental nature. Whether understanding veganism as "a new form of social movement" (Elizabeth Cherry qtd. in Wright, *The Vegan Studies Project* 32), "an accepted health choice" (Claire Suddath qtd. in Wright, *The Vegan Studies Project* 33), or a form of pro-animal activism (Wright, *The Vegan Studies Project* 32; Suddath in Wright, *The Vegan Studies Project* 33), veganism is an essential part of environmentalism. It helps not only to protect the environment but also to reimagine our own role on this planet, challenging the meaning of being human. These are similar questions that have already been raised in postcolonial studies—"What does 'human' refer to? Who counts as 'human'? What are the histories of this designation? And who speaks for the human?" (Jackson 19)—that veganism draws our attention to today, yet this time with regard to animals and the environment in general, foregrounding the criminal, barbaric actions of humanity to colonized Nature. Veganism helps reestablish the very idea of "human identity" and has a potential to "change current critical-theoretical practices" (Emelia Quinn and Benjamin Westwood qtd. in Wright, "Introducing" 732). Alongside veganism's theoretical challenges to the human/animal divide, it can considerably minimize "food-related greenhouse gas emissions by 29–70 percent" (Marco Springmann et al. qtd. in Wright, "Introducing" 728). The power of veganism is profound. Veganism functions both as an ideology through which to criticize the current anti-environmental reality and as a tool through which environmentalism can be exercised. These are essentially the two perspectives on veganism that are illustrated in Atwood's "MaddAddam" trilogy.

Tatiana Prorokova-Konrad

Speciesism and apocalyptic thinking in *Oryx and Crake*

The "MaddAddam" trilogy tells the story of humanity's obsession with power, abuse, production, and consumption that leads to an apocalypse. The few survivors of a human engineered pandemic search for ways to adjust to the new reality and build a new home. Veganism is an essential part of each novel in the trilogy, for its presence allows readers to question humanity's actions in the pre-apocalyptic times and conditions one's adaptation in the new, post-apocalyptic world.

Oryx and Crake is the first novel in the trilogy that focuses on Jimmy (known as Snowman in the post-apocalyptic world) and his friend Crake. When the boys grow up, Jimmy attends the Martha Graham Academy and studies humanities, whereas Crake goes to the Watson-Crick Institute to study bioengineering. Crake then gets a prestigious job in a corporation where he creates the Crakers—herbivorous humanoids who mate at specific times. In addition, Crake creates the BlyssPluss pill, which, as he explains, can improve sexual health and intercourse. This pill in the end causes a pandemic and leads to an apocalypse. Another important character in the book is Oryx—an Asian woman who is sexually assaulted during her childhood and appears in a number of pornographic films that Jimmy watches as a teenager. Crake later hires Oryx to help teach the Crakers. Oryx ultimately becomes a lover to both Crake and Jimmy. In the end, Jimmy is the only character of the three to survive the apocalypse.

The novel raises a whole panoply of issues—from reproduction and overpopulation, to child pornography, to genetically modified products, and beyond. Veganism, I argue, functions as a prism through which to understand the idea of collapse that is deeply entwined in the novel. The collapse happens rather rapidly and is essentially the result of various practices that allude to capitalism; the experiments on animals and the creation of new kinds of animals that can exist in the wild, be turned into pets, or used as food; the creation of the Crakers that are metaphorically portrayed as new, better humans; the interference in reproduction—these are the examples of humanity's intervention in various natural processes that lead to Nature's enslavement. Acutely sensing "environmental pollution and the impacts of capitalism," Atwood's trilogy is what Heather I. Sullivan terms as "the dark pastoral"—"a formula for navigating the textual and material contradictions of the Anthropocene" (47–48). *Oryx and Crake* comments on capitalism, based on production and consumption, as a destructive policy. This critique of capitalism is achieved through the images of abused and exploited animals and women.

Rachel Stein claims that in *Oryx and Crake*

> Atwood sets forth ... implicitly misogynist, anti-sex, and anti-human environmental positions in order to expose the horrifying repercussions of the belief that sex itself is an assault on nature, and that nature can only survive and recover from human depredations in a world without us. (185)

Here, Stein obviously refers to Crake's obsession to exclude sex from life as illustrated, first, through the Crakers who mate only in specific seasons and, second, through the BlyssPluss pill that Crake manages to successfully distribute globally, as the majority of people are eager to improve their sex lives—the effect that the pill promises to bring, even as the pill also causes an intentional unadvertised side effect, sterility. Through the pandemic that originates from the pill, the novel comments on "the apocalyptic disappearance of humans as the only way to preserve the natural environment" (185). Sex is also portrayed as evil through Oryx who, as a small girl, is sexually assaulted by men and forced to perform in pornographic films. And while the first two examples are interesting to analyze with regard to the questions of reproduction and the environment, I would like to address the misogynist, humiliating, and simply illegal situations that Oryx finds herself in throughout the novel. These situations help raise the issue of ethics in general, and illustrate what Wright terms as "a vegetarian ethic" in particular (*The Vegan Studies Project* 33).

Oryx's real name is not known to the reader. She is called "Oryx" by Crake who through this name equates her to an animal, even more so, to a herbivore. The violence and abuse that Oryx suffers throughout the novel, I argue, parallels violence inflicted on animals. I draw on Carol J. Adams' groundbreaking theory of patriarchal abuse of women that essentially mirrors humanity's abuse of animals. Adams contends: "Through butchering, animals become absent referents. Animals in name and body are made absent *as animals* for meat to exist" (20; italics in original). Adams singles out three ways through which the process of "becoming absent referents" are enabled: first, "through meat eating they [animals] are literally absent because they are dead"; second, "definitional: when we eat animals we change the way we talk about them, for instance, we no longer talk about baby animals but about veal or lamb"; third, "metaphorical," i.e., "[a]nimals become metaphors for describing people's experiences" (21). This violence, according to Adams, on various levels enables "the rendering of animals as consumable bodies" (xxxv). But in a similar way, women have been turned by patriarchy into consumable bodies, too. Adams writes: "[T]he women raped, butchered, and eaten … are linked by an overlap of cultural images of sexual violence against women and the fragmentation and dismemberment of nature and the body in Western culture" (20). Seeing the parallels in the two institutionalized practices of abuse, "Carol J. Adams has put forth a feminist defense of veganism based on the argument that meat consumption and violence against animals are structurally related to violence against women, and especially to pornography and prostitution" (Hamilton 112). The abuse of Oryx in the novel vividly illustrates Adams's concern regarding female oppression (Oryx being molested and sexually harassed as a child and later by Jimmy and Crake as she becomes their lover) and animal abuse (Oryx being nicknamed as a herbivorous animal and slaughtered at the end of the novel by Crake who slits her throat with a knife).

The story of Oryx uncovers the complexity of (patriarchal) abuse that has been conducted systematically and perceived generally as a norm. Yet while in the story of Oryx's abuse is gendered to convey the problems of sexism and misogyny, the images of genetically modified animals send more apparent and, from an animal rights perspective, more scandalous messages. I would like to specifically focus on the animals that in the novel are cultivated exclusively for consumption, as new kinds of meat. When Jimmy visits Crake at the Watson-Crick Institute, he witnesses the new way of producing meat:

> What they [Jimmy and Crake] were looking at was a large bulblike object that seemed to be covered with stippled whitish-yellow skin. Out of it came twenty thick fleshy tubes, and at the end of each tube another bulb was growing.
> "What the hell is it?" said Jimmy.
> "Those are chickens," said Crake. "Chicken parts. Just the breasts, on this one. They've got ones that specialize in drumsticks too, twelve to a growth unit."
> "But there aren't any heads," said Jimmy. He grasped the concept—he'd grown up with *sus multiorganifer*, after all—but this thing was going too far. At least the pigoons of his childhood hadn't lacked heads.
> "That's the head in the middle," said the woman. "There's a mouth opening at the top, they dump the nutrients in there. No eyes or beak or anything, they don't need those."

> "This is horrible," said Jimmy. The thing was a nightmare. It was like an animal-protein tuber.
> "Picture the sea-anemone body plan," said Crake. "That helps."
> "But what's it thinking?" said Jimmy.
> The woman gave her jocular woodpecker yodel, and explained that they'd removed all the brain functions that had nothing to do with digestion, assimilation, and growth.
> "It's sort of like a chicken hookworm," said Crake.
> "No need for added growth hormones," said the woman, "the high growth rate's built in. You get chicken breasts in two weeks—that's a three-week improvement on the most efficient low-light, high-density chicken farming operation so far devised. And the animal-welfare freaks won't be able to say a word, because this thing feels no pain." (202–3; italics in original)

This new way of producing meat is perhaps the most vivid illustration of what a vegan ethic condemns. What Jimmy sees is neither an animal nor a piece of meat but is an illustration of what Adams describes as turning animals into "absent referents" and thus "consumable bodies." Jimmy's shock that emerges as he sees these creatures and his inability to identify them as either meats or animals uncovers the artificiality of these bioengineered objects. Crake, in principle, experiences a similar problem, first calling them "chickens" and then immediately correcting himself saying that these are "chicken parts" rather than animals in their complete, natural form. The new invention reduces chickens to consumable bodies only, interpreting certain parts (e.g., breasts and drumsticks) as necessary and the rest as useless. The new creatures directly respond to demand: people only want to eat certain parts of a chicken, whereas the rest is thrown away. The profit can be made by recreating those parts that humans like to consume. From an animal, a chicken is turned into a deformed, mutilated object, for only those parts are preserved that are essential to sustain life and enable better growth, including the mouth and brain. The aim of this project is to create more meat and thus gain more profit. And while the woman tries to rehabilitate this invention, suggesting that the process is painless for these creatures, it is obvious that these are *animals* that have been transformed into beings that are more profitable for humanity. In the end, Jimmy is disgusted with these bioengineered chickens (and, as it seems, with the very idea of making such an experiment), yet he does not fully reject the possibility of eating such meat: after all, "as with tit implants—the good ones—maybe he wouldn't be able to tell the difference" (203). Thus, while at the beginning of the scene Jimmy's reaction to this experiment is indignation and bewilderment, which suggests how unnatural the very idea of creating such chickens is, in the end he is no longer concerned with the ethical side of the question, joining the majority who think that chickens are only good for human consumption.

The idea of meat as food of the privileged (and thus desired by everyone) is further developed in the novel when Jimmy eats with Crake at his Institute:

> The food in Crake's faculty dining hall was fantastic—real shrimps instead of the CrustaeSoy they got at Martha Graham, and real chicken, Jimmy suspected, though he avoided that because he couldn't forget the ChickieNobs he'd seen; and something a lot like real cheese, though Crake said it came from a vegetable, a new species of zucchini they were trying out.
> The desserts were heavy on the chocolate, real chocolate. The coffee was heavy on coffee. No burnt grain products, no molasses mixed in. It was Happicuppa, but who cared? And real beer. For sure the beer was real. (208)

The difference between meat and meat substitutes is made apparent in this excerpt. And while Jimmy is fascinated with literally every product being "real," including nonanimal foods like coffee, the emphasis on *realness* of all these foods undermines any types of substitutes and thus portrays them as cheap, unhealthy, and generally suspicious. Jovian Parry's idea of "[t]he [p]restige of [m]eat" effectively reinforces the contrast that the characters make between vegan and nonvegan diets, considering the former a survival strategy rather than a true hedonistic way to enjoy life—the latter is believed to be the only correct choice one should make (243). Yet as it might seem at first sight, despite this disadvantageous interpretation of substitutes, the novel energetically "pursue[s] deeper inquiry into whether and how fake meat leverages more responsive and responsible environmental ethics" (McHugh 83). Indeed, although the food that Jimmy eats at Crake's institute looks much more appetizing to him, its very production, conveyed through the images of bioengineered chickens, is revolting and deeply unethical. There is a clearly articulated difference between "real" shrimp, "real" chicken, "real" cheese, and other "real" products that are available to Crake at his prestigious Institute on the one hand, and the products that are served to Jimmy at a lower-class academy as well as the food that he finds in the post-apocalyptic times (these are soya products; meat can no longer be preserved in fridges since there is no electricity and is thus unsuitable for consumption) on the other. Introducing consumption of meat and other animal products as a privilege of the representatives of the upper class or those who are physically stronger (consider, e.g., the final scene in the novel when Snowman observes a group of people frying an animal), the novel raises the question of power, suggesting that veganism is an effective yet largely undermined way through which humanity can acknowledge animal rights and nature as, indeed, a *being* that should be treated with respect.

The novel also engages with veganism directly: the Crakers are vegan as are the God's Gardeners (who are much more prominent in the second novel in the trilogy). Bernice, Jimmy's roommate at college, burns his fake leather shoes for impersonating leather. Yet these images reveal how *Oryx and Crake* never fully commits to veganism, treating it often as a kind of joke. The Crakers are described as some alternative humans, with "their irritating qualities" that include "their naive optimism, their open friendliness, their calmness, and their limited vocabularies" (153). Bernice is referred to as

> a fundamentalist vegan ... who had stringy hair held back with a wooden clip in the shape of a toucan and wore a succession of God's Gardeners T-shirts, which—due to her aversion to chemical compounds such as underarm deodorants—stank even when freshly laundered. (188–89)

Bernice also behaves rather weirdly. For example, she burns not only Jimmy's sandals just for looking like leather but also his underwear because she thinks it is inappropriate to be sexually involved with several girls. God's Gardeners are described as "*a crazed mob*," and their actions taken to "*liberat[e] a ChickieNobs production facility*" are considered "*hilarious*" because "*those ChickieNob things can't even walk*" (340; italics in original). Vegans are thus portrayed as mentally ill people; what they do to allegedly make the world pro-animal is viewed as amusing and, in some instances, even dangerous. While *Oryx and Crake* never undermines the power of veganism, its choice to create humor through references to vegans and veganism does not allow the novel to fully uncover the potential of veganism and persuade the characters and readers in its essentialist nature. Through this ambiguous stance on veganism, however, *Oryx and Crake* evidently reflects the existing, diverse attitudes to veganism. Nevertheless, over the course of the trilogy, veganism evolves to become more serious and is no longer satirized; instead, it becomes the way to survive in the times of crisis and one of the most important means through which to build a new world.

Through consumption, Atwood's novel depicts the horrors of humanity's enslavement of nature that has ultimately led to an apocalypse. Scholars recognize that "the relation of humans to other animals is a matter of pressing environmental, social, economic and philosophical concern" (Cook 587). And while Jimmy/Snowman tells the story of his life before the apocalypse, he does so being "constantly under the threat of being eaten himself" (Parry 242). *Oryx and Crake*'s stance on the human–animal relationship is thus profoundly re-envisioned when Snowman, telling about his food preferences before the apocalypse, risks himself to become someone's prey (a similar effect is achieved through the animalistic nicknames of Jimmy and Glenn—Thickney and Crake—which in the game symbolically called Extinctathon hint at their vulnerability). One might wonder if his "desire to become something more," as interpreted by Mark S. J. Bosco, reflects the reconsideration of his actions that contributed to the collapse (166). Jimmy/Snowman is the survivor of the catastrophe that was inevitable because, as the novel skillfully illustrates, humanity has never had enough and has always wanted more—food that is tastier, sex that is more enjoyable, benefits that are abundant—and being unable to stop this hedonistic, selfish existence, was doomed to fall.

Veganism and survival in *The Year of the Flood* and *MaddAddam*

Oryx and Crake is followed by two other novels, *The Year of the Flood* and *MaddAddam*. While *The Year of the Flood* is closer to *Oryx and Crake* in a sense that it is set during the same time and thus parallels the events described in Atwood's first novel, I examine *The Year of the Flood* together with *MaddAddam*—the final novel in the trilogy that explicitly focuses on the post-apocalyptic world. I argue that the two novels speak about veganism more overtly, as compared to *Oryx and Crake*. They discuss veganism through the lens of survival, making the issue of ecoethics more pronounced and sketching out tight linkages between veganism and environmentalism. Both novels portray speciesism as a perverse and deeply unethical practice through which humanity justifies its dominance over nature and consumption of animals. In doing so, the novels promote the idea of veganism "as an aspect of anti-speciesist practice" (Matthew Cole and Karen Morgan qtd. in Wright, *The Vegan Studies Project* 32). *The Year of the Flood* and *MaddAddam* gradually reveal the criminal nature of meat-eating, acknowledging, through religious references and overt similarities between humans and animals, that survival is the aim of *both* humans and animals, and one way it can be achieved is through humanity's choice of the vegan diet.

The trilogy gets more "vegan" in the second book. This turn to veganism is particularly apparent through the novels' references to fish. Thus, *Oryx and Crake* provides the reader with multiple images of fish-eating, particularly so in the scenes of Snowman's routine consumption of this food: "The women are carrying his [Snowman/Jimmy] weekly fish, grilled the way he's taught them and wrapped in leaves. He can smell it, he's starting to drool" (100). The opening pages of *The Year of the Flood* make a curious reference to fish-eating, too. Toby—one of the protagonists—contemplates the idea that soon in the abandoned pool there might appear fish: "Is she thinking of eating these theoretical future fish? Surely not" (4). The novel adds immediately: "Surely not yet" (4). The attitude to eating fish is apparently different here compared to *Oryx and Crake*; and while it is hinted that Toby might have to eat fish later, such a choice is clearly described as strictly for the purpose of survival. With this example, the tone of the trilogy changes dramatically, as veganism becomes the only right, ethical way of thinking about the world in which the characters find themselves—the world that is collapsing (and later, collapsed) because of humanity's disrespect toward the environment and nonhumans that manifests itself, among multiple other practices and actions, through consumption of animals.

The Year of the Flood becomes even more preachy as it involves various religious events and makes multiple religious references to elucidate why veganism is the only true way to show respect to nature and the environment and survive the apocalypse. These references come from God's Gardeners, a religious group that appears in the second novel in the trilogy, promoting environmentalism through careful, ecofriendly actions, veganism being one of them. Membership in the vegan God's Gardeners is the thing that allows people to survive the plague. God's Gardeners proclaim, "God has given Adam free will, and therefore Adam may do things that God Himself cannot anticipate in advance. Think of that the next time you are tempted by meat-eating or material wealth!" (12). The novel censures capitalism by means of rejecting the imposed ideas of consumption, including consumption of animals and profiting in general.

Consuming animals in particular is described as a repulsive and morally wrong practice akin to cannibalism. Another protagonist of the novel, Ren, shares her experience of eating a rabbit while being among God's Gardeners:

> Zeb went on with the skinning. Amanda helped with the part where the furry green skin turned inside out like a glove. I tried not to look at the veins. They were too blue. And the glistening sinews.
>
> Zeb made the chunks of meat really small so everyone could try, and also because he didn't want to push us too far by making us eat big pieces. Then we grilled the chunks over a fire made with some old boards.
>
> "This is what you'll have to do if worst comes to worst," said Zeb. He handed me a chunk. I put it into my mouth. I found I could chew and swallow if I kept repeating in my head, "It's really bean paste…" I counted to a hundred, and then it was down.
>
> But I had the taste of rabbit in my mouth. It felt like I'd eaten a nosebleed. (140)

Here, the focus is on the rabbit's biological/anatomical closeness to a human being: it has skin, veins, and sinews. And no matter how much Ren is trying to imagine the cooked rabbit meat to taste like a vegan dish, it does taste like a piece of a human to her: "a nosebleed." Comparing the rabbit to a human being, the novel raises the question of ethical consumption, suggesting that a nonvegan diet is essentially similar to cannibalism, thus rejecting speciesism and accentuating that animals should have rights just as humans do because both are living beings.

The narratives equate animals to humans in both *The Year of the Flood* and *MaddAddam*, reinforcing the unethical nature of animal consumption. In *The Year of the Flood*, for example, genetically modified caterpillars are described as having "a baby face at the front end, with big eyes and a happy smile, which makes them remarkably difficult to kill" (16). Yet an even more illuminating example is given in *MaddAddam*, when a group of people encounters pigs. The pigs appear carrying something, at first sight unrecognizable, with them. They are also making sounds. Toby speculates: "If they were people, … you'd say it was the murmuring of a crowd" (325). The people soon realize that the ceremony that they are witnessing is "a funeral," organized in a very similar way as the characters would do in a pre-apocalyptic world (327). Through these attempts to compare animal and human rituals, the novel reimagines animals as social beings. Yet their closeness to humans is particularly effectively reinforced through various linguistic references to these animals as humans. For example, piglets are called "pig babies" (327). As the pigs have left, having complained to humans about the murder of their piglet, Toby notices: "'They've forgotten their…' She almost said *their child*. 'They've forgotten the little one'" (329; italics in original). Such a stark association of the little pig with a human child makes the characters later decide not to eat the piglet but to bury it, just as they would do with a human corpse. Indeed, Ren says that eating this piglet "would be like eating a baby" (331). Toby decides, too, that they "'should bury the piglet,' ... 'It would be right. Under the circumstances'" (334). These associations of animals with humans are helpful to defend and even promote veganism.

Nevertheless, such comparisons are largely de-animalizing, as through them consumption of animals is realized as unethical not because animals are recognized as beings who have rights. These scenes do not foreground the rights of nonhumans but rather continue to promote the speciesist views on human rights, suggesting that only humans (or those who are like humans) deserve to be treated with respect and survive. Through attributing human qualities to animals, both *The Year of the Flood* and *MaddAddam* promote veganism yet in a de-animalizing way, thus turning animals into, what Adams terms as, "absent referents." By making this statement, I do not reject the idea that animals can think, feel, and behave just as humans do. Indeed, scholars outline similarities between the two. For example, in his analysis of Chris Noonan's 1995 film *Babe*, Nathan Nobis argues that the film "helps us get the facts right about animal minds and see better methods of engaging in moral reasoning," thus identifying "a strong, inspiring case for vegetarianism" in this film, despite its exclusively "sentimental" portrayal of animals (59). What I wonder about is what happens to those animals that for certain reasons one cannot so easily associate with humans. I therefore claim that promoting veganism through *humanization* of animals, while indeed might influence some individuals, is essentially incorrect. I concur with Timothy Morton's argument regarding the peculiar nature of animals. Morton writes: "Instead of 'animal,' I use *strange stranger*. This stranger isn't just strange. She, or he, or it—can we tell? how?—is strangely strange. Their strangeness itself is strange. We can never absolutely figure them out" (41; italics in original). Acknowledging the differences between humans and animals *and concomitantly* recognizing animal rights is the true task for humanity today.

Toward the end of *MaddAddam*, peace is proclaimed between humans and pigs: "We [humans] agree to keep the pact. None of you, or your children, or your children's children, will ever be a smelly bone in a soup. Or a ham, she [Toby] added. Or a bacon" (451). With that, the novel, and the trilogy in general, celebrates the human–animal relationship that is allegedly made equal, for humans no longer consume animals (although it would probably be more correct to say *pigs* rather than generalize in this instance). Bearing in mind that "the ethics of eating meat has become framed as part of a wider debate on global sustainability and climate change" (Savvas 213), the "MaddAddam" trilogy can be considered an effective literary narrative that addresses environmentalism through veganism and vice versa. Indeed, as Wright states regarding *The Year of the Flood*, and I expand her argument and claim that the trilogy "specifically ask[s] that we act with regard to how and what (and who) we eat, before it is too late" ("Vegans" 3). And while the novels recreate the well-known "patriarchal versions of human dominance refracted through evolutionary science and ecology" (Keck 25–26; italics in original), they do so to intensify the narrative of exploitation and domination that permeates our culture and makes us every day closer to an inevitable collapse. Veganism and ecoethics are seen in the trilogy as solutions that humanity is reluctant to employ yet should recognize as constructive.

Conclusion

In *The Vegan Studies Project*, Wright says,

> [T]o live one's life without consuming or wearing animal products ... is such a major shift that to choose such a lifestyle essentially is to place oneself perpetually on the extreme margins of society. It is to invite questions, criticism, alienation, suspicion, and misunderstanding. (32)

Through this personal confession/observation, Wright shrewdly pinpoints the dual perception of veganism. On the one hand, veganism is (among other things) a pro-animal and pro-environmental practice. Yet, on the other, the misinterpretation and misuse of veganism and vegan narratives in media have led to a distortion of the notion to such an extent that it has become associated with something abnormal, unhealthy, repulsive, and even evil. Unlearning those meanings of veganism and recognizing its pro-environmental nature is particularly important today, in the era of ecological decline, environmental degradation, and climate change.

Atwood's *Oryx and Crake*, *The Year of the Flood*, and *MaddAddam* illustrate the positive aspects of veganism through their harsh critique of capitalism and endless, mindless consumption. While these novels, to a certain degree, parody veganism, they promote animal rights, call for mindful and ethical actions of humanity toward the environment, and recognize the current crisis that we find ourselves in as an exclusively human-made catastrophe. The trilogy vividly illustrates that co-existence and respect between humans and nonhumans is the only way to go on from now. After all, as Donna J. Haraway has wittingly pointed out in *When Species Meet*: "To be one is always to *become with* many" (2; italics in original). These are the recognition of animal rights and reevaluation and reimagination of what it means to be human that Atwood's trilogy energetically calls its readers to do, hoping for those significant changes that should be made to save the planet and its human and nonhuman inhabitants today.

Works cited

Adams, Carol J. 1990. *The Sexual Politics of Meat: A Feminist-Vegetarian Critical Theory*. New York: Bloomsbury, 2015.
Atwood, Margaret. *MaddAddam*. London: Virago, 2013.
———. *Oryx and Crake*. New York: Anchor Books, 2003.
———. *The Year of the Flood*. New York: Anchor Books, 2009.
———. "Writing Oryx and Crake." *Writing with Intent: Essays, Reviews, Personal Prose: 1983–2005*. 284–286. New York: Carroll & Graf Publishers, 2005.
Bosco, S. J. Mark. "The Apocalyptic Imagination in *Oryx and Crake*." *Margaret Atwood: The Robber Bride, The Blind Assassin, Oryx and Crake*, edited by J. Brooks Bouson, Continuum, 2010, pp. 156–171.
Cook, Guy. "'A Pig Is a Person' or 'You Can Love a Fox and Hunt It': Innovation and Tradition in the discursive Representation of Animals." *Discourse & Society*, vol. 26, no. 5, 2015, pp. 587–607.
Doyle, Julie. "Celebrity Vegans and the Lifestyling of Ethical Consumption." *Environmental Communication*, vol. 10, no. 6, 2016, pp. 777–790.
Emmerman, Karen S. "What's Love Got to Do with It? An Ecofeminist Approach to Inter-Animal and Intra-Cultural Conflicts of Interest." *Ethical Theory and Moral Practice*, vol. 22, 2019, pp. 77–91.
Greenebaum, Jessica Beth. "Questioning the Concept of Vegan Privilege: A Commentary." *Humanity & Society*, vol. 41, no. 3, 2017, pp. 355–372.
Greenebaum, Jessica, and Brandon Dexter. "Vegan Men and Hybrid Masculinity." *Journal of Gender Studies*, vol. 27, no. 6, 2018, pp. 637–648.
Hamilton, Carrie. "Sex, Work, Meat: The Feminist Politics of Veganism." *Feminist Review*, vol. 114, 2016, pp. 112–129.
Haraway, Donna J. *When Species Meet*. University of Minnesota Press, 2008.
Jackson, Mark. "For New Ecologies of Thought: Towards Decolonising Critique." *Coloniality, Ontology, and the Question of the Posthuman*, edited by Mark Jackson, Routledge, 2018, pp. 19–62.

Keck, Michaela. "Paradise Retold: Revisionist Mythmaking in Margaret Atwood's *MaddAddam* Trilogy." *Ecozon@*, vol. 9, no. 2, 2018, pp. 23–40.

McHugh, Susan. "Real Artificial: Tissue-cultured Meat, Genetically Modified Farm Animals, and Fictions." *Configurations*, vol. 18, no. 1–2, 2010, pp. 181–197.

Morton, Timothy. *The Ecological Thought*. Cambridge: Harvard University Press, 2010.

Nobis, Nathan. "The *Babe* Vegetarians: Bioethics, Animal Minds, and Moral Methodology." *Bioethics at the Movies*, edited by Sandra Shapshay, Johns Hopkins University Press, 2009, pp. 56–71.

Parry, Jovian. "*Oryx and Crake* and the New Nostalgia for Meat." *Society and Animals*, vol. 17, 2009, pp. 241–256.

Savvas, Theophilus. "Vegetarianism in the Anthropocene: Richard Powers and Jonathan Franzen." *Textual Practice*, vol. 33, no. 2, 2019, pp. 213–228.

Stein, Rachel. "Sex, Population, and Environmental Eugenics in Margaret Atwood's *Oryx and Crake* and *The Year of the Flood*." *International Perspectives in Feminist Ecocriticism*, edited by Greta Gaard, Simon C. Estok, and Serpil Oppermann, Routledge, 2013, pp. 184–202.

Sullivan, Heather I. "The Dark Pastoral: Goethe and Atwood." *Green Letters*, vol. 20, no. 1, 2016, pp. 47–59.

Szeman, Imre. "Energy, Climate and the Classroom: A Letter." *Teaching Climate Change in the Humanities*, edited by Stephen Siperstein, Shane Hall, and Stephanie LeMenager. *Routledge*, 2017, pp. 46–52.

Wright, Laura. "Doing Vegan Studies: An Introduction." *Through a Vegan Studies Lens: Textual Ethics and Lived Activism*, edited by Laura Wright, University of Nevada Press, 2019, pp. vii–xxiv.

———. "Introducing Vegan Studies." *ISLE: Interdisciplinary Studies in Literature and Environment*, vol. 24, no. 4, 2017, pp. 727–736.

———. *The Vegan Studies Project: Food, Animals, and Gender in the Age of Terror*. University of Georgia Press, 2015.

———. "Vegans, Zombies, and Eco-Apocalypse: McCarthy's *The Road* and Atwood's *Year of the Flood*." *Interdisciplinary Studies in Literature and Environment*, vol. 21, no. 4, 2014, pp. 1–18.

8
Vegan Cervantes
Meat consumption and social degradation in *Dialogue of the Dogs*

José Manuel Marrero Henríquez

Introduction

A traditional scholar would consider this chapter an impossible endeavor from its very beginning, for the title leads to a vegan Cervantes that never existed. In a strict reading, this observation is certainly true. In the age of Cervantes, veganism was far from being the dietary issue, philosophical movement, and sociological phenomenon that currently exists. Indeed, veganism has not been a topic of interest in Cervantine literary criticism, and the study of the role of animals in *Dialogue of the Dogs* (1613) has been the closest that literary critics have approached veganism in his works. Animal ethics have not been at the center of attention of *Dialogue*, and studies have mostly been limited to the relationship of the protagonist Berganza, a talking dog, either with the slave Aesop, who was also given the gift of speech, or with the main character's adventures that follow the tradition of the picaresque novel in which the protagonist continually goes from one master and job to another. Similarly, some of Plutarch's writings offer animals who have served to illustrate moral propositions useful in everyday life or clever strategies in political battles.

There is no assertion in *Dialogue of the Dogs* that leads to an explicit affirmation of veganism, not even a mild vegetarianism. And there is no advocacy of any green diet devoid of products coming from the exploitation of animals. Nothing seems to justify a vegan reading of Cervantes's *Dialogue*, a reading that from the start could be dismissed and considered a misreading full of unforgivable anachronies, historical incoherences, and a variety of capricious inexactitudes. Working with a universal classic of literature, a traditional scholar would assertively argue that Cervantes does not need veganism and that he has already won a permanent place in the history of Western literature; in short, *Dialogue* neither requires "original" readings nor hermeneutical "audacities."

Contrary to its fixed meaning, "permanence" is always changing. No solid argument exists that can support that Cervantes's *Dialogue of the Dogs* is a cultural monument set in stone, maintaining a significance that cannot and should not be found beyond a historicist approach. Nevertheless, *Dialogue of the Dogs* is not only connected to the remote past of the Greek and Latin classics and to its immediate present in Renaissance and Baroque, it is also connected to its future in such a vivid way that it continuously keeps alive the treasure of potential readings.

Hans Robert Jauss asserts that these readings emerge in the great works of art once unexpected circumstances and new horizons for their reception arise.

A vegan Cervantes flourishes with energy in *Dialogue of the Dogs* when contemporary thought arises regarding animal ethics, climate change, overexploitation of natural resources, abuse of the poor, and the political ills of the global dimension of a market economy. Every issue involved in the concept of the Anthropocene, and veganism is no doubt one of them, revitalizes *Dialogue of the Dogs* and upgrades its Horatian poetics, thereby making it again *dulce et utile* for the contemporary reader. Indeed, all of the above-mentioned topics are explicit or implicitly touched on by *Dialogue of the Dogs*, and all the conflicts they entail are figuratively incarnated in the role of meat and in the extreme desire to possess and consume it, which is a driving force seen in many characters of the *Dialogue*. Without a doubt, meat is the most profitable commodity in *Dialogue of the Dogs* and, consequently, greed is the primary subject of concern.

To justify a vegan reading of Cervantes's *Dialogue of the Dogs* in a way that will be acceptable to both open-minded readers as well as those of a more conservative attitude, such a reading will not only be supported by the horizon of expectations of contemporary environmental circumstances and sensibility toward animals and ecological issues, but also be founded on the *auctoritas* of Plutarch, one of the Hellenistic classics, and on a subterranean cultural flow that questions the division of language and rationality between humans and animals. This cultural flow becomes visible when Plutarch and the Cynic School are immersed in a wider non-anthropocentric Western tradition, from Maimonides to St. Francis of Aquinas, from Spinoza to Montaigne, Feijoo, and Wordsworth, from Stuart Mill to Thoreau and Whitman, from Richard Ryder and Peter Singer to Arne Naess and the Deep Ecology Movement.

A vegan Cervantes does not come out of a capricious personal reading of *Dialogue of the Dogs*; rather, it arises as the result of a strong connection with a tradition that has been marginalized by the dominant currents of Western thought and reaches the present time. A renewed Cervantes is being awakened when fully installed in not only what Jorge Bergua Cavero calls the "intense debate that was unleashed throughout Europe during the 17th-century and part of the 18th-century based on the thesis of Descartes according to which animals are automatons "deprived completely of thought and reason" (Plutarco 258), but also in the animal ethics of Tom Reagan, Peter Singer, or J.M. Coetzee and contemporary debates about meat industry practices and their relationship with the domination in politics of capitalism and market economy.[1] *Dialogue of the Dogs* goes deep into most of the topics that are pertinent to contemporary veganism, from the fundamental rejection of any kind of exploitation and cruelty to animals in slaughterhouses, to a more general stance against the "consumer mandate of capitalism," which, in the words of Laura Wright, promotes interest in "examining the ways that oppressions—of peoples, of nature, of animals—are enmeshed and reinforcing" (728, 729).

Aesop and the Picaresque tradition

All beings belong to the same ecosystem and all play a role in the homeostasis of life. The social recognition of this fact has prevented maltreatment of animals, and the vindication of their rights has been framed in what Subercaseaux calls "emergent human rights," a new generation of rights that Subercaseaux considers "akin to alterity and difference; that is, the right of autodetermination of the original people [of America] and ethnic minorities, reproductive rights, sexual minorities rights [and] animal rights" (42). With this conceptual frame at hand, it is curious that studies about the role of the dogs in the Cervantine *Dialogue* have not gone further than establishing relationships between *Dialogue of the Dogs* and those literary metamorphoses in which humans are transformed into animals (*The Golden Ass*) or mute people are given the gift of speech (*Life of Aesop*), the protagonists of the picaresque novel who are constantly changing work and master (figures like Lazarillo and Guzmán de Alfarache), and animals that appear in Polyantheas and treatises of emblems from the Renaissance. Read under the light of "emergent human rights" and with an ecocritical perspective, those relationships can lead much further than formal coincidences and moral lessons about temperance, valor, and patience in everyday life and politics, to a challenging reading that turns the Cervantine story into a text in favor of animal rights and vegan attitudes. As *dulce et utile* as always, the Horatian poetics is now attuned to the animal ethics and environmental awareness of the current time.

Marrero Henríquez (2018) has highlighted two features of the picaresque mode that have been a common ground in the philological studies of the relationship of *Dialogue of the Dogs* with the classics, and these two points are both of special interest to show the animalist and vegan pedagogical potentials of *Dialogue*. The first one is the autobiographical character of the *Life of Aesop* and of the Spanish picaresque tradition (*Lazarillo*, *El Buscón*, *Guzmán de Alfarache*, *Periquillo sarniento*). The second is that, at the beginning of his life, Aesop was a mute slave who, through a metamorphosis, acquires "magically the gift of talking, and afterwards [proceeds] to work for different lords as a servant, philosophical interlocutor and solver of all kinds of problems" (Carranza 142).

The autobiographical nature of Berganza's narration, who as if by magic is given the gift of speech, suggests that, just like Aesop the slave, Berganza and his dog friend Cipión already have the intellectual and sentimental qualities that they demonstrate as talking servants before they were given the ability of speech. With this possibility, the text challenges the separation of intelligence and reasoning from the possession of natural language. Appealing to readers' affection, the autobiographical character of *Dialogue* acts in favor of such challenge, for emotion invites readers to see *Dialogue of the Dogs* not only as a dialogical autobiography of Aesopic inspiration but also as the personal allegation of a dog in favor of animal ethics and rights based upon a series of relevant facts in both the context of *Dialogue* and in real-life: Dogs communicate and talk figuratively; they are faithful and have memory; they decide, have feelings, learn, and do their work with precision and honesty; they plan and foresee according to their experience and contribute to the social well-being. These qualities are without any need of further justification in the so-called "argument of the marginal cases".[2]

Plutarch and Cervantes's "gossip dogs"

It is unknown what books formed a part of Cervantes's library, and it is not clear whether Cervantes was able to read the original works in Greek or Latin; nonetheless, he surely had knowledge of Plutarch by one or all of the three channels at his disposal: the direct reading of primary fonts, the reading of secondary sources (translations, partial translations, and miscellany), and the common knowledge of his time. Not only was Plutarch a favorite reading of the Christian Humanism (Vega 263), Cervantes was educated with López de Hoyos and the Jesuits; and as Muñoz Gallarte brings to light, the Jesuit studies of *ratio studiorum* included Plutarch in the fourth course in which Plutarch was studied in relation to the moral teachings of the patristics (197).

Plutarch's *Parallel Lives* was well known in Spain through Alfonso López de Palencia's romance version published in 1491 in Seville and re-edited in 1508 and 1592. There is documentation on the translation by Juan Castro de Salinas (1562) and of other partial versions with interpolations and personal commentaries by Francisco de Enzinas in *El primero volumen de las vidas de los ilustres y excelentes varones griegos y romanos* (1551) and by Francisco de Quevedo in his *Vida de Marco Bruto* (1644). There are also several Latin and romance translations of *Moralia*, one of them, by

Diego Gracián, counts with two editions close to Cervantes, the first one in Alcalá de Henares (Juan de Brocar 1548) and the second one in Salamanca (Alejandro de Cánova 1571).[3]

The *Dialogue*'s relationship to some of the texts found in Plutarch's *Moralia*, namely "On the Intelligence of Animals," "Animals are Rational or 'Gryllus'," and "On Meat Eating" will serve as the impulse needed to give a step forward from animal ethics into a vegan Cervantes. Criticism has pushed this possible reading of Cervantes and this Plutarchian connection to the side and has instead focused on the influence of those texts from Plutarch that have a presence in treatises of education of princes. In these texts

> are found the examples from *Parallel Lives* that offer models of moral and political virtue to the clergymen and Erasmist and intellectual counter-reformers, committed to the education of princes and governors [and also examples from] *Moralia*, a work with a broad cultural spectrum dominated by pedagogical, theological, philosophical, ethical, religion and apothegm essays or dialogues, as appropriate for gender as for the didactic pretensions of its cultivators. (Pérez Jiménez 2003a: 176)[4]

Cervantine criticism has not considered *Dialogue* relevant for vegan studies, and it has discarded the influence of the texts about animal rationality and meat consumption in favor of other texts from *Moralia* and biographical examples from *Parallel Lives*. In fact, all of the twelve references to Plutarch (far fewer than Virgil's ninety four) with no translation *ad litteram* that Barnés Vázquez (28–39) finds in *Don Quijote* are related to figures found in Plutarch's *Parallel Lives,* and the moral lessons of *Dialogue of the Dogs* relate to the group of twenty-two biographies from relevant historical figures from Greece and Rome that shape *Parallel Lives* (Sáez 152). Nonetheless, there are compelling reasons to consider that specific texts from Plutarch's *Moralia*, such as "On the Intelligence of Animals," "Animals are Rational or 'Gryllus'," and "On Meat Eating," are of great relevance in *Dialogue*. Berganza the dog is intelligent and has feelings. Not only does his story begin in a slaughterhouse, but relevant episodes of his life's adventures revolve around meat as an object of greed, which leads to oppression, and to individual and social corruption.

Berganza was born near the "Door of the Meat," in a slaughterhouse in Seville. His first owner, a butcher named Nicolás el Romo, teaches him how to bite bulls and perform other cruelties. Berganza is in charge of carrying stolen pieces of meat in a basket to Nicolas's concubine. When a woman steals Berganza's meat, Nicolás believes that the dog had illicitly eaten it, and his violent reaction prompts Berganza's wandering life and varied stories with different owners and jobs, which Berganza later relates to Cipión, his dog friend. Indeed, not only is meat the narratological motive that originates the dialogue between Berganza and Cipión, but meat is also a main *leit motif* embodying the issues of greed and social corruption that are of the most relevance in *Dialogue*.[5]

Especially pertinent in two episodes of Berganza's life, meat plays an integral role when he works for a group of shepherds and again when he serves a sheriff. Just after Berganza runs away from Nicolás el Romo and the slaughterhouse of Seville, destiny leads him to a group of shepherds who adopt him and name him Barcino. His new task is taking care of a flock and defending it from wolves. Several attacks occur, and the shepherds order him to search for the wolves; however, Berganza always returns without finding one. One night, Berganza discovers that it is the shepherds themselves who are killing the sheep, stealing the best part of its flesh, and then blaming the wolves. Ignorant of their devious trick, the owner of the flock orders that the dogs be punished, and Berganza decides to flee. Later on in his narrative, Berganza begins to work with a sheriff who recognizes him because he was a friend of his first owner, Nicolás el Romo. Corrupt and allied with a group of thugs who take advantage of multiple robberies and frauds, the sheriff bribes the judges with meat.

Meat is the reason why the shepherds kill the sheep and falsely accuse wolves of the offense. Meat is the object that is stolen in the slaughterhouse and the commodity that the sheriff uses to bribe court clerks, lawyers, and judges. Murderers and thieves go unpunished with the complicity of lawyers and judges who are bought by stolen meat. Indeed, every criminal has a "guardian angel in St. Francis Plaza, gained with loins and tongues" (283). The plaza, located in Seville, is where, as Mariano Baquero Goyanes affirms, the center of justice is found, for there were "the halls of the Cabildo and of the Court" (283). Meat incites a corruption that takes possession of every element of the social body, from the most humble to those that possess the judicial, political, and social power.

In spite of the relevance of meat as a vehicle of corruption and a symbol of animal abuse, criticism has not taken into account the influence of topics like animal rationality, meat consumerism, and veganism that are present in Plutarch's *Moralia* in Cervantes's *Dialogue of the Dogs*. For example, Adrián J. Sáez highlights the relationship of *Dialogue of the Dogs* with the episode of Alcibiades's dog that appears both in *Parallel Lives* and *Moralia*. Alcibiades is a valiant soldier but also a traitor who sometimes saves Athens and on other occasions favors its destruction. He buys a beautiful dog for a considerable amount of money and immediately after cuts off his tail to set him free in the city so that people could gossip about the dog instead of going into more serious subjects about Alcibiades. Sáez considers that Alcibiades's dog is a primary influence on the dogs from the *Dialogue*, for both Cervantine dogs, Berganza and Cipión, not only talk about the ills of seventeenth-century Spanish society but also talk about the vice of gossip itself (151).

To justify the vegan reading of *Dialogue of the Dogs*, it is crucial to mention two facts about the way Cipión and Berganza understand the word "gossip." First, *Dialogue* warns against gossip, but on a significant number of occasions while the Cervantine dogs discuss gossiping they metafictionally refer to the breaking of the story-line and how digressions work against well-structured story-telling. Berganza might lose his capacity to talk at any time and Cipión advises him not to waste his time with gossip but rather guard against talking about his life before it might be too late. Although Sáez rightly considers that "the principal vice that Alcibíades attacks is the gossiping, [...] one of the scourges of 17th-century Spain, as depicted in *The Dialogue of Dogs* and in many other contemporary texts" (155), far from a minor extent, gossiping in *Dialogue* refers to digressions that disturb the order of a story. When Berganza tells the story of his adventures with the shepherds text name him Barcino, he is resting looking for the flock and

> occupied my memory by recalling many things, especially the life I had in the slaughterhouse [...] Oh, what I could tell you now from what I learned in the school of that butcher, my master's wife! But I'll shut them up, why don't you ignore me and consider me a gossip. (306)

A similar reflection occurs at the beginning of chapter XLIV in the second part of *Don Quijote*, a beginning that Marrero Henríquez has characterized as "errata sheet," for it is here that the translator of the original text by Cide Hamete considers that the interpolated novellas that appear in the first part of *Don Quijote* not only distract the reader from the adventures of Don Quijote and Sancho but also do not receive the attention that they, by their own qualities, deserve. Thus, the translator, with great ability and intelligence to discuss the whole universe, decides to keep the narration close to Don Quijote and Sancho's adventures and asks the reader "to praise him, not for what he writes, but for what he has left unwritten" (II, 367).[6]

Most relevant for the vegan reading of *Dialogue of the Dogs* is the fact that the term "murmurador" ["gossiper"] is also related to the exposition of uncomfortable truths and to the challenging thinking of the Plutarchian Cynical tradition. Cynics were identified with dogs for two main reasons: they barked at people and said exactly what they thought, without fear or favor, and they rejected conventional values and lived in accordance with nature, having the most basic necessities covered. Cervantes's dogs Berganza and Cipión are conscious of this Plutarchian canine descendancy. Berganza affirms that

> they sin just as much, the one who says *latines* in front of the one who ignores Latin and the one who says them ignoring [Latin, and declares that he has heard] say a foolishness in Latin as in a Romance language and [that he has seen] silly lawyers and heavy grammarians [that with their Latin lists of words...] very easily can annoy the world not once, but many times. (318–319)

Cipión then warns him that these commentaries not only distract from the line of the story, making it seem like an octopus "as you go adding tails" (319), but they are also dangerous for people can give them the name of "Cynics, which is to say gossiping dogs" (319).

In short, in terms of the structure of the narration, the main vice of the *Dialogue* is gossiping (understood as a digression) and, in moral terms, gossiping means the exposition of plain and uncomfortable truths. Gossip is far from being the main topic of the *Dialogue*, for it is greed incarnated in meat ownership and consumption, which is a central issue of the *Dialogue*. Along these lines, the Plutarchian texts that are most relevant for a vegan reading of *Dialogue of the Dogs* are to be found not in *Parallel Lives* but instead in *Moralia*, especially in the essays about the intelligence of animals and on flesh eating.

Cervantes's *Dialogue of the Dogs* and Plutarch's *Moralia*

As María Luisa Barcallet Pérez affirms when referring to Plutarch's work, in *Dialogue of the Dogs*, Cervantes not only "transgresses [...] our comfortable prejudices regarding the animal, [he also] calls into question the very way we usually contemplate the world, know it and systematize it" (24). For Barcallet Pérez, like Plutarch, Cervantes's *Dialogue* answers the question of "why have we given the place that we have given to animals" and why does animality have the place it has as a mere defense of "human particularity against the undifferentiated" (24), in a kind of work of "anthropogenesis" (25) based on the definition of the human against the animal "to find an essential and permanent nature of the human" (25).[7]

Dialogue of the Dogs invites the reader to an ethical reflection on the status of the animals and about our relationship with them, and like Plutarch's *Moralia*, Cervantes affirms the idea that the animals feel, remember what they felt, try it if it was pleasant, avoid it if it was unpleasant, show expectation or fear in the face of events, flee if necessary, and participate in reason, not, however, in the same way as humans, because animals do not require in their reason detours, theories, or abstractions. Like Plutarch, Cervantes finds in animals the example to follow for the human being "in what prudence, courage, love, continence and sociability refers" (Barcallet Pérez 26) and does not hesitate to make the animal an example of virtue, of courage, loyalty and continence, and despite recognizing the imperfection of the animal in terms of thought, it does not hesitate to find in animal reason a more natural element, more attached to the *logos* expressed in the cosmos. (Barcallet Pérez 28)

Both Cervantes and Plutarch put into question defective dichotomies like rational/irrational or sensation/reason and point out that there is no opposition or disparity between animals and human beings. On the contrary, when participating in reason, animals cannot be debased, devoured, or tortured with impunity. Just as Plutarch affirms in "Gryllus" and in Berganza's autobiographical testimony, man can be considered "the most miserable and calamitous of so many animals that exist in the world" (Barcallet 28). In Plutarch and Cervantes, the good savage of Rousseau exists because in both "the animal already points to a return to a nature alien to the corruptions of civilization and education" (Barcallet Pérez 29).[8]

Toward a vegan Cervantes
Animals talk

Defended by Pico della Mirandola in *On Human Dignity* (1486) and Descartes in *Discourse on the Method* (1637), the relationship of speech and reasoning as an exceptional nature of the human being is confronted by Berganza who suggests the possibility that dogs can possess understanding without having speech. He has

> heard great prerogatives being said [...] that we have a different nature, so alive and so sharp in many things, that it gives indications and signs of missing little to show that we have an *I-don't-know-what* understanding, which is capable of discourse. (280)

Figuratively stated, Berganza admits that perhaps the animals "speak" even though they do not have articulated language and, in doing so, *Dialogue* makes problematic the relationship of humans' ability to speak with the rationality and intelligence attributed to them and distances them from animals. Moreover, it presents the idea that speaking is not a guarantee of correct moral and social behavior. Nothing is evident, Cervantes seems to say, neither the intelligence and rationality of the human animal, nor the unconsciousness and mechanism without reflection of the nonhuman animal.

Dogs are faithful and remember

Berganza shares a wide range of qualities with people, and with respect to many of them, he even proves to be at an advantage, such as with the case of faithfulness and memory. The dog is an animal that stands out for its "great memory [and for] gratitude and great fidelity" (280) so much so that it is painted as a symbol of friendship and "in the alabaster graves, where lie the figures of those who are buried, they put a dog figure between husband and wife at their feet, as a symbol of the friendship and faithfulness that were inviolable in life" (280). In Berganza the dog, memory and fidelity are united—one quality of intellectual character and the other moral in nature. Without a doubt, judging by the social fresco that Cervantes paints in *Dialogue*, the dog is at this point very superior to the human beings with whom he interacts.

Dogs make decisions based on their experience

Wandering from one place and master to another does not happen by chance because Berganza makes multiple decisions. The first, which gives rise to his autobiographical account, is the decision to abandon Nicolás el Romo, his first master, not only because el Romo tries to stab him when he discovers that the meat he had stolen for his concubine did not reach its destination but also because Berganza, of good nature, does not feel comfortable among butchers because "all those who exercise butchery [are] people lacking conscience, heartless, fearless of the King or his justice; most of them living in sin; they, birds of prey, butchers, keep from their friends what they steal" (282–283) and he prefers to find a better place and company with whom to live.

Dogs have feelings

After leaving Nicolás el Romo and spending a night in the open, "another day's fate brought him a herd or flock of sheep and rams" (285). The owner of the flock appeals to Berganza's feelings to get him to stay and he tells a shepherd to "pet him, because he loves the herd and stays with it" (286). Although motivated by interest, the shepherds treat him well and then properly feed him and name him Barcino, and, in return, in his new job he looks "well fed and happy, [appearing] solicitous and diligent guarding the flock" (286). Berganza matches the attention that shepherds give him and decides to stay there on his own accord and responsibly perform his job there.

Dogs learn

Extremely versatile and adaptable, on one of his adventures, Berganza finds a company of soldiers and decides to stay with them. With the drummer, Berganza gives proof of his understanding and learns "to dance to the sound of the drum and to do other endearing things" (316). His new owner calls him "the wise dog" because Berganza is extremely intelligent:

> In less than fifteen days, with my good ingenuity and the diligence of the one I had chosen as my patron, I learned how to jump for the King of France and not jump for the bad tavern, he taught me how to prance like a Neapolitan horse and walk around as a grain mill mule, among other things that, if I did not think about not showing them, he would have wondered if I were a demon in a dog-figure that did these things. [...] I also learned to imitate the Neapolitan steed. He made me some covers of embossed leather and a small chair that I carried on my back, and on it he put a light figure of man with a ring runner and taught me to run straight to a ring between two sticks. (316–317, 318)

Berganza is versatile, capable not only of carrying out the trades of his domestic nature, such as grazing and guarding livestock but also of urban and artistic crafts. Not surprisingly, as the days go by, he finds a theater company and becomes an actor. In a month, he says, "I left a great skit actor and a great faker of silent figures" (341).

Dogs do their job well

Berganza is a good shepherding dog, excellent guardian, attentive caretaker, accomplished artist, and rehearsed actor. Solicitous in all his jobs, he is always skilled and, if in the end he has to leave his post, it is not because of his clumsiness, but because of the hand of the man who threatens him. He is guided more often than not by circumstances in which some moral vice like greed or envy plays a role. These vices foster distrust and are the sin that Cipión considers incompatible with social welfare because "it is impossible for people to have a good life in the world if they do not trust and confide" (291–292).

Dogs contribute to social welfare

Berganza is a faithful dog, even with Nicolás el Romo, his first master the butcher, and he is later with the shepherds, the merchant, the students, the drummer, the actors, and with all the masters he serves. His noble attitude, even with those who lack nobility, is of great social utility because mutual trust is essential for the foundation of community welfare. Both in honesty and in the good performance of his tasks, Berganza is superior to the human beings with whom he relates, who, mean and greedy offenders, use good faith for theft and defile justice with extortion and bribery. One can trust Berganza, and his behavior in society is exemplary and worthy of imitation. As Cipión has already pointed out trust and confidence are a must for having a healthy and happy society (291–292).

Meat consumption, greed, and social corruption

Through the character of Berganza, Cervantes is with Plutarch when he, in the character Gryllus in *Moralia*, shows his surprise before "the arguments with which sophists made animals to be considered irrational and stupid with the exception of humans" (Plutarco 367). Plutarch considers that "Nature is rational in its entirety—it is inspired by a universal logos—[and that] animals also will participate in it in greater or minor measure" (Plutarco 365). In front of Ulysses, Gryllus continues in his pig condition.

Berganza and Cipión have a high intellect. They show feelings and are of great social value. They have a dignity shared with humans that turns eating animals into an act of cannibalism. Meat consumption is but a clear symptom of human degradation, for in Plutarch's words

> first, a wild and predatory animal was sacrificed; then, it was a bird or a fish that was dismembered. And, once our criminal inclination was exercised in the tasting of the blood of the aforementioned animals, then came the ox that plows the earth, the meek lamb and, finally, the rooster guardian of the house. And so, gradually, yielding to our insatiable thirst, we have reached crimes, wars and murders. (Plutarco 394–395)

Furthermore, for Plutarch,

> the ingestion of meat is unnatural not only for the body but also makes the spirit greasy due to satiety and tiredness [...]—because of a numb body, heavy and full of incompatible foods—the light and glow of the spirit [become] weak and confused. (Plutarco 386–387)

It is not a coincidence that the canine protagonist of the Cervantine *Dialogue* was born in a slaughterhouse of Seville, that his first owner was a butcher, and that some relevant dangers the dog goes through during his life with different masters and jobs come after the greed of the immoral behavior that different characters demonstrate in order to possess and consume meat. Everybody can easily be bought with meat and, as shown above, meat is the currency by which judges and sheriffs are corrupted in Seville. And to delve into the Plutarchian connection, it is certainly significant that the very beginning of *Dialogue of the Dogs* comes after Berganza decides to abandon the slaughterhouse of Seville where he was born and his first owner, Nicolás el Romo, a cruel butcher.

Conclusion

Given the figure of Berganza, anthropocentrism and the exceptional nature of the human being are questioned. Neither language nor reasoning can stop the degeneration to which society is directed when arrogance is incapable of sympathizing with the suffering of animals in particular and of the humble in general: of animals that do not speak, or, in other words, of those who speak the unknown language of the colonized slave. Notably, Aesop and Diogenes, who were sold as slaves, guided their owners, and Berganza, who speaks to tell his life from his canine point of view, guides the Horatian potential of the *Dialogue of Dogs* for the benefit of animal rights and, to that end, brings to the forefront the clarity of understanding, sentimentality and social exemplarity of its dog behavior.

In *Dialogue of the Dogs*, there is a vegan Cervantes, a Cervantes that is against the maltreatment of animals and the exploitation of the humble. No doubt the tradition of the Cynics and Plutarch's *Moralia* were an inspiration for *Dialogue*; however, an autobiographical event must have also been of no minor relevance for writing *Dialogue of the Dogs*. Cervantes himself must have felt like an animal, or a "mute" native from the recently discovered America by the Spaniards, like a rational, intelligent, and sentimental animal devoid of language, frequently tied like a dog, when he spent five years, from 1575 until 1580, imprisoned in Argel under the power of the Turkish Empire.[9]

Notes

1. All translations are my own and Ellen Skowronski-Polito.
2. This argument is based on the idea that if all human beings have the same rights, including those that were born with intellectual or physical abilities extremely lessened, then animals of superior intelligence should also enjoy those rights. For this issue see Íñigo de Miguel Beriain (2009). On the development of a justice inspired by animal ethics see Pablo Lora Deltoro (2003).
3. See Adrián J. Sáez and Israel Muñoz Gallarte for further information on Plutarch editions in the Spanish Golden Century.
4. See also Pérez Jiménez (2003b, 2003c, 2005).
5. Economic and social values of meat make of it a nutritious product of symbolic wealth. See Negrín de la Peña for a study on gastronomy and on the role of food in the picaresque novel in the context of the economic history of Spain during XVIth and XVII centuries.
6. See Marrero Henríquez (1990) for a study of this and other structural preoccupations of Cervantes in *Don Quijote*.
7. For the origin of this thinking on animality see Elisabeth de Fontenay.
8. See Bernat Castany Prado for a study on the influence of the Cynics in the building of the good savage.
9. See de Cervantes (2019).

Works cited

Adrados, Francisco R. "La Vida de Esopo y la Vida de Lazarillo de Tormes." *La picaresca: orígenes, textos y estructuras. Actas del I Congreso Internacional sobre la Picaresca organizado por el Patronato "Arcipreste de Hita"*, edited by Manuel Criado de Val, Fundación Universitaria Española, 1979, pp. 349–357.

Bacarlett Pérez, María Luisa. "Plutarco y los animales." *La Colmena*, vol. 65–66, 2010, pp. 23–30.

Barnés Vázquez, Antonio. "Traducción y tradición clásica en el *Quijote*." *Estudios Clásicos*, vol. 138, 2010, pp. 49–72.

Beusterien, John. *Canines in Cervantes and Velázquez: An Animal Studies Reading of Early Modern Spain*. Routledge, 2016.

Carranza, Paul. "Cipión, Berganza and the Aesopic Tradition." *Cervantes: Bulletin of the Cervantes Society of America*, vol. 23, no. 1, 2003, pp. 141–163.
Castany Prado, Bernat. "*Perros en el paraíso*: la influencia de la filosofía cínica en la construcción del mito del buen salvaje." *Anales de la literatura hispanoamericana*, vol. 44, 2015, pp. 221–251.
Castro García, Ricardo José. "La locura y los ladridos. El cinismo en las *Novelas ejemplares* de Miguel de Cervantes." *Caracol*, vol. 6, 2013, pp. 178–202.
de Cervantes, Miguel. *Novelas ejemplares*, edited by V. II, Mariano Baquero Goyanes. Cátedra, 1976.
———. *El ingenioso hidalgo Don Quijote de la Mancha*. 2 vols, edited by Luis Andrés Murillo Castalia, 1978.
———. *Información de Argel*, edited by Adrián J. Sáez, Cátedra, 2019.
Coetzee, J. M. *The Lives of Animals*. Princeton University Press, 2017.
Derrida, Jacques. "L´animal que donc je suis (à suivre)." *L´animal autobiografique*, en Marie-Louise Mallet. París: Galilée, 1999, pp. 251–301.
Descartes, René. *Discurso del método*. Alianza, 2011.
Feijoo, Benito Gerónimo. *Teatro crítico universal*, Tomo III. Madrid: Imprenta de Ayguals de Izco Hermanos, 1845.
de Fontenay, Elizbeth. *Le silence des bêtes. La philosophie à l'éreuve de l'animalité*. Fayard, 1998.
Haussleiter, Johannes. *Der Vegetarismus in der Antike*. Verlag von Alfred Töpelmann, 1935.
Jauss, Hans Robert. *Toward and Aesthetic of Reception*. Minneapolis: University of Minnesota Press, 1982.
Lora Deltoro, Pablo de. *Justicia para los animales. La ética más allá de la humanidad*. Alianza, 2003.
Lope, Hans-Joachin. "La racionalidad de los brutos. El Padre Feijoo ante el problema de la vivisección." *Actas del X Congreso de la Asociación Internacional de Hispanistas*, en Antonio Vilanova (coord.), Vol. 2. Barcelona: Promociones y Publicaciones Universitarias, 1992, pp. 1185–1192.
Marrero Henríquez, J. M. "Affection, Literature, and Animal Ideation." *Spanish Thinking about Animals*, edited by Margarita Carretero-González. Michigan State University Press, 2020, pp. 3–20.
———. "Ética animal en *Coloquio de los perros*." *Ocnos*, vol. 17, no. 3, 2018, pp. 86–94.
———. "Animalismo y ecología: sobre perros parlantes y otras formas literarias de representación animal." *Castilla. Estudios de Literatura*, vol. 8, 2017, pp. 258–307.
———. "La crítica como refugio: animales, plantas y enclaves literarios en peligro de extinción." *Lecturas del paisaje*, edited by José Manuel Marrero Henríquez, Universidad de las Palmas de Gran Canaria—Gabinete Literario, 2009, pp. 17–32.
———. "El héroe frente a la preceptiva en el *Quijote*." *Anales Cervantinos*, vol. 28, 1990, pp. 63–71.
Miguel Beriain, Íñigo de. "¿Derechos para los animales?" *Dilemata*, vol. 1, 2009, pp. 15–31.
Mirandolla, Pico della. *Sobre la dignidad del hombre*. Editorialpi, 2006.
Montaigne, Michel de. "Apología de Raimundo Sabund." *Ensayos de Montaigne seguidos de todas sus cartas conocidas hasta el día*, 1898. http://www.cervantesvirtual.com/obra-visor/ensayos-de-montaigne--0/html/fefb17e2-82b1-11df-acc7-002185ce6064_84.html#I_85, pp. 290–391 Accessed August 2 2017.
Negrín de la Peña, José Antonio. "La mesa del Dómine Cabra: comida y vino en la novela picaresca del siglo de oro español." *Estudios Avanzados*, vol. 18, 2012, pp. 75–99.
Pérez Jiménez, Aurelio. "Los animales de Plutarco en la emblemática europea de los siglos XVI-XVII." *Les Grecs de l'Ántiquité et les animaux. Le cas remarkable de Plutarque*, edited by J. Boulogne, Université Lille 3, 2005, pp. 63–94.
———. "El Plutarco de los *Moralia* en la literatura emblemática hispánica." *Literatura hispanoamericanana del siglo XX. Mímesis e iconografía*, coordinated by Mª. G. Fernández Ariza, University of Málaga, 2003a, pp. 169–195.
———. "Las Vidas paralelas de Plutarco en la emblemática hispánica de los siglos XVI-XVII." *Humanitas*, vol. 55, 2003b, pp. 223–239.
———. "Los heroes de Plutarco como modeolo en la literature emblemática europeaen los siglos XVI-XVII." *Modeli eroici dall'Antichità alla cultura Europea*, edited by A. Barzanó et al., L'Erma di Bretschneider, 2003c, pp. 375–402.
———. "Plutarco y el Humanismo español del Renacimiento." *Estudios sobre Plutarco: obra y tradición. Actas del I Simposio Español sobre Plutarco (Fuengirola 1988)*, edited by Aurelio Pérez Jiménez y Gonzalo del Cerro Calderón, Universidad, 1990, pp. 229–248.
Plutarco. *Moralia. Obras morales y de costumbres*, edited by Vicente Ramón Palerm y Jorge Bergua Cavero, Gredos, 2002.
Ryder, Richard. *Victims of Science*. Davis-Poynter, 1975.
Sessions, George, editor. *Deep Ecology for the 21st Century*. Shambala, 1995.
Sáez, Adrián J. "Más sobre Cervantes, Plutarco y los cínicos: una anécdota de Alcibíades y el *Coloquio de los perros*." *Anales Cervantinos*, vol. 46, 2014, pp. 149–160.

Subercaseaux, Bernardo. "Perros y literatura: condición humana y condición animal." *Atenea*, vol. 509, 2014a, pp. 33–62.

———. *El mundo de los perros y la literatura. Condición humana y condición animal*. Santiago de Chile: Ediciones Universidad Diego Portales, 2014b.

Wordsworth, William. *The Collected Poems of William Wordsworth*. Wordsworth Editions, 1998.

Wright, Laura. "Introducing Vegan Studies." *ISLE. Interdisciplinary Studies in Literature and Environment*, vol. 24, no. 4, 2017, pp. 727–736.

9
A quiet riot
Veganism as anti-capitalism and ecofeminist revolt in Han Kang's *The Vegetarian*

Liz Mayo

In Han Kang's novel *The Vegetarian*, South Korean wife Yeong-hye decides abruptly to give up meat, eggs, and dairy and to stop wearing leather after a series of disturbing dreams. This change happens to her husband's chagrin, as his mild-mannered wife now practices "sheer obstinacy" (22) by refusing to eat, buy, or cook meat. The text is told in three parts: through Yeong-hye's husband's perspective, through her brother-in-law's, and through her sister's. The first two narratives include alternating views of Yeong-hye's new lifestyle: her husband sees her veganism as an aggressive act of insubordination, which angers and revolts him; her sister's husband, by contrast, becomes obsessively aroused and uses her weakened state for his own artistic gain. Yeong-hye's sister's perspective in the third part of the novel expresses her complicity in the crimes against the new vegan—a collusion she can't see until she recognizes her own lack of autonomy. Yeong-hye's veganism angers her abusive father who force-feeds her meat in front of her gawking family, and it prompts male healthcare practitioners to restrain and abuse her body in the name of wellness.

All of these characters are a foil to vegan, anti-materialist Yeong-hye; they present an encroaching patriarchal and capitalist force. This ethos links meat consumption with masculinity—one cannot exist without the other—and the men in Yeong-hye's life are drawn by Kang as agents of rape culture who use meat as their weapon; those opting out of this consumption—manifested here in Yeong-hye's refusal to engage in the meat industry, and by extension, the capitalist system—are destroyed and discarded. The men force Yeong-hye to eat flesh, sexually exploit her body, isolate, and abandon her when she does not comply, and condemn her to a realm of the pornographic and mentally insane when she refuses to *ingest* their authority. The women, including Yeong-hye's sister, mother, sister-in-law, and other judgmental female dinner patrons, offer little support to her. Perhaps fearing their own loss of autonomy, they shame and shun her. These women align themselves with those in power not only because they, too, are often the silenced and abused but also because this allegiance ensures they won't stand out and be destroyed. These characters become players in the furthering of a capitalist cause with Yeong-hye running away from consumerism and escaping into the natural world.

When viewed theoretically through a vegan studies perspective, Yeong-hye represents the natural world, and the oppressive men in her life are the push for industrialization. As Wright puts it, this theoretical frame posits a vegan body as "contested" and bound by confining "assumptions" (xv)—a truth made manifest in Kang's portrayal of Yeong-hye. She is the land, and the corporations—the men who hold the power—pillage it; their preconceived notions of her clear a path toward this abuse. As Gaarder notes, "Societies that see nature as inferior to culture (most Western societies) devalue and oppress persons and groups identified with nature" (5). Moor also details this trend away from respecting the land and its creatures the more a place becomes westernized (214). Yeong-hye is in Seoul—a westernized urban setting—and she falls prey to what Martin Hultman calls "industrial breadwinner masculinity." Proponents "see the world as separated between humans and nature. They believe humans are obliged to use nature and its resources to make products out of them" (qtd. in Gelin). Yeong-hye turns away from her prescribed role, using veganism as her personal riot, which is linked with her revelation that her lot is not unlike the animals beaten into meat. She is exploited; she is told to dress up for outsiders so as to improve her capital; she is controlled, violated, and wrangled; and she is destroyed. In short, Yeong-hye does not merely change her diet; she asserts the importance of bodily autonomy, whether it be animal or mineral, which is an insurmountable battle juxtaposed against capitalist gain.

As a disempowered wife of a controlling man in a burgeoning capitalist system, Yeong-hye must quietly revolt. South Korea is an apt site for this revolution, as it is a "strange country where capitalism, socialism, and communism blend and coexist…a land of contradictions" (Seong-kon). While there is a capitalist economic system, there is a decidedly communist mindset, generating friction between individual desires and collectivist obligations. As Seong-kon asserts, Koreans are both revolted by capitalist wealth while secretly envious of prosperity; thus, they "constantly compare [themselves] to others." This drive toward material gain places Yeong-hye in a perilous position. She operates in contrast to the manic consumerist model around her. And because South Korea has grown into one of the wealthiest nations in the world, especially in Asia, her veganism is an affront to the imperialist maxim Carol J. Adams identifies: "if the meat supply is limited, white people should get it; but if the meat is plentiful all should eat it" (8). As the wife of a professional, meat is readily available to Yeong-hye. Her refusal to partake is not only a shift in diet but, more importantly, an affront to capitalist tendencies. Yeong-hye represents something different: she is the anti-consumer. She expresses no desire for *things*, choosing to live in a bare space and often forgoing clothing. She opts out of the system; thus, she is seen as a rebellious denier of her feminine role, a petulant child, a vulnerable activist, and, finally, someone who must return to nature to heal after being assaulted within the unflinching capitalist economic system. In place of being the consumer, she becomes consumable.

The first part of the novel, entitled "The Vegetarian," is told not by Yeong-hye but by her husband, Mr. Cheong. He is attracted to her "passive personality" (11), noting that he enjoys interacting with people who he perceives are beneath him, thus ensuring his role of "ringleader" (12). Yeong-hye's passivity makes him less concerned about the diminutive size of his penis, and her silence along with her lack of demands make her, initially, the perfect wife to his weak ego. It is through his perspective that we view Yeong-hye, yet Kang ensures that his neuroses are apparent to readers. In Mr. Cheong's view—this being the only name we learn, which establishes his authoritarian role—his wife has little to offer by way of looks and personality, yet she makes him feel like a bigger man as they progress without fanfare up until the day that Yeong-hye declares her new diet. These changes create a fault line in her already unbalanced marriage; her husband is used to being unchallenged by an "ordinary wife who went about things without any distasteful frivolousness" (12). Initially, this "frivolous" decision to change her diet is seen as just that: a woman's silly whim or a ploy to lose weight. As Yeong-hye transitions from veganism to a food ascetic, however, she evolves from complacent wife to a woman who silently revolts against a life of abusive men.

Five years into their marriage, Mr. Cheong encounters his wife in her pajamas staring into the refrigerator, incapable of responding to his touch. Put off by this shift in routine, he finds this change "chilling" (15). Her mutiny continues as she throws all of their expensive meat into the trash, the capital waste angering him. He exclaims, "Have you lost your mind?" and begins to yank the bags from her. He is "stunned" that she is "tugging back against" him (18). Adams writes that "people with power have always eaten meat" (4), so it is no wonder that a man who seeks ultimate domestic authority would feel slighted by the removal of the meat that reinforces his masculine power. If a woman is trying to lose weight, in Mr. Cheong's mind, then the diet is founded on "reasonable grounds" (22), but this is not the case with Yeong-hye. He can't sanction a stance against masculinity, patriarchal power, and capitalist accomplishment, nor will he allow his wife to make these decisions for herself. Thus far in the marriage, Yeong-hye's only discernable rebellion was in the form of her refusal to wear a bra. This initially aroused him when they were dating, but he notes his desire to have her now wear a "thickly padded" brassiere so he can "save face" in front of others (13). Indeed, he wishes to control everything about Yeong-hye—be it her diet or appearance or her sensuality or celibacy—now that she is perceived as his property.

Yeong-hye's veganism is prompted by a disturbing, recurring dream, and it is through her stream-of-consciousness that bleeds into her husband's narrative that we learn about these images. She vividly sees scenes of cooking meat and remembers a feeling of shame and guilt: "*Blood in my mouth, blood-soaked clothes sucked onto my skin. …In that barn, what had I done?*" (20). We later learn that Yeong-hye's childhood included a traumatic incident with a dog who bit her. Her father, an overbearing and sadistic Vietnam War veteran who makes Yeong-hye the family whipping boy, tortures the dog then cooks and feeds it to her. She remembers the incident in her dreams, noting that she did "scoop up a mouthful" of dog meat after looking into the dog's eyes during the torture (49). She now claims she "really didn't care" about any of it (50), but it is clear that this trauma numbs Yeong-hye to the point that her dreams prompt waking action. Caruth writes that "traumatic dreams and flashbacks…resist cure to the extent that they remain…literal" (5). She continues by noting that the dream's "insistent return…constitutes trauma" and "the traumatized…carry an impossible history within them" (5). Yeong-hye has been beaten into submission by her sadist father and her controlling husband. These flashbacks awaken something disturbing yet powerful within her, exhibited in her staunch resolve to be vegan. Moreover, Elizabeth Cherry finds that vegans have greater long-term compliance when their decision is prompted by an "epiphanic moment" (156). Clearly, Yeong-hye's new way of eating is more than a fad or a quick dalliance; it is a response to trauma brought on by an epiphany of her buried past. Her veganism is an insurgency avoiding the feminine proclivity to use "apologetic strategies of dissociation and avoidance" for her lack of meat eating (Rothgerber). When asked by Mr. Cheong how long she'll go without meat, she responds "I suppose…forever" (21). And for the first time in their marriage, when he rages at her, she feels nothing—certainly not the usual distress: "*Why didn't this agitate me like it should have done? Instead, I became even calmer*" (27).

The abuse doesn't end at home for Yeong-hye who is at the mercy of others' disdain at a business dinner she's forced to attend. Mr. Cheong's boss says "My word, so you're one of those 'vegetarians,' are you?" His wife adds, "But surely it isn't possible to live without eating meat?" (30). The conversation "naturally continued" (30) on the topic of Yeong-hye's diet with fellow patrons remarking that veganism "isn't natural," is "narrow-minded," and leads to an "[un]balanced mind" (31). Having angered her husband because she did not dress up for the dinner, Yeong-hye stokes his rage by refusing "pleasantries" with the other wives (29) and by declining non-vegan food, stating that she quit eating meat because she "had a dream" (31). Her silent confrontation renders her "utterly unknowable" (33) to her husband. A vegan studies approach shows that like anything in the natural world when viewed through a consumer-driven lens, she appears wild and untamed, which is terrifying to a capitalist if not exploited. Yeong-hye refuses to follow the rules of polite human interaction, so she is dismissed as mentally incompetent, alien, selfish, or remote.

Because the default is that meat eating is natural, the dinner guests engage in what Alka Arora refers to as "uncritical carnism" (30). Amy Calvert asserts that "Rhetoric saturated with connotations of the 'natural' and 'normal' deems meat-eating socially acceptable, thus evading critique, and avoiding moral and ethical arguments contesting it" (19). Vegan Yeong-hye is the minority at the table; as the dinner is for business networking, she is outnumbered by people who are there for economic gain, and she's expected to adhere rigidly to gendered marital roles. The men are there to work, and the women should support that pursuit. The wives are just as critical of Yeong-hye as the husbands because they sense her contempt for the means of production via her refusal to *consume*. She skirts what Steven G. Kellman calls "anti-vegetarian bigotry" and "belligerent banter by the dinner-party smart alecks intent on discrediting a guest who prefers lettuce and tomato" (534–535). She contrasts the flesh-eaters who believe "to eat meat is also to consume, and thus embody, dominance" (Calvert 19).

At a family dinner, Mr. Cheong immediately begins appraising his sister-in-law, In-hye, taking note of her "nicely filled-out figure" and "demure manner of speaking" (42). In addition to his desire for her body, he admires her work ethic, which has brought wealth to their family, thus allowing In-hye's husband to "spend his whole life messing about with 'art'" (42). By contrast, Yeong-hye is quiet and, to her husband's vexation, doesn't waste words "complimenting the house nor thanking her sister for taking the trouble to prepare the food" (42). This dinner occurs after Yeong-hye emerges wearing no bra—effectively freeing herself on her own terms. Mr. Cheong views his wife's change in eating as a "plight" he must bear (42) while lusting after her sister's body and meat-heavy cooking. He co-opts his wife's lifetime of abuse and attempts to gaslight her into believing that *he* is the victim.

The criticism against Yeong-hye continues at the dinner table when In-hye remarks that her sister didn't eat the oysters she specially prepared for her. Yeong-hye's sister-in-law comments on her appearance and says "…I never would have guessed that going vegetarian could damage your body like that" (43). Her mother adds "How could you have got into this wretched state…?" (44). She continues by placing pork up to Yeong-hye's mouth. As a long-suffering wife of an overbearing husband, Yeong-hye's mother aligns with the masculine status quo. She wants her daughter to conform because she signals compliance as security; however, Yeong-hye defies them all with a simple "I won't eat it" (45). It is Yeong-hye's father who becomes the most insistent that she eat meat, shoving the flesh near her mouth. Rather than being offended or put off by the poor treatment of his wife, Mr. Cheong is "moved to tears" by Yeong-hye's father's "fatherly affection" (46). Barbara McDonald et al. assert that family and friends of vegans "keep individual autonomy within strict and narrowly defined boundaries… one could eat whatever one wants as long as it supports the ideology of speciesism," and Yeong-hye is subject to these food-compliance rules. It is not only the men in the room but also the women who wish for Yeong-hye to just "behave" (47), pleading that she not upset the patriarch. Amenability has been bred into the women through their traditional wifely roles. In Korean culture, vocal women are bullied until they "stay in their place" (qtd. in Kuhn). Even women with perceived capital power in Korean culture, such as famous female performers, are not immune to restrictive gender norms; some commit suicide to escape social judgment (Kuhn).

Kang's dinner table scene is a violent retelling that is reminiscent of a passage Adams highlights from Mary McCarthy's *Birds of America*. In it, Adams notes a "fictional illustration of the intimidating aspect to a man of a woman's refusal of meat," as it depicts a female vegetarian dining at a NATO general's home; when she refuses meat, he forces the meat onto her plate and continues a conversation celebrating the war in Vietnam (Adams 16). Like the General in this tale, Yeong-hye's father is a product of the war who boasts about his service in Vietnam, during which Koreans served to repay Americans for the Korean War—a thank you note for capitalism—and to make money. Like the General, Yeong-hye's father is unhinged by his daughter's veganism, seeing her refusal to eat flesh as an insubordinate act that doesn't align with his militaristic values of conquering and compliance.

Kang's scene, though, is far more violent than McCarthy's. Yeong-hye's father hits her when she says "Father, I don't eat meat" (46). He calls over Mr. Cheong and Yeong-hye's brother—the other men in the room—to assist him in force-feeding his daughter: "Take hold of Yeong-hye's arms, both of you," he commands (46). Her brother urges her to comply, pleading "Sister, just behave, okay? Just eat what he gives you" (47) as the father approaches with the meat now in his bare hands in place of the chopsticks. What follows is a violent display of abuse narrated by Mr. Cheong:

> My father-in-law mashed the pork to a pulp on my wife's lips as she struggled in agony. Though he parted her lips with his strong fingers, he could do nothing about her clenched teeth. Eventually he flew into a passion again, and struck her in the face once more. ... The instant that the force of the slap had knocked my wife's mouth open he'd managed to jam the pork in...My wife growled and spat out the meat. An animal cry of distress burst from her lips. (47–48)

Men use the "absence of meat" as a "pretext for violence against women" and as "an excuse for their violence" (Adams 17). The image of her father's fingers forcing Yeong-hye's mouth open and shoving in the meat is reminiscent of the sexual assaults Yeong-hye endures from both her husband and, later, from her brother-in-law. It is no wonder that she responds like a trapped animal fighting her way to safety before grabbing a knife and slicing her wrist. The narrative shifts to her stream-of-consciousness recall of the day her father killed the dog that bit her, linking her self-harm to her traumatic memory of eating a tortured animal and allowing her to dissociate from the present abuse.

At the end of part one, Yeong-hye is a broken shell. She has been raped by her husband who believes his "physical needs" are "unsatisfied" (38). He is annoyed that her face looks like a "woman of bitter experience, who had suffered many hardships" (39). To Mr. Cheong, Yeong-hye is overly dramatic when she fights back against his sexual abuse. He feels the same way about her physical struggle as he does her dietary revolt: both are unnecessarily histrionic. Yeong-hye's family, along with complete strangers, have shamed and verbally abused her, and she has nothing left to lose. She is swallowed by a healthcare system that cannot adequately treat her lifetime of trauma. Practitioners misunderstand her veganism as the cause of her odd behavior without realizing that this is her last right—to choose what to consume. Even her mother attempts to trick Yeong-hye into eating meat at the hospital. When Yeong-hye vomits the concoction, her mother is concerned not with her daughter's health but with the cost: "do you know how much this is worth?. ... Money scraped together with your own parents' sweat and blood!" (55). Yeong-hye feels a "*lump*" inside of her, claiming "*the lives of the animals I ate have all lodged there*" (56). While her mother's focus is on the cost of the meat for which she paid with "blood," to Yeong-hye, it is the animals' sacrifice that haunts her and for which she must atone.

For Yeong-hye to escape the "butchered bodies" that "still stick stubbornly" within her (56), she must leave the animal kingdom completely and become part of the vegetable world. Like a plant, she begins to sun herself in the nude. Yeong-hye moves from what Shantz calls "mainstream environmentalism" wherein "humans are conceptually separated out of nature" and given dominion over "non-human constituents" (43) and evolves toward "radical" and "deep ecology" where "the emphasis is upon human embeddedness within nature" (44). She is fully aligned with the natural world and is no longer a product of worth to her husband; he exploits all that she offers and divorces her. Her mental health never improves from this moment forward in the novel.

In part two entitled "Mongolian Mark," another man uses Yeong-hye's body for personal gain. Her brother-in-law is an artist who has been creatively stunted for several years until he becomes inexplicably obsessed with Yeong-hye's birthmark—knowledge of which causes him to have an erection. He wants to film two lovers covered in painted flowers with the female subject being his sister-in-law, Yeong-hye; he decides, with little confliction, to be the male subject. The proposition to an emotionally distressed Yeong-hye presumably feeds into her desire to be a plant, and it renews his artistic passion while, in *his* mind, rejuvenating Yeong-hye. This part recalls Richard Slotkin's "divine king myth" wherein the king's health is dependent upon his link to the land. This wellness can be ensured through a "ceremonial sexual union with the goddess of the woods…after the barrenness of winter" (299). This is how the brother-in-law sees himself: as the king of his own story in need of a goddess. His "barrenness" comes in the form of his artistic dearth, and Yeong-hye is the exotic creature who can "regenerate" him.

While he appears as the opposite of Yeong-hye's corporate-driven husband, the brother-in-law is just another man seeking to "profit" from Yeong-hye's body. Aph Ko and Syl Ko comment on women as objects of "perpetual beauty" who are "*exploitable*" because they are "distanced from subjecthood…alien and *different*, mystical creatures, passive beautiful things" (31). Vegans Ko and Ko connect culture's exploitation of women to the exploitation of animals and nature—all kept at a "distance" so as to be "perpetual object[s] of beauty" (31). While Yeong-hye is described by her husband as unattractive and foreign to him, her brother-in-law finds her alluring. Yet he just watches Yeong-hye at a distance as if she were a *thing* and not a *being*. Seeing nature as part of us—like seeing Yeong-hye as an autonomous person—would render exploitation of both entities taboo. Corey Lee Wrenn echoes the sentiment that stereotypes about women as alternately "beautiful, fertile, bountiful, inspirational, maternal, or romanticized" are "qualities applied to both nature and women" (133). The brother-in-law is mesmerized by oddness and aroused by the thought of Yeong-hye's naked body. He is fascinated, if shallowly ashamed, by the oddness of sex with his family member, a tormented artist who seeks a beautiful subject. The overlap here is clear through a vegan studies perspective: she *becomes* nature for him, and he exploits that status, believing that he is her savior and unlike the husband who plundered her.

Like Mr. Cheong, Yeong-hye's brother-in-law is self-conscious and self-absorbed. He sees in his reflection a "receding hairline" and a "paunch" (65), and he hides his "balding crown" (69) with a cap. After not working as an artist for two years and living in a house funded fully by his wife's salary, he receives an ego boost from pursuing the weaker of the two sisters. While his previous work focused on "people worn down by the vicissitudes of late capitalist society" (67), his new vision of a man and woman covered in flowers copulating depicts a divergence from his early art. Yeong-hye appears to him "like a tree that grows in the wilderness" (71) with a birthmark that looks "like a small blue petal" (67). She embodies his romanticized return to nature and artistic wealth; even her diet intrigues him, as it reminds him of the birthmark "so that the one could not be disentangled from the other" (79). He fetishizes Yeong-hye's body and assuages his conscious by claiming that the sex between them is "more vegetal than sexual" (90).

While the brother-in-law does have more sympathy for Yeong-hye, referring to her as a "cornered animal" (74) when her father tries to force meat into her mouth, his actions are not motivated by a desire for her well-being. Carretero-Gonzalez views this section of the novel as an experience for Yeong-hye that "breathes new life into her" (171), noting that she is not a "passive muse" (171). What Carretero-Gonzalez fails to fully acknowledge, however, is Yeong-hye's mental illness that renders her consciously incapable of sexual consent. The brother-in-law enters Yeong-hye's apartment and is aroused to see her emerge unabashedly nude. He tells himself that "she wasn't as far gone as all that" (83), yet a mentally well person would not lose the natural tendency to cover up in front of a family member's eyes. He chastises himself "for having used her as a kind of mental pornography" then imagines undressing her (84); his confliction is undermined by his titillation. When he first talks to Yeong-hye about his project, he does not reveal his motives, instead stating that he wants her to "model" (85). He plies her with ice cream as if she were a child, and she responds without emotion to his request. His fixation with Yeong-hye is revealed when passers-by view him as "this man who looked possessed" (90). When he allows himself to consider her mental illness, he admits that her eyes "reflect a kind of violence that could not simply be dismissed as passivity or idiocy or indifference" (93). To him, Yeong-hye "could not be called a 'person'" (95). As Young-hyun Lee states, "the failure of people around [Yeong-hye] to recognize her suffering is a failure to recognize her very being." Yeong-hye is part of the "patriarchal narrative" that "depicts male quests and female passivity" (Adams 78). The brother-in-law does not view Yeong-hye as an equal collaborator on his art because he does not validate her traumatic past or recognize her fragile mental state; to him, she holds no personhood status.

Like Mr. Cheong, the brother-in-law is an abusive husband who sees his relationship with his wife In-hye as that of "business partners" (88). That night, he covers In-hye's mouth and rapes her while fantasizing about his sister-in-law. In-hye mutters to him "*You're scaring me*" (89) but, as with Yeong-hye, he fails to acknowledge her pain. In-hye discovers her husband and sister naked together after filming the plant sex video, which ends her marriage. Carretero-Gonzalez comments that In-hye's response is limited in some way—that "she can only see the images…as an instance of sexual abuse, exerted by her husband on the body of her mentally weak sister" (173). If we trust the limited perspective of part two as told through the brother-in-law, then certainly one could construe the events as artistic experimentation. But after the sex, Yeong-hye "burst into tears" (120) and asks "Will the dreams stop now?" (121). The brother-in-law's dismissal of his wife's feelings, his crazed look revealed through outsiders' perspectives, and his projection of his artistic viewpoint upon his "model," draw him as just another swindler exploiting female bodies—a perfect capitalist confidence man.

In the final part of the novel, "Flaming Trees," Kang fully circles around to connecting both Yeong-hye's and In-hye's abused bodies to a wild natural world contrasted with an industrialized system. From a vegan studies perspective, Kang offers a "mainstream" interdisciplinary space for "women's utterances of displacement, abuse, and unequal treatment" (Wright 260). Yeong-hye is now imprisoned by a mental health system that cares little for her rehabilitation. At the facility, she stands beside a window mumbling and "bare[s] her breasts to the sun" (144). Yeong-hye no longer speaks or exhibits human traits, which fully alienates her from readers. The narrative then transitions to In-hye's perspective. Notably, the dissolution of In-hye's marriage allows her to see clearly what she hadn't yet comprehended: her own lack of agency and her culpability in Yeong-hye's abuse. In-hye believed, when her father forced the meat into Yeong-hye's mouth, that he was elderly and "not so bad" (51). She suggests then that Yeong-hye should have complied with eating the meat because "she is his daughter" (51). As failed advocate for her sister, In-hye questions the role she played in Yeong-hye's descent into madness. In-hye now views their father as "heavy-handed" (135), and her husband's "unforgivable" deed also makes her question her actions: "Wasn't there something she could have done to prevent it?" (142) and "Could she have found a way to impress on him that Yeong-hye was still...ill?" (143). Yeong-hye had "been perfectly cheerful and sociable" (135) but was now "retreating from herself" (136). The vulnerable seek protection through allegiance to the violator, explaining In-hye's failure to intervene on Yeong-hye's behalf. In-hye was loyal to the men who kept her in stunted adulthood: her fidelity to things that are "decaying" (167) is a trait she's carried her whole life.

In-hye has been nearly as damaged as Yeong-hye in the capitalist model. She reflects on her marriage as "utterly devoid of happiness and spontaneity" (166) and notes "the feeling that she had never really lived" (167). It is only in reflection and after witnessing her sister's suffering that In-hye is acutely aware of her own life lived as a "child" simply trying to "endure" (167). She remembers the night her husband forced himself onto her, telling her to "just put up with it for a minute" (169), an image that causes her to consider self-harm. Through these difficult months, she forces herself to smile at the customers at work, but night time brings back a "gaping black wound still sucking at her" (168). She looks at all of the "objects" in her apartment and feels that "they did not belong to her. Just like her life had never belonged to her" (170).

This is the crux of In-hye's story. Much like animals in captivity, she has never owned the rights to her body, but unlike Yeong-hye, it takes her much longer to see the trappings of capitalist culture. She realizes the hollowness of the beauty posters she displays at her cosmetics store, and she gains no fulfillment from the things she's accumulated. She finally *sees* and *acknowledges* Yeong-hye's deep depression—something no other character does—noting "Yeong-hye had simply let fall the slender thread that had kept her connected with everyday life" (172). In-hye closes her eyes and envisions Yeong-hye surrounded by "summer trees" and "only fragments of cities, small towns and roads are visible" (174); even in her fantasies, she wishes for her sister to be in nature. When the doctor forces a feeding tube down Yeong-hye's throat—another man invading Yeong-hye's body without her consent—In-hye rushes in and screams at him. Shirking her passive femininity, she "grabs Yeong-hye's doctor by the shoulder...and yanks him back" (180), which is reminiscent of Yeong-hye's early struggle against her husband in part one. It's as if the sisters have traded places. In-hye's revelation in that moment is that "It's your body, you can treat it however you please. The only area where you're free to do just as you like. And even that doesn't turn out how you wanted" (182). Whereas before she commanded Yeong-hye to comply and behave, In-hye now sees her sister as a sovereign being struggling against the encroachment of outsiders. Val Plumwood identifies two narratives: An individualist view that means "you 'own' your own body and have the right to exclusive use and control of it." The other view, the one we reserve for disenfranchised humans and animals, affirms that a "life is more like a book borrowed from the library and subject to immediate recall by other borrowers" (317). Both sisters' bodies have never been their own because they've been claimed and colonized, taken out for use when men see fit. At the close of the novel, In-hye "stares fiercely at the trees... as if protesting against something" (188); nature, again, is linked with revolution.

Perhaps the only other human who advocates for Yeong-hye is another female patient being treated for alcoholism at the hospital. Because of her in-betweenness—not fully human due to her mental illness and not fully animal due to her verbal skills—she becomes another part of the social-animal hierarchy who is willing to help for the right price, as she is paid pocket money to take care of Yeong-hye. Like a lab animal, Yeong-hye is subjected to the horror of being forced to eat through a tube. She has no allies in an expanding metropolitan area that is quickly aligning with new capitalist values; high rise corporate buildings have replaced trees, and apartments have replaced animal habitats. She has no saviors in the broken healthcare industry—only fellow patients, also caught in the system, who crowd around the doctor begging him for help, as if they'd "just discovered their Messiah" (177). Gary L. Francione writes about "similar-minds" theory (124), which means we give preferential and humane treatment to creatures that seem the most like us. With humans who suffer from mental illness, they fall further from our human realm and closer to the animal world. As she starves herself to death, Yeong-hye opts out completely, escaping what Caruth notes is common in trauma survivors: the *"crisis"* of merely existing (9). In the end, a vegan studies reading posits that all entities not validated as part of the human capital status quo are dismissed as less "worthy" of human consideration.

Yeong-hye absconds from the hospital to the mountains, appearing "deep in the woods… standing there stock-still and soaked with rain as if she herself were one of the glistening trees" (131). She baptizes herself in a place of pre-industrialized, capitalist gain before she is captured and returned to the facility. Selam remarks that as "mechanization grew, so did the urge to dominate and control this unpredictable…nature" and to turn it into, like in industrialized nations, "dead and passive matter" (77–78). Confined and medicated, Yeong-hye is made to comply like the other passive patients at the hospital. Because nature in industrialized society is a place of "confusion, wickedness, and suffering" (Moor 224), all extensions of the natural world must be confined. Calarco highlights the dangers of "anthropocentricism," which posits that humans are superior to all other forms of life. We reinforce this hierarchy through "the construction of our cities that are hostile to many modes of animal life" and through the "daily habits we have that aim to push away those portions of ourselves associated with animality" (419). With her initiation into the nonhuman animal and plant kingdoms that commenced with her veganism and ended in her fleeing to the woods, Yeong-hye is forced back into the realm of cage-able and controllable.

Won-Chung Kim acknowledges that Yeong-hye's "suffering asks for our attention and provocatively challenges us to lessen suffering of other beings." Yeong-hye memorializes all that has been pillaged from her body; she is a monument to the dead she's consumed and a vigil for those yet to be destroyed. To outsiders, she is the unknowable wilderness, and no one will shield her from the overreach of westernization. Because we barely hear her voice, it is through onlookers' perspectives and her limited, frenetic communication that we cobble together her essence. Selam writes that "a feminist response has always been about making the invisible visible" (75). And Wright asserts the importance of vegan studies as it creates "an articulation and conversation about oppression" (260). In depicting the raped and silenced, Kang forces people to look, painful though it may be. Animal rights activists have always employed this model to disrupt inhumane animal agricultural practices. They show what so many people have suppressed in order to eat without guilt because the story of animal and environmental abuse is a real horror story, and fighting mainstream anthropocentrism is, as Calarco notes, a "formidable" task (419). With empathy comes a loss in profit.

We can't hear animals' voices. We can't hear the trees and the land speak to us, but none of this makes them any less worthy of protection. It is the traumatized woman who can adeptly empathize with animals' lack of agency. Capitalism offers no refuge to Yeong-hye; thus, with veganism, she absented herself from the human realm and linked her plight to the animal and natural world. She is the activist rioting quietly as we readers writhe uncomfortably through her narrative of trauma.

Works cited

Adams, Carol J. *The Sexual Politics of Meat: A Feminist-Vegetarian Critical Theory*. Bloomsbury, 2015.
Arora, Alka. "Justice for Just Us? Spiritual Progressives and Carnism." *Tikkun (Duke University Press)*, vol. 31, no. 1, 2016, pp. 30–33. doi:10.1215/08879982-3446879.

Calarco, Matthew. "Being toward Meat: Anthropocentrism, Indistinction, and Veganism." *Dialectical Anthropology*, vol. 38, no. 4, 2014, pp. 415–429, www.jstor.org/stable/43895116.

Calvert, Amy. "You Are What You (M)eat: Explorations of Meat-Eating, Masculinity and Masquerade." *Journal of International Women's Studies*, vol. 16, no. 1, 2014, pp. 18–33.

Carretero-Gonzalez, Margarita. "Looking at the Vegetarian Body: Narrative Points of View and Blind Spots in Han Kang's *The Vegetarian*." *Through a Vegan Studies Lens: Textual Ethics and Lived Activism*, edited by Laura Wright, University of Nevada Press, 2019, pp. 165–179.

Caruth, Cathy, editor. *Trauma: Explorations in Memory*. Johns Hopkins University Press, 1995.

Cherry, Elizabeth. "Veganism as a Cultural Movement: A Relational Approach." *Social Movement Studies*, vol. 5, no. 2, 2006, pp. 155–177. doi:10.1080/14742830600807543.

Francione, Gary L. *Animals as Persons: Essays on the Abolition of Animal Exploitation*. Columbia University Press, 2008.

Gaarder, Emily. *Women and the Animal Rights Movement*. Rutgers University Press, 2011.

Gelin, Martin. "The Misogyny of Climate Deniers." *New Republic*, 28 August 2019, newrepublic.com/article/154879/misogyny-climate-deniers.

Kang, Han. *The Vegetarian*. Translated by Deborah Smith, Hogarth, 2015.

Kellman, Steven G. "'The Only Fit Food for a Man Is Half a Lemon': Kafka's Plea and Other Culinary Aberrations." *Southwest Review*, vol. 95, no. 4, 2010, pp. 532–545.

Kim, Won-Chung. "Eating and Suffering in Han Kang's The Vegetarian." *CLCWeb: Comparative Literature and Culture*, vol. 21, no. 5, 2019, p. NA.

Ko, Aph and Syl Ko. *Aphro-Ism: Essays on Pop Culture, Feminism, and Black Veganism from Two Sisters*. Lantern Books, 2017.

Kuhn, Anthony. "Death of a K-Pop Singer Leads to Discussion about Online Bullying." *National Public Radio*, 17 October 2019, www.npr.org/2019/10/17/771095252/death-of-k-pop-singer-leads-to-discussion-about-online-bullying.

Lee, Young-Hyun. "The Different Representation of Suffering in the Two Versions of *The Vegetarian*." *CLCWeb: Comparative Literature and Culture*, vol. 21, no. 5, 2019, p. NA.

McDonald, Barbara, et al. "An Ecological Perspective of Power in Transformational Learning: A Case Study of Ethical Vegans." *Adult Education Quarterly*, vol. 50, no. 1, 1999, pp. 5–23. doi:10.1177/07417139922086885

Moor, Robert. *On Trails: An Exploration*. Simon & Schuster, 2016.

Plumwood, Val. "Integrating Ethical Frameworks for Animals, Humans, and Nature: A Critical Feminist Eco-Socialist Analysis." *Ethics and the Environment*, vol. 5, no. 2, 2000, pp. 285–322. www.jstor.org/stable/40338997.

Rothgerber, Hank. "Real Men Don't Eat (Vegetable) Quiche: Masculinity and the Justification of Meat Consumption." *Psychology of Men & Masculinity*, vol. 14, no. 4, 2013, pp. 363–375. doi:10.1037/a0030379.

Selam, Ophelia. "Ecofeminism or Death: Humans, Identity, and the Environment." *Atenea*, vol. 26, no. 1, 2006, pp. 75–92.

Seong-kon, Kim. "Is Korea a Capitalist Country?" *The Korea Herald*, 18 November 2014, www.koreaherald.com/view.php?ud=20141118001115.

Shantz, J. "The Talking Nature Blues: Radical Ecology, Discursive Violence and the Constitution of Counter-Hegemonic Politics." *Atenea*, vol. 26, no. 1, 2006, pp. 39–57.

Slotkin, Richard. *Regeneration through Violence: The Mythology of the American Frontier, 1600–1860*. Harper, 1973.

Wrenn, Corey Lee. "The Role of Professionalization Regarding Female Exploitation in the Nonhuman Animal Rights Movement." *Journal of Gender Studies*, vol. 24, no. 2, 2015, pp. 131–146. doi:10.1080/09589236.2013.806248.

Wright, Laura, editor. *Through a Vegan Studies Lens: Textual Ethics and Lived Activism*. University of Nevada Press, 2019.

10
Causal impotence and veganism
Recent developments and possible ways forward

David Killoren

Introduction

It is often assumed by activists and even by many philosophers that, as soon as we come to understand that (1) animals matter morally just as humans matter morally,[1] and we accept that (2) animals are victims of extreme and unnecessary violence in modern farms and slaughterhouses[2]—then we've done nearly all of the work needed to soundly reach the conclusion that (3) each of us morally ought to refrain from purchasing and consuming a variety of different animal products (such as meat, dairy, eggs, wool, leather, and so on). However, a number of philosophers have laid an obstacle along the path from (1) and (2) to (3): the so-called "causal impotence problem." In this chapter, I'll discuss and evaluate a number of ways that philosophers have dealt with the causal impotence problem and I will discuss how the philosophical debate over the causal impotence problem might bear on the ethics of veganism.

Mark Budolfson has perhaps done more than anyone to develop the causal impotence problem. His explanation of the problem begins with a pair of grisly cases:

> [I]n the first case, a dumpster diver snags a T-bone steak from the garbage and eats it; in the second case, a diner enjoys a T-bone steak at Jimmy's You-Hack-It-Yourself Steakhouse, where customers brutally cut their steaks from the bodies of live cows, which are kept alive throughout the excruciating butchering process. (Once a cow bleeds to death, customers shift their efforts to a new live cow.)[3]

Budolfson proposes, not unreasonably, that the behavior in the first case is far less ethically objectionable than that in the second case. He continues:

> Conventional wisdom among consequentialist moral philosophers [such as Peter Singer] says that the effects [of purchasing animal products at a supermarket or restaurant] are more like eating at Jimmy's [than like acquiring a steak through dumpster diving]; however, the empirical facts suggest that they may be more like dumpster diving, because it is virtually impossible for an individual's consumption of animal products at supermarkets and restaurants to have any effect on the number of animals that suffer and the extent of that suffering,

just as it is virtually impossible for an individual's consumption of products acquired through dumpster diving to have any effect on animal welfare.

If consumers' choices have no effect on the degree of animal suffering, as is asserted in the above paragraph, then consumers are, according to the accepted jargon, "causally impotent." And if consumers are causally impotent in this way, then it's unclear, at least initially, why one would hold that their choices are *wrong*. This is a problem because it's paradoxical: specifically, it's paradoxical to grant (as Budolfson and others in this literature do grant) that animal agriculture is immensely harmful to animals, while maintaining that any given individual consumer who contributes financially to animal agriculture is not causally responsible for any of that harm.

But hold on a minute. This problem only gets off the ground if we agree that individual consumption patterns have no consequences for animals. Why would anyone believe that to be true?

Some have argued that our modern food economy is simply too vast, and too complex, to be sensitive to individual consumption choices.[4] The idea is that producers pay attention to trends in the behavior of millions or billions of consumers and are unaware of any given individual's choices, and therefore *your* behavior as a single consumer makes no appreciable difference to what producers do, just as your behavior as a dumpster diver (referring to Budolfson's example above) makes no difference to what producers do.

Budolfson offers a particular version of that line of thought. He says that "many products we consume are delivered by a massive and complex supply chain in which there is waste, inefficiency, and other forms of *slack* at each link," and this slack "serves as a *buffer*" to absorb any effects that individual choices might have. For example, according to this line of thought, some significant amount of beef that is produced each year goes unsold and is thus discarded; so, when demand for beef increases by some small fraction of a percent, this only means that less beef goes to waste—not that more beef gets produced. So, even if your decision to purchase beef increases demand by some non-zero percentage, this only has the effect of ever-so-slightly reducing "slack," thus reducing waste, and does not increase the number of animals raised, harmed, and killed in farms and slaughterhouses.

The causal impotence problem is, in a certain way, a larger-scale version of a problem that has faced vegans for just about as long as vegans have been around. Consider the choice whether to eat a leftover beef sandwich that would otherwise be discarded. Many philosophers who are very concerned about the welfare of animals will say that even if there's something wrong with *purchasing* a beef sandwich, there's probably nothing wrong with eating the *leftover* sandwich. For it seems that eating the sandwich would only prevent waste and would have no harmful effects. In fact, some philosophers, such as Bob Fischer, have argued that we morally *ought* to eat leftover meat. Yet those of us who count ourselves as vegans won't do so—because veganism includes a general prohibition against consuming animal products. Thus, veganism has its own version of a causal impotence problem that arises independently of any considerations about economic complexity and "slack." I'll come back to this in the final section of the chapter.

Given the causal impotence problem, if you want to defend the view that certain consumptive acts—for example, the act of going into a grocery store and purchasing a pound of chicken that you know has come from a place where chickens are treated in the cruelest ways imaginable—are immoral, then you have two main options.

First strategy: Try to *dissolve* the causal impotence problem by showing that our consumptive behaviors do in fact make a difference. Argue that purchasing a pound of chicken from a grocery store, for example, can result in more harm to chickens than would otherwise occur.

Second strategy: Grant that omnivores' consumptive behaviors do *not* make a difference—and go on to argue that such behaviors are immoral anyway.

I'm going to argue that the second strategy is unlikely to work (Section 2). Then (in Section 3) I'll explain a line of reasoning that aims to dissolve the causal impotence problem, paving the way for the first strategy above. Then I'll discuss how this reasoning bears on questions about the ethics of veganism, and I'll lay out what I take to be some crucial issues that need to be examined in future work on this topic.

Complicity and respect

In this section I'll assume that consumers are in fact causally impotent in the ways discussed above. (This assumption will be jettisoned later.) According to this assumption, for example, purchasing a pound of chicken from the supermarket makes no difference to what happens to any chickens or other animals in the future. My purpose in this section is to explore ways that one might argue that purchasing that pound of chicken might be wrong *despite* such causal impotence. I'll consider two possible approaches here. The first has to do with the relationship between the consumer and the institutions that inflict animal suffering. The second has to do with the relationship between the consumer and the animals themselves.

Complicity

The assumption that consumers are causally impotent does not, of course, entail that *other* agents—for example, farmers, abattoir workers or owners, grocery store managers, restaurateurs, collective agents such as businesses and governments, etc.—are causally impotent. All should agree that farmers, for example, could treat their animals better, and could even free their animals by placing them in sanctuaries—even if the *consumers* who purchase those farmers' products are powerless to affect the lives of those same animals. Given that farmers and other sorts of agents are able to make a difference for animals, it is entirely reasonable to think that they are guilty of wrongdoing (in many if not all cases) when they fail to do so. In light of these points, Tristram McPherson has argued that consumers bear certain relationships with the individuals and institutions who are guilty of wrongdoing, and that those relationships could make acts of consumption morally objectionable, even granting the assumption that consumers are causally impotent and their choices make no difference to animals.

To spell out those relationships, McPherson writes:

> First, the omnivore [i.e., the omnivorous consumer] *benefits from* this wrongdoing: the food she chooses to consume is a product of this wrongdoing, and would not be available—or at least, it would be available only in much smaller quantities at much higher prices—absent such wrongdoing. Second, the omnivore is *complicit* with the wrongdoing, in the sense of cooperating with the wrongful plans of the more immediate wrongdoers. [e.g., farmers, businesspeople, etc.].[5]

The hypothesis McPherson advances is that, even assuming causal impotence of consumers, the above relationships between consumers and wrongdoing can make acts of consumption wrong.

To evaluate that hypothesis, let's consider the first relationship: the consumer benefits from wrongdoing. Can this relationship be sufficient to establish that the consumer's consumptive acts are wrong? I doubt it. There are excellent reasons to doubt that the *mere* fact that an action involves benefiting from wrongdoing can make that action wrong.

Most (perhaps all) of us owe our greatest fortunes and successes and even our existence to the occurrence of atrocities and disasters. (For example, I would not have been born if the Korean War had not occurred.) Observing this fact, Saul Smilansky has compellingly argued[6] that we should "regret the history of the world that includes our existence."

Yet this plausible claim about what we should *regret* doesn't mean that we have an obligation to *forego the benefits* that come to us as a result of that history, given that we are unable to alter the past. After all, if benefiting from wrongdoing were in and of itself immoral, then it would be immoral to work at or attend Harvard University (which in its early days participated in use and sale of American slaves, among other wrongs) or drive a Volkswagen (given Volkswagen's Nazi past). But that is simply implausible. We can and should regret and address (as best we can) the wrongdoing of the institutions that benefit us—yet, at the same time, it seems clear that there are certain ways that we can engage with those institutions to our benefit.

To make this point vivid, consider the following case. Robert was enslaved in the early days of Harvard University's existence and forced to work on a construction project there. Mike is a modern-day descendent of Robert. Suppose Harvard University today decides to issue a large payment to Mike in order to recognize the injustice that was done to Mike's ancestor Robert. If benefiting from wrongdoing were wrong, then it would be wrong for Mike to accept that payment. But it is not wrong for Mike to accept that payment. So, benefiting from wrongdoing is not in and of itself wrong. And if benefiting from wrongdoing is not in and of itself wrong, then the mere fact that consumers of animal products benefit from wrongdoing cannot by itself make their consumptive acts wrong.

Now, as McPherson clearly recognizes and emphasizes, consumers of animal products do not *only* benefit from wrongdoing; they're also *complicit* in wrongdoing. To examine the significance of complicity, he defines complicity and offers a general principle:

> Call knowingly and voluntarily fulfilling a role that needs to be fulfilled in order for a wrongful plan to work being *complicit* with the plan. One might suggest the following principle: Complicity: Other things being equal, it is wrong to be complicit with others' wrongful plans.

If (as is plausible) the institutions (farms, slaughterhouses, corporations, etc.) that produce animal products have a wrongful plan (specifically: a plan involving extreme violence against animals on a massive scale for the sake of cheap gustatory pleasure and other such trivial benefits), and if (as is also plausible) consumers are typically complicit (according to the above definition) in that plan, then it follows from Complicity that consumers are guilty of wrongdoing even given the assumption of causal impotence.

In assessing this line of reasoning, the crucial question, of course, is whether Complicity is true. So let's examine that question.

The idea that complicity is wrong (all else equal) is intuitively attractive when applied in certain cases. Imagine a case discussed by Peter Singer: someone volunteers to be a guard at Auschwitz in order to avoid going to the Russian Front.[7] Once being appointed as a guard, this person commits many acts of extreme violence against innocent people. Suppose the guard knows that if he had not volunteered, someone else—someone who would have been even more brutal—would have taken his place. Then he can reasonably say that the victims of his violence are not worse off as a result of his having chosen to fill the role of their oppressor (just as, given the assumption of causal impotence, farmed animals are not worse off as a result of omnivores filling the role of consumer). Yet for many people, it still seems wrong in such a case to volunteer to be a guard at Auschwitz, and Complicity (if true) can explain why it is wrong.

The explanation furnished by Complicity is straightforward: Nazis had a wrongful plan; they needed guards in order for it to work; so anyone who volunteers to be a Nazi guard is complicit with a wrongful plan and therefore guilty of wrongdoing. The fact that Complicity is explanatorily useful in this way is a decided advantage for it.

However, I think further reflection will reveal that mere complicity in wrongdoing is not sufficient for wrongdoing. Consider the following. It is plausible that *nearly everyone* in German society during the Nazi period was, by McPherson's definition, either complicit in wrongdoing, or a victim of Nazi oppression, or both. Think about ordinary people who went about their business during this period as shopkeepers, businesspeople, teachers, researchers, clerks, janitors, and so on. These people fulfilled economic roles that needed to be fulfilled in order for the Nazis' plans to succeed. (For these people were necessary for the functioning of the German economy, and if the German economy had ceased functioning, the Nazis could not have started a war or even held onto power.) Thus, these ordinary people were complicit in wrongdoing according to McPherson's definition. But it seems implausible to suppose they might for that reason have been guilty of wrongdoing in simply living their lives and doing ordinary, ostensibly harmless jobs.

More broadly, Complicity is inconsistent with a general principle that many people consider to be quite attractive: "No Harm (or Failure to Benefit), No Foul: If an action does not make anyone worse off and is not a missed opportunity to benefit anyone, then it is not wrong."[8]

Complicity is inconsistent with that principle because it says that even if your action does not hurt anyone or fail to help anyone—i.e., even if your action has *no victims*[9]—the action can still be wrong in virtue of complicity considerations. To bring out a problem for this, think about a civilian medical doctor in Germany during the Nazi period who devotes herself completely to serving the health of her neighbors in her community. Suppose she never hurts anyone and never fails to help anyone. Despite this she is still complicit in Nazi plans in McPherson's sense (because she's filling the role of medical doctor; and German society could not have functioned without medical doctors; and the Nazis could not have succeeded in their wrongful plans if German society had not functioned). But such complicity seems utterly irrelevant, precisely *because* her actions do not hurt anyone and because (we are supposing) she never fails to help anyone she's in a position to help. In this case, the implication of No Harm (or Failure to Benefit), No Foul is far more plausible than the implication of Complicity.

If we accept No Harm (or Failure to Benefit), No Foul and therefore reject Complicity, then clearly we cannot rely on Complicity to explain what's wrong with omnivorous consumption. Further, even if we reject No Harm (or Failure to Benefit), No Foul for whatever reason, the case of the medical doctor above still looks like a counterexample to Complicity, and thus undermines the use of Complicity in critiques of omnivorous consumption.

Respect

An alternative way of explaining why consuming animal products might be wrong even given the assumption of causal impotence is developed by Blake Hereth, who offers two lines of reasoning:

> First, [purchasing or consuming immorally produced animal products] fails to treat moral losses as moral losses, wrongs as wrongs, and thereby fails to show minimally required respect for violated rights. Second, doing so rewards prior wrongdoing, which is likewise wrong.[10]

To support the idea that failure to treat wrongs as wrongs is wrong (independently of the consequences), Hereth considers a series of cases, two of which are as follows: (1) You pay for entry to an exhibit where corpses of people are on display. The corpses are of people who were murdered for the sole purpose of using their bodies in this way, though the murders were not committed by the current owners of the exhibit, and paying for entry won't cause more people to be murdered in the future. (2) A young woman has parents who got rich through ownership and exploitation of human slaves; she accepts her parents' offer to pay her college tuition.

It is not clear to me that these cases support Hereth's view. For it is not clear to me that the agents in these cases are themselves guilty of wrongdoing, given the assumption that their actions will not cause further harm to anyone.

Take the second case. In the second case, I readily grant, the daughter is required to do a number of things in relation to the victims of her parents' slave ownership: for instance, she should speak out against her parents' slave ownership, join in efforts to end slavery, and (if she can) help her parents' slaves to find freedom. But it is not at all clear why she should not take her parents' money for her college tuition, given that doing so will not causally contribute to slavery.

Further, it is unclear that using her parents' money fails to treat the wrongs done to her parents' slaves as wrongs. Indeed, if by going to college she is in a better position to fight against slavery in the future, then it would seem that going to college might be a *way* to recognize the wrongs of slavery.

Hereth's claim that there is an obligation to treat wrongs as wrongs strikes me as highly plausible, but it is not clear that this claim supports an obligation to avoid animal products given causal inefficacy. The obligation to treat wrongs as wrongs probably involves at least the following: (1) not acting wrongly oneself; (2) intending to avoid acting wrongly in the future; (3) trying to persuade others to avoid wrongdoing; (4) speaking out against wrongdoing; (5) refraining from actions that cause others to engage in wrongdoing. If purchasing and consuming animal products really is causally inefficacious and therefore does not cause any harm or other wrongs against animals, it's unclear why consuming animal products is inconsistent with doing all of (1)–(5).

Let's turn now to Hereth's second line of argument, which proceeds from the view that rewarding wrongdoing is wrong (independently of the consequences). To develop this view and its implications, Hereth provides this case:

> Imagine that a community wants Sawyer dead, and hit-man Hugo is ideally suited to conduct the assassination. Huge is hired and kills Sawyer. The town's citizens are pleased; they have what they want. The community, however, has not yet raised the funds to reimburse Hugo for his now-completed work. You overhear that countless citizens will donate tomorrow, and you know this to be true. Whether you donate or not, Hugo will be reimbursed for killing Sawyer.[11]

Hereth suggests that putting money into the donation box is wrong because it involves rewarding wrongdoing. It clearly *is* an instance of rewarding wrongdoing. And Hereth's claim that it is wrong to put money into the donation box in this case is plausible. Further, the fact that it is an instance of rewarding wrongdoing seems to *explain* why it is wrong.

On the one hand, we have (a) the intuitively attractive judgment that donating for Hugo's reimbursement is wrong; on the other hand, we have (b) a general principle discussed earlier: No Harm (or Failure to Benefit), No Foul. These two claims, (a) and (b), are inconsistent (given the assumption that donating to Hugo's reimbursement will neither harm anyone nor fail to benefit anyone). So, one of them has to be abandoned, even though both seem attractive.

This means that anyone who accepts No Harm (or Failure to Benefit), No Foul should reject the judgment in (a). Those who follow this path need to explain away the intuitive appeal of the judgment in (a). Here's one way that they might do so. Ordinarily, when you reward someone for wrongdoing, this encourages further wrongdoing. Typically in such cases, rewarding wrongdoing *is* harmful, and thus the judgment that it is wrong is fully consistent with No Harm (or Failure to Benefit), No Foul. Given this, we are naturally suspicious of any case in which someone rewards wrongdoing, especially when there are no benefits of doing so (and there are no benefits specified in Hereth's case). Thus, it can be proposed, the intuitive appeal of the judgment in (a) derives only from a general suspicion that is fully consistent with No Harm (or Failure to Benefit), No Foul. If that's right, then the intuitive appeal of the judgment in (a) does not, in fact, support Hereth's proposal that rewarding wrongdoing is in and of itself wrong even when it does not cause any harm. And then it would be reasonable to reject Hereth's proposal, at least until further arguments in favor of it are adduced.

Veganism in a world of causally efficacious consumption

Recall that in the Introduction, I mentioned two ways of responding to the causal inefficacy problem. One of these was to accept causal inefficacy and try to argue that consumption of animal products is nevertheless immoral. Thus far in the discussion of this chapter, this strategy has seemed to be quite difficult to pursue. We've considered a complicity-based version of this strategy (pursued by McPherson) and a respect-based version of this strategy (pursued by Hereth) and they have both run into serious problems. My own considered opinion is that this general strategy simply cannot succeed. I believe that if consumer behavior *really is* causally inefficacious in the sense that it truly makes no difference whatsoever to the lives of animals, then it cannot be wrong.

So now let's consider the other strategy that we discussed in the Introduction. That strategy is to try to *overturn* causal inefficacy and show that our consumptive behaviors do in fact make a difference. In what follows, I'll explain how we can do this and then I'll discuss what it means for veganism.

The threshold model

The most widely discussed and influential response to the causal inefficacy problem derives from what is known as the *threshold model*. The threshold model is illustrated in the following vignette offered by Shelly Kagan:

> [T]here are, perhaps, 25 chickens in a given crate of chickens. So the butcher looks to see when 25 chickens have been sold, so as to order 25 more. Here, then, it makes no difference to the butcher whether seven, 13, or 23 chickens have been sold. But when 25 have been sold this triggers the call to the chicken farm, and 25 more chickens are killed, and another 25 eggs are hatched to be raised and tortured.[12]

If you purchase a chicken from this butcher every day for a long enough period of time, you will *on average* trigger the birth, suffering, and killing of one chicken for every purchase.

The key claim of the threshold model is that the butcher scenario is *structurally* analogous to meat purchasing in the real world. Specifically, the claim is that whenever we purchase meat, we take a *small chance* of triggering a *large increase* in production—and the probability of triggering such an increase is inversely proportional to the size of the triggered increase; i.e., any given purchase has some small chance of being what we may call a *triggering purchase*—a purchase that triggers some large increase in production and (hence) causes a lot of animal suffering.

Importantly, this model accommodates uncertainty. The model is silent about how probable it is that any given purchase is a triggering purchase, and equally silent about how large the effect of any given triggering purchase will be.

If the threshold model describes consumption in the real world, then it answers the causal inefficacy problem. That's because the threshold model implies that some of our purchases, namely triggering purchases, do indeed have victims, contrary to what the argument that generates the causal inefficacy problem implies. A consumer will typically be unable to know which of her purchases are triggering purchases but, if she purchases animal products regularly, she'll have reason to believe that some number of her purchases are triggering purchases and thus have victims. Moreover, the view implies that when a purchase does have victims, it has *many* victims, and thus does a lot of harm. On this type of view, the decision to purchase animal products is *risky* from a moral point of view. Similarly, given that (under normal circumstances) we have no weighty reasons[13] to purchase meat, it is wrong to purchase meat (under normal circumstances) because doing so risks causing great harm, according to a view that I will call the *market threshold view*.

The market threshold view is not just a tidy story. There is good reason to believe that it is at least approximately true, as Steven McMullen (an economist) and Matthew Halteman (a philosopher) have explained.[14] After critically examining the arguments of philosophers who have promoted the causal inefficacy problem, they conclude by endorsing the standard threshold view: "if there is some probability (1/n) that any given purchase will occur on a threshold [i.e., will be a triggering purchase], then the threshold action will trigger a reduction in production of around n units, yielding an expected impact equal to 1," and so, for example, "there will be a close to 1-1 relationship between the purchase of a chicken and the expected impact on production." In short, on a long enough time scale, a consumer of meat can expect to cause the existence, suffering, and death of about as many animals as she consumes, and similarly for consumers of milk, eggs, and other animal products.

Additionally, McMullen and Halteman observe that shifting consumption away from animal products can be especially beneficial due to several different additional causal roles of consumption beyond those specified in the threshold model. These include effects on supply chains (when the number of animals killed decreases, this also decreases the number of animals needed elsewhere in the supply chain, e.g., animals used for breeding purposes), network effects (consumers' choices affect other consumers' choices: e.g., rising tofu consumption makes tofu more visible and available, thus potentially causing additional consumers to consume more tofu and less meat), and scale effects (as the market for vegan alternatives increases, economies of scale kick in, prices drop, and veganism becomes more affordable, hence more attractive).

Causal efficacy and the "Why be vegan?" question

Suppose it is really the case that purchases are causally efficacious in the way that McMullen and Halteman argue. By consuming animal products, we can cause—via mechanisms of supply and demand as captured in the threshold model—an increase in the number of farmed animals who are born, suffer, and die in miserable conditions.

Many philosophers accept that this is true. And yet few philosophers are vegan. Most philosophers seem to accept an approach that Neil Sinhababu once described on his blog (edited for concision):

> I divide meats into three categories: the Normal, the Weird, and the Fallen. Unethically farmed meats that someone else would eat if I didn't eat them are Normal. Weird meats are

those where the animals live under non-cruel conditions. Fallen meat is any kind of meat, Normal or Weird, that would go to waste if I didn't eat it. By eating only Weird and Fallen meat, I generate no economic demand pressures on factory farming. So that's what I do.[15]

In a similar vein, Bob Fischer recently argues that if consumption of animal products can negatively affect the lives of animals via mechanisms of supply and demand, this doesn't support the view that we ought to be *vegan*; it only supports the view that we ought to "eat unusually":

> You should be eating some animal products from the "animal-friendly" farm; you should be scavenging from dumpsters and department fridges; you should be pulling mussels out of their shells; and you should sample some crickets, termites, and their ilk.[16]

The approaches described by Sinhababu and Fischer are motivated by considerations about causal effects: some ways of consuming animal products economically cause[17] animal suffering and thus ought to be avoided; but ways of consuming animal products that do not economically cause animal suffering are acceptable. Such approaches are instances of a view that we might call *market freeganism*. Veganism, I believe, represents a very different approach from market freeganism.

Specifying the nature of veganism is a tricky matter.[18] Veganism is often defined by reference to a definition provided by the Vegan Society: "veganism is a way of living which seeks to exclude, as far as possible and practicable, all forms of exploitation of, and cruelty to, animals for food, clothing or any other purpose." However, I believe that this definition is of almost no value in explaining what veganism is. The problem with the definition is that its key terms—*exclude, practicable, possible, exploitation, cruelty*—are radically underspecified. Because of this lack of specificity, nothing can be derived from the definition on its own. My distinct impression as a practicing vegan is that the role of the Vegan Society definition in vegan thought is mostly ornamental or perhaps aspirational.

I see veganism as a rule-governed movement or community (accepting a loose conception of these terms): As vegans, we have certain rules that we live by, and our submission to those rules is how we gain admission into the community. If that's right, then in order to understand veganism, we need to understand its rules and their origins. My view—which I merely advance for consideration here, since I do not have the space to defend it—is that as vegans we get our rules directly from one another, i.e., from what may be called *vegan culture* as constituted by practicing vegans themselves. Thus, for example, consumption of honey is against the rules of veganism just because a rule against honey has been adopted by the community of practicing vegans.

If veganism's rules arise from the vegan community in the way that I've just proposed, there is probably no general principle from which all of veganism's rules are or can be derived. I don't intend this as a criticism of veganism. In fact, veganism is in good company in this respect.

Consider democracy. In a democratic society, laws are crafted and modified by different legislative bodies at different times. Because different legislators have different beliefs and aims, they tend to produce a messy and often inconsistent jumble of laws. The laws in a democratic society are rarely straightforwardly derivable from any single general principle. And that's as it should be. Most people understand that governing a society messily yet democratically is better than governing a society with a rigorous, consistent, orderly set of laws that have been determined by some non-democratic (e.g., autocratic) process. Something similar, I'd like to suggest, may be true of veganism: it may be better for veganism's rules to arise from the vegan community than for veganism's rules to be laid down by some single authority, even if this inevitably means that the rules will be more chaotic or less rational than they could be.

These considerations raise a number of different questions. One of those questions is whether veganism's rules can be improved by making them more consistent or more rational. It may be the case—indeed, I think it probably is the case—that veganism's rules are suboptimal. Some of its rules may be too restrictive (e.g., one might argue that bee nervous systems are incapable of producing conscious suffering and therefore veganism's prohibition against consumption of honey is too restrictive) and in other ways veganism may be too permissive (e.g., one might argue that consumption of palm oil ought to be against the rules of veganism, even though it is not). Veganism's rules can evolve over time, and even vary somewhat from place to place. There may be a role for philosophers to play in that evolutionary process.

A different question—which I believe is separable from the previous question—is whether each of us as individual consumers have an obligation to abide by the rules of veganism. As I've mentioned, I think most philosophers think that market freeganism is all that is required of us, and that veganism represents a step beyond the call of duty. To raise a problem for that view, I want to consider an analogy with labor union activity.

Suppose the union at your workplace calls a strike to begin on Tuesday. This is, in effect, to impose a rule: *Don't work on Tuesday and don't resume until the strike ends*. Suppose you happen to know that calling this strike was the wrong call. The union should have continued negotiations. In this case, the union has imposed a suboptimal rule.

Despite this imposition, you might well be obligated to join the strike. In fact, if the union's goals are worthwhile, I think it will *typically* be the case that you are obligated to join the strike. For the union derives its power from its ability to credibly threaten strikes and other similar actions, and it cannot credibly make such threats if workers do not strike when a strike is called. Such considerations may strongly support joining the strike even if you are quite sure that the strike shouldn't have been called in the first place. Indeed, the fact that the strike shouldn't have been called in the first place seems irrelevant to the question of what you ought to do now that the strike has in fact been called.

Veganism, I propose, is relevantly similar to a labor union. Veganism's power derives from its ability to credibly threaten producers: *We won't buy your product unless you make it according to our rules*. Such threats have power to push producers in a vegan direction if (1) the number of practicing vegans is large and (2) vegans strictly adhere to a common, publicly available set of rules that producers can easily identify and cater to.

Given these points, violating vegan rules by, for example, eating honey can undermine the ability of veganism as a social movement to credibly threaten producers, just as crossing a picket line is prone to undermine the ability of a union to credibly threaten the employer. If so, then just as crossing a picket line may often be immoral, so too may violating veganism's rules be immoral—*even if* veganism's rules are suboptimal. For even if veganism's rules are suboptimal, violating its rules may still do harm by undermining veganism's bargaining position in the marketplace. These considerations suggest that a concern with harmfulness of our choices—a concern that, as discussed above, commonly motivates philosophers to be market freegans—might be deployed to argue in favor of a strict requirement to be vegan rather than a (mere) market freegan. But a full elaboration of that line of argument is beyond the scope of this chapter.

Notes

1 There are many different views about what it means for animals to matter morally. On one influential view, which is prominently defended by Tom Regan among many others, animals matter morally in the sense that they have many of the same moral rights that humans have, including the right to life. On a different and equally influential view, defended by Peter Singer among many others, animals matter morally in the sense that their interests have moral weight that should be taken into account in moral deliberation, just as human interests should be taken into account. There are other views as well. For discussion of these views, refer to entry elsewhere in this volume on Singer and Regan.

2 For an extremely clear overview of routine treatment of farmed animals contained in chapter 1 of Fischer 2019, refer also to relevant entries in this volume.
3 Budolfson (2015).
4 See, for example, Frey (1985).
5 McPherson (2018).
6 Smilansky (2013).
7 Singer (2015, pp. 52–3).
8 This principle will be endorsed by utilitarians such as Peter Singer [refer to Chapter 4], but it is not a uniquely utilitarian principle. For example, this principle is consistent with the view that we ought to show a high degree of partiality toward our friends and family than to strangers—a decidedly non-utilitarian view. All that this principle says is that, from the moral point of view, there are no "victimless crimes."
9 Here I am assuming that S is a *victim* of a given action only if S is made worse off, or deprived of a chance to have been made better off, as a result of the action. In other words, if your level of well-being would have been the same no matter what I'd chosen to do in a given circumstance, then you are not a *victim* of my choice in that circumstance. Whether this definition fits with ordinary language is a question I do not have the space to address.
10 Hereth (2016, pp. 36–7).
11 Hereth (2016, p. 44).
12 Kagan (2011).
13 See Andrew (2020) for relevant discussion.
14 McMullen and Halteman (2018).
15 https://ethicalwerewolf.blogspot.com/2004/07/enter-meatrix.html.
16 Fischer (2019, p. 86).
17 Let's say X *economically causes* Y when, via a threshold-structured supply-and-demand mechanism, X affects the behavior of producers, suppliers, or other economic agents and thus causes Y.
18 Refer to other entries in this volume that address the nature of veganism.

Works cited

Andrew, J.P. "The Insignificance of Taste: Why Gustatory Pleasure Is Never a Morally Sufficient Reason to Cause Harm." *Southwest Philosophy Review*, vol. 36, 2020, pp. 153–160.
Bramble, Ben and Mark Fischer, editors. *The Moral Complexities of Eating Meat*. Oxford University Press, 2015.
Budolfson, Mark. "Is It Wrong to Eat Meat from Factory Farms? If so, Why?" *The Ethics of Eating Animals: Usually Bad, Sometimes Wrong, Often Permissible*, edited by Ben Bramble and Mark Fischer, Oxford University Press, 2015, pp. 80–99.
Frey, R.G. *Rights, Killing and Suffering: Moral Vegetarianism and Applied Ethics*. Oxford, 1985.
Hereth, Blake. "Animals and Causal Impotence: A Deontological View." *Between the Species*, vol. 19, 2016.
Kagan, Shelly. "Do I Make a Difference?" *Philosophy and Public Affairs*, vol. 39, no. 2, 2011, pp. 105–141.
McMullen, Steven and Matthew C. Halteman. "Against Inefficacy Objections: The Real Economic Impact of Individual Consumer Choices on Animal Agriculture." *Food Ethics*, vol. 2, no. 2–3, 2018, pp. 99–110.
McPherson, Tristram. "The Ethical Basis for Veganism." *The Oxford Handbook of Food Ethics*, edited by Barnhill, Budolfson, and Doggett. Oxford University Press, 2018.
Singer, Peter. *The Most Good You Can Do*. Yale University Press, 2015.
Smilansky, Saul. "Morally, Should We Prefer Never to Have Existed?" *Australasian Journal of Philosophy*, vol. 91, no. 4, 2013, pp. 655–666.

11

By any means of persuasion necessary

The rhetoric of veganism

Christopher Garland

Introduction

Rhetoric is a centuries-old discipline, and there may be no clearer definition than Aristotle's own, where he describes it as "the faculty of observing in *any given case the available means of persuasion.*" From classical Greece through the 1960s, rhetoricians had largely concerned themselves with "traditional" written and oral texts (e.g., a newspaper article or a political speech). However, in 1970, National Conference on Rhetoric participants recommended that the study of rhetoric "may be applied to any human act, process, product or artifact … [that] may formulate, sustain, or modify attention, perceptions, attitudes, or behavior." This broadening of rhetoric's purview came about in large part due to the work and influence of Kenneth Burke, who encouraged analysis of multiple symbolic forms including, but not limited to, "music, sculpture, architecture, painting, dance, architectural styles, and so on" (Burke qtd. in Foss 141). While not explicitly named, other human actions—such as what we do or do not eat and the justifications for those choices—fall under the purview of rhetoric. This chapter presents the rhetoric of veganism by highlighting rhetorical positions taken and appeals made in a select set of wide-ranging texts. Thinking about three key rhetorical appeals—*ethos* (ethics/credibility), *pathos* (emotion), and *logos* (logic)—as entry points into analysis of the aforementioned texts, this chapter reflects the reach of rhetoric and its applicability as a theoretical lens to examine the discourse of veganism. This chapter will look at a number of different articles, their rhetorical positions, and the way they intersect with various different contexts. While the three rhetorical terms will be the framework for my analysis, I am interested in putting these important texts into conversation with each other.

Veganism as "new" rhetoric

It is worth noting, however, that thinking about rhetoric as part of a range of human activities—including, as this chapter focuses on, the rhetoric of dietary choice—isn't necessarily a "new" idea. In the second chapter of his *Rhetoric*, Aristotle presents the reader with the notion of rhetoric as universal. Early on in *Rhetoric*, Aristotle is concerned with positing rhetoric as a "counterpoint" to dialectic. The latter is conceived as the art of logical discussion, while the former, in terms of Aristotle's focus, is the art of public speech. Aristotle claims that "all men make use, more or less, of both" because to some extent "all men attempt to discuss statements and to maintain them, to defend themselves and attack others" (19). Aristotle asserts that in terms of rhetoric,

> we look upon [it] as the power of observing the means of persuasion on almost any subject presented to us; and that is why we say that, in its technical character, it is not concerned with any special or definitive class of subjects. (24)

Before delving into the intersection of rhetoric and contemporary vegan discourse, I want to establish the primary concern of this chapter. There is countless vegan and vegetarian rhetoric produced and circulated on a daily basis, whether in social media posts, press releases by national organizations, articles in online magazines, or the innumerable other locations available for publication in the digital age. This chapter can only represent a small extract of the far-reaching discourse of this subject; however, what unifies this set of texts is how they foregrounded the use of rhetoric through readily identifiable means of persuasion.

A review of the literature that focuses on an analysis of vegan and/or vegetarian rhetoric reveals a wide-ranging set of texts that cross disciplines, purposes, and intended audiences. But in these texts that deal with the discourse of veganism/vegetarianism, rhetorical analysis is used in a variety of ways on a number of subjects related to the issue of eating animals (or not). Before introducing a selection of these vegan/vegetarian rhetoric, I want to clarify my use of the terms "rhetoric" and "rhetorical analysis" as they pertain to critical academic inquiry. For this purpose, I will use the example of visual rhetoric: feature and documentary film—the latter for a reason that will come clear once we later look at a vegan rhetoric text, Beth Jorgensen's article, "To Meat or Not to Meat? An Analysis of On-line Vegetarian Persuasive Rhetoric," which includes analysis of the People for the Ethical Treatment of Animals (PETA)-produced film, *Meet Your Meat* (2002). While viewed as entertainment, the feature film is a rhetorical object, with the filmmakers (or rhetors) employing a range of persuasive appeals to engage the audience. As rhetorician Wendy Hesford argues, "All of your responses to the movie—emotional and intellectual, individual and communal—are actually responses to rhetoric. The emotional, ethical, or logical responses you share with other members of the audience constitute a rhetorical vision" (2). Hesford later states that rhetoric *is* the "art of persuasion. In order to persuade somebody, rhetorician Kenneth Burke tells us, you have to 'talk his [sic] language by speech, gesture, tonality, order, image, attitude, idea, identifying your ways with his" (2). The rhetorical triangle is the commonly used theoretical lens to further explore how the rhetor doesn't exist in a vacuum but is tethered to the text and the audience.

Thus, the feature film is a prime subject for rhetorical analysis—as a textual object or artifact. As Elizabeth Losh and Jonathan Alexander assert in *Understanding Rhetoric* (2017):

> When we see images in a work of art in a film, we pay attention to the craft of intentional composition. We may need to look very closely and invest time to understand how the visual elements tell a story ... Increasingly, a variety of arguments are being made. (16–17)

Take then, say, a documentary film, a form much more explicitly associated with a consciously constructed argument (rhetoric). In this scenario, let's imagine that the film is about a specific fast food chain and its practices; as the filmmakers put together shots, sequences, and scenes that make up the visual language of the documentary, the filmmakers may also be involved in their own rhetorical analysis: considering, for example, the kinds of persuasive appeals that the fast food restaurant uses in advertising to engage its own audience of consumers. Then, to add another layer, the critic writing about the documentary is creating a text that is bound to rhetoric: examining the documentary film's use of a set of rhetorical appeals and considering the effectiveness of those appeals. While this simplistic example only scratches at the surface of the layers of rhetoric involved in critical analysis of a particular subject, I hope it is starting point for understanding what Jonathan Alexander and Susan A. Jarrett identify—and which I think applies directly to vegan/vegetarian rhetoric—as the "complex mix of bodies, technologies, discourses, and even histories that need to be considered collectively so as to guide a new understanding of contemporary rhetorical interventions within and across numerous spheres" (4). A sample of these vegan rhetorics demonstrates the interdisciplinary nature of the intersection of rhetoric and vegan and/or vegetarian discourse. This is in no means an exhaustive list—or indeed anything close to it— but rather an attempt to show how various texts have brought together veganism and/or vegetarianism and rhetoric.

A brief tour of the vegan rhetoric canon

While this chapter can only focus on a very select group of different forms of vegan rhetoric, I would be remiss not to mention some of the seminal works that deserve chapters all of their own—due to their multilayered rhetorical analyses, temporal and locational contexts, and scope. Indeed, these texts are both analyzed and referred to in other chapters in this book. Peter Singer's *Animal Liberation* is one of these canonical texts. Despite the *New York Times Review*'s claim that the book is "unrhetorical and unemotional," Singer's book is made up of a complex structure of explicitly rhetorical appeals, ranging from ethos to logos to *ekphrasis* (e.g., descriptive passages about the horrific treatment of animals). While Singer's tone might be cool, he masterfully combines rhetorical appeals. Take this passage from early on in the book, where the author lays bare his rhetorical movements:

> So far I have said a lot about inflicting suffering on animals, but nothing about killing them. This omission has been deliberate. The application of the principle of equality to the infliction of suffering is, in theory at least, fairly straightforward ... pains of the same intensity and duration are equally bad, whether felt by humans or animals. (17)

In synthesizing ethos, logos, and pathos, Singer continues to build his case for the ethical treatment of animals. In the final chapter of the book, Singer makes the *New York Times Book Review*'s claim that *Animal Liberation* is "unrhetorical" seem even more off-base and misleading. Returning again to address the "speciest"—one who views humans as superior to other animals—Singer makes clear his argument:

> Ignorance ... is the speciest's first line of defense. Yet it is easily breached by anyone with the time and determination to find out the truth. Ignorance has prevailed so long only

because people do not want to find out the truth. "Don't tell me, you'll spoil my dinner" is the usual reply to an attempt to tell someone just how their dinner was produced. (217)

Throughout *Animal Liberation* Singer is committed to persuading the reader to not only consider the rights of animals but also to act upon his call to action. The book's effect on the discourses of diet, animal rights, and the way that people think about "food" cannot be underestimated.

Equally important and rhetorically nuanced as Singer's book, Carol J. Adams *The Sexual Politics of Meat: A Feminist-Vegetarian Critical Theory*, first published in 1990, is a centerpiece of vegan studies, interweaving vegetarianism, feminism, and critical theory. In the book's classic opening salvo, Adams employs the rhetorical appeal of ethos, opening up to her reader about the intersection of the personal and the political. Foregrounding her own voice, Adams establishes her place as rhetor and provides both background and signposts to the argument to come:

My becoming a vegetarian had seemingly little relationship to my feminism—or so I thought. Now I understand how and why they are intimately connected, how being a vegetarian reverberates with feminist meaning. I discovered that what appeared to me as isolated concerns about health and ethics were interrelated and illumined by feminist insights. (34)

In the preface to the twentieth anniversary edition of the book, Adams discusses one of the primary concerns of the project: activism as engaged theory, the type of theory that "arises from anger at what is; theory that envisions what is possible. *Engaged theory makes change possible*" (xvi). As opposed to the ethos that marked her describing the progression in her thought and her research interests that led to this project, Adams employs the rhetorical question to tease out the real-world implications of engaged theory, which, she contends, "doesn't just sit down next to you at a dining table and ask, 'Do you know what you are participating in as you choose what to eat?'" (xvi).

Employing the evocative rhetorical appeal of pathos, Adams then writes evocatively of a situation that calls to mind Kenneth Burke's use of the salon as metaphor for discourse. Adams writes, taking on the voice of the contrarian at the average dinner table: "There is something more exciting, more fulfilling, more honest than eating a dead animal as hamburger or pork loin" (xvi). Then, in a move that calls to mind Aristotle's own claim about rhetoric's presence in a wide gamut of subjects, Adams takes the notion of critique from theoretical to concrete: we can engage in "critique of sexist ads on behalf of animal activism or a vegan strip club, or sexist ads from Burger King, or a 'Gentlemen's' steak club" (xvi). At its core, with its demand for change, *The Sexual Politics of Meat* is unabashedly rhetorical. And, in its use of a range of rhetorical appeals, engaged theory "exposes problems, but also offers solutions," "makes resistance empowering," and creates a culture of "engagers" who "understand that everything is connected" (xvi). As with a number of the vegan rhetorics referenced in this chapter, the interconnectivity is central to veganism and our study of it.

As compelling and controversial as both *Animal Liberation* and *The Sexual Politics of Meat*, Laura Wright's *The Vegan Studies Project: Food, Animals, and Gender in the Age of Terror* (2015) pulls these dynamic conversations concerning animal rights, feminism, and wider culture into the contemporary moment. Early on in *The Vegan Studies Project*, Wright uses the rhetorical appeal of *kairos* (timeliness), acknowledging that up to that moment there had been an "abundance of texts that deal with veganism and vegans" in various ways, but "there is no cultural studies text that examines the social and cultural discourses that imagine the vegan body and vegan identity" (23). Employing an interdisciplinary approach, Wright's book begins with a clear goal: "veganism and vegan identity, as well as the popular and academic discourse that constructs those categories, need to be explored, understood, and challenged" (1). In order to "frame"—to use Wright's term—this project, she first needed to establish definitions for these two terms: "vegan" and "studies." Wright identifies the latter as a process involving "the devotion of time to the acquisition of knowledge about and explication of a subject"; however, when it comes to "veganism" and "vegan identity," the definition is not so clear cut (1). That requires the kind of time and explication that one would see in the aforementioned academic sub-disciplines "that have emerged and been codified since the 1970s" (Wright 1). I highlight this particular part of the introduction in order to show that through Wright's methodical approach she immediately establishes her ethos, building credibility through careful reasoning. Wright does not intend to reduce veganism merely to another object of study for academics, but rather that due to the increased prominence of the practice (and the associated representation of the identity in many forms of popular culture and media), veganism deserves thorough and sophisticated exploration. And, in this cultural studies-informed academic inquiry, Wright places rhetoric front and center: "My study," she writes, "not only examines the reasons for the often negative and inflammatory discourse surrounding vegan identity but also explores the sexualization and often-contradictory gender-specific rhetorical constructions of both vegan and animal bodies" (22).

Through Wright's mapping out one of the main threads of the project, one can also see the line of influence back to *The Sexual Politics of Meat*. But there is also an important distinction that is part of the overall rhetorical appeal and significance of *The Vegan Studies Project*: the very adjective that sits in the book's title. Unlike Adams work, which deals with the discourse of vegetarianism, Wright is concerned primarily with veganism and vegan identity. At the very outset of the book, when dealing with the aforementioned definitions ("vegan" and "studies"), Wright takes issue with the "official" definition of a vegan put forth in a memorandum of association of the Vegan Society (2). Wright contends the definition is limiting because of its emphasis on the ethical reasons for this dietary choice, rather than the other important causes for someone to become vegan, including for health and religious reasons. But this analysis goes beyond finding the "right" definition for "vegan"; for Wright, the "tension between the dietary practice of veganism and the manifestation, construction, and representation is of primary importance ... particularly as vegan identity is both created by vegans and interpreted, and, therefore, reconstituted by and within contemporary (non-vegan) media" (22).

The specificity of Wright's language is central to not only her rhetorical positioning but also her critique of the various texts that she analyzes: whether it be a logo for an animal rights group, or a photograph of an American soldier, or a filmic adaptation of a novel (all examples of visual rhetoric that Wright probes in the book); an academic study of celebrity in America; or an editorial on a major news website. By engaging with these various texts and their representation and/or relationship to vegan identity, Wright's criticism is grounded in nuanced close reading. As with the "engaged theory" that marks Adams' work, in Wright's one can see a form of "local criticism." I draw this concept from Wendy Brown's *Edgework* (2005), in which she discusses the utility of "local criticism," an approach that asks for specificity rather than attempting to overhaul a social totality. Brown claims that "naming practices" are "among the objects of local criticism; interrogation, challenge, discernment, and displacement are among its actions" (viii). In the case of *The Vegan Studies Project*, Wright begins with addressing the "naming" of the vegan and then proceeds into a sophisticated interrogation of texts ranging from the television series *Buffy the Vampire Slayer* and *True Blood* to Margaret Atwood's *The Year of the Flood* to

Cormac McCarthy's *The Road*. The depth of rhetorical analysis that is on display in *The Vegan Studies Project* reflects the breadth and complexity of vegan discourse, making it a singular text in the field.

Further examples of contemporary vegan rhetoric in the academy

In her 2015 article "To Meat or Not to Meat? An Analysis of On-line Vegetarian Persuasive Rhetoric," Beth Jorgensen begins by referencing PETA-produced documentary, *Meet Your Meat* (2002). Running just 12 minutes long and narrated by famous film and television actor Alec Baldwin, *Meet Your Meat* is used by Jorgensen as an example of the development of the argument for the ethical treatment of animals. Jorgensen traces the trend of prominent vegan/vegetarian rhetoric back to the 1970s, a pivotal decade where "a number of seminal works were published that encouraged [at the least] reduced consumption of animal products" including Frances Moore Lappé's *Diet for a Small Planet* (1971), which was the "first bestseller to take a hard look at the food system"; what is "now considered the seminal text of the animal rights movement," Peter Singer's *Animal Liberation* (1975); and Ancel Keys et al.'s 1980 groundbreaking study, *Seven Countries: A Multivariate Study of Death and Coronary Heart Disease*, which made the argument that "countries whose native diets are lower in animal fats have lower incidence of coronary disease" leading to a widespread encouragement for "consumers [to] reduce dietary animal fat" (1–2). Jorgensen's measured description of these important text-based works stands in contrast to her use of *ekphrasis* (evocative writing that describes a visual object in a particularly potent manner) when writing about *Meet Your Meat*, a purposefully shocking piece of visual rhetoric that reflects the increased use of image-based arguments for animal rights. In the documentary, Jorgensen writes, the documentary filmmaker's use *pathos* (the appeal to emotions) from the first sequence onward:

> Two chickens, their feathers bedraggled, huddle together in apparent fear. The actor Alec Baldwin narrates, "What you are about to see is beyond your worst nightmares." A startling montage begins—a poultry worker herding birds against a wall as an injured hen struggles to stand, pigs in crates unable to roll over, rows of chickens on a conveyor line. So, begins *Meet Your Meat* … (1)

Jorgensen proceeds to summarize the effects of Lappé, Singer, and Keys et al.'s respective works, before addressing the different ways that these authors (rhetors) motivate their audiences to "go meatless" (3). Jorgensen argues that vegan/vegetarian rhetoric that advocates non-consumption of animals is most efficient when singular motivation (such as the "health aficionado" who is not concerned with the environmental fallout of mass animal farming) is supplanted by understanding a multitude of motivations, namely "connecting diet to a sustainable global food system" and taking "into account a number of factors: environmental, economic, cultural, anthropological, humanitarian, and nutritional" (4). In her use of logos—by specifically naming the intersectional nature of dietary choices—Jorgensen continues her analysis, synthesizing texts that demonstrate the kinds of pro-vegan arguments being made online.

Jorgensen is far from alone in, to use Wendy Brown's term again, "local criticism" about veganism, vegan identity, and rhetoric in the academic sphere. In "The Rhetoric of Food: Precedent Food Texts as Inventio," Adrienne P. Lamberti uses one of the fundamental canons of rhetoric, *inventio* (the method used for the discovery of argument) in order to analyze the genre of contemporary food writing. Using rhetorical theory and applying it to the depiction of veganism in the media, Ryan J. Phillips' article "Frames as Boundaries: Rhetorical Framing

Analysis and the Confines of Public Discourse in Online News Coverage of Vegan Parenting" considers the production and circulation of media concerning parental choices about their children's diets. In surveying the intersection of rhetoric and vegan/vegetarian discourse, one sees a return to the rhetorical appeal of ethos as an entry point into a range of texts. For example, in "Green Looks Good on You: The Rhetoric and Moral Identity of Conscious Consumption Blogs," Abigail O'Brien considers how vegan/vegetarian rhetoric is produced and consumed in a particular medium: the "conscious consumption" blog. Luca Simonetti's "The Ideology of Slow Food" employs a range of rhetorical devices in order to explore Italy's adoption of the slow food movement; in the course of this investigation, Simonetti encounters vegan discourse and the arguments for that dietary practice. Lori Gruen and Robert C. Jones's article, "Veganism as an Aspiration," is a text that returns to the idea of using pathos (appeals to the audience's emotion) as a primary aspect in the construction of pro-vegan arguments. The authors caution against an overindulgence in ethos, suggesting that "in avoiding the rhetoric of moral purity or superiority, [vegan aspiration] increases the likelihood that non- vegans will be open to embracing the nonviolence that grounds veganism." In this brief overview of the kind of work that is being done in regard to analyzing the rhetorical moves occurring in vegan discourse.

An example of vegan rhetoric in the blogosphere

As mentioned at the outset of this chapter, the rhetoric of veganism in the digital age constitutes, to put it plainly, a massive repository of text and images. It encompasses Instagram hashtags, YouTube documentaries, memes circulated on Facebook, comments on websites, and screeds of blogposts. This rhetoric is produced and circulated at a dizzying rate: from a "vegan" keyword hashtag to a user-produced video to self-published manifesto on one's own website. Googling the term "vegan rhetoric," which I did after looking at academic articles in edited collections and journals about the subject, yielded a range of results that crossed from social media to online magazine articles to the aforementioned blogposts. Rather than confined to the physical published book, the rhetoric of veganism truly embodies rhetorician Kenneth Burke's vision of the "unending conversation"—mentioned briefly earlier in the chapter—where discursive exchange is imagined through the metaphor of physical social interaction:

> Imagine that you enter a parlor. You come late. When you arrive, others have long preceded you, and they are engaged in a heated discussion, a discussion too heated for them to pause and tell you exactly what it is about. In fact, the discussion had already begun long before any of them got there ... You listen for a while, until you decide that you have caught the tenor of the argument; then you put in your oar. (110–11)

In the case of vegan rhetoric, the "heated conversation" includes (often lengthy) references to animal rights, human health and wellness, environmental concerns, philosophical ideas, and spiritual beliefs (to name just a few aspects). To be clear, this has been true of dietary discourse throughout the course of human history. However, the kind of mass connectivity between rhetors and potential audiences that is made possible by the Internet alters the way the conversation takes place. Here, though, I do not mean to present a utopian view of cyberspace: I have no doubt that many well-researched and intended blogs go unread; and, I am sure, facile comments on a social media post find an enthusiastic audience. While this is true of many subject areas, the intersection of dietary choices and animal rights appears to provoke particular "heat." Take, for example, the findings from my initial Google search using the search terms "vegan rhetoric." The first result was a post from *Medium*, an online publishing platform that was founded by one of the cofounders of Twitter, Evan Williams, and which launched in 2012. *Medium* is a perfect example of the shape of Burke's salon today.

The *Medium* article that appeared first in the search results was titled, "Anti-Vegan Rhetoric" and was written by Constantine Sandis, a professor of philosophy at the University of Hertfordshire and Fellow of the Royal Society of the Arts. Much like "traditional" websites, these blogs use the appeal of ethos by providing a biography that mentions the author's credentials: this is critical to platforms like *Medium* that attempt to find a larger audience for their writers than the traditional personal blog due to their large readership. Sandis begins his August 1, 2018 piece by addressing France's recent amendment to their agricultural bill that would ban the use of "so-called 'meat' and 'dairy' terms to describe plant-based products that serve as meat substitutes." In practical terms, this would punish companies/farms who use meat and dairy terms—sausage, steak, milk, cheese, etc.—for vegan products (fines could be enforced of up to 300,000 euros). Sandis quotes from the French politician and farmer, Jean Baptiste Moreau, who in support of the bill tweeted the following: "it is important to combat false claims. Our products must be designated correctly." Using this statement as a jumping off point, Sandis asserts that false claims exist but they belong to those who support the bill: "*All* uses of the expressions targeted by the new bill are perfectly meaningful and informative and explicitly designed and marketed to appeal to people actively seeking to *avoid* animal products, not to deceive others into buying such things in ignorance." Sandis states that the anti-vegan rhetoric purported by Moreau and others who support the bill is grounded in the assumption that "there is no such thing as non-dairy milk, or that sausages contain animal flesh by definition." By composing his argument with logical appeals, such as informing the reader of the non-scientific basis of the bill's supporters' claims, Sandis begins to dismantle the anti-vegan rhetoric. Sandis pushes his argument through his use of a popular practice in rhetorical theory: discursive analysis. Specifically, Sandis is concerned with the power of naming:

> Language evolves naturally alongside our behavioral practices and the rise of new uses and meanings of words cannot be stopped through legislation and it is wrong to try to do so. If one really wants to remain stuck in the past it is worth remembering that the English word 'sausage' and the French 'saucisse' are both derived from the Latin 'salsus' meaning salted. Perhaps Moreau would also like to ban unsalted sausages?

By addressing the etymology of sausage, Sandis provides both historical context for his claim while also employing pathos: in this case, the emotional appeal of humor. He makes light of the politician's notion that the language of vegan food undermines meat-based products in terms of authenticity. Again, returning to pathos, Sandis identifies what he calls the "real motive" behind this anti-vegan rhetoric. For Sandis, the need for "correct designation of agricultural products" is a red herring, designed to shift the rhetor's audience's (in this scenario, the French public's) attention away from what they are really doing: instilling "plain old fear." As Sandis states, from "museology to agriculture, fear lies behind most attempts to conserve the status quo in the face of progress." However, in a number of the results I found in my "vegan rhetoric" Google search, one is reminded of the second half of Burke's extended conversation metaphor. Namely, the emphasis on the back-and-forth nature of sharing ideas. Once the rhetor has joined the conversation, the real work has only just begun:

> Someone answers; you answer him; another comes to your defense; another aligns himself against you, to either the embarrassment or gratification of your opponent, depending upon the quality of your ally's assistance. However, the discussion is interminable. The hour grows late, you must depart. And you do depart, with the discussion still vigorously in progress. (Burke 110–11)

Part of the conversation of veganism is the critique of the practice. In cyberspace, one doesn't need to go far to find disagreement on any topic, and the rhetoric of veganism is no different. Just a few results down from Snadis's pro-vegan piece is a blog post titled, "On Specious Rhetoric by Vegan Advocates." The author of the post begins with a bold claim, immediately placing ethos at the forefront of his argument. "One of *my* biggest problems with vegan advocates," the author writes, "is the fallacious rhetoric they employ to achieve their goal of getting somebody to stop using animals." The author, a blogger named Dave Dandelion, acknowledges that the optimist in him is willing to give these advocates the benefit of the doubt due to the fact "[vegan advocates] don't see the logical errors" in their own thinking, but he admits that the "tiny misanthropist part [in him] suspects blatant deception." To again return to Burke's metaphor of the salon and the discussants, Dandelion identifies to whom he is responding: Erik Marcus, a prominent writer and public speaker who authored two popular vegan books, *Vegan: The New Ethics of Eating* (1998) and *Meat Market: Animals, Ethics, & Money* (2005). Dandelion had read a piece on *vegan.com*, a popular website that claims to offer "the web's most helpful information about a vegan lifestyle and plant-based eating with no clickbait, fluff, or intrusive ads." Dandelion provided a link to a (no longer available) article penned by Marcus titled "Oregano May Reduce Methane from Cattle." Dandelion claims that in the piece an argument is made that vegans "might actually find solutions" to specific environmental issues. Dandelion goes on to describe the arguments for veganism—"moral," "environmental," and "health"—as "vegan sophisms" that he dismisses without reference to any clear logos, citing, for example, the "fact" that "If eating animals the way we do is bad for our health how is it that mortality rates are dropping and we're living better than ever?" Continuing his logical fallacy, Dandelion, in his critique of how not eating meat lessens specific health risks, states that it's "like saying you should stop drinking water because it causes hyponatremia." In just this one example of competing ideas on the Internet, it appears that Burke's salon is alive and well, even if the discussants never come face-to-face.

Conclusion: a future of vegan rhetoric

In my tour of vegan rhetoric, I looked for potential new trends that might indicate where the argument for animal rights and non-consumption of animals is headed. Looking back to what changes have occurred since the emergence of these particular texts discussed earlier in the chapter might indicate what comes next. In the preface to the fortieth anniversary of *Animal Liberation*, Peter Singer reflects on his initial goal for the rhetoric contained within the book. "In my more pessimistic (or realistic) moments," Singer writes, "I understood the enormity of the task facing the movement that I envisaged. How can one change habits as widespread and as deeply ingrained as eating meat? It would first be necessary to transform people's attitudes towards animals …" (1). Here, Singer acknowledges the plainly rhetorical purpose of *Animal Liberation*: to persuade people to stop eating animals. This was also connected to a desire to see animals treated more humanely. To this end, Singer believes he has seen some success, though we are from the utopia one might imagine from the pages of Singer's book:

> We can rightly deplore the fact that today, 40 years on, animals are still being mistreated on a vast scale, but we should not despair of making a positive difference in the lives of animals. In many parts of the world, including Europe and the United States, there has been a huge shift in attitudes toward animals. (2)

Singer backs up this claim by employing logos: the animal movement, Singer states,

> has challenged the huge agribusiness industry with remarkable success, forcing producers of meat and eggs across the entire European Union—all twenty-eight member nations—to give hens and pigs and veal calves more space and conditions better suited to their needs. (2)

By marking the changes Singer has seen in the forty years since the publication of his seminal animal rights rhetoric, one is not only prompted to think of the contemporary moment, but to also consider the future.

Bearing in mind the current milieu, where issues of race and ethnicity have been put front and center in the discourses of everything from the workplace to academia to myriad forms of popular culture, one can't help but think about the intersection of race and vegan rhetoric. In Julia Feliz Brueck's *Veganism of Color—Decentering Whiteness in Human and Nonhuman Liberation* (2019), we see the discussion of race, animal rights, and systemic oppression come together. Brueck's edited collection is an example of one direction the conversation of veganism and vegan identity might be headed. Contributors to *Veganism of Color* come from around the world and include a diverse range of educational and vocational backgrounds: authors, hip-hop artists, musicians, community organizers and activists, independent scholars, and teachers.

The theme of the chapters in *Veganism of Color* reflects this variety and what follows is a selection from the collection intended to display the intricate and pressing concerns for veganism of color. Towani Duchsher's "The Shift from Hierarchy to Interconnection: My Path to Veganism," where the author traces her path to veganism back to viewing media representations of the murder of Eric Garner. Duchsher's powerful use of pathos is apparent as she describes Garner's treatment by the police.

> The public watched the act of oppression and its result: the pressing out of a man's life onto the dirty sidewalk. We watched it over and over again. I will never forget that. Nor should I. That video will haunt me forever. (81)

Duchsher goes on to provide the narrative of her path to veganism, including an evocative passage where she talks about her resistance to watching the documentary *Earthlings* (2005), the incisive and brutal condemnation of speciesism. She makes a connection between watching Garner's death and the annihilation of living beings in *Earthlings*, stating that she couldn't watch the film all at once because it was "too much" and each viewing left her "dissolved in tears," but, she concludes, "I felt that was an appropriate response to watching a being die … I will never forget that. Nor should I" (83).

In another particularly engrossing chapter in the collection, "Decentering Whiteness as the Narrative," by Dr. Linda Alvarez, the author asserts that as more People of Color (PoC) have become vegan, there has been a "pushback" against the notion that "veganism is a 'white thing'" (8). This pushback, Alvarez asserts, "stems from the recognition that a dominant, white narrative, which remains an extremely problematic aspect of this movement, has crafted the vegan movement, especially in the United States" (8). Alvarez says that is similar to the pushback that has occurred in other social movements (e.g., in feminist discourse). In her critique of the place that PoC have held in vegan discourse, Alvarez launches into a skillful and crucial analysis of a kind of visual rhetoric used in vegan discourse: images of PoC being physically violated, tortured, and/or killed being placed alongside images of animals being subjected to "seemingly similar types of violence in order to create a 'mental link' between human and nonhuman suffering" (8). The goal, Alvarez writes, is that this "link" will "push people towards veganism" (8–9). But in a discourse that has been dominated by white voices, this particular juxtaposition of black and brown bodies against animals cannot go unchecked. Using the rhetorical question, Alvarez challenges both the reader and the white-centric discourse of veganism: "Why do the attempts at forging this 'mental link,' this emotional connection, always involve People of Color and nonhuman animals in contexts of violence?" (9). Alvarez's subsequent rhetorical analysis of a particularly common/popular piece of visual rhetoric—an image of an unnamed, lynched Black person juxtaposed with a photograph of a presumably dead pig hanging from its back leg—is a stunning rebuke of the way PoC have been employed in vegan discourse. Other parts of *Veganism of Color* pose similarly challenging questions about the meaning of veganism and vegan identity in a moment where inclusivity is both increasingly encouraged and necessary. After reviewing the landscape of vegan rhetoric, traveling from Peter Singer's call to arms about the human practice of eating other animals through to the new technologies that allow dialectic to occur through the more immediate concerns of race and veganism, there is little doubt that the conversation about animal rights, dietary practice, and cultural identity will continue unabated.

Works cited

Adams, Carol J. *The Sexual Politics of Meat: A Feminist-Vegetarian Critical Theory*. New York: Bloomsbury Academic, 2015.

Alexander, Jonathan, et al. *Unruly Rhetorics: Protest, Persuasion, and Publics*. University of Pittsburgh Press, 2018. search.ebscohost.com/login.aspx?direct=true&AuthType=ip,uid&db=cat04364a&AN=ufl.036555929&site=eds-live.

Baldwin, Alec. *Meet Your Meat*. [Videorecording]. Updated, PETA Video, 2003. search.ebscohost.com/login.aspx?direct=true&AuthType=ip,uid&db=cat04364a&AN=ufl.023291245&site=eds-live.

Brown, Wendy. *Edgework: Critical Essays on Knowledge and Politics*. Princeton, NJ: Princeton University Press, 2005.

Brueck, Julia F., editor. *Veganism of Color: Decentering Whiteness in Human and Nonhuman Liberation*. Sanctuary Publishers, 2019.

Burke, Kenneth. *The Philosophy of Literary Form*. Berkeley: University of California Press, 1941.

Dandelion, Dave. "On Specious Rhetoric by Vegan Advocates." *Davedandelion.com*, 15 September 2010, https://www.davedandelion.com/?p=409. Accessed 21 March 2020.

Foss, Sonja K. "Theory of Visual Rhetoric." *Handbook of Visual Communication: Theory, Methods, and Media*, edited by Ken Smith, Sandra Moriarty, Gretchen Barbatsis, and Keith Kenney, Mahwah, NJ: Lawrence Erlbaum, 2005, pp. 141–152.

Gruen, Lori and Robert C. Jones. "Veganism as an Aspiration." *The Moral Complexities of Eating Meat*, edited by Ben Bramble and Bob Fischer, Oxford University Press, 2015, pp. 153–171.

Hesford, Wendy and Brenda Jo Brueggemann. *Rhetorical Visions: Reading and Writing in a Visual Culture*. New York: Longman, 2007.

Jorgensen, Beth. "To Meat or Not To Meat?" *Poroi: An Interdisciplinary Journal of Rhetorical Analysis & Invention*, vol. 11, no. 1, 2015, pp. 1–19. doi:10.13008/2151-2957.1220.

Lamberti, Adrienne P. "The Rhetoric of Food." *Poroi: An Interdisciplinary Journal of Rhetorical Analysis & Invention*, vol. 11, no. 1, 2015, pp. 1–6. doi:10.13008/2151-2957.1219.

Lappé, Frances Moore. *Diet for a Small Planet*. 10th anniversary ed., Completely rev. & Updated, Ballantine Books, 1982. search.ebscohost.com/login.aspx?direct=true&AuthType=ip,uid&db=cat04364a&AN=ufl.025668177&site=eds-live.

Losh, Elizabeth M., et al. *Understanding Rhetoric: A Graphic Guide to Writing.* 2nd edition, Bedford/St. Martin's, 2017. search.ebscohost.com/login.aspx?direct=true&AuthType=ip,uid&db=cat04364a&AN=ufl.036271453&site=eds-live.

Lunceford, Brett. *Naked Politics: Nudity, Political Action, and the Rhetoric of the Body.* Lexington Books, 2012. search.ebscohost.com/login.aspx?direct=true&AuthType=ip,shib&db=cat06429a&AN=gso.9913748617702931.

McAuley, James Brad. "Adventures in Modern Rhetoric." *Society for the Academic Study of Social Imagery, March 2019 in Greeley, Colorado,* edited by Thomas G. Endres, The Society for the Academic Study of Social Imagery, July 2019.

O'Brien, Abigail. *Green Looks Good on You: The Rhetoric and Moral Identity of Conscious Consumption Blogs.* 2018. Claremont C, Senior Thesis. https://scholarship.claremont.edu/scripps_theses/1161

Roberts, W. Rhys, et al. *Rhetoric.* 1st Modern Library ed.]. ed., Modern Library, 1954.

Phillips, Ryan. "Frames as Boundaries: Rhetorical Framing Analysis and the Confines of Public Discourse in Online News Coverage of Vegan Parenting." *Journal of Communication Inquiry,* vol. 43, 2018, pp. 152–170. doi:10.1177/0196859918814821.

Sandis, Constantine. "Anti-Vegan Rhetoric." *Medium,* 1 August 2018, https://medium.com/@constantinesandis/anti-vegan-rhetoric-7df0410027fa Accessed 20 March 2020.

Simonetti, Luca. "The Ideology of Slow Food." *Journal of European Studies,* vol. 42, no. 2, 2012, pp. 168—189. doi:10.1177/0047244112436908.

Singer, Peter. *Animal Liberation.* 2nd edition. New York, NY: Random House, 1990.

Wright, Laura. *The Vegan Studies Project: Food, Animals, and Gender in the Age of Terror.* Athens: University of Georgia Press, 2015.

12
Veganism and the U.S. legal system

Tim Phillips

Instead of providing a definitive concept of "vegan lawyering," this chapter describes where in the U.S. legal system vegans are often found; i.e., which legal cases involve people who have adopted a vegan diet, whether they are lawyers filing lawsuits to protect animals or defendants facing criminal prosecution related to their activism.

Introduction

Like others in the U.S. legal system, vegans can either be on the offense or defense. As to offensive maneuvers, particularly lawsuits, much of that work summarized below has been performed by attorneys, most or all of whom are vegan, with nonprofit organizations such as the Animal Legal Defense Fund (ALDF), the Nonhuman Rights Project, People for the Ethical Treatment of Animals, Mercy for Animals, and Compassion Over Killing. As to defending vegan activists when they are charged with crimes or incarcerated, this work has generally been performed by private criminal defense attorneys, defense committees, and individuals dedicated to supporting activists. Instead of providing a definitive concept of "vegan lawyering," this chapter describes where in the U.S. legal system vegans are often found; i.e., which legal cases involve people who have adopted a vegan diet, whether they are lawyers filing lawsuits to protect animals or defendants facing criminal prosecution related to their activism.

Requesting public records

The federal Freedom of Information Act (FOIA) and state public records laws have been powerful tools for vegans in their struggle for animal liberation. In particular, FOIA "was intended to facilitate transparency about the government's policies even—or perhaps especially—when members of the public are disturbed by those policies and are fighting to end them" (*National Day Laborer Organizing Network* 93). It "calls on government employees to diligently and honestly respond to requests even from people with whom they disagree," for the "purpose of engendering a more informed public and a more accountable government" (93).

In February 2017, four nonprofit organizations used FOIA to sue the United States Department of Agriculture (USDA) for purging reports from its website that documented animal cruelty in laboratories, zoos, circuses, and puppy mills, and by animal transporters. "Animal advocates, journalists, and the public long relied on these documents to," among other things, "build cases against facilities that neglect animals, and against the USDA for failing to properly administer the law" ("Exposing Animal Abusers"). The U.S. Court of Appeals for the Ninth Circuit concluded in August 2019 that FOIA provides district courts with the authority to order that an agency post certain public records online, such as the reports at issue (*Animal Legal Defense Fund v. United States Department of Agriculture*, 935 F.3d 858, 869). In February 2020, the USDA "restored pertinent animal welfare records under its searchable Animal and Plant Health Inspection Service (APHIS) public database for the duration of at least three years" (Starostinetskaya).

In another example, in December 2018, eight organizations filed a lawsuit challenging the Farm Service Agency's failure to conduct any environmental analysis before granting loans for medium-sized concentrated animal feeding operations (CAFOs) (*Dakota Rural Action v. United States Department of Agriculture*). As CAFOs confine hundreds to tens of thousands of cows, pigs, turkeys, or chickens for the purpose of producing animal products, they contribute to climate change and contaminate air and water ("Challenging FSA's"). The evidence on which this lawsuit was based was gathered via a FOIA request.

Lawyers have also used FOIA requests in criminal cases where activists have been targeted by the government. For example, from the summer of 2004 until January 2006, a paid FBI informant lured a vegan activist named Eric McDavid and two others into an ill-defined, politically motivated plot to bomb targets in Northern California (Aaronson and Galloway). McDavid was convicted in 2007 of conspiring to use fire or explosives to damage corporate and government property, and he was sentenced to nearly 20 years in prison.

Yet, as reported by Aaronson and Galloway, multiple FOIA requests were filed with the federal government on McDavid's behalf, and in late 2014, records the government had said did not exist were turned over to McDavid's lawyers. The prosecution admitted that, under the federal rules of evidence, at least some of these documents should have been provided before trial:

> When McDavid and his lawyers discovered that the FBI and federal prosecutors had withheld approximately 2,500 pages of discovery, they negotiated a settlement that allowed for McDavid's release with time served in exchange for changing his conviction to a lesser charge of general conspiracy. (Aaronson and Galloway)

Thus, records from government agencies have "been essential in defending activists facing government surveillance and repression, uncovering gross … rights violations, and arming movements with the information they need to fight powerful interests" ("Guide"). Several organizations provide further information for people interested in learning more about submitting FOIA requests, such as the Center for Constitutional Rights and the Reporters Committee for Freedom of the Press ("Guide"; "FOIA and Federal").

Challenging ag-gag laws

While many companies have taken steps to eliminate the worst forms of cruelty to animals, undercover investigations have revealed that abuse is still routine, especially in CAFOs and slaughterhouses. To prevent people from learning about such abuse, some states have passed laws that seek to silence (or "gag") would-be whistleblowers or undercover activists. These laws, dubbed "ag-gag" laws by critics, punish people for recording what goes on in animal agriculture.

Yet prohibiting people from recording conditions at factory farms or slaughterhouses clearly violates the First Amendment. In 2013, the first lawsuit challenging such legislation targeted Utah's ag-gag law. Four years later, the law was declared unconstitutional by a federal judge:

> What the [ag-gag law] appears perfectly tailored toward is preventing undercover investigators from exposing abuses at agricultural facilities ... Utah undoubtedly has an interest in addressing perceived threats to the state agricultural industry, and as history shows, it has a variety of constitutionally permissible tools at its disposal to do so. Suppressing broad swaths of protected speech without justification, however, is not one of them. (Chappell)

In the meantime, another ag-gag lawsuit was filed against the state of Idaho. Mercy for Animals had released "a secretly-filmed exposé of the operation of an Idaho dairy farm" in October 2012. The Idaho legislature responded by enacting an ag-gag law in February 2014 that criminalized "making misrepresentations to access an agricultural production facility as well as making audio and video recordings of the facility without the owner's consent" (*Animal Legal Defense Fund v. Wasden* 1189).

The U.S. Court of Appeals for the Ninth Circuit reviewed Idaho's ag-gag law. The court concluded that Idaho's law violated the First Amendment by criminalizing misrepresentations to enter an agricultural production facility and by banning audio and video recordings of the operations of such a facility (1189). But the Ninth Circuit concluded that portions of Idaho's ag-gag law did not violate the Constitution: making it illegal to (1) obtain the records of an agricultural facility by misrepresentation, or (2) obtain employment by misrepresentation with the intent to cause economic or other injury (1189).

Following these lawsuits, ag-gag laws have been challenged in Iowa, North Carolina, Kansas, and Arkansas ("Challenging Iowa's"; "Challenging North Carolina's"; "Challenging Kansas's"; "Challenging Arkansas's"). A federal judge declared Iowa's March 2012 ag-gag law unconstitutional in January 2019 (*Animal Legal Defense Fund v. Reynolds* 824–27); but three weeks later, the Iowa legislature passed a second ag-gag law. In response to a lawsuit challenging Iowa's second ag-gag law, a federal judge granted a preliminary injunction in December 2019 preventing Iowa officials from enforcing the law while the lawsuit proceeds (Eller).

Approximately one month later, in January 2020, a federal judge declared provisions of Kansas's 1990 ag-gag law unconstitutional (Hegeman). But in February 2020, another federal judge dismissed a challenge to an ag-gag law in Arkansas, concluding that the organizations that initiated the lawsuit had not shown that they had been, or would be, harmed by the law (Satter). Those organizations subsequently filed an appeal.

As photographs and video footage from factory farms and slaughterhouses show that these places are a nightmare for animals, workers, and the environment, several states have passed laws attempting to criminalize undercover investigations. Animal protection organizations have generally been successful in asking courts to declare such laws unconstitutional. This litigation also shows the activist community that there are lawyers who support their organizing efforts, including undercover investigations and related campaigns.

Using environmental laws to protect animals

Many practices that cause tremendous animal suffering also destroy the environment or negatively impact endangered species. Thus, environmental laws provide one possible route to stop such practices. These laws include citizen suit provisions, which "generally allow private individuals or groups to file lawsuits that seek to enforce federal environmental laws, regulations, or permits against private and public entities" (Mogharabi et al.)—an important tool in attempting to hold such entities accountable.

Endangered Species Act

One factor animal protection organizations take into account when deciding whether to file a lawsuit is the opportunity to set a legal precedent; i.e., a ruling that could potentially be used over and over again, helping animals in similar situations around the country. For example, in a lawsuit against Cricket Hollow Zoo, a roadside zoo in Manchester, Iowa, the U.S. Court of Appeals for the Eighth Circuit confirmed in April 2018 that the Endangered Species Act (ESA) applies not only to an endangered species in the wild but also in captivity (*Kuehl* 851–54). This case has been a useful legal precedent for animal protection organizations, because the ESA makes it unlawful to harass or harm an endangered species. Lawyers have used this precedent not only to have animals removed from Cricket Hollow Zoo but also to address neglect of captive wildlife at similar facilities in other states.

National Environmental Policy Act

The National Environmental Policy Act (NEPA) requires federal agencies to consider the environmental effects of any proposed action. Using this law, the ALDF and the American Wild Horse Campaign filed a lawsuit in October 2018 challenging the Forest Service's plan to round up and sell nearly 1,000 horses living in the Devil's Garden Wild Horse Territory in California's Modoc National Forest, without any limitation protecting them from slaughter ("Devil's Garden Sale"). While the Forest Service's "long-standing policy [has been] to sell some of the horses rounded up in Devil's Garden and other federally managed lands," previously these horses were sold with a restriction that they could not be resold for slaughter ("Challenging the Sale of Wild Horses").

Like requests for public records and opposition to ag-gag laws, the use of NEPA continues a theme of transparency, of vegans attempting to uncover the hidden impacts of certain facilities or projects on nonhuman animals. Pushing in the opposite direction, toward secrecy, President Donald Trump has proposed narrowing the scope of NEPA (Kaufman and D'Angelo). This proposal "will almost certainly face legal challenges" (Eilperin and Dennis).

The laws that exist to protect animals sometimes—paradoxically—do the opposite, by failing to address certain practices that cause animal suffering. By using environmental laws instead, lawyers have been able to help some animals who would not otherwise be protected.

Joining legal efforts to protect human rights and the environment

Lawyers working for animal liberation have not limited their efforts to challenging practices that affect only nonhuman animals. Instead, they have filed or joined lawsuits against the government to protect people, animals, and the environment. For example, three organizations filed a lawsuit challenging President Donald Trump's emergency declaration to construct a wall along the U.S.–Mexico border. The groups argued that the proposed border wall "threatens animals—including endangered species—in numerous ways, such as restricting their movement and passage, which could lead to 'extirpation' or localized extinction," and by taking funds "from programs to combat wildlife trafficking" ("Challenging Emergency Declaration").

Threats to animals were not the only reason to oppose construction of the border wall, of course. It would also negatively impact people: "when barriers are erected along the border, people attempt to cross at more remote and dangerous locations" ("The High Cost"). In addition, it would put thousands of acres of habitat at risk, increase soil erosion, and potentially exacerbate flooding (Parker). In another case, the ALDF filed a lawsuit to compel federal government action on the climate crisis, stating: "this case brings together the animal protection community, environmentalists, and human rights advocates. Animals, the environment, and human beings are all threatened by climate change" ("Protecting Our"). Veganism and anti-authoritarianism ought to, and frequently do, go hand-in-hand (crow and Harper). People who oppose speciesism should naturally "oppose all forms of domination, exploitation, and oppression" (Dixon 3). This opposition impacts how vegans operate within the legal system, often attempting to use legal pathways to further movements for collective liberation. While these lawsuits have not stopped climate change or construction of the border wall, they illustrate how vegans in the legal system can attempt to stand in solidarity with other struggles.

Legislation and ballot initiatives banning various forms of animal cruelty

Aware that existing laws related to nonhuman animals are inadequate, animal protection organizations have also collaborated to pass new laws. Once such laws exist, vegans can act directly or indirectly to make sure they serve their intended purpose.

California has led the way regarding animal protection laws, passing several in recent years. In August 2016, California banned the use of bullhooks on elephants (O'Brien). One month later, California banned captivity and breeding of orcas and their use in entertainment (Hugo). In October 2017, California became the first state to prohibit pet stores from selling dogs, cats, or rabbits unless they came from an animal shelter or rescue group, beginning in 2019 (Hauser). In November 2018, California voters approved a ballot initiative establishing new standards regarding the confinement of egg-laying hens, calves raised for veal, and breeding pigs. "The new law built upon a prior measure adopted in 2008 and effective [in] 2015 (Proposition 2) which also imposed space requirements but did not reach products produced out-of-state but sold in-state" (Simpson).

After the U.S. Supreme Court declined to review an opinion from the U.S. Court of Appeals for the Ninth Circuit, California's ban on foie gras went back into effect in January 2019 ("California foie gras ban"). In September 2019, California enacted the first statewide ban on commercial or recreational fur trapping for animal pelts on public or private land (Sahagun and Willon). In October 2019, California passed the first statewide ban on the manufacture and sale of new animal fur products, including fur coats, beginning in 2023 (Allen).

Other states have also enacted groundbreaking animal protection laws. For example, in 2017, Illinois and New York passed the first two statewide bans on the use of elephants in entertainment (Pallotta, "Illinois and New York"). In November 2018, Florida voters approved a state constitutional amendment that essentially bans greyhound racing (Rosica). In May and August 2019, Washington and Oregon passed similar laws that will end cage confinement of hens by 2023 and 2024, respectively (Krantz; Bugga). Finally, beginning on January 1, 2020, California,

Illinois, and Nevada became the first states to ban the sale of cosmetic products and ingredients that have been tested on animals (Linse).

Following the passage of new laws regarding the treatment of animals, activists have used such laws in various ways. To encourage criminal prosecution of animal abusers, the ALDF "provides free legal assistance to prosecutors, law enforcement, and veterinarians handling animal cruelty cases," including legal research, professional trainings, grant funding, and expert witnesses ("Criminal Justice"). On the civil side, and as discussed further below, an individual can potentially use a lawsuit to identify violations of animal cruelty laws and thereby demonstrate that such violations make the animal abuser a "public nuisance."

"Look behind the label"—labeling food appropriately

People often do not want to purchase products from cruel factory farms. Yet words and imagery can mislead consumers, causing them to purchase products they would otherwise avoid. For example, consumers tend to believe the word "natural" relates to how animals were raised, treated, or fed. When a product's label is false, lawyers can sometimes use deceptive advertising laws to attempt to hold the company accountable.

In 2012, for example, the ALDF filed a lawsuit against Hudson Valley Foie Gras, the largest U.S. producer of foie gras, for defining itself as "The Humane Choice" in its promotional materials. The owner of the Regal Vegan, a Brooklyn-based company that produced a humane and plant-derived foie gras alternative (called "Faux Gras"), was a co-plaintiff in the suit. Hudson Valley Foie Gras subsequently removed its deceptive "humane" language ("Foie Gras").

In 2018, the ALDF successfully resolved a similar lawsuit against Trader Joe's. The suit alleged that Trader Joe's was violating multiple California consumer protection laws by selling cage-free eggs in cartons with imagery that misrepresented the conditions in which egg-laying hens were confined. The cartons had images of hens foraging outdoors in green, wide-open pastures, while in reality, the eggs came from hens who spent their entire lives in massive industrial hen houses, without any outdoor access. Trader Joe's quickly discontinued the use of this misleading packaging nationwide ("Challenging Trader Joe's"). These cases can be an effective way to keep companies more honest than they would otherwise be.

Another deceptive marketing lawsuit—this time a class action—was filed in November 2019, after an undercover investigation documented egregious animal cruelty at Fairlife dairies ("Challenging Fairlife's"). In a separate class action case involving an eyewitness report, a federal judge concluded in February 2020 that Nellie's Free Range Eggs' marketing, showing "hens frolicking in elysian pastures," was sufficiently deceptive for the lawsuit to proceed ("Judge Gives"). As discussed above, ag-gag laws tailored toward preventing undercover investigations threaten to prevent the exposure of these kinds of abuses at agricultural facilities. Protecting activists' right to expose animal abuse, which ag-gag litigation has successfully done, is conducive to accountability in various forms, ranging from protest to possible deceptive advertising lawsuits.

While vegans work to guarantee that animal products are labeled appropriately, some states have taken steps to protect companies from their plant-based competition. As "sales of vegetarian and vegan alternatives are growing at a rapid clip," several states have passed "laws saying that only foods made of animal flesh should be allowed to carry labels like 'meat,' 'sausage,' 'jerky,' 'burger' or 'hot dog'" (Selyukh). Lawsuits challenging this kind of legislation have had mixed results.

In October 2019, a federal judge declined to temporarily "block a Missouri law that bans companies from labeling plant-based meat products or meat substitutes as meat" ("Judge Declines to Block"). The judge concluded that companies that disclose that their products are plant-based would not be affected by the law. The coalition that filed the lawsuit appealed the judge's decision, arguing that the law violates the Constitution. By contrast, in December 2019, a federal judge in Arkansas issued a preliminary injunction temporarily blocking a law that prohibits "the use of terms like 'burgers,' 'sausage' and 'steak' on plant-based foods" (Grzincic). The judge concluded that a plant-based meat producer, Tofurky, was likely to prevail on its claim that the law was an impermissible restraint on its First Amendment rights.

In February 2020, plant-based dairy company Miyoko's Kitchen filed a lawsuit against the California Department of Food and Agriculture. The lawsuit claims that California's Milk and Dairy Food Safety Branch violated the company's First Amendment rights when it

> ordered Miyoko's to remove truthful messages and images from its website and its product labels—including the phrase "100 [percent] cruelty and animal free," the use of the word "butter" in the phrase "vegan plant butter," and even an image of a "woman hugging a cow." (Miyoko's Kitchen v. Karen Ross)

On the dietary side of veganism, these are some of the most important ongoing legal cases, as they protect the existence of alternatives to animal products. Of course, states are not the only entities trying to thwart vegan competitors to companies that sell animal products. For example, the egg industry unlawfully "launched a secret two-year campaign"—reported in September 2015 due to a public records request by FOIA expert (and vegan) Ryan Shapiro—to crush a vegan mayonnaise competitor called Just Mayo (Mohan). Continuing the theme of transparency, these cases show further attempts by vegans to reveal the hidden impacts of certain products on nonhuman animals.

Advocating for vegans who are incarcerated

Jails and prisons are generally not required to provide someone who is incarcerated with vegan food, unless the person's veganism is a genuine religious dietary practice. Under the First Amendment, people who are incarcerated are entitled to "reasonable accommodation of their religious dietary needs" (*Sisney* 846; *Bass* 99; *LaFevers* 1119). Moreover, the Religious Land Use and Institutionalized Persons Act (RLUIPA) specifically contemplates that the law "may require a government to incur expenses in its own operations to avoid imposing a substantial burden" on religious exercise (42 U.S.C. section 2000cc-3(c)). Thus, the fact that a vegan diet may be more costly than a non-vegan diet is not, by itself, a compelling governmental interest that might justify not providing it to someone who is incarcerated (*Willis* 778).

Atheism may, in the specialized sense of applying First Amendment protections, be considered a religion (*Kaufman* 681–82). A person's religious beliefs need not be based on a mainstream faith, but should deal with issues of ultimate concern, occupying a place parallel to that filled by God in traditionally religious people (*Kaudman* 681; *Frazee* 834). In addition, the First Amendment protects genuine religious dietary practices even if they are not a central tenet of the person's religion or doctrinally required (*Cutter* 725; *Hernandez* 699). No court in the United States, however, has made a definitive ruling regarding whether veganism should be considered a protected class or religion.

A person's religious dietary practice is substantially burdened when a jail or prison forces them to choose between their religious practice and adequate nutrition (*Civil Liberties for Urban Believers* 760–61; *Love* 689–90; *McElyea* 198). If a person who is incarcerated observes a vegan diet based on sincere beliefs related to issues of ultimate concern, they arguably have a right to vegan food while in jail or prison. If, however, a person who is incarcerated observes a vegan diet based on "purely secular" concerns such as health or animal suffering, that person probably does not have a right to receive vegan food (*Thomas* 713–14; *Wisconsin* 215–16; *Koger* 797; *Vinning-El* 594).

There may be future litigation in the United States in an attempt to establish that ethical veganism is a protected class akin to religion under one or more anti-discrimination laws. This was established in the United Kingdom in January 2020 (Heil). For the time being, however, the status quo in the United States is further evidence that incarceration "is by its very nature destructive of human dignity, and the best antidote is for society to use it less often" (Horn). In an attempt "to ensure that … prison vegan diets are nutritionally sound and that vegan clothing, hygiene and bodycare products are made available or can be ordered or sent in to vegan prisoners," the Vegan Prisoners Support Group was formed in the United Kingdom in April 1994 (*Vegan Prisoners Support Group*). A similar effort in the United States, called Support Vegans in the Prison System, is "a volunteer based group working to help vegan individuals live a healthy vegan lifestyle, which is an expression of their deeply held ethical values" ("Mission Statement"). These groups try to support incarcerated vegans, who are often political prisoners. In the words of Ashanti Alston:

> We need to honor those who laid it down before us. Especially those who are still alive but are just in these dungeons. We need to let the system know that they are on the front of our minds. We want them out. ("An Interview")

Litigating to change animals' legal status

Animals are alive and feel pain just like human beings. Yet the U.S. legal system still considers animals to be "property," meaning they lack fundamental legal protections. This makes it difficult to present an animal's mistreatment to a judge or jury through a lawsuit. The entity initiating a lawsuit must have what the law calls "standing." This is a requirement that the party initiating a lawsuit has been, or will be, harmed by the entity being sued—the "defendant"—and that the court can remedy this harm. As the legal system does not recognize animals' personhood, they generally do not have standing, and thus they lack the legal capacity to bring a lawsuit or assert a claim in court.

The Nonhuman Rights Project (NhRP) is a U.S. civil rights organization dedicated solely to securing rights for nonhuman animals. Their lawyers file petitions for writs of habeas corpus, meaning they seek court determinations regarding the lawfulness of the incarceration of a specific animal, whether it is a great ape, elephant, dolphin, or whale. They also file affidavits from scientists and other experts that address why the specific animal is entitled to a recognition of their legal personhood, does not belong in captivity, and is entitled to a fundamental right to bodily liberty ("Litigation: Confronting the core issue"). The NhRP has filed several petitions for writs of habeas corpus, but attempts to create legal standing for animals have failed thus far. One NhRP case, however, resulted in a remarkable concurring opinion from Judge Fahey of the New York Court of Appeals, which included the following:

> Does an intelligent nonhuman animal who thinks and plans and appreciates life as human beings do have the right to the protection of the law against arbitrary cruelties and enforced detentions visited on him or her? This is not merely a definitional question, but a deep dilemma of ethics and policy that demands our attention. To treat a chimpanzee as if he or she had no right to liberty protected by habeas corpus is to regard the chimpanzee as

> entirely lacking independent worth, as a mere resource for human use, a thing the value of which consists exclusively in its usefulness to others. Instead, we should consider whether a chimpanzee is an individual with inherent value who has the right to be treated with respect. … (Nonhuman Rights Project 1058)

In a similar vein, the ALDF sought records under FOIA in May 2017 related to the health and well-being of Tony the Tiger, who was confined at the Tiger Truck Stop in Grosse Tete, Louisiana, for 16 years ("Animal Legal Defense Fund Demands"). The ALDF sought expedited processing, as it was reasonable to expect that delayed disclosure of the records could pose an imminent threat to Tony's life or physical safety. The ALDF subsequently sued the USDA for refusing to recognize Tony as an "individual" under FOIA whose safety could be at risk by delayed disclosure of the records sought ("Animal Legal Defense Fund Sues USDA"). The U.S. Court of Appeals for the Ninth Circuit concluded in August 2019, however, that the plain meaning of the word "individual" was "human being" (*Animal Legal Defense Fund v. United States Department of Agriculture*, 933 F.3d 1088, 1094).

Finally, in May 2018, the ALDF filed a similar lawsuit in Oregon on behalf of a mistreated horse. The case combined

> two uncontroversial, well-established legal principles: first, that animals are properly considered the victims of animal cruelty crimes, and second, that victims of crimes have a right to sue their abusers in civil court for damages for injuries caused by the defendant. (Pallotta, "Advocating for Justice")

Predictably, the lawsuit was dismissed (Thomas); but the ALDF subsequently appealed. Therefore, neither lawsuits nor petitions for writs of habeas corpus have successfully changed animals' legal status, though efforts to do so continue in various forms.

Filing public nuisance lawsuits

Regardless of whether cruel practices violate a specific animal protection law, they may still satisfy the legal definition of a public nuisance: any "activity or thing that affects the health, safety, or morals of a community," such as "a factory that spews out clouds of noxious fumes" ("Public Nuisance"). In August 2016, the ALDF filed a nuisance lawsuit to end a coyote-killing competition based in WaKeeney, Kansas, arguing that it met the state's definition of illegal commercial gambling. Participants, including children, paid money for the opportunity to win prizes by killing the most coyotes in one day. The ALDF represented Western Plains Animal Rescue (WPAR), the local organization that rehabilitated injured wild animals, as WPAR had incurred costs rehabilitating the coyotes who were injured but not killed during the competition. In October 2016, the organizer of the competition agreed to never host or organize another killing contest in Kansas, and the coyote-killing competition has not been held since ("Challenging Smoky Hill").

In July 2018, the ALDF filed another nuisance lawsuit to shut down four backyard slaughter operations outside Fort Myers, Florida, arguing that the operations violated the state's animal cruelty and slaughter laws ("Challenging Backyard Butchers"). The ALDF represented a neighbor who ran a produce stand nearby. A court ordered that these operations be shut down, marking "one of the first times in the country where a private citizen presented violations of animal cruelty and humane slaughter laws to demonstrate that animal abusers are a public nuisance—and used a civil lawsuit to enjoin the violations" ("Animal Legal Defense Fund Lawsuit Shuts Down").

In September 2018, the ALDF filed a similar nuisance lawsuit against Cricket Hollow Zoo in Manchester, Iowa, arguing that the roadside zoo chronically violated the state's animal cruelty standards ("Challenging Cricket Hollow"; "Animal Legal Defense Fund Lawsuit Aims"). In November 2019, the court ordered that the animals at Cricket Hollow Zoo must be transferred to sanctuaries, and barred the zoo's owners from owning exotic animals or wildlife ("Court Orders Animals From Cricket Hollow Zoo"; "Animals Rescued and Removed"). In light of these victories, public nuisance lawsuits are another important tool lawyers have used to end cruel practices that violate community standards.

Defending vegan activists in the criminal legal system

People who actively challenge the basic premises on which society is based, such as the exploitation of nonhuman animals, frequently end up in court:

> Debates over the rule of law too often seem to focus on whether the law went astray. Yet a body of law designed to protect property and political power need not stray very far in its application, if at all, to discredit and destroy those who seek to voice alternatives to the assumptions that underlie the prevailing social order. Few, if any, who have even come remotely close to having an audience for such change have escaped the courtroom.
> (Sayer 230)

Whether arrested at a protest or charged with liberating animals, vegan activists have fought criminal charges most effectively when they have combined legal and political strategies (Tilted Scales Collective). A group called Direct Action Everywhere (DxE), for example, "advocates for animal rights—often by breaking into farms and slaughterhouses to whisk away animals its members think are being raised in crowded and unsafe conditions" (Avila). Yet in addition to fighting the subsequent criminal charges, activists helped get a resolution passed by the Berkeley City Council in December 2019 supporting the people "facing serious criminal charges for giving animals aid in factory farms" ("Recent Updates"). This combination of legal and political strategies caused an attorney for biomedical research facilities and animal-related businesses to posit that:

> If such unlawful conduct were to become accepted by the mainstream and offenders were not properly punished, animal enterprises will be in great jeopardy. Instead, perhaps these offenses should be considered violations pursuant to the Animal Enterprise Terrorism Act. (Halpern)

The Animal Enterprise Terrorism Act (AETA) was signed into law by President George W. Bush on November 27, 2006, replacing its predecessor, the Animal Enterprise Protection Act (AEPA) of 1992. Industry groups espousing free-market, limited-government policies, such as the American Legislative Exchange Council and the Center for Consumer Freedom, pushed the AETA through Congress (Dye; "The Animal Enterprise Terrorism Act"). Even though the AETA arguably violates the First Amendment by punishing advocacy related to animal enterprises, legal challenges to date have been unsuccessful ("Blum v. Holder;" "United States v. Johnson").

The most notable criminal case under AETA's predecessor, the AEPA, was a felony case against six organizers participating in "an international, grassroots animal rights campaign" called Stop Huntingdon Animal Cruelty (SHAC) ("U.S. v. SHAC 7"). The goal of SHAC was to shut down Huntingdon Life Sciences (HLS), a research corporation that performed tests on animals at three laboratories—two in the United Kingdom and one in New Jersey (Monaghan and Walby). Several undercover investigations of HLS documented cruelty to animals (Bright).

The SHAC campaign pressured companies and individuals associated with HLS (e.g., investors, suppliers, customers, and stockbrokers) to cut ties with HLS, pushing HLS to the brink of bankruptcy ("The SHAC Model"). Anonymous activists contributed to this effort by breaking windows, burning vehicles, and engaging in other forms of politically motivated property destruction (Tomlinson). In March 2006, six SHAC activists (who were not alleged to have damaged any property) were convicted of, among other things, conspiring to violate the AEPA, convictions that were upheld because the activists allegedly coordinated electronic civil disobedience and disseminated the personal information of individuals employed by HLS or affiliated companies (*U.S. v. Fullmer* 153–56).

After the AETA replaced the AEPA, it appeared as though even more advocacy related to animal enterprises could be punished, and punished even more aggressively. This is still what is referred to as the "chilling effect" of the AETA ("ACLU Letter"). Yet the first prosecution under the AETA was a win for the animal rights movement.

On March 12, 2009, the U.S. government filed an indictment charging four animal rights activists in California with violating the AETA (*U.S. v. Stumpo*). The activists allegedly attended "home demonstrations"—protests outside the homes of, in this case, biomedical researchers who conducted experiments on animals (Potter). Lawyers for the activists filed a motion asking the court to dismiss the indictment, and the court did, concluding that the indictment lacked sufficient specificity and that "picketing and political protest are at the very core of what is protected by the First Amendment" (*U.S. v. Buddenberg* 6).

Through theory, action, reflection, and more action (defined as "praxis") (Russell), vegan activists are continuing to push the envelope despite draconian laws. They are exercising their most basic rights, such as the right to advocate for a cause or remain silent when questioned by law enforcement ("If An Agent Knocks"). It should be no surprise that some of their tactics will be deemed illegal, as "history is full of social upheavals in which true believers decided the cause was so great that they would step beyond the boundaries of law" (Rasmussen). Yet when laws criminalize even activism intended to comply with the law, as occurred in the SHAC campaign, the legal system is not a justice system, but "simply the means by which [the ruling] class defends its self-interest" (Honderich 32).

Conclusion

There is no shortage of time and energy that vegans—sometimes as lawyers and sometimes as defendants—spend in the legal system. These efforts no doubt improve the lives of animals. Vegan activists find themselves facing criminal charges for liberating animals or engaging in other forms of protest against animal cruelty. The assistance they receive in fighting these charges shows other activists the level of support they will receive if they break the law to help animals (or did so unintentionally, or are alleged to have broken the law, even if they did not). Meanwhile, vegan lawyers seek recognition from judges that specific nonhuman animals are individuals with inherent value, and recognition that animals have the right to be treated with respect.

Works cited

Aaronson, Trevor and Katie Galloway. "Manufacturing Terror: An FBI Informant Seduced Eric McDavid Into a Bomb Plot. Then the Government Lied About It." *The Intercept*, 19 November 2015, theintercept.com/2015/11/19/an-fbi-informant-seduced-eric-mcdavid-into-a-bomb-plot-then-the-government-lied-about-it/. Accessed January 15 2020.

"ACLU Letter to Congress Urging Opposition to the Animal Enterprise Act, S. 1926 and H.R. 4239." *American Civil Liberties Union*, aclu.org/letter/aclu-letter-congress-urging-opposition-animal-enterprise-act-s-1926-and-hr-4239. Accessed 18 January 2020.

Allen, Jonathan. "California bans sale, manufacture of fur products from 2023." *Reuters*, 12 October 2019, reuters.com/article/us-california-fur/california-bans-sale-manufacture-of-fur-products-from-2023-idUSKBN1WR0KQ. Accessed January 16 2020.

"An Interview with Ashanti Alston." *In the Middle of a Whirlwind*, inthemiddleofthewhirlwind.wordpress.com/an-interview-with-ashanti-alston/. Accessed 17 January 2020.

"Animal Legal Defense Fund Demands Feds Recognize Tony the Tiger as an 'Individual' Protected by the Freedom of Information Act." *Animal Legal Defense Fund*, 24 May 2017, aldf.org/article/animal-legal-defense-fund-demands-feds-recognize-tony-the-tiger-as-an-individual-protected-by-the-freedom-of-information-act/. Accessed January 17 2020.

"Animal Legal Defense Fund Lawsuit Aims to Rescue Remaining Animals from Iowa Roadside Zoo." *Animal Legal Defense Fund*, 27 September 2018, aldf.org/article/animal-legal-defense-fund-lawsuit-aims-to-rescue-remaining-animals-from-iowa-roadside-zoo/. Accessed January 18 2020.

"Animal Legal Defense Fund Lawsuit Shuts Down Florida Backyard Slaughter Operations." *Animal Legal Defense Fund*, 26 August 2019, aldf.org/article/animal-legal-defense-fund-lawsuit-shuts-down-florida-backyard-slaughter-operations/. Accessed January 18 2020.

"Animal Legal Defense Fund Sues USDA for Denying Tony the Tiger is an 'Individual' Protected by FOIA." *Animal Legal Defense Fund*, 11 July 2017, aldf.org/article/animal-legal-defense-fund-sues-usda-for-denying-tony-the-tiger-is-an-individual-protected-by-foia/. Accessed January 17 2020.

Animal Legal Defense Fund v. Reynolds, 353 F.Supp.3d 812 (S.D. Iowa 2019).

Animal Legal Defense Fund v. United States Department of Agriculture, 933 F.3d 1088 (9th Cir. 2019a).

Animal Legal Defense Fund v. United States Department of Agriculture, 935 F.3d 858 (9th Cir. 2019b).

Animal Legal Defense Fund v. Wasden, 878 F.3d 1184 (9th Cir. 2018).

"Animals Rescued and Removed from Manchester, Iowa, Roadside Zoo." *Animal Legal Defense Fund*, 9 December 2019, aldf.org/article/animals-rescued-and-removed-from-manchester-iowa-roadside-zoo/. Accessed January 18 2020.

Avila, Yuriria. "The Berkeley activist who puts her body on the line to fight animal cruelty." *Berkeleyside*, 12 December 2019, berkeleyside.com/2019/12/12/the-berkeley-activist-who-puts-her-body-on-the-line-to-fight-animal-cruelty. Accessed January 18 2020.

Bass v. Coughlin, 976 F.2d 98 (2d Cir. 1992).

"Blum v. Holder." *Center for Constitutional Rights*, 3 August 2016, ccrjustice.org/home/what-we-do/our-cases/blum-v-holder. Accessed January 18 2020.

Bright, Martin. "Inside the labs where lives hang heavy in the balance." *The Guardian*, 20 January 2001, theguardian.com/uk/2001/jan/21/martinbright.theobserver. Accessed January 18 2020.

Bugga, Hannah. "Progress: Oregon Bans Cage Confinement of Hens Used for Eggs." *Mercy for Animals*, 14 August 2019, mercyforanimals.org/progress-oregon-bans-cage-confinement-of. Accessed January 16 2020.

"California foie gras ban goes into effect after Supreme Court rejects challenge." *Los Angeles Times*, 7 January 2019, latimes.com/business/la-fi-foie-gras-prohibition-court-ruling-20190107-story.html. Accessed January 16 2020.

"Challenging Arkansas's Ag-Gag Law." *Animal Legal Defense Fund*, 27 December 2019, aldf.org/case/challenging-arkansass-ag-gag-law/. Accessed January 15 2020.

"Challenging Backyard Butchers in Florida." *Animal Legal Defense Fund*, 12 September 2019, aldf.org/case/challenging-backyard-butchers-in-florida/. Accessed January 18 2020.

"Challenging Cricket Hollow Zoo's Treatment of Animals (2018)." *Animal Legal Defense Fund*, 12 September 2019, aldf.org/case/challenging-cricket-hollow-zoos-treatment-of-animals-2018/. Accessed January 18 2020.

"Challenging Emergency Declaration for Border Wall." *Animal Legal Defense Fund*, 15 April 2019, aldf.org/case/challenging-emergency-declaration-for-border-wall/. Accessed January 16 2020.

"Challenging Fairlife's Deceptive Marketing Practices." *Animal Legal Defense Fund*, 14 November 2019, aldf.org/case/challenging-fairlifes-deceptive-marketing-practices/. Accessed January 16 2020.

"Challenging FSA's Medium-sized CAFO Exemptions." *Animal Legal Defense Fund*, 12 September 2019, aldf.org/case/challenging-fsas-medium-sized-cafo-exemptions/. Accessed January 15 2020.

"Challenging Iowa's Ag-Gag 2.0 Law." *Animal Legal Defense Fund*, 26 September 2019, aldf.org/case/challenging-iowas-ag-gag-2-0-law/. Accessed January 16 2020.

"Challenging Kansas's Ag-Gag Law." *Animal Legal Defense Fund*, 27 December 2019, aldf.org/case/animal-legal-defense-fund-et-al-v-coyler-et-al/. Accessed January 15 2020.

"Challenging North Carolina's Ag-Gag Law." *Animal Legal Defense Fund*, 27 December 2019, aldf.org/case/challenging-north-carolinas-ag-gag-law/. Accessed January 15 2020.

"Challenging Smoky Hill Calling Contest." *Animal Legal Defense Fund*, 20 October 2016, aldf.org/case/challenging-smoky-hill-calling-contest/. Accessed January 18 2020.

"Challenging the Sale of Wild Horses from Devil's Garden, California." *Animal Legal Defense Fund*, 27 December 2019, aldf.org/case/challenging-the-sale-of-wild-horses-from-devils-garden-california/. Accessed January 16 2020.

"Challenging Trader Joe's Misleading Egg Carton Labeling." *Animal Legal Defense Fund*, 21 June 2018, aldf.org/case/challenging-trader-joes-misleading-egg-carton-labeling/. Accessed January 16 2020.

Chappell, Bill. "Judge Overturns Utah's 'Ag-Gag' Ban on Undercover Filming at Farms." *National Public Radio*, 8 July 2017, npr.org/sections/thetwo-way/2017/07/08/536186914/judge-overturns-utahs-ag-gag-ban-on-undercover-filming-at-farms. Accessed January 16 2020.

Civil Liberties for Urban Believers v. City of Chicago, 342 F.3d 752 (7th Cir. 2003).

"Court Orders Animals from Cricket Hollow Zoo Be Transferred to Sanctuaries." *Animal Legal Defense Fund*, 25 November 2019, aldf.org/article/court-orders-animals-from-cricket-hollow-zoo-be-transferred-to-sanctuaries/. Accessed January 18 2020.

"Criminal Justice." *Animal Legal Defense Fund*, aldf.org/how_we_work/criminal-justice/. Accessed January 16 2020.

crow, scott and Josh Harper. "Animal Liberation and Anarchism." scottcrow.org/animal-liberation-and-anarchism-a-talk-by-josh-harper-and-scott-crow. Accessed 16 January 2020.

Cutter v. Wilkinson, 544 U.S. 709 (2005).

Dakota Rural Action v. United States Department of Agriculture, Complaint. *Public Justice*, 5 December 2018, publicjustice.net/wp-content/uploads/2018/12/FSA-NEPA-Complaint.pdf. Accessed January 15 2020.

"Devil's Garden Sale 'Without Limitation.'" *American Wild Horse Campaign*, americanwildhorsecampaign.org/devils-garden-sale-without-limitation. Accessed 16 January 2020.

Dixon, Chris. *Another Politics*. University of California Press, 2014.

Dye, Alan. "Pro-Business Advocacy." *New York Times*, 19 July 2012, nytimes.com/2012/07/20/opinion/pro-business-advocacy.html?_r=2&. Accessed January 18 2020.

Eilperin, Juliet and Brady Dennis. "Trump proposes change to environmental rules to speed up highway projects, pipelines and more." *Washington Post*, 9 January 2020, washingtonpost.com/climate-environment/white-house-wants-to-change-rules-to-speed-up-highway-projects-pipelines-drilling/2020/01/08/4e248fda-325a-11ea-9313-6cba89b1b9fb_story.html. Accessed January 16 2020.

Eller, Donnelle. "Judge issues order preventing enforcement of Iowa's new 'ag-gag' law." *Des Moines Register*, 2 December 2019, desmoinesregister.com/story/money/agriculture/2019/12/02/federal-judge-stops-enforcement-iowas-new-ag-gag-law/2591453001/. Accessed January 16 2020.

"Exposing Animal Abusers: Update on the Animal Welfare Blackout." *Animal Legal Defense Fund*, 18 September 2019, aldf.org/article/exposing-animal-abusers-update-on-the-animal-welfare-blackout/. Accessed January 15 2020.

"FOIA and Federal Open Government." *Reporters Committee for Freedom of the Press*, rcfp.org/foia/. Accessed 15 January 2020.

"Foie Gras." *Animal Legal Defense Fund*, aldf.org/issue/foie-gras/. Accessed 16 January 2020.

Frazee v. Illinois Dept. of Employment Security, 489 U.S. 829 (1989).

Grzincic, Barbara. "Judge puts Arkansas' plant-based meat labeling law on hold." *Reuters*, 12 December 2019, reuters.com/article/tofurky-lawsuit/judge-puts-arkansas-plant-based-meat-labeling-law-on-hold-idUSL1N28M2CQ. Accessed January 16 2020.

Guide: FOIA Basics for Activists. *Center for Constitutional Rights*, 28 May 2019, ccrjustice.org/foia-basics-activists. Accessed January 15 2020.

Halpern, Nancy. "The Right to Rescue or Criminal Trespass and Theft?" *Fox Rothschild*, 25 December 2019, animallaw.foxrothschild.com/2019/12/25/the-right-to-rescue-or-criminal-trespass-and-theft/. Accessed January 18 2020.

Hauser, Christine. "California Forces Pet Stores to Sell Only Dogs and Cats from Shelters." *New York Times*, 2 January 2019, nytimes.com/2019/01/02/us/california-pet-store-rescue-law.html. Accessed January 16 2020.

Hegeman, Roxana. "Court: Kansas 'Ag-Gag' unconstitutionally bans free speech." *AP News*, 22 January 2020, https://apnews.com/b897b5d3ec2364cfd60fc58bd56948f3. Accessed March 5 2020.

Heil, Emily. "'Ethical veganism is a protected class akin to religion in the U.K. after a landmark ruling." *Washington Post*, 3 January 2020, https://www.washingtonpost.com/news/voraciously/wp/2020/01/03/ethical-veganism-is-a-protected-class-akin-to-religion-in-the-u-k-after-a-landmark-ruling/. Accessed March 5 2020.

Hernandez v. Commissioner of Internal Revenue, 490 U.S. 680 (1989).

Honderich, Ted, editor. *Oxford Companion to Philosophy*, 2nd edition. Oxford University Press, 2005.

Horn, Martin. "Rights of City Inmates." *New York Times*, 28 July 2014, nytimes.com/2014/07/29/opinion/rights-of-city-inmates.html?_r=0. Accessed January 17 2020.

Hugo, Kristin. "Orca Shows and Breeding Banned in California." *National Geographic*, 14 September 2016, nationalgeographic.com/news/2016/09/california-bans-SeaWorld-orca-breeding-entertainment/. Accessed January 16 2020.

"If An Agent Knocks (the booklet)." *Center for Constitutional Rights*, 25 September 2009, ccrjustice.org/if-agent-knocks-booklet. Accessed January 18 2020. ("It is always best to not talk without an attorney present.")

"Judge Declines to Block Fake-Meat Law; Appeal is Filed." *Iowa PBS*, 4 October 2019, iowapbs.org/mtom/story/34939/judge-declines-block-fake-meat-law-appeal-filed. Accessed January 16 2020.

"Judge Gives Green Light to Lawsuit Against Nellie's Eggs." *People for the Ethical Treatment of Animals*, 24 February 2020, https://www.peta.org/media/news-releases/judge-gives-green-light-to-lawsuit-against-nellies-eggs/. Accessed March 5 2020.

Kaufman, Alexander and Chris D'Angelo. "Trump's Latest Environmental Rollback Is a Middle Finger to Common Sense." *Mother Jones*, 12 January 2020, motherjones.com/environment/2020/01/trumps-latest-environmental-rollback-is-a-middle-finger-to-common-sense/. Accessed January 16 2020.

Kaufman v. McCaughtry, 419 F.3d 678 (7th Cir. 2005).

Koger v. Bryan, 523 F.3d 789, 797 (7th Cir. 2008).

Krantz, Rachel. "Victory! Washington Ends Cage Confinement of Hens Used for Eggs." *Mercy for Animals*, 8 May 2019, mercyforanimals.org/victory-washington-ends-cage-confinement. Accessed January 16 2020.

Kuehl v. Sellner, 887 F.3d 845 (8th Cir. 2018).

LaFevers v. Saffle, 936 F.2d 1117 (10th Cir. 1991).

Linse, Jessica. "CA, IL, NV Ban Animal-Tested Cosmetics." *Duane Morris*, 3 February 2020, https://blogs.duanemorris.com/animallawdevelopments/2020/02/03/ca-il-nv-ban-animal-tested-cosmetics/. Accessed March 5 2020.

"Litigation: Confronting the core issue of nonhuman animals' legal thinghood." *Nonhuman Rights Project*, nonhumanrights.org/litigation/. Accessed 17 January 2020.

Love v. Reed, 216 F.3d 682 (8th Cir. 2000).

McElyea v. Babbitt, 833 F.2d 196 (9th Cir. 1987).

"Mission Statement." *Support Vegans in the Prison System*, supportvips.org/about/. Accessed 17 January 2020. I am the Legal Advisor for this organization.=

Miyoko's Kitchen v. Karen Ross, Complaint for Declaratory and Injunctive Relief. *The Brooks Institute*, 6 February 2020, https://thebrooksinstitute.org/sites/default/files/article/2020-02/Miyoko%27s%20Complaint%20-%20To%20Accompany%202020-02-10%20Issue%20No%2016.pdf. Accessed 5 March 2020.

Mogharabi, Sara, et al. "Environmental Citizen Suits in the Trump Era." *American Bar Association*, 22 January 2018, americanbar.org/groups/environment_energy_resources/publications/natural_resources_environment/2017-18/fall/environmental-citizen-suits-trump-era/. Accessed January 16 2020.

Mohan, Geoffrey. "The egg industry launched a secret two-year war against a vegan mayonnaise competitor." *Los Angeles Times*, 7 October 2016, latimes.com/business/la-fi-egg-board-investigation-20161007-snap-story.html. Accessed January 16 2020.

Monaghan, Jeff and Kevin Walby. "The Green Scare is Everywhere: The Importance of Cross-Movement Solidarity." *Upping the Anti*, 26 October 2009, uppingtheanti.org/journal/article/06-the-green-scare-is-everywhere. Accessed January 18 2020.

National Day Laborer Organizing Network v. United States Immigration and Customs Enforcement Agency, 877 F.Supp.2d 87 (S.D.N.Y. 2012).
Nonhuman Rights Project, Inc., on Behalf of Tommy v. Lavery, 31 N.Y.3d 1054, 1058 (N.Y. Ct. App. 2018).
O'Brien, Brendan. "California Governor Brown signs law banning use of bullhooks on elephants." *Reuters*, 30 August 2016, reuters.com/article/us-california-elephants/california-governor-brown-signs-law-banning-use-of-bullhooks-on-elephants-idUSKCN1150ET. Accessed January 16 2020.
Pallotta, Nicole. "Advocating for Justice in Oregon: Neglected Horse Sues Former Owner." *Animal Legal Defense Fund*, 13 September 2018, aldf.org/article/advocating-for-justice-in-oregon-neglected-horse-sues-former-owner/. Accessed January 18 2020.
Pallotta, Nicole. "Illinois and New York Pass First Statewide Bans on the Use of Elephants in Entertainment." *Animal Legal Defense Fund*, 17 November 2017, aldf.org/article/illinois-new-york-pass-first-statewide-bans-use-elephants-entertainment/. Accessed January 16 2020.
Parker, Laura. "6 ways the border wall could disrupt the environment." *National Geographic*, 10 January 2019, nationalgeographic.com/environment/2019/01/how-trump-us-mexico-border-wall-could-impact-environment-wildlife-water/. Accessed January 16 2020.
Potter, Will. "Animal Rights Activists Indicted as 'Terrorists' For Home Protests." *Green is the New Red*, 19 March 2009, greenisthenewred.com/blog/animal-rights-activists-indicted-as-terrorists-for-home-protests/1657/. Accessed January 18 2020.
"Protecting Our Constitutional Right to Liberty." *Animal Legal Defense Fund*, 27 December 2019, aldf.org/case/protecting-our-constitutional-right-to-liberty/. Accessed January 16 2020.
"Public Nuisance." *Nolo's Plain-English Law Dictionary*, nolo.com/dictionary/public-nuisance-term.html. Accessed January 18 2020.
Rasmussen, Matt. "Green Rage." *Orion Magazine*, 1 January 2007, orionmagazine.org/index.php/articles/article/6/. Accessed January 18 2020.
"Recent Updates." *Right to Rescue*, 11 December 2019, righttorescue.com/. Accessed January 18 2020.
Religious Land Use and Institutionalized Persons Act of 2000, 42 U.S.C.A. § 2000cc-1 *et seq*.
Rosica, Jim. "Losing their 'heritage': Ban on dog racing unconstitutional, federal lawsuit says." *Florida Politics*, 7 October 2019, floridapolitics.com/archives/307665-ban-dog-racing-unconstitutional. Accessed January 16 2020.
Russell, Joshua Kahn. "Praxis makes perfect." *Beautiful Trouble*, beautifultrouble.org/principle/praxis-makes-perfect/. Accessed 18 January 2020.
Sahagun, Louis and Phil Willon. "California becomes first state to ban fur trapping after Gov. Newsom signs law." *Los Angeles Times*, 4 September 2019, latimes.com/california/story/2019-09-04/fur-trapping-ban-california-law. Accessed January 16 2020.
Satter, Linda. "Challenge to state law on undercover farm investigations dismissed." *Northwest Arkansas Democrat Gazette*, 15 February 2020, https://www.nwaonline.com/news/2020/feb/15/challenge-to-law-on-undercover-farm-inv-1/. Accessed March 5 2020.
Sayer, John William. *Ghost Dancing the Law: The Wounded Knee Trials*. Harvard University Press, 1997.
Selyukh, Alina. "What Gets To Be A 'Burger'? States Restrict Labels on Plant-Based Meat." *National Public Radio*, 23 July 2019, npr.org/sections/thesalt/2019/07/23/744083270/what-gets-to-be-a-burger-states-restrict-labels-on-plant-based-meat. Accessed January 16 2020.
Simpson, John. "Voters Approve Two Key Animal-Related Ballot Initiatives." *Duane Morris*, 14 November 2018, blogs.duanemorris.com/animallawdevelopments/2018/11/14/voters-approve-two-key-animal-related-ballot-initiatives/. Accessed January 16 2020.
Sisney v. Reisch, 674 F.3d 839 (8th Cir. 2012).
Starostinetskaya, Anna. "USDA Restores Critical Animal Welfare Database After Three-Year Blackout." *VegNews*, 24 February 2020, https://vegnews.com/2020/2/usda-restores-critical-animal-welfare-database-after-three-year-blackout. Accessed March 5 2020.
"The Animal Enterprise Terrorism Act (AETA)." *Center for Constitutional Rights*, 19 November 2007, ccrjustice.org/home/get-involved/tools-resources/fact-sheets-and-faqs/animal-enterprise-terrorism-act-aeta. Accessed January 18 2020.
"The High Cost and Diminishing Returns of a Border Wall." *American Immigration Council*, 6 September 2019, americanimmigrationcouncil.org/research/cost-of-border-wall. Accessed January 16 2020.
"The SHAC Model: A Critical Assessment." *Rolling Thunder*, 1 September 2008, crimethinc.com/2008/09/01/the-shac-model-a-critical-assessment. Accessed January 18 2020.
Thomas v. Review Bd. of Indiana Employment Sec. Div., 450 U.S. 707 (1981).

Thomas, Virginia. "For Your Entertainment: Researching Animal Cruelty Under the Big Top." *Michigan Bar Journal*, December 2018, at 40 n.9, michbar.org/file/barjournal/article/documents/pdf4article3552.pdf. Accessed January 18 2020.

Tilted Scales Collective. *A Tilted Guide to Being a Defendant*. Combustion Books, 2017, tiltedscalescollective.org/a-tilted-guide/. Accessed January 18 2020.

Tomlinson, Heather. "Huntingdon delays listing after attacks." *The Guardian*, 8 September 2005, theguardian.com/business/2005/sep/08/research.animalrights. Accessed January 18 2020.

"United States v. Johnson." *Center for Constitutional Rights*, 8 November 2017, ccrjustice.org/home/what-we-do/our-cases/united-states-v-johnson. Accessed January 18 2020.

U.S. v. Buddenberg, 2010 WL 2735547, at *6 (N.D. Cal. July 12, 2010). I assisted the activists' attorneys as support counsel.

U.S. v. Fullmer, 584 F.3d 132, 153-56 (3d Cir. 2009).

"U.S. v. SHAC 7." *Center for Constitutional Rights*, 3 August 2016, ccrjustice.org/home/what-we-do/our-cases/us-v-shac-7. Accessed January 18 2020.

U.S. v. Stumpo, Defendant's Notice of Motion and Motion to Dismiss Indictment; Memorandum of Points and Authorities in Support Thereof, https://ccrjustice.org/sites/default/files/assets/Motion%20to%20dismiss%20April%202010.pdf. Accessed 5 March 2020.

Vegan Prisoners Support Group, vpsg.org/. Accessed 17 January 2020.

Vinning-El v. Evans, 657 F.3d 591 (7th Cir. 2011).

Willis v. Commissioner, Indiana Department of Correction, 753 F.Supp.2d 768 (S.D. Indiana 2010).

Wisconsin v. Yoder, 406 U.S. 205 (1972).

13
Vegan studies in sociology

Elizabeth Cherry

Introduction

In *The Vegan Studies Project*, Laura Wright proposed delineating a field of vegan studies—a field devoted to understanding the identity and practice of veganism as it appears in popular discourse and media texts. Vegan studies "is focused on what it means to be vegan, a singular identity category that may or may not be linked to an ethical imperative with regard to one's feelings about and advocacy for animals" (14). In the introduction, Wright distinguishes vegan studies' other, related interdisciplinary fields. Critical animal studies centers on ethics and animal rights, and human–animal studies focuses on the wide variety of relationships between human and nonhuman animals. Posthumanism seeks to understand species, including the human species. And though ecofeminism critically engages societal relations with the environment, Wright argues that ecofeminist contributions about animals have been ignored or rebranded within animal studies in ways that have erased earlier ecofeminist contributions. Vegan studies, in comparison, "examines the mainstream discourse surrounding and connecting animal rights to (or omitting animal rights from) veganism" (Wright 19). By centering vegans and the practice of veganism in a particular time, place, and cultural milieu, Wright established a new field of study devoted to the identity and practice of veganism.

The goal of this chapter is to present an overview of the work of sociologists studying veganism. To clarify this task, this chapter includes sociologists who publish their scholarship in academic books, in sociology journals, or in interdisciplinary journals related to vegan studies, such as animal studies journals or food studies journals. This chapter further focuses on sociology's empirical contributions to vegan studies, rather than theoretical or conceptual works, since valid and reliable empirical data is a strength that the discipline of sociology can bring to the interdisciplinary field of vegan studies. While the studies featured in this essay may contribute to other interdisciplinary fields, such as critical animal studies, human–animal studies, or ecofeminism, those distinctions matter less than the fact that they ultimately contribute to an understanding of empirical sociological work in vegan studies. Finally, while many more studies of vegetarianism exist in sociology, in keeping with this volume's focus on vegan studies, this chapter likewise centers on sociological work on veganism.

This chapter starts by explaining how sociological thought evolved to get to vegan studies, after which it considers studies of institutions and issues related to vegan studies, but which do not fit into vegan studies proper. The bulk of the chapter highlights major areas of study within sociology that contribute to vegan studies: symbolic interactionist studies, sociology of culture, inequality (race and gender), and social movements. The chapter ends by outlining the myriad paths for sociologists to further contribute to vegan studies. While sociology is a strong contributor to the interdisciplinary field of vegan studies, there still exist many empirical gaps to fill.

Precursors to vegan studies in sociology

To engage in vegan studies requires that humans consider nonhuman animals. This endeavor requires decentering humans. This task proved difficult and time-consuming, as sociology began as a wholly anthropocentric field. Early sociologists, seeking to establish sociology as a social science, endeavored to demonstrate the unique qualities of human interaction and human society. To accomplish this, they contrasted human and animal behavior as a way of differentiating between the social sciences and the natural sciences. While animals merely follow instinct, they argued, humans possess agency, or free will. Thus, they concluded that we need sociology to study human society.

Karl Marx's "species being" described in *Capital* exemplifies this approach:

> We presuppose labour in a form in which it is an exclusively human characteristic. A spider conducts operations which resemble those of the weaver, and a bee would put many a human architect to shame by the construction of its honeycomb cells. But what distinguishes the worst architect from the best of bees is that the architect builds the cell in his mind before he constructs it in wax. (Marx 283–84)

To Marx, humans are superior to animals because we ponder and plot in our minds before putting a plan into action.

Perhaps the best-known example of anthropocentrism in sociology comes from George Herbert Mead, in his writing on the development of the self. While symbolic interactionists later took up Mead's work to argue that humans and animals engage in shared meaning-making, Mead himself argued that animals differed from humans since animals' interactions did not use shared symbols. Mead explained: "We do not assume that the dog says to himself, 'If the animal comes from this direction he is going to spring at my throat and I will turn in such a way'" (42). In contrast, Mead argued that humans use "significant symbols" (47) that evoke the same meaning from the sender and the receiver. Thus, Mead claimed animals cannot share meanings since they do not use significant symbols.

Sociology remained a wholly anthropocentric field until the 1970s, when environmental sociologists began to argue that sociologists should study relationships between the social and natural worlds. Moving from what William Catton and Riley Dunlap called the HEP to the NEP, or from the Human Exemptionalist Paradigm to the New Ecological Paradigm, environmental sociology allows for seeing human society as interconnected with the natural world, and as subject to the laws of nature (Catton and Dunlap). This move foreshadowed food studies and animal studies in sociology, which, in turn, opened the door for vegan studies in sociology.

Although studies of food practices flourished for decades in anthropology, it was not until well after the environmental turn in sociology that food studies began in earnest in the field of sociology (see, e.g., the early work of Mennell and Murcott). These scholars did not yet consider veganism, much less vegan studies—they saw vegetarianism as one choice among many, studying the history of vegetarianism (Maurer, "Meat as a Social Problem") and the reasons to be vegetarian (Beardsworth and Keil, "The Vegetarian Option"; Beardsworth and Keil, *Sociology on the Menu*; Fiddes). Other early work in sociological food studies considered identity construction via food choices in vegetarians and vegans (Willetts), and the organizational strategies of vegetarian movement leaders (Maurer, *Vegetarianism*). After this, vegetarianism moved from being considered a "fad" or simply a dietary choice in food studies. These developments, in concert with the evolution of animal studies, paved the way for vegan studies in sociology.

Around the same time as the environmental turn in sociology, Clifton Bryant encouraged sociologists to study the "zoological connection," or the relationships between humans and animals. Sociological animal studies began with people's closest connections to animals, their companion animals (Arluke and Sanders; Sanders; Irvine). This shift led to studies of other "categories" of animals, including wildlife and farmed animals. Once sociology opened up to studying food and animal issues, and specifically veganism and farmed animals, vegan studies in sociology could emerge.

Adjacent work and institutions

A significant amount of sociological work facilitates vegan studies—and veganism itself—but falls outside the definition of vegan studies. The empirical work of sociologists on institutions that use animals, such as slaughterhouses, cattle ranching, and animal testing, unveil the world of animal uses that vegans critique. Research on legal protections and movements to protect animals, while not focused on vegan identity and practice, illuminate the work of vegan activists. Environmental sociologists who study environmental issues related to meat consumption further add to sociologists' understanding of a variety of issues related to veganism. Thus, while these works may not contribute to vegan studies in the strictest sense of the term, they provide empirical evidence to better understand the broader social world in which vegan studies exists.

As society moved into modernity, with its concomitant manners and rules for comportment, slaughterhouses moved out of sight, so as to not offend (Agulhon; Elias; Nibert, *Animal Oppression*). These centralized, industrial slaughterhouses, now hidden from sight, inspired the famous quote (famous, at least, to vegans) from Paul and Linda McCartney, "If slaughterhouses had glass walls, everyone would be a vegetarian" (McCartney). Empirical work on slaughterhouses illuminates this now-hidden world of slaughterhouses (Fitzgerald). Such work has documented the spillover effect from killing animals (Fitzgerald et al.), by showing that communities with slaughterhouses have higher arrest rates for violent crimes than do comparable communities with industrial workplaces like manufacturing.

Before the cattle reach the slaughterhouse, researchers have also demonstrated the often contradictory emotional connections ranchers have to their cattle. Ranchers must remind themselves to treat the cattle like economic entities (Ellis). They accomplish this process through de-individualizing the animals (Wilkie). This process resembles another institution built on animal use, that of animal testing. Researchers who test on animals draw symbolic boundaries between humans and nonhuman primates, and between their own companion animals and laboratory animals, so that they do not connect emotionally to the animals they use in their tests (Arluke and Sanders).

Research on activists fighting for nonhuman animal legal rights and protections may not always fall under the purview of "vegan studies" as defined as focusing on vegan identity and practice, but this work likewise helps vegans and vegan studies researchers understand activists fighting to create a vegan world. Early research on the animal rights movement explored the importance of emotions in activism (Jasper), and how activists purposefully use shocking images to get people to oppose practices like animal testing (Jasper and Poulsen). Other research on tactics has found that gender plays a role in the reception of tactics, such as when men dismiss women activists' critiques of animal issues as being "overly emotional" (Einwohner), or when women animal rights activists critique PETA's sexualized advertising campaigns promoting animal rights as demeaning and disrespectful to women and women animal rights activists (Gaarder 120).

As the fields of environmental sociology and animal studies in sociology intermingle, their work increasingly becomes relevant to vegan studies. A cross-national comparison of meat and fish consumption found that economic development spurs on the expansion of both consumption rates. Geography and culture both played a role, where Asian regions consumed more fish as their economic development grew, and non-Asian regions consumed more meat as their economic development grew (York and Gossard). Other environmental sociologists have studied what factors influence support for policies that promote plant-based diets (Whitley et al.). Comparing four different policies aimed at reducing meat consumption (environmental, animal welfare, public health, and direct meat reduction), they found that different factors affected support for each policy differently; i.e., it matters how those policies are presented, or framed, to the audience. These works, while not focusing on what it is like to be a vegan in contemporary society, still contribute to an understanding of what factors influence meat consumption and how to promote veganism.

Finally, as noted in the introduction above, sociologists have contributed to theoretical and conceptual work on vegan and animal rights issues, which likewise helps develop vegan studies in sociology. Nik Taylor and Richard Twine's edited volume *The Rise of Critical Animal Studies* presents several theoretical arguments for animal rights and veganism (Taylor and Twine), and Corey Wrenn's abolitionist theoretical analysis of animal rights advocacy takes a critical lens to a variety of animal rights organizations and their tactics (Wrenn, *A Rational Approach*). These adjacent empirical studies illuminate the institutions that use animals and the activists who fight for animals, and these theoretical works provide critical foundations for the empirical animal studies presented in the remainder of the chapter.

Symbolic interactionism

Identity and practice are linked—and are expected to be linked—with activist identities, especially environmental identities. Those who consider themselves environmentalists perform—and are expected to perform—environmentally friendly behaviors. The relationship between identity and practice has been well documented with environmental identities (see, e.g., Gatersleben and Murtagh 2014; Kashima, Paladino, and Margetts 2014; Stapleton 2015; Whitmarsh 2010). The same holds true for vegan identities. Those who identify as vegan are expected to perform vegan practices in their diet and lifestyle.

Most of the sociological work on the links between identity and practice uses a symbolic interactionist theoretical perspective. Symbolic interactionists argue that no identity or object holds inherent meaning, but instead its meaning is created, and recreated, in interaction. People can, however, manage the meanings they project through their presentation of self and impression management, seeking to control the image of themselves that they present to others (Goffman,

The Presentation). The myriad selves people perform comprise their multifaceted identity. For vegans, their veganism becomes one part of that identity that they perform for others and for themselves.

Becoming a vegan involves taking on a vegan identity, which can be so significant that it can be considered a "status passage," or an important process within a person's life, such as when they move from adolescence to adulthood (Larsson et al.). Once becoming vegan, vegans then engage in symbolic interactions in their everyday encounters with others, especially non-vegans. Ethical vegans avoid all animal products in food and other areas of consumption, such as clothes, household goods, beauty products, medicine, and entertainment. Thus, vegans try to present an "authentic" vegan self to others through presentational aspects such as their clothing (J. Greenebaum, "Veganism, Identity"). Wearing vegan shoes aligns identity and practice and also serves as a preventative measure against non-vegans asking, "Are your shoes leather?" when they seek to "catch" vegans engaging in a non-vegan practice.

Because most vegans' interactions will be with non-vegans, they prepare for many different types of fraught moments, such as when someone challenges their veganism, ignores basic facts about food production and mammal biology, or when non-vegans ask about veganism at the dinner table. At these times, vegans may engage in face-saving techniques (Goffman, *The Presentation*), such as avoiding confrontation, waiting until the appropriate time to engage in such a discussion, or promoting the health benefits of veganism as a tactic to avoid discussing the more controversial topic of animal rights (Greenebaum, "Managing Impressions").

When engaging with non-vegans close to home, such as partners or housemates, vegans may also engage in boundary maintenance, such as separating the vegan cookware from non-vegan cookware, winning over friends and family to accept their veganism and accommodate it, such as by cooking vegan meals for them, and performing veganism in a demonstrative manner, such as sharing delicious vegan food with non-vegans (Twine, "Vegan Killjoys").

Vegans' interactions with non-vegans are not always so successful or positive. Vegans experience stigma (Goffman, *Stigma*), or being labeled as odd, different, or deviant. These negative impressions of veganism may come from the news media (Cole and Morgan), which ridicule veganism through stereotypes, and engaging in derogatory discourses such as characterizing veganism as nothing more than asceticism or a fad, or as difficult and impossible to sustain. These media also alternately describe vegans themselves as overly sensitive, or as hostile.

With the recent emphasis on "clean eating" and veganism as a healthy "diet," vegans who do not conform to the *Skinny Bitch* (Freedman and Barnouin) stereotype also experience stigma from other vegan activists. Fat vegans report experiencing fat discrimination (including fat-shaming, healthism, sizeism, and thin privilege) in the vegan movement (Wrenn, "Fat Vegan Politics"). This sizeism may come from PETA billboards promoting veganism as weight loss, such as a "Save the Whales" billboard campaign that reads "Lose the blubber: go vegetarian." Thus, fat vegan activists turn to online activism as a way to avoid stigma they experience in offline vegan communities. The various interactions described here are not only informed by non-vegans' sensibilities; they are also informed by the broader culture, as described below.

Culture

Until the cultural turn, sociologists tended to view culture as an enabling force, as an area in which people were free to act agentically. Foundational cultural theorists (Bourdieu; Giddens; Sewell) took up the anthropological view of culture as a restricting and empowering structure (Lévi-Strauss). As Sharon Hays put it, "Culture is both constraining and enabling. Culture is a social structure with an underlying logic of its own" (Hays 65). Studies of veganism that focus on food rules and classifications exemplify this classic structuralist argument. Following Lévi-Strauss, and Mary Douglas's theory of impurity (Douglas), which argues that beliefs about purity and pollution are central to cultural life, vegan foods may be seen as "pure" and non-vegan foods are "impure," or forbidden. While many vegans may view meat and animal products as "impure" foods to be avoided, such dietary rules alone are not sufficient to explain vegan practice (Arppe et al.).

Seeing culture as a structure helps sociologists doing vegan studies better understand how mainstream views may impede veganism, and also how culture might act as an enabling tool for activists. Studies of "vegaphobia" in the media cited above (Cole and Morgan) demonstrate how mainstream culture structures ideas about veganism and provides cultural constraints to veganism. The news media often portray veganism as difficult and impossible to maintain, thus creating a cultural barrier to seeing veganism as a possible lifestyle to pursue.

At the same time that it acts as a constraining force, culture can also provide opportunities for vegan activism and identity development. Music-based subcultures, such as punk and hardcore, can provide opportunities to learn about veganism and animal rights through the political discourse in the music scene and through providing supportive social networks for vegans (Cherry, "Veganism as a Cultural Movement"). Social networks more generally also provide opportunities for recruitment to veganism and retention of vegan identity and practices. Through supportive social networks, vegans gain a sense of community, support, and new cultural tools, such as cooking skills, information on veganism, and other resources to help them live a vegan lifestyle (Cherry, "I Was a Teenage Vegan").

If culture provides tools to maintain a vegan lifestyle, practice theory further specifies those tools. Following Shove et al., who delineate practices as comprised of competencies, materials, and meanings, a practice theory approach helps explain how vegans learn to be vegan, how they understand what veganism means, and how to use new materials such as new vegan food items. These new competencies about meanings and materials help people successfully become and stay vegan (Twine, "Materially Constituting"; Twine, *A Practice Theory*).

Cultural sociology can also help explain why vegans may engage in the face-saving strategies described above (Greenebaum, "Managing Impressions"). While vegans may believe that veganism is a collective moral imperative, they strategically deploy individualized explanations for veganism, presenting their morals as an individual choice or experience (Turner). Individualism is a readily available discourse or tool in the United States, and thus it can easily be deployed to diplomatically discuss veganism with non-vegans. As shown in this section, the broader culture can contribute to negative stereotypes about vegans. However, vegan identity does not exist in a vacuum. It also intersects with other important aspects of a person's identity, such as gender and race.

Inequality: gender and race

Research on inequality—most often in terms of race, class, and gender—is a core foundation of contemporary sociology. In addition, obviously, to standalone courses on each subject, the study of inequality remains central to introductory sociology courses, graduate training in sociology, and scholars of race, class, and gender comprise some of the largest sections of the American Sociological Association. However, within empirical sociological vegan studies, this remains an understudied area. This may be due to the significant theoretical work already done in the area (see, e.g., Twine, "Ecofeminism and Veganism"; J. Greenebaum, "Questioning"; Nibert, *Animal Oppression*).

While most vegans are women ("Find out How Many"; Millum), empirical research on gender has focused on men and masculinity. This may be due to the demographic and cultural minority status of men in a culture that equates meat with masculinity and virility. To wit, empirical research on vegan men has reiterated the importance of those dominant cultural discourses about gendered food norms to vegan men, such as their need to engage with the importance of meat as a cultural foundation of masculinity, sexuality, and strength (Nath). Other research has shown that vegan men challenge this narrow definition of hegemonic masculinity, instead redefining their compassion for other animals as an act of courage, and holding up vegan athletes as examples of strength (Greenebaum and Dexter). Thus, while legitimating veganism as a "masculine" endeavor, these vegan men fall short of challenging gender inequalities.

Similarly, while most vegans are white (Millum), empirical research on race has focused on vegans of color. Jessica Greenebaum ("Vegans of Color") found that vegans of color reported they had to navigate race in relation to their veganism in a variety of ways. Vegans of color had to confront the stereotype of veganism as a white, economically privileged practice. Simply by virtue of their veganism, they were accused of "acting white." They also had to fight the notion that veganism was incompatible with their ethnic food identity. Vegans of color pushed back against these negative stereotypes and assumptions by focusing on simple, affordable, plant-based foods that aligned with their ethnic cuisines. These acts seeking to normalize and universalize veganism play a role in more than simply facilitating one's personal practice of veganism—they also contribute to veganism as a social movement.

Social movements

As noted above, sociologists have long studied the animal rights movement, even though most of the empirical research on animal rights would not fall under the rubric of vegan studies, as those studies do not focus on vegan identities or practices. Two related areas in social movement studies focus on the relationships between identities and practices: lifestyle movements and prefigurative politics (or prefiguration).

Research on lifestyle movements focuses on cultural goals and tactics used by activists, centering on people's everyday lifestyle and consumption choices. In lifestyle movements, the goals and the means of the movement are purposefully interchangeable (Haenfler et al.). As such, lifestyle movements align with prefigurative politics, as the tactics must be consistent or at least compatible with a movement's goal (Brienes). Through their actions, lifestyle activists create, in the moment, the world they wish to see in the future. Lifestyle movement activists make changes in their identities, lifestyles, consumption practices, and ways of speaking about the world. By encouraging individual, private, ongoing actions, which participants see as part of their personal identity, lifestyle activists see their work as working toward larger social changes (Haenfler et al.).

In their generative work on lifestyle movements, Haenfler et al. used veganism as an example of a lifestyle movement, alongside green living, straight edge, and voluntary simplicity. It is easy to see why veganism exemplifies a lifestyle movement. Culture structures food norms so that people consider it "normal" to consume animals and animal products and to use animals for other purposes, such as clothing, testing, or entertainment. Veganism as a lifestyle movement aims to end such uses of animals through prefiguration, or making the changes vegans wish to see in the world in the here and now.

These vegan movements are international. Interviews with vegan activists in France demonstrate the importance of prefiguration and everyday life in vegan activism, such as sharing food at pop-up events like "Vegan Place" (Véron). Creating these alternative spaces, in public, facilitates vegans being the change they wish to see. Further, in countries that still largely view veganism as a weird and unhealthy diet, such public displays of veganism demonstrate the possibility of an alternative, vegan lifestyle to non-vegans.

Just as culture provides tools for vegans, vegan food itself provided a tool for animal rights activists when promoting veganism. However, the utility of vegan food as a tool depends on how readily available it is. Animal rights activists in the United States easily used vegan food as a cultural resource in their work, bringing store-bought foods to events to showcase the ease of eating vegan (Cherry, *Culture and Activism*). Animal rights activists in France, in contrast, had a more difficult time using food as a cultural resource, due to the lack of vegan food options. Instead, French activists focused on promoting homemade vegan versions of traditional French foods and emphasizing the conviviality of communal vegan meals (Cherry, *Culture and Activism*).

When studying the animal rights movement in Italy, Niccolò Bertuzzi (Bertuzzi) demonstrated the importance of veganism to animal advocates—not as a "purity test" for activists, but as an abolitionist practice to live the changes they wish to see in the world. Bertuzzi divided the movement into three areas: animal care (companion animal rescues), protectionism (national NGOs focused on lobbying), and antispeciesism (grassroots organizations engaged in radical activism). He found that antispeciesist activists were much more likely to be vegan than were animal care or protection activists. He also found that veganism was more of a practice among left-wing activists, followed by centrists, and with the smallest number of vegans among right-wing activists, a finding similar to Corey Lee Wrenn's post-2016 election survey of U.S. vegans and their political beliefs ("Trump Veganism"). These findings on the relationship between veganism and progressive politics concur with other demographic studies of vegans conducted by nonprofit research institutes for animal advocacy organizations (Millum).

Conclusions and future directions

This chapter provided an overview of the development and scope of vegan studies in sociology. It has shown how field-wide trends, such as the development of environmental sociology, sociology of food, and sociology of animals and society paved the way for vegan studies in sociology. These movements allowed sociology to break from its anthropocentric foundations and consider nonhuman animals in their work, which, in turn, allowed for vegan studies to thrive in the field of sociology.

Empirical work is a strength that sociology brings to the interdisciplinary field of vegan studies as a whole. While each disciplinary field has contributed to the broader body of theoretical work in vegan studies, sociology (and other social sciences) helps further understandings of the contemporary social world and activism for animals through its methods of collecting empirical data. Such empirical work is crucial for shaping activist strategies and public policy seeking to create a vegan world.

While this chapter has shown that vegan studies greatly contributes to sociology, and sociology to vegan studies, there remain areas to be further developed. Vegan studies has its strongest empirical foothold in sociology in symbolic interactionist studies, sociology of culture, inequality, and social movements. Some of these important areas, like inequality, need much more empirical research. Other areas central to sociology likewise would benefit from more vegan studies research, such as socialization, deviance, work, the media, medical sociology, education, and the family. As the field of vegan studies grows, there is plenty of room for more sociological vegan studies.

Works cited

Agulhon, Maurice. "Le Sang Des Bêtes: Le Problème de La Protection Des Animaux En France Aux XIXème Siècle." *Romantisme*, vol. 31, 1981, pp. 81–109.
Arluke, Arnold, and Clinton R. Sanders. *Regarding Animals*. Temple University Press, 1996.
Arppe, Tiina, et al. "Living Food Diet and Veganism: Individual vs Collective Boundaries of the Forbidden." *Social Science Information*, vol. 50, no. 2, 2011, pp. 275–297. doi:10.1177/0539018410396618.
Beardsworth, Alan, and Teresa Keil. *Sociology on the Menu: An Invitation to the Study of Food and Society*. Routledge, 1997.
Beardsworth, Alan. "The Vegetarian Option: Varieties, Conversions, Motives and Careers." *The Sociological Review*, vol. 40, no. 2, 1992, pp. 253–293. doi:10.1111/j.1467-954X.1992.tb00889.x.
Bertuzzi, Niccolò. "Veganism: Lifestyle or Political Movement? Looking for Relations beyond Antispeciesism." *Relations*, vol. 5, no. 2, 2017, pp. 125–144. doi:10.7358/rela-2017-002-ber1.
Bourdieu, Pierre. *Outline of a Theory of Practice*. Cambridge University Press, 1977.
Brienes, Wini. *Community and Organization in the New Left*. Praeger Publishers, 1982.
Catton, William R., and Riley E. Dunlap. "Environmental Sociology: A New Paradigm." *The American Sociologist*, vol. 13, no. 1, 1978, pp. 41–49.
Cherry, Elizabeth. *Culture and Activism: Animal Rights in France and the United States*. Routledge, 2016.
———. "I Was a Teenage Vegan: Motivation and Maintenance of Lifestyle Movements." *Sociological Inquiry*, vol. 85, no. 1, 2015, pp. 55–74.
———. "Veganism as a Cultural Movement: A Relational Approach." *Social Movement Studies*, vol. 5, no. 2, 2006, pp. 155–170.
Cole, Matthew, and Karen Morgan. "Vegaphobia: Derogatory Discourses of Veganism and the Reproduction of Speciesism in UK National Newspapers." *British Journal of Sociology*, vol. 62, no. 1, 2011, pp. 134—153. doi:10.1111/j.1468-4446.2010.01348.x.
Douglas, Mary. *Purity and Danger*. Routledge, 1966.
Einwohner, Rachel L. "Gender, Class, and Social Movement Outcomes: Identity and Effectiveness in Two Animal Rights Campaigns." *Gender and Society*, vol. 13, no. 1, 1999, pp. 56–76.
Elias, Norbert. *The Civilizing Process*. Urizen Books, 1978.
Ellis, Colter. "Boundary Labor and the Production of Emotionless Commodities: The Case of Beef Production." *The Sociological Quarterly*, vol. 55, no. 1, 2014, pp. 92–118.
Fiddes, Nick. "Declining Meat: Past, Present...and Future Imperfect?" *Food, Health and Identity*, edited by Pat Caplan, Routledge, 1997, pp. 252–266.
"Find out How Many Vegans There Are in Great Britain." *The Vegan Society*, 2016, https://www.vegansociety.com/whats-new/news/find-out-how-many-vegans-there-are-great-britain.
Fitzgerald, Amy J. "A Social History of the Slaughterhouse: From Inception to Contemporary Implications." *Human Ecology Review*, vol. 17, no. 1, 2010, pp. 58–69.
———. "Slaughterhouses and Increased Crime Rates: An Empirical Analysis of the Spillover from 'The Jungle' into the Surrounding Community." *Organization & Environment*, vol. 17, no. 1, 2009, pp. 58–69.
Freedman, Rory, and Kim Barnouin. *Skinny Bitch*. Running Press, 2005.
Gaarder, Emily. *Women and the Animal Rights Movement*. Rutgers University Press, 2011.
Gatersleben, Birgitta, et al. "Values, Identity and pro-Environmental Behaviour." *Contemporary Social Science*, vol. 9, no. 4, 2014, pp. 374–392.
Giddens, Anthony. *The Constitution of Society: Outline of the Theory of Structuration*. University of California Press, 1984.
Goffman, Erving. *Stigma: Notes on the Management of Spoiled Identity*. Simon & Schuster, 1963.
———. *The Presentation of Self in Everyday Life*. Doubleday, 1959.
Greenebaum, Jessica. "Managing Impressions." *Humanity & Society*, vol. 36, no. 4, 2012a, pp. 309–325. doi:10.1177/0160597612458898.
———. "Questioning the Concept of Vegan Privilege." *Humanity & Society*, vol. 41, no. 3, 2017, pp. 355–372. doi:10.1177/0160597616640308.
———. "Veganism, Identity and the Quest for Authenticity." *Food, Culture and Society*, vol. 15, no. 1, 2012b, pp. 129–144. doi:10.2752/175174412X13190510222101.
———. "Vegans of Color: Managing Visible and Invisible Stigmas." *Food, Culture and Society*, vol. 21, no. 5, 2018, pp. 680–697. doi:10.1080/15528014.2018.1512285.
Greenebaum, Jessica, and Brandon Dexter. "Vegan Men and Hybrid Masculinity." *Journal of Gender Studies*, vol. 27, no. 6, 2018, pp. 637–648. doi:10.1080/09589236.2017.1287064.

Haenfler, Ross, et al. "Lifestyle Movements: Exploring the Intersection of Lifestyle and Social Movements." *Social Movement Studies*, vol. 11, no. 1, 2012, pp. 1–20.
Hays, Sharon. "Structure and Agency and the Sticky Problem of Culture." *Sociological Theory*, vol. 12, no. 1, 1994, pp. 57–72.
Irvine, Leslie. *If You Tame Me: Understanding Our Connection with Animals*. Temple University Press, 2004.
Jasper, James M. *The Art of Moral Protest: Culture, Biography, and Creativity in Social Movements*. University of Chicago Press, 1997.
Jasper, James M., and Jane D. Poulsen. "Recruiting Strangers and Friends: Moral Shocks and Social Networks in Animal Rights and Anti-Nuclear Protests." *Social Problems*, vol. 42, no. 4, 1995, pp. 493–512.
Kashima, Yoshihisa, et al. "Environmentalist Identity and Environmental Striving." *Journal of Environmental Psychology*, 2014, pp. 64–75.
Larsson, Christel L., et al. "Veganism as Status Passage: The Process of Becoming a Vegan among Youths in Sweden." *Appetite*, vol. 41, no. 1, 2003, pp. 61–67. doi:10.1016/S0195-6663(03)00045-X.
Lévi-Strauss, Claude. *Structural Anthropology*. Basic Books, 1963.
Marx, Karl. *Capital: A Critique of Political Economy*. Penguin Books, 1876.
Maurer, Donna. "Meat as a Social Problem: Rhetorical Strategies in the Contemporary Vegetarian Literature." *Eating Agendas: Food and Nutrition As Social Problems*, Aldine de Gruyter, 1995, pp. 143–163.
———. *Vegetarianism: Movement or Moment?* Temple University Press, 2002.
McCartney, Paul. *If Slaughterhouses Had Glass Walls, Everyone Would Be Vegetarian*. https://www.paulmccartney.com/news-blogs/charity-blog/if-slaughterhouses-had-glass-walls-everyone-would-be-vegetarian. Accessed April 20 2020.
Mennell, Stephen. *All Manners of Food: Eating and Taste in England and France from the Middle Ages to the Present*. Basil Blackwell Inc., 1985.
Millum, Joseph. "Who Are the Vegetarians?" *Faunalytics*, 2018, https://faunalytics.org/who-are-the-vegetarians/.
Murcott, Anne. *Sociology of Food and Eating*. Aldershot Gower, 1983.
Nath, Jemál. "Gendered Fare?: A Qualitative Investigation of Alternative Food and Masculinities." *Journal of Sociology*, vol. 47, no. 3, 2011, pp. 261–278. doi:10.1177/1440783310386828.
Nibert, David A., editor. *Animal Oppression and Capitalism*. Praeger Publishers, 2017.
———. *Animal Oppression and Human Violence: Domesecration, Capitalism, and Global Conflict*. Columbia University Press, 2013.
Sanders, Clinton R. *Understanding Dogs: Living and Working with Canine Companions*. Temple University Press, 1999.
Sewell, William. "A Theory of Structure: Duality, Agency, and Transformation." *American Journal of Sociology*, vol. 98, no. 1, 1992, pp. 1–29.
Shove, Elizabeth, et al. *The Dynamics of Social Practice: Everyday Life and How It Changes*. Sage, 2012.
Stapleton, Sarah Riggs. "Environmental Identity Development through Social Interactions, Action, and Recognition." *Journal of Environmental Education*, vol. 46, no. 2, 2015, pp. 94–113. doi:10.1080/00958964.2014.1000813.
Taylor, Nik, and Richard Twine, editors. *The Rise of Critical Animal Studies: From the Margins to the Centres*. Routledge, 2014.
Turner, Ryan. "Veganism: Ethics in Everyday Life." *American Journal of Cultural Sociology*, 2019. doi:10.1057/s41290-017-0052-8.
Twine, Richard. "A Practice Theory Framework for Understanding Vegan Transition." *Animal Studies Journal*, vol. 6, no. 2, 2017, pp. 192–224.
———. "Ecofeminism and Veganism - Revisiting the Question of Universalism." *Ecofeminism: Feminist Intersections with Other Animals and the Earth*, edited by Carol Adams and Lori Gruen, Bloomsbury Academic, 2014a, pp. 191–207.
———. "Materially Constituting a Sustainable Food Transition: The Case of Vegan Eating Practice." *Sociology*, vol. 52, no. 1, 2018, pp. 166–181. doi:10.1177/0038038517726647.
———. "Vegan Killjoys at the Table—Contesting Happiness and Negotiating Relationships with Food Practices." *Societies*, vol. 4, no. 4, 2014b, pp. 623–639. doi:10.3390/soc4040623.
Véron, Ophélie. "(Extra)Ordinary Activism: Veganism and the Shaping of Hemeratopias." *International Journal of Sociology and Social Policy*, vol. 36, no. 11–12, 2016, pp. 756–773. doi:10.1108/IJSSP-12-2015-0137.
Whitley, Cameron, et al. "Public Receptiveness to Policies Promoting Plant-Based Diets: Framing Effects and Social Psychological and Structural Influences." *Journal of Environmental Policy & Planning*, vol. 20, no. 1, 2018, pp. 45–63.

Whitmarsh, Lorraine, and Saffron O'Neill. "Green Identity, Green Living? The Role of pro-Environmental Self-Identity in Determining Consistency across Diverse pro-Environmental Behaviours." *Journal of Environmental Psychology*, vol. 30, no. 3, 2010, pp. 305–314.

Wilkie, Rhoda. "Sentient Commodities and Productive Paradoxes: The Ambiguous Nature of Human-Livestock Relations in Northeast Scotland." *Journal of Rural Studies*, vol. 21, 2005, pp. 213–230.

Willetts, Anna. "'Bacon Sandwiches Got the Better of Me': Meat-Eating and Vegetarianism in South-East London." *Food, Health and Identity*, edited by Pat Caplan, Routledge, 1997, pp. 111–130.

Wrenn, Corey. *A Rational Approach to Animal Rights: Extensions in Abolitionist Theory*. Palgrave Macmillan, 2016a.

———. "Fat Vegan Politics: A Survey of Fat Vegan Activists' Online Experiences with Social Movement Sizeism." *Fat Studies*, vol. 6, no. 1, 2016b, pp. 90–102.

Wright, Laura. *The Vegan Studies Project: Food, Animals, and Gender in the Age of Terror*. University of Georgia Press, 2015.

York, Richard, and Marcia Hill Gossard. "Cross-National Meat and Fish Consumption: Exploring the Effects of Modernization and Ecological Context." *Ecological Economics*, vol. 48, no. 3, 2004, pp. 293302. doi:10.1016/j.ecolecon.2003.10.009.

14
Psychology and vegan studies

Adam Feltz and Silke Feltz

In the past 40 years, there has been a surge in research attempting to identify some of the psychological factors involved in vegan and vegetarian identities. In this chapter, we review some of those factors. We group these psychological factors into three broad categories: non-cognitive factors, cognitive factors, and cognitive skills. We situate efforts to change people's behaviors concerning animal consumption by influencing some of these psychological factors. Then, we provide some avenues for future directions by illustrating one way that the disparate results could be unified in a single framework, focusing on changing behaviors in ethically defensible ways.

A few clarifications and caveats are worth mentioning. First, it is somewhat difficult to have precise and accurate measures of vegan or vegetarian identities. Some people do not know what the terms "vegetarian" and "vegan" mean. For example, some who self-identify as vegan or vegetarian still consume animal products or animal flesh (Nezlek and Forestell 46; Richardson et al. 1; Rosenfeld and Tomiyama 2; Wright 5). Second, there are a number of different ways to measure vegan and vegetarian identities including asking what category one belongs to (e.g., vegan) or by asking how frequently one consumes various animal products (e.g., cheese). Because of these different ways of measuring vegan identities, we sometimes refer to studies that ask people to self-identify and other studies that measure animal consumption. Third, we do not make any claims that the general categories that we use to identify the psychological factors are exhaustive or exclusive. Rather, the groupings are meant to be one helpful way to conceptualize the different psychological factors involved in vegan and vegetarian identities. Fourth, we will only review studies that explicitly explore psychological factors. We will not review factors that are associated with vegan and vegetarian identities such as demographic, social, or cultural factors (e.g., sex or social settings (Nezlek and Forestell 48; Ruby 43).

Non-cognitive factors

Non-cognitive psychological factors involve mental states that have contents that can neither be true nor false; such as emotions, motivations, and attitudes. In this section, we review some of the prominent non-cognitive factors that have been associated (i.e., correlated) with vegetarian and vegan identities.

Motivation

Motivation generally refers to mental states that provide impetus to perform (or intend to perform) some action (Mele "Motivation and Agency" 78). People's motivations not to consume animal products appear to be diverse. Rothgerber found that when people were asked to offer justifications for their dietary patterns, self-identified vegetarians cited that they desired that their food to be ethically produced at a higher rate (63 percent) compared to the justifications offered by meat eaters (29 percent) ("Comparison of Attitudes" 103). This general pattern has been replicated in other studies (Piazza et al. "Rationalizing Meat" 121; Verain et al. 6) and in diverse countries (e.g., Finland) (Vanhonacker et al. 9).

Another motivational factor is how committed one is to consuming animals. Those who report being very committed and desiring to eat animal products are more likely to consume animal products than those who are not committed to eating animal products (Dhont and Hodson 13; Graca et al. "Moral Disengagement" 357; Piazza et al. "Cruel Nature " 114; Piazza et al. "Rationalizing Meat" 125).

Emotions

Disgust is one prominent emotion that has been related to vegan identity and reduction of animal consumptions. The body of research suggests that to the extent that one is more disgusted by meat and animal products, the less likely one is to consume those products. The rationale for the relation is likely to be something like the following. Disgust is an aversive reaction. Those who experience disgust are likely to avoid the thing that causes disgust. The tendency to avoid disgusting things is likely to be evolutionary advantageous for people since things that are found to be disgusting to humans also tend to be harmful to humans (e.g., have harmful pathogens) (Rozin and Haidt 367). The relation between disgust and reduction of animal consumption has been reproduced a number of times using different measures, samples, and techniques (Kunst and Hohle 760; T. Lund et al. 92; Piazza et al. "Cruel Nature " 112; Piazza et al. "Rationalizing Meat"118; Rothgerber "Can You Have Your Meat" 199; Rothgerber "Comparison of Attitudes" 101; Rothgerber "Underlying Differences"254; M. Ruby et al. 342).

Empathy has been shown to be connected to a reduction of animal consumption behaviors. For example, even among those omnivores who want their products to be ethically produced, there is a reduction in empathy for animals used for products compared to self-identified vegetarians (*Cohen's d* = 0.36, or 64 percent of the vegetarians will have higher empathy scores than the average omnivore) and vegans (*Cohen's d* = 1.01, or 84 percent of vegetarians having higher empathy than the average omnivore) (Rothgerber "Underlying Differences" 254; Rothgerber and Mican 14). This basic pattern has been replicated (Rothgerber "Can You Have Your Meat" 199) by other researchers (Graca et al. "Moral Disengagement" 357; Kunst and Hohle 760).

Other emotions have also been explored, but less intensively. For example, there is some evidence that feeling more guilty about eating animals is associated with being more likely to be vegetarian (Graca et al. "Moral Disengagement "357; Rothgerber "Can You Have Your Meat" 199).

Attitudes

One way to conceptualize attitudes is that they are settled dispositions toward various objects, typically containing an evaluative component (Albarracin et al. 16). On this conceptualization, attitudes can be composed of beliefs, feelings, normative judgments, and motivational states.

While some components of any particular attitude could be true or false (e.g., beliefs), typically the attitude is thought to be neither true nor false. For example, one's political attitudes are commonly neither thought to be true nor false even if some of the contents of those attitudes can be (e.g., beliefs about actual distributions of wealth).

Several attitudes have been shown to be related to vegan identities and reduction of consumption of animal products. One consistent predictor of vegetarian identities is whether consuming animals is thought to be *normal, necessary, natural, and nice* (the 4Ns) (Piazza et al. "Rationalizing Meat" 118). Those who have stronger 4N attitudes are more likely be omnivores than those with weaker 4N attitudes (correlation of about .25, a moderately strong relation). This general effect has been replicated in a number of studies using the 4Ns (Feltz et al.; Feltz and Feltz "Knowlege" 40) and with similar items (Cordts et al. 103). (For related work on Carnism, see Monteiro et al. and other related work on Meat Attachment see Graca et al. "Attached to Meat 118.)

Speciesism has become a focus of research. Speciesism is the general view that the interests of some creatures count more morally because of membership in a specific species and for no other reason (Ryder 158; Singer 35). On anti-speciesist accounts, identical pain is an equally bad thing no matter where that pain exists. If one prefers the experience of pain in one creature over an equivalent pain in another creature only because the former creature is a member of a different species, then that would be a speciesist attitude. There have been various ways of measuring speciesism (Caviola et al. 1020; Graca et al. "Moral Disengagement" 358; Piazza et al. "Rationalizing Meat" 120), with all of them giving the same general pattern that there is a moderate relation between speciesist attitudes and increased animal consumption (Everett et al. 792). Relatedly, stronger attitudes about human supremacy have been shown to predict increased animal consumption behaviors (Dhont and Hodson 15; Graca et al. "Moral Disengagement" 358).

Two related attitudes, Social Dominance Orientation (Pratto et al. 753) and Right-Wing Authoritarianism (Altmeyer 45), have also been linked to animal consumption behaviors. Social Dominance Orientation is characterized by attitudes that support social hierarchies and in-group and out-group differences. Right-Wing Authoritarianism is characterized by attitudes in favor of deferring to authority and opposed to dissent. Those who are higher in Social Dominance Orientation (Dhont and Hodson 15; Graca et al. "Moral Disengagement" 358; Jackson and Gibbings 156; MacInnis and Hodson 738; Veser et al. 1953) along with those who are higher Right-Wing Authoritarianism (De Backer and Hudders 71; Dhont and Hodson 15; MacInnis and Hodson 736; Ruby et al. 344; Veser et al. 1953) are more likely to consume more animal products that those who are lower in those attitudes. One possible explanation for those relations is that those who are high in Right-Wing Authoritarianism or Social Dominance Orientation feel especially threatened by vegan ideologies because vegetarians can be seen as deviant or consisting of an out-group (Dhont and Hodson 15; MacInnis and Hodson 738; Ruby et al. 344).

Political orientation and associated moral foundations have been linked to tendencies to consume animal products. Those who are more politically liberal are less likely to consume animal products than those who are politically conservative (Lusk and Norwood 238; MacInnis and Hodson 736; Pfeiler and Egloff "Personality and Attitudinal" 297). Political orientation has been found to be linked to different moral foundations on which one makes judgments (Graham et al. "Moral Foundations" 107; Graham et al. "Liberals and Conservatives" 1035). Those who are liberal tend to focus on *individualizing foundations* involving harm to others and fairness. Those who are conservative tend to focus on *binding foundations* that involve respect for authority, purity, and in-group/out-group differences. It stands to reason that moral foundations associated with political conservatism would also predict increased animal consumption since political conservatism predicts increased animal consumption. But in this case, there are some puzzling relations. Some research suggests that those stronger in *binding foundations* (purity, authority, and in-group/out-group) typically associated with being politically conservative predict less animal consumption (Ruby et al. 345). More in line with what would be predicted, those who identified as vegetarian also were more likely to endorse the *individualizing* foundations (harm, fairness) typical of more liberal orientations compared to omnivores. Other work suggests that the only foundation that reliably differentiated vegetarians from meat eaters (in this case, flexitarians) was the harm foundation (De Backer and Hudders 70).

Other attitudes that have not received as much attention in the literature include attitudes about environmental concern (Ruby et al. 345), thinking that eating animals is good (Saba and Di Natale 72), and general sympathetic, caring, or concerned attitudes toward animals (Abrams et al. 497; Diaz 271; Herzog 16; Herzog et al. 188). Some personality traits are also associated with reduced animal consumption behaviors. One common conceptualization of personality is the Big Five Factor model. The Big Five Factor model of personality includes the global personality traits extraversion, agreeableness, openness to experience, emotional stability, and conscientiousness (John and Srivastava 27). Some evidence suggests that those who are high in agreeableness are less likely to consume animal products than those low in agreeableness (Pfeiler and Egloff "Personality and Attitudinal" 298; Pfeiler and Egloff "Personality and Eating" in press). Other research suggests those who are high in openness to experience tend to consume fewer animal products than those who are lower in openness to experience (Keller and Siegrist 132).

Values

By one prominent definition, values are something by which meaningful comparisons can be made (Chang 26). One common way to measure values' relations to animal consumption is by using the Schwartz Value Survey (Schwartz and Bilsky 559). The Schwarz Value Survey identifies 10 basic human values. Among these 10 values, Universalism (preference for fair, inclusive application of values) predicted favorable attitudes toward reducing animal consumption, whereas Power (valuing power and prestige) and Security (valuing reduction of potential threats) predicted less favorable attitudes toward reducing consuming animal products (Hayley et al. 104; Kalof et al. 506). Other research suggests that meat eaters and vegetarians rely on different kinds of moral reasoning. Perhaps counterintuitive, Lund et al. found that there was a relation between moral reasoning that focuses on maximizing overall good outcomes or values (e.g., utilitarianism) and being a meat-eater. This relation between utilitarian value maximization was weaker for vegetarians. Vegetarianism also tended to predict animal rights viewpoints, a relation that was much weaker for meat eaters. Related work using the Ethics Position Questionnaire (Forsyth 180) found that in college undergraduates, idealism (the view that following correct moral principles will lead to good outcomes) was related to increased concern for animals measured by the Animal Attitudes Scale (Herzog 17).

Cognitive factors

We define cognitive factors as psychological states with contents that can be either true or false (e.g., belief is a psychological state, and the content of that psychological state can be true or false). We will review two main kinds of cognitive factors: perceptions and beliefs.

Perceptions

Perceptions can either be accurate or inaccurate (akin to visual perceptions). Among the most explored perception is the perception of human-like traits in nonhuman animals (e.g., intelligence, ability to experience pain). For example, Rothgerber ("Underlying Differences" 255) found associations (correlations between = .22-.44, indicating a moderate to strong relation between the two) between the attribution of human-like mental states to animals and reduced permissibility of killing animals for food. Similar results were found by Ruby and Heine whose data suggested that perceived intelligence of animals is one of the major predictors of reactions of disgust to eating animals (see also Diaz 270; Piazza et al. "Cruel Nature" 118).

Some perceive that barriers to reducing meat consumption are difficult to overcome, and that perception is linked to increased consumption of animal products. Some of these perceived barriers involve estimating the difficulty of preparing vegetarian meals (Pohjolainen et al. 1159) or the perception that any one individual cannot have much of an impact on food production, sustainability, or the environment (Tobler et al.; Vanhonacker et al. 678).

Beliefs and justifications

One prominent set of beliefs that has been linked to increased animal consumption is justificatory beliefs for consuming animals. Rothgerber ("Real Men" 370) developed the Meat Eating Justification scale, which asks participants to respond to a series of questions that could offer possible justificatory beliefs for eating meat (e.g., animals don't feel pain). Higher scores on the Meat Eating Justification scale have been linked to a tendency to eat more animals and to identify as an omnivore (Piazza et al. "Rationalizing Meat" 122; Rothgerber "Underlying Differences" 255). Other research suggests that beliefs about how vegetarianism relates to the environment are a predictor of being vegetarian (Kalof et al.; Richardson et al. 507). Those who believe that eating a vegetarian or vegan diet can help reduce global warming and pollution tend to eat fewer animal products.

Finally, there is gathering research about the role that objective knowledge has on animal consumption behaviors. Objective knowledge is often contrasted with subjective reports of knowledge. Subjective knowledge typically involves how much people *think* they know about some topic (Verain et al. 379). Objective knowledge measures how much people *actually* know about factual information. Subjective reports of knowledge can result in overestimations or underestimations of what one actually knows (Ybarra et al.). Research suggests that those who have more knowledge about the facts of animal consumption are less likely to consume animal products (Feltz and Feltz "Knowlege" 27).

Cognitive skills

Probably the least explored psychological factors associated with animal consumption are cognitive skills. Cognitive skills refer to the mental skills and abilities, such as reading, writing, and arithmetic (but not limited to those). Cognitive skills are of central importance to cognitive psychology as they are essentially bound to how people process information (including emotional and attitudinal information). In many instances, cognitive skills can have an impact on the integration of one's cognitive and non-cognitive states resulting in judgments and actions. To illustrate, one might be empathetic to animals, know that reducing animal consumption will reduce animal suffering, but not have the skills to understand the magnitude of the difference the reduction of animal consumption might have.

One kind of cognitive skill is IQ. There is some evidence linking early childhood IQ to decreased consumption of animal products in adult life. In one study, having a childhood IQ of 115 (one standard deviation higher than average) led to a greater chance that one would be a vegan or vegetarian in adult life compared to a person who had an IQ of 100 (average IQ) (*odds ratio* = 1.42, or having a 1.42 greater odds of being vegetarian or vegan) (Gale et al. 245).

Higher numeracy has been linked to factors associated with a reduction of animal consumption. Numeracy is the ability to understand and use statistical information in context (Cokely et al. 481). For example, those who are high in numeracy and are given an intervention attempting to increase knowledge of animal consumption behaviors learned the most (Feltz and Feltz "Knowlege" 27). Those who were more numerate were also more likely to be able to accurately identify nutritional differences between plant-based and animal-based products and know more about the conditions that impact animals used as food (Feltz and Feltz "Consumer Accuracy" 98). While there is currently little data suggesting that those who are more numerate consume fewer animal products, these data are suggestive that a relation exists (that is probably mediated by other factors, see discussion of Skilled Decision Theory below).

Interventions

There is substantial interest in using some of the insights from psychological science to help bring about changes in behavior concerning animal consumption behaviors (Cooney 53). Here, we review evidence from experiments that provide some causal evidence that interventions can change animal consumption behaviors and associated psychological states.

First, there is some evidence that educating people about the facts and conditions of animals used as food can alter behaviors and animal-related psychological factors. Those who were given an article by a famous nutritionist explaining why reducing meat consumption is desirable had an effect at one week and four weeks in reducing animal consumption behavior (Loy et al. 607). This effect was even larger for participants who were asked to write down intentions to reduce meat, identify obstacles to reducing animal consumption, and identify ways to overcome those obstacles. In similar work, participants who were asked to read a fictional newspaper article about the negative impact on animal welfare had increased intentions to reduce animal consumption behaviors. The impact of animal welfare information was greater than the estimated effect of environmental messaging, human health implications, and graphic images on animal consumption behaviors (Cordts et al. 97).

Second, some researchers have found evidence that increasing perceptions of human-like traits in nonhumans can decrease consumption of animal products (Kunst and Hohle 768; Rothgerber "Efforts to Overcome" 39). Other work suggests that the causal relation can go the other way: making animal consumption salient reduces perceptions of human-like traits in animals (Bastian et al. 252; Bilewicz et al. 205).

Other evidence suggests that generalized ethics education can have an impact on vegetarian identities and behavior. For example, Schwitzgebel reports that those who read and discuss an article about the ethics of vegetarianism purchased fewer animal products subsequently (as measured by University Purchase Card receipts) than those who were in a control group. Other work suggests that college undergraduates who learn about animals used as food and have lower 4Ns or speciesist attitudes consume fewer animal products over time (e.g., 1 week) (Feltz et al.).

Opportunities and future directions

So far, attempts to model animal consumption behaviors have been fragmented. One likely fruitful avenue for future exploration is to provide a unifying, causal model for psychological factors involved in animal consumption behaviors. The unifying theory would not only identify psychological factors that predict animal consumption but also help understand the interactions of those factors. The identification of factors and their interactions would help future researchers and activists design interventions that are likely to be the most effective. For example, if one were only to focus on emotional or attitudinal changes, then these changes (even if possible and lasting) would not necessarily in and of themselves change behaviors. Tiplady et al. measured the effect of a nationally televised program about the cruelty animals undergo when exported to another country (875). The footage was very graphic (e.g., 20 percent of the sample though the footage was too graphic). Over 98 percent of the sample had a negative emotional reaction to the video (primarily pity for the animals), but that emotional reaction did not translate into much behavioral change. Only eight out of the 156 people sampled reported having stopped eating meat (~ five percent).

There have been some attempts at unification (see, e.g., Rosenfeld and Burrow 1). The most common causal model that has guided researchers is the Theory of Planned Behavior (Ajzen 195; Saba and Di Natale 76; Verain et al. 380). The Theory of Planned Behavior gives a central role to intentions in the initiation, sustaining, and controlling of actions (see also Mele "Springs of Action"). On the Theory of Planned Behavior, there are a variety of factors that go into the intention formation including attitudes, subjective norms, and perceived control one has over a potential action.

While the Theory of Planned Behavior offers an efficient and powerful approach to help understand important aspects predicting vegetarian identities and behaviors, there are potentially important features missing. First, common models of a Theory of Planned Behavior do not include cognitive skills (e.g., numeracy, intelligence) that predict vegetarian identities, attitudes, behaviors, and change. More than that, there is no natural place in the model for objective knowledge (rather than perceptions and beliefs). Finally, depending on the precise model of a Theory of Planned Behavior, it is sometimes difficult to incorporate emotions into the model. All of these potentially missing factors have been associated with vegetarian identity and behaviors, so a unifying theory should be able to account for them in some way (or indicate why they are not necessary to understanding, predicting, and controlling vegetarian identities and behaviors).

There are many possible unifying models that could be useful depending on a researcher's goals. Here, we mention one potential unifying framework: The Framework of Skilled Decision Theory (Cokely et al. 500). The Framework of Skilled Decision Theory (specific relations and factors represented in Figure 14.1) offers a powerful yet simple approach to causally modeling animal consumption behaviors amidst the multitude of factors. The psychological factors included in the framework are thinking carefully (i.e., deliberation), being sure that one has come to the right conclusion (i.e., confidence), having the relevant set of true beliefs (i.e., knowledge), and having the appropriate feelings and motivations when acting (i.e., affect/attitudes). Each of these factors has somehow been represented in the reviewed literature about animal consumption behaviors.

The Framework for Skilled Decision Theory also provides avenues for estimating and evaluating the practical and ethical impacts of educational interventions. For example, some authors suggest that we should take advantage of some of the factors identified in order to persuade people to become vegetarian or reduce animal consumption behaviors (Cooney 65). We could engage in these persuasive behaviors by increasing emotional reactions or taking advantage of cognitive biases (e.g., framing effects, setting defaults intentionally) to persuade people to become vegetarian or adopt vegan behaviors (e.g., with Libertarian Paternalistic policies, or Nudges (Sunstein and Thaler 1189; Thaler and Sunstein 177)). But there are ethical costs

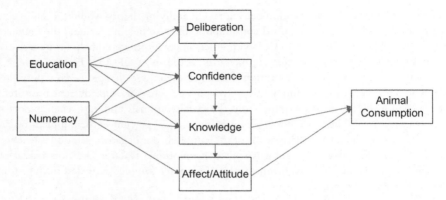

Figure 14.1 Framework for skilled decision making. Arrows represent hypothesized causal pathways. Nodes in the model represent hypothesized psychological factors influencing animal consumption behavior.

associated with all libertarian paternalistic policies, and typically that cost is a reducing (or not promoting) autonomy, or one's ability to be self-governed (e.g., undue influence, restriction of freedom) (Gert and Culver 203; Hausman "Behavioural Economics" 59; Hausman "Efficacious and Ethical" 270). If there was a way to influence people's choices that did not infringe on autonomy, or in some instances promote it, then that alternative method would be better than a paternalist policy (everything else being equal).

The Theory for Skilled Decision Making offers a helpful alternative to only endorsing potentially ethically problematic interventions that undermine or do not promote autonomy. Among other factors, the Theory for Skilled Decision Making features cognitive skills and knowledge, two factors that have traditionally been taken to be necessary for, and in many cases promote, autonomous decision making (Mele "Autonomous Agents" 68; Mele "Motivation and Agency" 54). Some of the evidence we have reviewed suggests that those who are knowledgeable about the facts and conditions of animals have reduced animal consumption behaviors (Feltz and Feltz "Knowlege" 36). Other work indicates that knowledge is *causally* efficacious in bringing about a reduction in animal consumption behaviors (Feltz et al.). These results suggest that we can change people's animal consumption behaviors while at the same time using interventions that are most likely not to be ethically problematic and likely to be ethically desirable (educating and promoting autonomy rather than persuading and not promoting autonomy) (Feltz and Cokely 320).

Works cited

Abrams, Katie et al. "Communicating Sensitive Scientific Issues: The Interplay between Values, Attitudes, and Eupemisms in Communicating Livestock Slaughter." *Science Communication*, vol. 37, 2015, pp. 485–505.
Ajzen, Icek. "A Theory of Planned Behavior." *Organizational Behavior and Human Decision Processes*, vol. 50, 1991, pp. 179–211.
Albarracin, Dolores et al. "Attitudes: Introduction and Scope." *Handbook of Attitudes*, edited by Dolores Albarracin et al., Taylor & Francis Group, 2005, pp. 3–19.
Altmeyer, Robert. *The Authoritarian Specter*. Harvard University Press, 1996.

Bastian, Brock et al. "Don't Mind the Meat? The Denial of Mind to Animals Used for Human Consumption." *Personality and Social Psychology Bulletin*, vol. 38, no. 2, 2012, pp. 247–256.

Bilewicz, Michal et al. "The Humanity of What We Eat: Conceptions of Human Uniqueness among Vegetarians and Omnivores." *European Journal of Social Psychology*, vol. 41, 2011, pp. 201–209.

Caviola, Lucius et al. "The Moral Standing of Animals: Towards a Psychology of Speciesism." *Journal of Personality and Social Psychology*, vol. 116, no. 6, 2019, pp. 1011–1029.

Chang, Ruth. "Introduction." *Incommensurability, Incomparability, and Practical Reason*, edited by Ruth Change, Harvard University Press, 1997, pp. 1–34.

Cokely, Edward et al. "Skilled Decision Theory: From Intelligence to Numeracy and Expertise." *Cambridge Handbook of Expertise and Expert Performance*, edited by Anders Ericsson et al., Cambridge University Press, 2018, pp. 476–505.

Cooney, Nick. *Change of Heart: What Psychology Can Teach Us About Spreading Social Change*. Lantern Books, 2011.

Cordts, Anette et al. "Consumer Response to Negative Information on Meat Consumption in Germany." *Interational Food and Agribusiness Managment Review*, vol. 17, no. 4, 2014, pp. 83–106.

De Backer, Charlotteand Liselot Hudders. "Meat Morals: Relationship between Meat Consumption and Consumer Attitudes Towards Human and Animal Welfare and Moral Behavior." *Meat Science*, vol. 99, 2015, pp. 68–74.

Dhont, Kristof and Gordon Hodson. "Why Do Right-Wing Adherents Engage in More Animal Exploitation and Meat Consumption." *Personality and Individual Differences*, vol. 64, 2014, pp. 12–17.

Diaz, Estela. "Animal Humanness, Animal Use, and Intention to Become Ethical Vegetarian or Ethical Vegan." *Anthrozoos*, vol. 29, 2016, pp. 263–282.

Everett, Jim et al. "Speciesism, Generalized Prejudice, and Perceptions of Prejudiced Others." *Group Process Intergroup Relat*, vol. 22, no. 6, 2019, pp. 785–803.

Feltz, Adam and Edward Cokely. "Informing Ethical Decision Making." *Handbook of Neuroethics*, edited by K. Rommelfanger and L.S. Johnson, Routledge, 2017, pp. 314–327.

Feltz, Adam et al. "The Effectivness of Animal Ethics Education." *Northwest Philosophy Conference*, October 25, 2019.

Feltz, Silke and Adam Feltz. "Consumer Accuracy at Identyfing Plant-Based and Animal-Based Milk Products." *Food Ethics*, vol. 4, 2019a, pp. 85–112.

Feltz, Silke. "The Knowlege of Animal as Food Scale." *Human–animal Interaction Bulletin*, vol. 7, 2019b, pp. 19–45.

Forsyth, Donelson R. "A Taxonomy of Ethical Ideologies." *Journal of Personality and Social Psychology*, vol. 39, no. 1, 1980, pp. 175–184.

Gale, Catherine R. et al. "IQ in Childhood and Vegetarianism in Adulthood: 1970 British Cohort Study." *BMJ*, vol. 334, no. 7587, 2007, p. 245.

Gert, Bernhard and Charles M. Culver. "Justification of Paternalism." *Ethics*, vol. 89, no. 2, 1979, pp. 199–210.

Graca, João et al. "Attached to Meat? (Un)Willingness and Intentions to Adopt a More Plant-Based Diet." *Appetite*, vol. 95, 2015, pp. 113–125.

Graca, João et al. "Situating Moral Disengagement: Motivated Reasoning in Meat Consumption and Substitution." *Personality and Individual Differences*, vol. 90, 2016, pp. 353–364.

Graham, Jesse et al. "Moral Foundations Theory: The Pragmatic Validity of Moral Pluralism." *Advances in Experimental Social Psychology*, vol. 47, 2013, pp. 55–130.

Graham, Jesse "Liberals and Conservatives Rely on Different Sets of Moral Foundations." *Personality Processes and Individual Differences*, vol. 96, 2009, pp. 1029–1046.

Hausman, Daniel M. "Behavioral Economics and Paternalism." *Economics and Philosophy*, vol. 34, no. 1, 2018a, pp. 53–66.

———. "Efficacious and Ethical Public Paternalism." *Review of Behavioral Economics*, vol. 5, no. 3–4, 2018b, pp. 261–280.

Hayley, Alexa et al. "Values, Attitudes, and Frequency of Meat Consumption: Predicting Meat-Reduced Diets in Australians." *Appetite*, vol. 84, 2015, pp. 98–106.

Herzog, Harold A. "Gender Differences in Human–Animal Interactions: A Review." *Anthrozoos*, vol. 20, 2007, pp. 7–21.

Herzog, Harold A. et al. "Gender, Sex Role Identity and Attitudes toward Animals." *Anthrozoos*, vol. 4, 1991, pp. 184–191.

Jackson, Lynne M. and Aaron Gibbings. "Social Dominance and Legitimizing Myths About Animal Use." *Anthrozoos*, vol. 29, 2016, pp. 151–160.

John, Oliver P. and Sanjay Srivastava. *The Big-Five Trait Taxonomy History, Measurement, and Theoretical Perspectives*. University of California, 1999.

Kalof, Linda et al. "Social Psychological and Structural Infuences on Vegetarian Beliefs." *Rural Sociology*, 1999, pp. 500–511.

Keller, Carmen and Michael Siegrist. "Does Personality Influence Eating Styles and Food Choices? Direct and Indirect Effects." *Appetite*, vol. 84, 2015, pp. 128–138.

Kunst, Jonas R. and Sigrid Møyner Hohle. "Meat Eaters by Dissociation: How We Present, Prepare and Talk About Meat Increases Willingness to Eat Meat by Reducing Empathy and Disgust." *Appetite*, vol. 105, 2016, pp. 758–774.

Loy, Laura S. et al. "Supporting Sustainable Food Consumption: Mental Contrasting with Implementation Intentions (Mcii) Aligns Intentions and Behavior." *Frontiers in Psychology*, vol. 7, 2016, p. 607.

Lund, Thomas B. et al. "A Multidimensional Measure of Animal Ethics Orientation – Developed and Applied to a Representative Sample of the Danish Public." *Plos One*, vol. 14, no. 2, 2019, p. e021165.

—— "Animal Ethics Profiling of Vegetarians, Vegans, and Meat-Eaters." *Anthrozoos*, vol. 29, 2016, pp. 89–106.

Lusk, Jason L. and Norwood Bailey. "Some Vegetarians Spend Less Money on Food, Others Don't." *Ecological Ecnomics*, vol. 130, 2016, pp. 232–242.

MacInnis, Cara C. and Gordon Hodson. "It Ain't Easy Eating Greens: Evidence of Bias toward Vegetarians and Vegans from Both Source and Target." *Group Processes & Intergroup Relations*, vol. 20, 2017, pp. 721–744.

Mele, Alfred. *Autonomous Agents: From Self-Control to Autonomy*. Oxford University Press, 1995.

——. *Motivation and Agency*. Oxford University Press, 2003.

——. *Springs of Action: Understanding Intentional Behavior*. Oxford University Press, 1992.

Monteiro, Christopher A. et al. "The Carnism Inventory: Measuring the Ideology of Eating Animals." *Appetite*, vol. 113, 2017, pp. 51–62. doi:10.1016/j.appet.2017.02.011.

Nezlek, John B. and Catherine A. Forestell. "Vegetarianism as Social Identity." *Current Opinion in Food Science*, vol. 33, 2020, pp. 45–51.

Pfeiler, Tamara M. and Boris Egloff. "Personality and Attitudinal Correlates of Meat Consumption: Results of Two Representative German Samples." *Appetite*, vol. 121, 2018, pp. 294–301.

Pfeiler, Tamara M. "Personality and Eating Habits Revisited: Associations between the Big Five, Food Choices, and Body Mass Index in a Representative Australian Sample." *Appetite*, vol. 149, in press.

Piazza, Jared et al. "Cruel Nature: Harmfulness as an Important, Overlooked Dimension in Judgments of Moral Standing." *Cognition*, vol. 131, no. 1, 2014, pp. 108–124. doi:10.1016/j.cognition.2013.12.013.

—— "Rationalizing Meat Consumption. The 4ns." *Appetite*, vol. 91, 2015, pp. 114–128.

Pohjolainen, Pasi et al. "Consumers' Perceived Barriers to Following a Plant-Based Diet." *British Food Journal*, vol. 117, 2015, pp. 1150–1167.

Pratto, Felicia et al. "Social Dominance Orientation: A Personality Variable Predicting Social and Political Attitudes." *Journal of Personality and Social Psychology*, vol. 67, 1994, pp. 741–763.

Richardson, Nicola et al. "Meat Consumption, Definition of Meat and Trust in Information Sources in the Uk Population and Members of the Vegetarian Soceity." *Ecology of Food and Nutrition*, vol. 33, 1994, pp. 1–13.

Rosenfeld, Daniel L. and Anthony L. Burrow. "The Unified Model of Vegetarian Identity: A Conceptual Framework for Understanding Plant-Based Food Choices." *Appetite*, vol. 112, 2017, pp. 78–95.

Rosenfeld, Daniel L. and A. Janet Tomiyama. "When Vegetarians Eat Meat: Why Vegetarians Violate Their Diets and How They Feel About Doing So." *Appetite*, vol. 143, 2019, p. 1–9.

Rothgerber, Hank. "Can You Have Your Meat and Eat It Too? Conscientious Omnivores, Vegetarians, and Adherence to Diet." *Appetite*, vol. 84, 2015a, pp. 196–203.

——. "A Comparison of Attitudes toward Meat and Animals among Strict and Semi-Vegetarians." *Appetite*, vol. 72, 2014a, pp. 98–105.

——. "Efforts to Overcome Vegetarian-Induced Dissonance among Meat Eaters." *Appetite*, vol. 79, 2014b, pp. 32–41.

——. "Real Men Don't Eat (Vegetable) Quiche: Masculinity and the Justificatino of Meat Consumption." *The Psychology of Men and Mascuilinty*, vol. 14, 2013, pp. 363–375.

——. "Underlying Differences between Conscientious Omnivores and Vegetarians in the Evaluation of Meat and Animals." *Appetite*, vol. 87, 2015b, pp. 251–258.

Rothgerber, Hank and Frances Mican. "Childhood Pet Ownership, Attachment to Pets, and Subsequent Meat Avoidance. The Mediating Role of Empathy toward Animals." *Appetite*, vol. 79, 2014, pp. 11–17.

Rozin, Paul and Jonathan Haidt. "The Domains of Disgust and Their Origins: Contrasting Biological and Cultural Evolutionary Accounts." *Trends Cogn Sci*, vol. 17, no. 8, 2013, pp. 367–368.

Ruby, Matthew B. "Vegetarianism. A Blossoming Field of Study." *Appetite*, vol. 58, 2012, pp. 141–150.

———. "Too Close to Home. Factors Predicting Meat Avoidance." *Appetite*, vol. 59, no. 1, 2012, pp. 47–52.

——— "Compassion and Contamination: Cultural Differences in Vegetarianism." *Appetite*, vol. 71, 2013, pp. 340–348.

——— "Attitudes toward Beef and Vegetarians in Argentina, Brazil, France, and the USA." *Appetite*, vol. 96, 2016, pp. 546–554. doi:10.1016/j.appet.2015.10.018.

Ryder, Richard D. "Speciesism." Privately Printed Leaflet. Oxford, 1970.

Saba, Aanna and Roberto Di Natale. "A Study on the Mediating Role of Intention in the Impact of Habit and Attitude on Meat Consumption." *Food Quality and Preferences*, vol. 10, 1999, pp. 69–77.

Schwartz, Shalom H. and Wolfgang Bilsky. "Toward a Universal Psychological Structure of Human Values." *Journal of Personality and Social Psychology*, vol. 53, 1987, pp. 550–562.

Schwitzgebel, Eric. "Ethics Classes Can Influence Student Behavior: Students Purchase Less Meat after Discussing Arguments for Vegetarianism." *The Splintered Mind*, 2019. http://schwitzsplinters.blogspot.com/2019/07/ethics-classes-can-influence-student.html.

Singer, Peter. "All Animals Are Equal." *Animals Rights and Human Obligations*, edited by Tom Regan and Peter Singer, Prentice-Hall, 1989, pp. 148–162.

Sunstein, Cass R. and Richard H. Thaler. "Libertarian Paternalism Is Not an Oxymoron." *University of Chicago Law Review*, vol. 70, no. 4, 2003, pp. 1159–1202.

Thaler, Richard and Cass Sunstein. "Libertarian Paternalism." *American Economic Review*, vol. 93, no. 2, 2003, pp. 175–179. doi:10.1257/000282803321947001.

Tiplady, Catherine M. et al. "Public Response to Media Coverage of Animal Cruelty." *Journal of Agricultural and Environmental Ethics*, vol. 26, 2013, pp. 869–885.

Tobler, Christina et al. "Eating Green. Consumers' Willingness to Adopt Ecological Food Consumption Behaviors." *Appetite*, vol. 57, no. 3, 2011, pp. 674–682.

Vanhonacker, Filiep et al. "Flemish Consumer Attitudes Toard More Sustainable Food Choices." *Appetite*, vol. 62, 2013, pp. 7–16.

Verain, Muriel C. et al. "Sustainable Food Consumption. Product Choice or Curtailment?" *Appetite*, vol. 91, 2015, pp. 375–384.

Veser, Petra et al. "Diet, Authoritarianism, Social Dominance Orientation, and Predisposition to Prejudice: Results of a German Survey." *British Food Journal*, vol. 117, 2016, pp. 1949–1960.

Wright, Laura. *The Vegan Studies Project: Food, Animals, and Gender in the Age of Terror.* University of Georgia Press, 2015.

Ybarra, Vincent et al. "Rethinking the Bias Blind Spot: Numeate People Are Less Biased and They Know It." *Society for Judgment and Decision Making*, 2018.

15
Vegan studies and food studies

Jessica Holmes

Introduction

The Food and Agriculture Organization of the United States (FAO) estimates that well over 70 billion land animals are slaughtered annually for consumption.[1] Though veganism and vegetarianism are on the rise, more animals are being killed and eaten than ever before. Given the commodification and designation of these nonhuman beings as "food" (something vegans inherently oppose), conversations in the field of vegan studies overlap considerably with conversations in the field of food studies. This chapter discusses the relationship between these two emerging spheres of scholarly and pedagogical discourse. I will begin by giving a brief overview of food studies before digging into some of the shared inquiries as well as important distinctions between food studies and vegan studies. Through my identification and discussion of these distinctions, I argue that vegan studies challenges normative interpretive assumptions surrounding human-nonhuman animal relations and calls into question the very nature of food. Though writers, teachers, and scholars across the world are engaged in vibrant work in each respective field, the scope of this chapter is limited primarily to the United States.[2] Because of its foundation in ecofeminism and intersectionality, and its grounding in a social justice movement, I argue that vegan studies offers an adaptable, interdisciplinary approach which can be taught alongside or in conversation with food studies, but without overlooking the fundamentally different underlying principles and future goals of each field.

What is food studies?

The still emerging field of food studies advances scholarship related to food topics ranging from sustainability to health to economics, as well as the history of food systems and food policy, the prevalence of food insecurity and food injustice, the ethics of food consumption, and the relationship of food to cultural, political, and social identity. In "Food studies programs," gastronomy scholar Rachel Black characterizes food studies as "an interdisciplinary approach to studying where food comes from, how it is prepared, consumed, and disposed of. It is this holistic approach that sets food studies apart from other academic pursuits that focus on food such as nutrition, food policy and agricultural studies" (201–2). Emily Contois, a leading voice in contemporary food studies and editor of the *Graduate Journal of Food Studies*, similarly emphasizes the integrative qualities of food studies curricula and scholarship, defining the area as a "burgeoning, interdisciplinary, inherently politicized field of scholarship, practice, and art that examines the relationship between food and all aspects of the human experience, including culture and biology, individuals and society, global pathways and local contexts."

The tradition from which food studies emerges aligns loosely with that of gender studies and American studies, but, as the above characterizations indicate, contemporary academic work in food studies draws on a wide variety of disciplines and encompasses an array of methodologies. As for any cross-disciplinary field of academic discourse, particularly one still in the process of establishing itself within the academy, it is difficult to pinpoint a precise origin or starting point. Black traces food studies to 18th-century lawyer and politician Jean Anthelme Brillat-Savarin's *La Physiologie du Goût* (*The Physiology of Taste*, published in 1825 just before his death), a work responsible for elevating the professional status of culinary discourse and the role of food in society (201). In its contemporary iteration, we might trace the commencement of food studies to the 1980s and 1990s. An emerging canon of food studies scholarship includes anthropologist Sidney Mintz's *Sweetness and Power: The Place of Sugar in Modern History* (1985), which examines the role of sugar in the development of colonialism and capitalism, and American studies historian Warren Belasco's *Appetite for Change: How the Counter Culture Took on the Food Industry* (1990). Belasco also served as chief editor for *Food, Culture & Society*, one of the first food studies journals (originally called *Journal of the Association for the Study of Food and Society*, founded in 1996), and is considered by some to be the "grandfather" of food studies. Ethnographic anthropologist Carole Counihan is also considered a pioneer of the field for her work on food and gender; alongside Penny Van Esterik she edited *Food and Culture: A Reader* (1997), which further codified food studies as a legitimate academic field. For more expansive coverage of key scholars, methodologies, and central discourses in food studies, I recommend referencing the *Routledge International Handbook of Food Studies*.

Since the 1980s food studies' existence within the academy has been further legitimized by programmatic and departmental institutional inclusion, peer reviewed journals, and the expansion of conference presence across multiple disciplines. Founded in 2012, the quarterly journal *Food Studies: An Interdisciplinary Journal* seeks to provide "an interdisciplinary forum for the discussion of agricultural, environmental, nutritional, health, social, economic, and cultural perspectives on food"; and the annual International Conference on Food Studies seeks to foreground approaches to food production, nutrition, politics, and place. *Gastronomica: The Journal for Food Studies*, *Food and Foodways*, and *Food Studies: An Introduction to Research Methods* are among the many journals and publications at the forefront of ongoing food studies scholarship and discourse. Programmatic and departmental inclusion of food studies has also become more prevalent across higher education institutions. Some of the first academic programs included Boston University's Gastronomy program, founded in 1993, New York University's Steinhart School's Nutrition and Food Studies program, founded in 1996, and Indiana University Bloomington's Anthropology of Food program, founded in 2007. As a 2015 article in *The Atlantic* on "The Rise of Food-Studies Programs" points out, emerging food studies programs often take on the attributes and priorities of their surrounding demographics; the article examines how the development of an academic food studies curriculum at Hostos Community College in New York has been informed by the prevalence of racialized food insecurity in the Bronx (Cosgrove).

Today food studies continues to develop and define itself as an academic field; in addition to a rich, expanding foundation of scholarship, food studies teaching and writing also explore popular works of literature such as Michael Pollan's *The Omnivore's Dilemma: A Natural History of Four Meals* (2006) and *In Defense of Food: An Eater's Manifesto* (2008), and Eric Schlosser's *Fast Food Nation: The Dark Side of the All-American Meal* (2001), as well as a myriad of food-related documentaries, advertisements, and representations in popular culture.

The relationship between food studies and vegan studies

Given that one key component of veganism is avoidance of animal products in the diet, vegan studies and food studies naturally share a number of key thematic inquiries; many food studies scholars discuss veganism, animal welfare, animal agriculture, and the ethics of eating. Indeed, a list of frequently used texts in vegan studies courses would very likely contain some overlap with a respective list in food studies courses. Because a "vegan" or plant-based diet is more particular than an omnivorous "food" diet, an undiscerning observer of these terms might conclude that vegan studies should comprise a sub-category or specialization within the field of food studies. However, a closer look at the guiding foundations of and evolving criterion (as expounded by their central participants) for each respective field highlights important divergences between the two. While vegan studies and food studies scholars alike advocate against oppression at the hands of global food and agriculture systems, vegan studies is distinct from food studies in that its fundamental organizing principle opposes the exploitation of animals. Where food studies scholars may raise ethical questions about the consumption of animals (and some specific scholars may argue against that consumption[3]), vegan studies scholars categorically cease to presume animal subjects (or their bodies) as constituting food commodities. The works of founder Laura Wright and fellow vegan studies scholars lean on concepts such as Carol J. Adams' "absent referent": "Animals in name and body are made absent as *animals* for meat to exist" (*The Sexual Politics of Meat* 40). Veganism as an imaginative, integrative frame of reference rejects this translation of live individuals, through slaughter, into "food," and furthermore respects the rights of nonhuman animals to live free from exploitation and violence.

Emily Contois discusses the inherent politicization of food studies in her editor's note for the *Graduate Journal of Food Studies*: "Food studies scholars often assert that food—food culture, food access, and food sovereignty—is a human right." I argue vegan studies is even more politicized, as it calls into question the very translations and categorizations underlying the term "food," and thus challenges the dominant interpretive assumptions latent in terms such as "food culture," "food access," and "food sovereignty." Furthermore, as Laura Wright discusses in her foundational text *The Vegan Studies Project: Food, Animals, and Gender in the Age of Terror*, vegan studies scholarship attempts to define and to deconstruct "vegan" as an evolving identity category (1). While this undertaking may fall under the more general inquiry into food's relationship to human identity often pursued by food studies scholars, vegan studies' grounding in animal rights as well as in a specific identity category differentiates it from food studies on the basis of assumptive principles. Lastly, any study of veganism by nature extends well beyond the realm of food; while vegans indeed eat a plant-based diet, ethical *veganism* delineates a holistic commitment to refrain from all forms of animal exploitation and violence toward animals, not simply in terms of food consumption.

According to The Vegan Society, "Veganism is a way of living which seeks to exclude, as far as is possible and practicable, all forms of exploitation of, and cruelty to, animals for food, clothing or any other purpose." While this definition is aspirational in nature, food studies scholars must be careful not to collapse veganism and vegetarianism into any single generalized category (as mainstream media and culture frequently do); while vegan studies certainly draws on the traditions of feminist-vegetarianism, veganism is by no means an extension of vegetarianism. In their modern iterations, vegetarianism constitutes a diet, whereas (as indicated by The Vegan Society's definition above), veganism comprises an ethical stance or ideology carried out through lived behavior (or rather abstinence from certain lived behaviors). For instance, in addition to eating eggs, dairy, cheese and/or honey, many vegetarians also wear animal skins, use products tested on animals, and/or attend zoos or rodeos. Because veganism functions as a lived ideology, it should not be categorized as a solely food-based topic like vegetarianism and plant-based diets; likewise it is illogical to position vegan studies under the umbrella of food studies.

In discussing the relationship of vegan studies to food studies, it is also important to acknowledge distinctions between vegan studies and veganism. While veganism as an aspirational paradigm seeks to end animal exploitation (and while vegan studies as a discipline contributes to that pursuit), the intentions and objectives of vegan studies differ from those of the vegan movement itself. As Wright's work exhibits, vegan studies seeks to explore and deconstruct vegan *identity*. While the treatment of veganism by food studies scholarship engages questions of dis-ease with and morality of killing and eating animals, the work of vegan studies scholars in particular interrogates the widespread cultural animosity so frequently directed at veganism and vegans in mainstream media and culture. For example, *The Vegan Studies Project* engages constructions of the vegan body in relation to "terror" in the post-9/11 era; additionally, in her 2019 talk entitled "The Dangerous Vegan," Wright further elucidates and dismantles the charges of extremism, militarism, and threat often attributed to vegans. Similarly, Richard Twine unravels the notion of the vegan "killjoy," in his essay "Vegan Killjoys at the Table": "Veganism constitutes a direct challenge to the dominant affective community that celebrates the pleasure of consuming animals. It questions the assumptions of shared happiness around such consumption raising the prospect of a cruel commensality" (628).

This potential opposition between dominant omnivorous practice and minority vegan practice (especially as highlighted and sometimes heightened in mainstream media) is of course being examined from a number of angles in both vegan studies and food studies. But at times, by characterizing vegans as "strict" or "puritanical," food studies scholars misrepresent an ethical and political commitment to nonviolence on the part of vegans as a social constraint, dietary inhibition, or personal preference. In "Food Studies and Animal Rights," Carol Helstosky contends that "for many ethical vegans, food choice can become a point of tension or discord with the broader community. Food studies scholars understand food quite differently. They enjoy chronicling the expansion, not the restriction, of diet" (306). This common portrayal of veganism as restrictive betrays the inclusiveness at the heart of an ideology and lifestyle which aims to further extend rights to human and nonhuman animals alike. No other social justice movement is subject to such widespread critiques of exclusion or restriction. The mainstream media and culture, and even some examples of the most visible vegan activism,[4] are of course in large part responsible for ongoing anti-"expansion" (to use Helstosky's term) portrayals of veganism. Nevertheless, in their treatment of veganism, food studies scholars would do well to consider the integrity of veganism as a social justice movement, its inherent resistance to an oppressive status quo, and the context of what Shanti Chu describes as "the intersectional relationship between racism, colonialism, capitalism, and speciesism" (190).

In this respect, food studies and vegan studies *are* deeply aligned insofar as they both espouse pro-justice education and action; as Bradley and Herrera state, the food justice movement is "fundamentally a social justice movement. It takes issue with inequalities in access to food, exploitative labor practices in the food system, and environmental degradation" (100). Veganism likewise opposes exploitation (of both human and nonhuman animals), and a more plant-based agricultural system will be integral to stagnating and reversing the environmental degradation and climate change that currently threatens all species on the planet. Furthermore, as many intersectional vegan studies scholars assert, veganism expands (not restricts) revolutionary traditions of nonviolence and in doing so serves as a force for social and ecological transformation. Chu argues specifically in favor of vegan practice and identity as a means to dismantle hegemonic food systems and decolonize the body. Drawing on A. Breeze Harper's "Going Beyond the Normative White 'Post-Racial' Vegan Epistemology" and *Sistah Vegan*, Chu contends: "Nonviolent daily practices can be a means of decolonization. More specifically, women of color can decolonize their bodies through veganism as a means of resisting institutionalized racism and sexism" (190).[5] Chu goes on to dispel widespread myths and misrepresentations of contemporary veganism as exclusive or elitist:

> Although veganism has the unfortunate reputation of being for the privileged in the West, it has been a way of life for many indigenous and pre-colonized populations and can still be used today as a means of resisting the Eurocentric, capitalist patriarchy. Such revolutionary ways of existing are even more of a necessity within the current politically tumultuous context and the reality of climate change. (197)

Scholars such as Shanti Chu and Aph Ko illustrate the relevance and power of veganism in post-colonial contexts and across racial and gender lines. Works such as these clearly evince that a study of veganism is much more expansive than a study of food choices or an argument for (solely) nonhuman animal rights. As Chu writes, veganism "disrupts the violence of the oppressor" and returns agency to "bodies marked by the social and historical context of colonization, slavery, sexism, capitalism, and racism" (195–6).

Morality, animal rights, and affect

Carol Helstosky's portrayal of the seeming opposition between animal rights advocates and food studies scholars in "Food Studies and Animal Rights" highlights the role of morality in dictating food choices and food production (and by extension in the *study* of food choices and food production). According to Helstosky, food scholars are generally more focused on examining "how taste, not ethics, motivates food choices and they tend to see food as a unifying, not dividing element in society" (207). This is of course a generalization and does not apply to every food studies scholar, but the statement rightfully suggests that it is the ethical commitment underlying vegan food choices, rather than food itself, which proves divisive; to return to Twine's vegan "killjoy," a vegan ethical disposition disrupts the (supposedly unified) "shared happiness" of the "dominant affective community" (628). With regard to affect in particular, Helstosky ultimately participates in an outdated (though familiar) dualistic mindset by dismissing vegan writers (and animal rights writers) on account of their supposed overreliance on emotion and embodied experience in making their respective arguments;

> Whether one is appalled by or grateful for the death of an animal, descriptions of such experiences offer little in the way of a critical perspective on one of the most significant issues facing communities and societies today: That our current system of meat production hurts our health, the environment, and our sense of morality. (313)

To detach affect, emotion, and embodied experience from critical questions of morality, health, and consumption, however academic the context, is to ignore both the reality of human physiology and decision-making and decades of ecofeminist scholarship by writer-scholars such as Carol J. Adams, Greta Gaard, and Vandana Shiva on the unproductive (and sexist) feminization by those in power of qualities such as empathy, compassion and nonviolence. In "A Hunger for Words: Food Affects and Embodied Ideology," Tom Hertweck presents a theory of affective eating that understands food as *embodied ideology* (133); by combining food studies with affect theory, Hertweck offers an example of the way in which food scholars might engage in discursive questions of identity, justice, and the marketplace, without erasing the materiality and embodied experiences (those of both human and nonhuman animals, as well as ecological bodies) that shape our interactions with and surrounding food.

Though Helstosky suggests above that food studies scholars prefer to focus on "taste, not ethics," this is not to say that morality is not ever a consideration of food studies scholars; many food studies scholars interrogate the moral dimensions and consequences of food choices, but food studies as a field does not operate under any particular moral stance regarding the consumption of nonhuman animals as food, nor does it categorically reject the classification of those beings as food products. Julia Abramson in "Food and Ethics" affirms that

> at present, food and ethics come into relation within the contexts of the global industrial food system, a transformed scientific landscape, and intensified conditions of higher global population and greater exploitation than ever before of natural resources for agricultural and other purposes. (372)

Abramson makes no mention of veganism here—perhaps because a vegan standpoint disturbs the very notion of what and who qualifies as "food" or "resources," and contends that living beings do not—rather they possess rights.

Again, there are important distinctions between vegan studies and the animal rights movement, but the understanding that animals possess inherent moral rights is the cornerstone of vegan practice. As for the perceived (and often real) separation between an academic discipline and a social justice or activist-led movement, Laura Wright states in the introduction to *Through a Vegan Studies Lens* that the compendium of activist-scholars and scholar-activists contributing to the emerging field of vegan studies marks it "as a pedagogy and scholarly venue that is not exclusive and that owes its existence to lived animal rights activism" (xxi). In this way, vegan studies is perhaps most closely aligned with the field of critical animal studies, which argues for an "interdisciplinary and multidisciplinary intersectional and multi-movement approach for a total liberation field of study" (Nocella et al. xxii). Just as food scholars too often group or collapse the categories of vegetarianism and veganism, likewise there is often little differentiation made between the animal rights and animal welfare movements. While both, as Helstosky points out, have "shaped attitudes towards using animals as food sources" (307), they are two fundamentally different ideologies. Veganism is defined by a rights-based position against all exploitation (i.e. total liberation), not a welfarist position advocating for less exploitative forms of exploitation. Food studies is also arguably connected to a rights-based ideology in the sense that the field generally argues for food as a human right (Contois); so while exceedingly compatible and aligned in their rights-based objectives, these separate ideologies (veganism and food justice) delineate distinct fields of discourse and study.

Jessica Holmes

Future directions

In "The Greatest Cause on Earth: The Historical Formation of Veganism as an Ethical Practice," sociologist Matthew Cole discusses the foundational aspirations of veganism, hearkening back to the creation of The Vegan Society in 1944 by Donald Watson and his fellow pioneers:

> [Veganism] combines compassionate non-exploitation of other animals with an emancipated vegan self *and* a more compassionate human society. Vegan ethics, from the beginning, was directed towards these interconnected goals of transforming human beings and transforming human society, with both flowing from the foundational reconfiguration of human-nonhuman animal relations. (220)

As evidenced by popular food narratives both inside and outside the academy, veganism continues to be largely overlooked as a rights-based social justice movement in the interests of both human and nonhuman animals, too often being regarded as a restrictive dietary and/or (at best) lifestyle preference. Of course, one is hard pressed to think of any social justice issue that has not at some point (and usually for extended periods of time) been misunderstood or misrepresented; it is no surprise that the field of vegan studies has so far been perceived by food scholars and general readers alike as divisive or radical. Vegan studies, in comparison to food studies, builds on and deconstructs a more clearly defined ideology; though of course all matters of food are inextricably caught up in identities and ideological attachments, and thus there is bound to be some overlapping discussion between the two fields. The distinctions between vegan studies and food studies explicated in this chapter are by no means an attempt to paint food studies in a negative light or to suggest that veganism is necessarily the antidote to all systems of oppression, but rather to distinguish vegan studies as its own area of scholarship—one which builds on and recontextualizes what the founders of modern veganism proposed; i.e., a vision for humanity, not just for food. If veganism constitutes a lived social, political, and ethical stance against violence, vegan studies is the study of that stance and its relationship to identity (both self-constructed identity and identities constructed by culture, media and history). As vegan studies and food studies carry forward their ongoing efforts to define and substantiate themselves within the academy, more alignment and exchange between the two fields, particularly with regard to social justice and the demystification of vegan identity, is likely to prove beneficial for all parties, as well as for the social sciences and humanities at large.

Notes

1 Fish and aquatic animals are left out of this statistic because they are measured in tons rather than lives.
2 This is in part because both food studies and vegan studies higher education programs (at least in their recent form) officially began in the United States; for a fuller global picture of vegan studies, I recommend referencing the other chapters of this volume, as well as *Through a Vegan Studies Lens*, and for a fuller global picture of food studies, I recommend referencing the *Routledge International Handbook of Food Studies* and *Food and Culture: A Reader* (see bibliography).
3 Examples include John Robbins in *Diet for a New America* (1987), Mark Braunstein's *Radical Vegetarianism* (1981) and Dudley Gehl's *Vegetarianism* (1979). Food studies courses often include popular contemporary pro-vegetarian or pro-veganism texts such as Jonathan Safran Foer's *Eating Animals* (2009) and David Foster Wallace's "Consider the Lobster" (2005).
4 PETA is a well-known example of vegan activism that is not always aligned with the furthering of social justice for human animals, especially women.
5 Chu goes on to quote pattrice jones, saying "One must dismantle the 'dietary colonialism' 'that began when Europeans forcibly replaced subsistence crops with cash crops…that make it cheaper for poor people to eat [at] fast-food restaurants owned by multinational corporations that to buy healthy food from local farmers'" (195).

Works cited

Abramson, Julia. "Food and ethics." *Routledge International Handbook of Food Studies*, edited by K. Albala, New York, NY: Routledge, 2013, pp. 371–378.
Adams, Carol J. *The Sexual Politics of Meat*. Bloomsbury Publishing, 2015.
Albala, Ken editor. *Routledge International Handbook of Food Studies*. Routledge, 2014.
Black, Rachel. "Food studies programs." *Routledge International Handbook of Food Studies*, edited by K. Albala, New York, NY: Routledge, 2013, pp. 201–208.
Black, Rachel. "Editor's Note." *Graduate Journal of Food Studies*, vol. 5, no. 1, 2018.
Bradley, Katharine, and Hank Herrera. "Decolonizing Food Justice: Naming, Resisting, and Researching Colonizing Forces in the Movement." *Antipode*, vol. 48, no. 1, 2016, pp. 97–114.
Chu, Shanti. "Nonviolence through Veganism." *Through a Vegan Studies Lens: Textual Ethics and Lived Activism*, edited by Wright, Laura, University of Nevada Press, 2019, pp. 180–201.
Cole, Matthew, and Richard Twine. "The Greatest Cause on Earth: The Historical Formation of Veganism as an Ethical Practice." *The Rise of Critical Animal Studies*, edited by Nik Taylor, Routledge, 2014, pp. 223–244.
Contois, Emily. "From the Editor: Defining Food Studies and the Next Four Years." *Graduate Journal of Food Studies*, vol. 4, no. 1, 2017.
Cosgrove, Emma. "The Rise of Food-Studies Programs." *The Atlantic*, 2 June 2015, www.theatlantic.com/education/archive/2015/06/the-rise-of-food-studies-programs/394538/.
"'Definition of Veganism.'" *The Vegan Society*, www.vegansociety.com/.
Food and Agriculture Organization of the United Nations. "Livestock Data." https://www.fao.org/. Accessed 15 February 2020.
Helstosky, Carol. "Food studies and animal rights." *Routledge International Handbook of Food Studies*, edited by K. Albala, New York, NY: Routledge, 2013, pp. 306–317.
Hertweck, Tom. "A Hunger for Words: Food Affects and Embodied Ideology." *Affective Ecocriticism*, 2018, pp. 133–154.
Nocella II, Anthony J., Sorenson, John, Socha, Kim, and Matsuoka, Atsuko. "The Emergence of Critical Animal Studies." *Defining Critical Animal Studies: An Intersectional Social Justice Approach for Liberation*, Peter Lang Inc., 2013, pp. xix–xxxv.
Twine, Richard. "Vegan Killjoys at the Table-Contesting Happiness and Negotiating Relationships with Food Practices." *Societies*, vol. 4, no. 4, 2014, pp. 623–639.
Wright, Laura. "The Dangerous Vegan: The Politics of Scholarship, Identity & Consumption in the Anthropocene." Talk, 10 October 2019a, Appalachian State University.
——. "Doing Vegan Studies: An Introduction." *Through a Vegan Studies Lens: Textual Ethics and Lived Activism*, edited by Wright, Laura, University of Nevada Press, 2019b, pp. vii–xxi.
—— editor. *Through a Vegan Studies Lens: Textual Ethics and Lived Activism*. University of Nevada Press, 2019c.
——. *The Vegan Studies Project: Food, Animals, and Gender in the Age of Terror*. University of Georgia Press, 2015.

Part 3
Vegan studies in the disciplines
Religion

Part 3

16
Veganism and Christianity

Allison Covey

Introduction

Lions, lambs, locusts, and even a leviathan—Christianity and its texts are full of animals, from the mundane to the mystical, and at its center, a Good Shepherd. Despite centuries of all creatures great and small depicted in Christian art and literature, it remains rare that Christianity directly addresses nonhuman animals as more than symbols and metaphors. The study of animals in Christianity is a relatively new academic pursuit but one that has experienced significant growth with the "animal turn" of the late 20th and early 21st century.[1] This chapter begins by outlining the theological challenges that have historically impeded the development of a Christian concern for animals and continue to act as stumbling blocks for the integration of veganism into Christian thought and practice. Having established the stakes of the debate, the chapter traces the involvement of Christians in the earliest animal welfare movements and eventually, the advent of Christian animal theology.

The *Imago Dei* and human uniqueness

In 1967, historian Lynn White, Jr. published an article entitled "The Historical Roots of Our Ecologic Crisis," in *Science*. White's article, the most cited, most re-published piece in the 140-year history of the journal, made the provocative claim that "especially in its Western form, Christianity is the most anthropocentric religion the world has seen" (1205). White credits the Creation stories of the Hebrew Bible's book of Genesis with encouraging in Christianity (through its roots in Judaism) a belief that the natural world had been created by God "explicitly for man's benefit and rule: no item in the physical creation had any purpose save to serve man's purposes" (1205). Not only do these stories, White argues, promote a divinely-ordained androcentrism, but they set up a dangerous dichotomy. On one side sits the natural world and, on the other side, sits God and the only species made in God's own image—humanity. The world of nature is imminent, material, and finite. Humanity, imaging God's own transcendence, immateriality, and infinity, is not a part of this world and indeed is meant to exploit it (1205).

What White points to is the Christian doctrine of the *Imago Dei*. In its most basic sense, this doctrine asserts that humanity was created in the image and likeness of God. The text of the first Creation story of Genesis reads:

> Then God said, "Let us make humankind in our image, according to our likeness; and let them have dominion over the fish of the sea, and over the birds of the air, and over the cattle, and over all the wild animals of the earth, and over every creeping thing that creeps upon the earth." (New Revised Standard Version, Gen. 1:26)

This explicit coupling of the *Imago Dei* with human dominion over the other animals may seem, at first glance, to preclude the possibility of an authentic Christian veganism. Certainly, White understood pericopae like this to offer carte blanche to humanity in a way that left little room for redemption. Biblical scholars and systematic theologians—both Jewish and Christian—however, have long debated the meaning of these texts. Fueling the theological debate is the fact that the Biblical texts offer no explanation of what it means to be made in the image and likeness of God. That this language is meant to establish the supremacy and dominance of the human species over all others is far from settled theology.

In response to White's article and following broader societal interest in the Western environmental movement of the late 20th century, Christian theologians from a variety of denominations recognized the need for a theological response to environmental degradation. Christian ecotheology was born, bringing with it a reinterpretation of Biblical dominion that understood the *Imago Dei* as a benevolent stewardship of the natural world. Ecotheologians expressly rejected previous notions of humanity as dominator and exploiter of the earth and advocated instead for a reading of Genesis that positioned humanity as divinely appointed caretakers of the planet. Pope Francis, leader of the world's largest Christian denomination, the Catholic Church, embraced this language of stewardship and care in his 2015 environmental encyclical *Laudato Si'*.

Understanding the *Imago Dei* as an obligation of stewardship has facilitated Christian concern for environmental issues, linking them to Biblical roots as deep as Adam and Eve. Notably, however, this newfound Christian enthusiasm for issues such as pollution and climate change has rarely included any explicit concern for other animal species. Moral theologian John Berkman has noted a complete absence of animals in a variety of contemporary textbooks and academic volumes on moral theology and Christian bioethics, including those specifically dedicated to environmental concerns (Berkman 15). Considering this absence, Berkman and systematician Celia Deane-Drummond together conclude that ethical concern for other animals demands "more immediate and radical change" on the part of humanity, change that some believe comes at the cost of humanitarian interests (4). Though the doctrine of the *Imago Dei* has been reframed in an ecologically promising way, the desire to preserve a Christian understanding of human uniqueness and a hierarchy of creatures remains.

Animals and the problem of pain

Christianity's insistence on a dualism of man and brute beast was influenced in no small part by the work of the 17th-century French philosopher René Descartes' *Discours de la Methode*. The human being, Descartes argued, is made up of both a corporeal animal spirit and an incorporeal immortal soul that interact with one another through the pineal gland. The animal spirit and the rational soul, he believed, were ontologically distinct from and independent of one another. It was theoretically possible then for the body and mind to exist separately (Descartes 55). A body without a mind, an animal spirit without rational soul, was how nonhuman animals exist, Descartes argued. He famously proposed that, if humans only had the right material, it would be possible to construct a *bête-machine* indistinguishable from a real animal. Descartes writes,

> that if there had been such machines, possessing the organs and outward form of a monkey or some other animal without reason, we should not have had any means of ascertaining that they were not of the same nature as those animals. (38)

Descartes is often identified as the arch-villain in the history of animal philosophy, credited with the advancement of what has become known as the Monstrous Thesis—that "animals are without feeling or awareness of any kind" (Smith 136, 140). Contemporary scholars of Descartes, however, dispute this view. Despite his mechanistic understanding of other animal species, Descartes nevertheless acknowledged their ability to experience subjective sensation through sense organs similar to those found in human beings (Hatfield 421). Though it is not rightly attributed to Descartes himself, the Monstrous Thesis does find roots in Cartesian thought. Some of Descartes' disciples, such as philosopher priests Nicolas-Joseph Poisson and Nicolas Malebranche, built upon Descartes' work, arguing that in addition to being incapable of rational thought, animals are also incapable of suffering and pain (French 27). This belief in animal automatism was used to justify the practice of vivisection, one held to be necessary for scientific advancement, among other invasive uses of animals (27).

The pseudo-Cartesian notion of the unfeeling *bête-machine* had a particular appeal to Christian audiences, not only because it affirmed a sense of human superiority and justified the anthropocentric use of other animals but also because it made good theological sense. According to Christian hamartiology, suffering and death were not an original part of God's plan for Creation but entered the world as a consequence of human sin. In the letter of Paul to the Romans, Paul writes that "sin came into the world through one man, and death came through sin, and so death spread to all because all have sinned" (Rom. 5:12). Sin, understood as a free and conscious offense against God, requires rational thought. Other animal species, being both without rational capacity and the divine gift of free will—given only to human beings and to angels—are incapable of personal sin by definition.

The claim that animals are sentient, for Christian thinkers like Poisson, undermined a core tenant of the Christian faith—belief in a just and merciful God. Following Poisson, Malebranche writes of nonhuman animals that

> being innocent, as everyone agrees and I assume, if they were capable of feeling, this would mean that under an infinitely just and omnipotent God, an innocent creature would suffer pain, which is a penalty and a punishment for some sin. (323–24)

Both Poisson and Malebranche cite the work of Augustine, defending the axiom "sub justo Deo, quisquam, nisi mereatur, miser esse on potest" (under a just God, nobody can be miserable unless he deserves it). Malebranche insists that, despite the way an animal appears to cry out in pain in response to a beating, "to hold that beasts feel, desire, and know, although their souls are corporeal, is to say what is inconceivable and what contains a manifest contradiction" (324). What is observed is not real suffering but merely instinct; to claim otherwise would be to deny the justice of God. This perspective—what philosopher Lloyd Strickland has dubbed the "argument from divine justice"—was popularized by Poisson and used to argue against the sentience and ensoulment of animals (Strickland 293).

As Strickland notes, the *bête-machine* debate had fizzled out by the early 18th century, in part due to what he calls the "argument from deception" (304). This counter to the argument from divine justice claims that if God has designed other animal species with bodies that only *appear* to be animated by souls, then God has deceived humanity. God's intentional deception of human beings would also be an undermining of divine justice. Parson-naturalist John Ray, rejecting the notion of God as a deceiver, noted that the belief of automatists like Poisson and Malebranche leads understandably to a strong teleological anthropocentrism. Ray writes,

> If this is true, it is doubtless why man elevates himself and takes pride in himself, and rightly boasts that this world was founded for his cause alone, for it does not seem that there would be any further use for it if men were wiped out or moved elsewhere. (30)

Christian support for the Monstrous Thesis, though perhaps puzzling to contemporary readers, contains within it a useful theodicy for those who would advocate for Christian veganism. In rejecting the possibility of animal suffering, thinkers like Malebranche and Poisson take for granted that undeserved suffering, even of nonhuman animals, is an affront to God's just ordering of Creation. Animals do not suffer because the suffering of innocent creatures is theologically unthinkable. Accepting, as most would in good faith do today, that the majority of animal species are, in fact, demonstrably sentient, might the concerned believer not still espouse that Georgian conclusion that their suffering is an affront to divine justice? The Victorian era brought with it a new Christian interest in precisely this question.

Christians and the antivivisection movement

As biomedical experimentation on animals became more widespread in 19th-century Britain, public apprehension about vivisection grew. When the passing of the 1876 Cruelty to Animals Act failed to fully satisfy the moral objections of lobbyists, the antivivisection movement was birthed in earnest (Li 142). Historian Chien-hui Li points out that this early movement for animal defense had a decidedly religious, specifically Christian character that is often overlooked (142). The early 19th century was a period of moral reform in which Christians took a new interest in social issues, framing them in theological terms. Among the concerns of reformers were the challenges of gambling, prostitution, prison reform, and cruelty to children and animals (143). Li argues that the majority of the antivivisection movement was comprised of Christians who saw their activism as informed by Christian morals. One Scottish group for the abolition of vivisection proclaimed that they "took their stand on religious grounds, believing that the Almighty had decreed that all His creatures should be treated with mercy and kindness" (144). Antivivisection activists saw animal experimentation as a cruel infliction of suffering on innocent creatures and, more specifically, as sinful.

Several years earlier, in 1847, the world's first Vegetarian Society was founded in the United Kingdom to promote the adoption of a diet free from meat. Members of the Bible Christian Church, known as Cowherdites after Reverend William Cowherd, were among the founding members of the society (Davis). Vegetarianism, for the Cowherdites, was a means of practicing the Christian virtue of temperance, inseparable from their teetotalism, sexual ethics, and general emphasis on asceticism (Gregory 21, 99). Historian James Gregory has argued that the vegetarian movement, from its origins, has had "an internal genealogical impulse." The Cowherdite vegetarians published essays purporting to trace the origins of their diet back through Christian history, making claims to its antiquity through the construction of a vegetarian canon of Biblical and classical sources (5).

As contemporary veganism has grown, so too has an interest in identifying resources for veganism within religious traditions, not unlike the genealogical efforts of the Victorian Cowherdites. Activists and authors alike have noted that Christians have, for centuries, practiced forms of fasting and dietary restriction that involve abstinence from animal products. Saints who followed ascetic diets are in particular held up as historical examples of Christian vegetarianism and veganism.[2] The temptation to harmonize veganism and Christianity no doubt has a dual motivation—the preexisting dedication of some vegans to both and the desire of activists to present veganism not as a mere complement to but rather an historical part of authentic Christianity. Demonstrating that veganism has always been a part of the Christian tradition offers a neat solution to faith-based objections to the adoption of a plant-based diet and moral concern for animals. Despite the obvious strategic advantages of being able to identify an historically rooted tradition of Christian veganism, one must proceed with caution.

A note on anachronism

An understanding of the practices and motivations of contemporary ethical veganism reveals important incongruities with the practices and motivations of fasting and abstinence in the Christian tradition. To ignore these incongruities would be to undermine the contextual credibility of the very sources the inquirer hopes to draw upon. Though many resources for Christian compassion for animals have been identified within the New Testament and other early Christian texts, one must recognize the novelty of ethical veganism as it is practiced today.

The term "vegan" was coined by British animal activists Donald and Dorothy Watson, co-founders of the Vegan Society, in 1944 ("History"). Initially, the term referred primarily to the dietary practice of abstaining from animal products; an expansion of the familiar notion of vegetarianism to include byproducts such as eggs and milk. Although the parameters of a vegan diet were well established, it was not until 1949 that the then vice president of the Vegan Society, Leslie J. Cross, encouraged the group to offer an official definition of "veganism" ("History"). Cross's definition has undergone numerous amendments and clarifications over the years but the core elements of veganism have remained stable through these refinements—veganism is a philosophy that actively seeks, insofar as it is practicable, an end to human exploitation of other animals.

Contemporary veganism then takes as its primary motivation an ethical concern for other animals. The chief interest of the ethical vegan is the avoidance and, ultimately, the eradication of animal oppression as far as is "possible and practicable" ("Definition"). Veganism is the conscious rejection of a teleological and ethical anthropocentrism that views other animal species as mere means to human ends. It encourages an expansion of the circle of moral concern and a deliberate challenging of the dominant culture, in large part through pressures applied to the market. Veganism might be thought of as a sustained boycott undergirded by a particular philosophical and ethical position on human identity vis-à-vis other animal beings.

This understanding of contemporary ethical veganism stands in contrast to historical practices of Christian abstinence and asceticism. Where Christian ecclesiastical practices of fasting and abstinence or individual fasts by particular saints resemble veganism, they are rarely, if ever, motivated by the same concerns as ethical veganism. Lenten prohibitions on the consumption of animal products in Catholicism and Eastern Orthodoxy assume the high value of these foods in the human diet. Abstaining from animal products during Lent is understood as a sacrifice, a penance endured by the human sinner as a means of atonement for wrongdoing. It represents also a spiritual discipline, meant to bring the faithful into solidarity with the poor and vulnerable

(NCCB). A plant-based diet is viewed therefore as a mortification of the body, a deprivation that calls to mind the anguish of both the spiritually and financially impoverished.

Tales of Christian saints subsisting on meat-free diets or even on the Eucharist alone are likewise poor parallels for contemporary ethical veganism. The motivation behind these fasts is not the liberation of animals from temporal suffering but the mortification of the human soul in preparation for its encounter with God. The ascetic practice of these saints is an expression of their desire for transcendence of the natural world rather than a show of solidarity with the suffering of animals within it.

The New Testament and vegan anachronism

Another common attempt to link veganism to Christianity, championed by activist organizations such as People for the Ethical Treatment of Animals, claims that Jesus belonged to a first-century Jewish sect called the Essenes (Green). Though the New Testament only makes mention of the dominant Jewish groups of the day—the Pharisees and the Sadducees—classical Jewish historian Josephus notes that the Essenes numbered in the thousands and existed in communities throughout Roman Judea (Mason 269). Comparatively little is known about the Essenes, but scholarly interest in the sect was piqued in the 1940s by the discovery of the Dead Sea Scrolls in the caves of Qumran. The records of Josephus and Jewish philosopher Philo suggest that, unlike the larger two Jewish groups, the Essenes were highly sectarian, rejecting the authority of the Pharisees and Sadducees and refusing participation in Temple life out of concern for purity (Burns 261). The Essenes espoused a strongly dualist, apocalyptic theology, believing in the immanence of divine warfare that would wipe out their enemies (Ehrman 77).

Those who argue that Jesus was an Essene argue that Josephus has written that the Essenes followed a Pythagorean way of life and that a Pythagorean lifestyle necessarily involved vegetarianism.[3] Reading the Gospel of Matthew, they note that Jesus' cousin, John the Baptist, was said to have eaten a diet of locusts and wild honey (Mt. 3:4). This diet, they argue, sounds similar to vegetarianism so John the Baptist must have been an Essene. Each of the three Synoptic Gospels records the baptism of Jesus by John the Baptist. They conclude that if John the Baptist was an Essene, then Jesus' baptism can be understood as a baptism into the Essene sect. Instances in the New Testament in which Jesus and the Apostles are said to fish or to consume meat are mistranslations or even intentional redactions, they argue (Rosen 28). This theory, despite its popularity in a minority of activist circles, has been thoroughly discredited by Biblical scholars, classicists, and archeologists alike.

Historian of Christian origins and Second Temple Judaism Joan E. Taylor, an expert in the Dead Sea Scrolls, has pointed out that there is no evidence from the classical sources that the Essenes were vegetarian. Archeologists have unearthed charred animal bones at Essene settlements including Qumran, pointing to the regular use of animal flesh as food in these communities (16). One does not need to be a religionist, however, to note that dining on locusts and wearing camel hair and leather does not point to John the Baptist having been a vegetarian let alone a vegan by today's definitions (Mt 3:4). New Testament scholar and animal theologian Richard Alan Young echoes scholarly consensus that Jesus's observance of Judaism, as described in the New Testament, is significantly dissimilar to what is known about the Essenes. Jesus routinely rejected Jewish purity laws by practicing table fellowship with outcast tax collectors and sinners and by and touching lepers (7). He preached in the Temple and His followers took His message to the Gentiles, a group outside even the bounds of the existing Jewish covenant. These historically credible characteristics do not point to Jesus having been a member of an insular, puritanical, apocalyptic sect that rejected Temple rituals let alone to His having been an ethical vegan.

The suggestion that the New Testament has been mistranslated or purposely redacted to remove mention of Jesus's vegetarianism has been similarly discredited by scholars. It is well documented that the early Church actively worked to condemn what it considered heterodoxy. The Johannine epistles, for example, warn of the threat of Gnostisicm, painting its adherents as antichrists and deceivers (1 Jn 2:18–26). Throughout the second century, the nascent Church issued fervent condemnations of heresies such as Arianism and Docetism and formulated creeds to express orthodox belief. Despite the concerted effort of figures such as Athanasius of Alexandria to ban and destroy heterodox texts, numerous copies of Gnostic manuscripts survive from antiquity, giving scholars a window into the competing theologies of the era. It is difficult to imagine that, despite such well-documented offensive maneuvers against other rejected views, the Church was simultaneously destroying evidence of early Christian veganism by redacting its manuscripts in complete silence. Neither proclamations against Christian veganism nor declarations mandating Christian meat eating were penned and no manuscripts containing alternate, pro-vegan versions of the New Testament texts have ever been discovered.

A biblical case for Christian veganism

Rather than seeking evidence for the veganism of Jesus himself in the New Testament, animal theologians look back to the book of Genesis to build a case for Christian veganism. The Priestly Creation story of Genesis 1 depicts God proclaiming to Adam and Eve, "See, I have given you every plant yielding seed that is upon the face of all the earth, and every tree with seed in its fruit; you shall have them for food." With death yet to enter the world through human sin, the prescribed diet of the Garden of Eden is plant-based. It is not until after the Flood, in Genesis 9:3, that God declares, "Every moving thing that lives shall be food for you; and just as I gave you the green plants, I give you everything." It is worth noting, however, that this relaxing of dietary standards is immediately followed by God's entering into the Noahic covenant with Noah, Noah's descendants, "and with every living creature that is with you, the birds, the domestic animals, and every animal of the earth with you, as many as came out of the ark" (Gn 9:10). Despite this later permission to consume animals, one might argue that it is the earlier, prelapsarian state of original peace in Eden to which Christians aspire and that God originally intended.

This vegan-friendly hermeneutic has a certain appeal both for the way it depicts nonviolence as the intended order of Creation and for its faithful reading of Scripture. There is neither need to alter existing theology nor to suspect a conspiracy for which there is no evidence; one needs only to return to the beginning. In the Hebrew Bible, Isaiah 11 is read through this same hermeneutic as an eschatological promise of the restoration of original peace:

> The nursing child shall play over the hole of the asp, and the weaned child shall put its hand on the adder's den. They will not hurt or destroy on all my holy mountain for the earth will be full of the knowledge of the Lord as the waters cover the sea. (Is 11:9)

Christian theologians advocating for animal compassion seek not to reinterpret or revise Christian history in a way that reads contemporary ethical veganism back into the 2000 year history of the faith. Instead, they aim to retrieve resources from within the tradition that can be used today to justify ethical veganism in light of contemporary systems of animal use and abuse. It is not a problem for Christian animal ethics that Christ Himself did not practice ethical veganism in the same way that it is not a problem for contemporary theologians that He did not preach directly on slavery and colonialism, the rights of women, or the dignity of LGBTQ persons. One of the primary contentions of the Christian faith is that the Bible is a living document, available for synchronic readings that speak to contemporary problems despite the distance of centuries between authors and readers.

Christian animal theology

The birth of the contemporary animal rights movement is often credited to the work of philosophers Peter Singer and Tom Regan. Singer's *Animal Liberation* (1975) and Regan's *The Case for Animal Rights* (1983) have prompted countless responses and provided valuable intellectual groundwork for the concept of animal rights. During this same era, British theologian Andrew Linzey published *Animal Rights: A Christian Perspective* (1976), offering a Christian argument for the moral consideration of animals and the practice of vegetarianism. Linzey condemned anthropocentric readings of humanity's dominion and argued that an instrumentalist use of other animals was contrary to Christianity's intended focus on God. Theocentrism, not anthropocentrism, ought to orient the Christian. Despite the timing of these major publications, Linzey has labored throughout his career to distinguish his work from that of secular animal rights theorists, particularly Singer and Regan. He is not, he insists, merely dressing up animal rights philosophy in Christian garments but offering his own, very different approach to the moral worth of other creatures ("Divine Worth" 120).

Linzey's 1994 monograph *Animal Theology* represents a pioneering theological argument for animal rights and one of the first attacks on Christian anthropocentrism from within the theological community. In it, Linzey argues for serious theological consideration of nonhuman animals as religious subjects, not religious objects designed to be used by humanity on its singular quest toward God. Rather than rejecting or re-writing the Christian tradition, as suggested by White, Linzey holds that Christian teachings on the *Imago Dei* and human dominion need not be at odds with a theological recognition of the goodness of other animal species. Because animals have been created by God and are valued by God, their goodness is theocentric rather than anthropocentric (*Animal Theology* 95). Linzey cautions however that "the Biblical principle that all life has value is not to hold that all being has the same value or to hold that there are not morally relevant distinctions between one kind of being and another" (23).

In keeping with these distinctions, Linzey rejects Singer's equality-based approach to animal rights. Equality paradigms do not, Linzey argues, go far enough to establish the unique moral obligations of humanity with regard to other creatures (39). Linzey sees in the Christian doctrine of the *Imago Dei* resources for a rejection of anthropocentrism and the recognition of human moral duties toward animals. He proposes that humanity's unique status in Creation establishes not a hierarchy of privilege but a set of moral obligations that require of humanity a kind of self-costly service to other species. To insist that humanity's interests always come first, he contends, is an idolatrous raising of human beings to a status reserved only for God (40). "Our special value in creation consists in being of special value to others," Linzey writes (33). Christianity is a religion in which the weak are afforded priority and their liberation from both earthly and eternal suffering becomes the central concern of the strong.

While Linzey's work circulated among Christian theologians, interest in nonhuman animals was growing in other religious traditions and scholarly circles as well. Recognizing a set of organizing questions unique to the study of animals and religion, ecofeminist ethicist Marti Kheel and religionist Anwar Ghazzala first proposed a formal Animals and Religion consultation at the American Academy of Religion (AAR) in 2001. Their proposal was initially rejected but a new proposal was submitted the following year leading to the creation of the formal Animals and Religion consultation at the AAR in 2003, co-chaired by religionists Paul Waldau and Laura Hobgood-Oster (Van Horn 236). For the first time, the American Academy of Religion's annual meeting included panels devoted to animal questions arising within the fields of Religious Studies and Theology. This recognition of animals and religion as an academic research area unto itself, separate from the study of religion and ecology, marked a milestone in scholarly acceptance of the field.

In 2013, theologian David Clough, an active member of the AAR's Animals & Religion group, published the first portion of a two-volume theological work on animals. Clough's efforts have been hailed as "the most significant Christian theological and ethical treatment of animals in the history of Christian ethics as an academic discipline" ("On Animals"). Intending to write a manuscript on Christian animal ethics, Clough notes that

> the doctrinal foundations for such a project were radically underdetermined. If we are not sure where other animals belong in God's work of creation, reconciliation and redemption, it seems to me, we can make little headway with a plausible account of what our responsibilities might be in relation to them. (*On Animals: Volume I* x)

Instead, Clough found it necessary to begin with a volume on systematic theology to lay the foundation for his second volume on Christian ethics, published in 2018.

On Animals, like Clough's earlier work on the topic, argues that Christian concern for animals does not necessitate the reconceptualization of God or significant revisions to existing theology. This is due, at least in part, to the fact that very little has been said that would need to be undone. Clough responds as much to lacunae in theology as to anthropocentric doctrine. Where animals do appear in Christian theology, Clough notes that they tend to serve as devices by which human authors can discuss human creatureliness. Theologians have used other animals "to prop up constructions of the human and are usually not discussing 'animals' even when they appear to be doing so" ("Angels" 68). Like Linzey, Clough argues against the temptation among some animal advocates to deny humanity a uniqueness that is not merely arbitrary. Human uniqueness, he suggests, lies in its imaging God to the world (*On Animals: Volume I* 101). This uniqueness is not, however, a denial of the uniqueness of other animal species nor evidence of the superiority of humanity ("On Thinking" 765–766).

Conclusion

Today's animal theology recognizes ethical veganism as a contemporary contribution to both philosophy and theology. It is a response to the systemic use and abuse of nonhuman animals in systems of agribusiness, scientific research, and entertainment that began to develop with the dawning of modernity. That Jesus, His Apostles, and the Christian saints of history were not vegans says little about the way Christians ought to respond to the destruction of anthropocentrism in the 21st century. Instead, it is the compassionate concern of Christ for the poor and vulnerable and His self-costly sacrifice for the sake of others that inspire Christian veganism. It is an attempt to bring about God's desire for peace, on earth as it is in Heaven. An approach to Christianity and veganism that respects the rich intellectual traditions of Theology and Religious Studies can only help to further the cause.

Notes

1 See Weil, especially Chapter 1, for an overview of the animal turn.
2 See Roberts for an example of this trend.
3 See Vaclavik for an example.

Works cited

Berkman, John. "From Theological Speciesism to a Theological Ethology: Where Catholic Moral Theology Needs to Go." *Journal of Moral Theology*, vol. 3, no. 2, 2014, pp. 11–34.
Berkman, John and Celia Deane-Drummond. "Introduction: Catholic Moral Theology and the Moral Status of Non-Human Animals." *Journal of Moral Theology*, vol. 3, no. 2, 2014, pp. 1–10.
Burns, Joshua Ezra. "Essene Sectarianism and Social Differentiation in Judaea After 70 C.E." *The Harvard Theological Review*, vol. 99, no. 3, 2006, pp. 247–274.
Clough, David. "Angels, Beasts, Machines, and Men: Configuring the Human and Non-human in Judeo-Christian Tradition." *Eating and Believing: Interdisciplinary Perspectives on Vegetarianism and Theology*, edited by Rachel Muers and David Grummett, T&T Clark, 2008, pp. 60–72.
———. *On Animals: Volume I, Systematic Theology*. Bloomsbury T&T Clark, 2013.
———. *On Animals: Volume II, Theological Ethics*. Bloomsbury T&T Clark, 2018.
———.. "On Thinking Theologically About Animals: A Response." *Zygon*, vol. 49, no. 3, 2014, pp. 765–766.
Davis, John. "Early History of the Vegetarian Society." *Vegetarian Society*, August 2011, www.vegsoc.org/about-us/history-of-the-vegetarian-society-early-history. Accessed March 22 2020.
"Definition of Veganism." *The Vegan Society*, www.vegansociety.com/go-vegan/definition-veganism. Accessed 22 March 2020.
Descartes, René. *Discourse on Method and Meditations*. Translated by Elizabeth S. Haldane and G.R.T. Ross, Mineola, Dover Publications, Inc., 2003.
———. *Meditations on First Philosophy with Selections from the Objections and Replies*. Translated by Michael Moriarty, Oxford University Press, 2008.
Ehrman, Bart. *The New Testament: A Historical Introduction to the Early Christian Writings*. 7th edition, Oxford University Press, 2020.
Francis. "Laudato Si'" *The Holy See*, June 2015, www.vatican.va/content/francesco/en/encyclicals/documents/papa-francesco_20150524_enciclica-laudato-si.html.
French, William C. "Beast-Machines and the Technocratic Reduction of Life." *Good News for Animals? Christian Approaches to Animal Well-Being*, edited by Charles Pinches and Jay B. McDaniel, Orbis Books, 1993, pp. 24–43.
Green, Joshua. "Was Jesus a Vegetarian?" *Slate*, October 13, 2000, slate.com/news-and-politics/2000/10/was-jesus-a-vegetarian.html. Accessed March 18 2020.
Gregory, James. *Of Victorians and Vegetarians: The Vegetarian Movement in Nineteenth-Century Britain*. Tauris Academic Studies, 2007.
Hatfield, Gary. "Animals." *A Companion to Descartes*, edited by Janet Broughton and John Carriero, Wiley-Blackwell, 2011, pp. 404–425.
"History." *The Vegan Society*, www.vegansociety.com/go-vegan/definition-veganism. Accessed 22 March 2020.
Li, Chien-hui. "Mobilizing Christianity in the Antivivisection Movement in Victorian Britain." *Journal of Animal Ethics*, vol. 2, no. 2, 2012, pp. 141–161.
Linzey, Andrew. *Animal Rights: A Christian Perspective*, London, SCM Press, 1976.
———. *Animal Theology*. Chicago, University of Illinois Press, 1995.
———. "The Divine Worth of Other Creatures: A Response to Reviews of *Animal Theology*." *Review and Expositor*, vol. 102, 2005, pp. 111–124.
Malebranche, Nicolas. *The Search After Truth*. Translated by Thomas M. Lennon and Paul J. Olscamp, Ohio State University Press, 1980.
Mason, Steve. *Josephus, Judea, and Christian Origins: Methods and Categories*. Ada, Baker Academic, 2008.
McLaughlin, Ryan Patrick. "A Meatless Dominion: Genesis 1 and the Ideal of Vegetarianism." *Biblical Theology Bulletin*, vol. 47, no. 3, 2017, pp. 144–154.
National Conference of Catholic Bishops. "Pastoral Statement on Penance and Abstinence." *United States Conference of Catholic Bishops*, November 18, 1966, www.usccb.org/prayer-and-worship/liturgical-year/lent/us-bishops-pastoral-statement-on-penance-and-abstinence.cfm. Accessed March 20 2020.

"On Animals Volume II: Theological Ethics." *Bloomsbury*, www.bloomsbury.com/us/on-animals-9780567660862. Accessed 20 March 2020.

Regan, Tom. *The Case for Animal Rights*. University of California Press, 2004.

Roberts, Holly H. *Christian Vegetarian Saints*. Anjeli Press, 2004.

Rosen, Steven. *Diet for Transcendence: Vegetarianism and the World Religions*. Torchlight Publishing, 1997.

Singer, Peter. *Animal Liberation: The Definitive Classic of the Animal Movement*. Harper Perennial Modern Classics, 2009.

Smith, Norman Kemp. *New Studies in the Philosophy of Descartes*. Macmillan, 1952.

Strickland, Lloyd. "God's Creatures? Divine Nature and the Status of Animals in the Early Modern Beast-Machine Controversy." *International Journal of Philosophy and Theology*, vol. 75, no. 4, pp. 291–309.

Taylor, Bron, et al. "Lynn White and the Greening of Religion Hypothesis." *Conservation Biology*, vol. 30, no. 5, 2016, pp. 1000–1009.

Taylor, Joan E. *The Essenes, the Scrolls, and the Dead Sea*. Oxford University Press, 2012.

Vaclavik, Charles P. *The Vegetarianism of Jesus Christ: The Pacifism, Communalism and Vegetarianism of Primitive Christianity*. Kaweah Pub Co, 1989.

Van Horn, Gavin. "The Buzzing, Breathing, Clicking, Clacking, Biting, Stinging, Chirping, Howling Landscape of Religious Studies." *Inherited Land: The Changing Grounds of Religion and Ecology*, edited by Whitney A. Bauman, et al., Pickwick Publications, 2011, pp. 230–250.

Weil, Kari. *Thinking Animals: Why Animal Studies Now?* Columbia University Press, 2012.

White, Lynn, Jr. "The Historical Roots of Our Ecologic Crisis." *Science*, vol. 155, no. 3767, 1967, pp. 1203–1207.

Young, Richard Alan. *Is God a Vegetarian? Christianity, Vegetarianism, and Animal Rights*. Open Court, 1998.

17
Yes, but is it Kosher?
Varying religio-cultural perspectives on Judaism and Veganism

Barry L. Stiefel

"Kashrut"[1] is the set of Jewish religious dietary laws on what is fit (kosher) or unfit (treif) to eat. Until recent decades, kashrut was primarily concerned with the biblical prohibition of certain animal species (pork, shellfish, fish without scales, insects) and the proscribed separation of permitted meats and dairy products that are not to be eaten together (so no cheeseburgers, though cheese and hamburgers can be kosher when not eaten together). Based on these restrictions one might assume that veganism—an entirely plant-based diet—is kosher since it is devoid of animal products. As indicated in a report by *The Guardian* from 17 March 2018, a Jewish public consensus investigation found that "Vegan food is, by most accounts, naturally kosher so is seen as a safe food choice for many Jews." Moreover, "In September [2017], more than 70 rabbis from around the world signed a declaration urging Jews to choose veganism" (Holmes). But rabbis and Jewish communities are not entirely in agreement. According to some very respected Orthodox rabbis "a vegan restaurant can be just as complex as a meat or dairy restaurant when it comes to kashrus" (Teichman).

How can there be such varying perspectives on what is permissible under Jewish dietary rules related to veganism? Since Judaism has the religio-cultural dietary tradition of kashrut (the practice of kosher), what can vegan studies and Jewish Studies learn from one another about cultural perspectives of dietary practices, consumer goods pertaining to animals, and environmental ethics based on their respective values? The intersection with Jewish Studies is an interesting one, for Jewish Studies was established in the early 19th century to critically question the accepted portrayal of Judaism in Western society (Heschel 101–115), even though Jewish ethics have been greatly influenced by European thought due to the long sojourn of Jews in the West. By learning about those who are different from ourselves can we understand more about who we are and what it means to consume or not to consume certain things? Therefore, this chapter seeks to use a vegan studies approach to explore dietary permissibility within Judaism. Comparison studies are an important approach to reflect upon since kashrut and veganism are evolving constructs that adapt to changes in the way food is produced as well as the politics, economics, and social values associated with it (LeVasseur 154). After all, we are what we eat, both physically and intangibly.

The intersection of Jewish studies and vegan studies: literature review

Eastern European Jewish vegetarianism began out of necessity due to impoverished conditions during the Middle Ages and Early Modern period when kosher meat was sometimes unattainable. Not until the twentieth century did Jewish vegetarianism become political, most significantly as a form of protest when anti-Semitic régimes in Tsarist Russia, the Second Polish Republic, and Nazi Germany outlawed kosher meat (Underwood 25–27). Contemporary Jewish interest in plant-based eating emerged in the 1980s, most notably with the publication of *Vegetarianism and the Jewish Tradition* by Louis A. Berman, which established the first academic Jewish perspective on the practicality, health, moral principles, and religious references of plant-based diets. In 2001, Richard H. Schwartz authored *Judaism and Vegetarianism*, which explored how Jewish ethics in combination with vegetarian living provides guidance for the humane care for animals, human health, and environmental responsibility. Most recently, in 2019, Jacob Ari Labendz and Shmuly Yanklowitz co-edited *Jewish Vegetarianism and Veganism*, asserting that "veganism is a significant, complex, and meaningful development in the history of Jewish culture, religion, and practice" (xiii). Labendz also observes that "veganism resembles *kashrut*. That is why it works so well as an embodied cultural technology for crafting transcendent Jewish identities" (298).

What is missing from the Jewish Studies interest in vegetarianism and veganism is the scholarship coming out of vegan studies that emphasizes ethical veganism. Examples include Laura Wright's *The Vegan Studies Project: Food, Animals, and Gender in the Age of Terror* and *Through a Vegan Studies Lens: Textual Ethics and Lived Activism*; as well as earlier works from Animal Studies (such as *The Sexual Politics of Meat* by Carol J. Adams) regarding animal rights, social justice, public health, and environmental conservation. Wright describes veganism as a dietary and life choice, a form of identity for people who choose to abstain from the exploitative consumption and use of animals and animal products, such as food and clothing (*The Vegan Studies Project* 1). Kashrut is also a dietary and life choice and is sometimes part of Jewish identity. Echoing previous scholarship, Wright describes that Veganism is conceptualized by some as an identity orientation, and research encountered the term "Jewish Vegan" (Labendz and Yanklowitz ix) being used in a similar way to "Jewish American," "Jewish LGBTQ+," or "Jewish Feminist;" so the concept resonates among Jews too. This chapter responds to Wright's call for more "cultural studies text[s] that examines the social and cultural discourses that imagine the vegan body and vegan identity" (*The Vegan Studies Project* 23). Jews and Judaism are an intriguing instance to compare with vegans and veganism, because Wright identifies vegans as living "perpetually on the extreme margins of society" which "is to invite questions, criticisms, alienation, suspicion, and misunderstanding" (*The Vegan Studies Project* 32). This observation is equally applicable to Jews when one considers the last two thousand years of their history and anti-Semitism.

The kosher diet

About 22 percent of American Jews maintain a kosher diet (Weiss). Labendz and Yanklowitz also identify a demographic of Jews who also identify as vegan, but the reasons for doing so differ. Not all vegan Jews observe the religious lifestyle of kashrut. They include secular Jews who may only identify with the Jewish people culturally or ancestrally; as well as adherents of some movements within Judaism, such as Reform and Humanistic, that have officially abandoned kashrut as a practice. Veganism, on the other hand, is not always religiously or culturally specific. While there are some faiths, such as Buddhism, Hinduism, and Seventh Day Adventism that have many adherents that are vegan or vegetarian, vegans do not necessarily have to subscribe to one of these faiths. Thus, veganism can transcend religious, cultural, and ethnic boundaries. At the same time, in places like Canada and the United Kingdom, veganism is a protected category akin to religion. This study will focus on the overlap of Jews who simultaneously adopt both kosher and vegan diets, lifestyles, and philosophies where each is of equal importance to that person.

Kashrut begins in the Hebrew Bible with the first dietary prohibition given to Noah after the flood, where he and his descendants (the one kashrut regulation that applies to non-Jews) are ordered by God not to eat flesh torn from a living animal (Genesis 9:4). Before this admonition, the Jewish Biblical tradition suggests that the world was vegan, for both people and animals. Additional regulations are given in Leviticus and later books, which are expounded upon in great detail by the rabbis in the Talmud from the third through sixth centuries C.E., and which continue to be debated. Kashrut is more complex than simply abstaining from a particular thing, such as animals and animal products as is the case with veganism. To summarize, kosher food includes all plants and fungi, mammals that have a cleft hoof and chew their cud, fish that have fins and scales, specifically mentioned birds (chicken, geese, duck, quail, etc.), specifically mentioned locusts (the Desert Locust), and honey. However, simply killing an animal identified as kosher does not make its meat kosher. There are decreed ways the animal must be treated before, during, and after slaughter in order for it to be morally and ethically kosher. These include a relatively high state of health before death, no duress approaching the moment of slaughter, and draining the blood after death. Blood even from kosher-slaughtered animals is prohibited for consumption because the blood is where it is believed that the intangible soul resides. Another restriction is that meat and dairy must never be cooked or consumed together, with flesh representing death and milk representing life. From a religious perspective, kashrut is done because it was mandated by God as an aspect of how to live a proper spiritual life regarding diet. To willingly eat treif is to cause oneself to become spiritually impure (Forst 45).

These guidelines reveal the religion-based standard for the treatment of animals within kashrut observance. Food that is neither flesh nor milk based, such as plants and fungi, is neutral in these respects, and the term used is "parve." However, while all vegan food is parve, there are also parve food items that come from animals, including fish (which is considered a separate kind of animal from mammals and birds), eggs, honey, and the permitted locusts. There are also sub-traditions to kashrut, such as those nuanced traditions found between Ashkenazi and Sephardi Jews. Regarding edible plants and fungi, the only item where there are kashrut restrictions is the grape and associated products, such as juice, wine, vinegar, and liquor (Stiefel 116–17). The reasons for these specifications are that grape juice and wine are sacred to Jewish ritual, and that in the ancient Levant some non-Jewish peoples used wine for idol worship. Therefore, the use of non-Jewish grape juice and wine is considered inappropriate by the rabbis.

Are vegan restaurants and certified foods kosher?

Based on this foundational knowledge of kashrut will be explored the complexities of the intersection between kashrut and veganism. Richard Rabkin, Managing Director for the very well-respected Kashruth Council of Canada (COR), posed the question, "can kosher consumers rely on vegan or vegetarian certification, for example?" (36–39). His concerns about vegan restaurants and food products are as follows:

1. Vegan restaurants do not always sufficiently clean and inspect their produce for insects.
2. Jewish involvement is required in the cooking of food, a term called Bishul Yisroel (does not apply to raw foods).

3. Cooking and serving equipment must not have previously come into contact with non-kosher food, or feature meat-dairy cross contamination.
4. If the vegan establishment is owned by someone who is Jewish, the facility and proprietor must also adhere to the additional kashrut restrictions during the Passover holiday. The establishment exclusively owned by a Jewish person must also be closed on the Sabbath and major religious holidays.

Based on a survey of other kashrut certifying agencies, Rabkin's opinion constitutes the majority. However, what is the minority opinion of rabbinic authorities, especially those that are specialists on kashrut? Regarding insect inspection, Rabbi Haim Ovadia, who received his semicha (training) from Israel's Chief Sephardic Rabbi (Mordechai Eliyahu, term 1983–1993) has stated that "when preparing foods one should only look for what is easily seen to the naked eye" (Ovadia "Koshering"), a practice that vegan restaurants would also observe in their choice to refrain from eating bugs.

Jewish involvement in cooking (Bishul Yisroel) may seem strange or unusual for those not familiar with kashrut, but is far more common and simple than many would assume. For example, all kosher-certified cooked foods have had at least one Jewish person involved in their preparation at some point in their creation. Within industrial and commercial food processing this involvement might entail simply flipping a machine switch that begins manufacturing thousands of units for any particular product, thus achieving Bishul Yisroel can be relatively easy. Notably, Bishul Yisroel is not mentioned anywhere in the Hebrew Bible. The prohibition of eating food cooked by non-Jews (called Bishul Akum) was codified in the Talmud. The reason for this prohibition was to prevent the development of close personal relationships between Jews and non-Jews that could lead to their intermarrying, as Judaism traditionally practices endogamy (Forst 44).

According to Rabbi Ovadia, foods served at a vegan restaurant by a non-Jewish chef are kosher because this person is not looking to marry all of their Jewish customers. Therefore, Bishul Akum does not apply. By extension, those who work at industrial or commercial food processing facilities also never knowingly meet the consumers of the products they make. However, within a more private setting, such as a non-Jewish vegan cook inviting their vegan Jewish friends over for a meal for the purpose of having a romantic relationship constitutes a Bishul Akum problem. Even the most lenient rabbi would object because in Judaism only endogamy is practiced. Conversion does exist but Judaism is not a religion that seeks converts.

In a parallel manner to how food preparation must be mindful of avoiding cross contaminating food allergens, such as peanuts, tree nuts, or gluten, so too must treif foods, or even kosher meat and dairy items, not be prepared or served on the same equipment or dishes. There is a re-kashering sanitation process so that equipment once used for treif, or kosher meat, or kosher dairy can be made "neutral," or parve, again. Where we see the status of cooking equipment play out further in the kosher consumer world is when we see next to a kosher symbol on a consumer product—called a hechsher—the initials "D.E.", an abbreviation for dairy equipment. In these D.E. instances, from a kashrut perspective, even if the food ingredients are vegan (parve) they may not be used or mixed with another dish or ingredients that are "M.E." (meat equipment), even if here everything is also vegan. An example is when plant-based milk products made from oat, soy, hemp, or various nuts with a kosher D.E. demarcation on the container cannot be added to a vegan entrée made in a pot that once cooked meat, because the plant-based milk was once on equipment that had mammal-based dairy. Kashrut sterilization is different from sanitation sterilization, so the product may be perfectly fine hygienically or allergically for non-kosher vegan purposes. The rabbis have prescribed how cooking and serving equipment can be re-kashered, but the details of this are tangential because the processes vary according to materials, size, shape, and composition. The issue of cooking equipment classification (meat vs. dairy vs. parve) can be problematic for vegan restaurants, commercial, and industrial food processing facilities that acquire used equipment instead of new. The concern is that the flavor (and by extension residue) of non-Kosher food has been absorbed into the equipment, thus making any kosher food cooked on the equipment treif. From a kashrut perspective, the ideal strategy is for the proprietor to work with a local rabbi experienced in kashrut supervision in order to have the establishment certified kosher. However, this is not a one-time interaction but a continued relationship entailing inspection and oversight. This course of action would also address the previous concern of Bishul Yisroel.

Kashrut industry: food for thought in the emerging vegan industry

Worldwide there are over 1,400 kosher symbols (hechshers) and supervising agencies (Fishbane "Directory"), with most concentrated in North America and Israel, and to a lesser extent in Europe, Latin America, Australia, and Africa, reflecting the distribution of world Jewry. Most of the supervising agencies are small, though a handful are large, such as the Orthodox Union (or O-U for short) that oversees more than 1,000,000 products from 8,500 food preparing facilities across the globe. According to the *Times of Israel*, less than two percent of the American population is Jewish (and even fewer observe kashrut), yet 41 percent of American food products are certified kosher, creating a growing $12.5 billion industry (Lempel). The big business of kosher-supervising today came about due to two key events during the twentieth century. The first was in 1915 when New York state passed the country's first Kosher Food Law prohibiting commercial establishments passing off non-kosher food as kosher. The other was with the immigration of Holocaust survivors to North America, who brought with them stricter kashrut standards, and consequently increased the market demand for kosher certified foods (OK Kosher Certification). Prior to this time, restaurants, bakeries, and other eateries only had the endorsement of their local rabbi. There were no big kosher supervising groups because food establishments were simply trusted by their customers. Israel as well as other countries with large Jewish populations also frequently have kosher consumer laws to try to prevent fraud.

Based on this information about kashrut, there are experiences that can be learned by the emerging vegan certification sector. Mentioned on more than one occasion was Rabbi Ovadia's minority opinion on kashrut, which comes from both a sincere and qualified perspective. If his position was more universally applied, it would both cause a great financial loss to and undermine the authority of some rabbis who specialize in kashrut, especially those employed by the larger supervision agencies. These rabbis—as well as their inspection assistants, called mashgiach—can only charge a fee if an establishment or facility is under their supervision, and so we begin to see a structural conflict of interest that results in the over $12.5 billion industry in the United States where less than two percent of American consumers observe kashrut. The large supervising agencies have also lost trust within the politics of the kashrut world, as they declare that only their supervision is reliable (TOI Staff). Organizations such as the Chicago Rabbinical Council have created directories of recommended and non-recommended agencies (Fishbane "Understanding"). This situation is challenging when we consider that beyond the specific texts defining kashrut in the Hebrew Bible and Talmud, kashrut is largely subjective (Heilman). This subjectivity contrasts with the fees of a local pulpit rabbi often being lower since their primary employment is with a synagogue, so they are less likely to be endorsed by a large group like the Chicago Rabbinical Council.

Nowhere within the Hebrew Bible or the Talmud is it declared that kashrut of what is plant-based food must be overseen by a third party. Therefore, does (or should) vegan food and other products need third-party certification, and if so, to what extent? This question is significant due to the prolific emergence of vegan-certifying groups as well as whether vegan self-certification is acceptable or problematic in terms of conflict of interest. Within kashrut self-certification occurs on occasion, but is not the accepted standard practice. In Israel there has emerged an "alternative kashrut" initiative of private supervision, called Hashgacha Pratit, without the rabbinate, which many Israelis "view as a corrupt and inefficient bureaucracy" (TOI Staff). In order to remain compliant with Israel's strict laws prohibiting kashrut fraud, similar to New York's kosher laws, a business can only claim that it obtains its ingredients from kosher sources and that meat and dairy do not mix. The beginning for Hashgacha Pratit in Israel started at vegetarian and vegan restaurants because there were no meat products to complicate the kitchens. In Israel, the overlap between kashrut and veganism is significant when we consider that "Israel is arguably the vegan capital of the world, with more vegans per capita than any other country" (Hendelman), more so than countries with large Hindu and Buddhist populations where vegetarianism is widespread (Figure 17.1).[2]

Kashrut supervision is very patriarchal. The Conservative movement of Judaism does accept women as Rabbi (it is more liberal despite its name), but the majority who live a kosher lifestyle are Orthodox, which is in fact the most conservative form of Judaism. In more progressive circles of orthodoxy, the position of Rabbanit for ordained women has emerged, sometimes called Rabba or Maharat since "Rabbi" is a masculine word in Hebrew. But because Rabbanit positions are fringe from centrist patriarchal Orthodox practice, they are not widely employed in the kashrut sector. Nor do many of the major kashrut agencies employ women in supervisorial mashgichot (female for mashgiach) positions. Starting in 2009, the major kashrut agency Star-K began holding kashrus training seminars specifically for women and is open about employing them (Pensak). While still a minority, mashgichot are more commonly found at smaller, more local kashrut agencies (Feder; Yanover). Women are also involved in the counterculture Hashgacha Pratit in Israel (Ilnai).

The significance of gender and kashrut to the emerging vegan food supervision industry and vegan studies field is awareness behind who vegan consumers are in relation to those providing

Figure 17.1 The Village Green is the oldest vegan restaurant in Jerusalem, Israel, which has been serving its customers since 1992. It is under the kashrut supervision of the Badatz Machzikei HaDat (see certificate on the right). Photographs by the author.

vegan supervision and product preparation services. There is a very real perception that the majority of vegans in the North America are white, female, and from socio-economic affluence, including Jewish vegans (Wright, *The Vegan Studies Project* 31). As a matter of contrast, the adoption of a vegan lifestyle among African Americans is growing at an increasing rate (McBride). Therefore, is demographic diversity among workers in the vegan supervision food service and product sectors, whether by race, gender orientation, or something else, structurally important for inclusivity? Diversity considerations have not been done in the kashrut supervision sector and have, among other inequalities, led to great employment imbalances between Jewish men and women. The lack of ethics in respect to fairness and equality may have also contributed to the conflicts of interests that were previously encountered, such as the unnecessary kashrut supervision of products that don't require it and the lack of trust between some supervising agencies. Data on these dynamics within the vegan certification world should be collected to ascertain what the realities of the situation really are.

Religion, culture, and history beyond food

A Jewish person who observes a kosher diet and lifestyle can have a vegan diet without issue, though where they are willing to eat will vary depending on their comfort level. Contemporary Judaism is also a faith where certain ritual objects are made from animals. Most significantly, Torah scrolls and other sacred texts, such as for mezuzah, megillah, and tefillin are made from animal parchment. The casings for tefillin are also made of leather. Tefillin are traditionally worn by men during weekday morning worship and are a reminder to focus ones prayers toward God. The Hebrew word for prayer is tefillah, so there is a shared semantic root. The shofar musical instrument is made from a hollow Bovidae horn, with sheep and goats being preferred (Figure 17.2). In all instances the animal does not have to have been kosher slaughtered; so the material could hypothetically come from animals that died naturally (Eisenberg 223; Montagu 61). Some people might even reflect that the reuse of an animal for parchment or shofar could be a means to honor its memory, such as a former beloved inhabitant of a Farm Sanctuary. However, no parchment or shofar suppliers offering this cruelty-free option could be found. Ritual prayer shawls (tallit) are frequently made from wool, though linen is an acceptable albeit sometimes difficult traditional vegan alternative to find. Cotton and synthetic are non-traditional materials, and wool and linen must not be mixed in order to be a kosher garment (Yitzhak 217–21).

Figure 17.2 The Jewish scribe Shlomo Washadi writing the Torah on animal parchment in the traditional way that has been done for thousands of years (left). Abram Ajwar blowing the shofar, as well as wearing tallit and tefillin (right). Both photographs taken in Jerusalem. Library of Congress Prints and Photographs Division.

Tefillin are a special intersection with Jewish feminism and a conflict with the eco-feminist discourse of veganism. Like kashrut certification, the making and use of animal-based Jewish ritual objects has predominantly been the purview of men. Therefore, female use of tefillin can be a means of asserting Jewish feminism, which until the twentieth century was almost unheard of. So too was the synagogue predominantly a Jewish male space. In traditional synagogues, especially Orthodox, men and women pray in separate spaces. In more liberal Jewish communities, women began to proactively assert themselves instead of sitting passively in the synagogue, which by extension entails the more frequent use of ritual objects made from animals, including tefillin, torah scrolls, shofar, and tallit. As some have argued, "in a broader culture in which women's lower social status was assumed, it would have made a mockery of tefillin and their purpose to impose it on the socially inferior." Therefore, from a liberated feminist perspective, Jewish "women can - and must - lay tefillin" (Friedman) because they are equal to men, which complicates the feminist and defense of animals arguments (Adams 202).

Women wore tefillin in ancient times. Not until the 13th century did Rabbi Meir of Rothenberg declare the prohibition of women wearing tefillin, which was echoed and codified by Rabbi Moshe Isserles in the 16th century. The premise was that women must cease using tefillin because of their frequency of spiritual impurity caused by their monthly menstruation cycle. Since this prohibition also extended to post-menopausal women (no exception was made for them), these declarations by Rothenberg, Isserles, and other rabbis were structured to control Jewish women in the public spiritual sphere. While there is a scarcity of quantitative information on women who wore tefillin in ancient times, the repeated instances of rabbinic decrees against the practice suggests that some women continued to wear tefillin in defiance of the changed rule (Hauptman 165). Thus, it was Medieval and Early Modern rabbis who disempowered women by taking away tefillin, forcing them into a spiritually vegetarian existence against their choice. If feminism is about the equalities of the sexes than putting on animal-based tefillin is what they should do. This is an inverted situation argued by Adams, where men disempowered women by compelling them to be omnivores instead of their preferred state of vegetarianism (125–26).

Judaism is a faith that once had a very strong historical animal-based past that continues to have a lasting legacy. While Judaism presently does not practice animal sacrifice, there is a desire to return to it after the messianic redemption and the rebuilding of the Holy Temple in Jerusalem, according to late Biblical prophecies. While cruelty-free ritual objects made of animals are possible, the infrastructure needed to provide these things is virtually non-existent. Sacred objects made from animals is where Vegan Studies needs to consider the dynamics and limitations of its worldview as it encounters traditional cultures where animals and animal products have a long enduring relationship. Judaism began as an agrarian religion thousands of years ago, whereas veganism is a postmaterialist, post-Green Revolution movement that is heavily impacted by animal rights/welfare and environmental ethics debates—debates that did not exist when the kosher laws were written. In other words, the concerns of contemporary vegans would not have been present in an agrarian society of over 3,000 years ago.

Peoples who have deep connections with animals, such as hunter-gatherers and pastoralists, offer a challenge to Vegan Studies approach to Judaism. To disregard alternative worldviews and values of indigenous and non-Western people will only perpetuate the shortcomings of Western hegemonic elitism, albeit with a new contingent that only eats plants (Stobie 132). This Jewish example of veganism is also a situational instance where flexible understanding should be considered, since even though Jews today are predominantly Western and urban, much of Jewish heritage comes from an ancient Levantine pastoral legacy. The founding patriarchs of Judaism, Abraham, Isaac, and Jacob were shepherds, the matriarch Rachel a shepherdess (signifying that it was not exclusively a male occupation), as well as the prophets Moses, Amos, and King David.

God is likened to a shepherd in Psalm 23 among other important scriptural texts. To this day, religious leaders in Judaism and other monotheistic faiths are still referenced to as "shepherds" and congregations "flocks" based on this foundational experience. Judaism forbids cruelty to animals, which is a position that aligns with veganism. The continued consumption of kosher meat is a carryover from ancient times when meat was consumed because there is ambiguity on what cruelty exactly is since slaughtering animals for sacrificial worship is biblically mandated. This is made more complex as well because Jewish mysticism from the Lurianic tradition accepts that animals have a form of soul (Gold 169).

Conclusion

A vegan diet is kosher, though how a kosher-keeping vegan decides to live this way varies due to their comfort level. This is an important example for mainstream vegans in Western Christian- based societies to understand even if their lives are agnostic, secular, or something else because of how values rooted in Jewish concepts of spirituality are different. Other religious and cultural groups also come with varying histories and legacies that can complicate their relationships with animals, animal rights, and the Animal Studies aspects of vegan studies. This is especially significant when there has been occasional rhetoric that is dismissive of another culture or religious group's worldview and values of animals that may be centuries if not millennia in age (Wright, "Conclusion" 257–65). Proverbs 3:17–18 describes how the Hebrew Bible, called the Torah, "is a tree of life to all who grasp it, and whoever holds onto it is happy; its ways are ways of pleasantness, and all its paths are peace." While the Torah is an intangible cannon of knowledge that has been passed on for many generations, it has been ever since its beginning physically represented as a double-roll scroll made of animal parchment; a product of a pastoralist past stemming from the founding patriarchs and prophets. An entire people with that kind of enduring history is not going to simply walk away from this heritage.

In response to the question "[s]ome people believe that vegetarians should aspire to become vegans. How can an Orthodox Jew be a vegan since he would not be able to use tefillin, a shofar (ram's horn), a Sefer Torah, and other ritual items that are made from animals[?]", Richard H. Schwartz, President of the Jewish Vegetarians of North America and co-founder and coordinator of the Society of Ethical and Religious Vegetarians responded, "If a person became a vegetarian but not a vegan, he or she would still do much good for animals, the environment, hungry people, and the preservation of his or her health. If a person embraces veganism except where specific mitzvot [commandments] require the use of some animal product, more good will be done. It is important to emphasize that, for hiddur mitzvah [enhancement of good deeds], it is preferable for the religious items mentioned above to be made from animals that were raised compassionately and died natural deaths" (120–21). Schwartz exemplifies the Jewish value of continually improving oneself and the world around them as a noble virtue, and that absolutes can be problematic. Jews and Judaism can learn a lot from vegan studies, such as how to make the world a better place for all species and the environment; but there is much vegans and vegan studies can learn from minority religions, cultures, and ethnic groups like Jews and Judaism, like why they perceive the relationship between people, animals, and ecology differently.

Notes

1 תּוֹרְשַׁכ is the Hebrew for Kashrut/Kashrus, which is pronounced differently depending on the dialect used. Kashrut, as used by the author, is used in the Israeli and Sephardic dialect. Kashrus is used in the Ashkenazic dialect.
2 In terms of gross population India and some other countries do have more vegans than Israel.

Works cited

Adams, Carol J. *Sexual Politics of Meat*. New York: Bloomsbury Publishing, 2015.
Berman, Louis A. *Vegetarianism and the Jewish Tradition*. New York: KTAV Publishing House, 1980.
Davis, Moshe. "Kosher," *Brith Sholom Beth Israel Synagogue*, 2018. https://www.bsbisynagogue.com/about/kosher-food-in-charleston/.
Chu, Shanti. "Nonviolence through Veganism: An Antiracist Postcolonial Strategy for Healing, Agency, and Respect." *Through a Vegan Studies Lens: Textual Ethics and Lived Activism*, edited by Laura Wright, University of Nevada Press, 2019, pp. 180–202.
Eisenberg, Ronald L. *Dictionary of Jewish Terms: A Guide to the Language of Judaism*. Schreiber Publishing, 2011.
Feder, Shira. "Orthodox Women May Be Kashruth Experts at Home, But Are Rarely Accepted As Professional Kosher Inspectors." *Forward*, 28 March 2018. https://forward.com/food/396902/orthodox-women-may-be-kashruth-experts-at-home-but-are-rarely-accepted-as/.
Fishbane, Sholem. "Understanding the Reliability of Kosher Agencies." *AMI Magazine*, Issue 189, 12 November 2014.
———. "Directory of Kosher Certifying Agencies." *Chicago Rabbinical Council*, 28 October 2019, http://www.crcweb.org/agency_list.php.
Forst, Binyomin. *The Laws of Kashrus: A Comprehensive Exposition of Their Underlying Concepts and Applications*. Mesorah Publ, 2004.
Friedman, Will. "Why Women Can—And Must—Lay Tefillin." *Forward*, 22 January 2014, https://forward.com/opinion/191430/why-women-can-and-must-lay-tefillin/.
Gold, Michael. *Three Creation Stories: A Rabbi Encounters the Universe*. Wipf & Stock, 2018.
Hauptman, Judith. "Women and the Conservative Synagogue." *Daughters of the King: Women and the Synagogue*, edited by Susan Grossman and Rivka Haut, Jewish Publication Society, 1992.
Hendelman, Ariel Dominique. "Kosher Vegan: Bringing two values together – under God?" *The Jerusalem Post*, 10 August 2018. https://www.jpost.com/Magazine/Kosher-Vegan-564532.
Heschel, Susannah. "Jewish Studies as Counterhistory." *Insider/Outsider: American Jews and Multiculturalism*, edited by David Biale, Michael Galchinsky, and Susannah Heschel, University of California Press, 1998, pp. 101–115.
Holmes, Oliver. "'There is no kosher meat': the Israelis full of zeal for going vegan." *The Guardian*, 17 March 2018, https://www.theguardian.com/world/2018/mar/17/there-is-no-kosher-meat-the-israelis-full-of-zeal-for-going-vegan.
Ilnai, Itay. "Women working to break Rabbinate's monopoly over kashrut supervision." *Y-Net News*, 2 February 2017. https://www.ynetnews.com/articles/0,7340,L-4925644,00.html.
Jerusalem Post Staff. "Israel's largest fast food chain is going vegan." *Jerusalem Post*, 2 July 2019, https://www.jpost.com/Israel-News/Israels-largest-fast-food-chain-is-going-vegan-594353.
Kashrus Magazine. *The Kosher Supervision Guide: 2019–2020 Edition*, Vol. 40. New York: Kashrus Magazine, 2019.
Labendz, Jacob A. "Jewish Veganism as an Embodied Practice: A Vegan Agenda for Cultural Jews." *Jewish Veganism and Vegetarianism: Studies and New Directions*, edited by Jacob A. Labendz and Shmuly Yanklowitz, State University of New York Press, 2019, pp. 298–313.
Labendz, Jacob A. and Shmuly Yanklowitz. *Jewish Veganism and Vegetarianism: Studies and New Directions*. State University of New York Press, 2019.
Lempel, Jesse. "More than holy, healthy and halal, Big Kosher is big money." *The Times of Israel*, 16 November 2014. https://www.timesofisrael.com/more-than-holy-healthy-and-halal-big-kosher-is-big-money/.
LeVasseur, Todd. *Religious Agrarianism and the Return of Place*. State University of New York Press, 2017.
Montagu, Jeremy. *The Shofar: Its History and Use*. Rowman & Littlefield Publishers, 2016.
Pensak, Margie. "Other News From The STAR-K." *Kashrus Kurrents*, Fall 2009. https://www.star-k.org/articles/kashrus-kurrents/660/star-k-side-bar-8/.
McBride, Suzanne. "More African Americans adopting vegan diet to combat health problems." *Chicago Sun Times*, 19 June 2019. https://chicago.suntimes.com/2019/6/19/18637414/vegan-vegetarianism-african-americans-healthy-diet-ron-reid-chicago.
OK Kosher Certification. "Timeline of Kosher." *The OK Story*, 2019. http://www.ok.org/about/our-ongoing-story/a-timeline-of-kosher/.
Orthodox Union. "The World's Largest Kosher Certification Agency Certifying Over 1 Million Products Worldwide." *OU Kosher*, 2019. https://oukosher.org/.

Ovadia, Haim. "May one eat at a Vegan or Vegetarian Restaurant that does not have a Kosher Certification?" *Shamayim: Jewish Animal Advocacy*, 2019a. http://www.shamayimvaretz.org/vegan-restaurants-dont-need-certification.html.

———. "Koshering Dishes in Modern Times," Addendum to Halakha of the Day, 2019b. http://files.constantcontact.com/64c06db0201/e0c28217-2deb-444c-9e34-f3089c5fb520.pdf?ver=1458240790000.

Rabkin, Richard. "Are Vegan Restaurants Kosher?" *Kashrut Magazine*, vol. 38, no. 3, 2018, 36–39.

Schwartz, Richard H. *Jewish Vegetarianism*. Lantern Books, 2001.

Stiefel, Barry L. "Kosher Wine." *Alcohol in Popular Culture: An Encyclopedia*, edited by Rachel Black, Greenwood, 2012, pp. 116–117.

Stobie, Caitlin. "South Africa: 'My Culture in a Tupperware': Situational Ethics in Zoë Wicomb's *October*." *Through a Vegan Studies Lens: Textual Ethics and Lived Activism*, edited by Laura Wright, University of Nevada Press, 2019, pp. 131–145.

Teichman, Yakov. "Keeping Kosher When Vegan." *Kosher Spirit*, Spring 2018, http://www.ok.org/ja/kosherspirit/spring-2018/keeping-kosher-ina-vegan-restaurant/.

TOI Staff. "Restaurants okayed to say food kosher without rabbinate's approval." *The Times of Israel*, 13 September 2017. https://www.timesofisrael.com/restaurants-okayed-to-say-food-kosher-without-rabbinates-approval/.

Underwood, Nick. "Vegetarianism as Jewish Culture and Politics in Interwar Europe," in *Jewish Veganism and Vegetarianism: Studies and New Directions*, Jacob A. Labendz and Shmuly Weiss, Elizabeth. "Kosher for Gentiles," *The New Yorker*, 11 April 2014, https://www.newyorker.com/business/currency/kosher-for-gentiles.

Wright, Laura. "Conclusion: Dinner With Beatriz: The Enmeshed Rhetoric of Vegan Studies." *Through a Vegan Studies Lens: Textual Ethics and Lived Activism*, edited by Laura Wright, University of Nevada Press, 2019a, pp. 257–265.

———, ed. *Through a Vegan Studies Lens: Textual Ethics and Lived Activism*. University of Nevada Press, 2019b.

———. *The Vegan Studies Project: Food, Animals, and Gender in the Age of Terror*. University of Georgia Press, 2015.

Yanklowitz, S. eds. Albany: State University of New York Press, 2019, 23–48.

Yanover, Yori. "The Mashgiach Wore a Dress: The Fight over Opening Kosher Supervision to Women." *The Jewish Press*, 26 November 2012. https://www.jewishpress.com/news/breaking-news/the-mashgiach-wore-a-dress-the-fight-over-opening-kosher-supervision-to-women/2012/11/26/.

Yitzhak, Hertzel Hillel. *Tzel Heharim: Tzitzit*. Jerusalem: Feldheim Publishers, 2006.

18
Veganism, Hinduism, and Jainism in India
A geo-cultural inquiry

Saurav Kumar

This chapter has two purposes. First, it aims to critically analyze the geo-cultural development of veganism in India. Second, it contemplates how the emerging vegan theory and criticism can intervene in the discourses that constitute the present Indian culture. Indian religions such as Jainism, Buddhism, and Hinduism have long traditions of vegetarianism. Vegetarianism in India is chiefly based on the teachings of *ahimsa* embedded in these religions (Ramchandran 37, 39). *Ahimsa* is a Sanskrit word for non-violence or the avoidance of violence (*himsa*). *Ahimsa* is the Indian doctrine of non-violence that "affirms that all forms of life are sacred, and thus it prohibits violence in thoughts, words, and actions under any circumstances." It also says that "all life forms, including plants and animals, are equal, possess souls, and are capable of attaining salvation" (Bouchard 18).

Hinduism, the most ancient of Indian religions, in its early days was not inclined toward vegetarianism (Sen, *Feasts and Fasts* 36-37, Ramchandran 39). The essence of the early form of Hinduism (1700-1100 BCE), sometimes also called Vedism or Brahmanism, was animal sacrifice. In this period, animal sacrifice was deemed to be the sole way of appeasing gods and supernatural forces. People used to consume the meat of the sacrificed animals. Meat was a normal diet for all the sections of society (Sen, "India" 133). In the sixth century BC, however, a collective dissent against eating meat evolved in Indian masses. This dissent was rooted in the birth of two new philosophical and religious movements in North India: Jainism and Buddhism (133–134). Jainism was founded by Vardhamana Mahavira (540–468 BCE), while Buddhism was founded by Gautama Buddha (563–483 BCE).

In the times when Buddhism and Jainism were spreading their roots in India (500 BCE to 500 CE), the promoters and advocates of the movements placed great emphasis on the preservation of plant and animal eco-systems. Compassion for all living beings and leading life in harmony with nature were central to these two religions. Out of the two, Jainism took its compassion toward other creatures and nature in general to "extreme logical conclusion," believing that each component of nature (even stone and soil) contains *jiva* (a soul). This extreme level of the observance of non-violence in daily life seems to have made an impregnable impact on Indian society in the form of the rise and wide proliferation of vegetarianism in Indian subcontinent (Gadgil and Guha 77–78).

In *My Experiments with Truth* (first published in two volumes; Vol. I in 1927; Vol. II in 1929), Mahatma Gandhi, a supreme advocate of *ahimsa*, vehemently criticized the violence and suffering meted out to animals, and emphasized vegetarianism and abstinence from milk (discussed later in the chapter). Despite the efforts of Gandhi, the wide-ranging uses of milk in Jainism, Buddhism, Hinduism, and Sikhism kept scholars from imagining veganism in India for a long time. In India, what one eats or drinks is essentially a religious matter. It is religion that prescribes what to eat and what not to eat. Hinduism divides food into three categories in terms of levels of spirituality: *sattvik* (acquired following the ideal of truthfulness or *ahimsa*), *rajasi* (the lavished food consumed by kings and their families) and *tamasik* (food that leads to spiritual barrenness). Out of the three, *sattvik* food is considered to be sacred. *Sattvik* food is vegetarian in nature. In Hinduism and other Indian religions that have originated from Hinduism, milk is considered to be *sattvik* and therefore vegetarian. Historically, in India, vegetarianism has never been conceived of as a choice, but as a prescriptive and proscriptive category. Indians generally adopt vegetarianism as a religious dietary code.

Veganism as a belief and philosophy could permeate Indian society around 50 years after the vegan movement began—only after the awareness about the adverse impact of animal agriculture on Indian ecosystems grew among common people. A report published by World Bank in 1999 mentions livestock as an important cause of environmental degradation in India. The report confirms "[t]he growth in livestock populations, coupled with shrinking grazing areas, has put intense pressure on existing pastures, encouraging encroachment into forest lands, and contributed to the degradation of land resources" (World Bank xvi). The growing public awareness about the harmful effects of livestock agriculture on the environment combined with the already existing notion of *ahimsa* made way for a vegan movement in India. In an article, "Veganism in India: How the Dairy-Loving Country is Embracing a Plant-Based Diet," Joslyn Chittilapally reports that "a new movement is growing in India—veganism" (Chittilapally).

From cookbooks to restaurants to e-commerce: tipping points for an *Indian* vegan culture

A range of literatures focusing on Indian vegan recipes have played a pivotal role in the rise of veganism as an alternative foodway in India. Cookbooks have not merely remained confined to recording a collection of recipes; they have also served as a tool to discipline one's dietary routine. In a way, they have functioned as treatises envisioning multiple philosophies of life. For example, in many vegetarian cookbooks, the reasons for adopting a vegetarian diet matter as much as the recipes mentioned in them. The reasons authors offer for suggesting vegetarianism range from animal rights to religion to health consciousness (Phillips 75). The last two decades have witnessed a *flood* of vegan cookbooks, "catering to the newly health-conscious and appealing to young people who are embracing alternative and ethical lifestyles" (79). Like their predecessors, vegan cookbooks also describe in detail why and how individuals should adopt vegan food as a part of their lives.

In 2009, Madhu Gadia published *The Indian Vegan Kitchen: More Than 150 Quick and Healthy Homestyle Recipes*. Gadia notes that "A majority of the traditional Indian vegetarian recipes are vegan by design. Eggs, hard cheeses, and honey are not a part of a typical Indian vegetarian diet, and therefore not an issue. You will find recipes from appetizers to desserts" (Gadia "Introduction"). In 2012, Anupy Singla's *Vegan Indian Cooking: 140 Simple and Healthy Recipes* appeared. The vegan spirit of the book is apparent from its opening lines: "[i]t's not a book that forces a lifestyle upon you. It's not a book that tells you what you should be eating on any given day." By writing this book, Singla recognizes that "everyday Indian recipes that are traditionally vegan," and "give

[...] South Asians a new way to think about the foods [they] grew up with." Singla speaks about how she looked forward to vegan food:

> I first began my journey following a predominantly vegan diet (meaning no meat or dairy) back in the mid-1990s, when I was a graduate student at the East—West Center and the University of Hawaii. I fell ill with walking pneumonia and found that I had no energy. My immune system was shot. I went to see a naturopath, who suggested I give up milk, cheese, meat, and seafood for a period of six months so I could cleanse my system and better assess any possible food allergies. (Singla "Introduction")

She recognizes that beans, lentils, and grains are the prime sources of nutrients and protein in a traditional Indian diet, which means that Indian diets already recognize that meat is not essential. Further, she notes that "Any Indian can cite hundreds upon hundreds of vegetarian dishes and preparations—*most of them vegan*" (Singla "Getting Started," emphasis added).

In 2013, Anuradha Sawhney's *The Vegan Kitchen: Bollywood Style!* was published by Westland. The back cover of the book claims that the book is "[o]ne of the first books for the growing vegan population of India." Further, the book "brings together recipes from no less than 50 leading names from the world of Bollywood, fashion and music" as a means of "showing how it's possible to incorporate a delicious, healthy vegan diet with no cholesterol—in other words, one with no animal products, including dairy—into your life" (Sawhney back cover). In Jackie Kearney's *Vegan Street Foods: Foodie Travels from India to Indonesia*, the writer chiefly attempts to show "There's a reason veganism is so popular among the Hollywood elite. You'll live longer (so will the planet). Over half of the planet's population lives on a vegan diet and it isn't food to be endured for health reasons." The aim of Kearney's 2015 book is "to celebrate vegan food in all its health-giving glory" (Kearey "Introduction") by recording a vast number of vegan varieties of street food available in India, Sri Lanka, Thailand, Laos, Vietnam, Malaysia, and Indonesia.

Recently, "[t]here has been an exponential increase in fully vegan restaurants in cities like Mumbai, Pune, Hyderabad, Bangalore and Goa" (Chittilapally). Veganism as a dietary choice has even reached Siliguri, a small town in West Bengal. "While there is Ubuntu Community Café in Calcutta, there is Vegan Nation in Siliguri" (Saha) (both of the restaurants specialize in serving vegan dishes). Initially visited by tourists who used Siliguri as the starting point for their journeys toward North East, "Vegan Nation now sees locals dropping in while in search of something new to explore." Talking about how to adopt vegan food, Abhishek Mittal, aka Dylan, a 33-year-old chef who runs Vegan Nation, says "[i]t is very important to keep an open mind and not aim to stop or change completely overnight. Reduce your [non-vegan] intake and see how you are doing" (Saha). The menu at Ubuntu Community Cafe at Dhakuria, Kolkata offers Fysh Fry, Grilled Shrymp, Kosha Mangsho—all plant-based versions of non-vegan dishes. The restaurant uses soy, wheat, and seaweed to prepare the basic ingredients for the Fysh Fry, while the Kosha Mangsho is cooked with "vegetarian meat" manufactured by a brand called Good Dot which provides a country-level delivery facility. The main ingredients used for preparing the vegetarian meat are soy, wheat and South American cereal quinoa (Saha).

In India, many food establishments have begun labeling their food items as "vegan" and "veganizable." Veganizable items are those that "can be altered to make them vegan." Many supermarkets now have separate "vegan aisles." Also, vegan e-commerce stores are flourishing, "making vegan products accessible even in small cities and towns" (Chittilapally). In India, Raw Pressery, Urban Platter, Jus' Amazin, Broke Mate, Amayra Naturals, and Disguise Cosmetics are some brands that actively promote vegan products on Amazon. Raw Pressery sells tetra packs of almond milk and bottled juices; Urban Platter sells various flavors of vegan milk powder (soy, almond, etc.); Jus'Amazin sells dairy-free butters (cashew butter, almond butter, peanut butter); Broke Mate provide vegan handbags; Amayra Naturals and Disguise Cosmetics sell vegan cosmetics. These brands have also linked to vegan awareness initiatives like Veganuary India and the Save Movement India.

Jainism and veganism

Jainism is one Indian religion that closely mirrors the beliefs of ethical veganism. Jainism considers all of nature to be alive: Jains believe that each and every component of nature, right from rocks and trees to gods, contains an immortal soul, or *jiva*. This belief is at the helm of *ahimsa*—the Indian concept of non-violence (Sen, *Feasts and Fasts* 53). Mahavira, the founder of Jainism, propounded a "pure unchanging eternal law" for his followers. The law also defines what *ahimsa* means. According to Mahavira, "all things breathing, all things existing, all things living, should not be slain or treated with violence." The prohibition on killing animals has been so extreme in Jainism that Jains are not allowed to take up farming as a profession. Jains believe agriculture involves activities that can destroy insects in the soil (53).

In Jainism, some food items are absolutely forbidden, such as meat and meat products, fish, eggs, alcohol, and honey. Jains detest alcohol for two reasons. First, the process of fermentation multiplies and destroys living organisms. Second, alcohol blinds one's conscience and may inspire violence. Honey is forbidden since removing honey from a comb kills bees. Jain monks and nuns never eat fruits and vegetables containing many seeds (figs, aubergines, guava, and tomatoes), since seeds consist of the germ of life. They never consume vegetables that grow as roots (potatoes, turnips, radishes, mushrooms, fresh ginger, and turmeric), since uprooting them kills the plants as well as millions of *jivas* living in soil. In addition, they eschew garlic and onions, since they invoke carnal passions; yeast-containing foods and fermented foods; cauliflower and cabbage, since insects live within the leaves of these vegetables; and buds and sprouts (Sen, *Feasts and Fasts* 53). Renouncers practice non-violence (*ahimsa*) more strictly than laypeople. For example, they are not allowed to use vehicles such as planes, trains, and automobiles "because of the small living beings (such as insects) that are killed by these vehicles." They "walk barefoot wherever they go." They remain "careful not to step on and kill any small creature on the ground." Monks and nuns carry "soft brooms." They use these brooms "to sweep the ground in front of them while walking in the dark so that they will avoid stepping on any small insects on the ground" (Fohr 42).

Veganism and Gandhi

In the foreword to the 20th anniversary edition of Carol J. Adams's *The Sexual Politics of Meat*, Nellie Mckay comments, "Gandhi was a vegetarian decades ahead of his time" (35). Gandhi was born in a Vaishnava family, which meant that he was a vegetarian by birth. In *My Experiments with Truth*, Gandhi explains the vegetarianism inherent in his family: "Gandhis were Vaishnavas. ... The opposition to and abhorrence of meat eating that existed in Gujarat among the Jains and Vaishnavas were to be seen nowhere else in India or outside in such strength" (19–20). In *The Sexual Politics of Meat*, Adams says,

> When he arrived in London, Gandhi's discovery of the writings of his British contemporary, Henry Salt, specifically his *A Plea for Vegetarianism*, provided the ethical grounding he

needed to continue his vegetarianism. Gandhi reported, "From the date of reading this book, I may claim to have become a vegetarian by choice". (121)

Gandhi always believed milk was not a natural diet for human beings. When he came to know that the cows and buffaloes were forced to undergo the cruel process of *phooka* (blowing of air into cow's vagina for gaining more milk), he shunned milk completely (Gandhi 418). At a later stage of life, when the ailing Gandhi was instructed by his doctor to consume goat's milk, Gandhi felt guilty of breaking his vow to never consume milk: "The memory of this action even now rankles in my breast and fills me with remorse, and I am constantly thinking how to give up goat's milk" (418). Gandhi explains how he broke the vow. He says that "his intense eagerness to take up the Satyagraha fight" had generated in him "a strong desire to live." Therefore, he eased himself "adhering to the letter of my vow only" and gave up to its spirit. He clarifies his giving up to the spirit of his vow: "although I had only the milk of the cow and the she-buffalo in mind when I took the vow, by natural implication it covered the milk of all animals" (418). Though "veganism as a political concept for liberation and non-violence" had not gained impetus by that time, Gandhi surely "had some notion that an *ahimsic* lifestyle must reject the consumption of all animal products, including lactation" (Narayanan 144).

Cow milk, Hinduism, and vegan feminism

In the hymns of the Vedas (2nd to 1st millennium BCE), the cow was related to "the sacred, though not completely sacrosanct." With the passage of time, the cow "has undergone a gradual apotheosis, becoming over time a key symbol of all that is sacred to, and unifies, Hindus" (Nelson 180). Hinduism sees the cow's udder (that part of the cow where her milk gets collected) as the microcosm of universal order, a treasure full of resources that takes care of the health of the Hindu world. The recent vegan feminist critiques of cow milk subvert "the singular emphasis on meat alone as responsible for violence to animals, including their slaughter." These critiques "explicitly highlight milk and eggs as also profuse with harms" (Narayanan 134).

In the preface to the 10th anniversary edition to *The Sexual Politics of Meat*, Adams states that *The Sexual Politics of Meat* introduces a particular conceptual term to signify "the exploitation of the reproductive processes of female animals": "milk and eggs should be called *feminized protein*, that is, protein that was produced by a female body" (21). In a chapter of the same book, "Masked Violence, Muted Voices," she argues that female animals such as cows suffer oppression on account of "their femaleness." These female animals are mostly treated as "surrogate wet-nurses." When their productiveness declines, they are slaughtered and turn into "animalized protein." Adams proposes that each and every vegan should reject "feminized *and* animalized protein" (112). In "Why Feminist-vegan Now?," Adams defines "feminized protein" as "protein produced through the abuse of reproductive cycle of animals," and she emphasizes that "the unique situation of domesticated animals," under which "their reproductive capacity is manipulated for human needs" is "a sexual slavery" with cows and hens. She says, "even though the animals are alive, dairy products and eggs are not victimless foods" (305).

Yamini Narayanan analyzes the legend of the child Krishna's love of butter churned from cow milk from the perspective of vegan feminism. While the legend of Krishna's great love of milk and butter extracted from cow milk are profusely used by dairy industry for promoting the consumption of cow milk and by Hindu narratives for glorifying cow as mother, the legend discounts Krishna's separation from his biological mother (Devaki) immediately after his birth in jail, even before his first lactation from Devaki. The fate of Krishna here is not different from that of a male calf in dairy industry—both are deprived of lactation from their biological mothers. This erasure in the legend is suggestive of a deep silence that envelopes "the harms to dairy cows, whose lactation (and biological children) are directed to serve their 'adopted' human progeny." The "biological" cow-mother-to-calf relationship suffers deletion, while the "adoptive" and "forced" cow-mother-to-human-being relationship is venerated (134).

Narayanan also argues that the holiest milk in Hinduism is not bovine, but vegan and plant-derived (144). The legend of the churning of the great ocean, popularly known as *samudramanthana*, is one of the most important Hindu mythologies on the sacredness of milk. A core feature of the legend—that it was the mixing of the sap from herbs and weeds with water that made the ocean milky—has been almost entirely ignored (Narayanan 135). The vegan nature of *kshirasagara* or the ocean of milk formed as a result of *samudramanthana* challenges the co-option and commercialization of cow milk as sacred among Hindus (Narayanan 144).

According to the legend, both gods and anti-gods (demons) craved nectar (*amrita*), the liquid that could make them immortal. The two sides came to know that they needed to churn the ocean to achieve nectar. In *Milk: A Local and Global History*, Deborah Valenze narrates the legend in the following words: with the help of a snake (as a rope) and a mountaintop (as a churning stick), the gods and the demons began churning the ocean. As they "pulled and writhed," "the sap from the mountain mixed with water from the sea." "*As the swirling progressed, the ocean water turned to milk and then—following laws of an ordinary dairy—butter*" (13, emphasis added). In *The Body of God: An Emperor's Palace for Krishna in Eighth-Century Kanchipuram*, D. Dennis Hudson discusses "a *Mahabharata* version of the churning story": "the 'bucket of the Ocean' that surrounds the inhabited world becomes milky from the juices of herbs and resins of trees on the golden mountain Mandara that flow into it when it is churned" (547).

Narayanan cites as an example of vegan milk the *soma*, a sacred drink in the *Rigveda* extracted from herbs and plants (146). The *Rig Veda* consists of a chapter of 114 hymns dedicated to *soma* (Sen, *Feasts and Fasts* 38). In the states of Bihar, Jharkhand, and West Bengal, *soma* has for a long time been extracted from palm and date trees (due to its hallucinatory property, Bihar has recently put a ban on the use of *soma*). This *soma* happens to be milky in color and texture. In these areas, *soma* is sometimes also referred to as "milk without an offspring" (meaning the milk not yielded from an animal). Further, coconut milk is highly popular in South India and is prepared through the churning of the white part of coconut fruit. It is either used as a drink or as an ingredient in the preparation of many South Indian dishes.

Vrata as vegan rite

There are a number of *vratas* observed in the eastern part of the Gangetic plains (Bihar, Jharkhand, and Bengal), which are vegan in nature: Bishua, Teej, Karma, and Juitia. Kunal Chakrabarti discusses two kinds of *vratas*: *Puranic* and *asastriya*. Chakrabarti defines *vrata* as "a vowed observance, a religious act of devotion and austerity, performed for the fulfilment of specific desires" (218). *Puranic vratas*, as the name suggests, originated from the *Puranas* (Hindu religious codes, expressed in the form of stories). Since cow milk is considered to be *sattvik* (sacred) food in *dharmasutras* (Hindu religious codes), *Puranic* vratas involve the use of cow milk as diet and oblation. A *Puranic vrata* stands for a complex ritual that involves procedures like *snana* (ritual bath), morning prayer, *samkalpa* (vow), *homa* (sacrifice), *upavasa* (fast), and the customary observance of some fixed restrictions during *vrata* (218-219). With the rise of vegetarianism among Hindus after the advent of Buddhism and Jainism, combined with opposition to the killing of animals in the name of sacrifice, the *homa* no longer (popularly) meant (animal) sacrifice, but the offering to the holy fire of milk, ghee, curd, honey, coconut, and black lentil. What differentiated Jainism and Buddhism from earlier beliefs was the "institutionalization of ascetic practices" in the newer religions (Sen, *Feasts and Fasts* 55). "Vegetarianism as a widespread ethical and moral idea" evolved in India with the flourishing of Jainism and Buddhism (46). Condemnation of animal sacrifice on the ground of *ahimsa* was at the center of the asceticism in Jainism and Buddhism. One legend says that when the king of Kosala had decided to organize a great sacrifice of 500 oxen, 500 male calves, 500 female calves, and 500 sheep, Buddha forbade him to do so (55).

Unlike *Puranic* vratas which are *sastryia* (mentioned in didactic brahminical scriptures), *vratas* like Bishua, Teej, Karma, and Juitia are "*asastriya*" (not mentioned in didactic brahminical scriptures). *Asastriya* vratas, also popularly called "*meyeli* (belonging to women) *vratas*," are "not half as elaborate as the one noted above and certainly much less 'religious.'" *Asastriya vrata* involves

> *aharana* or collection of commonly available and inexpensive articles of daily use for the observance of the rite, *alpana* or drawing of standard motifs on the floor, *chada* or recitation of doggerel verses from memory which express the desire behind the performance of the rite, and *katha* or listening to the story which establishes the justification of the rite.

In the place of brahmana priest and sacred hymns in such observances, in *asastriya vratas*, maidens and married women assemble at one place to perform the *vrata* "for the fulfilment of rather mundane and unostentatious wishes such as a desirable husband or a happy and modestly prosperous life" (220). Since the ritual of *homa* (sacrifice) is absent from *asastriya vratas*, milk plays no role in Bishua, Teej, Karma, and Juitiya.

Bishua *vrata*, most often identified as a community festival, is observed in Bihar on the first day of the month of *baisakha*. On this day, *sattu* (gram flour) and green mangoes are used as food. Women take bath in a river or a pond, and the ritual is called Bishua *Snana*. Teej *vrata* is observed by women for the safety of their husbands. Women-vratis, on this day, abstain from any kind of food for 24 hours. In some cases, *vratis* at most take sherbet (water mixed with sugar). On this day, women observing the fast build the clay idols of Lord Shiva, Parvati, and Ganesha and worship them. Karma *vrata* is observed by women for the safety of brothers on the 11th day of the *shukla paksha* of *Bhadra* month. On this day, women prepare the idols of Shiva, Parvati, and Ganesha with clay. Women observing Karma fast also observes abstinence from food for 24 hours. In evening, after worshipping Shiva, Parvati, and Ganesha, women essentially take sherbet. Juitiya fast is kept by women for the safety of their children on the ninth day of *Krishna Paksha* of *Ashwina* month. On this day, women remain *nirjala* (complete abstention which includes avoiding even water) for 24 hours and worship *pitars* (the souls of deceased ancestors). On the next day, Women who have observed the fast prepare a plant-based diet which includes *kushi keraaw* (dry small peanuts), *golwa saag* (a leafy vegetable that tastes salty), *kanda* (a kind of yam), and rice. They eat the diet as *prasada* (oblation) along with other members of her family.

One salient feature of *asastriya vratas* is that they are essentially agrarian by character and primarily involve locally available seasonal crops as oblations. Anthropologically, all these *vratas* signify different phases of the Indian agricultural year and thus can be seen as regeneration rites. Also the role of women as *vratis* (those who perform *vratas*) embodies a tridimensional approach to the harmonious relation between nature and human life where women, family, and nature coordinate with one another—a woman performs *vratas* involving easily available crops and plants for the well-being of her family, while the family acts as a single unit to make this happen.

Vata Savitri vrata is one *Puranic vrata* which is vegan in nature. The women perform this vrata for the health and long life of their husbands and sons. The procedure of this *vrata* is quite simple: women sprinkle water at the root of the banyan tree, surround it with cotton threads, and perform its worship. Next, they offer worship to Savitri "mentally or in an image," and pray to her for freedom from widowhood in this and subsequent lives. The story of Savitri is found in the *Mahabharata*: Savitri was a brave woman who had won the life of her already dead husband, Satyavan, from Yama, the Hindu god of death.

Conclusion

Writing on H. Jay Dinshah, the founder of American Vegan Society and an excellent advocate of the practical aspect of *ahimsa*, Lida Hudgins still finds *ahimsa* at the center of vegan philosophy. Dinshah wrote what he meant by *ahimsa* in the form of an anagram: Abstinence from animal products/Harmlessness with reverence for life/Integrity of thought, word, and deed/Mastery over oneself/Service to humanity, nature, and creation/Advancement of understanding and truth. From 1960 to 2000, the journal of American Vegan Society was published under the title, *Ahimsa* (In 2000, the journal was renamed as *American Vegan*, "in an effort to attract a more mainstream audience"). Currently, "the journal still retains the motto, 'Ahimsa lights the way'" (Hudgins 81–82). The motto is an English translation of a famous Sanskrit thought—*ahimsa paramo dharamah*—and means that *ahimsa* is the ideal *dharma* or way of life.

Interestingly, *ahimsa*, despite being an Indian notion, could not invoke veganism in India alone (the vegan movement could only begin in India in the beginning of the 21st century, when the role of excessive animal agriculture in the degradation of environment became a global concern). One strong factor behind this limitation of *ahimsa* in the Indian context is the blurring of the subjecthood of animals in Indian religious traditions in the name of either transcendence or sacrifice. In "'A Very Rare and Difficult Thing'—Ecofeminism, Attention to Animal Suffering and the Disappearance of the subject," Carol Adams posits that human contemplation of animal's suffering is a "very rare and difficult thing" (591). Adams states: "Behind every meal of meat is an absence: the death of the nonhuman whose place the product takes. The *absent referent* is that which separates the consumer from the animal and the animal from the end product." According to Adams, "the function of the absent referent is to keep our 'meat' separated from any idea that she or he was once an animal" (595).

In India, animals are not (merely) "animals." Sometimes, they are divine beings (Vishnu's incarnations as *matsya* (a fish), *kurma* (a tortoise), *varaha* (a boar), *narasimha* (half lion, half human); *garuda* (a bird akin to eagle but bigger in size) worshipped as the king of birds; *shukdev* (half parrot, half human) as the narrator of *Shrimad Bhagvad Purana*). Sometimes, animals also *transcend* as the carriers of various gods and goddesses (a mouse in the case of Ganesha, a lion in the case of Durga, *Nandi*, an ox, in the case of Shiva, *eiravat* (an elephant) in the case of Indra, a peacock in the case of Kartikeya, *hans* (a swan) in the case of Saraswati, an owl in the case of Lakshmi, *Shesha Naga* (a giant snake), and *garuda* in the case of Vishnu). Many times, animals like goats, sheep, hens, pigeons, and buffaloes are treated as oblations to deities. Cows need a special mention, since they are revered as goddesses. Cow is the earth goddess responsible for nourishing the entire Hindu universe with her produce. These transcendences (when they are treated as divine beings) and reductions (when they are seen as oblations) play an important role in the blurring of the original subject-hood of animals. This blurring of the original subject-hood makes human contemplation of the suffering of these animals "highly rare and difficult." Another factor behind the blurring of animal's subject-hood is the Hindu concept of "transmigratory journeying" of the same self (the soul) between different species in pursuance of *moksha* or salvation. Hindus believe in *punar janma* (re-birth). One's rebirth into a particular species or *yoni* (*yoni* is Sanskrit word for "womb") depends on the kind of *karma* (doing) one has done in previous births. In the hierarchy of *yonis* (species), human beings are at the top, followed by animals, birds, and insects. The superiority of human beings among various *yonis* makes them a "natural" patron of all other *yonis* and leads to the marginalization of other species (Nelson 180-182).

The vegan nature inherent in *asastriya vratas* consolidates the claim that the spirit of veganism exists in Indian cultural memory from the beginning, though in the form of small patches. Preservation of the indigenous nature of *asastriya vratas* by different local communities can be one effective way of retaining veganism in India. *Asastriya vratas*, unlike *Puranic*, have been more often conceived as an "activity," rather than as a "moral code." India is quite fertile for the propagation of veganism, given the availability of numerous vegan recipes and a strong presence of vegetarianism aligned with *ahimsa* in the region. Emelia Quinn and Benjamin Westwood caution that, as veganism spreads more widely within "public discourse," it may get reduced to "proscriptive dietary practices or pragmatic goals." Such a reduction is destructive to the "useful ambiguity" of veganism (5). Indians are particularly vulnerable to this reduction, as it is mainly religion that decides what is prescriptive and what is forbidden in India. In India, religion is interpreted as *dharma* or a collective way of life. The word—*dharma*—originated from Sanskrit root verb, *dhri*, which means "to possess or hold." That which is worth-possessing is called *dharma*. In order to *preserve* veganism's potential to invoke reactions, discussions, and initiatives that transgress the socio-cultural homogenizations of people's appetite and way of living, it is essential that veganism is kept from being understood as a kind of food ethics or a set of moral conducts.

Works cited

Adams, Carol J. *The Sexual Politics of Meat: A Feminist-vegetarian Critical Theory*. 20th anniversary ed., Continuum, 2010a.
Adams, Carol J.. "'A Very Rare and Difficult Thing': Ecofeminism, Attention to Animal Suffering and the Disappearance of the subject." *A Communion of Subjects: Animals in Religion, Science and Ethics*, edited by Paul Waldau and Kimberley Patton, Columbia University Press, 2006, pp. 591–604.
———. "Why Vegan Feminist Now?" *Feminism and Psychology*, vol. 20, no. 3, 2010b, pp. 302–317.
Bouchard, Jen Westlandmore. "Ahimsa." *Cultural Encyclopedia of Vegetarianism*, edited by Margaret Puskar-Pasewicz, Greenwood, 2010, pp. 17–18.
Chakrabarti, Kunal. "Textual Authority and Oral Exposition: The *Vrata* Ritual as a Channel of Communication in Early Medieval Bengal." *Studies in History*, vol. 10, no. 2, 1994, pp. 217–241.
Chittilapally, Joslyn. "Veganism in India, How the Dairy-loving Country is Slowly Embracing a Plant-based Diet." *LifeGate*, 27 December 2019. https://www.lifegate.com/people/lifestyle/veganism-in-india. Accessed March 23 2020.
Fohr, Sherry. *Jainism. Guides for the Perplexed*. Bloomsbury, 2015.
Friedman, Jerold D. "Protests and Activisms." *Cultural Encyclopedia of Vegetarianism*, edited by Margaret Puskar-Pasewicz, Greenwood, 2010, pp. 1–8.
Gadia, Madhu. *The Indian Vegan Kitchen: More Than 150 Quick and Healthy Homestyle Recipes*. Electronic ed., Penguin Group, 2009.
Gadgil, Madhav, and Ramchandra Guha. *This Fissured Land: An Ecological History of India*. 1992. Oxford University Press, 2013.
Gandhi, M. K. *An Autobiography or The Story of My Experiments with Truth*. Translated by Mahadev Desai, Navajivan Publishing House, 1927.
Hudgins, Lisa. "Dinshah, H. Jay (1933–2000)." *Cultural Encyclopedia of Vegetarianism*, edited by Margaret Puskar-Pasewicz, Greenwood, 2010, pp. 81–82.
Hudson, D. Dennis. *The Body of God: An Emperor's Palace for Krishna in Eighth-century Kanchipuram*. Oxford University Press, 2008.
Korom, F. J. "Holy Cow! The Apotheosis of Zebu, or Why the Cow Is Sacred in Hinduism." *Asian Folklore Studies*, vol. 59, no. 2, 2000, pp. 181–203. doi:10.2307/1178915.
Kearney, Jackie. *Vegan Street Foods: Foodie Travels from India to Indonesia*. Electronic ed., Ryland Peters and Small, 2015.

Mckay, Nellie. "Foreword by Nellie Mckay: Feminists Don't Have a Sense of Humour." *The Sexual Polities of Meat: A Feminist-vegetarian Critical Theory*, by Carol J. Adams, 20th anniversary ed., Continuum, 2010, pp. 33–37.

Narayanan, Yamini. "Animal ethics and Hinduism's Milking, Mothering legends: Analysing Krishna the Butter thief and the Ocean of Milk." *Sophia*, vol. 57, no. 1, 2018, pp. 133–149. doi:10.1007/s11841-018-0647-8

Nelson, Lance. "Cows, Elephants, Dogs, and Other Lesser Embodiments of Ātman: Reflections on Hindu Attitudes Toward Nonhuman Animals." *A Communion of Subjects: Animals in Religion, Science and Ethics*, edited by Paul Waldau and Kimberley Patton, Columbia University Press, 2006, pp. 179–193.

Olson, J. "Soma." *Hinduism and Tribal Religions: Encyclopedia of Indian Religions*, edited by Pankaj Jain et al., Springer, 2018, pp. 1–3. https://doi.org/10.1007/978-94-024-1036-5_207-1

Phillips, Cedar. "Cookbooks." *Cultural Encyclopedia of Vegetarianism*, edited by Margaret Puskar-Pasewicz, Greenwood, 2010, pp. 75–79.

Quinn, Emelia, and Benjamin Westwood. "Introduction: Thinking Through Veganism." *Thinking Veganism in Literature and Culture: Towards a Vegan Theory. Palgrave Studies in Animals and Literature*, Palgrave Macmillan, 2018, pp. 1–24.

Ramchandran, Ammini. "Asia." *Cultural Encyclopedia of Vegetarianism*, edited by Margaret Puskar-Pasewicz, Greenwood, 2010, pp. 37–41.

Saha, Shrestha. "Viva las Vegan: A Philosophy and a Lifestyle." *Telegraph*, 18 January, 2020. https://www.telegraphindia.com/health/viva-las-vegan-a-philosophy-and-a-lifestyle/cid/1736950. Accessed March 23 2020.

Sawhney, Anuradha. *The Vegan Kitchen: Bollywood Style!*. Westland, 2012.

Sen, Colleen Taylor. *Feasts and Fasts: A History of Food in India*. Reaktion Books, 2015.

——. "India." *Cultural Encyclopedia of Vegetarianism*, edited by Margaret Puskar-Pasewicz, Greenwood, 2010, pp. 131–137.

Singla, Anupy. *Vegan Indian Cooking: 140 Indian Healthy and Simple Recipes*. Electronic ed., Surrey Books, 2012.

World Bank. *India Livestock Sector Review: Enhancing Growth and Development*. World Bank and Allied Publishers, 1999.

19

The interface between "identity" and "aspiration"

Reading the Buddhist teachings through a vegan lens

Joyjit Ghosh and Krishanu Maiti

He prayeth well, who loveth well
Both man and bird and beast.

S.T. Coleridge, *The Rime of the Ancient Mariner*

What is veganism? There is no easy answer to this question. Veganism is not merely a dietary habit or practice; it is a philosophy and a lifestyle; it is a "pedagogy" but at the same time "owes its existence to lived animal rights activism" (Wright, *Through a Vegan Studies Lens* xxi). While theorizing veganism, Lori Gruen and Robert C. Jones in "Veganism as an Aspiration," speak of two distinct ways of being vegan: one is a way of life that becomes an integral part of one's identity and the other is directly related to the question of aspiration. Ethical vegans adopt veganism as a lifestyle and are often dedicated to their struggle against all forms of cruelty and violence. They ardently believe that those who have put it into practice have achieved a kind of integrity as well as purity. But there is another form of veganism, called "Aspirational Veganism," that views veganism not as a lifestyle or identity, but rather as a type of practice/process of eliminating or minimizing violence against and domination over the nonhuman other. It therefore speaks of an ongoing process of moral awakening. There is, however, no rigid line of demarcation between the two forms of veganism because in different contexts, someone who appreciates veganism as an aspiration may also believe in a vegan lifestyle. Actually, these two forms/ways of veganism overlap at a significant point where both of them "oppose the systematic cruelty toward and destruction of other animals" (Gruen and Jones 155–158). This is exactly where the Buddhist idea of *Dharma* becomes relevant. *Dharma* is a Sanskrit word loaded with meanings. *Dharma* is the other name of truth. Its Pali equivalent is *Dhamma*. It refers to the Buddhist doctrine that teaches the limitless path of spiritual awakening and enlightenment. Buddhists believe that to follow the *Dhamma,* one must practice non-violence to sentient beings. In our present study of the Buddhist teachings available in *The Dhammapada,* and other *Sutras* including *Lankavatara Sutra, Mahaparinirvana Sutra, Surangama Sutra,*[1] and the *Jataka Tales,* we explore that these teachings anticipate the essentialist notions of both "Identity" and "Aspiration," which are central to the discourse on Vegan Studies discussed above by Gruen and Jones.

Before we read the teachings of Gautama Buddha (scattered over different realms of Buddhist literature) through a vegan lens, let us first explore why people in increasing numbers resort to veganism in the present-day world. In the first place, people seem to have an inclination to a vegan "way of living which excludes all forms of exploitation of, and cruelty to, the animal kingdom, and includes a reverence and compassion for all life".[2] In order to satisfy the human appetite, animals, and other sentient creatures are slaughtered every day. But that is not the whole story. The farmed animals that we kill for our daily consumption are often kept in inhospitable surroundings. Vegans across the world are always vocal about this issue, and social media[3] plays a very important role in this regard. Vegans make us conscious of the systemic torture and cruelty we inflict on sentient creatures in farms. All these contribute to, what Melanie Joy and Jens Tuider describe in their "Foreword" to *Critical Perspectives on Veganism* as, "the visibility of farmed animal suffering" (vi). But Joy and Tuider also speak of "the *viability* of veganism as a personal and thus moral choice" (vi). To quote their words, "due to the modernization of food production, unless one is geographically or economically unable to make her or his food choices freely, eating animals is no longer a necessity and is therefore a choice. When a behavior becomes a choice, it takes on a much more significant ethical dimension" (vi). Veganism as an ideology thus poses a viable moral alternative to carnism in which people support the ethics of meat-eating and consumption of animal products.

More and more people across the world embrace veganism not for ethical reasons alone. There are two other reasons: health reasons and environmental reasons. Let's first briefly talk about the health reasons for embracing veganism as a lifestyle. Epidemiological research has found substantial correlations between consumption of animal fat and meat to "an elevated incidence of heart disease, stroke, cancer of the colon and breast, liver and kidney disease, depletion of the bone mass, arthritis and a host of other afflictions."[4] In comparison with animal products, plant-based foods are higher in fiber, free of cholesterol, and low in calories. In addition, a vegan diet which comprises a wide variety of fruits, vegetables, whole grains, cereals, pseudocereals, seeds, seaweeds, nuts, and legumes is rich in vitamins, minerals, and antioxidants, and there is evidence that it might help consumers live "longer" and "healthier lives" (Tarchichi 146).

In terms of environmental impact, advocates of veganism assert that eating a vegan diet could be the "single biggest way" to reduce environmental impact on the earth. Researchers at the University of Oxford found that cutting meat and dairy products from one's diet could reduce an individual's carbon footprint from food by up to 73 percent. Not only would this dietary change result in a significant drop in greenhouse gas emissions, it would also free up wild land lost to agriculture, one of the primary causes for mass wildlife extinction (Petter, "Veganism Is 'single Biggest Way'"). Vegan environmental advocates also very often speak of the harmful impact of animal agriculture and livestock industry in terms of land degradation, air pollution, water shortage, water pollution, and loss of biodiversity (Steinfeld et al. xx). They offer veganism as a solution to some of the practical problems caused by animal agriculture and vindicate the rise of veganism as "a realistic, and even commendable, option" (Joy and Tuider, "Foreword" v).

But the vegan movement/ideology has provoked a lot of criticism from time to time. It is argued that vegan diets have "welfare footprints" in the form of widespread indirect harms to animals, harms often overlooked or obscured by the champions of veganism. Industrialized culture harms and kills a large number of sentient field animals in the production of fruits, vegetables, and grains produced for human (and livestock) consumption (Gruen and Jones 157). It would be relevant if we quote a passage from Hardy's *Tess of the d'Urbervilles* in this context as it offers a poignant representation of the suffering of field animals during the harvesting:

The narrow lane of stubble encompassing the field grew wider with each circuit, and the standing corn was reduced to smaller area as the morning wore on. Rabbits, hares, snakes, rats, mice, retreated inwards as into a fastness, unaware of the ephemeral nature of their refuge, and of the doom that awaited them later in the day when, their covert shrinking to a more and more horrible narrowness, they were huddled together friends and foes, till the last few yards of upright wheat fell also under the teeth of the unerring reaper, and they were everyone put to death by the sticks and stones of the harvesters. (68)

The "teeth of the unerring reaper" (a synecdochic reference to the reaping machine) is obviously a signifier of the industrialized culture. The vegan diet is therefore scarcely innocent. Whether we are vegans or not, we cannot live without killing others or, at best, letting them die (Gruen and Jones 157–58).

Harold Fromm who favors vegetarianism but opposes veganism (both in theory and practice) remarks that vegans are "enlisted in an open-ended but futile metaphysic of virtue and self-blamelessness that pretends to escape from the conditions of life itself" ("Vegans and the Quest for Purity"). Fromm is therefore highly dismissive about the vegan way of living which he finds to be a "futile metaphysic of virtue." He seems to have no faith in the argument that "adopting a vegan diet constitutes environmental activism, whether or not the vegan intends such activism" (Wright, "Introducing Vegan Studies" 728). In addition, he only makes a passing reference to J.M. Coetzee, Michael Pollan, and Peter Singer while approving of "their revulsion at the brutal treatment of animals raised for our consumption" (Fromm). But nowhere he speaks of issues like animal rights/liberation; nowhere he touches upon the question of compassion and reverence for sentient creatures of the earth that vegans do. One may in this connection remember that the second "pillar" of *Ahimsa* propounded by H. Jay Dinshah, the founder of the American Vegan Society, is "Harmlessness with Reverence for Life" (qtd. in Moran 31). Victoria Moran beautifully illustrates the idea of *Ahimsa* when she argues, "It does not mean that a person can live and never do any harm at all (i.e. killing no plants or microbes) but actions are to be weighed carefully. Reverence for life is not animal worship but respect for life itself" (Moran 31). It is worth exploring the teachings in the Buddhist literature (which constitute a vast field of study) that lucidly address all these issues.

Let us start our discussion on the dialogue between Buddhism and veganism with reference to *The Dhammapada*,[5] which is the most widely known in Buddhist scripture. In Chapter XIX of *The Dhammapada* ("Dhammatthavaggo") we have a discourse on the *Righteous* where we read that a man is not noble (or elect) if he injures living creatures (Radhakrishan 143). In the words of the Dalai Lama: "We can say that an act is immoral or improper to the extent that it causes harm to others."[6] The act of a nobleman is free from deliberate harm to his fellow-creatures. At this point, one may very well remember the first Buddhist precept which is "Do not kill." This is perhaps the most significant of the five precepts that Buddhist practitioners follow because it throws light on boundless compassion for all sentient beings, which is at the center of the Buddhist discourse. There is another chapter (X) in *The Dhammapada* which is relevant to us in this context. The chapter is called "Dandavaggo" which means *punishment*. Here we read that all men love life and tremble at punishment. Likening others to oneself, one should neither slay nor cause to slay. He who seeks his own happiness yet inflicts pain (strikes with a stick) on beings who like himself are desirous of happiness does not obtain happiness after death (Radhakrishan 103). *The Dhammapada* thus speaks of a moral philosophy which is committed to ending the suffering of all living beings, whether human or nonhuman. The basic idea is that one must liken oneself to all sentient beings. The sense of affinity with them can only help one conquer the killing instinct. This is precisely where the doctrine of Buddhism and that of Jainism come close to each other. Let us quote a relevant portion from *Acaranga Sutra* at this point: "to do harm to others is to do harm to oneself. "Thou art he whom thou intendest to kill! Thou art he whom thou intendest to tyrannize over!" We corrupt ourselves as soon as we intend to corrupt others. We kill ourselves as soon as we intend to kill others" (Tatia 18). The principle of *ahimsa* (nonviolence), therefore, strikes the essential point of connection between two very ancient religions of the world. *The Dhammapada* that contains the cardinal teachings of the Buddha always speaks of reverence for animal life. In his Introduction to *The Dhammapada*, S. Radhakrishnan writes, "A good Buddhist does not kill animals for pleasure or eat flesh. They are his humble brethren and not lower creatures over whom he has dominion by divine right. Serenity of spirit and love for all sentient creation are enjoined by the Buddha" (22–23). The quoted observation is insightful for two reasons: first, it addresses the question of compassion and love for all creatures without a sense of dominion over the nonhuman world; secondly, it obliquely criticizes the bad faith of those Buddhist monks and lamas who eat the flesh of animals and thereby mislead the followers of the precepts of Gautama Buddha.

There is a debate centering around the issue of flesh-eating in the Buddhist teachings. The debate basically addresses two questions: (1) Did the Buddha take meat in the last meal? (2) Did he sanction meat-eating to his disciples in the scriptures? Before entering into this debate, we would like to quote a passage from Chapter 8 of the *Lankavatara Sutra* where the Buddha tells Mahamati, the interlocutor:

> Again, Mahamati, there may be some unwitted people in the future time, who, beginning to lead the homeless life according to my teaching, are acknowledged as sons of the Sakya, and carry the Kashaya robe about them as a badge, but who are in thought evilly affected by erroneous reasonings. ... Being under the influence of the thirst for [meat-] taste, they will string together in various ways some sophistic arguments to defend meat-eating. They think they are giving me an unprecedented calumny when they discriminate and talk about facts that are capable of various interpretations. Imagining that this fact allows this interpretation, [they conclude that] the Blessed One permits meat as proper food, and that it is mentioned among permitted foods and that probably the Tathagata himself partook of it. (Suzuki 217–218)

A close reading of the passage reveals that the Buddha could predict that after his death the "unwitted people" among his disciples might resort to "sophistic arguments" in order to vindicate meat-eating; and in their "thirst" for meat they might even go the extent of concluding that the Buddha himself partook of meat on occasions.

Let us first attempt to resolve the first question whether the Buddha took meat in the last meal and died from eating poisonous pork. The dispute here revolves around the phrase "sukara-maddava." Tashi Nyima, an ordained monk in the Jonang lineage of Vajrayana (Tibetan) Buddhism, observes that the term used in the (Pali) *Mahaparinirvana Sutta* literally means "pig's delight," a clear reference to a type of mushroom that pigs are keen to eat, and not pig meat ("sukara-mamsa"). And the monk categorically states that unless one is grossly ignorant of the Pali language, or is wilfully misleading others, it is impossible to assert that "pig's delight" means "pork meat" (Nyima 225).

The second question in the debate mainly arises from a doctrine in the *Jivaka Sutta* wherein Buddha addresses the issue of permissibility regarding the consumption of meat by a *bhikkhu*. A *bhikkhu* is an ordained member of the Buddhist Sangha who has devoted himself to the task of following the Path by renunciation of all mundane distractions, and who relies for his sustenance upon the gifts of lay disciples.[7] Let's read the *sutta*:

> Jivaka, I say that there are three instances in which meat should not be eaten: when it is seen, heard, or suspected that the living being has been slaughtered for the bhikkhu. I say that meat should not be eaten in these three instances. I say that there are three instances in which meat may be eaten: when it is not seen, not heard, and not suspected that the living being has been slaughtered for the bhikkhu, I say that meat may be eaten in these three instances. ("MN 55 Jivaka Sutta: To Jivaka")

The authenticity of this doctrine has been questioned not only by certain Buddhist monks but also by staunch followers of vegan action. David Blatte who was a co-founder of Dharma Voices for Animals and who has lived and practiced at Vipassana monasteries in Myanmar and Sri Lanka observes, "Much could be questioned about this doctrine, including its authenticity, but even if taken as authentic, its purpose was not to generally condone the eating of animals but instead to narrowly proscribe circumstances under which this was allowed—when the eating of an animal does not contribute to the killing of an animal" (31). James J. Stewart, who belongs to the School of Philosophy in the University of Tasmania, however, does not debate the authenticity of the clause. In his opinion, "this directive is designed to ensure that the monk is not connected directly with the animal slaughter as such. Rather, his connection to the slaughter is only tacit and indirect. Hence, the monk cannot be blamed for the killing since the animal would have been slaughtered anyway" (Stewart 113). This "permissibility clause," according to Stewart, was included in the Buddhist teaching "only under political duress"; the Buddha appears to allow the practice of meat-eating "in order to prevent monastic schism" (115). We, however, had best not press this interpretation because we can never really know whether or not the Buddha sanctioned meat-eating under any circumstances. Rather a close study of the Buddhist scriptures reveals that there is no equivocation regarding the issue of meat-eating on the part of a *bhikkhu*. The *Mahaparinirvana Sutra*, for example, categorically states:

> Let yogis not eat any animal flesh. Animal flesh eating is forbidden by me everywhere and for all time for those who abide in compassion. (qtd. in Blatte 30)

Animal flesh is, therefore, never pure for a Yogi who seeks the truth by means of self-discipline. The underlying argument is that a *sattvic* diet will make a *sattvic* person and a *sattvic* person will always "abide in compassion" (Dale 214).

In the section entitled "Prohibition against killing" of *Surangama Sutra* Buddha asks the monks: "How can those who practise great compassion feed on the flesh and blood of living beings?" (Yü 153–154). This is a crucial question addressed to those who follow the Buddhist teachings yet partake of meat. The Buddhist discourse brings home the point perfectly well that one cannot understand the essence of the *Dhamma* if one does not refrain from eating flesh. In the *Brahmajala Sutra* we read:

> Pray, let us not eat any flesh or meat whatsoever coming from living beings. Anyone who eats flesh is cutting himself off from the great seed of his own merciful and compassionate nature. ... Someone who eats flesh is defiled beyond measure.[8]

In the *Lankavatara Sutra* we have a detailed discussion of how flesh-eating may defile the consumer. One may in this context quote a relevant section from the *Lankavatara Sutra* (Chapter Eight) in which the Buddha tells Mahamati about the vice of meat-eating:

> For the sake of love of purity, Mahamati, the Bodhisattva should refrain from eating flesh which is born of semen, blood, etc. For fear of causing terror to living beings, Mahamati, let the Bodhisattva who is disciplining himself to attain compassion, refrain from eating flesh. To illustrate, Mahamati: When a dog sees, even from a distance, a hunter, a pariah, a fisherman, etc., whose desires are for meat-eating, he is terrified with fear, thinking, "They are death-dealers, they will even kill me." (Suzuki 213)

This quotation touches upon certain points that are central to the discussion on the vegan way of living and identity. The "love of purity," to which the Buddha alludes in his conversation with Mahamati, is an integral part of the vegan lifestyle. The diet is obviously an important point of consideration here because eating, like all of our actions, has moral implications (Blatte 32). While discussing on the value of a "Buddhist Vegan diet," Norm Phelps in his book *The Great Compassion: Buddhism and Animal Rights* (2004) observes that this diet is "undertaken out of compassion for the suffering of animals," and he continues:

> Every morsel of meat that we eat, every slice of cheese, every omelette comes at the price of cruel, unnatural confinement and childhood death. We cannot eat animal products even occasionally without supporting the torture and killing of innocent animals. Every retreat from veganism toward "moderation" or a "middle way" is a step farther into cruelty and killing. (129–130)

So, the argument posited by Phelps is that a vegan way of living avoids cruelty to and killing of all living creatures of the earth. This is exactly where the Buddhist teaching in the *Lankavatara Sutra* sounds relevant: "If … meat is not eaten by anybody for any reason, there will be no destroyer of life" (Suzuki 217). We also read here that the Buddha condemns meat-eating because "in the majority of cases the slaughtering of innocent living beings is done for pride and very rarely for other causes" (217). This statement demands a critical examination in the context of vegan studies. In their "Introduction" to *Thinking Veganism in Literature and Culture*, Emilia Quinn and Benjamin Westwood draw our attention to the fact that in the present world the animal body is increasingly coming to the fore, and the new culture revels in and celebrates the relation of meat to the slaughtered animal (14). Vegans vehemently resist this politics of meat.

However, as Laura Wright argues, there are many reasons why people choose to become vegan, and there are reasons why others choose not to be. The observation of Wright is that veganism continues to be a largely white, upper-middle class identity, and it's often depicted as an elitist endeavor (Wright, "Introducing Vegan Studies" 728). While speaking of the growing public reception of vegans, Gruen and Jones also touch upon the sense of superiority (often moral) cherished by vegans as they often exhibit a kind of self-righteous zealotry and promulgate veganism as the universal and one-and-only way to fight systemic violence against animals (Gruen and Jones 155). But we need not exaggerate the issue of moral elitism with reference to the vegan attitude and identity. Rather we may argue that we cannot always afford to be prejudiced against the vegan way of living because it often reveals an enlightened attitude. And this attitude certainly speaks of love and respect for all sentient life. Tony Page in *Buddhism and Animals* observes, "Every person who feels any affinity with the Bodhisattva ideal, particularly, will surely feel the necessity of speaking out on behalf of the oppressed and victimized—whether they may be in human or animal form" (175). Bodhisattva is one whose inner nature is compassion itself and who has made significant progress toward developing *bodhichitta* meaning an *enlightened mind*. A vegan is not necessarily a Buddhist. But when a vegan chooses not to wear fur, leather, wool, or silk or use cosmetics or household products containing ingredients that are derived from animals, one realizes the perennial appeal of a doctrine in *Surangama Sutra* ("Prohibition against killing"):

> If bhiksus do not wear garments made of silk, boots of local leather and furs, and refrain from consuming milk, cream and butter, they will really be liberated from the worldly; after paying their former debts, they will not transmigrate in the three realms of existence. (Yü 153–154)

This doctrine thus teaches that a *bhiksu*[*bhikkhu*] can liberate himself from *Samsara* (which is imagined as the wheel of existence comprising life, death, and rebirth) by non-injury to all sentient beings. He should not only refrain from harming and killing animals, but at the same time should take caution that his livelihood does not depend on animal products. This obviously points toward the moral goal of "Aspirational Veganism" which, as defined by Gruen and Jones, is "something that one works at rather than something one is" (156). But the question is inevitable: Can vegans entirely avoid animal products in their day-to-day existence? Harold Fromm, who has a great reservation for a vegan's quest for purity, sarcastically observes:

> The grandstanding of vegans for carefully selected life forms, to serve their own sensitivities—through their meat-and dairy-free diets, their avoidance of leather and other animal products—doesn't produce much besides a sense of their own virtue. As they make their footprint smaller and smaller, will they soon be walking on their toes like ballet dancers? And if so, what is the step after that? (Fromm)

The observation of Fromm on the aspirations of vegans is indeed caustic and smacks of politics of exclusion as the critic tends to alienate vegans from the mainstream by using the loaded expressions like "their own sensitivities," "their own virtue," etc. But can the protest of a vegan against the world that has normalized the cruelty to nonhuman life be suppressed or even silenced by othering the vegan identity? Can the vegan aspiration be dismissed in such a crass fashion particularly when it is close to achieving profound compassion and respect for all life? The answer, we believe, would be largely in the negative.

When we read the *Jataka Tales*,[9] we find at their center tremendous compassion, loving-kindness (*metta*), and reverence for all living creatures of the earth. Vicky Seglin in her essay "May All Beings Be Happy" persuasively remarks, "Increasingly, the Buddhist and the vegan paths feel like two aspects of one interconnected path, each leading back to the other, and providing guidance and encouragement for each other. They are both sources of joy, creative challenge, and harmony" (139). The *Jataka Tales* are an integral part of the Buddhist canon and they narrate the previous births of Tathagata Buddha in both human and animal form to drive home didactic messages. Sinhala Buddhists regard it as *Buddhavacana*—Buddha's own words, and it is treated as being a part of *Sutra Piṭaka*.

The *Jataka* stories occupy a privileged space in the domain of Buddhist literature as animals, to echo Christopher Chapple, "are presented in a very positive manner" (220). The argument made by Chapple is twofold: (1) While narrating the tales drawn from his past lives the Buddha portrays himself as a rabbit, a swan, a fish, a quail, an ape or an elephant, to name a few creatures; (2) Animals are said to have contributed to his [Buddha's] desire for *nirvana*; seeing animals and humans suffer caused Buddha to seek enlightenment. Both the points are illuminating. In the context of posthumanist discourse, however, the first point seems to be more interesting than the second one. Posthumanism, in the words of Derek Ryan, "attends to ontological entanglements between human bodies and nonhuman animals, and opens up non-anthropocentric worldviews, *in the present*" (69, italics in original). The worldview of the *Jataka Tales* is largely non-anthropocentric and the appeal of the stories often lies in their vivid response to and respect for nonhuman worlds. The stories urge and exhort the readers to be more and more sensitive to the sentient beings of the earth. They promote *ahimsa* and provide examples of non-violence towards animals. They even illustrate the idea of evil connected to animal slaughter.

Nigrodhamiga Jataka is a classic case in point. King Brahmadatta, the ruler of Benares, loved deer hunting and had meat at every meal. Every day he advised his cohorts to hunt down deer, even when they did not enjoy it. Eventually, when Bodhisattva became the king of all these deer, he came to know the plight and fear of his fellow beings and became very anxious about their fate. He approached king Brahmadatta with an agreement to negotiate. The treaty states that instead of hunting the deer, one will be sacrificed everyday with its consent. But one day a pregnant doe faces her turn to be slaughtered. Bodhisattva takes her place, and goes to sacrifice his life. The king is shocked at such willing sacrifice and awestruck by this demonstration of compassion; he takes a vow never to slay any deer in future. But Bodhisattva is not satisfied with his vow and asks the king to release all the deer, and at the same time, to refrain from killing other four-footed animals of the forest. The king happily negotiates with Bodhisattva and provides full freedom not only to four-footed animals but also birds and fish from the hunt. This story exemplifies that (1) animal hunting is wrong and unethical; and (2) the violence can be overcome through acts of compassion and self-sacrifice. This story also leaves a profoundly valuable message: "to free others is to free ourselves; to free ourselves is the beginning of freeing others" (Martin 24).

Jataka Tales contain many examples in which we find abundant references to the instrumental use (abuse, exploitation, and slaughter) of animals, particularly elephants (Waldau 176–177). The stories can be read from the theoretical perspectives of Vegan Studies as it interrogates and critiques all sorts of animal exploitation and raises questions relating to animal welfare. The elephant-related stories[10] in *Kuddāla Jataka* and *Mahājanaka Jataka*, *Taṇḍulanāli Jataka* and *Dummedha Jataka* provide instances where animals suffer from infinite pain inflicted on them by humans when they are used as means of transport. In *Bhīmasena Jataka*, an elephant is used in the war between a hostile king and Bodhisattva who warned Bhimsena while he fouled the elephant's back. In *Alīnacitta Jataka*, *Palāyi Jataka*, *Kuṇāla Jataka*, and *Mahā-Ummagga Jataka* we also find that elephants are used for the purpose of warfare. In *Palāyi Jataka*, the clamorous cry of the elephants is terribly disturbing as the men on elephants' back in the battlefield exhort them to trumpet:

> Rush against them—fall upon them! shout the war-cry—loudly sing! While the elephants in concert raise a clamorous trumpeting! (Cowell 153)

So, the animals are represented here as mere instruments at the hands of war-mongers.

In *Kaka Jataka*, we find awful examples of ill-treatment of sentient creatures at the hands of humans. The story narrates that elephants are kept in small stables, and unfortunately when the stables catch fire the elephants are badly injured; to cure them the king plans to slaughter nearly 80,000 crows, because he thinks that the crows' fat will cure the injured elephants. Bodhisattva then rushes to the king and beseeches "him to shield all living creatures from harm" by saying,

> In ceaseless dread, with all mankind for foes, Their life is passed; and hence no fat have crows. (Cowell 302)

The king is obviously outwitted by the shrewd intelligence of Bodhisatta and thus the crows' lives are saved from the imminent destruction.

Dubbalakaṭṭha Jataka shows terrible violence involved in the process of animal domestication. Elephants suffer both physical torture and mental stress when they are tied up against their will by the trainers:

> And they tied the elephant up fast to a post, and with goads in their hands set about training the animal. Unable to bear the pain whilst he was made to do their bidding, the elephant broke the post down, put the trainers to flight, and made off to the Himalayas. (Cowell 248)

This is an eloquent representation of torture and pain to which the animals are subjected when they are trained. The word "training" is crucially loaded with significance; it entails a sense of systematic violence inflicted on animals for the purpose of domesticating them. The "post" and "goads" constitute the symbols of persecution. But the message of the story is that animals may revolt against cruelty and oppression at the hands of human beings and thereby deconstruct the whole discourse of human sovereignty on the planet.

In *Indasamānagotta Jataka* Bodhisattva advises the eponymous Brahmin not to keep the elephants as pets, or to treat them as domesticated animals, because these animals do not like to be captivated. The captivity of animals is also a vital issue in *The Dhammapada*. In *Nāgavaggo* ("The Elephant Chapter" of *The Dhammapada*), we read of an elephant (named Dhanapalaka) who "is hard to control when the temples are running with a pungent sap (in the time of rut)." Dhanapalaka "does not eat a morsel (of food) when bound. The elephant thinks longingly of the elephant-grove" (Radhakrishnan 161). This poignant representation of the suffering of a captive elephant offers a powerful message against all forms of animal exploitation and makes us think of the right of an animal to roam freely and with dignity on the face of the earth.

Buddhism is often viewed as an animal rights religion of a great order. Buddhist teachings reveal that animals are ethically relevant and they deserve/demand our loving-kindness and respect. The teachings of Buddha exhort us to embrace a right livelihood that in the first place opposes exploitation/oppression of animals at the hands of humans for human-centered reasons. The Buddhist teachings seem to have a considerable bearing on veganism as it extends the "ethical concern to every aspect of our relations with animals" and all other sentient creatures of the earth (Tuttle 56). Vegans acknowledge that they cannot wholly escape from their complicity in the acts of violence to their fellow-creatures but they seek to exclude, as far as possible and practicable, all forms of cruelty to and exploitation of animals and other living creatures in their day-to-day existence. They continually subject themselves to self-definition and aspire for a way of living which is commendable both as an ideology and practice loaded with "fundamental ethical, political, and cultural ramifications" (Joy and Tuider "Foreword" xiv). Imagining and advocating oneself to be a vegan is therefore not altogether an illusion. Because a vegan is true to his/her own *Dhamma* and he/she knows that one has miles to go before one's mission is achieved.

Notes

1 Buddhism has two primary traditions, Theravada and Mahayana. The older Theravada traditions which are found today in Thailand, Cambodia, and Sri Lanka are based on the *Arhat* (one who has attained enlightenment or *Bodhi*) ideal. The Mahayana traditions which are found mainly in China, Korea, Japan, and Central Asia are based on the *Bodhisattva's* aspiration, i.e., to attain liberation for the benefit of all living beings. The sutras referred to in this context belong to the Mahayana tradition, and they contain the most explicit passages advocating vegan ideals. See Will Tuttle, "Do Buddhist Teachings Mandate Veganism?," Introduction to *Buddhism & Veganism: Essays Connecting Spiritual Awakening & Animal Liberation*, pp. 20–21.

2 See, The Vegan XX (Spring 1964): Frontispiece. Quoted in Victoria Moran, *Compassion: The Ultimate Ethic*, p. 18.

3 https://www.onegreenplanet.org/, https://www.aspca.org/, https://www.vegansociety.com/.
4 See [Alex Hershaft], *Vegetarianism Like it Is* (Washington, DC: Vegetarian Information Service, n.d.), p. 1. Quoted in Victoria Moran, *Compassion: The Ultimate Ethic*, p. 67.
5 All references to the *Dhammapada* are from *The Dhammapada, with Introductory Essays, Pali Texts, English Translation and Notes* by Sarvepalli Radhakrishan, Oxford University Press, 1966.
6 See, The Dalai Lama, *Beyond Dogma: Dialogues and Discourses*, North Atlantic Books, Berkley, 1996, p. 67. Quoted in Norm Phelps, *The Great Compassion*, p. 46.
7 The idea of "bhikkshu" is largely taken from Christmas Humphreys's *A Popular Dictionary of Buddhism*, pp. 25–26.
8 See, "The Scripture of Brahma's Net", in *Buddhist Writings*, translated by Rev. Hubert Nearman, O.B.C. Shasta Abbey, California, 1994, pp. 127–128. Quoted in Tony Page, *Buddhism and Animals*, p. 131.
9 All the references to the *Jataka Tales* are from Edward B. Cowell's translation *The Jataka or Stories of the Buddha's Former Births, Six vols.* Cambridge University Press, 1957.
10 According to Waldau, among the nonhuman animals, elephants are most commonly referred to in the *Jataka Tales*. See Waldau, *The Specter of Speciesism*, p. 177.

Works cited

Blatte, David. "Vegan Dharma." *Buddhism & Veganism: Essays Connecting Spiritual Awakening & Animal Liberation*, edited by Will Tuttle, Vegan Publishers, 2018, pp. 25–34.
Castricano, Jodey, and Rasmus R. Simonsen, editors. *Critical Perspectives on Veganism*. Palgrave Macmillan, 2018.
Chapple, Christopher. "Noninjury to Animals: Jaina and Buddhist Perspectives." *Animal Sacrifices: Religious Perspectives on the Use of Animals in Science*, edited by Tom Regan, Temple University Press, 1988, pp. 213–236.
Cowell, Edward B., editor. *The Jataka or Stories of the Buddha's Former Births*. Six Vols., Cambridge University Press, 1957.
Dale, Alan. "Born to this World a Bodhisattva." *Buddhism & Veganism: Essays Connecting Spiritual Awakening & Animal Liberation*, edited by Will Tuttle, Vegan Publishers, 2018, pp. 207–216.
Fromm, Harold. "Vegans and the Quest for Purity." *The Chronicle of Higher Education*, 4 July 2010, www.chronicle.com/article/Vegansthe-Quest-for/66090. Accessed December 25 2019.
Gruen, Lori and Robert C. Jones. "Veganism as an Aspiration." *The Moral Complexities of Eating Meat*, edited by Ben Bramble and Bob Fischer, Oxford University Press, 2015, pp. 153–171.
Hardy, Thomas. *Tess of the d'Urbervilles: An Authoritative Text, Backgrounds and Sources Criticism*, ed. Scott Elledge, Norton, 1991.
Humphreys, Christmas. *A Popular Dictionary of Buddhism*. Routledge, 2005.
Joy, Melanie and Jens Tuider. "Foreword." *Critical Perspectives on Veganism*, edited by Jodey Castricano and Rasmus R. Simonsen, Palgrave Macmillan, 2018, pp. v–xv.
Martin, Rafe. *Before Buddha Was Buddha: Learning from the Jataka Tales*. Wisdom Publications, 2018.
"MN 55 Jivaka Sutta: To Jivaka." *suttas.com*, www.suttas.com/mn-55-jivaka-sutta-to-jivaka.html. Accessed 10 February 2020.
Moran, Victoria. *Compassion, the Ultimate Ethic: An Exploration of Veganism*. American Vegan Society, 1985.
Nyima, Tashi. "Dark Alleys and Bright Aisles." *Buddhism & Veganism: Essays Connecting Spiritual Awakening & Animal Liberation*, edited by Will Tuttle, Vegan Publishers, 2018, pp. 217–226.
Page, Tony. *Buddhism and Animals: A Buddhist Vision of Humanity's Rightful Relationship with the Animal Kingdom*. UKAVIS, 1999.
Petter, Olivia. "Veganism Is 'single Biggest Way' to Reduce Our Environmental Impact on Planet, Study Finds." *The Independent*, 1 June 2018, www.independent.co.uk/life-style/health-and-families/veganism-environmental-impact-planet-reduced-plant-based-diet-humans-study-a8378631.html. Accessed December 27 2019.
Phelps, Norm. *The Great Compassion: Buddhism and Animal Rights*. Lantern Books, 2004.
Quinn, Emilia, and Benjamin Westwood, editors. *Thinking Veganism in Literature and Culture*. Palgrave Macmillan, 2019.
Radhakrishan, Sarvepalli, editor. *The Dhammapada, with introductory essays, Pali text, English translations and notes*. Oxford University Press, 1966.
Ryan, Derek. *Animal Theory*. Edinburgh University Press, 2015.

Seglin, Vicky. "May All Beings Be Happy." *Buddhism & Veganism: Essays Connecting Spiritual Awakening & Animal Liberation*, edited by Will Tuttle, Vegan Publishers, 2018, pp. 133–139.
Steinfeld, Henning, et al. *Livestock's Long Shadow: Environmental Issues and Options*. Food and Agriculture Organization of The United Nations, 2006.
Stewart, James J. "The Question of Vegetarianism and Diet in Pali Buddhism." *Journal of Buddhist Ethics*, vol. 17, 2010, pp. 100–140.
Suzuki, Daisetz Teitaro, translator. *The Lankavatara Sutra: A Mahayana Text*. Foreword by Moti Lal Pandit. Munshiram Manoharlal Publishers, 2013.
Tarchichi, Paul. "Birthday Crashing and Spiritual Awakening." *Buddhism & Veganism: Essays Connecting Spiritual Awakening & Animal Liberation*, edited by Will Tuttle, Vegan Publishers, 2018, pp. 141–153.
Tatia, Nathmal, editor. *Acaranga Sutra* 1.1.2, 1.5.5. *Studies in Jaina Philosophy*. Jain Cultural Research Society, 1951.
Tuttle, Will, editor. *Buddhism & Veganism: Essays Connecting Spiritual Awakening & Animal Liberation*. Vegan Publishers, 2018.
Waldau, Paul. *The Specter of Speciesism: Buddhist and Christian Views of Animals*. Oxford University Press, 2002.
Wright, Laura. *The Vegan Studies Project: Food, Animals, and Gender in the Age of Terror*. University of Georgia Press, 2015.
———. "Introducing Vegan Studies." *ISLE: Interdisciplinary Studies in Literature and Environment*, volume 24, issue 4, 2017, Oxford University Press, pp. 727–736, https://doi.org/10.1093/isle/isx070.
———, editor. *Through a Vegan Studies Lens: Textual Ethics and Lived Activism*. University of Nevada Press, 2019.
Yü, Lu K'uan, trans. *The Surangama Sutra*. B. I. Publications, 1978.

20
Veganism and Islam

Magfirah Dahlan

In *The Vegan Studies Project*, Laura Wright traces veganism to its ecofeminist foundation. She explains that similar to ecofeminism, veganism is based on the belief that "the various forms of oppressions are the result of the devaluing of those things that are designated inferior in a binary construction of the world" (16). She analyzes the process of this devaluation rhetorically, where certain words and names are used to enable and justify such oppression. Drawing from Carol J. Adams's work, *The Sexual Politics of Meat*, Wright notes Adams's formulation of the "absent referent" as a means of showing how the term "meat" renders "animals" absent and "can constitute a dangerous erasure that removes from view that which is of primary importance" (Wright 16). Originally published in 1990, Adams's work compares the hierarchical gender relationship to the hierarchical relationship between humans and other animals. She uses the term "absent referent" in her work to refer to the concealment and erasure of the individuality of animals, as well as the pain and suffering they experience. Human consumption of animals, Adams argues, "acts as a mirror and representation of patriarchal values" where "[t]he patriarchal gaze sees not the fragmented flesh of dead animals but appetizing food" (178). Veganism, in short, seeks to challenge this patriarchal hierarchy by making visible the pain and suffering of the animals consumed by humans.

Although current discourse on veganism is not inherently linked to religion, there are an increasing number of practitioners of many religions who find ways to reconcile their religious values with those of veganism. This chapter discusses the teachings of Islam as well as the ways contemporary Muslims interpret and practice those teachings through the lens of veganism. A starting point for this discussion is the scriptural basis found in the Qur'an, the main authoritative text in Islam. On the one hand, historically, Muslims in general consider consuming animals to be permissible. Several of the Qur'anic verses that specifically allow Muslims to consume and use animals are as follows:

> And cattle He has created for you (men): from them ye derive warmth, and numerous benefits, and of their (meat) you eat. (Qur'an 16:5)

> It is He Who has made the sea subject, that ye may eat thereof flesh that is fresh and tender, and that ye may extract therefrom ornaments to wear… (Qur'an 16: 14)

> And in cattle (too) ye have an instructive example: from within their bodies We produce (milk) for you to drink; there are, in them, (besides) numerous (other) benefits for you; and of their (meat) ye eat. (Qur'an 23:21)

On the other hand, the overall practice of such consumption and use of animals is subject to strict regulations. These regulations can be found in the Qur'an, as well as the sayings and examples set by Prophet Muhammad (hadith), that speak to the importance of recognizing and respecting the animals' capacity to suffer physical and mental pain. In his work, *Animal Welfare in Islam*, Masri discusses several examples of these sayings and practices that focus on the importance of being kind to animals. They include the example of the Prophet reminding his wife A'ishah against rough handling of her camel; his condemnation of branding cattle on their faces as the face is a sensitive part of the body; and his order to his companions to return young birds to their mother because their removal has caused the mother-bird emotional distress (48–49).

Islamic dietary laws, in particular, specify not only the type of animals that Muslims are permitted to consume but also the method of slaughtering them:

> Forbidden to you (for food) are: dead meat, blood, the flesh of swine, and that on which hath been invoked the name of other than Allah; that which hath been killed by strangling, or by a violent blow, or by a headlong fall, or by being gored to death; that which hath been (partly) eaten by a wild animal; unless ye are able to slaughter it (in due form); that which is sacrificed on stone (altars); (forbidden) also is the division (of meat) by raffling with arrows; that is impiety. (Qur'an 5:3)

> Say: "I find not in the Message received by me by inspiration any (meat) forbidden to be eaten by one who wishes to eat it, unless it be dead meat, or blood poured forth, or the flesh of swine—for it is an abomination—or, what is impious, (meat) on which a name has been invoked, other than Allah's." But (even so), if a person is forced by necessity, without willful disobedience, nor transgressing due limits—thy Lord is Oft-forgiving, Most Merciful. (Qur'an 6: 145)

While the end of the verse above allows Muslims to consume animal product normally prohibited in the case of severe hunger, the following verses forbid Muslims to prohibit what Allah has permitted:

> O ye who believe! Make not unlawful the good things which Allah hath made lawful for you, but commit no excess: for Allah loveth not those given to excess. Eat of the things which Allah hath provided for you, lawful and good; but fear Allah, in Whom ye believe. (Qur'an 5: 87–88)

Taken together, these verses can be interpreted as not only allowing Muslims to consume and use products made of and by animals but also prohibiting Muslims from making such consumption illegal.

As discussed previously, however, veganism rests on the assumption that the immorality of consuming animals is the result of the exploitation involved. If vegans view consuming animals per se as exploitation, then there seems to be a clear contradiction between veganism and the permissibility of consuming animals found in the Qur'anic scripture. However, if vegans view the exploitation comes from the particular way the animals are consumed, there can be reasons based on Islamic teachings to reject such exploitation.

In advanced industrial countries such as those in North America and Western Europe, some Muslims have taken this concern of animal welfare into consideration when interpreting the religion's permissibility of consuming animals. In general, they believe that ensuring that animals they consume are raised in humane living conditions is as important as following the slaughter requirement explicitly outlined in the Qur'an. Some of them prefer animals raised on smaller-scale local farms than those raised in the industrial animal farming system. Some of the concerns regarding the welfare of animals raised in the industrial farming system include packed feedlots, inhumane long-distance transportation of live animals, the use of hormones, the spread of diseases, mutilation such as the burning of the beaks of chicks, and the mechanized slaughter process. For many Muslims, the problem with contemporary meat-eating lies in the way animals are treated in the historically particular system of industrial farming.

A smaller, but growing, number of Muslims have taken a stronger opposition against industrial animal farming. They argue that the permissibility of consuming animals in the Qur'an was based on the assumption that such consumption was a necessity given the context of seventh-century Arabia at the time of the revelation of the verses. More specifically, the earliest Muslims to whom the verses were revealed had a very different human–animal relationship that was not characterized by the sufferings of industrial animal farming. Moreover, the original audience of the Qur'anic revelation did not have access to the abundance of plant-based food that many Muslims in contemporary industrial societies do, and their reliance on animals for sustenance was arguably more justifiable.

In her article in which she interviews a number of vegan Muslims around the world, Ebrahim finds that this rejection of the suffering experienced by animals in the industrial farming system is an important reason for the adoption of their vegan practice. Their answers reflect their awareness of the contrasting conditions between when the Qur'anic verses were first revealed and what today's Muslims are experiencing. A Muslim living in the Netherlands, Anissa Buzhu explains, "the meat industry and consumption today is completely different compared to how our prophets have been treating and consuming animals." The Muslims that Ebrahim interviewed also describe the challenges they face from their families and community for practicing veganism. Ya'eesh Khan, from South Africa, for example, describes the following experience:

> it's not easy being a vegan Muslim. I have been ridiculed for the way I live and shunned by my friend groups. People also tend to think I have denounced my faith for veganism and follow it as a religion.

Similarly, Baya Tellai from Algeria explains the accusations that she and her family receives,

> We face some criticism: we're being influenced by a foreign culture, our ancestors never gave up meat. We get asked questions like: where do you get your protein from? Why are you going against religion? When we give evidence of veganism along the evolution of cultures and humans (using health studies, Qur'an, Sunnah, evidence from history) they usually say we won't last long, we're isolating ourselves from the society, it's not practical.

The experience of being ridiculed and considered as an apostate or going against the religion is common among many vegan Muslims because of the textual basis for the permissibility of consuming animals.

This permissibility, however, is subject to different interpretations. Among academics who analyze Islamic approaches to animal ethics, Foltz is one who argues that the Qur'anic injunction to permit consuming animals was not absolute. He argues that people who live in contemporary industrial societies do not depend on consuming animals for their survival, given the abundance of dietary alternatives. Following the religion's principle of compassion would compel Muslims living in this context to refrain from slaughtering animals and practice vegetarianism instead.

Another type of Islamic argument for vegetarianism is framed in feminist ethics. Ali's argument for Islamic vegetarianism is much more similar to Wright's argument for veganism. Both scholars draw from the work of Carol J. Adams by outlining the similarities between violence toward women and that toward nonhuman animals. Ali approaches the Qur'anic verses that allow Muslims to consume animals similarly to those that are ostensibly supportive of gender inequality. She argues that those verses are best understood in terms of Islam's original intention of promoting justice and equality. More specifically, she argues that Muslims who accept the feminist critical approach to the hierarchical relationship between genders are compelled to be critical of the hierarchical relationship between human and nonhuman animals as well. Overall, her argument for Islamic vegetarianism emphasizes Islamic teachings that speak to the importance of the virtues of sympathy and care, which are central to the discourse of feminist ethics.

A discussion of Islam and animal consumption cannot be limited to that of individual consumption. Traditionally, with the ritual of animal sacrifice, Muslims practice meat-eating as part of their communal obligation. There are a number of reasons for Muslims to practice animal sacrifice, including a simple act of charity (sadaqah) and to celebrate the birth of a newborn (aqiqah). The most widely practiced animal sacrifice is the annual festival of Eid al-Adha, which Muslims observe during the season of pilgrimage (hajj) at the end of Islamic calendar.

Some of the Qur'anic verses that serve as the foundation for this practice are as follows:

> And complete the Hajj or 'umrah in the service of Allah. But if ye are prevented (from completing it), send an offering for sacrifice. ... (Qur'an 2: 196)

> That they may witness the benefits (provided) for them, and celebrate the name of Allah, through the Days appointed, over the cattle which He has provided for them (for sacrifice): then eat ye thereof and feed the distressed in want. (Qur'an 22:28)

> The sacrificial camels We have made for you as among the Symbols of Allah: in them is (much) good for you: then pronounce the name of Allah over them as they line up (for sacrifice): when they are down on their sides (after slaughter), eat ye thereof, and feed such as (beg not but) live in contentment, and such as beg with due humility: thus have We made animals subject to you, that ye may be grateful. (Qur'an 22: 36)

Those who argue that Muslims should practice vegetarianism call for the end of the practice of animal sacrifice. Foltz, for example, argues that the essence of the ritual of animal sacrifice is the act of charity. This can be fulfilled by substituting the giving of the meat of the sacrificial animals with money or other non-meat food to the poor.

Ebrahim's interview with vegan Muslims also provides some examples of the different ways the festival of Eid al Adha (Qurbani) is celebrated. Their explanations illustrate Foltz's claim that the essence of the ritual is the act of charity. Anissa Buzhu explains that as a butcher's granddaughter, her family traditionally celebrated the festival by sacrificing an animal whose meat was then distributed in the neighborhood and community. In today's condition of overconsumption of meat, however, she believes that the traditional way of practicing the ritual has become redundant. She chooses to substitute the animal sacrifice by purchasing and donating plant-based groceries. According to her,

> *Qurbani* symbolizes what the essence of Islam means to me: i.e. submission. The expression of that submission comes with practices from ancient traditions, which in itself have a lot of value and wisdom. *Qurbani* goes beyond the sacrifice of an animal: it's about connecting with your Maker, reflecting on yourself and serving God by serving people. Helping others, I perceive as something you can do without animal products.

Similarly, R K, a vegan Muslim in France describes his/her observance of Eid al Adha as follows:

> To me, *Qurbani* means the sacrifice of Abraham to obey Allah to show him his true faith. It means an important day for me to show that we have to prove our faith to Allah by praying, doing *duaa* (prayer) and giving charity. On Eid-al-Adha, I wake up early, pray the Eid prayer, and pray the five mandatory prayers through the day. Sometimes I give money to charity organizations.

This act of substituting animal sacrifice has also been done in practice, for example, in the context of Muslims who live as minority in Western countries. In his work, Masri describes this substitution as follows:

> According to the laws in the West, no animal can be slaughtered for trade except under supervision and only under licensed abattoirs. [...] In the Welfare State of Europe there are hardly any "poor" to be found. [...] Muslims in the West are now more inclined to donate an equivalent amount of case to some charitable institution ... (122)

In other words, while the ritual of sacrifice has traditionally taken the form of slaughtering sacrificial animals and sharing their meat with the needy, the essence of the ritual can take different forms given different contemporary context.

There is a difference, however, between those who believe that such substitution is acceptable because Muslims live as a minority group in an industrial society and those who argue that such substitution is preferable since it does not involve pain and death of sacrificial animals. In my previous work, I analyzed this preference of not causing certain pain and suffering to animals that we consume as well as doing away with the practice of religious animal sacrifice. I argued that arguments against religious slaughter and animal sacrifice are best understood in the context of Western colonialism and the spread of industrialization. The shift from religious to modern methods of animal slaughter is often presented as a story of moral progress because it minimizes the pain that animals experience at the moment of slaughter. Arguments for ethically abstaining from consuming animals are framed largely as an extension of this civilizing narrative, where the desire to minimize pain and suffering is taken to its logical conclusion. In this narrative, religious method of animal slaughter as well as rituals of animal sacrifice are considered as inhumane and uncivilized.

Donaldson and Kymlicka, for example, argue that a society in which humans do not kill animals for their meat is a more humane society. They distinguish between mixed human–animal society (which includes companion animals such as cats and dogs) and wild animal society. In a wild animal society, meat-eating is an ethically justifiable practice because there is no alternative to the natural predator–prey relationship. They argue that mixed human–animal society, however, has the capacity to transcend the barbarity of the violent predator–prey relationship. Moreover, humans have the moral obligation to transcend this violence.

The argument that humans are morally obligated to transcend the violence that is considered to be natural for other animals is not without its critics. Lavin, for example, argues that the ethical argument to abstain from animal consumption is essentially an aspiration rooted in Western enlightenment values to transcend human nature. He describes the ethical choice to adopt a diet that is "free of violence and cruelty endemic to meat eating, often signals mastery of the human appetite" as an aspiration for "a superhuman status" (119–120). He explains,

> Despite the significance differences between Tom Regan's claim that eating meat violates the moral rights of animals, Peter Singer's utilitarian argument that a vegetarian diet is preferable for its minimizing the amount of suffering in the world, and Carol J. Adams's feminist comparison of the meat and dairy industries to the enslavement and subjugation of women and people of color, what is consistent across the literature is an appeal to the terms of a political liberalism in which the enslavement and slaughter of animals violates the universal principle of freedom from cruelty. (120—121)

This notion of a universal principle of freedom from cruelty, however, is best understood in terms of its historical specificity. More specifically, the modern nation of humaneness is central to the civilizing narrative that underlies European Enlightenment as well as its spread to other parts of the world through colonialism.

In his work *Formations of the Secular*, Asad explains that the ostensible goal of the civilizing project of European colonialism was to bring about "moral improvements in behavior" in the colonies by eliminating cruel and barbaric practices (109). The real goal, however, was not to avoid or eliminate all types of pain and suffering. Instead, he argues that the civilizing project involved a re-categorization of what types of pain and suffering are considered to be acceptable. He explains,

> only some kinds of suffering were seen as an affront to humanity, and their elimination is sought. This was distinguished from suffering that was necessary to the process of realizing one's humanity—that is, pain that was adequate to its end, not wasteful pain. Inhumane suffering, typically associated with barbaric behavior, was a morally insufferable condition. (111)

Asad gives an example of how colonial reforms made illegal punishments that are considered as inhumane—such as flogging—and replaced them with such options as imprisonment (including solitary confinement), which is considered as humane punishment.

Among the colonial laws that were introduced in the late 19th century were the humane treatment of animals laws. In his work *The Animal in Ottoman Egypt*, Mikhail argues that the British colonial laws on humane treatment of animals were part of the modern European civilizing project, where punishing the colonized people for committing violence (as defined by the colonial standard) against animals was considered progress toward a more civilized society. He explains,

> Many British anti-cruelty advocates in colonial Egypt expressed their animal welfare politics through violence against other humans to protect nonhumans. [...] The emergence of a new discourse about animal rights at the end of the nineteenth century [...] put in stark relief the contradictory ways colonial ideas about the hierarchy of humanity stood unproblematically alongside imperial support for animal welfare. In these colonial hierarchies, nonhumans often stood above certain kinds of (nearly always non-European) humans. (179)

The re-categorization of acceptable pain and suffering is evident in the discourse on colonial laws on animal welfare. For example, the humane treatment of animal laws are the basis of outlawing religious methods of animal slaughter, including the Islamic method, in many countries in Europe to date. This law deems the modern method of animal slaughter with prior stunning as humane and the religious methods as barbaric.

Secular modern approaches to animal ethics are ostensibly sensitive to animal pain and suffering and assume that the civilizing narrative of progress would result in their minimization or even elimination. However, these approaches define humans as being fundamentally different from other nonhuman animals in a way that does not recognize human vulnerability and dependence. On the one hand, arguments against human consumption of animals rest on the premise that humans are able to—and therefore morally obligated to—transcend their animality. On the other hand, the same arguments often challenge the hierarchy between humans and nonhuman animals. Furthermore, these arguments often position religion, more specifically the Judeo-Christian Biblical view, as one of the sources of such hierarchy. More specifically, the focus is often on the Biblical narrative in which God gives humans dominion over nonhuman animals. Tlili, however, argues that there is a significant difference between this Biblical view of human–animal relationship and the one found in the Qur'an. While the Biblical view espouses hierarchy, Tlili argues that "no verse in the Qur'an gives humans dominion over other creatures" (13 of 18). Following her analysis of several terms used by the Qur'anic verses that are often interpreted as promoting anthropocentrism, Tlili concludes that overall the Qur'an views humans as being vulnerable and that their need to consume animals as food is part of this vulnerability that Muslims should constantly remember.

Tlili argues that this emphasis on human vulnerability is what distinguishes the Qur'anic view of human–animal relationship as different from the Biblical view found in the Old Testament. She explains,

> Far from highlighting humans' special status, the verse seems rather to highlight their inherent vulnerability and utter dependence on Gold on one hand and their failure to show gratitude for God's grace toward them on the other. (14 of 18)

The act of invoking God's name at the moment of slaughter can be understood as a reminder of the vulnerable nature of being human—a reminder that in order to live, one must consume what God has provided and recognize the subsequent responsibility to show gratitude. This reminder is evident in the various Qur'anic verses quoted earlier in this chapter, which link human use and consumption of animals such as cattle with the virtue of humility and gratitude.

While permitted to use and consume animals, Muslims are also subject to various regulations concerning such consumption. An argument can be made that the teachings of Islam would consider problematic the consumption of animals raised and slaughtered in advanced industrial societies. One reason is the way industrial animal farming and slaughter do not allow for the recognition of the suffering experienced by the animals. The act of invoking God's name can also be interpreted as a reminder of the individuality of the animals whose lives are sacrificed for human benefit. On this point, Islamic teachings are consistent with the vegan principle of making visible the individuality and suffering that animals experience. The goal of this visibility, however, is not to prohibit what God has permitted, but to cultivate gratitude and humility for one's vulnerability.

In my previous work, I have discussed Muslim farming and slaughtering practices that promote visibility and proximity, such as a particular type of halal slaughterhouses where customers are encouraged to get to know the animals they are going to consume. At Madani halal slaughterhouse in Queens, New York, animals are slaughtered following the traditional Islamic guidelines. They are hand-cut without prior stunning by a Muslim who pronounces the name of God for each animal at the moment of slaughter. Animals are slaughtered in a separate room, away from the other animals that are still alive to minimize their psychological pain. Describing the customer experience at Madani, Falkowitz explains,

> Customers spend as much as an hour with chickens or goats to pick out the best specimens for their dollar. Some ask to slaughter the animals themselves, which Uddin [the owner] obliges. While saying a traditional Muslim prayer, he guides customers' hand with a knife to ensure a clean, fast, and low-pain kill.

Witnessing or partaking in the traditional Islamic practice of animal slaughter encourages Muslims to acknowledge both the animals' individuality as well as one's own vulnerability; a sharp contrast to the way industrial animal farming and slaughter erase the animals' individuality and conceal their suffering.

Works cited

Adams, Carol J. *The Sexual Politics of Meat*. Bloomsbury Publishing, 2015.
Ali, Abdullah Yusuf. *The Holy Qur'an*. Wordsworth Publishing, 2000.
Ali, Kecia. "Muslims and Meat-Eating." *Journal of Religious Ethics*, vol. 43, no. 2, 2015, pp. 268–288. doi:10.1111/jore.12097.
Asad, Talal. *Formations of the Secular: Christianity, Islam, Modernity*. Stanford University Press, 2003.
Dahlan, Magfirah. *Sacred Rituals and Humane Death: Religion in the Ethics and Politics of Modern Meat*. Lexington Books, 2019.
Donaldson, Sue and W. Kymlica. *Zoopolis: A Political Theory of Animal Rights*. New York, NY: Oxford University Press, 2011.
Ebrahim, Shaazia et al. "How Vegan Muslims Observe Qurbani." *The Daily Vox*, 12 November 2019, www.thedailyvox.co.za/how-vegan-muslims-observe-qurbani-shaazia-ebrahim/.
Falkowitz, Max. "An Inside Look at a Halal Slaughterhouse." *Serious Eats*, 9 December 2011. https://www.seriouseats.com/2011/12/inside-look-halal-slaughterhouse-madani-queens-what-is-halal.html
Foltz, Richard. *Animals in Islamic tradition and Muslim cultures*. Oneworld, 2006.
Lavin, Chad. *Eating Anxiety: The Perils of Food Politics*. Minneapolis, University of Minnesota Press, 2013.
Masri, A.B.A. *Animal Welfare in Islam*. The Islamic Foundation, 2009.
Mikhail, Alan. *The Animal in Ottoman Egypt*. Oxford University Press, 2014.
Tlili, Sarra. "Animal Ethics in Islam: A Review Article." *Religions*, vol. 9, no. 9, 2018, p. 269, doi:10.3390/rel9090269.
Wright, Laura. *The Vegan Studies Project: Food, Animals, and Gender in the Age of Terror*. University of Georgia Press, 2015.

Part 4
Theoretical engagements

21
A vegan ecofeminist queer ecological view of ecocriticism
A Costa Rican natureculture walk in literary/environmental studyland

Adriana Jiménez Rodríguez

Three events marked the last stages of writing this piece: the devastating Australian fires of 2019, the reading of an LGBTQ+ fairytale to our children, and taking our kittens, Sparkles and Sprinkles, to the vet for sterilization. The profound implications of the interconnectedness between these events finally landed my intention(s) to problematize and challenge the field of ecocriticism via a vegan studies, ecofeminist analysis. Severely distressed by media images of thousands of suffering burnt nonhuman animals, the last drop for me was listening to an injured koala wail. The sound that came out of him was heartbreaking, a cry of absolute despair. *His* heart was broken. I pulled myself together and decided to read *Prince and Knight*, a non-heteronormative fairytale that I got them for Christmas,[1] to Kaelan and Kellas. So we read about the Prince rejecting all the Princesses, until we get to page ten and the appearance of an "evil" dragon: "All the villagers ran in fear! Even the soldiers hid and fled. 'This vicious beast is far too great. We must retreat or we'll be dead!'" (Hack and Lewis). The Prince, aided by Knight, proceed to trap and tie the dragon up. My four-year-old son was very upset: "Mommy WHY did they not just calm her or him down!"[2] After a discussion on whether or not the dragon was murdered by the "brave" (handsome, able-bodied, white, rich) gay protagonists, Kaelan, my six-year-old concluded that, indeed, yes, she or he was dead "because look at the X's in her or his eyes." We talked a little about the fact that just because a story is LGBTQ+ inclusive does not necessarily mean that it addresses other forms of oppression and/or violence, especially toward nonhuman animals. They liked the gay wedding ending but were quite upset about the dragon's unjust murder for days.

For some reason this experience made me think about my father's comment about the cats' sterilization appointment. He holds that sterilization is "cruel" because the cats themselves are not choosing it. I typically ask him if he wants to care for all the kittens in the universe, both financially and emotionally.[3] He says no, and so on. I believe sterilization of domestic nonhuman animal companions is the one ethical, *humane* (whatever that means), environmentally friendly choice for a planet facing overpopulation of unwanted nonhuman animals that suffer under horrifying conditions. However, I did freely decide to bring two new little human animals into the world, and a considerable number of my friends believe that that choice is irresponsible and unethical for the very same reason I just stated for cats. Moral complications notwithstanding, I would like to read my children stories that address at least several types of intersecting oppressions.[4] I expect the same level of intersectionality in other areas of creative and scholarly inquiry, ecocriticism included. It is indeed very difficult to comment on a survey of the field of ecocriticism. I was recently told, to my mild surprise, that I am an ecocritic. I do not identify as such but rather as a vegan ecofeminist queer ecologist of color, but the remark helped me to note that I have discovered that one main cornerstone of ecocriticism is definition. The other is affiliation. The third is white people—men, overwhelmingly. I am none of these things.

I have written about what I call vegan ecofeminist queer ecologies before. In my study of ecofeminism and queer ecologies I wanted to put them together in a way that was simple, specific, and inclusive enough because I was not finding such connections anywhere else. Technically, ecofeminism is considered a sub-section of ecocriticism, although both fields originated independently around the same time[5]; queer ecologies is one of the most radical strands of ecocriticism. It becomes difficult to separate the theoretical and methodological strands, and it may even be unnecessary except affiliation is crucial, apparently. In her 1996 foundational collection *The Ecocriticsm Reader*, Cheryll Glotfelty defines ecocriticism as "the study of the relationship between literature and the physical environment" (xviii). Greg Garrard adds to the definition by referring to the activist aspect of ecocriticism: "Most of all, ecocriticism seeks to evaluate texts and ideas in terms of their coherence and usefulness as responses to environmental crisis" (4). I was initially perplexed by Lawrence Buell's affirmation that "an ecocritic may be an ecofeminist, but only a fraction of ecofeminists would be thought of as ecocritics" (n.p.). I dislike passive voice precisely because it allows "be thought of"s such as his. I want to ask by who? Who would not think (a large) faction of ecofeminists are not ecocritics? Then I concluded that I agree with him, but in an entirely different dimension. Ecocriticism is almost like an environmental church, and membership requires a certain… *civility* that most ecofeminists pointedly *lack*. "Although there is something potentially noble about human attempts to speak ecocentrically against human dominationism," says Buell, "unless one proceeds very cautiously there soon becomes something quixotic and presumptuous about it" (n.p.). All the ecofeminists I respect speak passionately against human domination of the nonhuman.[6] Perhaps this passion marks the divide between ecofeminism and ecocriticism—and perhaps the admonition that doing so is quixotic and presumptuous is a sexist assertion from a key male scholar in a field that predominantly recognizes the work of men.

Ecocriticism initially brought together academics in the humanities who wrote about the relationship between literature and the environment. Originally focused on the Romantic tropes of the pastoral, aesthetics, and on a (conservative) nature preservation agenda, ecocriticism has never exercised radical activism, academically or politically, even if lately it has ventured into more contemporary literary genres alongside climate change (and planetary devastation) theory. Fundamentally, I feel that the question of the representation of nature is paramount to most ecocritics; the *question of representation*, not *nature* itself, the nature that is on its deathbed because of human intervention. It is ultimately an issue of perspective, what ecocritics choose to focus their gaze upon. The Association for the Study of Literature and the Environment (ASLE) originated in 1992 as a laudable effort to bring together environmental literary critics in order to have a base for action. Scholars in the humanities had nowhere to go with their interest in environmental issues. ASLE offers room for everyone, but is not in itself particularly radical. It is very civilized. A brief look at ASLE's journal *ISLE*'s last Editor's Choice reveals a very interesting variety of research topics.[7] As far as I can see, to put it bluntly, ASLE is not vegan. Vegans (and other Others) are welcome, but veganism is not part of ASLE's or ecocriticism's core ideology, not even an option in the "areas of interest" section, for instance. In order to concisely discuss the relationship between vegan studies and ecocriticism, I decided to focus on four major ecocritics to map the possibilities of connection with ethical veganism.[8] There were none. If an alien came to visit and read those four *major* books, she would never know that veganism exists or that it is even remotely relevant to ecocriticism/environmental studies. I definitely cannot speak about all of ecocriticism; the field is immense. The present work is, however, a careful attempt to visualize ecocriticism's (definitely male) bone structure, so to speak, at its most general, in the following works: *The Song of the Earth* by Jonathan Bate (2000), *The Future of Environmental Criticism: Environmental Crisis and Literary Imagination*, by Lawrence Buell (2005), *Ecocriticism* by Greg Garrard (2012), and *Ecocriticism on the Edge: The Anthropocene as a Threshold Concept* by Timothy Clark (2015).

Buell's *The Future of Environmental Criticism* is an excellent overview of ecocriticism. He explains with both clarity and authority the difference between first wave and second wave ecocritics,[9] and discusses the field's issues with definition/representation and lack of methodological basis at length. He is less clear about ecofeminism (s), and a little less comfortable with the weaknesses of the field inasmuch as I think he does point to them but then relapses into what I have begun to call the political *politeness* of ecocriticism. Firstly, his definition of ecofeminism ("ecofeminism … is an umbrella term for a range of theoretical and practical positions that share the view that the 'twin dominations of women and nature' are artifacts of patriarchal culture instituted in antiquity") does not even mention speciesism—perhaps assuming that nonhuman animals are somehow included in "nature."[10] One could argue that nonhumans (or ecofeminism or queer ecologies or veganism) are not really the focus of the book, that they are not really the focus of ecocriticism at large. This is precisely my point. As a matter of fact, Buell himself mentions that his overview of the chronology of ecocriticism has "relegated a number of significant ethico-political positions to the sidelines, most notably the discourses of animal and other nonhuman rights and a range of local-global interaction from liberal green reform to anticapitalist critiques of consumerism" (n.p.).[11] The other books I discuss in this chapter do the same, more or less. Why must "animal and other nonhuman rights" texts be separate from ecocriticism? For instance, why does Buell not answer his own question: "Should the outer circle of moral consideration be extended to include only 'higher' animals, all sentient beings, all forms of life, or somewhere beyond that?" That surely is an interesting question. After stating that all ecocentric strains "define human identity not as free-standing but in terms of its relationship with the physical environment and/or nonhuman life forms" he strips that relationship from due (human) responsibility by tepidly arguing that 'sustainability' as an ethical position is hard to pin down, not the least of which reasons being that it requires guesswork about what the future generations will be like and that it runs contrary to the known fact that nature itself does not remain stable" (n.p.)

Sustainability is not that hard to pin down and nature's lack of stability has not much to do with our ethical responsibility to reduce and repair damage as much as is humanly possible—protect water sources, plant trees, acknowledge minorities, work for food sovereignty, protect seeds, and stop eating nonhumans, for example. And these all should also be vegan concerns as well. Ethical veganism needs to problematize the issues of (white) privilege, capitalist consumerism, and pervasive sexism, classism, ableism and hetero and homonormativity, to name just a few. Ecocriticism, however, has to take a stronger, perhaps *impolite*, stand in the face of all of these issues and recognize their interconnectedness.

In my opinion, Buell's most interesting idea is that of "environmental unconscious." Buell argues that "an individual text must be thought of as environmentally embedded at every stage from its germination to its reception" and that "a text's environmental unconscious is more deeply embedded even than its 'political unconscious'" (n.p.). I wish he would speak more about the ways in which we can work to become more environmentally conscious, and perhaps even in terms of veganism, specifically. Assumptions about nonhuman animals and socially sanctioned eating practices are part of this environmental unconscious, and they are certainly worth investigating in any vegan-oriented literary analysis. Buell also makes a revealing observation about the place of environmental studies scholars in academia when he comments that "[e]nvironmental criticism in literature and the arts clearly does not yet have the standing within the academy of such other issue-driven discourses as those of race, gender, sexuality, class, and globalization" (n.p.). I think the key is bringing all of these together, changing the "standing" altogether and striving for much more inter-issue discourses, complicating things a bit and fighting against theoretical compartmentalization. Why not? When Buell speaks about communities, he reminds me of Daly's consciousness of one: "Always the read text is being engaged by at least one solitary mind/body poised somewhere in space; the experience becomes communal via a reading group or formal class; and these reading contexts matter" (n.p.). However, in this particular now, communities must include nonhuman animals and our shared contexts. The power of communal thinking is undeniable, just as is the power and possibility that we as teachers have to support and encourage our students in environment-oriented tracks. I deeply believe in the transformational potential of the classroom, where place and time offer an unlimited diversity of possibilities in the transactional process of teaching, especially via the lens of feminist pedagogies. In the end, Buell does identify the main weakness of the field of ecocriticism in general:

> Unless ecocriticism can squarely address the question of how nature matters for those readers, critics, teachers, and students for whom environmental concern does not mean nature preservation first and foremost and for whom nature writing, nature poetry, and wilderness narrative does not seem the most compelling forms of environmental imagination, then the movement may fission and wane. (n.p.)

Traducido al guatuso[12] as my mother would say: until ecocriticism can start to exercise its imagination to think about the ways in which people of color think about naturecultures, it will remain a White Person Thing, and therefore of no practical use. People of color also have to think about veganism, as scholars and activists like A. Breeze Harper and Aph and Syl Ko have, as a means of social action, decolonization, and self-care. Surviving in the ruins is not about anybody shirking responsibilities; it is about finally getting over our privilege (whatever this might mean for different humans) and thinking together in ways that we can all connect to in some way.

The Song of the Earth

Jonathan Bates's *The Song of the Earth* at least has a chapter with the word "animals" in it ("Poets, Apes, and Other Animals"), but his instrumentalization of nonhuman bodies is disappointing in the extreme.[13] The opening is straightforward enough:

> This is a book about why poetry continues to matter as we enter a new millennium that will be ruled by technology. It is a book about modern Western man's alienation from nature. It is about the capacity of the writer to restore us to the earth which is our home. (ix)

A vegan ecofeminist queer ecological view of ecocriticism

While it is monumentally clear that he writes from and for the category Man in all its splendor, and his focus *is* ecopoesis, he fails at explaining how this romantic restoration (in the actual world) can take place. If "mortals dwell in that they save the earth and if poetry is the original admission of dwelling, then poetry is the place where we save the earth" (283) is quite bizarre indeed: metaphors are not going to stop the ice from melting, clearly. Any environmental criticism of literature and/or society should definitely connect to concrete reality, to ways in which we believe that the humanities can contribute to actually effecting change in the world.

However, Bates' analysis of John Clare and his poetry is quite moving, and speaks, in a way, of a type of connection with the environment which is still highly relevant to an ecocritical approach to literature: "A human being can do anything except build a bird's nest. What we can do is build an analogue of a bird's nest in a poem" (160). Unfortunately, monkeys and bears do not produce the same sympathy in him, as when he speaks about Byron's exotic pets. In his reading of the relationship between "man and animal" he also makes some regrettable comparisons that show a startling lack of sensitivity: "The animal liberation movement is premised on the idea of an increasingly extended circle of rights: first the emancipation of the unpropertied and the poor, then that of women and children, next to slaves and so to animals" (177).[14] While he agrees that Byron was inconsiderate in how he treated his monkeys and his bear (they apparently survived in filthy cages and were traipsed all over Europe), the patronizing implications in his comparison become clearer when he says about the nonhuman pets that, *however*, "[l]ike his servant Fletcher, they are part of the family" (185). What a relief, then! Bates believes that animal rights belong to the field of ethics, not poetry: "My argument in this chapter is not about animal rights, but about how animals make us think about our own animalness, our embodiedness in the world" (187). For him, then, nonhumans are useful to human imagination only because of the representational projections that they can facilitate. This is confusing because just a few pages earlier he states that ecological criticism sees nature for itself, not as a reflection of human emotions (180). This argumentative contradiction shows that he somehow separates "animal" from "nature." He closes the chapter by openly mocking Snyder and his poetry. "The cause of ecology," he writes, "may not necessarily be best served by poets taking the high moral ground and speaking from the point of view of political correctness" (199). So poetry is *higher* than high moral ground, according to him. I find that Bates' ethical compartmentalization of poetry, animals, and nature is not uncommon in ecocriticism as a field, and this lack of (inter) connection(s) is intrinsic to the ideological *politeness* that I mentioned earlier.

Ecocriticism: The New Critical Idiom

Greg Garrard's *Ecocriticism* is a valuable overview of the field under study. He uses tropes to cover the main elements of ecocriticism, and the organization is useful.[15] His criticism of the idealization of the "Ecological Indian" figure, particularly, is both pertinent and culturally sensitive, and his analysis of deep ecology is quite detailed. However, like Buell, when Garrard hits ecofeminism he gets shaky: "Deep ecology identifies the anthropocentric dualism humanity/nature as the ultimate source of anti-ecological beliefs and practices, but ecofeminism also blames the androcentric dualism man/woman" (26). The emphasis on "blame" and basic binary oppositions disregards ecofeminism's huge contribution to intersectional, multidimensional theory and activism; at times it seems to me he compares it excessively and inaccurately with deep ecology even if he admits that ecofeminism is more closely related to environmental justice movements. This is significant because a more adequate understanding of ecofeminism would necessarily bring speciesism to the fore.[16] Thus, I find that he is still ambiguous about the place of nonhumans in the theory of ecocriticism and remains silent on veganism. He spends considerable time wondering about the relationship between human animals and nonhuman animals, but he never takes up a concrete position in terms of the human eating of nonhumans; he vacillates. For instance, Garrard seems uncomfortable with capitalist farm factories when he commends Berry's portrayal of a nonhuman animal's slaughter in a more traditional farmer-murders-nonhuman context:

> The preoccupation here is not the welfare of the animal in itself, but rather the authenticity of the encounter and the gratitude and respect evinced by the killer. Properly carried out, the slaughter does not erode but enhances his humanity. (123)

And, again, in discussing Berger's work, Garrard shows typical macho disdain of emotion by claiming that the "relationships of humans and domestic animals in *Pig Earth* are funny, compassionate and humane without sentimentality or anthropomorphism" (126). I suppose vegan ecofeminists possess a *sentimental* compassion, then, when we point out that however (debatably) "humane" a murder, the nonhuman animal still ends up very *dead*, and that no amount of human "gratitude" validates such an unnecessary death. According to his reading, nonhuman dead bodies serve two functions, the standard capitalist one, human economic profit, and a second, more or less spiritual one that honestly sounds quite sentimental, "enhancing" humanity. Nonhuman animals apparently not only live because and for human animals, but die because and for them as well; their existence is thus viewed as exclusively human. In celebrating a distance from a perceived anthropomorphism Garrard ends up displaying a troubling anthropocentrism.

Garrard adheres to ecocriticism's solemn separation of itself from other fields of study that would actually confront its practitioners with their apathy for the analysis of simultaneous forms of human oppression and how it directly speaks to planetary devastation. "Since intensive livestock farming is objectionable on both environmental and welfare grounds," he says, "animal studies may be seen as an important ally of ecocriticism if not strictly a branch of it" (149). This theoretical separation weakens ecocriticism; it follows Bates in the sense that it places nonhuman rights *elsewhere*. Garrard, like the others, remains obsessively within the realm of language and the philosophical scope of representation[17] (Descartes and Derrida *ad nauseum*) when it comes to the relationship between human and nonhuman animals. He comments on Donna Haraway's work in thinking about companion nonhumans such as dogs: "Animals, in other words, make us human in a continual process of reshaping, just as we affect the evolution of both domesticated and wild species" (151). Yes, but human animals (selectively) eat nonhuman animals; it is as convenient as it is dangerous to speak of this relationship as equally reciprocal. His reflection on therapy dogs, dogs and inmates, and how people with autism might interpret the world similarly to dogs is somewhat confused and confusing. He is almost trying to convince himself of something, perhaps that nonhuman animals are more than tropes? He therefore ends up with startling sentences such as: "Humans can both be, and be compared to, animals" (153). Garrard then goes briefly back to eating nonhumans, touches on queer animals momentarily,[18] and then suddenly moves to an impassioned ridiculing of human love of dolphins and Disney's nonhuman characterizations.

His ethical ambiguity is also reflected in the strange thematic organization of his chapter. He juxtaposes lackluster conclusions such as "there is no necessary or even predictable relationship between representational forms and moral valuations" (156) with slightly melodramatic sentiments like the following one: "'Humans' are like 'animals,' but 'animals' are not 'animals'" (2010: 41). Certainly humans should not be treated 'like animals', but why should animals be treated 'like animals'?" (160) Nonhuman animals are vital to ecocriticism, so much so that one of the three challenges to the field that he offers at the end of his book highlights it:

> There are three key challenges for the future. One is the relationship between ecocriticism and animal studies. The extended treatment of animals in this edition has barely kept pace with research in this area, which is proceeding largely independently of the other developments discussed in this book. (203)

I would precisely challenge the need for this to happen "independently." However, what becomes clear in Garrard's conclusion is that the vegan unconscious continues to function in these ecocritics' writing, pointing to the undeniable fact that an ecological analysis that does not seek to examine an ethical position of the human eating of nonhumans, along with its catastrophic environmental consequences and its imbrication(s) with other types of patriarchal violence, simply will not *do* in the present planetary context.

Ecocriticism on the Edge

Finally, Timothy Clark's *Ecocriticism on the Edge* is, more than an overview, a challenge to the field in terms of its impact on the current environmental crisis. Framed in the Anthropocene,[19] and displaying a significantly less polite tone, this critic looks for answers in chaos. While he briefly acknowledges the catastrophic consequences of the meat industry on the planet, he refrains from engaging with veganism. This omission is shocking, quite frankly, but in line with ecocriticism on the whole. Indeed, according to him, "[m]any of the tensions and intellectual fragilities of ecocriticism come from the drive to reconcile increasingly incompatible claims under one diagnostic framework, despite a context that must render them more and more at odds with one another" (12). Perhaps it is worthwhile to stop and analyze those "incompatible" claims carefully because in the planet's present context, I do not think being "more and more at odds" serves any purpose; I believe a lot more in integration and interconnectedness. One of Clark's main concerns is the problematic move from individual to communal action, an important element of which is the (very real) sense of the irrelevancy of personal choices in the face of global disarray: "Environmental issues such as climate change entail the implication of the broadest effects in the smallest day-to-day phenomena, juxtaposing the trivial and the catastrophic in ways that can be deranging or paralyzing—for what can I do?" (14) His description of scale framing can possibly place us at a very useful starting point—in spite of the fact that for Clark the risks of falling into "evasion" or "oversimplification" are huge. I agree with him in that it is impossible to comprehend and engage with the magnitude of planetary devastation all at once; however, I do not think that immediately sliding into derisive qualification of "trivialities" really adds to the discussion, as when he says that "[v]iewed in terms of the deceptive rationality and scale of day-to-day life, environmental activists seem condemned to get everything out of perspective, to veer between a general priggishness about trivialities and an emptily apocalyptic rhetoric" (54).

It is risky to think that individual choices are trivial, especially in terms of consumer choices of who we eat or do not eat. However much he is targeting mainstream environmental slogans (specifically the vegetarian "eat less meat and save the rainforest"), the lack of serious consideration of veganism as an individual/communal response to environmental crisis makes me wonder about his intentions. While I do appreciate that at least he takes a position, his (unconscious or purposeful?) anti-vegan stance strikes me as unproductive, especially since he never actually brings it up to the fore and remains in the realm of "[t]his may be why environmental moralism, targeted at any individual, always seems over the top as it tries to implicate that person in damaging the Earth" (75). We all are implicated in damaging the Earth. The question is firstly one of intensity; that is, some humans are more implicated than others. And the second one is more related to what we choose to actually *do* about it. Who I choose to eat and how I choose to relate to that act and the ways in which I speak of it to the world, all of these actions matter.

When Clark speaks about social ecological strains of ecocriticism, he makes some dangerous claims. "For several decades," he says, "demographic concerns came increasingly to be tinted as latently racist, anti-woman, anti-immigrant and anti-poor" (83). He is irritated by thinkers who try to represent the ecological violence of overpopulation as entirely a matter of excessive consumption in the 'developed' world [who] look increasingly like people attempting to keep the arguments on more ethically comfortable and intellectually convenient terrain" (86). Well, most "demographic concerns" of white men are in fact racist, anti-woman, anti-immigrant, and anti-poor. Universal education, healthcare, and fair wages would significantly reduce population growth in the Global South; alas, these are not political or "economic growth" priorities. Furthermore, excessive consumption in the Global North is the other side of the overpopulated, poverty-stricken, environmentally exploited Global South, two sides of the same coin. Is this only obvious to Third-World humans and perhaps First-World thinkers who at least attempt something akin to global sensitivity? Migration, one of the unfortunate children of Third-World overpopulation is a much more useful phenomenon to consider ecocritically, anyway. After all, like Latour says,

> [m]igrations, explosions of inequality, and New Climatic Regime: these are one and the same threat. Most of our fellow citizens underestimate or deny what is happening to the earth, but they understand perfectly well that the question of migrants puts their dreams of a secure identity at risk. (9)

I think Clark's secure identity is probably at risk when, for example, he attacks queer ecologist critic Andil Gosine and his main thesis in "Non-White Reproduction and Same-Sex Eroticism: Queer Acts against Nature," which is basically that the reproduction of humans of color and non-reproductive (queer) sex freak White People out. Clark does appear very freaked out, frankly: "Intellectually at least, arguments as extreme as Gosine's are reassuring even in their evasiveness, for they force the terms of discussion back into such familiar and well-practised fields of debate as prejudice about race and sexuality" (89).[20] Not only does he insist on compartmentalizing (and minimizing!) issues that impact the environmental crisis, but he refuses to move past the *you-cannot-say-anything-anymore-because-everything-is-racist* excuse. We can basically substitute "racist" for "sexist," "homophobic," "ableist," and "speciesist," as I have been insisting throughout this chapter. Even if the fields of race and sexuality are allegedly well-practiced, I do not think that racism, sexism, or homophobia has been even remotely overcome. What is more, we have to further problematize them by including ableism and speciesism intersectionally in the discussion. There is very little time for (literally) outdated academic tantrums; the planet is dying. If we cannot critically interrogate our ideological position in the face of our human or ability privileges, to name just two, then our moral authority remains dubious, at best.

Clark's concluding remarks are symptomatic of the categorical refusal of many ecocritics (and countlessly *more* in other fields of academic study) to engage intersectionally with environmental criticism. "An ecological overview," he suggests, "is in danger of feeding a reductive green moralism, keen to turn ecological facts into moral imperatives on how to live" (108). Such a liberalist concern speaks loudly about the urgent need for a more integrated approach to the global crisis.[21] How can we *not* adapt the way we live given the context? Can he argue that queer vegan ecofeminists are urging humans to stop eating nonhumans out of "green moralism" with a straight face? I think he can, and he does.[22] He goes on to contemptuously speak about a "widespread working hypothesis in ecocriticism: this is that given forms of human 'oppression' make up a unitary monolith, of which ecophobia, racism, sexism and unjust hierarchy are all co-conspiring and mutually supporting parts, such that to question or call on one must be at once to implicate the others'" (109). *Exactly*, except he does not even mention speciesism, maybe because he is not comfortable with admitting how it is the same as homophobia, xenophobia, xenophobia, or "[o]ther forms of human prejudice or bigotry" (Idem). However, since he clearly understands the intricate workings of the unjust system of patriarchy, he is halfway there. Toward the end of his book, I feel that Clark does begin to alter his sarcastic tone, especially when he goes back to his introductory query of the possible impact of moving from the space of the individual choice to the space of the communal transformation: "My act of condemnation is likewise spectralized, that is, it will remain an ineffective gesture of empty anger unless somehow also generalized, duplicated by innumerable others in innumerable times and places, and carried over into action" (143). He enumerates actions that may appear simple, and which he has earlier referred to as part of the difficulty in living under a "green moralist" regime, such as turning a light on, buying certain types of pineapples[23] or flying to conferences… how about not eating nonhumans? He does admit the importance of the work at hand when he asks: "how can the increasingly felt need to read a text or issue in relation to—effectively—almost everything else retain some kind of coherence and discipline?" (145) It can be done. I managed a fairly decent approximation when I read Ozeki's *My Year of Meats* using vegan ecofeminist queer ecologies.[24] This methodology only seems impossible if someone has never experienced a combination of oppressions at the same time. When you have, the simultaneity of "almost everything" is perfectly understandable. Even if Clark backtracks almost immediately by clarifying that "[i]t is hard, however, to endorse here the assumption that knowledge of interconnection must somehow lead to an ethic of care" (189), he does finish what almost seems to be advice for himself: "Environmental readings of literature and culture may need to engage more directly with delusions of self-importance in their practice, keeping alert to the need for more direct kinds of activism" (198). I could not agree more. Perhaps it is time for ecocriticism to become a better version of itself.

The need for vegan studies is urgent, perhaps precisely because of its *glaring* omission from ecocriticism. Indeed,

> in term of crises brought about by human activity, of primary concern at present is human-engineered environmental devastation and the earth's backlash reactions to it (in the form of global warming and dramatic weather events), as well as the planet's increasing inability to support human and nonhuman life in the wake of environmental destruction. (Wright 68)

We need a space in academia where we can focus on vegan ecofeminist queer ecologies; I believe this is the place to begin. We have to point to theoretical and methodological problems within ethical veganism, of course, but this does not negate the acute need to speak openly about the planetary consequences of continuing to unnecessarily abuse/murder/exploit/eat nonhumans. I think that it is true that PETA wants a vegan world without touching capitalism and while participating and promoting blatant sexism. Greenpeace wants world peace and the end of climate change without attacking the meat industry… and so on. Unless vegan/environmental activism starts addressing all forms of oppression at the same time, fighting to dismantle the social system of patriarchy that produced it all then there is no hope. I have found, in my experience, that all-oppressions-at-once-is-impossible complainers have one thing in common: they have not experienced any multi-oppression themselves. *No les pasa por el cuerpo*.[25] Therefore, they could not care less. Most ecofeminist critics understand the importance of the actual *body* in any body of theory, and this is not essentialist. We speak about a diverse body of bodies, and about the many and very complex ways in which culture intervenes in their construction. Choosing to keep our bodies, our experience, our *emotions* in our theoretical writing is a courageous political choice[26]:

> We—the animal and I—are chosen, fixed and invested with purpose, constructed as things to devour and be devoured. Objects for and of consumption. To tolerate speciesism is to tolerate sexism is to consent to the obliteration of subjective agency (for eating-disordered women, for farmed animals). What else can I do but to use my voice, my words, to rectify these atrocities? No more silence. (Morr qtd. in Wright 161)

The establishment does not enjoy this breaking of silence. In fact, the very frequent violent reactions to veganism, vegan feminists/queers, vegan feminist academics are an expression of a generalized social crisis of masculinity, in my opinion. In the Anthropocene all borders are collapsing and signifiers like *man*, or *white*, which used to provide a certain stability (however frail) are not holding.[27] Maybe men are responding hysterically to calls of intersectionality (in and out of academia) because these by force require critical self-examination in the face of the bodies, human and nonhuman alike, that have been getting fucked over for centuries so that their privileges can exist in the first place.

Ecocriticism fails in not putting ethical veganism front and center. In general, I feel the field displays a very strange avoidance of engaging with the concrete consequences of the brutality that human animals inflict on nonhuman animals. If queer ecologies remains the most radical subgenre of ecocriticism (although barely acknowledged even as such) and it still also resists addressing ethical veganism I see very little hope that real action can be taken to survive in the planetary ruins that humanity has created. What is missing from ecocriticism is an emphasis on *emotion*, an addressing of the unmeasurable pain that human animals have caused nonhuman animals, a discussion that engages with the suffering of wailing koalas in Australia, tortured cows, chickens and pigs in slaughterhouses, suffering wild animals in illegal food markets, starving wild birds, homeless and displaced orangutans, dying bees, abused domestic dogs and cats, all of them. This suffering connects to human animals' suffering, in so many very ways. We need, as environmental critics, to be brave enough to look at all of this pain in the face, to understand that our food choices *matter*. To not leave this pain behind when we look at naturecultures in context[28] or when we suggest ways in which literature and theory can aid human animals in discovering ways to manage and deal with the consequences of humanity in an injured planet. Ethical veganism involves a political commitment to do this, at the same time that it understands the deep interconnections between who we eat and planetary devastation. Fromm has the audacity to say that "however delicate our moral sensibilities, it still remains that to be alive is to be a murderer" (n.p.). As a queer vegan ecofeminist queer ecologist woman of color living/surviving/struggling/loving in a tiny third-world country in the Global South I do not feel insulted by his arrogant accusation of "moral sensibility." I say to him, speak for yourself. Hiding behind such an overstated, grandiose excuse is your choice. In the current planetary *situation*, to so viciously attack ethical veganism, speaking from a deeply unexamined position of privilege, is as shameful and violent as it is typical.

Yes, veganism needs to reject soy monoculture because it has terrible environmental consequences that harm the nonhuman, animals, and other(s), to mention just one problematic area. We need to work hard to achieve a functioning articulation of the multiple ways in which multilayered forms of cruelty remain in vegan diets around the world. We need to talk about sexism, racism, classism, colonialism, and ableism in ethical vegan discourse(s) and theory. This is precisely why we desperately need vegan studies departments, everywhere, *now*. But this does not disqualify our intention: we want to inflict as little suffering as possible in the particular time and space where we stand; we want to actively exercise empathy as an act of imagination, and mostly, as an act of love. We must do this intellectually but also *emotionally*; we have to integrate vegan ecofeminist queer ecologies into our individual daily lives, into an interdisciplinary and transnational academy, and into our communities with responsibility and rigor. However much it is very true that it is already too late, we must embrace the very fragility of our future on earth, and do everything that we still can to creatively procure hope, peculiar little non-monkeys that we human animals are.

Notes

1 In Costa Rica, I have no options of bookstores that have an LGBTQ+ children's books section in English. The ONE independent bookstore that has such section is *Libros Duluoz* in San José downtown, and they only carry books in Spanish (excellent books—we own quite a few). I order books for my children via Amazon, and members of my U.S. extended-blended family bring them over when they come to visit. Feel free to think about the (vegan) queer ecological implications of *that*.
2 It is difficult enough to explain "soldier" to them, let alone "knight." Costa Rica does not have an army. I think ecocritical research into the impact of military culture on the environment is a really interesting project both for people from military cultures and people from non-military cultures; perhaps a comparative endeavor would reveal meaningful details about the imbrications of both and the perception of the construction of military ecosystems, especially through an integrated vegan ecofeminist queer ecological perspective.
3 I have spent much of my life trying to help abandoned nonhuman animals. I know a bit about the time, love, and money that goes into that kind of labor.
4 Murdering a dragon is so unnecessary, by the way, speciesist and look-ist—nobody ever murders unicorns in the same socially sanctioned manner. And why can authors not imagine a *Latino* Prince? How about a transgender Prince? Why am I not seeing enough diversity of body types and abilities in children's books? Is it impossible for vegan story books to acknowledge that human animals' "cultures" are enmeshed in nonhuman animals' "natures"?
5 "Ecofeminism" was coined by Françoise d'Eaubonne in her book *Le Féminisme ou la Mort* in 1974 while "ecocriticism" was coined by William Ruekert in 1978 in his essay "Literature and Ecology: An Experiment in Ecocriticism."
6 I am certainly not alone:
Greta Gaard takes up the omission of female writers like Adams in a 2010 article in Isle in which she advocates for a more feminist ecocriticism, one that addresses the ecocritical revisionism—by such writers as Garrard and Lawrence Buell—that has rendered a feminist perspective largely absent. (Wright 17)
7 Indeed, "the quality of the best work now published in ASLE's flagship journal, *ISLE*, is at least equal to that of the articles published in Environmental History, the journal of the American Society for Environmental History, even though the latter (both the journal and the organization itself) has been in existence twice as long" (Buell n.p.).
8 I do not read male authors by choice, so this was an unusual and difficult thinking exercise for me.
9 Basically, as Buell explains it, first-wave ecocritics saw nature as opposed to culture, analyzed only certain types of literature, tended to see nature as a vehicle/receptacle/mirror of man's condition at the same time that they ironically rejected anthropocentrism, especially in terms of literary representation. Second-wave ecocritics recognize that nature and culture are inevitably enmeshed in complicated co-construction/destruction, focus more on social ecology, take into account urban and degraded landscapes side by side with "natural ones," and are somewhat closer to environmental justice movements. This in spite of the fact that, as he points out, many people have said that "ecocriticism's lack of a strong environmental justice component" shows a "deep crisis" I would add that environmental justice movements are lacking a vegan component. I agree with Buell that "Second-wave environmental critics would define the proper mission of greenspeak as centered more on environmental equity among humans than on interspecies harmony" and this is a mistake. Until all issues are addressed with equal urgency, no permanent change will take place.

10 A simple definition does not have to delete fundamental elements to achieve readability. Try this one: "the ecofeminist position offers that as all oppressions are linked and codependent, there can be no freedom from one form of oppression unless there is freedom from all of them ... What ecofeminism does not do is hold that these divisions are in any way essential or natural, despite many theorists' dismissal of ecofeminism based on such inaccurate readings" (Wright 17).

11 Chronologically, then, it seems that ecocriticism became interested in the "animal" question in the 2000s and that in the 2010s the vegan issue began to intervene ecocriticism (what I have called the vegan unconscious), in spite of an overt effort to *not* address it.

12 This a colloquial expression loosely meaning "in simple words," but oh, so much is lost in translation.

13 This is, after I could procure the book; Amazon politely told me they could not *sell* it to me because of "zone restrictions." There is such a thing as Third World Research Issues Especially in English.

14 When Wright develops a similar idea, she does so with remarkable ethical sensibility: "This work also links vegetarianism to other social movements, like abolition, noting that 'unlike today, when social movements tend to stand apart from one another, during the Jacksonian era reformers of various causes were united in their views'" (62). She does not use the word "slaves," but focuses on "abolition," the movement against the brutal use of humans as slaves, and I appreciate it. White men casually saying "slaves" always distresses me in the extreme (must be my "radical" vegan diet, based on "unusual sensibility" mixed with my Latina woman "temper"). In any event, words matter.

15 I also agree with his intention: "Only if we imagine that the planet has a future, after all, are we likely to take responsibility for it" (116).

16 When Wright discusses Fraiman she discusses the concern "with the revisionist history that places Derrida at the fore as the father of legitimate animal studies and erases from that discourse the voices of pioneering women—like Adams, Lori Gruen, Marti Kheel, and Greta Gaard. What Derrida did was to remove the gendered component from the analysis, to take animal studies away from various lineages at the point at which it had maintained established linkages with women's studies" (18). These ecocritics, in a similar way, by erasing ecofeminist theory, avoid dealing with the speciesism at the heart of their discussion of nonhuman animals.

17 I think that this is why male ecocritics like (and quote) Plumwood so much. She has always seemed to me the least ecofeminist ecofeminist. Maybe they also like the time and dedication that she devotes to proving Carol Adams "wrong."

18 "Queer animals," he says, "are a fascinating and genuinely subversive phenomenon. At the same time, though, heterosexual copulation is a precondition for the survival of species incapable of asexual reproduction. Homosexuality therefore remains a puzzle in evolutionary terms, which can be resolved through a constructive encounter between queer theory and biological science" (172). I am as always perplexed by this fascination with "origins" of queer animality. Who cares? We exist.

19 "Anthropocene," he explains, "to use the currently still informal term for the epoch at which largely unplanned human impacts on the planet's basic ecological systems have passed a dangerous, if imponderable, threshold" (1).

20 White people only get called "extreme" or "radical" when they are feminist, queer or vegan, to name a mere three.

21 For example, he defends "[s]imply things like the desire for improved health and living conditions (and subsequent population increases), better travel facilities and the need for food production that drive destructive behaviours such as overfishing, the destruction of the habitats of other species or rising carbon emissions" (111).

22 He holds that position in spite of the fact that he (obviously) knows the environmental facts about the global human eating of nonhumans: "Today, animal agriculture has been argued to be a greater source of greenhouse gases, directly and indirectly, than all the world's transportation systems" (123). Later, he says: "Human beings could not exist and cannot be understood without other species, whatever the tendency of modern societies to keep livestock hidden away in factory-like enclosures while people live as if red meat were on tap, like water from a reservoir" (123). Yet he does not write a single word on veganism.

23 He is correct in worrying about that. Pineapple (produced strictly as monoculture unless labeled as certified organic) in Costa Rica is about the *last* product anyone should support. A good example of the undeniable interconnectedness of patriarchal exploitation, pineapple farming combines environmental racism with sexism, speciesism and the exploitation of undocumented Nicaraguan workers. It is, truly, an atrocity, which is invisibilized behind the greenwashing of the Costa Rican government and the general apathy of the Costa Rican population.

24 Joaquin Phoenix did it in under a minute during his acceptance speech at the Oscars recently. It is really not that difficult.
25 This could be literally translated as: *It does not cut across their bodies.*
26 I could not agree more with Wright when she says that "personal narrative should also be a part of the vegan studies project, as the personal provides nuance and depth to the incomplete and ever-shifting nature of the public narrative" (159). The personal, as we have been saying for decades, is political. It is even more urgent that we understand this in 2020, that we actively incorporate it in our vegan ecofeminist infiltration of academia, for instance.
27 "The Anthropocene blurs and even scrambles some crucial categories by which people have made sense of the world and their lives. It puts in crisis the lines between culture and nature, fact and value, and between the human and the geological or meteorological" (Clark 9). Men should be talking about the impact of the environmental crisis on hegemonic and non-hegemonic masculinity.
28 Plumwood's arguments for contextual veganism as opposed to what she calls ontological veganism are interesting, but in my opinion, she does not address the concrete suffering of nonhuman animals enough. I also prefer analyses that foreground the social construction of nature and its direct (very complex) relationship (s) with dissident sexualities, speciesism, and ableism, to mention just a few. Furthermore, that "sacred eating" bit... I think we would need first-hand nonhuman animal opinions on that. Perhaps if human animal "sacred eating" of other human animals was on the menu I would be more open to the possibility of such an analysis.

Works cited

Aymerich, Thalita. *From Pastoral to Ecophobia: Stations of Ecocriticism in Anglophone Poetry.* University of Costa Rica. (To Be Defended in 2020).
Bates, Jonathan. *The Song of the Earth.* Picador, 2001.
Buell, Lawrence. *The Future of Environmental Criticism: Environmental Crisis and Literary Imagination.* Kindle ed., Blackwell, 2008.
Clark, Timothy. *Ecocriticism on the Edge: the Anthropocene as a Threshold Concept.* Kindleed, Bloomsbury Academic, an Imprint of Bloomsbury Publishing Plc, 2015.
Garrard, Greg. *Ecocriticism.* Kindle ed., Routledge, 2012.
Glotfelty, Cheryll, and Harold Fromm, eds. *The Ecocriticism Reader: Landmarks in Literary Ecology.* University of Georgia Press, 1996.
Haack and Lewis. *Prince and Knight.* Little Bee Books, 2018.
Jiménez, Adriana. "'Strange Coupling': Vegan Ecofeminism and Queer Ecologies in Theory and in Practice. Chapter 2: Queer Ecologies, Complications and Possibilities in Coupling with Queer Vegan Ecofeminism(s)." *Revista de Lenguas Modernas,* vol. 1, no. 28, 2018, pp. 403–425. doi:10.15517/RLM.V0128.34847.
———. "'Strange Coupling': Vegan Ecofeminism and Queer Ecologies in Theory and in Practice. Chapter 3: A Vegan Queer Ecological Reading of Ruth Ozeki's My Year of Meats." *Revista de Lenguas Modernas,* vol. 1, no. 29, 2019, pp. 69–91. doi:10.15517/RLM.V0129.36542.
Latour, Bruno. *Down to Earth: Politics in the New Climatic Regime.* Kindle ed., Polity, 2019.
Plumwood, Val. "Integrating Ethical Frameworks for Animals, Humans, and Nature: A Critical Feminist Eco-Socialist Analysis." *Ethics and the Environment,* vol. 5, no. 2, 2000, pp. 285–322. www.jstor.org/stable/40338997.
Wright, Laura. *The Vegan Studies Project: Food, Animals, and Gender in the Age of Terror.* Kindle ed., University of Georgia Press, 2015.

22
Veganism in Critical Animal Studies
Humanist and post-humanist perspectives

Jonathan Sparks-Franklin

What does it mean to engage in a "Critical" Animal Studies? Critical Animal Studies (CAS) scholars continue to productively debate the fundamental meaning and function of its defining descriptive term. Yet in the midst of these debates, one aspect of it remains clear:

> to engage in a *Critical* Animal Studies is to engage in a *political* and *normative* Animal Studies (McCance; Taylor and Twine; Nocella II et al.). Contrary to the descriptive and apolitical tasks of Anthrozoology, Animal Studies, or Human Animal Studies (DeMello), CAS is not merely concerned with the "question" of the animal. Its primary concern is the "condition" of the animal (Pedersen and Stanescu in Socha ix–xii). "What defines critical animal studies," as Claire Jean Kim puts it, "is that it is fiercely, unapologetically political. Critical animal studies scholars aim to end animal exploitation and suffering and have little patience for work that just happens to be about animals". ("Introduction" 464)

Moreover, given this radical political stance, veganism always has been, and will continue to be, a concern of CAS scholarship. A direct response to the most urgent, widespread, and concrete violence facing animals, veganism is a, if not the, primary site where CAS has explored and embodied its defining political commitment to animal liberation.[1] In this sense, CAS is, or at least should be, a form of vegan studies (Wright). The question, "Must Every Animal Studies Scholar be Vegan?" (Warkentin), for example, is very much at the center of contemporary developments in the field (see also Jenkins; Potts and Armstrong; King et al.).

Significantly, however, despite this shared allegiance to normative political activism, and thereby vegan praxis, there is no single approach to the latter in CAS. Conflicting philosophical commitments, particularly those concerning the nature of subjectivity and ethics, have resulted in various theorizations of what veganism is, why it makes a claim on us, and its relation to other ethical–political issues.[2] This chapter aims to provide a conceptual–historical survey of these diverse conceptions of veganism in CAS. To do this I follow standard philosophical divisions of the field into its humanist (analytic) and post-humanist (continental) trajectories (Calarco; Wolfe; Cavalieri *The Death*). This is not, of course, the only way to read the theoretical landscape of CAS. It is, however, a profoundly useful typology for broadly analyzing the two fundamental philosophical orientations informing contemporary scholarship in the field. As a result, I here suggest it provides an insightful heuristic framework for surveying prominent conceptual approaches to veganism. Grounded in fundamentally divergent accounts of the human subject and ethical responsibility, these two traditions have come to articulate and defend quite different understandings of vegan ethics.

Humanist veganism: perspectives from analytic philosophy

What I am here referring to as the humanist model is undoubtedly the most influential, perhaps because it is the most intuitive approach to veganism. It is, for example, the operative position assumed by the mainstream animal rights movement. In order to properly understand it one must first appreciate the general philosophical framework, and thereby operative approach to animal ethics, that it assumes. Located in the analytic philosophical tradition, this approach is grounded in what Gary Steiner calls a "reformed humanism" (5). Assuming the human, defined by its unique possession of various mental and cognitive capacities as regulative norm, analytic animal ethics argue that moral consistency requires the inclusion of all beings, regardless of species, proven to possess these abilities (even in diminished form) within the moral community. Be it an insistence upon sentience (Singer), subjectivity (Regan), intentional agency (Cavalieri), or flourishing (Nussbaum), this tradition argues that a failure to consider these capacities wherever they are found results in an arbitrary "speciesism" akin to the exclusionary dynamics of sexism and racism.

The humanist position thereby promotes a kinship ethics of recognition, a moral extensionism wherein logical consistency, a commitment to the science of universal Reason, mandates the equal consideration of interests, of "treating like alike" (Francione xxv). Consequently, animal ethics have little to do with affect or even necessarily caring for animals. Rather, they are the consequence of an abstract and formalistic deduction grounded in a referential understanding of language, knowledge, and objective truth (McCance 3). Motivated by the demands of a ubiquitously valid Reason, they thus typically manifest as a defense of quasi-universal, self-evident, and unambiguous rules, laws, and principles that apply to most (if not all) people in most (if not all) situations.

This is the philosophical framework, the fundamental approach to subjectivity and ethics, that informs the humanist approach to veganism. Here, and as with animal ethics in general, what Steiner calls "the vegan imperative" (203–9) is the outcome of a commitment to general principles informed by rational argument. Consider, for example, the pioneering work of Peter Singer. A utilitarian committed to maximizing utility, to promoting the greatest good for the greatest number, Singer's animal ethic follows Jeremy Bentham in identifying the interest that requires equal consideration with sentience, with the capacity to suffer and feel pleasure. Hence, "the question is not," as Bentham famously put it, "can they reason? nor can they talk? but, can they suffer?" And for Singer, as for Bentham, there is a host of irrefutable philosophical and scientific arguments permitting us to confidently calculate that they can (*Animal Liberation* 11–17). As a result, "the simple straightforward principle of equal consideration of pain and pleasure," concludes Singer, "is a sufficient basis for identifying and protesting against all the major abuses of animals that human beings practice" (17).

Significantly, Singer identifies vegetarianism as the primary form that this protest, what he often calls "boycott," must take (162). "I believe that applying the principle of utility to our present situation—especially the methods now used to rear animals for food and the variety of food available to us," he argues, "leads to the conclusion that we ought be vegetarian" ("Utilitarianism" 325). For Singer one need not appeal to rights to make his case. Rather, the equal consideration of interests is more than enough to require that we "cease to eat animals"

(*Animal Liberation* 159) Why? Because a rational calculation would reveal that, all things considered, this is the optimal way to maximize utility. First and foremost, the undeniable immense suffering on modern factory farms simply cannot be justified by the comparatively trivial pleasures that they produce. The former clearly outweighs the latter. Moreover, going vegetarian comes at no great cost to us: "it does not involve great sacrifices, not in our health, nor in our capacity to feed the growing world population, nor in the pleasures of the palate" ("Utilitarianism" 333). In fact, far from coming at a great cost, it actually allows us to "produce less suffering" *and* "more food at a reduced cost to the environment" (*Animal Liberation* 159). Vegetarianism is a net benefit, maximizing pleasure for all.

Singer's selective emphasis on "our present situation" and "factory farms" however, should not go overlooked. For Singer, the question is not whether it is "*ever* right to eat meat? But: Is it right to eat *this* meat" (160)? A utilitarian committed to the minimization of suffering, Singer cannot deny that it might be possible, say on a small or local level, to rear or even kill animals without causing suffering. He thus rejects a vegetarianism grounded in "moral absolutism" ("Utilitarianism" 328)."Nevertheless, these hypotheticals, argues Singer, are ultimately "quite irrelevant to the immediate question of our daily diet." "Whatever the theoretical possibilities of rearing animals without suffering may be," he continues, "the fact is that the meat available from butchers and supermarkets comes from animals who were not treated with any real consideration at all while being reared" (*Animal Liberation* 160). Consequently, while he rejects a certain moral absolutism, he ultimately embraces a quasi-absolutism as it concerns the need for most people to avoid consuming animals.

A similar, albeit far more radical, approach can be seen in the work of Tom Regan. A Kantian rather than a utilitarian, Regan appeals to a reformist deontology (see also Korsgaard) to promote an animal ethic based on their "right to life" (*The Case for*). According to Regan, Singer is correct to argue that it is the logical recognition of a shared capacity that makes us responsible to animals. He is wrong, however, about what that specific capacity is. Suffering, argues Regan, is not the primary issue. Rather it is the more complex criterion of having "positive interests" ("The Moral Basis"), what he theorizes as being a "subject of a life." And how does Regan know that animals, like us, are subjects of a life? Similar to Singer, he can confidently deduce this conclusion based on a calculation of physiological and behavioral similarities. "This is an empirical question," as he puts it, "to be answered on the basis of reasoning by analogy" (161).

It is this commitment to an equal consideration of a subject's positive interests that leads Regan to defend the necessity of vegetarianism. "Vegetarianism," he concludes, "is not supererogatory; it is obligatory" (*The Case for* 346). Significantly, however, Regan's Kantian framework requires a far more demanding vegetarianism. On his account, Singer's utilitarian allegiance to sentience results in a dangerous welfarism wherein the interests of an individual animal can easily be overridden by the interests of others (human or nonhuman). Indeed, for Regan there are a variety of situations wherein a utilitarian case could easily be made for the use and consumption of animals ("Utilitarianism, Vegetarianism").

Such utilitarian negotiations are entirely unacceptable for Regan (see also Nussbaum). Indeed, this is precisely why he turns to Kant rather than to Bentham. From this perspective we have a categorical imperative to treat animals, like other humans, as direct ends in themselves. This means that they have intrinsic, rather than instrumental, value protected by inviolable rights. As a result, there is no utilitarian calculus that could ever justify their commodified treatment as a means to an end. Contra Singer, killing *is* an issue. For Regan, the problem is not merely suffering and large-scale factory farms; the problem is the killing or instrumentalized use of animals in any situation. As a result, there are practically no circumstances, even on a small idyllic farm, where one is justified in using or eating them. Regan's vegetarianism is thereby a far more radical abolitionist vegetarianism (see also Francione) demanding empty, rather than larger, cages (*The Case for* 2004).

Post-humanist veganism: perspectives from continental philosophy

As we have seen, analytic approaches to vegetarianism are grounded in a reformed humanism, a moral extensionism based in a sovereign Reason's recognition of various capacities that have their origin in a normative humanity. From this perspective, one does not eat animals because they, like us, are objectively proven to possess some morally relevant ability such as sentience or positive interests that require equal consideration. Grounded in a commitment to logical consistency, they typically take the form of adherence to quasi-universal rules or principles.

What I am here calling post-humanist veganism takes nearly the exact opposite approach. Here the "critical" task of CAS is not just about praxis and the response to an urgent political *crises*. Rather, in the tradition of Adorno, Foucault, and Butler, it also bespeaks a commitment to *critique*, to the critical interrogation of "inherited conceptual frameworks and modes of actions they inform" (McCance 4). Weary of the analytic tradition's ironic tendency to assume and engage animals on the terms of an anthropocentric humanism, this approach to CAS argues that a genuinely critical response to animals can only be accomplished "*by way of* post-humanist theory" (Wolfe 207).

Consequently, grounded in the continental, rather than the analytic, philosophical tradition, this approach does not assume the sovereign subject of humanism as normatively given. To the contrary. It actually assumes, and begins with, its end. A post-humanist tradition committed to the deconstruction of what Heidegger called the metaphysics of subjectivity/presence, the entirety of modern continental philosophy can arguably be best read as one long engagement with Jean-Luc Nancy's famous inquiry, "Who Comes After the Subject?" Here, after metaphysics, the human subject is emphatically not the transcendental origin or foundation of the world, truth, or meaning. Rather, it is that which is subject to, or dependent on, an inaccessible exteriority, be it power, language, or the other. As a result, ethics can no longer be approached as the objective calculations of a self-sovereign being. The dizzying complexity of the non-rational, the aporetic, and the contextual replace the universal absolutes of self-evident foundations (Bauman 1993).

Consider, for example, recent work on a Foucauldian approach to veganism. As outlined by Chloe Taylor, the vast majority of scholarship on Foucault and CAS has tended to focus on animal agriculture as a site of sovereign power, biopower, disciplinary power, or pastoral power. Recently, however, scholars have also begun to explicitly explore the relevance of Foucault's project to veganism. As is well known, Foucault, contra analytic scholars, does not assume the Enlightenment subject as normatively given. He deconstructs it by way of power. The human is not a fixed essence or eternal substance. Rather it is a malleable form to be actively cultivated through a contingent set of power-laden performative practices or technologies of the self. As a result, ethics cannot be a matter of adherence to universal moral codes (scientific or religious). Rather, following the ancient Greeks, they must alternatively take the form of an intentional stylization of this fluid form that is the subject, a "politics of ourselves" (*About the Beginning* 76) or an "aesthetics of existence" ("An Aesthetics" 49).

The implications of this particular aesthetic account of the subject, and thereby ethics, for veganism has been explored by Chloe Taylor (see also Twine). In "Foucault and the Ethics of Eating" she argues that ethical vegetarianism should not, as is typically the case, be understood as a universal moral code. Rather, it functions as a type of "self-transformative practice" or "ethico-aesthetics of the self." The ethics of not eating animals, she argues, cannot be reduced to a static and legalistic list of "dos and don'ts." It is first and foremost a sort of spiritual exercise, a type of ascesis, aimed at the "care of the self." In fact, it is not just *a* disciplinary practice, but a unique form of *counter-disciplinary* self-constitution" ("Foucault and the Ethics" 75). Contrary to what Foucault called a "disgusting" ethic focused exclusively on the self, vegetarianism would be an altruistic form of self-constitution that "takes into account the pleasure of the other" (80) and thereby contests the aforementioned violent forms of agricultural power.

Significantly, such an approach to vegetarianism is not a matter of mere theoretical preference. For Taylor, it has profound practical and pragmatic political implications for the success of the animal liberation movement. On her account, standard approaches grounded in reason and moral argument, what I have called humanist veganism, have simply not been as effective as one would think. These positions have been around for decades. Moreover, they remain, at least from an analytic perspective, logically irrefutable. Yet people continue to eat animals. Why? According to Taylor this is because an exclusive focus on moral argumentation ignores the disciplinary, affective, and aesthetic dimensions of the issue. "What is at issue with food choices," she argues, "may be neither reason nor alimentary pleasure." "Not eating meat or eating it, although apparently a simple ethical choice," she continues, "is, for many, a momentous symbolic act, enacting a self-transformation into a different kind of subject" (82). And these alternative subjectivities, she suggests, are loaded with all sorts of complex (and often negative) gendered, cultural, and ethnic affective associations. For Taylor, this is not to say that moral argumentation does not matter. It is merely to recognize that it will inevitably remain incomplete and unpersuasive without equal consideration of the contested self that this practice constitutes.

Such a Foucauldian approach, however, is not the only, nor the most influential, way to theorize veganism from a post-humanist perspective. Rather, the vast majority of scholarship on this topic has been informed by the pioneering work of Jacques Derrida. Similar to Foucault, and as with any continental philosopher, Derrida too begins with deconstruction of the sovereign subject. Yet for Derrida the human is not dispossessed or decentered by power, but by the dynamics of *différance*, by language and the claim of the other. Constituted by the call of a radical exteriority, it is thereby not defined by its autonomous and unique possession of any power, capacity, or ability. Rather, the human is defined by the same fundamental thing that defines "the animal," namely, an ontological powerlessness, incapacity, or inability.

Defined by this fundamental weakness or incapacity, animal ethics cannot, contra the humanist model, take the form of a sovereign Reason calculating and recognizing morally relevant capacities. Rather, it here takes the form of one vulnerable creature being interrupted or addressed by an entirely other and different way of being a vulnerable creature. Think here of a post-humanist Levinas. In fact, this is precisely the dynamic and what Derrida is after in his animal ethic (*The Animal that Therefore*). I am not responsible for an animal because it is like me. I am responsible for an animal because it, in all of its unique animality, makes a claim on me. Moreover, a response to an "unsubstitutable singularity" (9), to *this* particular individual animal in *this* particular situation, animal ethics cannot be a matter of applying predetermined rules, laws, and principles. Rather, they must take the form of an incalculable decision, a risky response to the unrepeatable particularities of each unique instant.

What, then, does this account of the subject and ethics mean for veganism? Typically, conversations about this topic tend to begin, as well as end, with Derrida's own controversial and ultimately ambivalent claims about it. On the one hand, Derrida openly decries the "unprecedented violence" of modern animal agriculture (25). He declares his "sympathy" for those who "are in the right and have good reasons to rise up against the way animals are treated: in industrial production, in slaughter, in consumption, in experimentation" ("Violence Against" 64). Indeed, he even goes so far as to identify the "dominant schema of subjectivity itself," the very metaphysical account of the subject that his entire project aims to deconstruct, with the carnivorous eating of meat. This subject is "carnophallogocentric," it not only "accepts sacrifice and eats flesh" ("'Eating Well'" 281), but needs to do so in order to become a subject at all.

Yet on the other hand, when it comes to the necessary response to this undeniable violence, Derrida does not, as one might expect, proceed to explicitly promote vegetarianism. He admits to being a "vegetarian in his soul." But this frustratingly cryptic proclamation leads to no defense of the necessity of ethical vegetarianism. Why? Because "vegetarians, too," he argues, "partake of animals, even of men. They practice a different mode of denegation." As a result, he does "not believe in absolute vegetarianism, nor in the ethical purity of its intentions" (282). In fact, "a certain cannibalism remains unsurpassable" ("Violence Against" 67). Consequently, at least for Derrida, "the moral question is thus not, nor has it ever been: should one eat or not eat, eat this and not that, the living or the nonliving, man or animal." No, "since *one must* eat in any case and since it is and tastes good to eat, and since there's no other definition of the good," the proper question is, "*how* for goodness sake should one *eat well*?" ("'Eating Well'" 282).

Unsurprisingly, such an enigmatic response and refusal to promote any determinate principles has left many critics unsatisfied (Steiner). How, they rightly ask, can Derrida "talk animatedly about carnophallogocentrism while eating with gusto a plate of steak tartare" (Attridge 54)? First, it should be noted that Derrida's own relation to eating animals remains inclusive. Despite the ambiguity of the aforementioned comments, one of his biographers, for example, claims that Derrida himself actually identified as a "vegetarian who sometimes eats meat" (Peeters 427). Second, and far more importantly, it is necessary to emphasize that his primary issue is not with vegetarianism per se, but with a certain "elementary" understanding of it ("Violence Against" 71). He is concerned, that is, with vegetarianism as a discourse of moral purity and the good conscience that this informs. Here, the vegetarian thinks they are "cruelty free," that they have somehow transcended the violent dynamics of sacrifice and consumption. From Derrida's perspective, as for any post-modern ethicist, this belief is a fantasy. It is impossible to not "eat" the other. Eating, for Derrida, is not only a matter of the physical ingestion of food. It is a metonym for our structural relation to the other as such. From this perspective, all of our relationships assimilate, whether symbolically or literally, the other. Violence is inevitable. Justice is impossible. Ethics are inherently aporetic. Indeed, even in doing the right thing, in responding to the claim of *this* other, I am inevitably ignoring, and thereby sacrificing, the claims of *that* other (Derrida *The Gift*). My decisions are never fully justified. This is the reason that Derrida is hesitant to promote vegetarianism. Lulled to complacency by the self-assurance and good conscience of a justified rule, the vegetarian substitutes the infinite and uncertain task of *responding* to each unique moment with the *reactions* of a calculated program.

Yet would it not be possible to accept Derrida's justified concerns about good conscience and still defend the necessity of a deconstructive vegetarianism? This is the position of David Wood. A continental philosopher who is a vegetarian (King et al.), Wood argues that Derrida's comments border on needlessly "assimilating" "real and symbolic sacrifice so that real sacrifice (killing and eating flesh) becomes an instance of symbolic sacrifice" (*Comment* 31). Yes, both meat eaters and vegetarians inevitably engage in some type of "carnivorous" sacrifice. But is there not a profound difference between them? For Wood, there undoubtedly is. In fact, in refusing to recognize this difference and make a decision between the two Derrida himself ironically risks "the kind of good conscience that too closely resembles a beautiful soul" (32). Consequently, if "deconstruction is justice," as Derrida famously puts it in "Force of Law," an attempt to respond to the address of every other, then for Wood, "deconstruction is vegetarianism"

(33). While it, like justice, is impossible, an unattainable ideal that will always be "to come," it is precisely that which our excessive responsibility requires us to endlessly pursue.

Leonard Lawlor agrees. In his book about Derrida and animality he too begins with the recognition that violence is inevitable. The task of animal ethics is thereby not to eliminate it, but to pursue the least violence, a "more sufficient response" that avoids the "worst violence" (23). "You have to eat, after all," he says echoing Derrida, "but let us try to eat in the least violent way." And for Lawlor, this least violent way of eating well must take "some form of vegetarianism," albeit a vegetarianism that turns out to be a form of "minimal carnivorism" (2). Our task, he argues, is to "eat animals well," and to do this we must substitute their *literal* consumption with the *symbolic* internalization of the name (105). It is only through the violence of naming each animal, recognizing each one as an irreplaceable singularity, that we can avoid the worst violence of consuming their actual bodies. Significantly, Lawlor is not here providing a universal prescription. He is merely promoting what he calls a "recipe" for eating well that can only inform locally negotiated reforms. And none of these reforms, necessary as they are, will ever be "sufficient in responding to animal suffering" (2).

Derrida has thus come to inform a post-humanist approach to eating well that differs profoundly from someone like Donna Haraway. In her influential account of "companion species," Haraway, like Derrida, "recognizes the inevitability of sacrifice, that "there is no way to eat and not kill, no way to eat and not to become with other mortal beings to whom we are accountable, no way to pretend innocence and transcend to final peace" (*When Species* 295). Yet, whereas Wood and Lawlor take this inevitability as a call to pursue the least violence, Haraway and her ontology of entangled co-becoming accept it as an inescapable given. For her, eating well is not about the endless pursuit of nonviolence, but about "killing responsibly" (81). While she admits she is not "comfortable" eating meat, she also refuses to "renounce it" ("Science Stories" 161). Consequently, Haraway has been charged with what Stephanie Jenkins calls a "hypo-critical" apoliticism (2012) that does not apply to the Derridean trajectory of CAS.

Ultimately, what becomes clear in Wood and Lawlor's approach is that a deconstructive veganism is not, contra the position's critics, opposed to determinate principles or rules as such. In fact, and as with Derridean ethics in general, they are entirely necessary. Responsibility, as Derrida likes to put it, occurs in the undecidable aporia *between* the conditional (rule) and the unconditional (singularity), a response to each unique iteration of "rule and event" (Wolfe in Cavalieri 54). Rather, the issue is how we relate to these finite principles. In the context of eating, this means that "the question of what to eat," as Kelly Oliver puts it, "is never answered once and for all." "Eating well," she continues, "requires vigilance and must resist becoming merely a habit" (108).

This self-critical dimension of a deconstructive veganism has been most clearly picked up and developed by vegan continental philosopher Matthew Calarco (King et al.). Calarco agrees with Wood that deconstruction should inform a robust commitment to vegetarianism. It is the best way to eat well and begin dismantling the sacrificial economy of carnophallogocentrism. However, it would be a huge mistake, he argues, to equate the two. In "Deconstruction is not Vegetarianism: Humanism, Subjectivity, and Animal Ethics," he argues that our task is not, as it is for Wood, to merely "save vegetarianism" by differentiating between real and symbolic sacrifice (194). Derrida's intention, he argues, was not to assimilate these two types of sacrifice in order to lazily equate the vegetarian and the carnivore. Rather, his point was to complicate the distinction. "Vegetarians, too," as Derrida puts it, "partake of animals, even of men. They practice a *different mode of denegation*" ("'Eating Well'" 282).

Consequently, rather than merely attempting to convince Derrida, or anyone else for that matter, that deconstruction *is* vegetarianism, Calarco argues that our primary task should be to engage in a "deconstruction *of* vegetarianism" (*Zoographies* 134) and the "different mode of denegation" that it participates in. While the vegetarian ideal, like justice, is undeconstructable, its historical embodiment is not. A series of determinate practices and discourses that inevitably fall short of their motivating ideal, it, like any other finite construction, is fundamentally deconstructable. Accordingly, our primary concern should be the following: "In what ways do vegetarian discourses and practices continue to sacrifice animals, both in a real and symbolic sense, and human beings symbolically?" (198).

For Calarco, there are multiple dimensions to this deconstruction of vegetarianism. We could, for example, deconstruct the ways in which what I have called analytic approaches *symbolically* sacrifice the animality of nonhumans by only valuing them on the basis of their similarity to humans. From a more *literal* perspective, we could not only deconstruct the violence overlooked by vegetarianism in the name of a more radical veganism but also explore the ways in which the industrial production of even vegan food contributes to the very *real* sacrifice of the environment, animals, and even humans. And perhaps most importantly, a deconstruction of veganism must also extend so as to critically examine the complex ways in which it participates, both symbolically and literally, in other forms of systemic violence such as racism, sexism, and colonialism.

Calarco himself has provided an example of what this deconstructive approach might look like. Drawing on Nietzsche, Deleuze, and Val Plumwood, he defends a post-humanist veganism that appeals to the shared vulnerability of humans and animals in their common "being toward meat" ("Being Toward Meat"). However, I suggest that the clearest example of it can be found in the work of Cora Diamond. While Diamond herself addresses the issue by way of Wittgenstein rather than Derrida, Cary Wolfe has demonstrated the profound similarities between their respective approaches to animal ethics ("Exposures"). In essays like "Eating Meat and Eating People" (1991) and "Injustice and Animals" (2001), for example, she argues that animal ethics, contra Regan and Singer, have absolutely nothing to do with rights and the empirical calculation of morally relevant capacities and abilities. Rather, and as with Derrida, they are a response to our common *incapacity* or *inability* as embodied vulnerable beings. And while her early work located this response in a *recognition* of our shared finitude, she has more recently (2008) joined Derrida in emphasizing the way in which it befalls us like a trauma that transcends any comprehension.

Significantly, Diamond explores this approach to animal ethics through the vegetarianism of Elizabeth Costello, fictional protagonist of J.M. Coetzee's *The Lives of Animals*. Here, Diamond finds a vegetarianism as vulnerable as her own account of ethics. When pressed to defend her position, Costello famously makes no formal appeal to systematic argument. Her refusal to eat animals is not the outcome of self-evident calculations and philosophical consistency. There is no reference to universal obligations and not a hint of a utopian purity. Indeed, she openly recognizes the inconsistency of her position. She admits to wearing leather. Rather, her vegetarianism is the imperfect response of one finite vulnerable creature being haunted, what she calls wounded, by the vulnerability of another. It is an attempt to "save her soul" (Coetzee 43).

Conclusion: toward an intersectional veganism

The differences between what I have called humanist and post-humanist veganism should now be clear. For the former, veganism is a commitment to quasi-universal rules grounded in the rational recognition of sameness. For the latter, it is a finite, and thereby deconstructable, affective response to the singular address of the wholly other. Consequently, whereas analytic approaches tend toward an "identity veganism," continental theorists promote an "aspirational veganism"

(Gruen and Jones). As a result, the development of veganism in CAS has very much been a progressive evolution toward a greater appreciation of the inherent complexity and "messiness of eating" (King et al.). Indeed, I would argue that this, a self-critical intersectional recognition of the ways in which veganism itself is irreducibly connected to other forms of violence, is the most important outcome of recent developments in the field.

Fortunately, much promising scholarship has already been done in this area and I would like to conclude by briefly pointing to it as the way forward for the theorization of veganism in CAS. Long before Derrida, for example, vegetarian ecofeminists like Carol J. Adams and Greta Gaard had already deconstructed a carnophallogocentric account of the subject through an affective, situational, and intersectional vegetarianism that explored the constitutive intersections between eating animals and other hierarchical forms of oppression, particularly patriarchy (Gaard). Here, vegetarianism functions as a form of active resistance to the interrelated objectification of animals and women (Adams *Sexual Politics*). Yet despite this profound potential to deconstruct patriarchy and heteronormativity (Simonsen), much mainstream vegan scholarship unfortunately functions to reinforce them. The mainstream animal rights movement is not only defined by structural sexism (Wrenn) and frequent sexual abuse (Adams "The Second Class"), but is grounded in patriarchal theory. Feminist Care scholars, for example, have revealed the ways in which Singer and Regan's account of a rational, universal, and rule-oriented vegetarianism reinforces a problematic masculinity (Donovan and Adams). Consequently, they have worked to deconstruct this theoretical sexism by way of a contextual vegetarianism (Curtin) grounded in entangled empathy (Gruen).

Finally, scholars working at the intersection of animal studies and post-colonial theory have also revealed the mutually informative co-constitution of the discourse of species and race (Kim *Dangerous Crossings*). This work has come to inform the theorization of a multi-dimensional "black veganism" where the refusal to eat animals functions as a type of radical anti-racist and decolonial practice (Ko and Ko; Harper). Contrary to misguided concerns about a "performative whiteness" (Kymlicka and Donaldson 122), veganism is not the exclusive property of a white, western, and privileged elite, but a powerful way for marginalized people to reclaim a rich pre-colonial identity and heritage (Deckha). Unfortunately, however, this type of approach has not been centered or appreciated by mainstream vegan theory. In fact, the vast majority of it has not only been written by white men, but done so in a naively post-racial context that assumes that racism has ended and is a thing of the past (Kim "Abolition"). Here, animals become the latest and most urgent "frontier of justice" (Nussbaum) in a linear and single issue framework. Issues of race, if addressed at all, typically arise only by way of reductive and offensive comparisons between human and animal "slavery." Indeed, an intersectional focus on racism is often dismissed as being a distraction from the "real" issue of animal agriculture. Consequently, intersectional scholarship on black veganism has committed itself to "decentering whiteness" (Feliz Brueck) in mainstream conversations about the topic by grounding it in black experience and theory (Ko).

Notes

1 I will here be focused on veganism in relation to food and the ethics of consuming animals as this is the aspect of it that has received the most attention in the literature.
2 The reader will notice that the terms veganism and vegetarianism are used somewhat interchangeably in this chapter. This is not because I fail to appreciate the profound difference between the two. Rather, it is a consequence of the shifting and indeterminate terminology used by the authors analyzed. Many of them refer to vegetarianism but their understanding of it is quite similar to contemporary accounts of veganism.

Works cited

Adams, Carol J. "The Second Class Status and Exploitation of Women in the Animal Rights Movement." 2017. https://caroljadams.com/carol-adams-blog/the-second-class-status-and-exploitation-of-women-in-the-animal-rights-movement-ten-questions. Accessed April 30 2020.

———. *The Sexual Politics of Meat: A Feminist Vegetarian Critical Theory*. Continuum, 2011.

Attridge, Derek. *Reading and Responsibility: Deconstruction's Traces*. Edinburgh University Press, 2010.

Bauman, Zygmunt. *Postmodern Ethics*. Blackwell, 1993.

Calarco, Matthew. "Being Towards Meat: Anthropocentrism, Indisctinction, and Veganism." *Dialectical Anthropology*, vol. 38, 2014, pp. 415–429.

———. "Deconstruction is Not Vegetarianism: Humanism, Subjectivity, and Animal Ethics." *Continental Philosophy Review*, vol. 37, 2004, pp. 175–201.

———. *Thinking Through Animals: Identity, Difference, Indistinction*. Stanford University Press, 2015.

———. *Zoographies: The Question of the Animal From Heidegger to Derrida*. Columbia University Press, 2008.

Cavalieri, Paola. *The Animal Question: Why Nonhuman Animals Deserve Human Rights*. Oxford University Press, 2001.

———. *The Death of the Animal: A Dialogue*. Columbia University Press, 2009.

Coetzee, J.M. *The Lives of Animals*. Princeton University Press, 1999.

Curtin, Deane. "Toward an Ecological Ethic of Care." *Hypatia*, vol. 6, no. 1, 1991, pp. 60–74.

Deckha, Maneesha. "Postcolonial." *Critical Terms for Animal Studies*, edited by Lori Gruen. Columbia University Press, 2018, pp. 280–293.

DeMello, Margo. *Animals and Society: An Introduction to Human–Animal Studies*. Columbia University Press, 2012.

Derrida, Jacques. "'Eating Well,' or the Calculation of the Subject." *Points... Interviews, 1974–1994*, edited by Elizabeth Weber. Trans. Peggy Kamuf. Stanford University Press, 1995, pp. 255–277.

———. *The Animal That Therefore I Am*. Trans. David Wills. Fordham University Press, 2008.

———. *The Gift of Death*. Trans. David Wills. University of Chicago Press, 1996.

———. "Violence Against Animals." *For What Tommorow...* Stanford University Press, 2004, pp. 62–76.

Diamond, Cora. "Eating Meat and Eating People." *The Realistic Spirit: Wittgenstein, Philosophy, and the Mind*. Press, 1991, pp. 319–334.

———. "Injustice and Animals." *Slow Cure and Bad Philosophy: Essays on Wittgenstein, Medicine, and Bioethics*, edited by Carl Elliott, Duke University Press, 2001, pp. 118–148.

———. "The Difficulty of Reality and the Difficulty of Philosophy." *Philosophy & Animal Life*. Columbia University Press, 2008, pp. 43–90.

Donovan, Josephine, and Carol J. Adams, eds. *The Feminist Care Tradition in Animal Ethics*. Columbia University Press, 2007.

Feliz Bruek, Julia. *Veganism of Color: Decentering Whiteness in Human and Nonhuman Liberation*. Sanctuary Publishers, 2019.

Foucault, Michel. *About the Beginning of the Hermeneutics of the Self: Lectures at Dartmouth College 1980*. Trans. Graham Burchell. University of Chicago Press, 2016.

———. "An Aesthetics of Existence." *Michel Foucault: Politics, Philosophy, Culture: Interviews and Other Writings 1977–1984*, edited by Lawrence Kritzman. Trans. Alan Sheridan. Routledge, 1984, pp. 47–56.

Francione, Gary L. *Introduction to Animal Rights: Your Child or the Dog?* Temple University Press, 2000.

Gaard, Greta. "Vegetarian Ecofeminism: A Review Essay." *Frontiers: A Journal of Women Studies*, vol. 23 no. 3, 2002, pp. 117–146.

Gruen, Lori. *Entangled Empathy: An Alternative Ethic for our Relationship with Animals*. Lantern Books, 2015.

———. "Veganism as an Aspiration." *The Moral Complexities of Eating Meat*, edited by Ben Bramble and Bob Fisher, Oxford University Press, 2016, pp. 153–171.

Haraway, Donna. "Science Stories: An Interview with Donna Haraway." *The Minnesota Review*, vol. 73, no. 74, 2009, pp. 133–163.

Haraway, Donna. *When Species Meet*. University of Minnesota Press, 2008.

Harper, A. Breeze. *Sistah Vegan: Black Female Vegans Speak on Food, Identity, Health, and Society*. Lantern Books, 2010.

Jenkins, Stephanie. "Returning the Ethical and Political to Animal Studies." *Hypatia*, vol. 27, no. 3, 2012, pp. 492–526.

Kim, Claire Jean. "Abolition." *Critical Terms for Animal Studies*, edited by Lori Gruen. New York: Columbia University Press, 2018, pp. 15–32.

———. *Dangerous Crossings: Race, Species, and Nature in a Multicultural Age*. Cambridge University Press, 2015.

———. "Introduction: A Dialogue." *American Quarterly*, vol. 65, no. 3, 2013, pp. 461–479.
King, Samantha, et al., editors. *Messy Eating: Conversations on Animals as Food*. Fordham University Press, 2019.
Ko, Aph, and Syl Ko. *Aphro-ism: Essays on Pop Culture, Feminism, and Black Veganism from Two Sisters*. Lantern Books, 2017.
Ko, Aph. *Racism as Zoological Witchcraft: A Guide to Getting Out*. Lantern Books, 2019.
Korsgaard, Christine. *Fellow Creatures: Our Obligations to Other Animals*. Oxford University Press, 2018.
Kymlicka, Will, and Sue Donaldson. "Animal Rights: Multiculturalism, and the Left." *Journal of Social Philosophy*, vol. 45 no. 1, 2014, pp. 116–135.
Lawlor, Leonard. *This is Not Sufficient: An Essay on Animality and Human Nature in Derrida*. Columbia University Press, 2007.
McCance, Dawn. *Critical Animal Studies: An Introduction*. SUNY Press, 2013.
Nancy, Jean-Luc, Eduardo Cadava, and Peter Connor, editors. *Who Comes After the Subject?* Routledge, 1991.
Nokella, Anthony J., et al., editors. *Defining Critical Animal Studies: An Intersectional Social Justice Approach for Liberation*. Peter Lang, 2014.
Nussbaum, Martha. *Frontiers of Justice: Disability, Nationality, Species Membership*. Harvard University Press, 2006.
Oliver, Kelly. *Animal Lessons: How They Teach Us To Be Human*. Columbia University Press, 2009.
Peeters, Benoit. *Derrida: A Biography*. Polity Press, 2013.
Potts, Annie, and Philip Armstrong. "Vegan." *Critical Terms for Animal Studies*, edited by Lori Gruen, University of Chicago Press, 2018, pp. 395–409.
Regan, Tom. *Empty Cages: Facing the Challenge of Animal Rights*. Rowman & Littlefield, 2004a.
———. *The Case for Animal Rights*. University of California Press, 2004b.
———. "The Moral Basis of Vegetarianism." *Ethical Vegetarianism: From Pythagoras to Peter Singer*, edited by Kerry S. Walters and Lisa Portmess, SUNY Press, 1999, pp. 153–164.
———. "Utilitarianism, Vegetarianism, and Animal Rights." *Philosophy and Public Affairs*, vol. 9, no. 4, 1980, pp. 305–324.
Simonsen, R.R. "A Queer Vegan Manifesto." *Journal For Critical Animal Studies*, vol. 10, no. 3, 2012, pp. 51–81.
Singer, Peter. *Animal Liberation*. Harper Perennial, 2009.
———. "Utilitarianism and Vegetarianism." *Philosophy and Public Affairs*, vol. 19, no. 4, 1980, pp. 325–337.
Socha, Kim. *Women, Destruction, and the Avant-Garde: A Paradigm for Animal Liberation*. Brill, 2012.
Steiner, Gary. *Animals and the Limits of Postmodernism*. Columbia University Press, 2013.
Taylor, Chloe. "Foucault and Critical Animal Studies: Genealogies of Agricultural Power." *Philosophy Compass*, vol. 8, no. 6, 2013, pp. 539—551.
Taylor, Chloe. "Foucault and the Ethics of Eating." *Foucault Studies*, vol. 9, 2010, pp. 71–88.
Taylor, Nik, and Richard Twine. *The Rise of Critical Animal Studies: From the Margins to the Centre*. Routledge, 2014.
Twine, Richard. "Materially Constituting a Sustinable Food Transition: The Case of Vegan Eating Practice." *Sociology*, vol. 52, no. 1, 2018, pp. 166—181.
Warkentin, Traci. "Must Every Animal Studies Scholar be Vegan?" *Hypatia*, vol. 27, no. 3, 2012, pp. 499–504.
Wolfe, Cary. *Animal Rites: American Culture, the Discourse of Species, and Posthumanist Theory*. University of Chicago Press, 2003.
———. "Exposures." *Philosophy & Animal Life*. New York: Columbia University Press, 2008, pp. 1–42.
Wood, David. "*Comment ne pas manger* – Deconstruction and Humanism." *Animal Others: On Ethics, Ontology, and Animal Life*, edited by H. Peter Steeves, SUNY Press, 1999, pp. 15–36.
Wrenn, Corey Lee. *A Rational Approach to Animal Rights: Extensions in Abolitionist Theory*. Palgrave Macmillan, 2016.
Wright, Laura. *The Vegan Studies Project: Food, Animals, and Gender in the Age of Terror*. University of Georgia Press, 2015.

23
Vegan studies and queer theory

Emelia Quinn

In November 1970, in a document protesting their exclusion from the Black-Panther sponsored Revolutionary People's Constitutional Convention, a group referring to themselves as the Gay Male Vegetarians (GMV) set out a series of demands.[1] Positioning themselves as in solidarity with the Radical Lesbians, also denied a platform at the event, the "Demands of the Gay Male Vegetarians" calls for the recognition of both vegetarians and nonhuman animals as oppressed peoples. Their platform connects the oppression facing gay men to that facing animals, calling for "autonomy for all living species" and an acknowledgment that "the nuclear family is a microcism [sic] of the meat-eating state, where the men and animals are owned by, and their fate determined by, the needs of the family, in a meat-eating world." Advocating for the communal care of animals, under the direction of the GMV, as well as for the time and support necessary to research and report upon male vegetarian history and identity, the group's demands swiftly descend into a seemingly parodic register. Heteronormative gender roles are aligned with a form of "species role programming," the latter to be resisted through the "open enrollment of all schools to all animals, financial support to any animals who need it, and on-the-job training with pay for any animals attending schools and under apprenticeship." In addition to universal animal schooling, the group assert their right to the use of defense machinery and the need for a vegetarian militia with which to "defend the demands, rights, and interests of vegetarians struggling toward an unoppressive social system."

This somewhat bizarre archival document, providing a textual legacy for a group now otherwise entirely erased from the historical record,[2] blends seemingly earnest intersectional critique with the outlandish and satirical. It is unclear how we should read these demands. Is the document a sober call for animal rights, incorporating the nonhuman into the purview of human social reform? Or, if we are not to take this short piece too seriously, or at least not too literally, perhaps the accordance of basic education and employment to nonhuman animals aims to draw attention to the relative absurdity of such rights being denied to queers. The call for a vegetarian militia in such a reading draws attention to the all too real violence enacted against gay men, from both official and unofficial channels. On the other hand, there is also the possibility that the document is a parody. The GMV's alignment with the Radical Lesbians, stated at the outset, and the capitalized assertion that division by gender is "NOT ENOUGH DIVISION," could be read as a satirical critique of queer political movements and identitarian politics more broadly.

In evaluating such diverse readings of this document, we might take a lesson from queer theory and, in Eve Kosofsky Sedgwick's terms, move beyond a fixation on uncovering the relative truth or sincerity behind such demands.[3] Sedgwick critiques a certain paranoid mode within queer studies, in which the revelation of knowledge and truth takes place under a commonplace "hermeneutics of suspicion." She questions instead

> What does knowledge *do*—the pursuit of it, the having and exposing of it, the receiving again of knowledge and what one already knows? *How*, in short, is knowledge performative, and how best does one move among its causes and effects?. (Sedgwick 124)

In foregrounding the idea "that knowledge *does* rather than simply *is*" (124), Sedgwick encourages a shift in our reading practices. In the context of the archival legacy of the GMV, whether they were demanding schooling and paid apprenticeships for nonhuman animals in all earnestness is not necessarily the most important, nor the most interesting, question. We might think instead about the apt crystallization the document provides of the ways in which vegetarianism and veganism repeatedly rub up against queerness in the modern and contemporary period.

In the first instance, the text asserts the relationship between meat-eating and a heteronormative standard of masculinity. Second, it draws attention to the coding of vegetarian and vegan identities *as* queer; as radically disruptive to the heteronormative status quo. Third, it provides us with a route through which to consider the ways in which both queerness and veganism work to expand the definition of "the human," providing alternative modes of kinship and affiliation beyond those proscribed by the nucleic family structure. At the same time, the irrelevance of paid apprenticeships to the material needs of animals highlights the pitfalls of universalism in rights discourses. Fourth, it speaks to veganism's relationship to queer temporalities, aligned with a sense of impossibility and failure while aspiring toward a utopian vision of a future world. And finally, it draws attention to the ways in which the intersections between queerness and veganism seem always already at risk of descending into farce.[4] Akin to that which Richard Twine terms "intersectional disgust" ("Intersectional"), a concern for veganism appears to invalidate the seriousness or gravity of human social causes.[5]

Aligning queerness and veganism might appear on the surface as a problematic conflation of two distinct notions of identity and histories of oppression. Scholars such as Greta Gaard have however established the various ways in which incorporating queerness into ecocritical scholarship functions as a natural extension of the intersectional commitments that have motivated ecofeminism from its inception. Furthermore, in the introduction to *Thinking Veganism in Literature and Culture: Towards a Vegan Theory*, Emelia Quinn and Benjamin Westwood note the productive analogies to be drawn between a vegan theoretical position and queer theory, positing four key points of alignment:

> First, veganism challenges many of the same objects of critique found in queer theory, especially normative gendered and sexual identities. Second [...] veganism expands the scope of queer ideas of alternative affiliation to include relations with nonhuman animals. Third, 'vegan' structurally resembles the use of 'queer' as an umbrella term for a diversity of subject positions, which nonetheless rejects the stultifying logic of identity politics. Finally,

in its interest in maligned ideas of utopianism and failure, recent queer theory has engaged directly with issues that [...] undergo a productive rethinking through veganism. (3)

This chapter elaborates on these four key points of connection. What follows will establish that thinking queer theory with and alongside vegan theory provides important nourishment for vegan theoretical perspectives, providing new horizons for thinking about and negotiating vegan modes of being in the world.

Veganism and gender

In their concluding pronouncement "No longer will we bring home the bacon," the GMV make clear the link they observe between the performative force of meat consumption and its association with the role of male "provider." A critique of these associations has occupied a central position within the broad umbrella of animal studies, most famously in the work of Carol J. Adams and Jacques Derrida.[6]

In *The Sexual Politics of Meat* (1990), Adams argues that meat-eating is a male identified activity that reflects patriarchal dominance. Her conception of the "absent referent" forms the connective tissue linking the oppression of women and nonhuman animals within a patriarchal, meat-eating culture, both of whom are made absent through literal, definitional, and metaphorical modes of violence. Adams thus emphasizes vegetarianism and veganism as means of recovering the absent referent animal from structures that obfuscate its suffering. The relationship between meat-eating and patriarchal dominance, demonstrated by the central importance accorded to meat in male diets, means that vegetarianism becomes "de facto a rebellion against a dominant culture regardless of whether it was claimed to be a rebellion" (Adams, *Sexual Politics* 226). The rejection of meat offers a refusal of gender norms and roles, while meat itself becomes a fetishistic signifier of masculinity and virility.

Derrida's work, while skeptical of the ethical force of vegetarianism and veganism, addresses similar issues as Adams. As Matthew Calarco argues, both Adams and Derrida "*call explicit attention to the carnivorism that lies at the heart of classical notions of subjectivity*" (Adams xix). Such classical notions of subjectivity are premised here on heterosexuality. Of particular note is Derrida's coinage of the term "carno-phallogocentrism." Carno-phallogocentrism names the white, male, and carnivorous subject of Western culture and binds the question of subjectivity to the question of sacrifice, whether of the racialized, gendered, or nonhuman other. Akin to the dominant schema of "phallogocentrism," Derrida adds the prefix "carno-" as a sign of the necessary implication of the carnivorous virility of "the subject." Derrida's work is incisive for a queer vegan critique that seeks to unravel and disrupt a normative humanity premised on a carno-phallogocentric order. However, for Derrida, vegetarianism, and veganism by extension, are seen to offer only an illusion of "good conscience" that negates our ability to respond to the singularity of the nonhuman animal. This argument has been refuted in numerous important ways. Moral philosopher Gary Steiner, for example, argues that the reality of modern veganism is not the safeguard of the beautiful soul, but "a gnawing horror born of a recognition of what is being done to billions of animals *right now* and of the seeming futility of one's decision" (63). Steiner, while in agreement with the basic premise that a "felt sense of lived kinship with other sentient beings" is the origin of ethical principles, suggests that once this sense has been awakened "it becomes possible to develop principles that articulate that sense in rational terms" (154). David Wood also critiques Derrida's attack on vegetarianism but retains the idea that attempts to calculate our responsibility to nonhuman animals "would be to fail to grasp a responsibility that exceeds all calculation" (27). Contrary to Steiner's focus on principled reflection, Wood argues that vegetarianism might be better understood as a "willingness and capacity to respond, hence an indeterminable openness" (32). If carno-phallogocentrism is a "mutually reinforcing network of powers, schemata of domination, and investments that has to reproduce itself to stay in existence" then "Vegetarianism is [...]—at least potentially—a site of proliferating resistance to that reproduction" (Wood 33).

Veganism, in these terms, has the potential to subvert traditional gender roles, and, as demonstrated below, allows for a rethinking and refiguring of dominant models of desire. Adams's explicit focus on heterosexual role-programming risks sidelining a queer perspective, and the distinct intersections to be drawn between dead animal bodies and queer lives.[7] However, her work, along with Derrida's, draws attention to the need to think about the dual construction of our alimentary and sexual appetites.

Queer vegans

The relationship between meat-eating and masculinity sees carnivorism as deeply embedded within the maintenance and regulation of gender norms and compulsory heterosexuality, domains which queer theory has long sought to disrupt and challenge. With meat-eating associated with masculine virility, veganism finds itself positioned as a necessary antithesis: associated with femininity, passivity, and homosexuality. The controversial campaign tactics of groups such as PETA have sought to counter this association of veganism with a failed masculinity. A notable 2012 television advert, for example, celebrated a young woman in neck brace limping through city streets, suffering from, as the voiceover narration details, "my boyfriend went vegan and knocked the bottom out of me, a painful condition that occurs when boyfriends go vegan and can suddenly bring it like a tantric pornstar." While the evident parodic and ironic satirization of heterosexual culture at play in such adverts, and the fragile masculinity upon which it is built, is too often overlooked in vegan-oriented scholarship (the vegan boyfriend to whom the woman returns is notably presented as a pale, skinny, and bookish character), such campaigns demonstrate that veganism need not be, and indeed is not, always in alignment with radical politics.

However, there are important intersections to be found at the point at which one identifies oneself as vegan, and/or as queer. In his essay "A Vegan Form of Life," Robert McKay provides an example of the intersections between homophobia and a certain phobic response to those who refuse to abide by modes of eating deemed normal and desirable.[8] Reporting of the repeated jocular designation by his brother-in-law of his vegan fare as "your lesbian food!", McKay argues that "By equating two such apparently non-congruous categories, my host foregrounds the conceptual level on which he regards them as similar—they are weird, socially unintelligible—and, for a moment at least, he essentializes their meaning as such" (250–251). His brother-in-law's desire to keep lesbianism abject raises questions for McKay of "what anxiety about *his* subjectivity motivates both his parallel abjecting of veganism by saying 'lesbian food' and the nervous laughter that accompanies it? What position is in danger when it is confronted by veganism?" (251).

McKay's refusal of meat, as a man, is aligned here with a denigrated sense of femininity and passivity. Anxieties revealed in the media sensationalization of "vegan sexuality" in late 2007 provides a pertinent example of how such denigrations apply to the perception of vegan women. "Vegansexuality," a term used to describe vegans primarily sexually attracted to other vegans, emerged as a result of a report on the dietary practices of New Zealanders published in early 2007 by Annie Potts and Mandala White. Potts and Jovian Parry have since detailed the staunch public backlash against the term, a backlash that tapped into existing misogynistic and homophobic discourses. Vegansexuality was associated primarily with women and decried, predominantly by meat-eating heterosexual men, as little more than "a superficial cultural veneer of misguided abstinence, beneath which powerful, 'natural' carnal urges roil unabated" (Potts and Parry 60). In this conception of female desire as a tempest of carnal longing for men and meat, veganism is reduced to a superficial restriction that denies supposedly natural and beneficial appetites—carnivorous and heterosexual—in favor of a misguided asceticism. However, the subsequent embrace of the term by many vegans, choosing to publicly self-identify as vegansexual, suggests that the term allows for the reclamation and refiguring of one's relationship to desire. This sense of veganism as an orientation, rather than pure abstraction, has been forwarded by Laura Wright, defining veganism as "a delicate mixture of something both primal and social, a category [...] that constitutes for some people, just perhaps, something somewhat beyond one's choosing" (7).

Veganism's potential for establishing a way of desiring differently marks a significant alignment with queer modes of being and leads us to interrogate the active claiming of vegan food *by* and *for* queers. Indeed, one seems to encounter more vegans within LGBTQIA+ communities than anywhere else, a suspicion reinforced by the spatial geography of major cities, with gay districts often the best place to source vegan food.[9] This may appear as mere anecdotal stereotyping and we might question whether this is simply the product of homophobic discourse, the declaration of "lesbian food!" possessing a certain perlocutionary force. However, we might also ask if something more central to a queer veganism is at stake in such affinities, the result of: a resistance to gendered and sexual norms that is under less pressure to conform to a narrative in which meat-eating equates to heterosexual masculinity; a shared sense of injustice with nonhuman animals due to lives lived under threat from institutional oppression; or simply the consequence of an increased likelihood of engagement with other forms of political activism that would provide easier access to vegan protest movements?

For Rasmus Rahbek Simonson, veganism's queerness resides less in this coincidence of subcultural affiliation than in its ability to disturb the status quo. An affective involvement "with species other than the human directly expresses a desire to transverse not to say disrupt the boundaries that uphold and police the categories that separate the human from the non-human" (54). Simonsen notes, in particular, veganism's threat to the domestic dinner table as a traditional locus of familial coherence. Similarly, Quinn and Westwood suggest the relationship between the imagined queer presence at a heterosexual marriage ceremony, as theorized by Sedgwick, and the vegan's challenge to such a site of heterosexuality *and* its assumed carnivorous feast. These respective sites of familial and heterosexual coherence are challenged by the presence of the disruptive figure of that which Twine has coined the "vegan killjoy." Drawing on Sara Ahmed's conception of the "feminist killjoy," Twine explicates the ways in which the vegan exposes a normative order of happiness as anthropocentric, and "In willfully speaking up ... may engender anxiety, discomfort, guilt, and risks exclusion for doing so" ("Killjoys" 625). As with other minority positions, if the undermining of normative happiness figures as an important performative refusal, "In performing a practice that attempts to *re*construct happiness, pleasure and politics the vegan killjoy does what all politically willful killjoys attempt to do: create new meanings and practices that underline the shared joy in living outside and beyond social norms once thought fixed" (Twine, "Killjoys" 638). Here, veganism is coded as queer by a culture to whom the performative action of not eating meat, of refusing traditional Western modes of consumption, appears threatening and anxiety-inducing.

Emelia Quinn

Kinship and affiliation

For McKay, the coding of his dietary choices as "lesbian" operates as a function of carnophallogocentric discourse in which masculinity is associated with humanness: "when my carnivorous host names a vegan meal 'lesbian' he is citing the heterosexist designation of lesbianism as 'not fully human' and reapplying it in order to abject vegan identity; this in turn reassures his own humanity (and indeed sexuality)" (252). This then, for McKay, is a means of expressing "species panic via homosexual panic" (252) in which anxieties about lesbian and gay male identities intimately intersect with an anxiety about veganism as a challenge to one's understanding of human identity. McKay's desire to declare that "I am vegan, not human," speaks to the ways in which a vegan or vegetarian identity seems to expand the definitional limits of what we currently understand as the human animal. To be vegan rather than human is to recognize veganism as "an infinitely compound way of being in the world" (McKay 265) involving a never-ending series of actions, reactions, and interactions that open out onto affiliations with nonhuman animals.

While nonhuman animals remain absent from much contemporary queer theory, Dana Luciano and Mel Y. Chen argue that the foundational texts of queer theory have long sought to interrogate and unsettle the concept of "the human." They assert that "queer theory has long been suspicious of the politics of rehabilitation and inclusion to which liberal-humanist values lead [...] because 'full humanity' has never been the only horizon for queer becoming" (Luciano and Chen 188). If Enlightenment humanism is premised on drawing divisions between the human, the nonhuman, and the not-quite-human, McKay argues of a mode of "species dissidence" found within a vegan form of life, in which humanism comes to be seen, in Judith Butler's terms, as a regulatory ideal rather than an inherent essence of our species identity. Veganism, along with queer theory, allows for an expansion of our conception of the human, and an unravelling of the security of species boundaries.

This expansion of the human facilitates wider possibilities for kinship and affiliation. Questions of kinship have been central to the field of animal studies. As Agustín Fuentes and Natalie Porter argue, "If *kin* are those closest to us in space, time, and flesh, then *kinship,* by definition, is a multi-species endeavor" (183). The work of posthumanist feminist scholar Donna Haraway has been foundational in exploring the multispecies entanglements that constitute our lives with animals. The complexity of our daily interactions are seen by Haraway as irreducible to any preformed moral code or ethic principle, functioning as part of a complex and everchanging web of relations that is best conceptualized as a mode of becoming-with. Veganism is thus positioned as antithetical to Haraway's project of exploring and cultivating various networks of multispecies co-flourishing: a moral absolute that "would consign most domestic animals to the status of curated heritage collections or to just plain extermination as kinds and as individuals" (*Species* 80). That veganism fails to face up to living *and* dying, caring *and* killing, proceeds then as an anthropomorphic projection that fails to recognize the singular otherness of the nonhuman.

Haraway's argument against veganism forces us to reflect on the idea that reducing nonhuman animals to infantilized tokens, to whom we generously offer our protection, leaves our sense of human exceptionalism intact. Such thinking also increasingly plays on the "cutification" of animals, an aesthetic sensibility that, as Sianne Ngai notes, functions in contemporary culture as "an eroticization of powerlessness, evoking tenderness for 'small things' but also, sometimes, a desire to belittle or diminish them further" (3). I would add that a tendency in much veganoriented scholarship to establish the possibilities for human-nonhuman animal kinship through a valorization of the Child works to further negate veganism's ability to adequately engage with the complex negotiations required in the present. As in Graham Huggan and Helen Tiffin's assertion that children possess an inherent ability to view animals as "moral equivalents of themselves" (194), animals and vegans are often connected in their association with moral purity and a particular ideal of childhood innocence that cements vegan futures within the figure of an idealized past: the child to whom we grew up not to be.[10]

Veganism's relation to failure, insufficiency, and complicity, as detailed below, necessitates a step away from the Child as emblem of vegan futures, toward the very multispecies entanglements Haraway sees as adverse to a vegan positionality. Tom Tyler provides a concise summary of the ways in which recent vegan scholars have taken issue with Haraway's critiques:

> Eva Giraud has argued [...] that, far from being a totalizing moral imperative [... veganism] is "epistemologically disruptive," challenging traditional humanist hierarchies and unsettling the ways the certain groups are designated as legitimately exploitable [...] Moreover, [...] Anat Pick suggests that, in her caricature of vegans as dogmatic and otherwordly, Haraway misses the point that veganism is "in its very incompleteness and imperfection" a conscious participation in the world. Pick argues that veganism is a "labour of love and justice, no less worldly than Haraway's multispecies earthly entanglements," but it is one that works hard to see clearly not only the webs of interspecies relations as they are but also as they could be. (112–113)

Haraway's work thus asks questions of the state of our relationship to the nonhuman world that are of particular pertinence to the growing field of vegan studies and theory. As Haraway states, in our current disturbing times

> The task is to become capable, with each other in all of our bumptious kinds, of response. [...] The task is to make kin in lines of inventive connection as a practice of learning to live and die well with each other in a thick present. (Staying 1)

I assert, along with Giraud, Pick, and Tyler, that veganism is exactly this kind of continual response: of everyday choosing to respond and negotiate a world stacked against the nonhuman, a means of thinking through our entanglements with other beings, while not giving up on a world that might be figured differently in an-ever rescinding utopian vision. This assertion relates then to Lori Gruen's conception of "entangled empathy," a mode of ethical reaching that acknowledges both complexity and complicity in our relations with others.

If vegan theory is to learn from the lessons of contemporary queer theory, we need to consider what it means to reject the Child as emblem of futurity. This is an argument most famously put forward by the queer theorist Lee Edelman, who refuses the dominant cultural power of that which he terms "reproductive futurism." Reproductive futurism is that which enshrines the figure of the child as "the fantasmatic beneficiary of every political intervention" and preserves "the absolute privilege of heteronormativity by rendering unthinkable, by casting outside the political domain, the possibility of queer resistance to this organizing principle of communal relations" (Edelman 2–3). The anti-social turn in contemporary queer theory raises questions about the oppressive heteronormativity undergirding investments in futurity. For Sara Salih, critiquing the animal rights discourses of writers such as Jonathan Safran Foer which require us to justify ourselves against the enquiry of future generations into what we did to protect the animals, the imperative "to hold ourselves accountable even if only in our fantasies, to our accusing, ultra-moral children" (Salih 54) is one to be deeply skeptical of. The Child here is both an imperative to action as much as a stultification, in which the future embodies the social order's "traumatic encounter with its own inescapable failure" (Edelman 26).

In order to capture the "wondrous anarchy" of childishness lauded by J. Jack Halberstam, who describes a childlike relation to failure and disorder that "disturbs the supposedly clean boundaries between adults and children" (*Failure* 5), we must reject the Romantic idealization of childhood and embrace instead the presentism of responding constantly to a world of complex webs of harm. Indeed, if seeing ourselves in nonhuman animals is a cornerstone of much vegan activism, in which a fundamental *similarity* between the human and the nonhuman motivates ethical action, what happens to those animals not included under the categories of pets or "charismatic megafauna" that encourage such responses: cockroaches, mosquitoes, and snakes, for example? Queer theory provides us with the tools to evaluate what happens when we don't love all animals in an Edenic state of childhood innocence. Tim Dean's work, for example, offers a theory of sex and sexuality that doesn't require us to see anything of ourselves in others. As Dean argues, in relation to the queer subculture of barebacking, we might theorize an alternative mode of queer ethics based on the impersonal, "in which one cares about others even when one *cannot* see anything of oneself in them" (25, emphasis original). This impersonality is perhaps key to a queering of vegan attachments.

Fuentes and Porters's formulation of human–animal kinship sees significant overlap with Dean through a focus on "Reciprocity, touching, and infection [as] pathways to familiarity" (Fuentes and Porter 185). Their definition of kinship is seen to "depart from usual understandings of viral infection as foreign agent invading its host and instead narrate the same relational processes as a host inviting a virus into the fold of its relations: making kin" (Fuentes and Porter 185). Such reformulations of infection link to Dean's work, where his study of queer barebacking subcultures conceptualizes HIV/AIDs infection in terms of alternative modes of reproduction and community that can, counterintuitively, foster intimacy and forge connection between bodies. While these radically different theoretical contexts are not to be too readily conflated, offered here are alternative modes of kinship beyond a model of equivalency or similarity, with discourses of infection forming one possible radical alternative to our existing models for understanding community.

Failure and utopianism

While vegetarianism and veganism have functioned as exchangeable terms in the above analysis, I want to establish now the specific resonance of queerness for a distinctly "vegan" identity. To quote Quinn and Westwood, "Vegetarianism, by definition, is an abstinence from meat-eating. While its adherents may often object to other kinds of animal exploitation, perhaps leather or fur, the occupation of a vegetarian identity relies on a clearly defined limit in relation to animal flesh and ingestion. Veganism […] is attended instead by contradictions and inconsistencies" (4). The contradictions and inconsistencies of veganism's impossibly inclusive aspirations here provide it with an important, and ultimately productive, distinction from vegetarianism. For Gruen and Robert C. Jones, "to ascribe moral purity and clean hands to veganism is to make a category mistake" (156). An aspirational veganism, by contrast, has the power to make a difference, forging "a particularly empowering and grounded form of individual political commitment, [and] fostering a deeper understanding of intersecting injustices and oppressions" (Gruen and Jones 169). While veganism continues to be associated with a moral puritanism in mainstream culture, vegan studies has increasingly sought to reconceptualize veganism in relation to the lessons learnt from queer theory. Vegan forms of life are positioned by McKay as "complex lives rather than as realizations of a clearly articulated position" (266). Similarly, for Simonsen, veganism is an identity category, "but rather as a radically unassimilable force" (58) that "as a *pure* concept is always impossible to sustain or even arrive at" (73). And for James Stanescu, veganism is best conceptualized as a site of permanent becoming, "a practice that transforms the self and our relationship with others" (38).

An aspirational veganism, then, acknowledges at its core the impossibility of a fixed or secure vegan identity. This exemplifies the dilemma facing postmodern identity politics more broadly. For example, reflecting on the reclamation of the term "queer," Butler suggests the necessary violence enacted by identity categories in their attempt to totalize the individual. However, this does not negate the importance, or necessity, of identity categories as a means through which to subvert and reinvent political discourses. As Butler elaborates, "the temporary totalization performed by identity categories is a necessary error. And if identity is a necessary error, then the assertion of 'queer' will be necessary as a term of affiliation," even if one must acknowledge that "it will not fully describe those it purports to represent" (175). Rethinking the discursive security of the term "vegan," I follow Butler's argument that the political efficacy of terms such as "woman" or "queer" comes from understanding them as permanent sites of contest and refusing closure into an all-inclusive or substantive definition. Resisting attempts at discursive closure is seen to require "a double movement: to invoke the category, and, hence, provisionally to institute an identity and at the same time to open the category as a site of permanent political contest" (Butler 222).

The sense of veganism as a horizon of becoming, as opposed to a state at which one can successfully arrive, puts faith in the idea that failure need not be an impediment to action. In *The Queer Art of Failure*, Halberstam invests in the potential rewards of failure for queer theory. Failure appears as a possible strategy to bring down the mainstream establishment, a way of refusing to speak for others or directing all struggles into a normative logic that desires fulfilment, recognition, and achievement. This raises the question of how we might utilize queer theory to better understand veganism, not just as dietary practice or ethical response, but as a negotiation of normative understandings of success, adulthood, masculinity, and humanity. As Halberstam suggests of queer time, the acknowledgment or threat of having "no future" need not only suggest annihilation but might also be "about the potentiality of a life unscripted by the conventions of family, inheritance, and child rearing" (*Queer Time* 14).

José Esteban Muñoz's *Cruising Utopia* is instructive here for thinking about the intersections of failure and insufficiency with the utopian optimism that remains. For Muñoz, "Queerness is essentially about the rejection of a here and now and an insistence on potentiality or concrete possibility for another world" (1). Potentiality, in Muñoz's terms, is not simply the possibility of an event happening in the future, but the existence of that possibility within the present: "a certain mode of nonbeing that is eminent, a thing that is present but not actually existing in the present tense" (9). Muñoz positions queer as an "ideality" that we have not yet reached, a utopian longing and performative doing *for* the future. Moments of refusal, breakdown, and emotion, characteristic of vegan negotiations with the world, might equally signal such utopian potentialities, suggestive of the possibility of an alternative world, where veganism, as practice, enacts potential futures which renegotiate our current exploitative relations to nonhuman animals while acknowledging the inevitable disappointment of such visions.

Both queer theory and vegan theory have emerged under a shadow of death, though at different levels of proximity, in the context of HIV/AIDs and animal agribusiness respectively. As such, both struggle to balance trauma and grief with an account of the pleasure, optimism, and utopianism that remains. Veganism's resistance to a normative humanity responsible for systemic abuses of nonhuman animals requires an acknowledgment, in Muñoz's terms, of the co-existence of failure, inconsistency, and complicity, with hope and utopianism. As Joshua Schuster asserts, the inevitability of violence and the impossibility of a "fully vegan world" is "no reason to relent on a desire for utopian ways of living together" (216).

Conclusion

It is not the case that all vegans experience same-sex attraction or desire, nor that misogynist or homophobic vegans don't exist. Of course not all queers are vegan, nor all vegans queer. As Carrie Hamilton's insightful negotiation of her past experiences within queer leather communities demonstrates, queer practices of intrahuman intimacy, care, and community are often enacted through animal products. Nonetheless, veganism offers a challenge to a meat-eating world so closely linked to heteronormativity and refuses to sanction normative modes of happiness. It provides means by which to desire differently, to expand the parameters of the human and our understanding of kinship and community, and to acknowledge and embrace failure while striving for a utopian future. Through its building of community, it also offers up reparative means of engaging with the violence and hostility of a mass culture dependent on animal sacrifice.

Notes

1 With thanks to a tweet from @ShelleyAsquith for drawing this document to my attention. The original is held at the Stuart A. Rose Manuscript Archives & Rare Book Library at Emory University.
2 The only other reference to the Gay Male Vegetarians I have found is in a passing comment about the Revolutionary People's Constitutional Convention in a story from the *Chicken Soup for the Soul Cookbook* (Canfield et al.).
3 Acknowledgment is due here to Prof. Jason Edwards who provided this useful reflection on how we might approach the document.
4 In "Notes on Vegan Camp", I propose "vegan camp" as a means of harnessing this comedic potential, a possible reparative mode of vegan aesthetics that accounts for the pleasures of vegan life while performing a sense of complicity in mass violence (Quinn).
5 The rejection of the Gay Male Vegetarians by the Black Panther conference might also suggest further important intersections between veganism and race, with vegan identity frequently associated with whiteness and the marginalization of other disenfranchised peoples. Recent work by Aph and Syl Ko, and A. Breeze Harper has done much to think about veganism's intersections with critical race studies and the decolonization of diet.
6 For further analysis of the gendered nature of meat-eating, see Alex Lockwood's essay in this collection.
7 Carrie Hamilton's recent "Mourning Leather: Queer Histories, Vegan futures" provides an insightful corrective here.
8 Of at least anecdotal interest is the report by many of my close queer vegan friends that "coming-out" as vegan generated significantly more hostile responses from family members than coming-out as gay.
9 This latter point should be made under the proviso that veganism is not immune to what has been seen as "pink-washing" of queer culture, that intersects with the "green-washing" of environmental movements, working often alongside gentrification to produce perhaps its own form of muddy-grey-washing.
10 For more on how ghostly child figures informs adult queer identities, see Kathryn Bond Stockton's *The Queer Child*.

Works cited

Adams, Carol J. *The Sexual Politics of Meat: A Feminist Vegetarian Critical Theory*. 1990. Bloomsbury Academic, 2015.
Butler, Judith. *Bodies that Matter: On the Discursive Limits of "Sex."* Routledge, 2011.
Canfield, Jack, Mark Victor Hansen, and Diana von Welanetz Wenworth. *Chicken Soup for the Soul Cookbook: 101 Stories with Recipes from the Heart*. Simon and Schuster, 2012.
Dean, Tim. *Unlimited Intimacy: Reflections on the Subculture of Barebacking*. University of Chicago Press, 2009.
Derrida, Jacques. "'Eating Well', or the Calculation of the Subject: An interview with Jacques Derrida." *Points...: Interviews, 1974–1994*, edited by Elisabeth Weber, translated by Peggy Kamuf. Stanford University Press, 1995, pp. 255–287.

Edelman, Lee. *No Future: Queer Theory and the Death Drive*. Duke University Press, 2004.
Fuentes, Agustín, and Natalie Porter. "Kinship." *Critical Terms for Animal Studies*, edited by Lori Gruen. University of Chicago Press, 2018, pp. 182–196.
Gaard, Greta. "Towards a Queer Ecofeminism." *Hypatia*, vol. 12, no. 1, 1997, pp. 114–137.
Gruen, Lori. *Entangled Empathy*. Lantern Books, 2015.
Gruen, Lori, and Robert C. Jones. "Veganism as Aspiration." *The Moral Complexities of Eating Meat*. Oxford University Press, 2015, pp. 153–171.
Halberstam, J. Jack. *The Queer Art of Failure*. Duke University Press, 2011.
———. *In a Queer Time and Place: Transgender Bodies, Subcultural Lives*. New York UP, 2005.
Hamilton, Carrie. "Mourning Leather: Queer Histories, Vegan Futures." *Memory Studies*, 2019.
Haraway, Donna. *When Species Meet*. University of Minnesota Press, 2008.
Harper, A. Breeze. *Sistah Vegan: Black Female Vegans Speak on Food, Identity, Health, and Society*. Lantern Books, 2010.
Huggan, Graham, and Helen Tiffin. *Postcolonial Ecocriticism: Literature, Animals, Environment*. Routledge, 2010.
Jones, Robert C. "Veganisms." *Critical Perspectives on Veganism*, edited by Jodey Castricano and Rasmus R. Simonsen. Palgrave Macmillan, 2016, pp. 15–39.
Ko, Aph, and Syl Ko. *Aphro-ism. Essays on Pop Culture, Feminism, and Black Veganism from Two Sisters*. Lantern Books, 2017.
Luciano, Dana, and Mel Y. Chen. "Has the Queer Ever Been Human?" *GLQ*, vol. 23, no. 2–3, 2015, pp. 183–207.
McKay, Robert. "A Vegan Form of Life." *Thinking Veganism in Literature and Culture: Towards a Vegan Theory*. Palgrave Macmillan, 2018, pp. 249–271.
Muñoz, José Esteban. *Cruising Utopia: The Then and There of Queer Futurity*. New York UP, 2009.
Ngai, Sianne. *Our Aesthetic Categories*. Harvard University Press, 2012.
Potts, Annie, and Jovian Parry. "Vegan Sexuality: Challenging Heteronormative Masculinity through Meat-Free Sex." *Feminism & Psychology*, vol. 20, no. 1, 2010, pp. 53–72.
Quinn, Emelia. "Notes on Vegan Camp." *PMLA*, forthcoming.
Quinn, Emelia, and Benjamin Westwood. "Introduction: Thinking Through Veganism." *Thinking Veganism in Literature and Culture: Towards a Vegan Theory*. Palgrave Macmillan, 2018, pp. 1–24.
Salih, Sara. "Vegans on the Verge of a Nervous Breakdown." *The Rise of Critical Animal Studies: From the Margins to the Centre*, edited by Nik Taylor and Richard Twine. Routledge, 2014, pp. 52–68.
Schuster, Joshua. "The Vegan and the Sovereign." *Critical Perspectives on Veganism*, edited by Jodey Castricano and Rasmus R. Simonsen. Palgrave Macmillan, 2016, pp. 203–223.
Sedgwick, Eve Kosofsky. "Paranoid Reading and Reparative Reading, or, you're so paranoid, you probably think this essay is about you." *Touching Feeling: Affect, Pedagogy, Performativity*, edited by Adam Frank. Duke University Press, 2003.
Simonsen, R. R. "A Queer Vegan Manifesto." *Journal for Critical Animal Studies*, vol. 10, no. 3, 2012, pp. 51–80.
Stanescu, James. "Toward a Dark Animal Studies: On Vegetarian Vampires, Beautiful Souls and Becoming-Vegan." *Journal for Critical Animal Studies*, vol. 10, no. 3, 2012, pp. 26–50.
Steiner, Gary. *Animals and the Limits of Postmodernism*. Columbia University Press, 2013.
Twine, Richard. "Vegan Killjoys at the Table—Contesting Happiness and Negotiating Relationships with Food Practices." *Societies*, vol. 4, 2014, pp. 623–639.
———. "Intersectional disgust? Animals and (eco) feminism." *Feminism and Psychology*, vol. 20, no. 3, 2010, pp. 397–406.
Wood, David. "Comment ne pas manger—Deconstruction and Humanism." *Animal Others: On Ethics, Ontology, and Animal Life*. New York UP, 1999, pp. 15–35.
Wright, Laura. *The Vegan Studies Project: Food, Animals, and Gender in the Age of Terror*. The University of Georgia Press, 2015.

24
"You would betray your own mother for meat"
A postcolonial vegan reading of Tsitsi Dangarembga's Nervous Conditions

Sarah Rhu and Laura Wright

In *The Wretched of the Earth*, Algerian psychiatrist Frantz Fanon, whose work is foundational to the field of postcolonial studies, writes, "[t]he relations of man with matter, with the world outside, and with history are in the colonial period simply relations with food" (308). Fanon recognizes that control over one's means of sustenance is essential for survival and liberation. In this analysis, we apply

> a vegan studies approach [that] examines texts (broadly speaking) via an intersectional lens of veganism as practice, identity category, and theoretical perspective in order to complicate our understandings of, our relationships with, and our access to food, animals, the environment, and other humans. (Wright xv)

In doing so, we provide a postcolonial vegan reading which complicates our understanding of the roles of food and animals in Zimbabwean author Tsitsi Dangarembga's 1988 novel *Nervous Conditions*. This chapter places veganism in the context of the traditionally plant-based diet of the Shona culture, of which the characters in *Nervous Conditions* are a part. This approach suggests the return to the plant-based foodways of her ancestors as an alternative form of rebellion for the deuteragonist Nyasha, a Rhodesian girl who develops an eating disorder in a society on the verge of decolonial revolution.

Postcolonial studies

There is considerable debate over the precise parameters of the scope and the definition of the term "postcolonial." For the purposes of this essay, "postcolonial studies" consists of the study of the interactions between European nations and the societies they colonized—India, African countries, New Zealand, and the Caribbean, for example—both during the period of colonization as well as after independence. Postcolonial scholars explore issues of power, race, and gender with regard to colonial domination and engage with the following questions: How did the experience of colonization affect those who were colonized while also influencing the colonizers? What were the forms of resistance against colonial control? How did colonial education and language influence the culture and identity of the colonized? How did Western science, technology, and medicine change existing knowledge systems? What are the emergent forms of postcolonial identity after the departure of the colonizers? To what extent has decolonization (a reconstruction free from colonial influence) been possible? How do gender, race, and class function in colonial and postcolonial discourse? Are new forms of imperialism replacing colonization and, if so, how?

As a field that has been both politically controversial and markedly successful in its elevation of marginalized voices, postcolonial studies traces its beginnings to the Subaltern Studies Group of the early 1980s, following the publication of Edward Said's *Orientalism* in 1978. As a theoretical framework, postcolonial studies has sought to bring to the fore perspectives of marginalized and colonized peoples via a careful and sustained analysis of the ways that hierarchical power structures erase indigenous pre-colonial histories, cultural norms, and, in the context of this chapter, foodways. Postcolonial studies has always focused on literary analysis, as evidenced by one of the key moments in its theoretical history, when Nigerian author Chinua Achebe delivered his now famous "An Image of Africa" lecture at the University of Massachusetts in 1975, during which he declared Joseph Conrad a racist for his depiction of Africa and Africans in his canonical novella *Heart of Darkness*. This literary focus has, on the one hand, created opportunities for engagement with imagined precolonial histories and postcolonial encounters, while, on the other, allowed for criticisms of postcolonialism as a field interested in art as opposed to real-life politics and an academic exercise that has failed to achieve any real-world impact. Further, as a field, postcolonialism's engagement with ecocriticism and animal studies has been slow to manifest, in part because, as Rob Nixon notes, postcolonial critics have traditionally been less concerned with environmental issues, viewing them as "irrelevant and elitist" (716) as compared with the continuing human rights struggles of formerly colonized peoples. Nixon argues that in order to link the two fields of inquiry, scholars need to "rethink oppositions between bioregionalism and cosmopolitanism, between transcendentalism and transnationalism, between the ethics of place and the experience of displacement" (721). By the second decade of the 21st century, however, postcolonial ecocriticism entered the mainstream via a proliferation of scholarly interest in explorations of such issues as the "slow violence" of climate change's impact on postcolonial cultures, the environmentalism of the poor,[1] the creation of wildlife preserves and the subsequent resultant displacement of indigenous peoples, ecotourism, the privatization of water, and indigenous versus settler conceptions of environmentalism, sustainability, and land usage.

From within this theoretical nexus has also emerged scholarship that has engaged with the impact of colonialization and Western dietary practices on indigenous foodways. In *Affective Communities: Anticolonial Thought, Fin-de-Siècle Radicalism, and the Politics of Friendship*, Leela Gandhi notes in the chapter "Meat" that "equating beef with imperial virility" and plant-based diets with femininity and weakness was an "ideological tactic" pushed back against by M. K. Gandhi's lived vegetarian ethic and his rhetorical aligning of the partition of India with the vivisection of the continent. Carol J. Adams acknowledges this tactic, citing 19th-century physician George Beard's assertion that British imperialism was successful in part because of the proclivity of the British for beef: "the rice-eating Hindoo and Chinese and the potato-eating Irish peasant are kept in subjection by the well-fed English ... [a] nation of beef-eaters" (Beard qtd. in Adams 9). Aside from India, where Hinduism has led to the "lowest per capita meat consumption of all nations" (Muzaffar), vegetarianism and veganism are almost entirely absent from postcolonial ecocritical discourse except in cases where vegetarian/vegan diets are characterized as elitist and culturally insensitive. In her call for a more postcolonial posthumanist feminist theory, Maneesah Deckha addresses such criticisms and challenges the "growing chorus

... that charges vegetarian and vegan advocates with ethnocentrism/imperialism and elitism in their attempts to promote an animal-free diet," noting that such criticisms are often based in a "perception that antimeat advocates are ignorant of and/or unresponsive toward non-Western cultures whose traditional diets are animal-based. This critique is often advanced through the example of subsistence hunting practices of indigenous peoples" (534). Rather than uncritically accepting such assertions, Deckha suggests that such an

> elitist and ethnocentric characterization of vegetarianism/veganism obscures the reality that in many parts of the globe, it is more expensive to lead a nonvegetarian lifestyle than a vegetarian lifestyle, with animal flesh marked as a luxury item or indulgence. ... These arguments also discount the enormous amounts of plant and land resources that are required to sustain current Western levels of flesh consumption ... and ignore the richness of non-Western flesh-free food traditions and ideologies of nonviolence toward all living beings. (535)

Further, in *The Postcolonial Animal*, Evan Maina Mwangi calls for an examination of "the vegan unconscious" that situates veganism as useful to the studies of postcolonial—specifically African—literatures "where the texts do not even openly espouse vegetarianism" (7). While *Nervous Conditions* does not address plant-based eating as a means of postcolonial resistance, the text does engage with this vegan unconscious to place the Western meat-centric diet embraced by the novel's Westernized characters in stark contrast to the predominantly plant-based traditional diet of the Shona.

Nervous Conditions and Shona foodways

The title and epigraph of Tsitsi Dangarembga's *Nervous Conditions*, the first novel published in English by a Black Zimbabwean woman, derive from a line in Jean-Paul Sartre's introduction to Fanon's aforementioned *The Wretched of the Earth*: "The status of 'native' is a nervous condition" (Fanon 20). Thus, Dangarembga, who studied psychology, inherits from Fanon, a psychiatrist, by way of Sartre. She also develops, from a feminist perspective, Fanon's ideas about rebellion against colonization while showing how European modes of consumption colonize indigenous foodways. Many scholars have interpreted the eating disorders of Nyasha, the deuteragonist of *Nervous Conditions*, as forms of resistance to colonialism and patriarchy in 1960s Zimbabwe. They observe that the colonizers' texts are figured as food throughout the novel, and Nyasha, as in Fanon's description of the period of decolonization, "vomit[s] them up" (Fanon 43). However, Nyasha's resistance is to colonization and patriarchal control, not just of her body, but of her diet itself.

With her article "Disembodying the Corpus: Postcolonial Pathology in Tsitsi Dangarembga's *Nervous Conditions*" (1994), Deepika Bahri became the first scholar to describe Nyasha's eating disorders as a form of resistance to colonialism and patriarchy in the novel. Several similar essays have followed, but Bahri's remains one of the best. Her thesis is as follows: "Nyasha's diseased self suggests the textualized female body on whose abject person are writ large the imperial inscriptions of colonization, the intimate branding of patriarchy, and the battle between native culture, Western narrative, and her complex relationship with both" (para 1). Bahri uses the work of Western theorists, like Susan Bordo, and postcolonial ones, like Chandra Talpade Mohanty, to make her argument. She acknowledges that anorexia and bulimia are stereotypically disorders of Western white women. However, she also calls attention to the fact that hunger strikes, such as Gandhi's fasting, are a time-honored and cross-cultural form of protest. Bahri discusses the protagonist Tambu's mother Ma'Shingayi's refusal to eat as well as Nyasha's. Thus, she recognizes these women's agency to resist patriarchal and colonial structures.

Muzna Rahman places Nyasha's anorexia and bulimia in the context of the history of food scarcity in Zimbabwe. Chronic famine has plagued the country, but before colonization, mortality rates from hunger were relatively low. Lack of rain usually caused the food shortages, but the people would keep reserves and trade with one another. Only regions that were extremely vulnerable to weather-related challenges would struggle with a dearth of food. However, colonial forces' land requisition caused famine to spread from the susceptible areas to the entire population. The government provided aid, but it was just enough to keep people from starving to death, not to prevent chronic hunger among the nation's poor. Rahman shows how the characters who live on the Tambu's family's homestead in *Nervous Conditions* experience this food economy of subsistence and survival. The women in particular suffer from a lack of nutrition because they eat only after the men have had their fill. The family members at the missionary school, on the other hand, have plenty to eat, yet Nyasha refuses food from her father's table. Rahman discusses the mind-body dualism in the novel and reveals that most of the times that Nyasha rejects food, her attitude is introspective. Reading the narrative in light of Zimbabwe's history of hunger, she interprets Nyasha's body as "aligning itself with the starving bodies of her famished countrymen and their particular legacy of nutritional hardship" (286). Therefore, she argues that *Nervous Conditions* intervenes on distorted Western perceptions of African hunger, turning hunger into a choice, an act of political resistance.

In *Nervous Conditions*, Tambu's family lives on a homestead where their food is primarily plant-based. *Sadza*, a thick porridge made from grains, forms the staple of their diet. Tavuyanago et al. explain that *sadza* used to be comprised of native millet and sorghum; however, through colonization, maize has become its most common ingredient. The Portuguese introduced maize to the Shona in the 16th century, and the crop gained popularity because of whites' demand for it (Tavuyanago et al. 1). While Tambu's family sometimes eats millet (*rukweza*), they make their *sadza* from maize meal. They grow mealies, or corncobs, for their own consumption and to sell for a living. Tavuyanago et al. provide an overview of the scholarship on maize in Africa. For example,

> Zeleza (1993) highlights that many Africans ... took to the growing of [maize], not just because it was a useful addition to their stock of food crops, but also because the crop offered a vent through which Africans could raise funds to pay taxes imposed by the colonial government. Gakou (1987) argues that funds from the sale of the crop could also be used to pay school fees. (Tavuyanago et al. 1)

Tambu asks her parents for her own plot and seeds to grow mealies and sell them in order to raise money for her school fees. Her teacher recommends that she sell the maize to whites because they can afford to and will buy them at a much higher price than Black Africans will (Dangarembga 24). Tavuyanago et al. argue that European crops like maize cause food insecurity and upset social relations of production among the Shona (1). However, Manel I. Gomez includes maize in his "Resource Inventory of Indigenous and Traditional Foods in Zimbabwe" because while "not essentially 'indigenous' (of local origin)," the crop has "become part of the traditional diet" (54).

Tambu's mother supplements her family's staple *sadza* with vegetables which she cultivates in her garden: "rape, *covo*, tomatoes, *derere* and onions—which she grew on a plot that had been my grandmother's" (Dangarembga 8). *Covo* is a leafy green like kale, and *derere* is a "[g]eneric term for vegetables that are mucilaginous when cooked" (Gomez 62). The italicization of their names indicates that *covo* and *derere* are the Shona terms for these plants. Dangarembga leaves many nouns, especially words for foods, untranslated in *Nervous Conditions*, suggesting that the book's audience may be Zimbabweans who are familiar with these vegetables and fruits from their traditional diet. See, for example, the wild fruits which Tambu says her brother Nhamo could pick and eat on his walk home from the bus terminal: "matamba and matunduru. Sweet and sour. Delicious" (Dangarembga 3). Matamba are monkey oranges and matunduru mangosteens (Gomez 65). However, Nhamo does not like to walk home after attending his uncle's missionary school. After going to the mission herself, Tambu states that she and her cousins, including Nyasha, have become "too civilised … to be amused by eating *matamba* and *nhengeni*," or sour plums (Dangarembga 122, Gomez 65).

Western food has colonized their diets, and they can no longer enjoy their native fruits. Nevertheless, Tambu and the women in her family continue to eat mangoes, hute (or waterberries), peaches, guavas, and mulberries, which their neighbors offer them on their way to the Nyamirira River for water and washing (Dangarembga 136). Gomez explains that while mangos and mulberries are introduced species, they "have in some regions become 'naturalized' and are frequently encountered in the vegetation bordering forests and roadsides" (54). Such plant foods are linked to women in *Nervous Conditions*. In Shona culture, gardening is women's work; thus, the garden passes down the matrilineal side of Tambu's family. Tambu receives part of this plot to grow mealies. Tambu's mother is able to feed her family much more cheaply with plant-based meals because she can grow vegetables and pick fruits herself.

Milking cows, on the other hand, is a male job among the Shona.[2] While living on the homestead, Tambu's brother Nhamo must milk cows before and after school. However, he only does so "when a cow [is] in milk," unlike in industrialized agriculture where farmers keep cows constantly pregnant and separate them from their young (Dangarembga 21). Therefore, Tambu's family does not always have milk as part of their diet. Nevertheless, cattle are extremely valuable to the Shona. They provide dung for fertilizer and the construction of housing and labor for pulling plows in the fields as well as milk for consumption. Tambu's uncle and family patriarch Babamukuru reveals that he has forbidden her father Jeremiah from slaughtering his livestock (Dangarembga 124). As a poor man, Jeremiah cannot afford to lose his animals as sources of food, strength, and building materials. He must keep them rather than kill them for meat. The Shona also use cattle to pay the bride price that requires that the husband's family present the wife's with livestock in exchange for their daughter's hand in marriage. Thus, women become interchangeable with non-human animals as men employ both of them for their labor, homemaking, and reproductive capacities.

The Shona do not often consume meat. Solomon Murungu states, "it is not unusual for some [Shona] families to go for two weeks eating sadza with vegetables instead of meat. Thus eating sadza with meat becomes a bit of a treat." Tambu's family only eats meat on special occasions, particularly when male relatives return to the homestead: "On the days that Babamukuru came to visit we killed a cock. Or rather, we killed a cock if there was one to spare, otherwise just a hen. We also killed a fowl on the occasions that Nhamo came home" (Dangarembga 8). Cultures across the globe associate the consumption of meat with strength and therefore masculinity. Carol J. Adams asserts that "a mythology permeates all classes that meat is a masculine food and meat-eating a male activity" (Adams 3–4). Consequently, Tambu's family feels obligated to prepare chicken for the visits of their male relatives, especially powerful figures like Babamukuru. However, meat is more expensive than plant foods because it requires more resources to produce. Tambu's family must feed their livestock some of their grain and thus have less of it to eat themselves. If they slaughtered a cow, they would lose a source of milk and dung, and when they kill chickens, they lose their source of eggs. Therefore, they rarely slaughter their animals and eat meat.

Tambu detests having to kill chickens for her male relatives' visits:

> I hated the whole process of enlisting Netsai's help to head off the bird's escape, growing irritable as I lunged for its wings and clutched empty air until finally I caught it, protesting and cackling in its strident voice, until, sensing the inevitable, it was quiet. Nor could I bear the smell of blood that threatened to suffocate when boiling water was poured over the headless bird to loosen its feathers. Next time, I thought naively, Nhamo will catch it himself. If he wants to eat chicken, he will catch it and kill it. I will pluck it and cook it. That seemed a fair division of labor. (Dangarembga 12)

Tambu knows that her brother will not slaughter the fowl himself because he considers doing so to be a girl's job. Instead, she must have her younger sister assist her in capturing the bird. Children often express greater empathy toward nonhuman animals than adults do because they have not yet become desensitized to the violence inherent in their consumption. Vegan ecofeminists have theorized that women also experience a stronger connection to nonhuman animals because of their common oppression under patriarchy. Tambu reveals this link with her juxtaposition of the slaughter of chickens and the unequal gender division of labor in her culture.

Babamukuru often has to provide meat, even for his own visits, because Tambu's family cannot afford it. One Christmas, he brings the side of an ox to the homestead, although his wife Maiguru warns him it is too much food. She has a paraffin refrigerator, in which she can store a small amount of the meat. However, because Tambu's family does not regularly eat animals, they do not have a way to preserve all of the ox, and most of the side goes bad. Nevertheless, Tambu's family cannot afford to throw away the meat because they have to feed all of their relatives who are visiting for the holiday, so they continue to eat the spoiled ox. Tambu's aunt Gladys refuses to eat the bad meat and expresses her surprise that Babamukuru can consume it. Out of shame, Maiguru takes "to cooking, twice a day, a special pot of refrigerated meat for the patriarchy to eat as they planned and constructed the family's future" (Dangarembga 138). Gladys is able to obtain some of this good ox because she is Babamukuru's sister and therefore a member of the patriarchy. By her kinship with the male line of the family, she acquires higher status and better-quality food.

Women on the homestead usually do not receive as much meat, or food in general, as the men do. Their feminine role requires them to prepare the meal for and serve everyone else before they can eat it themselves (Dangarembga 136). They dish out food for the patriarchy first and then have whatever is left over. On Babamukuru's return from England, Tambu's aunt Mavis excitedly serves so much meat to the family members dining in the house that there is not enough left for the women and children in the kitchen: "As a result the youngest of us had only gravy and vegetables to go with our *sadza*. ... We, who rarely tasted meat, found no reason to complain" (Dangarembga 41). Adams reveals that women having less to eat than men is a cross-cultural phenomenon: "Women engage in deliberate self-deprivation, offering men the 'best' foods at the expense of their own nutritional needs" (4). Meat is considered one of the "best" foods because of its association with masculinity and wealth. According to Adams, "Women, second-class citizens, are more likely to eat what are considered to be second-class foods in a patriarchal culture: vegetables, fruits, and grains, rather than meat" (3). We see this pattern on the homestead in *Nervous Conditions* with the women in Tambu's family eating vegetables from her mother's garden, wild fruits, and *sadza* while reserving meat for the patriarchy. Adams explains that the unfair distribution of meat between the sexes occurs more frequently in circumstances of poverty because the resource-intensive nature of meat production renders it an expensive and rare commodity (4).

Tambu eats a piece of meat while preparing the feast for Babamukuru's return:

> The three-legged pot that on normal days contained *sadza*, but today was full of meat, splashed half of its juices into the embers. A piece of meat fell out too. I picked it out of the ashes and ate it. (Dangarembga 38)

Tambu then feels sick because she is thinking about her cousins' inability to speak Shona after living in England and Nhamo's attempt to speak English with them. Nyasha and her brother Chido become hybrid figures not only through the loss of their native language but through a change in their diet. White Westerners tend to eat more meat because they can afford it, and Tambu's cousins' family is wealthier than her own, so they begin to eat more meat while in England and continue to do so once back home. Adams defines "racism as the requirement that power arrangements and customs that favor white people prevail, and … the acculturation of people of color to this standard includes the imposition of white habits of meat eating" (7–8). Nyasha and Chido experience the imposition of white habits of more frequent meat eating because of the lack of access to their traditional plant-based foods while in England but also because Westerners consider animal products to be superior foods, so their family adopts these values while abroad. Thus, Tambu links the consumption of meat to the colonization of her cousins.

Meat, "The Englishness," and disordered eating

The food which Maiguru provides Tambu and her own children at the mission is Anglicized, and Tambu has trouble eating it at first. At her first meal at the mission,

> [t]he food looked interesting, which made me suspicious of it since I knew that food was not meant to be interesting but filling. Besides the rice, there was something that might have been potato: I could not be sure since it was smothered in a thick, white, tasteless gravy. Although I gallantly placed small portions of it in my mouth, it refused to go down my throat in large quantities. (Dangarembga 83)

Tambu is accustomed to eating for sustenance and survival, not pleasure. The potatoes she is used to become unrecognizable under a Western-style, notably *white* gravy. The dish exemplifies the colonization of her traditional plant-based Shona diet by the imposition of animal products. Tambu is barely able to eat it, and Maiguru sympathizes: "'When we first went to England,' she was saying, 'it was terrible. It took me months to get used to the food. It has no taste'" (Dangarembga 84). The process of acculturation to new foodways takes time, but Maiguru and her family have adjusted to the Western diet. Tambu, on the other hand, has not yet done so. Maiguru requests some *sadza* for Tambu to eat instead, and she is relieved to receive it.

After the meal, Tambu has a nightmare about the colonization of her brother's diet:

> Dribbling a ball gracefully through maize plants that had sprung up in the football field of our old school, he paused from time to time to pick a fat, juicy cob and stuff it into his mouth. The cobs were full of white gravy. … I saw him eat and became alarmed that he would make himself ill with the strange mealies. (Dangarembga 91)

The maize plants at their old school evoke the mealies Tambu sells to raise money for her tuition and over which she and Nhamo fight on the football field. However, white gravy has corrupted these mealies just as it did the potatoes at her previous meal. The dream implies that the colonization of Nhamo's diet may have led to his sickness and death. Critical race feminist A. Breeze Harper theorizes that the imposition of WESTERN foodways onto indigenous populations contributes to health disparities between white and Black people (157), and Tambu's nightmare supports this hypothesis in terms of both the physical and psychological health of the characters in the novel.

Unlike her family on the homestead, Tambu's relatives at the mission eat meat regularly because it makes up a large part of the English diet and they can afford it. The morning after her dream about Nhamo, Tambu witnesses Nyasha having bacon and eggs: "I found time to be impressed by these relatives of mine who ate meat, and not only meat, but meat and eggs for breakfast" (Dangarembga 93). The unequal distribution of animal products between men and women is not as obvious at the mission. Maiguru serves Babamukuru extra meat, but there is still enough for her, Nyasha, and Tambu to have some (Dangarembga 83). Adams clarifies that "[i]n situations of abundance, sex role assumptions about meat are not so blatantly expressed" (7). By the time she returns to the homestead for Christmas, Tambu has become accustomed to eating animal products for breakfast and is dissatisfied with her family's offerings: "Bread and margarine! I would have preferred egg and bacon!" (Dangarembga 136). The food at the mission has successfully colonized her diet and her thinking.

Tambu's mother Ma'Shingayi observes this change in her daughter and rebukes her:

> If it is meat you want that I cannot provide for you, if you are so greedy you would betray your own mother for meat, then go to your Maiguru. She will give you meat. I will survive on vegetables as we all used to do. And we have survived, so what more do you want? You have your life. Go to your Maiguru and eat sausage. (Dangarembga 143)

Ma'Shingayi values food for subsistence rather than enjoyment as Tambu did before she went to the mission. She references the traditional plant-based foodways of the Shona in contrast to the Western meat-laden diet. She also situates herself in opposition to Maiguru; Ma'Shingayi has given her children life, while she blames Maiguru, who feeds them animal products, for Nhamo's death at the mission. Nhamo and Tambu both gain weight from their diet at Maiguru's house, and Nhamo even appears closer to white from the nutrition: "Vitamins had nourished his skin to a shiny smoothness, several tones lighter in complexion than it used to be" (Dangarembga 52). The Western food colonizes him: he pretends to have, like his cousins, lost his ability to speak Shona. Ma'Shingayi attributes Nhamo's death and Nyasha's eating disorders to colonization: "'It's the Englishness,' she said. 'It'll kill them all if they aren't careful,' … She went on like this for quite a while, going on about how you couldn't expect the ancestors to stomach so much Englishness" (Dangarembga 207). Her ancestors could not stomach so much Englishness partly because of their plant-based diet.

Ma'Shingayi accuses Babamukuru of "fattening [her] children only to take them away, like cattle are fattened for slaughter" (Dangarembga 187). The word "cattle" comes from "chattel," meaning "property" ("chattel, n."). Babamukuru owns Nhamo and Tambu the way that he controls their father Jeremiah's livestock, instructing his brother on what to do with both the animals and his children. However, unlike Jeremiah, Babamukuru can afford to slaughter cattle. He does not depend, as Jeremiah does, on his children receiving an education so that they can support him in the future. Ma'Shingayi resists Babamukuru's patriarchal control through food. Each time Tambu leaves for a new missionary school, Ma'Shingayi refuses or is unable to eat. The lack of nourishment renders her incapable of sufficiently performing her womanly duty of breast-feeding her youngest child (Dangarembga 187). Ma'Shingayi's sister Lucia finally convinces her to eat by preparing a meat stew: "'Tambudzai,' she instructed me in my father's presence, 'make sure nobody touches this meat. Nobody besides your mother, who is ill and needs to regain her strength'" (Dangarembga 189). For the first time in the novel, meat is reserved for a woman rather than for men. Nevertheless, Lucia has a reputation for being rebellious, so she is able to go against the traditional distribution of meat and does so only because her sister is sick. Moreover, she brings the meat from the mission, where Babamukuru has gotten her a job. The Western food appeases Ma'Shingayi into letting Tambu leave for school without protestation.

Babamukuru wields even more power over Nyasha, including her diet, because she is his daughter. He often insists that she finish her meals and supervises her eating: "She must eat her food, all of it. She is always doing this, challenging my authority. I am her father" (Dangarembga 193). Nyasha resists this patriarchal control by refusing to eat or, when she does eat, throwing up what Babamukuru forces her to consume. After Tambu hears her purge for the first time, Nyasha explains: "Imagine all that fuss over a plateful of food. But it's more than that really, more than just food. That's how it comes out, but really it's all the things about boys and men and being decent and indecent and good and bad" (Dangarembga 193). Babamukuru and Nyasha both connect her eating habits to her sexuality. Young women sometimes develop anorexia to prevent the onset of puberty. They also do so in order to exercise control over some aspect of their lives, especially when they feel out of control of the rest of it. Tambu first observes Nyasha refuse food at the mission after Babamukuru confiscates her copy of *Lady Chatterly's Lover*—notably a British novel—because he thinks the book is too salacious for her (Dangarembga 82–85). While Babamukuru controls what she reads and considers the novel to be overly mature, Nyasha can decide how much she eats and make her body more childlike by starving herself. At the same time, she rejects the "ritual dishing" in which Babamukuru serves the plates and everyone waits for him to finish before they start eating. While Maiguru takes Babamukuru's old meal for herself because it is no longer fresh, Nyasha serves herself and says, "I don't like cold food" (Dangarembga 82–83). Thus, she resists the sexual politics that require women to accept lower-quality meals than men.

Tambu only witnesses Nyasha refuse food on the homestead once, shortly after her move back from England. Nyasha has a choice between milk and vegetables for lunch (Dangarembga 52). At first, she chooses milk because dairy is more familiar from the Western diet to which she has become accustomed than the native vegetables are. However, once she sees that everyone else is eating the vegetables, she remembers that the traditional Shona diet is plant-based and wishes to return to it. (Milk is usually a rarer commodity on the homestead than vegetables.) After this event, Tambu does not recount Nyasha refusing food on the homestead again. Nyasha only does so at the mission where her diet is Westernized. She also never purges on the homestead, where the meals are more traditional. Therefore, Nyasha resists the colonization of her diet by refusing and throwing up Western dishes while eating plant-based ones.

Harper promotes veganism as way for Black women in particular to "decoloniz[e] their bodies from the legacy of racialized colonialism" (157), and the return to the plant-based diet of their ancestors may enable them to heal from health issues. Thus, food serves as a tool of colonization and also one of resistance. In the novel, animals and meat operate as metaphors for the oppression of women and children under patriarchy. Nyasha rebels against this colonization and patriarchal control of her diet through her eating disorders but could do so more effectively through a return to the traditional plant-based diet of the Shona. The lens of vegan studies and a recognition of the "vegan unconscious" allow for this alternative reading of *Nervous Conditions*.

Notes

1 See in particular Rob Nixon's 2011 work *Slow Violence and the Environmentalism of the Poor*.
2 See Dangarembga 137: "two cows were in milk and the boys took their duty of milking them seriously."

Works cited

Achebe, Chinua. "An Image of Africa: Racism in Conrad's Heart of Darkness." *Heart of Darkness, An Authoritative Text, Background and Sources Criticism*, 3rd edition, edited by Robert Kimbrough, Norton, 1988, pp. 251–261.
Adams, Carol J. *The Sexual Politics of Meat: A Feminist-Vegetarian Critical Theory*. Bloomsbury, 2010.
Bahri, Deepika. "Disembodying the Corpus: Postcolonial Pathology in Tsitsi Dangarembga's *Nervous Conditions*." *Postmodern Culture*, vol. 5, no. 1, 1994.
Buchan, T. and L. D. Gregory. "Anorexia Nervosa in a Black Zimbabwean." *British Journal of Psychiatry*, no. 145, 1984, pp. 326–330.
"chattel, n." *Oxford English Dictionary*, Oxford University Press, 2019, https://www-oed-com.proxy195.nclive.org/view/Entry/30963?redirectedFrom=chattel#eid. Accessed September 28 2019.
Conrad, Joseph. *Heart of Darkness*. Norton, 2016.
Dangarembga, Tsitsi. *Nervous Conditions*. Ayebia Clarke Publishing, 2004.
Deckha, Maneesha. "Toward a Postcolonial, Posthumanist Feminist Theory: Centralizing Race and Culture in Feminist Work on Nonhuman Animals." *Hypatia*, vol. 27, no. 3, 2012, pp. 527–545.
Fanon, Frantz. *The Wretched of the Earth*. Grove Weidenfeld, 1961.
Gomez, Manel I. "A Resource Inventory of Indigenous and Traditional Foods in Zimbabwe." *Zambezia*, vol. 15, no. 1, 1988, pp. 53–73.
Harper, Breeze A. "Going Beyond the Normative White 'Post-Racial' Vegan Epistemology." *Taking Food Public: Redefining Foodways in a Changing World*, edited by Psyche Williams Forson and Carole Counihan. Routledge, 2012, pp. 155–174.
Muzaffar, Maroosha. "The State in 'Vegetarian' India Where 98 Percent of People Eat Meat." *Ozy*, 5 February 2019. https://www.ozy.com/acumen/the-state-in-vegetarian-india-where-98-percent-of-people-eat-meat/92383/. Accessed March 6 2020.
Nixon, Rob. "Environmentalism and Postcolonialism." *Postcolonial Studies and Beyond*, edited by Ania Loomba et al. Duke University Press, 2005, pp. 233–251.
———. *Slow Violence and the Environmentalism of the Poor*. Harvard University Press, 2011.
Rahman, Muzna. "Bodily Secrets: The History of the Starving Body in Tsitsi Dangarembga's *Nervous Conditions*." *Forum for Modern Language Studies*, vol. 50, no. 3, 2014, pp. 275–288.
Said, Edward. *Orientalism*. Vintage, 1979.
Tavuyanago, Baxter, et al. "Traditional Grain Crops in Pre-Colonial and Colonial Zimbabwe: A Factor for Food Security and Social Cohesion Among the Shona People." *Journal of Sustainable Development in Africa*, vol. 12, no. 6, 2010, pp. 1–8.
Thomas, Sue. "Rewriting the Hysteric as Anorexia in Tsitsi Dangarembga's *Nervous Conditions*." *Scenes of the Apple: Food and the Female Body in Nineteenth- and Twentieth-Century Women's Writing*, edited by Tamar Heller and Patricia Moran, State University of New York Press, 2003, pp. 183–198.
Wright, Laura, editor. *Through a Vegan Studies Lens: Textual Ethics and Lived Activism*. University of Nevada Press, 2019.

25
Radical recipe
Veganism as anti-racism

Marilisa C. Navarro

Start with the visceral, move to the intellectual, and end with the political.
—Bryant Terry

La comida es medicina y resistencia.
—Luz Calvo and Catriona Esquibel

Introduction: reframing vegan food politics

At the Decolonizing Foodways Conference (2015) held at the University of California, Berkeley, chef Bryant Terry and scholars/chefs Luz Calvo and Catriona Esquibel highlighted the importance of honoring ancestral foods and foodways from African American and Mexican communities. By drawing from their recent cookbooks, *Afro-Vegan* (2014) by Bryant Terry and *Decolonize Your Diet* (2015) by Calvo and Esquibel, these authors argued that food is a site for challenging racism and colonialism. Their San Francisco Bay Area-based cookbooks highlight African American and Mexican American foods to reframe veganism.

In this chapter, I argue that *Afro-Vegan* and *Decolonize Your Diet* are cookbooks that produce an anti-racist vegan critique. They do so by analyzing racialized food and health disparities, by privileging the knowledge of communities of color, and by contextualizing recipes within a longer history of struggle and survival. These cookbooks offer a critique of structural and systemic racism and, in doing so, produce subjectivity by highlighting the knowledge, experiences, and voices of African American and Mexican American communities.

The cookbooks give credence to the ways in which African American and Mexican American culinary traditions and histories have always engaged in veganism, rooted in the consumption of local, seasonal, plant-based, nutritious, and savory dishes. Rather than demonize and pathologize, these cookbooks celebrate and honor African American and Mexican American foodways. Analyzing how communities of color engage in veganism while simultaneously diverging from some of its ideals demonstrates how these communities claim their own stake in food politics.

When we center marginalized foodways, we privilege those knowledges as not only significant but also vital to understanding vegan food politics.

Cookbooks as case studies

Afro-Vegan and *Decolonize Your Diet* are unique case studies for analyzing veganism as anti-racist practice. Cookbooks written by communities of color have liberatory potential. Various scholars have shown how African American cookbooks retain cultural memory and resist stereotypes (Eves), confront racial inequities, build community, and reclaim tradition (Inness). African American cookbooks are used to define and redefine African American communities and knowledge (Witt) and to honor the historical contributions of African Americans (Bower; Tipton-Martin *The Jemima Code* and *Jubilee*). These cookbooks have sought the pursuit of equity, respect, and progress (Zafar) and reflect the intersections of race, gender, geography, joy, and meaning (Franklin). Mexican and Mexican American cookbooks are a means of resisting European colonialism (Pilcher "Recipes for Patria") and are sources of cultural capital (Pilcher "Voices in the Kitchen"). They are sites of independence for women and a means of challenging traditional ideas about authorship for Mexican women (Pilcher "Voices in the Kitchen"). Mexican and Mexican American cookbooks are forms of collective affirmation, modes of "self-articulation" and political assertion, and they connect the individual to a broader ethnic history (Goldman).

Thus, cookbooks do not solely transmit recipes; they are producers of knowledge. *Afro Vegan* and *Decolonize Your Diet* transmit histories of systemic racism and challenge that racism through recipes constructed by communities of color. While neither cookbook touts plant-based recipes as the only or best way of eating for everyone, both highlight the nutritional value of a plant-based diet. In *Afro-Vegan*, Terry writes,

> When you consider that for thousands of years traditional West and Central African diets were predominantly vegetarian—centered around staples like millet, rice, field peas, okra, hot peppers, and yams—and that many precolonial African diets heavily emphasized plant-based foods, a vegan cookbook celebrating the food of the African diaspora is perfectly fitting. (4)

Terry and Calvo state that while they had consumed vegetarian foods prior to Calvo's diagnosis of breast cancer in 2006, the cancer prompted them to shift to an exclusively vegan diet. In *Decolonize Your Diet* Calvo and Esquibel argue,

> We started to evaluate Mesoamerican cuisine and quickly found that foods from the pre-Hispanic era (i.e., before colonization) were among the healthiest foods on the planet… Meat was eaten only in small quantities. Our ancestors gathered and ate wild herbs and greens. They cultivated hundreds of different varieties of beans, squash, and corn, not just the few varieties now available at most grocery stores. (14)

The above quotations demonstrate an embrace of a plant-based diet to prioritize the knowledge, needs, and ailments of communities of color. Terry, Calvo, and Esquibel underscore that communities of color have historically consumed nutritious vegan foods. Yet this knowledge has not entered the mainstream of either vegan foods or African American and Mexican American foods. In their cookbooks, the authors return to this knowledge as a means of addressing health as well as racial and historical inequities.

Chefs, educators, healers: Bryant Terry, Luz Calvo, and Catriona Esquibel

Bryant Terry is a gourmet eco-chef, speaker, educator, and well-known figure in the food justice movement. His four single-authored cookbooks have garnered him accolades for their creativity, attention to detail, and privileging of Afro-diasporic foods. His activist work has focused on the intersection of poverty, malnutrition, and institutional racism. He is credited as instrumental in making vegan soul food popular as well as plant-based Afro-diasporic gourmet foods. *Afro-Vegan*, Terry's third single-authored cookbook, is critically acclaimed and has won several awards. In this cookbook, Terry combines ingredients and recipes from African, Caribbean, and U.S. southern regions for a wide range of diverse recipes.

Luz Calvo and Catriona Esquibel are academics in the San Francisco Bay Area. Calvo is a professor in Ethnic Studies at California State University, East Bay, while Esquibel is an associate professor of Ethnic Studies at San Francisco State University. Food justice and decolonization are a significant research focus, particularly in relation to reducing diet-related illnesses for Mexican Americans. *Decolonize Your Diet*, their first cookbook, emphasizes the importance of Mexican and Mexican American plant-based food for health and nourishment, while also highlighting local, native foods, and a "made from scratch" approach to cooking.

Decolonizing diets: food inequities, industrialization, and health disparities

Afro-Vegan and *Decolonize Your Diet* critique the ways in which racialized food inequities and industrialization result in disproportionately higher rates of health inequities for communities of color, including type 2 diabetes, hypertension, heart disease, and premature death. The cookbooks shift the culinary gaze by contesting the notion that African American and Mexican American foods are inherently "bad." Instead, they center medicinal recipes rooted in African American and Mexican American vegan cooking.

In *Afro-Vegan*, Terry discusses how black people have always eaten healthy foods and how it is in fact because Afro-diasporic people have strayed from historically Afro-centric foods that increased food-related conditions have arisen.

> Afro-diasporic foodways (that is, the shape and development of food traditions) carry our history, memories, and stories. They connect us to our ancestors and bring the past into the present day. They also have the potential to save our lives. As Afro-diasporic people have strayed from our traditional foods and adopted a Western diet, our health has suffered. … In the United States… African Americans suffer from some of the highest rates of preventable diet-related illnesses, such as heart disease, hypertension, and type 2 diabetes. Many factors contribute to the increase in chronic illnesses affecting African-American communities, and I would argue that disconnect from our historical foods is a significant contributing force. (2)

Terry frames African American dietary health inequities as resulting from the consumption of the Standard American Diet (SAD) and the lack of access to healthy, fresh, affordable foods. As a result of historical geographic segregation, redlining, and gentrification, many African American and Latino communities live in poor or working-class urban areas where fresh, affordable, nutritious food is not readily accessible. These regions are oversaturated with fried foods, and foods and beverages high in calories and sugars. These foods are sold in the fast food restaurants, corner stores, and liquor stores that overwhelm urban food deserts. The overabundance of low-quality, highly processed foods is exacerbated by the lack of stores that sell fresh, nutritious, affordable foods. As a result, low-income communities of color experience disproportionately higher rates of type two diabetes, hypertension, heart disease, and early death (Freeman; McClintock; Alkon and Agyeman; Alkon et al.; Kurtz; Brones; Reese).

These dietary food and health inequities are forms of structural racism built upon legacies of racial violence, oppression, and marginalization (Bronnes; Bradley; Vick). Racism is the differential access to health, resources, power, and life itself that is normalized into society, privileging whites over communities of color (Gilmore; Delgado and Stefancic). Though racial categories have been proven to be social constructions, they nonetheless result in material effects onto the body. Thus, the health disparities that result from food inequities demonstrate how racism results in biological vulnerabilities to disease and premature death (Guthman; Delgado and Stefancic).

Afro-Vegan critiques food oppression (Freeman) as structural racism by arguing that the health of African Americans is related both to the structural environment as well as to the consumption of animal by-products. These are framed as equally important nutrition issues for African American communities. Terry states,

> More and more, mainstream medical institutions have been acknowledging that the overconsumption of animal protein puts people at increased risk of preventable, diet-related illnesses, such as heart disease, type 2 diabetes, and hypertension, and an increasing number of medical professionals are endorsing plant-centered diets for optimal health. This book continues in the tradition of my previous work by keeping one eye on contemporary health concerns while presenting food that honors the flavors, ingredients, and heritage of the African diaspora. *Afro-Vegan* will further empower people to choose wholesome foods to improve the physical and spiritual health of their families and communities. (3)

Terry includes nutritious, vegan recipes as a counter-narrative to the notion that African American communities consume only death-producing foods. The recipe for Millet and Sweet Potato Porridge is one such example:

> When cooking soaked millet, if you stir it often while simmering and slightly overcook it, the seeds will burst and release starch, creating a creamy consistency that's ideal for breakfast porridge. The addition of baked sweet potato, almond milk, and pureed cashews adds silky richness. Pecans provide depth and texture. Because whole grains are digested slowly, releasing their sugars into the bloodstream gradually, eating a hearty bowl of porridge in the morning will give you sustained energy and tide you over until lunch. Millet is high in vitamin B6, niacin, and folic acid and also has significant amounts of magnesium, zinc, iron, calcium, and potassium. Note that if you make almond milk for this recipe, you should omit the sweetener. (162)

Terry's emphasis on the nutritional elements of the recipe—"sustained energy" and the note of the many vitamins and minerals in the dish—are examples of life-sustaining ingredients. The final sentence of the epigraph seems a direct intervention to the presence of sugar and sugar-sweetened food items that overwhelm low income African American communities. While the

Millet and Sweet Potato Porridge is intended as a sweet breakfast, it uses foods with natural sugars rather than artificial ones. It also discourages an excessive consumption of sugar —i.e., "if you make almond milk...omit the sweetener"—as a means to reduce the sugar intake in African American communities.

Decolonize Your Diet also intervenes in food disparities, by focusing on the industrial food system and the SAD. They argue that industrialization of food in the 21st-century United States led to an excessive consumption of meat, dairy, and processed foods:

> Most Americans do not eat a plant-based diet with plenty of fresh fruits, vegetables, and herbs. Instead, North Americans consume a lot of sugary, fried, or fake foods like sodas, energy drinks, chips and other bagged snacks, candy bars, and cookies, which contain considerable amounts of high fructose corn syrup, sugar and artificial sweeteners, corn and soybean oils, and sodium. (26)

In particular, Calvo and Esquibel emphasize how the SAD has been a colonial tool for U.S. Latin@s. For instance, when migrants move from Mexico to the United States, their health tends to deteriorate. Further alarming is that these migrants often enter a higher income bracket upon having arrived to the United States. This "paradox" has been attributed to the increased consumption of the sugary, fried, and high calorie foods that constitute the SAD (Saenz and Morales). *Decolonize Your Diet* asserts that the SAD is a form of colonization that causes premature death through "Americanization programs, school lunch programs, targeted advertising campaigns, and national food policies. Our communities are now riddled with the diseases of development—diabetes, high blood pressure, heart disease, and some cancers" (Calvo and Esquibel 26 and 37). Racialized targeted food marketing and school lunch programs have historically functioned to oppress communities of color, resulting in malnutrition and exploitation (Freeman). Additionally, national food policies benefit corporations and large farms through federal subsidies, and, in turn, injure communities of color through highly processed, toxic, poor quality, obesogenic foods that contain addictive-style flavoring (Guthman *Weighing In*).

In *Decolonize Your Diet*, the Kick-Ass Chayote Salad with Pickled Red Onions emphasizes energy and healing. The authors write,

> This simple, colorful salad is a nutritional powerhouse. The crunchy chayote is high in antioxidant phytochemicals that may help undo some of the damage caused by the Standard American Diet. This salad has benefits for all ages: the folate in the chayote is especially good for pregnant moms and for the brain health of our elders. Mint is an especially potent inhibitor of cancer cells. (81)

This recipe illustrates how Calvo and Esquibel work to counter the negative effects of the SAD and industrialization through the use of indigenous Mexican ingredients. This recipe seems particularly significant in that it addresses cancer, the disease with which Calvo had been diagnosed. The recipe contests the idea that Mexican American communities consume only foods that result in premature death and instead highlights foods that heal illness and produce vitality and life.

Terry's and Calvo and Esquibel's cookbooks are a direct challenge to the notion that African American and Mexican American foods are inherently unhealthy. Studies demonstrate that Americans believe soul food and Mexican food to be some of the unhealthiest foods in the United States (Miller 2). Although soul food and other Afro-diasporic foods have been demonized as the cause of rampant health problems in academic literature, among social reformers and health care professionals (Opie; Greenebaum; Witt) and in popular cultural televisions shows and movies like *Soul Food Junkies* (2014), *The Boondocks* (2006), and *Soul Food* (1997), Terry embraces foods that come from Africa and the African diaspora and highlights their nutritional value. He demonstrates how cooking made-from-scratch vegan foods is not antithetical to traditional African-descended foodways. Similarly, despite the perception that Mexican American foods are harmful (Saldivar; Ramirez et. al), Mexican immigrants confirm that it is the incorporation of a U.S.-based diet that results in food-related illness (Sussner et al; Batis et al). Calvo and Esquibel's recipes highlight the ways in which consuming Mexican and Mexican American foods actually helps to combat health disparities.

Decolonize Your Diet and *Afro-Vegan* contest the notion that African American and Mexican communities consume only death-producing foods. Their critique of food and health inequities are in fact critiques of structural racism. The cookbooks reveal that communities of color incorporate foods, recipes, and dishes that engender healing and wellness. These healthy food alternatives illustrate that communities of color have always produced vegan foods that produce vitality and life.

Dismantling whiteness in veganism: subjugated knowledges and racial difference

Afro-Vegan and *Decolonize Your Diet* challenge whiteness within the vegan movement. By highlighting ingredients, dishes, and recipes from African American and Mexican American communities, the cookbooks privilege the subjugated knowledge of these communities. While the dominant narrative in Western veganism has been to prioritize white bodies, histories, and experiences, these cookbooks contest that narrative, and instead focus on voices and histories of communities of color.

The mainstream vegan movement maintains and reinforces whiteness. Whiteness, or white supremacy, is a system of power that benefits those marked as white by placing them in a system of structural advantage through an accumulation of resources and privileges (Harris; Roediger; Wise' Lipsitz' DiAngelo; "Understanding Whiteness"). In other words, whiteness is a form of structural racism that gives white people unearned advantages and treats white experiences as normative (and people of color's experiences as deviations from that norm). Whiteness is preserved in mainstream and alternative food spaces through discourse and language, exclusionary practices, exploitative labor policies, marketing, and segregation (Slocum; Guthman "If they only knew"; Cooley). In particular, the vegan movement upholds whiteness by privileging the voices and experiences of whites (Harper *Sistah Vegan*; Harper "Vegans of Color"; Greenebaum), equating humanity with white bodies (Polish), supporting gentrification (Polish), stigmatizing veganism for communities of color (Greenebaum), failing to address issues of power and oppression, including racism and colonialism (Chatila), and emphasizing elitism and consumerism (Navarro).

Yet plant-based recipes are central to communities of color. People of color participate in veganism as a means of improving health, animal rights, and emotional and bodily healing. For vegans of color, veganism is a means to heal racial trauma, understand the intersectional relationship between race, gender, class, sexuality, animal rights, and food practices, work toward personal and community health, and as a means of bodily decolonization (Harper *Sistah Vegan*; Navarro). Vegan studies scholar Jessica Greenebaum argues that vegans of color who are stigmatized in their own communities attempt to thwart such exclusions by participating in "*differentiation* from white veganism and highlight[ing] how they do veganism differently [and]... engage in a process of *normalization* to show people of color that anyone can be vegan," (682). Veganism can be a strategy to achieve racial and social justice (Chatila) and offer possibilities for racial healing (Harper "Doing Veganism Differently"). Thus, vegans of color claim their own stake in vegan politics, despite racialized challenges.

Terry, Calvo, and Esquibel politicize veganism by bringing attention to, rather than obscuring, racial difference. They underscore the intergenerational knowledge of African American and Mexican American communities. In doing so, they uphold the subjugated knowledge of communities of color. Subjugated knowledges are those sources of knowledge, wisdom, and information that have been deemed illegitimate, incoherent, non-sensical, or unimportant (Foucault 6–8; Hartman). These cookbooks reclaim recipes, foods, and ingredients ignored within mainstream veganism. Terry's Dandelion Salad with Pecan Dressing upholds the health benefits of vegan cooking and underscores the importance of African American ancestral knowledge:

> While they are not often associated with Southern foodways in their popular imagination, dandelion greens are a staple in traditional African-American cooking. My family grew them, and we cooked them along with collard and mustard greens and other leafy vegetables. They are often used as a healing and preventative herb during the spring when they're at their peak, and they're a good source of vitamins A, B16, K, and E, as well as thiamin, riboflavin, calcium, iron, copper, and potassium. Tangerines, which are cultivated in Algeria, add a sweet counterpoint to the bitterness from the dandelion green in this salad, and the sugar-coated pecans add sweet crunch. (81)

Terry highlights the health benefits of African-descended foods, countering notions that African American foodways have nothing to contribute to healthy vegan eating. His description highlights the histories of African Americans and Algerians, demonstrating how blackness travels across space for innovative plant-based recipes.

Calvo and Esquibel call for the reclamation of native foods, including a range of grains, vegetables, fruits, and meats. The authors highlight how colonialism has impacted indigenous Mexican foodways—by deeming that knowledge invalid:

> Both of us have grandparents who spoke fondly of finding and preparing *quelites* (lamb's quarters) and *verdolagas* (purslane)... there is considerable archeological evidence of [verdolagas'] presence in the Americas before colonization.... Throughout the world, agribusiness considers both *quelites* and *verdolagas* to be weeds and uses herbicides, such as Monsanto's Roundup, to try to kill these nutritious plants. (24–25)

Agribusiness and food corporations have sought to suppress the native knowledge of communities of color or constructed it as unhealthy or backward (Harris). Calvo and Esquibel reclaim the subjugated knowledge of ancestors for health and healing with the Pickled Verdolagas recipe:

> During late summer months, when verdolagas (purslane) are plentiful, we like to pickle them so we can continue eating them during the fall and winter months. This plant [verdolagas] is a nutritional powerhouse. It is higher in omega-3 fatty acids than many other vegetables, protects the liver, and helps heal kidney damage caused by diabetes. You can use pickled verdolagas instead of Pickled Red Onions in any of our recipes as they add a similar acid note. (179)

Terry, Calvo, and Esquibel embrace racial difference as a means of passing down subjugated knowledge of communities of color and as a means of uniting African Americans and Mexican Americans across generations. Despite attempts to co-opt, exoticize, and/or appropriate the vegan recipes of communities of color (Harper "Vegans of Color"), *Afro-Vegan* and *Decolonize Your Diet* claim their stake, by embracing their histories and defining their own vegan culinary stories.

By privileging the knowledge of African- and Mexican-descended peoples, the cookbooks participate in "dietary decolonization," understanding the body as a site for change (Hayes-Conroy and Hayes-Conroy). Despite legacies of racism and colonialism, they contend that communities of color have long-standing knowledge about nutritious, healing, flavorful meals. In this way, decolonizing diets are not solely about individual transformation, but about communal, racial, and social change.

Spices, song, struggle, and survival: recipes for resistance and empowerment

As discussed in the aforementioned sections, *Afro-Vegan* and *Decolonize Your Diet* do not only transmit recipes but also critique racialized health inequities and preserve the subjugated knowledge of vegans of color. Additionally, these cookbooks communicate messages of resistance to legacies of racism, violence, and injustice by referencing histories of struggle and survival.

Afro-Vegan, like Terry's previous cookbooks, narrates histories of oppression and resistance through the inclusion of suggested soundtracks, books, and artwork that accompany recipes. These accompaniments enhance the cooking experience by referencing histories of colonialism, slavery, violence, and other injustices. Cooking becomes not just about replicating recipes and making meals, but about creating an experience of racialized consciousness and radical anti-racism.

The recipe for Spiced Persimmon Bundt Cake with Orange Glaze is an excellent example. The accompanying soundtrack is "A Piece of Ground" by Miriam Makeba, from *Miriam Makeba in Concert* and the suggested book is *To Us, All Flowers are Roses: Poems* by Lorna Goodison. Miriam Makeba was a South African singer and civil rights activist. Mentored by Harry Belafonte and married to Stokely Carmichael for ten years, Makeba critiqued apartheid in South Africa and capitalism and racism in the United States. "A Piece of Ground" is about white colonialism of black lands, exploited black labor, white capitalist greed, and black resistance ("A Piece of Ground, Miriam Makeba"). *To Us: All Flowers are Roses: Poems* analyzes chattel slavery, being a woman of color in the Caribbean, poverty in Jamaica, and motherhood and survival in oppressive conditions. These accompaniments to the Bundt Cake underscore that Terry wants the reader to analyze sexism, colonialism, capitalism, labor exploitation, in conjunction with songs and movements of resistance.

The Spiced Persimmon Bundt Cake with Orange Glaze (176–7) is dedicated to Edna Lewis, the acclaimed chef well known for her cookbooks on Southern food. Famously the grandchild of American slaves, this James Beard winner was known as the Grand Dame of Southern Cooking. Lewis' cooking became popular due to her made-from-scratch approach to local, seasonal, delicious meals. Her cookbooks include *The Edna Lewis Cookbook* (1972, 2016), *The Taste of Country Cooking* (1976, 2006), *In Pursuit of Flavor* (1988, 2019), and *The Gift of Southern Cooking* (2003). In *The Taste of Country Cooking*, Lewis discusses Freetown, a settlement of freed slaves in rural Southern Virginia and the idyllic upbringing she had there. Her introduction communicates a connectedness to land, community, hard work, and festivities. Her narratives about her upbringing are not about the horrors of being a black person, but about rejoicing and celebrating blackness—the pleasure, traditions, and love she shared with family and community members through farming, raising animals, and cooking. These stories recount the thriving and flourishing of a black community in a society that demeans and oppresses black people. Lewis showcases the joys of her upbringing, which included resistance to norms, practices, laws, and ideologies that understood black people to be inferior, deficient, and inept. As *New York Times Magazine* author Francis Lam argues, "[Edna Lewis] chose to see, and to show us, beauty; and under the shadow of oppression and slavery, that is a political act" (Lam).

Thus, when Terry writes his recipe for Bundt Cake, he cultivates a unique experience for the reader. The accompaniments include fights for civil rights in the United States and South Africa; critiques to colonialism, racism, and capitalism; poverty, gender discrimination, and violence; black successes, celebrating blackness and black life; and resistance to anti-black injustices. The recipe and its accompaniments communicate a history of struggle and survival for African Americans. By writing in this way, Terry explains food as a political mechanism to communicate shared histories of violence and the agency used by communities of color through music, poetry, and food.

Decolonize Your Diet similarly highlights a long-standing history of oppression, resistance, and empowerment through recipes. In particular, the Nopales "De Colores" Salad brings attention to the exploitation of farmworker labor in the San Joaquin Valley, California in the late 20th century. The salad mentions the United Farm Workers (UFW), the impactful farmworker union that has led the U.S. movement for better wages, safe working conditions, and treatment with dignity and respect. The epigraph reads:

> In the United Farm Workers' movement, the folk song "De Colores" uses the image of multiple colors to signal appreciation for biodiversity in the fields, in the people, and in the beauty of creation. We use this principle in creating the dish because we strive to eat fruits and vegetables of every color each day. Get your "five a day" in this zesty grilled salad, while at the same time benefiting from the blood sugar-stabilizing properties of the cactus. This is best prepared in the fall, when the vegetables are freshly harvested. (76)

The UFW has been heralded for its success in improving working conditions for farmworkers. Led by Cesar Chavez, Dolores Huerta, and Gilbert Padilla in 1962, the organization has fought against racism and exploitative pay and working conditions (Ferriss and Sandoval) and the poisonous use of pesticides (Gordon). It succeeded in leading local and nation-wide change, including strikes, protests, and boycotts against food corporation such as Safeway and Guimarra Vineyard Corporation (Araiza). The UFW built solidarity with other civil rights organizations, including the Black Panther Party (Araiza), founded the Rodrigo Terronez Memorial Clinic in Delano, California to organize and address the needs of the rural poor (Rudd), and fought for environmental justice (Pulido and Peña). Women in the organization engaged in feminist critiques and activism (Rose) as well as organizing and voting (Ferris and Sandoval). The reference here to the UFW emphasizes the empowerment of communities of color to band together to create long-lasting, meaningful change in relation to exploitation and subjugation.

The song "De Colores" is emblematic of the 1960s and 1970s Chicano/a movement. While it was traditionally a religious song, it became representative of the struggle for the political rights of Chicano/as (Ragland). Songs have been a means of expressing anguish, building solidarity among oppressed groups, and producing something meaningful that belongs to subjugated communities of color. In reflecting on her time with the UFW Jan Peterson states,

> There were many times on the UFW picket lines that songs were all that we had… We sang when we were sad or discouraged; we sang when we were angry or defiant; we sang when we were proud; we sang to lift our spirits. And we carried that singing with us everywhere: to meeting halls, to cities, to other countries, even to other continents. Many of these songs have traveled… to weave themselves into a single thread of truth; a soaring of the human spirit—a laughing, irreverent, spirit, at times—determined, in the face of the greatest odds, to take a stand for human dignity. (Peterson and Scott 6–7)

Music was (and is) a form of resistance, creativity, fortitude, solidarity, and hope amidst struggle. "De Colores," while religious in origin, signifies new beginnings, peace, hope, and love. Taken up by the UFW, it came to symbolize community and resilience among farm laborers (Murguía and Rivera 6–7).

Similar to the Spiced Persimmon Bundt Cake, the Nopales "De Colores" Salad produces a relationship between the dish itself, farmworker struggles and activism, music, racial pride, and healthy, nutritious vegan food. By highlighting the trials and triumphs of the UFW in the mid- to late 20th century, *Decolonize Your Diet* emphasizes the importance of the context in which food is grown, produced, and distributed before it gets to the plate.

Afro-Vegan and *Decolonize Your Diet* highlight ways in which communities of color have resisted structural racism and violent oppression. They demonstrate that African American and Mexican American communities use agency to engage in social action, through song, poetry, protest, celebrating life, farming/gardening, cooking, expressing racial and ethnic pride, and creating and sharing recipes. In doing so, they underscore how subjugated peoples beckon the past to inform the present and future. To situate the cookbooks in racialized histories of struggle, survival, and empowerment is to argue that the past is always with us, as a reminder of previous and contemporary injustice and possibilities for change.

Conclusion: cultivating an anti-racist vegan praxis

In this chapter, I argued that *Afro-Vegan* and *Decolonize Your Diet* produce an anti-racist vegan critique. They do so, first, by analyzing racialized health disparities, food inequities, and industrialized food as a critique of structural racism. By including healing and nutritious recipes, they intervene in discourses that pathologize the consumption of people of color. I argue that the cookbooks show how African American and Mexican American communities consume foods that address diet-related health conditions, such as type 2 diabetes, hypertension, heart disease, and premature death. Secondly, *Afro-Vegan* and *Decolonize Your Diet* highlight the subjugated knowledge of communities of color, contesting whiteness that permeates mainstream veganism. In doing so, they produce subjectivity in groups that have historically been constructed as objects of study, rather than agents of knowledge and action. Finally, the cookbooks situate recipes within the context of historical struggle, survival, and empowerment. This asks the reader to consider how historical injustices are linked with contemporary oppression. What we eat and how we eat is a political act, traced to the past, present, and future.

Through a critique of structural and systemic racism, the cookbooks provide an alternative vegan praxis to mainstream veganism: a way of understanding vegan foodways that is embedded in the knowledge and action of communities of color. They reframe pleasurable eating as an act of racialized politics that emphasizes African American and Mexican American histories. Rather than understand communities of color as objects to be educated and acted upon, they see these communities as narrators and producers of a radically anti-racist future. *Afro-Vegan* and *Decolonize*

Your Diet engage in a politics of representation that embraces racial difference to show how communities of color create their own cultural ownership and self-determination within veganism.

Works cited

Alkon, Alison Hope, and Julian Agyeman. *Cultivating Food Justice: Race, Class, and Sustainability*, edited by Alison Hope Alkon and Julian Agyeman. MIT Press, 2011.

Alkon, Alison, Daniel Block, Kelly Moore, Catherine Gillis, Nicole DiNuccio, and Noel Chavez. "Foodways of the Urban Poor." *Geoforum*, vol. 48, 2013, pp. 126–135.

"Understanding Whiteness." *Alberta Civil Liberties Research Centre*. www.aclrc.com/whiteness

Araiza, Lauren. "'In Common Struggle Against a Common Oppression': The United Farm Workers and the Black Panther Party, 1968–1973." *The Journal of African American History*, vol. 94, no. 2, 2009, pp. 200–223.

Batis, Carolina, Lucia Hernandez-Barrera, Simon Barquera, Juan A. Rivera, and Barry P. Popkin. "Food acculturation drives dietary differences among Mexicans, Mexican Americans and Non-Hispanic Whites." *The Journal of Nutrition*, vol. 141, no. 10, 2011, pp. 1898–1906.

Bower, Anne. "Recipes for History: The National Council of Negro Women's Five Historical Cookbooks." *African American Foodways: Explorations of History and Culture*, edited by Anne L. Bower, 2007, pp. 153–174.

Bradley, Katharine, and Ryan Galt. "Practicing food justice at Dig Deep Farms & Produce, East Bay Area, California: self-determination as a guiding value and intersections with foodie logics." *Local Environment: The International Journal of Justice and Sustainability*, vol. 19, no. 2, 2014, pp. 172–186.

Bronnes, Anna. "Food apartheid: The root of the problem with America's groceries." *The Guardian*, 15 May 2018. www.theguardian.com/society/2018/may/15/food-apartheid-food-deserts-racism-inequality-america-karen-washington interview?CMP=share_btn_link.

Calvo, Luz, and Catriona Rueda Esquibel. *Decolonize Your Diet: Plant-Based Mexican American Recipes for Health and Healing*. Arsenal Pulp Press, 2015.

Chatila, Iman. *Veganism through a Racial Lens: Vegans of Color Navigating Mainstream Vegan Networks*. 2018. Portland State University. Undergraduate Honors Thesis.

Cooley, Angela Jill. *To Live and Dine in Dixie: The Evolution of Urban Food Culture in the Jim Crow South*. University of Georgia Press, 2015.

Delgado, Richard, and Jean Stefancic. *Critical Race Theory: An Introduction*, 3rd edition, New York University Press, 2017.

DiAngelo, Robin. *White Fragility: Why it's so hard for white people to talk about racism*, Boston, MA: Beacon Press, 2018.

Eves, Rosalyn Collings. "A Recipe for Remembrance: Memory and Identity in African American Women's Cookbooks." *Rhetoric Review*, vol. 24, no. 3, 2005, pp. 280–297.

Ferriss, Susan, and Ricardo Sandoval. *The Fight in the Fields: Cesar Chavez and the Farmworkers Movement*. Harcourt Brace & Company, 1997.

Foucault, Michel. *"Society Must be Defended": Lectures at the Collège de France 1975–1976*. Picador Press, 1997.

Franklin, Sarah B., editor. *Edna Lewis: At the Table with an American Original*. The University of North Carolina Press, 2018.

Freeman, Andrea. "Fast Food: Oppression through Poor Nutrition." *California Law Review*, vol. 95, no. 2221, 2007, pp. 1–33.

"A Piece of Ground, Miriam Makeba." *Genius*, 2020. genius.com/Miriam-makeba-a-piece-of-ground-lyrics.

Goldman, Anne E. "I Yam what I Yam." *Take My Word: Autobiographical Innovations of Ethnic American Working Women*. Berkeley, CA: University of California Press, 1996, pp. 3–31.

Goodison, Lorna. *To Us, All Flowers are Roses: Poems*. University of Illinois Press, 1995.

Gordon, Robert. "Poisons in the Fields: The United Farm Workers, Pesticides and Environmental Politics." *Pacific Historical Review*, vol. 68, no. 1, 1999, pp. 51–77.

Greenebaum, Jessica. "Vegans of Color: managing visible and invisible stigmas." *Food, Culture and Society*, vol. 21, no. 5, 2018, pp. 680–697.

Guthman, Julie. "Doing Justice to Bodies? Reflections on Food Justice, Race, and Biology." *Antipode*, vol. 46, no. 5, 2014, pp. 1153–1171.

———. "'If they only knew': The unbearable whiteness of alternative food." *Cultivating Food Justice*, edited by Alison Alkon and Julian Agyeman. MIT Press, 2011a, pp. 263–282.
———. *Weighing In: Obesity, Food Justice, and the Limits of Capitalism*. University of California Press, 2011b.
Harper, Aimee Breeze. "Doing Veganism Differently: Racialized Trauma and the Personal Journey Toward Vegan Healing." *Doing Nutrition Differently: Critical Approaches to Diet and Dietary Intervention*, edited by Alison and Jessica Hayes-Conroy. Ashgate Publishing, 2013, pp. 133–150.
———, editor. *Sistah Vegan*. Lantern Books, 2010.
———. "Vegans of Color, Racialized Embodiment and Problematics of the 'Exotic'." *Cultivating Food Justice: Race, Class and Sustainability*, edited by Alison Alkon and Julian Agyeman. MIT Press, 2011.
Harris, Cheryl. "Whiteness as Property." *Harvard Law Review*, vol. 106, no. 8, 1993, pp. 1707–1791.
Harris, Jessica. *High on the Hog: A Culinary Journal from Africa to America*. New York, NY: Bloomsbury, 2011.
Hartman, Ann. "In Search of Subjugated Knowledge." *Journal of Feminist Family Therapy*, vol. 11, no. 4, 2000, pp. 19–23.
Hayes-Conroy, Allison, and Jessica. "Feminist Nutrition: Difference, Decolonization, and Dietary Change." *Doing Nutrition Differently*, edited by Allison and Jessica Hayes-Conroy. Ashgate Publishing Company, 2013.
Kurtz, Hilda. "Linking food deserts and racial segregation: Challenges and limitations." *Geographies of Race and Food*, edited by Rachel Slocum and Arun Saldanha, New York, NY: Routledge, 2013.
Inness, Sherri. "More 'than apple pie': Modern African American Cookbooks Fighting White Stereotypes." *Secret Ingredients: Race, Gender, and Class at the Dinner Table*. New York, NY: Palgrave Macmillan, 2005, pp. 105–126.
Lam, Francis. "Edna Lewis and the Black roots of American Cooking." *The New York Times Magazine*, 28 October 2015. www.nytimes.com/2015/11/01/magazine/edna-lewis-and-the-black-roots-of-american-cooking.html?smid=em-share.
Lewis, Edna, and Evangeline Peterson. *The Edna Lewis Cookbook*, Axios Press, 2016.
Lewis, Edna. *The Taste of Country Cooking*. Alfred A. Knopf Press, 1976.
Lipsitz, George. *The Possessive Investment in Whiteness*. Temple University Press, 2018.
McClintock, Nathan. "From industrial garden to food desert: demarcated devaluation in the flatlands of Oakland, California." *Cultivating Food Justice: Race, Class, and Sustainability*, edited by Alison Hope Alkon and Julian Agyeman, Cambridge: MIT Press, 2011.
Miller, Adrian. *Soul Food: The Surprising Story of an American Cuisine, One Plate at a Time*. University of North Carolina Press, 2013.
Navarro, Marilisa. *Decolonizing Our Plates: Analyzing San Diego and Vegans of Color Food Politics*. 2011. University of California, San Diego. Master's thesis.
Opie, Fredrick. *Hog and Hominy: African American Critics and Opponents of Soul Food*. Columbia University Press, 2008.
Pilcher, Jeffrey. "Recipes for Patria: Cuisine, Gender, and Nature in Nineteenth-Century Mexico." *Recipes for Reading: Community Cookbooks, Stories, Histories*, edited by Anne L. Bower, University of Massachusetts Press, 1997.
———. "Voices in the Kitchen: Mexican cookbooks as cultural capital." *Studies in Latin American Popular Culture*, vol. 14, 1995, p. 297.
Polish, Jennifer. "Decolonizing Veganism: On Resisting Vegan Whiteness and Racism." *Critical Perspectives on Veganism*, edited by Jodey Castricano and Rasmus R. Simonsen. Oxford, UK, Palgrave Macmillan, 2016, pp. 373–391.
Pulido, Laura, and Devon Peña. "Environmentalism and Positionality: The early pesticide campaign of the United Farm Workers' Organizing Committee, 1965–1971." *Race, Gender & Class*, vol. 6, no. 1, 1998, pp. 33–50.
Ragland, Cathy. Rolas de Atzlán: Songs of the Chicano Movement (Review) Produced, compiled and annotated by Estevan Cesar Azcona and Russell Rodríguez. *American Folklore Society*, vol. 121, no. 482, 2008, pp. 489–490.
Ramirez, A. Susana, et al. "Questioning the Dietary Acculturation of Paradox: A Mixed-Methods Study of the Relationship between food and ethnic identity in a group of Mexican-American Women." *Journal of the Academy of Nutrition and Dietetics*, vol. 118, no. 3, 2018, pp. 431–439.
Reese, Ashanté. *Black Food Geographies: Race, self-reliance and food access in Washington, D.C.*, University of North Carolina Press, 2019.
Roediger, David. *The Wages of Whiteness*. Verso Press, 2007.
Rose, Margaret. "Traditional and Nontraditional Patterns of Female Activism in the United Farm Workers of America, 1962–1980." *Frontiers: A Journal of Women Studies*, vol. 11, no. 1, 1990, pp. 26–32.

Rudd, P. "The United Farm Workers clinic in Delano, Calif.: a study of the rural poor." *Public Health Reports*, vol. 90, no. 4, 1975, pp. 331–339.

Saenz, Rogelio, and Trinidad Morales. "The Latino Paradox." *The Demography of the Hispanic Population: Selected Essays*, edited by Richard R. Verdugo, Information Age Publishing, 2012, pp. 47–73.

Saldivar, Steve. "If you think Mexican food is unhealthy, then you need to read this cookbook." *Los Angeles Times*. 22 April 2016. www.latimes.com/health/la-he-decolonize-your-diet-20160416-story.html.

Slocum, Rachel. "Race in the Study of Food." *Progress in Human Geography*, vol. 35, no. 3, 2011, pp. 303–327.

Sussner, Katarina M., Ana C. Lindsay, Mary L. Greaney, and Karen E. Peterson. "The Influence of immigrant status and acculturation on the development of overweight in Latino families: A qualitative study." *Journal of Immigrant and Minority Health*, vol. 10, 2011, pp. 497–505.

Terry, Bryant. *Afro-Vegan: Farm-Fresh African, Caribbean and Southern Flavors Remixed*. Random House Publishing, 2014.

Tipton-Martin, Toni. *The Jemima Code: Two Centuries of African American Cookbooks*. University of Texas Press, 2015.

Tipton-Martin, Toni. *Jubilee: Recipes from Two Centuries of African American Cooking: A Cookbook*. Clarkson Potter, 2019.

"The UFW: Songs and Stories, Sung and Told by UFW Volunteers." *University of California, San Diego Libraries*, libraries.ucsd.edu/farmworkermovement/media/Scott/INTRODUCTIONTOSONGSANDCOMMENTARY(FINAL).pdf

Vick, Karl. "L.A. Official wants a change of menu." *The Washington Post*, 13 July 2008.

Wise, Tim. *White Like Me*. Soft Skull Press, 2011.

Witt, Doris. 2007. "From Fiction to Foodways: Working at the Intersections of African Americans Literary and Culinary Studies." *African American Foodways: Explorations of History and Culture*. edited by Anne L. Bower. University of Illinois Press, 2007.

Zafar, Rafia. *Recipes for Respect: African American Meals and Meaning*. University of Georgia Press, 2019.

26
Vegan studies and gender studies

Alex Lockwood

You can imagine for a moment that gender is like a game of pass the parcel. A mystery package has been wrapped with many layers—by your parents, community, school, the media, advertising, the government—and is passed around over the course of your life. Each time the music stops you might take another layer off the wrapping to discover the prize inside.

The wrappings all look similar: if you identify as a woman, they might be pages from magazines such as *Vogue*, stills from movies such as *Legally Blonde*, or pages taken from *Wuthering Heights*. If you're a man, they are spreads from *The New York Post*, *Men's Health*, *Sports Illustrated*, *Woodworker's Weekly*, and the latest Robert Ludlum novel. While you're passing the parcel, Patriarchal Society—always playing with painful distractions to make you look the other way—keeps adding new layers. And because you've been taught to experience a kind of ersatz pleasure when handling a familiar package, providing a sense of where you fit in this circle, you're not worried that you never get to see what's inside. You're kept too busy playing a role. You fit into this social sphere that keeps passing you this parcel, at ever greater speeds. You look (enough) like the images on the paper (although never quite enough). More to the point, you *believe* you *want* to look like them. Why unwrap the recognizable for a dangerous mystery inside?

For men in Western societies, this game is so diversionary we die from it. In many countries, suicide is the biggest killer of men under the age of 45, and three quarters of all deaths by suicide in the United Kingdom are male (ONS). Men have higher cancer mortality rates in all forms of cancer that affect both men and women, often due to men's under-utilization of healthcare services. In terms of those taking their own lives, a major cause is that the male wrappings are dominated by stories where men are overwhelmingly reliant on one other person—often a non-male partner; conventionally a "wife"—for all of their emotional support; when that relationship breaks down, men in their midlife have no other safety net. The stories in the wrapping educate men on the socially constructed narrative we call masculinity: in this context, that it is "masculine" not to ask for help or develop emotional bonds with other men. Men's attempts to live up to what the U.K. charity the Samaritans call a "gold standard" of male experience, which "prizes power, control and invincibility" (Samaritans) is a major factor in why men fail to learn how to process emotions, refuse to get a cancer screening, and, critically for this chapter, consume certain kinds of foods (such as meat) and eschew others (such as "effeminate" or vegan foods).

Women's wrappings similarly educate and train women in the socially constructed narrative we call femininity. For women, in many cultures, this training includes the practice of submissive roles in relationships with men, the wearing of certain kinds of clothing and face paints, and, as with men, to consume certain kinds of foods and eschew others. The social, economic, health, and safety consequences for women are deleterious, evidenced in too many ways to capture here but including: gender pay gaps, domestic abuse, sexual violence and rape, forced marriage, genital mutilation, and lack of access to political and economic leadership. These are lives lived on alert to both the micro and macro aggressions and micro and macro inequalities (Sue) that structure the unjust and unequal ways in which those identifying and living as men and women experience life differently.

For the majority of our modern history in Western countries, there have been only two recognized parcels which you could legally handle. This limitation has changed to a certain degree, incorporating parcels that begin to offer alternative narratives to the cis-gendered binary of masculine/feminine. However, it is often difficult to handle these packages, and when seen in public domains, their handlers are often treated with fear, discrimination, and violence. The package most of us are handed at birth—and earlier—remains wrapped in dominant gender stories. The securing of identities and privileges that these gender stories shore up are threatened by other non-binary scripts. These gender stories are also implicated in how we explore ethical animal rights orientations at the heart of vegan praxis; and so, this chapter sets out to understand the different psychological and practical categories through which masculine, feminine, and non-binary identities are constructed in relation to vegan practices, particularly around food, and especially those food products derived from the exploitation of animals. For an in-depth exploration of queer theory and veganism, see Quinn (Ch. 24), and for a deeper unpacking of the role played by the film and television in these constructions see Stewart and Cole (Ch. 29), for media see Estok (Ch. 30), for advertising see Trauth (Ch. 31), and for social media see Aguilera-Carnerero (Ch. 32).

While I have been alive to these other parcels in social circulation, my personal experience has been of unconscious and conscious identification with the parcel wrapped in the narrative of "cis-gendered manhood." My wrapping is also printed on white, thickly rich and European paper. I am conscious enough to recognize the advantages this wrapping has given me, yet my worldview remains directed by forty-five years of this narrative. It has rarely felt as if the prize inside was worth the heavy burden requiring constant carrying effort. As Kimmel argued in his seminal work on the construction of manhood, the parcel is not always safe to handle and offers only a "perilous masculinity" which, as Ruby and Heine note, "is tenuous and fragile. That is, in most cultures, manhood is earned through social displays, competition and aggression, and is socially, rather than biologically determined" (450). As Vandello et al. have shown, manhood is a precarious state, easily lost and requiring constant validation. One of the key ways in which this constant validation is practiced is through the food we eat; and the broader exploitation of animals as nonhuman beings for those foodstuffs and the other products we gain benefit from, in reinforcing the stories of ourselves as gendered and speciated beings.

There is no way I can discuss with authority the experience of what it has been to identify, consciously or unconsciously, acceptingly or coerced, as a biologically sexed woman, with femininity as an identity, or as a person of color, a non-binary, gay, lesbian, queer or trans person; although, being raised for the majority of my early life in an all-female household has given me less "masculine" ideals to live up to, and more "feminine" modes of life as instruction (Lockwood *The Pig in Thin Air*). The outcome, at least for this chapter, is that while I learn from and engage with ecofeminist critical practices that underpin robust vegan scholarship, I do not write here comfortably on the experiences of feminine or feminized gender roles—nor on hypermasculine experiences. Yet a focus on masculinities is timely, with the need for more men to "do" critical gender work within vegan studies. As Wright told me in personal communication (Adams, Carol J. *The Sexual Politics of Meat: A Feminist-Vegetarian Critical Theory*, Personal Communication, 2019):

> Until straight, white men decide that they are willing to stand up to other straight, white men ... and call them out for their racism, sexism, speciesism, and homophobia, then this is where we are, and this is why most men aren't vegan. I can talk all day about veganism, but who cares? I'm just a woman.

If that is the case, we need to ask—all of us, "men" and "women," but especially "straight, white men"—who exactly does the construction of gender identities serve? If binary gender norms are a deranged and dangerous package of limiting experiences and beliefs, what price are we paying to play this game? And who suffers most from the imposition of these insane, controlling practices?

Gender and vegan studies under capitalism

Vegan studies as a practice has been engaged with issues of gender from its inception. Among others, ecofeminists such as Carol J. Adams, Josephine Donovan, and Greta Gaard whose animal-focused scholarship and research preconfigured the vegan studies field to follow, explored and revealed how gender norms are used as organizing differences in violent hierarchical relationships within patriarchal societies, often by positioning women and animals together as subordinate to men. As Yilmaz puts it, "meat has historically figured and continues to do so in interrelated oppressive structures, practices and meanings" (23) inscribed in society, particularly in reference to gendered identities. Laura Wright's foundational work for the field *The Vegan Studies Project* (2015) has the subtitle "food, animals, and gender in the age of terror" and grew out of what was originally called "the vegan body project." Wright's conception of vegan studies puts forth "that an ecofeminist approach to veganism allows for what ... is the most inclusive politics with regards to that position, and such theoretical grounding provides a scaffolding onto which I can build my concept of vegan studies" (18). This concept gives "specific attention to the construction and depiction of the U.S. [sic] vegan body—both male and female—as a contested site" (19) in texts of popular culture. The ecofeminist approach, which early on identified "rhetorical linkages [working] to establish the psychological justification of actual—not rhetorical—oppressions" (17) such as the identification of women as "pieces of meat" or colonized people as "brutes," has laid much of the groundwork for vegan studies practitioners in understanding how "the mythology of meat and the ways that a meat-based diet not only is cruel to animals but constitutes sexist and racist ideology" (19).

Ecofeminism, and especially the work of Adams, is covered in more depth elsewhere in this handbook. But ideas put forward by Adams and others first identified, as Cohoon succinctly summarizes, how the "violence inflicted upon women and animals is tacitly interpreted as something that is part of their nature" (526). Such validation of violence against animals and women is inherent in social constructions of both animality and femininity. That people whose identities are constructed as animal or female are open to violence from those wrapped up as masculine or "Human" (the epitome of "human" speciation being the white, Western, straight, Christian man) gives vegan studies a mandate to explore constructions of vegan bodies in relation to the construction of gender. It is, perhaps, also why a specifically "vegan ecofeminism" (Yilmaz) rejects, in the main, a rights-based approach to liberation for both women and animals.

The reductive (male) individualism within rights-based theories and policies obstructs our ability to think ourselves in relation with others, and other animals. As Wright puts it, a "vegan studies approach is theoretical, but it engages in a lived politics of listening care, emotion, and the empathetic imagination" (*Through a Vegan Studies* viii). A vegan ecofeminism has, in that sense, evolved from the "ethics of care" tradition that is itself a fundamental thread unpicking the traumatic exploitation of women and animals in our societies.

And these societies are generally capitalist. The study of veganism and gender together is also often, and perhaps best, situated within the critique of the capitalist systems of production. These systems of production render those outside the "Human" as consumable products, as for example "pieces of meat" or "chattel/cattle." As Corey Wrenn argues:

> in a capitalist system, power is concentrated through the exploitation of vulnerable groups, and this vulnerability is exemplified in 'meat'. Meat in this context refers not only to the butchered flesh of nonhuman animals but also the fragmented flesh of human women. ... Power rests on the consumption of feminized bodies, human and nonhuman alike. (201)

For Wrenn, the process of feminizing human and nonhuman bodies is a process without which capitalism could not function. Society "is structured to disadvantage and hurt women and other animals in the process of extracting value and privilege from them. Females are made into 'meat' [...] and the making and selling of 'meat' is a primary function of capitalism" (202). Indeed, and unsurprisingly, "foodstuff" is the commodity on which most money is spent, globally, by individual consumers (World Bank).

And as pattrice jones argues, we have always experienced life under a "gendered capitalist system" by which she means a binary gendered system, one that leaves no room for nonbinary, "queer or intersex animal bodies" (97) whether human or nonhuman animal. The binary gender parcels are primary products of capitalist systems, which create difference allowing for wildly different treatments of groups. This creation of difference is perhaps equally invidious in human and animal relations. Erika Cudworth has outlined in great detail how nonhuman animals are gendered in the agricultural system, and the majority of protein consumed, for example, is feminized protein in the form of eggs, dairy, and "meat" from the exhausted bodies of female reproductive cows and chickens.

The institution of human dominance itself is gendered as well. As Wrenn continues:

> In Western Culture, masculinity is a performance of domination, while femininity is a performance of subordination ... Femininity is defined by its powerlessness in relationship to masculinity, which in turn is defined by its domination of the feminine. The entire capitalist system in this sense is a patriarchal one, as nonhuman animals, women, and exploited workers are all feminized through subordination. (202)

The practice of a vegan studies scholarship cannot, for it to be a thorough vegan critique, avoid asking questions about how the gendering of bodies shapes the vegan or non-vegan body, and how gendered bodies are in turn shaped by capitalist forms of meaning and production. This is the case for the development of masculinity through industrialization. As Kimmel argues, the 19th century saw the emergence of a distinct form of modern masculinity, which, as Garlick suggests, is "embodied in an ideal of the 'Self-Made Man' [and] intimately connected to the competitive market relations of the emerging capitalist economy" (235). Kimmel's argument, and one that critical Marxist vegan feminists such as Wrenn would agree with, is that these constructions of masculinity remain dominant today. As Connell makes evident "the world in which neoliberalism rules is still a gendered world, and neoliberalism has an implicit gender politics. The 'individual' of neoliberal theory has the attributes and interests of a male entrepreneur" (51). For Garlick,

> masculine subjects are the main bearers of the neoliberal ideology of competition, and this means that men, in particular, tend to have an investment in the maintenance of current social and economic relations, insofar as they bolster or secure masculine identities. (235)

There is an explicit point here for a vegan feminist context and analysis. By expanding vegan critiques to incorporate the study of gender at every step, we see more easily that "Capitalism runs on females … Women's devalued status in the capitalist system is also functionally important in regard to the role they play in consumption" (209).

Gender and veganism: food practices as constant validation

Take a closer look at that wrapping around the "man" parcel and you'll see a lot of pictures of typically processed animal products such as burgers, bacon, sausages, and steak. You'll read stories of men in practices where the exploitation of animals is normal and rife. Staying with "meat" foods for now: foods are inscribed, perhaps like no other objects we have in human social life, with meanings "representing ethnicity, nationality, region, class, age, sexuality, culture, and (perhaps most importantly) gender" (Sobal 136). Numerous works (e.g., Adams 1990; Beardsworth and Keil 1997; Bentley 1998; Bourdieu 1984; Fiddes 1991; Greenebaum and Dexter 2017; Roe and Buser 2016; Roe and Hurley 2018; Nilsen 1995) have identified the ways in which foods are gendered as either masculine or feminine. One of the most referenced works on this is Jeffery Sobal's (2005) article "Men, Meat, and Marriage: Models of Masculinity," in which he surveys the literature, exploring how foods are gendered differently across cultures. As Sobal notes:

> Animal flesh is a consummate male food, and a man eating meat is an exemplar of maleness. Men sometimes fetishize meat, claiming that a meal is not a 'real' meal without meat. Men often hypermasculinize meat in male rituals. For example, men dominate meat cooking competitions, such as barbecue contests, and are the main contestants engaging in eating competitions, which often focus on meats. (138)

Plenty of men engage in the direct animal-exploitative behaviors they believe confer masculine identities upon them, and the benefits and status such behaviors bring: angling, hunting, betting on animal sports. But the vast majority of the abuse of animals comes through our food systems. There are almost no women working on the kill floors of slaughterhouses worldwide (Pachirat). Of course, the majority of the exploitation takes place where men, pleasurably wrapped up in images of what it means to be a man, continue to dominate the bodies of other animals through the heavy consumption of "meat" products. Globally men eat around 57 percent more meat than women (U.S. Department of Health). Most vegans are women—in the United Kingdom, about two-thirds of vegans identify as women, and the in United States it's more like four to one. Veganuary, the campaign to get people to choose vegan in January, attracts around 82–88 percent women every year, and only 10–15 percent men. For Luke the reason for this disparity is that those who identify as men continue to benefit from institutions of animal exploitations in ways that women do not. Those "ways" are wrapped up in what men see as the benefits of "meat" consumption in providing a social identity which is, using Joy's formation, Normal, Natural, and Necessary. And as Piazza et al. have added: Nice.

For women, the wrappings of femininity are loaded with pictures of salad, yoghurts, fruit, chocolate, and "white" "meats" such as chicken or fish, as well as contextualized by time and place; for example, Chaiken and Pliner's findings of single women choosing not to eat "steak" or other "red meats" on a date. Much of this socialization is done when we are children, specifically through our relations to animals (Cole and Stewart). As Sobal summarizes, "Western men are socialized into adopting beliefs and behaviours about masculinity by the active and passive efforts of other men and women, with fathers acting as examples of meat-eating men and mothers reinforcing those gendered values" (138).

Anat Pick divides meat eaters into three categories, with an explicit gendered expression. The categories are

> the "defaulters", who take what is and what ought to be as one and the same; the "new moralists" … who portray the consumption of animal flesh as an enlightened and conscientious choice, sensitive to both the lives of animals and to the higher value of human culinary discernment; and "bravado eaters" who insist on meat eating as an expression of manly superiority.

Sobal's work had already illustrated how masculine dominance shaped food practices within marriage, drawing on a considerable literature in psychology, sociology, and anthropology that provided evidence for how "men's food preferences dominate family food choices" (142) and provide a "patriarchal dividend" (Connell 25) that "both reflect and reproduce wider patterns of male dominance and female subordination (Sobal 142). There is no way, therefore, to explore the vegan or veganized body in these contexts without also exploring the shaping roles that gender plays in such relationships, and how gendered foods matter for building embodied identifications. As Sobel writes, "men and women 'do gender' by consuming gender appropriate foods. Meat, especially red meat, is an archetypical masculine food. Men often emphasize meat, and women often minimize meat, in displaying gender as individuals" (142).

Accomplishing a gendered masculine identity through food involves acts demonstrating and celebrating autonomy in the face of other demands, with men eating what they want, not what they should. This leads to Wright's finding in *The Vegan Studies Project* that "hegan" men feel a need to pass through the "masculine ritual" of cardiovascular disease and poor health to attain the right to adopt healthier plant-based diets. So much of the "power, control and invincibility" (Samaritans) that men practice in the constant validation process of maintaining their masculinity comes at the expense of those who are most easily controlled and overpowered: animals. According to Sobal, "to eat in a masculine way is to eat meat, accomplishing maleness by the relict behavior of eating animals that were (or at least could be) hunted" (138).

And yet as Wright established, veganism is, for men in general, "depicted as impossible to maintain" (*The Vegan Studies Project* 108). There was a moment, specifically in American culture, pre-9/11, where a discursive space "opened for the negotiation of new, nonnormative masculinities that challenge our traditional understandings of what it means to be manly" (108). But Wright's analysis of media and popular culture texts of the two decades either side of the 9/11 attacks convincingly depicts a backlash against vegetarianism and veganism as threats to established forms of masculinity, that the "War on Terror" successfully defended in its mission to reinstate patriarchal white male privilege as the dominant global operating system. Quoting numerous sources, Wright articulates how challenges to these entrenched "eating identities" (Parkinson, Twine, and Griffin) as formative of the larger gendering of identities, in their positions as either shoring up or challenging patriarchal structures, manifested as "a profound denunciation of vegetarian and vegan diets as indicators of weakness, ethnicity, and femininity, all of which have been constructed as threats to a traditional 'American' way of life" (Wright, *The Vegan Studies Project* 114). As such, the fifteen years or so following 9/11 were, for Wright, characterized by situating male veganism "within a space that exists by its virtue of its increasingly misogynist overdetermination of its difference from a veganism practiced by women" (155).

This is how veganism (and before it, vegetarianism) have constantly been viewed. "People attend to others' diets as a means of understanding them" (Ruby and Heine 445), and so when people are following vegan diets or lifestyles, understanding is inferred from these practices and, most comprehensively, understood through a gendered lens. Women have been found to be much more accepting than men of vegetarians; vegetarian men have also been regularly perceived as "less masculine than omnivorous men, underscoring the link between men, meat and masculinity" (Ruby and Heine 450). Omnivores also tend to rate vegetarians as good, but weak people (MacInnis and Hodson), suggesting already that omnivores would expect most vegetarians to be stereotypically women (where "weakness" is a hegemonically colored trait of femininity).

Such stereotypes, acceptances and refusals also filter sexual relationships. As Potts and Parry have analyzed, the threat of a vegan sexuality, where (mainly) vegan women expressed a desire not to have sex or relationships with non-vegan men, was felt most vehemently by heterosexual meat-eating men. Write Potts and Parry of those responding to their research findings, "meat and meat-eaters were assumed to forever prove a temptation to veg*n women. ... The language of abstinence was invoked to describe a vegan or vegetarian's decision to avoid animal flesh, echoing news coverage's portrayal of vegansexual women as 'abstaining' from sex with men who eat meat" (38). They concluded: "The particularly brutal remarks directed at women 'vegansexuals' may also be understood as an effect of masculinist meat-eating culture's relationship to certain forms of male violence perpetrated against both nonhuman animals ... and other humans" (42).

As noted above, this constant revalidation belies a fragility in the construction of gendered identities that vegan scholars and practitioners can attend to. As Adams told me in 2019, "I keep hearing the call for men to 'renew the man card.' Well I've had my library card for 30 years, why is the 'man card' so fragile it needs to be renewed every time they eat?"

But femininity is also constantly validated through acts around food practices. For example, women are more able to focus on the sociability involved in providing food for others, whereas men tend to emphasize the necessity of eating particular foods (and especially meat) (DeVault). Researchers found a gendered division between "food work" (considered in terms of masculinity and manhood as economic provision, e.g. "bringing home the bacon") and "feeding work," categorized as feminine and centered around household stocking, shopping, preparing, and cooking (DeVault). For Sobal, that food remains a "social performance" allows men and women both to decide how to "do marriage" and "do meat" simultaneously, including the "existence of options for hypermasculine cooking and eating ... using the plural models of masculinities as justifications for a diversity of forms, types, times, and quantities of meat consumption" (149).

Studying such pinch points in gendered constructions of masculinity and femininity may provide opportunities to advocate ways to improve lived experiences for nonhuman animals, and humans marginalized and outside of the dominant "Human" category. We can look at some of these other ideas, and recent research into the ways in which new identities are forming around the intersection of gender and veganism.

Plural masculinities, vegan feminisms, and hybrid identities

Sobal contrasts singular masculinity and plural concepts, which has helped shape the field to explore the gendered and contextual understanding of masculinities. For Sobal, "Multiple masculinities (and femininities) are assumed to be developed, learned, considered, selected and enacted as men (and women) engage in the continuous construction of gender in everyday life, including in their food choices" (136). Plural masculinities and femininities are a recognition that there is no "real," simple binary of gender, and even within dominant discourses they can be practiced in different ways. Recently, for example, whereas we already have ecofeminism, and perhaps plural ecofeminisms (e.g., queer ecofeminism) (Gaard, "Toward a Queer"), we now have "ecomasculinities" to challenge the idea of a hegemonic and always toxic masculinity. These ecomasculinities to explore and embody have been theorized by Martin Hultman and Paul Pulé. Their proposal is for a third and relationally focused pathway that they call ecological masculinities, which advocate and embody broader, deeper, and wider care for the global through to local commons.

This recognition of pluralities is perhaps an example of a new gender script, providing room for multiple forms of gendered identification inside the concept of masculinity or femininity, especially in relation to food practices. For Sobal, "multiple masculine scripts are invoked as sources for particular individuals to draw upon in specific contexts. Thus, masculinities are enacted situationally, such as a man lunching on hamburgers at work with his pals and sharing salad for dinner with his wife" (147). And while

> a hegemonic masculine, meat-eating model exists in contemporary Western societies … individual men may choose how they engage with that food script alone and with partners. Men who have access to and experience in using multiple models of masculinity have greater freedom and control in their food choices, and are less tightly bound by singular of hegemonic cultural prescriptions to consume meat. (149)

In the context of vegan studies, a form of engagement in regards to masculinity, Greenebaum and Dexter found that there was no hard line between femininity and masculinity for vegan men: "While hegemonic masculinity is defined in opposition to femininity, the vegans in our study do not reject associations with femininity" (1). Rather, they found vegan men practiced a form of "hybrid masculinity" constructed through three key themes from their worldview:

> First, they questioned traditional tenets of hegemonic masculinity, challenging a simplistic binary understanding of masculinity. Second, they claim their attitudes towards masculinity are different from other men, specifically non-vegans. Third, although veganism did not shape their definition of masculinity, it strengthened their identity as "good" men. (5)

However, one of the problematic issues of this focus on men, masculinity, and veganism are the ways in which "men legitimize veganism" (Greenebaum and Dexter 8). While compassion for animals and animal rights activism has been traditionally stereotypical feminine traits, they have been easily marginalized in patriarchal cultures. The majority of activists and donors within the animal rights movement are women, yet research continues to shows how men are considered necessary to legitimize the movement (Einwohner 1999; Gaarder 2011; Luke 2007). Such "legitimization" comes at the cost of marginalizing and silencing the women, particularly women leaders, in the movement (Luke 2007; Wrenn 2017). In my research (Lockwood, "How to Turn") I have found that men were likely to listen to or adopt the practices of other men over those of other women, echoing Greenebaum and Dexter's findings that,

> Non-vegan men are more likely to be encouraged to accept or consider becoming vegan when they see other men demonstrating masculinity within the context of

veganism. Whether desired or not, they still benefit from masculine privilege, when men legitimize veganism. (9)

So even vegan men, show Greenebaum and Dexter, don't refute masculinity; they don't totally unwrap the parcel. And this fact has long been problematic for the animal rights movement. Sadly, most vegan men engage in a hybrid form of masculinity that only modifies masculine associations—eating plant-based burgers, talking of "vegan gains" in the gym—and fall short, like most of us do, of challenging gender inequalities, which are transferred onto the suffering bodies of animals.

Conclusion

Not much has changed, then, since Carol Adams wrote in 1990 that "a mythology permeates all classes that meat is a masculine food and meat eating is a male activity" (26). Throughout the 2000s and into the 2010s, those wanting to promote veganism to men went mostly with the grain of masculinity, rather than against it. For example, Johnson found that veganism was predominantly promoted to men through magazines and books such as John Joseph's *Meat is for Pussies*, for its health benefits, accentuating and supporting the ideas of male domination and sexual conquest, explaining how plant-based diets could support new forms of masculinity without threatening older models (29). Such attitudes have also been seen, for example, in PETA's sexualized campaigns, which appease men's fears over the loss of their traditional masculine roles if they choose to adopt vegan life practices. For Thomas this might be a tactically sound decision, after finding that "choosing veganism, not veganism itself, is associated with lower levels of masculinity" (85). Yet Thomas's argument has held little truck with ecofeminists, who continue to clarify the ways such ongoing exploitative messages reinforce intersectional oppressions against both animals and women. As Gruen and Weil write in their introduction to a special issue of *Hypatia* on "Feminists Encountering Animals," there is a critical "need to maintain feminist, ethical, and political commitment within animal studies—commitments to reflexivity, responsibility, engagement with the experiences of other animals, and sensitivity to the intersectional contexts in which we encounter them" (493).

What is interesting in recent developments has been shifting beliefs held by social groups about veganism and plant-based diets. For example, in Bryant's research, he found that omnivores agreed that vegan lifestyles were healthier, more environmentally conscious, and more virtuous. Omnivores also agreed that veganism was socially acceptable. So Wright's suggestion that "male veganism only seems acceptable if it is not linked to animal welfare" (*The Vegan Studies Project* 129) has perhaps shifted somewhat with the rapid expansion of veganism across both Western and non-Western countries. Not enough to suggest that we have entered a fully open space where "the negotiation of new, nonnormative masculinities that challenge our traditional understandings of what it means to be manly" (108) can be had, but perhaps with renewed hope that this can begin.

If such negotiations do begin, however, they will still need a critical and patient vegan ecofeminist eye on developments. We should not forget Wrenn's reminder that "gender is difference, and difference is conjured to stimulate market growth" (203–4). We can see this in the way that foods continue to be gendered today, and how this drives marketing to predominantly either masculine- or feminine- identified audiences (Mogelonsky). What we need is to continue to expand our sense of vegan ecofeminist studies and, perhaps, encourage a new vegan ecomasculinist studies, both of which remain focused on critiquing and changing "a speciesist economic system that is not only capitalistic but patriarchal" (Wrenn 207).

One of the rich areas for future vegan studies research that intersects with gender is the construction of the male body and mental health, in relation to the masculine food and food practices men carry out. Some of this work has begun to be done (e.g. Richardson *Redefining*). If we can get men talking, finding emotional support and networks, and if we can help men understand that masculinity is a construction—no more than the wrapping on a parcel, not the gift inside—then we will also help nonhuman animals who men, mostly, in their desperate needs to be masculine, exploit. Living in these times of mass industrialization and climate change, driven by patriarchal standards of separation and domination, these are critical interventions to make. Perhaps someone will finally unwrap the parcel. Better yet, we will all throw them out the window.

Works cited

Adams, Carol J. "The Oedible Complex: Feminism and vegetarianism." *The Lesbian Reader*, edited by Gina Covina Laurel Galana, Amazon Press, 1975.

———. *The Sexual Politics of Meat: A Feminist-Vegetarian Critical Theory*. Continuum Publishing, 1990.

Beardsworth, Alan, and Teresa Keil. *Sociology on the Menu: An Invitation to the Study of Food and Society*. Routledge, 1997.

Bentley, Amy. *Eating for Victory: Food Rationing and the Politics of Domesticity*. University of Illinois Press, 1998.

Bourdieu, Pierre. *Distinction: A Social Critique of the Judgement of Taste*. Routledge & Kegan Paul, 1984.

Bryant, Christopher J. "We Can't Keep Meating Like This: Attitudes Towards Vegetarian and Vegan Diets in the United Kingdom." *Sustainability*, 11, 2019, pp. 1–17.

Chaiken, Shelly, and Patricia Pliner. "Women, But not Men, Are What They Eat: The Effect of Meal Size and Gender on Perceived Femininity and Masculinity." *Personality and Social Psychology Bulletin*, vol. 13, no. 2, 1987, pp.166–176.

Cohoon, Christopher. "Ecofeminist Food Ethics." *Encyclopaedia of Food and Agricultural Ethics*, edited by Paul Thompson and David M. Kaplan. Dordrecht: Springer, 2014.

Cole, Matthew, and Kate Stewart. *Our Children and Other Animals: The Cultural Construction of Human–Animal Relations in Childhood*. Routledge, 2016.

Connell, Raewyn W. *The Men and the Boys*. University of California Press, 2000.

Cudworth, Erika. *Social Lives With Other Animals: Tales of Sex, Death, and Love*. Palgrave McMillan, 2011.

DeVault, Marjorie L. *Feeding the Family: The Social Organization of Caring as Gendered Work*. University of Chicago Press, 1991.

Donovan, Josephine. "Animal Rights and Feminist Theory." *Signs: Journal of Women in Culture and Society*, vol. 15, no. 2, 1990, pp. 350–375.

Einwohner, Rachel L. "Gender, Class, and Social Movement Outcomes: Identity and Effectiveness in Two Animal Rights Campaigns." *Gender and Society*, vol.13, no.1, 1999, pp.56–76. doi:10.1177/089124399013001004

Fiddes, Nick. *Meat: A Natural Symbol*. Routledge, 1991.

Gaard, Greta. *Ecological Politics: Ecofeminists and the Greens*. Temple University Press, 1997a.

———. "Toward a Queer Ecofeminism." *Hypatia*, vol. 12, no. 1, 1997b, pp. 114–137.

Gaarder, Emily. "Where the Boys Aren't: The Predominance of Women in Animal Rights Activism." *Feminist Formations*, vol. 23, no.20, 2001, pp. 54–76.

Garlick, Steve. "Complexity, Masculinity, and Critical Theory: Revisiting Marcuse on Technology, Eros, and Nature." *Critical Sociology*, vol. 39, no. 2, 2011, pp. 223–238.

Greenebaum, Jessica, and Brandon Dexter. "Vegan Men and Hybrid Masculinity." *Journal of Gender Studies*, vol. 27, no. 6, 2017, pp. 637–648. http://dx.doi.org/10.1080/09589236.2017.1287064

Gruen, Lori, and Kari Weil. "Introduction: Feminists Encountering Animals." *Hypatia*, vol. 27, no. 3, 2012, pp. 492–493.

Hultman, Martin, and Paul Pulé. *Ecological Masculinities: Theoretical Foundations and Practical Guidance*. Routledge, 2019.

Johnson, Justine A. *Hegans: An Examination of the Emerging Male Vegan* (Unpublished master's thesis). Minnesota State University, 2011.

jones, pattrice. "Eros and the Mechanisms of Eco-Defense." *Ecofeminism: Feminist Intersections with Other Animals & The Earth*. Bloomsbury Academic, 2014, pp. 91–106.

Joy, Melanie. *Why We Love Dogs, Eat Pigs, and Wear Cows*. Conari Press, 2009.
Kimmel, Michael. *The Politics of Manhood*. Temple University Press, 1996.
Lockwood, Alex. *The Pig in Thin Air*. Lantern Books, 2016.
———. "How To Turn a Man Vegan: Interviews with 40 Vegan Men Who Overcame Obstacles to Change their Lifestyles". Unpublished manuscript, in press.
Luke, Brian. *Brutal: Manhood and The Exploitation of Animals*. University of Illinois Press, 2007.
MacInnis, Cara C., and Gordon Hodson. "It Ain't Easy Eating Greens: Evidence of Bias Toward Vegetarians and Vegans from Both Source and Target." *Group Processes and Intergroup Relations*, vol. 20, no. 6, 2015. doi: 10.1177/1368430215618253
Mogelonsky, Marcia. "*It's Time to Look Beyond 'Gendered' Food and Drink*." Mintel, 2019. https://www.mintel.com/blog/consumer-market-news/its-time-to-look-beyond-gendered-food-and-drink
Nilsen, Alleen Pace. "From Aunt Chilada's to Cactus Willy's: Gender Naming in the Marketing of Food in Arizona." *Names*, vol. 43, no. 1, 1995, pp. 29–52.
ONS (2019) Office for National Statistics: Suicides in the UK 2018 Registrations. https://www.ons.gov.uk/peoplepopulationandcommunity/birthsdeathsandmarriages/deaths/bulletins/suicidesintheunitedkingdom/2018registrations
Pachirat, Timothy. *Every Twelve Seconds: Industrializes Slaughter and the Politics of Sight*. Yale University Press, 2013.
Parkinson, Claire, Richard Twine and Naomi Griffin. *Pathways to Veganism: Exploring Effective Messages in Vegan Transition*. Edge Hill University, 2019.
Piazza, Jared, Matthew B. Ruby, Steve Loughnan, Mischel Luong, Juliana Kulik, Hanne M. Watkins, and Mirra Seigerman. "Rationalizing Meat consumption. The 4Ns." *Appetite*, 91, 2015, pp. 114–128.
Pick, Anat. "Fleshing out the Morality of Meat: Thoughts on the *New York Times*'s contest 'Calling All Carnivores'," 2012. https://www.cupblog.org/2012/05/04/anat-pick-fleshing-out-the-morality-of-meat-thoughts-on-the-new-york-timess-contest-calling-all-carnivores/
Potts, Annie, and Jovian Parry. The Vegansexual Challenge to Macho Meat Culture." *Feminism & Psychology*, 2010, https://doi.org/10.1177/0959353509351181.
Richardson, Michael. *Redefining Masculinity: Feminism, Family and Food*. Routledge, in press.
Roe, Emma and Michael Buser. "Becoming ecological citizens: connecting people through performance art, food matter and practices." *Cultural Geographies*, 2016. https://doi.org/10.1177/1474474015624243
Roe, Emma, and Paul Hurley. *The Man Food Project*, 2018. http://generic.wordpress.soton.ac.uk/man-food/
Ruby, Matthew B., and Steven J. Heine. "Meat, Morals and Masculinity." *Appetite*, 56, 2011, pp. 447–450.
Samaritans. *Middle Aged Men and Suicide*, 2012. https://www.samaritans.org/about-samaritans/research-policy/middle-aged-men-suicide/
Sobal, Jeffery. "Men, Meat, and Marriage: Models of Masculinity." *Food and Foodways*, vol. 13, no.1, 2005, pp. 135–158.
Sue, Derald W. *Microaggressions in Everyday Life: Race, Gender and Sexual Orientation*. Wiley, 2010.
Thomas, Margaret A. "Are Vegans the Same as Vegetarians? The Effect of Diet on Perceptions of Masculinity." *Appetite*, 97, 2016, pp. 79–86. doi:10.1016/j.appet.2015.11
U.S. Department of Health. *Dietary Guidelines 2015–2020*, 2020. https://health.gov/our-work/food-nutrition/2015-2020-dietary-guidelines/guidelines/chapter-2/a-closer-look-at-current-intakes-and-recommended-shifts/#figure-2-6
Vandello, Joseph. A, Jennifer K. Bosson, Dov Cohen, Rochelle M. Burnaford, and Jonathan R. Weaver. "Precarious manhood." *Journal of Personality and Social Psychology*, vol. 95, no. 6, 2008, pp. 1325—1339. https://doi.org/10.1037/a0012453
World Bank. Consumption Data, 2020. http://datatopics.worldbank.org/consumption/
Wrenn, Corey. "Toward a Vegan Feminist Theory of the State." *Animal Oppression and Capitalism Vol. 1*, edited by David Nibert, Praeger, 2017, pp. 201–230.
Wright, Laura. "Doing Vegan Studies: An Introduction." *Through a Vegan Studies Lens: Textual Ethics and Lived Activism*, University of Nevada Press, 2019, pp. vii–xxiv.
———. *The Vegan Studies Project: Food, Animals and Gender in the Age of Terror*. University of Georgia Press, 2015.
Yilmaz, Ayce F. "Contemporary Feminist Politics of Veganism: Carol J. Adams' The Sexual Politics of Meat and Alternative Approaches." *Global Media Journal—Canadian Edition*, vol. 11, no. 1, 2019, pp. 23–38.

Part 5
Veganism in the media

27
Screening veganism
The production, rhetoric, and reception of vegan advocacy films

Alexa Weik von Mossner

Vegan advocacy films work.[1] If people get around to watching them, they can change lives. This truism was recently confirmed for me by the most unlikely of sources: my own family. During one of our infrequent family dinners, my sister announced that she and her partner have been eating vegetarian for the past three months and were planning to do without meat for the rest of their lives. Asking what had brought about the change of mind, I learned that they had watched a film on Netflix, picking it randomly on their search for some mildly interesting evening entertainment. She couldn't remember the title of the movie, but when she started to describe its content, it took me less than a minute to provide it: Kip Andersen and Keegan Kuhn's vegan advocacy film *What the Health* (2017). According to my sister, she and her partner spent the evening looking at each other in surprise, or horror, asking each other the ever-same question: "Did you know about this?" Apparently, they didn't know about "this" before watching the film. None of it. They had known, of course, that animals were being slaughtered for meat and, because they both love animals, had been feeling bad about their meat consumption, and thus started to buy organic whenever that seemed possible and they were cooking at home. But they hadn't known about the serious health implications of meat and dairy consumption, that it has been related to cardio-vascular diseases, diabetes, even cancer. I listened in amazement, and not only because I might have mentioned those health implications once or twice myself over the years. None of what I said, however, or what had been all over the media at times, seemed to ever make an impact on my family. But *What the Health* did.

As someone who writes often about the rhetorical structure and (potential) impact of documentary films, this is a fascinating piece of anecdotal evidence. What I find particularly enlightening is the fact that my sister and her partner weren't seeking out this information. It is often considered a downside of documentary film that, because its audiences tend to be highly self-selected, it preaches mostly to the converted.[2] That wasn't the case here, as the choice was somewhat random. But then they found their interest piqued by Kip Andersen who, in the tradition of Morgan Spurlock and Michael Moore, goes on a personal quest for knowledge about the relationship between health and diet. Watching his interviews with dozens of doctors and nutrition experts, they were shocked to learn that the World Health Organization classifies processed meat as a Group 1 carcinogen, along with "cigarettes, asbestos and plutonium," that red meat is a Group 2 carcinogen, and that saturated fat is one of the main causes for diabetes. Moreover, they learned that organizations such as the American Cancer Society and the American Diabetes Association nevertheless recommend eating all of the above because they are sponsored by the meat and dairy industry. Given all this bad news, they were grateful for the information also provided in the film about the many health benefits of a whole-foods plant-based diet that isn't lacking in protein and other essential nutrients. They liked that *What the Health* was entertaining and that it didn't display too much animal suffering (which they find hard to digest). But what changed their mind about their own diet was the film's explicit focus on (human) health and how to improve it. And while they were aware that *What the Health* advocates veganism, not vegetarianism, they said that the idea of giving up cheese is still too radical for them right now, but they are taking steps to reduce their intake of dairy.

In attributing a sudden diet and/or lifestyle change to a film, my sister and her partner are not alone. In fact, it is remarkable how many vegans report similarly transformative viewing experiences.[3] Books such as Jonathan Safran Foer's *Eating Animals* (2009) are also frequently cited as the cause of lifestyle change, and I do not at all want to diminish the impact an immersive reading experience can have.[4] But in this chapter, I am interested in the remarkably large and diverse range of vegan advocacy films that have been conceived, financed, produced, distributed, and promoted over the past 15 years, from no-budget productions and crowd-funding campaigns to the involvement of streaming services and Hollywood celebrities. Moreover, the chapter will explore how such films tap into related discourses such as speciesism, animal rights, health, climate change, and celebrity culture to bolster their arguments for adopting a vegan diet and/or lifestyle. I am interested in the narrative strategies employed in these films and in whether their central emotional appeals are targeting viewers' self-interest, their capacity for trans-species empathy, their moral sense of social and ecological responsibility, or their sense of humor. Through these different routes of analysis, I hope to give insight into how vegan advocacy films get made and what narrative strategies they use in order to reach not only other vegans but also people who might happen upon them for whatever reason and find themselves challenged to change their lives.

Getting off the ground: financing the vegan advocacy film

Financing documentary films is a tricky business. On the one hand, filmmakers profit immensely from the digital revolution in camera technologies that have brought expenses down to a fraction of what they used to be while also allowing for much smaller crew sizes and more creative flexibility. On the other hand, raising money for a feature-length nonfiction film can nevertheless be difficult. The somewhat more traditional choice is to pitch the idea to a TV station or, in recent years, streaming service. If successful, this route promises relative financial security, but such commissions tend to come with a degree of editorial influence on content and style that some filmmakers find restrictive.[5] Possible alternative routes to the necessary funds lead (in some countries) through public funding agencies as well as private foundations, financers, and social-action entities like Impact Partners and Participation Media (Anderson 2016).[6] The most radical alternative, however, along with using personal funds, are the various crowdfunding schemes that have become popular in recent years. A remarkable number of vegan advocacy films were funded through a combination of the last two options. This includes some of the best-known movies, among them *Earthlings* (2005), which director Shaun Monson financed himself, and *Cowspiracy*, which was paid for by a mix of personal funds and crowdfunding after all four of its original funders dropped out when learning more about the subject matter of the film and the mainstream environmental organizations it was going to target, among them 350.org, the Sierra Club, and Greenpeace (Andersen 2016).

Crowdfunding has become increasingly important in recent years for issue-driven films. While the personal funds a documentary filmmaker can invest are often quite limited, crowdfunding websites such as Indiegogo allow them to raise large amounts through aggregated small donations. Andersen and Kuhn's first vegan advocacy film *Cowspiracy* (2014) acquired 1,449 backers through the website, who gave a total of $117,092, an amount that surpassed the filmmakers' original funding goal (Homewood). For their second film, *What the Health*, Andersen and Kuhn were able to raise more than $230,000, also through Indiegogo (Indiegogo.com). Such funding schemes have the obvious advantage of providing filmmakers with funding when major players decline or back out because of what they perceive as social undesirability and/or direct or indirect economic risks. But they are also affected by the same issue that Andersen detects as a general problem for documentary financing: in order to attract enough backers, filmmakers must present a project that is issue-driven and resonates with the current zeitgeist. That seems to be presently the case for vegan advocacy films, but not only can the tides change; it is also a fact that the amount of money raised through crowdfunding can only do so much to lift a film and its message into the public consciousness.

In this context, it is important to note that Netflix's eventual pickup of *Cowspiracy*—which is largely responsible for its wide popularity—was facilitated by Leonardo DiCaprio, who has also been involved in the production and promotion of *What the Health* and a whole range of other social and environmental issue films. DiCaprio's involvement is part of another growing trend in the production of vegan advocacy films: the engagement of affluent celebrities who support veganism as a social and environmental cause. In many cases, these celebrities are vegan themselves, and not only do they lend their glamor and visibility to these projects, but they also invest personal funds to get the message across. Joaquin Phoenix, who narrated *Earthlings*, was an executive producer on *What the Health*. Natalie Portman produced (and narrates) Christopher Dillon Quinn's *Eating Animals* (2018), which is based on Foer's book. Louie Psihoyos's *The Game Changers* (2018) lists Pamela Andersen, Arnold Schwarzenegger, Jackie Chan, and James Cameron as executive producers, along with sports stars Lewis Hamilton, Novak Djokovic, and Chris Paul, who are all also featured in the film (more on that below).

As scholars such as Laura Wright and Julie Doyle have pointed out, the "celebrity vegan project" (Wright, *The Vegan Studies Project* 130) is not without its problems. While celebrities certainly have done a lot to enhance the visibility and social acceptance of veganism, and some are without doubt driven by a genuine desire to use their status and financial means to support a cause they believe in, "these ethics are reworked through the commodity logic of celebrity culture to make it more marketable and thus consumable as a set of ideas and lifestyle practices" (Doyle 777). The enormous personal fortunes of some vegan celebrities make them an attractive source of funding, but, for the filmmakers, their involvement also runs the risk of getting "fully co-opted by the hegemonic processes that shape social ideology" (Wright, *The Vegan Studies Project* 130). And while it is unlikely that celebrity investors profit very much from the box office earnings of a vegan advocacy film, some critics have had an eye on indirect links between those investments and parallel investments in plant-based meat substitute companies such as Impossible Foods and Beyond Meat, which then profit from what passes itself off as a social issue film (Ng). Regardless of whether the rumors of indirect (corporate) payoffs are true, the larger question of how to successfully and responsibly finance a social issue documentary is one that remains prevalent for the makers of vegan advocacy films, and it without doubt also shapes those films' narrative strategies.

Alexa Weik von Mossner

Narrative strategies and visual tactics: from animal other to self and back

Over the years, the makers of vegan advocacy films have embraced different narrative strategies and visual tactics to get their message across. These strategies often overlap, but there are nevertheless some broad trends I want to highlight. The first and still most prominent strategy is an explicit focus on animal welfare and rights. Monson's *Earthlings*, Mark Devries's *Speciesism* (2013), and Chris Delforce's *Dominion* (2017) are all films that foreground animal suffering in combination with an animal rights argument and an appeal to trans-species empathy. These films are packed full of footage that exposes the horrific abuse in the meat and dairy industry, evidence that has often been obtained secretly and/or illegally.[7] The central aim of this investigative and revelatory approach is to push viewers into *empathic distress* by reminding them of the fact that the meat they eat used to belong to the body of a thinking, feeling, and suffering being not unlike themselves and nearly identical to their beloved pet. Empathic distress is a prosocial emotion that, according to psychologist Martin Hoffman (105), plays a central role in moral decision making and helping behavior. Cutting through the complex social, cultural, and egoistical factors that can lead to apathy and psychic numbing (Joy 18), films that rely on the shock-and-awe tactic of exposing animal abuse, suffering, and death can be powerful motivators for personal lifestyle changes. The potential downside of this tactic is that it requires an audience that (a) cares for animals and that (b) is sufficiently interested in learning the truth about the meat and dairy industry to be willing to endure painful emotions during and potentially also after the viewing experience. Clearly, not everyone is willing or able to do these things, not even when they are genuinely interested in a lifestyle change. And so while the focus on animal suffering can be very effective with some audiences, filmmakers have also used alternative strategies that allow them to reach people for whom animals aren't a primary concern and/or who are unwilling or unable to grapple with graphic visual evidence of their abuse.

One of those strategies is an explicit focus on the various health benefits of a diet that is vegan or "plant-based," as it is often called in films that use this strategy, perhaps to avoid alienating people who don't like the term "vegan" or its larger ethical connotations (Doyle 777). Invariably, these films highlight the potential of such a diet to halt or reverse serious health conditions that are known as the main killers in the industrialized West: cardiovascular diseases, diabetes, and cancer. Andersen and Kuhn's *What the Health* is a prime example, as are Or Shlomi and Shelley Lee Davies's *PlanEat* (2010), Joe Cross and Kurt Engfehr's *Sick, Fat, and Nearly Dead* (2010), Lee Fulkerson's *Forks Over Knives* (2011), and Paul David Kennamer's *Eating You Alive* (2018). Because of their central focus on the relationship between disease and diet, films in this category speak to viewers' concerns about their own health and that of their loved ones, and they are marked by the repeat appearances of a small but distinguished group of vegan health experts who advocate a plant-based, whole-food diet. They include the biochemist T. Colin Campbell, one of the co-authors on the famous *China Study* (2005), along with medical doctors Caldwell Esselstyn, Michael Greger, Michael Klaper, and Neal Barnard. Because of their healthy looks and old age, Campbell and Esselstyn are often presented not only as professional experts but also as living examples of the benefits of the diet they are advocating.

As has become clear in the example of my sister and her partner, the evidence presented in this type of vegan advocacy film can be very convincing for people who worry about their health or who just needed one more reason to finally give up meat. I have also made the experience of teaching *What the Health* to a group of students who were deeply impressed by its arguments. But most of these films have come under attack for cherry-picking scientific research (Berry; Purdy) and for promoting the careers and books of the health professionals that appear in them (Messina). Since their central message—that a plant-based whole-food diet has positive effects on human health—is hard to refute, critics have focused on rebutting individual (un) scientific claims presented by people who, supposedly, don't know any better. *What the Health*, which accuses major U.S. health and pharmaceutical organizations of deliberate disinformation due to the lobbying efforts of the meat and dairy industry, has been denounced as the irresponsible product of filmmakers who are "not nutrition scientists or trained in any aspect of medicine or science, therefore not trained or qualified to make sense of scientific research" (Berry). Often, the aim of such criticism is the spreading of doubt and confusion about the safety and actual health benefits of a plant-based diet. But the film has also been criticized from within the vegan community for "over-stat[ing] the data, highlight[ing] dubious stories of miraculous healing, and focus[ing] on faulty observations about nutrition science" (Messina). The fear that "the vegan movement's credibility is undermined when we make claims that are so easily refuted," combines here with the conviction that the ends cannot justify the means in vegan advocacy.

Worth mentioning in this context are two films that try out somewhat different strategies to convey the benefits of veganism. Marisa Miller Wolfson's *Vegucated* (2011) follows three omnivore Americans who have accepted a six-week vegan challenge and try to come to terms with what that means for their daily lives. In the process, they not only find out that eating plant-based significantly improves how they feel, but they also experience first-hand the unspeakable suffering of animals in industrial factory farming and the joy of engaging with the same types of animals at a farm sanctuary. At the end of the film, both their diets and their worldviews are transformed. The German documentary *Live and Let Live* (2013), directed by Marc Pierschel, further widens the scope by following the life stories of six individuals who made the choice to go vegan for different reasons and whose lives were also transformed, among them a committed animal rights activist, a former butcher who is now a vegan chef, and a former factory farmer who now runs a farm sanctuary. Through these individual perspectives, the film aims to convey the wide variety of reasons that can lead to and sustain veganism as a lived practice.

It bears mentioning that most of the featured individuals in *Live and Let Live* are male and that the same is true for many of the other films discussed so far. As Wright has observed, veganism is frequently "gendered as a female undertaking" (*Through a Vegan Studies Lens* xvi), and so one thing to note about vegan advocacy films is their explicit foregrounding of *male* veganism, be it that of the filmmakers themselves, the doctors that lend their medical expertise, or the protagonists of the individual "conversion stories" featured in them. One of the most obvious examples is Psihoyos's *The Game Changers*, which prominently features the hyper-masculine bodies of the likes of Arnold Schwarzenegger and Patrik Baboumian, while at the same time challenging the myth that animal products are necessary to nurture such bodies. As Schwarzenegger puts it in the film, the media keeps "selling the idea that real men eat meat. But you got to understand that's marketing." *The Game Changers* thus consciously participates in the discourse on veganism and masculinity with the aim to prove that when men choose a plant-based diet, this choice does not, in fact, "go against their essential dietary nature" (Wright, *The Vegan Studies Project* 108). At the same time, however, the film can easily be criticized for buying into, and perpetuating, the narrative that "real" men are either muscular hunks or vastly successful businessmen (and even the female athletes featured in the film say happily of themselves that they have become "like a machine" as a result of switching to a plant-based diet). The difference between the portrayal of masculinity in *The Game Changers* and *Live and Let Live*, notably, is that the latter film also makes room for more average men (and women) who, rather than aiming for optimal performance, have made an ethical choice in their lives and seem content with it.

Just as important, in terms of challenging problematic preconceptions, is that the American films *Vegucated* and *The Game Changers* both make a point of featuring vegan individuals who are non-white. Not only is veganism often coded female, it also—at least in the United

States—is constructed as "a largely white, upper middle-class identity" (Wright, *Doing Vegan Studies* xvi). But this is slowly beginning to change. The over 30 contributions to A. Breeze Harper's *Sistah Vegan* (2010), for example, embrace veganism as a feminist agenda while pushing back against the idea that all vegans are necessarily white and upper-class. In her introduction, Harper explains that "experiencing life as a working-class, black-identified female" led her to "practice *ahimse*-based veganism from a different point of entry that didn't initially involve animal rights as the catalyst to [her] 'awakening'" (xvii). Instead, it was a growing awareness of the continuities between "systematic racism, sexism, [and] nonhuman animal exploitation," and the effects these discriminatory practices had on her body and on those of others. Kenny and Jasmine Leyva's 2019 documentary *The Invisible Vegan* is equally aware of the colonial legacies that have defined the traditional African American diet and, more recently, led to the emergence of Black veganism. As Jasmine Leyva explains in the film, all she used to know was that "we turned scraps into soul food and … that was our only culinary legacy." Like so many people, she "identified veganism as a white thing," but that was only because she "didn't know [her] history." Consequently, the film harks back beyond Black Nationalism and the history of slavery to the traditional foods of West Africa, arguing that "eating fresh, healthy crops is part of our legacy and we should embrace it." *The Invisible Vegan* is also very conscious of the class and economic barriers that keep Black communities from eating more fresh vegetables as well as of the government subsidies that keep those barriers in place. With its explicit focus on African Americans, it offers an overdue corrective to the predominant whiteness of earlier vegan advocacy films.

The last trend I want to consider concerns films that not only draw a connection between veganism and various environmental issues—most of the above-mentioned films do that to some degree—but also aim to offer a *vision of the future* that is either dystopian or utopian. The dystopian mood certainly has been more prevalent in environmental documentaries across the board in recent years, and vegan advocacy films are no exception. This fact becomes particularly obvious in a film like *Cowspiracy* with its overt link between the carbon emissions of the meat and dairy industry and the ongoing climate catastrophe. Such links are risky because they layer one piece of bad news on top of the other, potentially overwhelming viewers who only wanted to learn about eating plants instead of animal products. If *Cowspiracy* is any indication, however, mixing vegan advocacy with other pressing environmental issues does not have to mean a less popular or effective movie. Relating her experiences in teaching the film at Florida Tech, Natalie Dorfeld affirms its "efficacy in engaging students in a discussion on the negative effects of livestock farming, and even in securing "their [theoretical] support for meat-free Mondays" (241). However, Dorfeld also reports that this support did not necessarily translate into personal action. "Many young people," she believes, "don't think 30 years into the future, but are concerned with the here and now," which is why they are unable to see how their habitual meat-based lifestyle will affect them and the planet in the future (254).

This lack of imagination is the reason why some climate change documentaries, like Franny Armstrong's *The Age of Stupid* (2009), present viewers with (fictional) dystopian images of a devastated future. But few vegan advocacy films will go as far as imagining such concrete visions. If they do, however, these visions tend to be utopian rather than dystopian, perhaps because, as far as our treatment of animals is concerned, our present is already a living nightmare. It is therefore no surprise that films like Marc Pierschel's *The End of Meat* (2017) and Liz Marshall's *Meat the Future* (2020) look forward to a better time in which we no longer need to torture and kill animals but can keep eating our beloved (cultured) meat. Despite or perhaps because of their sincere intentions, such films can appear naïve, and they also run the risk of ignoring the adverse health effects of meat, regardless of whether it is cut from an animal or cultured in a lab. But I want to dedicate the final pages of this chapter to a different utopian film, which also allows me to consider the (rare) use of irony and humor in vegan advocacy.

"It Just Had to Be Funny": a note on style and affect in the vegan advocacy film

Environmentalist films are a serious affair. "Even when leavened by a dose of humor," writes ecocritic Nicole Seymour, such films "tend to be underwritten by earnest beliefs" and thus "solicit serious affective responses from viewers, such as reverence, guilt, dread, and conviction" ("Irony" 61). This is certainly true for most vegan advocacy films. *Cowspiracy*, *What the Health*, and *Vegucated* are all examples of films that try to serve some comic relief along with their more dire fare. But since their central concern is the lives and deaths of animals and humans alike, along with the health of the entire planet, the general assumption seems to be that these things cannot be treated lightly and therefore necessitate precisely the "reverence, guilt, dread, and conviction" that Seymour considers problematic or at least ineffective. She has urged critics and filmmakers to embrace more irreverent approaches, arguing that the use of irony and humor "can foster a self-critical attitude that does not hinder but in fact enables environmentalist work" ("Irony" 62). One of her prime examples is a vegan advocacy film: the drama-documentary hybrid *Carnage* (2017) by the British writer, director, and stand-up comedian Simon Amstell.

Amstell's film, which was distributed via the BBC's online-only channel BBC3, has been called many things, among them a science fiction mockumentary and a speculative comedy (Seymour, *Bad Environmentalism* 226). But its narrative techniques are much closer to *The Age of Stupid*, which also mixes fictitious visions of the future seamlessly with documentary footage of the actual past. *Carnage*, as Brett Mills has noted, is a "future documentary" (179) that uses cinematic techniques we associate with fiction—actors, costumes, set design, a script—in order to confront viewers with the long-term consequences of their present practices and behaviors. However, Amstell's imaginary future isn't a wrecked and wretched planet that no longer sustains human life, as it is the case in *The Age of Stupid*. His vision of 2067 is a happy place where androgynous looking young people enjoy their plant food in a beautiful park and cannot even imagine—or endure the imagination—that people once ate other animals. It is only the older generation that still lives with, and is tortured by, the memories of their own meat and dairy consumption. The amount of guilt and shame they feel about the cruel and perverse behavior of their childhoods is so crushing that they are seeking help in support groups and psychotherapy.

Carnage thus relies on typical science fiction techniques such as extrapolation, defamiliarization, and estrangement (Otto 9). While the ostentatious purpose of the movie is to offer the people of 2067 an explanation of how it was possible that humans once ate animals, its actual purpose is to help contemporary viewers see their own normalized behavior from a different, unfamiliar angle. Unlike most of sci-fi films, however, and unlike most mockumentaries, much of its running time consists of actual archival footage. Starting with the founding of the Vegan Society in 1944, the film portrays the world's ever-growing desire for meat along with the marketing practices that propelled that growth and the industrial livestock farming practices it produced. Important for the overall effect of the film, the actual archival footage used to illustrate that process often meets or even surpasses in ludicrousness the fake archival material that is later used to portray the developments beyond 2017. "From its speculated future position," notes Seymour, "the film thus defamiliarizes and invites us to recognize the absurdities of meat and dairy consumption" (*Bad Environmentalism* 226). This is precisely the "job" of speculative storytelling. In the words of science fiction scholar Tom Moylan, it is "a fictive practice" that "has the formal potential to re-envision the world in ways that generate pleasurable, probing, and potentially subversive responses" (4). This combination of the subversive, the probing, and the pleasurable was of central importance for Amstell when making his film. "It just had to be funny," he explains in an interview with the British Film Institute, because

> otherwise the whole thing would stink... Because the problem with everything that you ever hear [about veganism] is that it is kind of a bit preachy and annoying, and there's a superiority to it, so the intention was to make something kind of self-deprecating and funny enough so you didn't mind when a new bit of information was presented. That you didn't mind too much when we tell you that male chicks get gassed or shredded. (Amstell)

At this point in the interview, Amstell visibly pauses to see whether his words have any effect on the interviewer and, when that doesn't seem to be the case, repeats the last line. This little moment says a lot about how he uses humor as a glove for the shocking graphic images of animal suffering that are scattered across the film and hit viewers at unexpected moments. It also says a lot about how this strategy can fail to achieve its goal since the interviewer remains unresponsive to the uneasy mixture of humor and horror.

As Seymour acknowledges in her book, "not everyone will 'get' these works" and they "may not necessarily succeed. For example, one might not necessarily go vegan after watching ... *Carnage*" (*Bad Environmentalism* 227). She argues that such irreverent and playful modes of narration are nevertheless worthy of our scholarly attention, "regardless of their effects" (227). I find myself agreeing with that, but for the makers of vegan advocacy films, the ultimate effects surely do play an important role. It is not only its use of humor, however, that makes *Carnage* special. The film is also remarkable because its temporal structure allows it to integrate all the pro-vegan arguments mentioned so far as it chronicles the development from the early days of the Vegan Society to our contemporary present and on to speculative future events and far-reaching decisions. In some instances, even people relatively familiar with the matter will likely wonder whether the information they are presented with is fact or fiction. That kind of cognitive estrangement, along with an often amusing depiction of a future in which there are no vegans anymore, just some poor old people who used to be carnists, can be mind-boggling at times, and in some viewers it might instill a desire for change.

Conclusion

Making a vegan advocacy film, then, is not without its challenges, regardless of whether one chooses to focus on the animal rights side of veganism, on its effects on human health and well-being, or on the larger environmental repercussions of meat and dairy consumption. Arguably it is getting easier because—at least in some countries and in some circles—the attitude toward veganism is changing rapidly and for the better, opening new funding opportunities and new audiences. What remains unclear, however, is whether more altruistic appeals—asking viewers to go vegan for the sake of other animals or for that of future human generations—are more successful than the more self-centered approaches that convinced my family members. Or whether utter sincerity is more effective than a more playful, humorous take on the matter. The current assumption is that different types of films and arguments resonate with different communities and even with the same individual at different moments in life. And so it is welcome that the number and variety of vegan advocacy films is steadily increasing.

An aspect that at times has come up in the discussion of such films is whether the people making them should (all) be vegan. Asked about how many people on his team he turned vegan, Simon Amstell flippantly responds that after editing "the bit where the cows are being taken away," his editor "switched to almond milk." He then adds that turning his team vegan wasn't his aim, it was "making sure that the whole thing looked real." Even the small production teams necessary for documentary films are still large enough to make any dietary or lifestyle requirements tricky if one is also trying to secure the best and/or affordable talent. Some films have nevertheless been realized by largely vegan teams, but such ethical consistency on the production level isn't always an option or even a priority. It is a reminder though, that we need not only films, but any form of advocacy we can get in order to make sure that by the time we reach 2067, there are no vegans left, only normal people and former carnists.

Notes

1 Research for this chapter was carried out with support from the project "Cinema and Environment: Affective Ecologies in the Anthropocene" (Reference PID2019-110068GA-I00 / AEI / 10.13039/501100011033).
2 While this is generally true, there are exceptions. Several documentaries by Michael Moore were considerable box office successes, attracting viewers that would not normally watch a nonfiction film. The same is true for some wildlife films and environmental documentaries such as Davis Guggenheim's *An Inconvenient Truth* (2006).
3 One of the most frequently mentioned films in this context is Shaun Monson's *Earthlings* (2005). Ellen DeGeneres attributed her going vegan to this film and the same is true for many other celebrities, influencers, and bloggers.
4 I have engaged with vegan advocacy in other media in Weik von Mossner (2019).
5 The British documentarist Franny Armstrong has explained that despite the obvious financial downsides, "it helps not to have a commission. Well, it helps that the copyright is owned by a small production company obsessed with getting the story out and not too bothered about making money" (quoted in Hockenhull 2017).
6 On funding opportunities for documentary films, see also Bershen (2006).
7 Another film in this category is Bruce Friedrich and Cem Akin's short film *Meet Your Meat* (2002), which was produced by PETA. Andersen cites the film as the reason why he decided to go vegan (2016).

Works cited

Amstell, Simon, director. *Carnage*. BBC3, 2017a.
Amstell, Simon. Interview on *Carnage*. British Film Institute. 2017b. https://www.youtube.com/watch?v=DMcli9vhM2I
Andersen, Kip. Room for Discussion Interview at the University of Amsterdam (May 18, 2016). https://www.youtube.com/watch?v=qSIJ6Ou10AM
Andersen, Kip, and Keegan Kuhn, directors. *Cowspiracy: The Sustainability Secret*. First Spark Media. Netflix, 2014.
———. *What the Health*. First Spark Media, Netflix, 2017.
Anderson, John. "Documentary Filmmakers Find that an Agenda Helps with Financing." *The New York Times*, 8 July 2016. https://www.nytimes.com/2016/07/10/movies/documentary-filmmakers-find-that-an-agenda-helps-with-financing.html
Armstrong, Franny, director. *The Age of Stupid*. Spanner Films, 2009. DVD.
Berry, Sarah. "What the Health: Netflix Documentary Trades on 'Alternative Facts' about Veganism." *Sydney Morning Herald*, 20 July 2017, https://www.smh.com.au/lifestyle/health-and-wellness/what-the-health-netflix-documentary-trades-on-alternative-facts-about-veganism-20170719-gxebwd.html
Bershen, Wanda. "Finding Funding: A Primer on Financing Your Documentary Film." *International Documentary Association Website*, 22 February 2006, https://www.documentary.org/feature/finding-funding-primer-financing-your-documentary

Campbell, T. Colin and Thomas M. Campbell II. *The China Study*. BenBella Books, 2005.
Cross, Joe and Kurt Engfehr. *Sick, Fat, and Nearly Dead*. Gravitas Ventures, 2010.
Delforce, Chris. *Dominion*. Aussie Farms, 2017.
Devries, Mark, director. *Speciesim: The Movie*, 2013.
Dorfeld, Natalie M. "Meatless Mondays: A Vegan Studies Approach to Resistance in the College Classroom." *Through a Vegan Studies Lens: Textual Ethics and Lived Activism*, edited by Laura Wright, University of Nevada Press, 2019, pp. 240–256.
Doyle, Julie. "Celebrity Vegans and the Lifestyling of Ethical Consumption." *Environmental Communication*, vol. 10, no. 6, 2016, pp. 777–790.
Foer, Jonathan Safran. *Eating Animals*. Little, Brown & Company, 2009.
Friedrich, Bruce, and Cem Akin, directors. *Meet Your Meat*. PETA, 2002.
Fulkerson, Lee, director. *Forks Over Knives*. Virgil Films, 2011.
Guggenheim, Davis, director. *An Inconvenient Truth*. Paramount Classics, 2006.
Hockenhull, Stella. *British Women Film Directors in the New Millennium*. Palgrave Macmillan, 2017.
Hoffman, Martin. *Empathy and Moral Development: Implications for Caring and Justice*. Cambridge University Press, 2000.
Homewood, Alison. "Beware *Cowspiracy*—and the Spread of the Vegan Virus." *New Nationalist*, 24 September 2015, https://newint.org/blog/2015/09/24/cowspiracy-documentary-vegan
IndiGoGo—*What the Health* Campaign. 7 March 2016. https://www.indiegogo.com/projects/what-the-health-movie-film#/
Joy, Melanie. *Why We Love Dogs, Eat Pigs and Wear Cows: An Introduction to Carnism*. Conari Press, 2010.
Kennamer, Paul David Jr., director. *Eating You Alive*. Garden Fresh Media, 2018.
Leyva, Kenny and Jasmine, directors. *The Invisible Vegan*. The Leyva Company, 2019.
Marshall, Liz, director. *Meat the Future*, 2020.
Messina, Virginia. "A Vegan Dietitian Reviews 'What the Health.'" *Vegan.com*, 27 July 2017, https://www.vegan.com/vegan-dietitian-review-what-the-health/
Miller, Wolfson, Marisa, director. *Vegucated*, 2011.
Mills, Brett. *Animals on Television: The Cultural Making of the Non-Human*. Palgrave Macmillan, 2017.
Monson, Shaun, director. *Earthlings*. Nation Earth, 2005.
Moylan, Tom. *Scraps of the Untainted Sky: Science Fiction, Utopia, Dystopia*. Westview, 2000.
Ng, Lance. "Is *Game Changers* Funded by Impossible Foods or Beyond Meat?" *Medium*, 17 November 2019, https://medium.com/@lancengym/is-game-changers-funded-by-impossible-foods-or-beyond-meat-d9f323133350.
Otto, Eric. *Green Speculations: Science Fiction and Transformative Environmentalism*. The Ohio State University Press, 2012.
Psihoyos, Louie, director. *The End of Meat: Black Rabbit*, 2017.
——, director. *The Game Changers*. Netflix, 2018.
——, director. *Live and Let Live*. Syndicado, 2013.
Purdy, Chase. "Hollywood Vegans Are Trying to Convince You Eggs Are as Bad as Cigarettes—That's Irresponsible and Wrong." Quartz, 8 August 2017, https://qz.com/1047900/hollywood-vegans-are-trying-to-convince-you-eggs-are-as-bad-as-cigarettes-thats-irresponsible-and-wrong/
Quinn, Christopher Dillon, director. *Eating Animals*. IFC Films, 2018. DVD.
Seymour, Nicole. "Irony and Contemporary Ecocinema: Theorizing a New Affective Paradigm." *Moving Environments: Affect, Emotion, Ecology, and Film*, edited by Alexa Weik von Mossner, Wilfrid Laurier University Press, 2014, pp. 61–78.
——. *Bad Environmentalism: Irony and Irreverence in the Ecological Age*. University of Minnesota Press, 2018.
Shlomi, Or and Shelley Lee Davies, directors. *PlanEat*. Studio At 58, 2010.
Weik von Mossner, Alexa. "How We Feel about (Not) Eating Animals: Vegan Studies and Cognitive Ecocriticism." *Through a Vegan Studies Lens: Textual Ethics and Lived Activism*, edited by Laura Wright, University of Nevada Press, 2019, pp. 28–47.
Wright, Laura. *The Vegan Studies Project: Food, Animals, and Gender in the Age of Terror*. Athens: University of Georgia Press, 2015.
——. "Doing Vegan Studies: An Introduction." *Through a Vegan Studies Lens: Textual Ethics and Lived Activism*, edited by Laura Wright, University of Nevada Press, 2019, pp. vii–xxiv.

28
(Mis)representing veganism in film and television

Matthew Cole and Kate Stewart

What does it mean to represent veganism in fictional media? In this chapter we argue that the answer to this question pivots on the meaning of "veganism" and the social construction of that meaning through fictional narratives. This is in recognition of the discursive drift, appropriation, and contestation of the meaning of veganism since it was first formally codified as "the doctrine that man [sic] should live without exploiting animals" by The Vegan Society, in 1951 (see Cole 203 for an extended analysis of the formulation of the first definition of veganism). Through a critical vegan studies lens (Wright, *The Vegan Studies Project*), the social reconstruction of veganism in the mainstream media has tended to undermine the implications of its founding definition (Cole and Morgan 136). This is unsurprising when it is considered that mainstream media in a capitalist context frequently legitimate exploitation, in all of its forms, none more so than the profitable exploitation of nonhuman animals for food and many other products (Almiron 371; Molloy 102).

Rather than trace this historical process of discursive contestation, in this chapter we posit applying an analytical polarity of ideal types of veganism, in terms of its contemporary social construction in fictional films and television programs. By "contemporary" we refer to examples largely drawn from the 21st century, with select culturally resonant and influential late 20th-century instances. The polarity posits that, on the one hand, veganism may be constructed so as to re-erase nonhuman animals and to enact a discursive death that compounds their conventional cultural status as "absent referents" (Adams 14). This "negative" ideal type constructs veganism as human narcissism, and vegans as disengaged from the lives and deaths of nonhuman animals, and from the struggles and sufferings of other humans. Such a construct inverts the impulse to species-humility that first animated veganism (Cole, "The Greatest Cause"). Instead, it projects conventional human supremacism onto veganism, such that veganism is inverted as elitist inauthenticity. Concomitantly, non-veganism is insulated from reflexive awareness of its own complicity in massive, systematic violence against nonhuman animals. For example, in the 2010 comic book-based film *Scott Pilgrim vs. the World*, the non-vegan titular protagonist portrayed by Michael Cera deceives a "vegan" antagonist named Todd Ingram (portrayed by Brandon Routh) into drinking half and half (a dairy product comprised of cow's milk and cream), leading to his arrest by "the vegan police" for failing to adhere to a construct of vegan purity: "You're under arrest for veganity violation, code number 827: imbibing half and half."

On the other hand, a "positive" ideal type constructs veganism through its engagement with the lives and deaths of nonhuman animals. This ideal-typical construct of veganism is a means by which to discursively reverse the absent referent and critique the victimization of nonhuman animals and its denial by mainstream culture. In other words, the impulse to species-humility is re-centered in this construction, so that veganism becomes a means through which to focus attention on nonhuman animals, and especially their systematic exploitation, which flows from human supremacism. For example, in Mike White's 2017 film *Year of the Dog*, Newt, a vegan animal shelter worker portrayed by Peter Sarsgaard, expresses his empathic connection with other animals: "Animals are like us; they live for love."

In the remainder of this chapter, we begin by outlining the polarity of ideal types, with reference to seven representational (vegan) theses and (anti-vegan) antitheses. We then briefly reflect on how this analytical schema can, in hindsight, illuminate some of our previous research. In that light, this earlier work has been overwhelmingly dominated by, broadly speaking, "negative" representations of veganism. Anti-vegan media abounds, and it would be easy to add to that catalog of disappointment here, so instead we have chosen to purposely seek out examples that gravitate toward the "positive" ideal type. To that end, we focus our analysis on two films written by vegan filmmaker Mike White, *Year of the Dog* (2007) and *Beatriz at Dinner* (2017) respectively. In conclusion to the chapter, we reflect on our methodological and ethical reasons for making these "positive" analytical choices.

A polarity of ideal types: vegan and anti-vegan representations

To ground the vegan vs. anti-vegan polarity of ideal types, in this chapter we adapt a set of seven vegan methodological principles as an analytical tool. They comprise the building blocks of the ideal type constructs. These principles were initially devised as a guide to conducting empirical social research from a vegan methodological standpoint. In this context, they are employed retrospectively to facilitate thematic analysis of film and televisual representations of vegans and veganism, including through the lens of the representation of nonhuman animals. The following table presents the set of seven principles and their theses and antitheses.

A "positive" ideal type would fulfill all seven theses from Table 28.1. A "negative" ideal type would fulfill all seven antitheses. As with all ideal types, a "pure" example of either positive or negative (or "vegan" vs. "anti-vegan") may not exist, though our previous research has revealed a plethora of close approximations to the "negative" pole (discussed below). We do not propose establishing ourselves or anyone else as vegan media police, ready to hand out veganity violations for deviations from the vegan ideal type. However, we do argue that the positing of a hypothetical "ideal" vegan fictional film or television program provides us an aspirational model that is simultaneously a tool for reflexive critique. By the same token, the positing of "ideal" anti-vegan media presents a model of what to avoid and simultaneously a tool with which to contest the misappropriation of veganism. The same holds for our original formulation of the principles in Table 28.1 in the context of social research methodology—the principles are not a stick to beat ourselves or others with for past failings, but a tool to guide us toward more effective vegan work. The same applies to the principles themselves, in that we recognize that they will inevitably be limited by our own experiences, disciplinary and personal biases, and can without doubt be further refined, elaborated, or added to, so as to be more effective still. We hope that this chapter contributes to iterative processes in vegan social research, vegan cultural critique, and vegan media production.

Table 28.1 A typology of vegan representational theses and their antitheses

Principle	Thesis	Antithesis
1. Representations support nonhuman animals	Vegan representations further the interests of nonhuman animals by challenging their oppression by human animals	NHAs are represented only insofar as they serve human needs, or at best NHA needs are ultimately subordinated to human interests
2. Representations promote species consciousness	Vegan representations raise consciousness of human species privilege	Human species privilege is unreflexively assumed and unquestioned
3. Representations align with social constructionist epistemology	Vegan representations critique speciesist knowledge claims about other animals that legitimate their oppression	Speciesist epistemology is unreflexively adopted and human supremacism is thereby reproduced
4. Representations facilitate awareness of socio-structural context	Vegan representations highlight the socio-structural conditions for the human oppression of other animals	Speciesist social structures are accepted as a reflection of a natural order of human superiority
5. Representations facilitate empathy	Vegan representations foreground nonhuman animals' own experiences and perspectives as much as is possible, while acknowledging difference and unknowability	Human ways of knowing are assumed to be superior to nonhuman ways of knowing. Nonhuman ways of knowing may be entirely denied or ignored
6. Representations highlight intersectionality and complexity	Vegan representations highlight the complex and intersecting relationships between the human oppression of other animals and intra-human forms of oppression on the basis of "race," gender, class and all "othered" social categories	Representations isolate "others," which may include playing off experiences of oppression against each other as well as obscuring or denying intersectionality
7. Representations reflexively critique their impact on nonhuman animals	Vegan representations reveal and critique any exploitation of nonhuman animals involved in the production process, and their likely impacts on nonhuman animals	The exploitation of nonhuman animals in the production process is ignored. The likely impact of representations on nonhuman animals is ignored

Previous research: hegemonic anti-veganism

This chapter represents our first conscious application of the representational typology in Table 28.1. However, it is salient to briefly reflect on how it is applicable to our previous research on film and television. In this earlier work, we have frequently focused on fictional representations of nonhuman animals, especially as characters in children's films (Cole and Stewart, *Our Children & Other Animals* 89; *Socialising Superiority* 1287). Our findings have been dominated by the theme of those representations serving human rather than nonhuman interests (antithesis 1). In other words, fictional nonhuman characters tend not to be used to leverage critique of the exploitation of their real-world counterparts, but may even be used to compound such exploitation. This can take the form of direct ideological justification for violence, such as the explicit legitimation of "meat"-eating for the target audience by Mufasa, the father of Simba, in Disney's 1994 animated film *The Lion King* (Stewart and Cole 466). Or it can take the more indirect form of diverting viewer empathy toward fictional representations and thereby away from their real counterparts, as in Dreamworks' 2000 film *Chicken Run* (Cole and Stewart, *Our Children* 3). Often the two forms are intertwined within the same media. The results are representations that gravitate toward the "negative" pole, according to our methodological principles in Table 28.1. This result is the case even when, overtly, nonhuman animals are represented as agential subjects (antithesis 2), because their apparent *nonhuman* agency is either only a cipher for *human* agency (the trap of unreflexive anthropomorphism), or because their apparent agency manifests in "voluntarily" serving human interests (such as animal companions' desire to remain as humans' "pets" in *The Secret Life of Pets* (2016)). There are exceptions of course, perhaps most famously in the CGI animated film *Babe* (see Stewart and Cole, "The Conceptual Separation" 469). It is therefore worth briefly revisiting our analysis of *Babe* in light of Table 28.1.

Unlike many films with nonhuman protagonists, Chris Noonan's 1995 live action CGI children's film *Babe* presents the celebration of order and hierarchy as constraining, exploitative, and legitimating of unjust violence. The plot of the film centers on Babe, a runt pig, and his journey from potential human food to recognition as a quasi-human family member by the end of the narrative. *Babe* therefore upsets our usual understanding of the meaning of pigs as farmed animals (thesis 3), whose experiences on farms and at slaughterhouses are generally invisible to us (thesis 1). Babe's early life in a factory farm is described as a "cruel and sunless world," and the farmers are shown only by their feet kicking the pigs or by their hands wielding canes (thesis 2). When Babe's mother is removed from the farm, Babe believes that she is leaving for a far-off happy land, while in reality she is being trucked to slaughter. Most of the other nonhuman characters in the film go on to express the same oppressive consequences of the prevailing order. *Babe* does have limitations in its critique of hierarchical species relations. Ultimately, Babe's salvation and recognition as a subject results from his transcendence of his pig-ness as a result of his ability to fulfill a "sheep-dog" role for the farmer (antithesis 1). So his fate is still dependent on the way that humans regard him in terms of his utility within that established speciesist order. There is some evidence that the film had an impact on both makers and audiences in terms of their consumption of animals (Stewart and Cole, "The Conceptual Separation" 471).

Film and television are produced in a largely non-vegan social context, and the vast majority of productions are therefore oblivious to vegan ethical principles. This context is true of media that features nonhuman animal characters (performed by real or animated nonhumans) and whether they do, or (more likely) do not feature vegan human characters. This non-vegan context becomes especially troublesome when the internal logic of the fictional world or characters impels vegan representational principles, but which fail to materialize (antithesis 3). We have examined two quite different fictional examples in recent research: the 2016 adult CGI animation film *Sausage Party* (Cole and Stewart, "Speciesism Party" 767), and the long-running British science fiction television series *Doctor Who* (Cole and Stewart, "I Need Fish Fingers and Custard" 198).

Our analysis of the surreal comedy *Sausage Party* describes how the film situates anthropomorphized food items (and other commodities) as heroic outsiders struggling against seemingly invincible opposition (in this case their human consumers). The premise—food items reanimated in the fictive world of the film—is squandered on juvenile scatological humor instead of leveraging critique of the absent referent. The "hero" of the film is an animated hotdog (voiced by Seth Rogan), horrified by his potential consumption as human food, but not by having been produced through the prior murder of "livestock" animals. Instead of giving voice to the real victims of speciesist oppression, *Sausage Party* provides an exemplary case study in the cultural reproduction of an intersected relational system of power. It celebrates ecocidal, oppressive consumption practices reflecting unequal power relations between humans and other species, and also how those power inequalities intersect with intra-human power relations along the lines of gender, sexuality, "race," age, class, faith, different experiences of embodiment, and so on.

Doctor Who, produced by the BBC (British Broadcasting Corporation), is the world's longest running television science fiction series, broadcast in the U.K. between 1963–1989, before going on hiatus, briefly revived in a TV movie in 1996, and then as an ongoing series in 2005. The titular Doctor is a member of an alien species, a Timelord from the planet Gallifrey, who has the technological capacity to travel through time and space. *Doctor Who* frequently engages a science fiction trope of exploding hubristic human "superiority" in the face of technologically and/or intellectually superior alien threats (thesis 2), as well as articulates empathy for other-than-human species (thesis 5). Yet it continues to retain a human exceptionalism inconsistent with its premise. For example, commenting on having averted disaster in the episode "Voyage of the Damned" (2007), the 10th Doctor refers to the Earth's population as six billion, affirming that only human lives enter into his calculations. This point recurs in the historical episode "The Fires of Pompeii" (2008), when the Doctor is only concerned for the imminent loss of 20,000 human lives in the volcanic eruption. By casting Jodie Whittaker in the titular role in 2017, *Doctor Who* responded positively to a long-standing critique of its gender politics. However, human exceptionalism remains as central, and illogical, as ever: In the 2020 episode "Praxeus," the Doctor and her human companions are faced with a bacterial pathogen that targets plastics and is fatal to living creatures who ingest them. Positioned as a commentary on the plastic pollution of oceans, the episode features both human and nonhuman life being killed by the pathogen. Yet when the threat becomes global in scale, as in "Voyage of the Damned" (2007) the doctor only tallies the loss of human life, stating "Planet Earth. Seven billion lives. Separate, and connected from the edge of the atmosphere to the depths of the ocean": two areas of the earth's ecosystem in which humans cannot naturally survive.

As this brief overview has shown, there are of course some hopeful spots in our recent cultural history, and much potential for more "positive" vegan representations to break through and help to heal some of our collective cognitive dissonance about other animals. With *Doctor Who*, for instance, it seems that a vegan script writer could make relatively subtle adjustments to the show, which would enable the character to realign with their espoused values through their speech and action. For instance, imagine Jodi Whittaker's iteration of the Doctor lamenting the potential deaths, not of 7 billion humans, but of "all life on earth," or "the trillions of earthlings in all their wonderful variety" in "Praxeus." That leap of imagination is made easier by considering what happens when a vegan filmmaker *does* have creative control, which is our focus for the remainder of this chapter.

The possibility of representing veganism

Notwithstanding *Babe* and some of our wish-fulfillment about a vegan *Doctor Who*, our previous research has been a catalog of approximations to the anti-vegan ideal type. Rather than add to that gloomy roster here, we turn to analysis of examples that approximate more closely to the vegan ideal type, specifically the work of vegan filmmaker Mike White. We begin with a discussion of White's 2007 directorial debut *Year of the Dog*, for which he also wrote the script. We then move forward by ten years to *Beatriz at Dinner*, written by White and directed by

Miguel Arteta. The films share some inter-textual references and thematic similarities, which we explore below. They also illustrate the possibility of representing veganism in divergent genres, as well as doing so either overtly, or more subtly. *Year of the Dog* is rated PG (Parental Guidance) in the United Kingdom and overtly explores veganism, primarily through whimsical comedy. *Beatriz at Dinner* is rated 15 in the U.K. and R in the U.S., and explores vegan themes more subtly through black comedy-drama.

Year of the Dog: "I'm a vegan now ... it's nice to have a word that can describe you"

Year of the Dog tracks the journey into veganism and animal activism of its protagonist, Peggy Spade (played by Molly Shannon). The film had a limited commercial impact and audience reach, taking only $1,606,237 at the worldwide box office, 96 percent of which was comprised of U.S. takings ("Year of"). Peggy is a white U.S. suburban office worker, living with her companion Beagle named Pencil (Pencil is played by two different real dogs in the film). Her significant human family relationships in the film are with her brother Pier (Tom McCarthy), sister-in-law Bret (Laura Dern), infant nephew, and pre-teen niece Lissie (Zoe and Amy Schlagel). She has a close friend and confidant at work, Layla (Regina King), and befriends Newt (Peter Sarsgaard), the vegan shelter worker, as the film progresses. She also has a complex, fractious relationship with her boss, Robin (Josh Pais), and her neighbor, Al (John C. Reilly). Newt is the only character who is vegan throughout the film, and his influence is instrumental in Peggy's own path toward veganism. Peggy's journey is impelled by the death of Pencil early in the film, which leads her to meet Newt (and through him, many other dogs), and subsequently to self-educate about veganism and then dive headlong into vegan activism. Rather than recapitulate the entire plot, our analysis proceeds by considering how the seven vegan principles play out within it.

Firstly, the representation of the vegan characters does foreground the interests of nonhuman animals. It is made repeatedly clear that both Newt's and Peggy's veganism is motivated by sincere concern for nonhuman animals. Peggy's journey toward veganism is hastened by Newt explaining his veganism to her over lunch. At the tail end of the scene, Peggy looks guiltily at her own lunch which includes chicken's flesh. The following scene shows Peggy flicking through a book entitled *Vegan and Humane*, showing photographs of intensive "livestock" farming. Afterward, Peggy resolves, "I'm gonna be a vegan." In a later scene at Pier and Bret's house, Peggy explains to Bret, "I'm a vegan now." This assertion elicits Bret's reply, "Is that healthy, Peg? You can eat free range." Peggy's rejoinder ignores the implied deflection from ethics onto personal health with a direct ethical critique of "free range": "you know, it's still murder." The scene proceeds with Peggy reflecting on identifying as vegan, "It's nice to have a word that can describe you, I've never had that before." The foregoing scenes have established the meaning of vegan, for Peggy, as implicitly close to its original formulation, introduced at the start of this chapter, as living without exploiting nonhuman animals. The representation of nonhuman characters also foregrounds *their* interests as being central to the meaning of veganism. For instance, Newt's job focuses on rehoming abandoned companion animals, and the intrinsic value of those animals is repeatedly asserted. For instance, when introducing Peggy to some of the dogs in his care, Newt invites her to, "look at his eyes, there's an old soul in him."

Secondly, the film promotes consciousness of human species privilege in a number of ways. This is most starkly represented through the powers of life and death over abandoned dogs in the city pound. Peggy's narrative journey takes her to the pound, and she is moved to rescue 15 dogs from almost certain euthanasia that day, deceiving the pound's staff that she is a shelter worker in order to secure release of the dogs into her care. Equally dramatic are Peggy's attempts to educate Lissie about the violent realities of human species privilege, and in so doing, subverting her conventional speciesist socialization (see Cole and Stewart, 2014). During an extended passage of the film while Peggy is baby-sitting, she first takes her niece and nephew to a nonhuman animal sanctuary named Paradise Farm (the DVD commentary reveals that the sanctuary was fictional), explaining to Lissie that "they rescue pigs like Babe," a direct reference to Noonan's influential film. This scene frames the sanctuary residents as individual subjects. But Peggy then resolves to drive to the local chicken slaughterhouse, explaining to Lissie that "there is a Holocaust going on up the road right now, and you need to know about it." The implication is that Peggy feels compelled to expose the violent consequences of objectification to Lissie, but she stops short of attempting to enter the slaughterhouse, after Lissie implores, "I don't want to see them hurt the chickens!"

Thirdly, it is possible to detect a social constructionist perspective in the film, insofar as speciesist knowledge claims are undermined. At Paradise Farm, nonhuman animals are subjectified, inverting their objectification as "food." The film repeatedly emphasizes that nonhuman animals have unique and highly variable personalities: Peggy reminisces of Pencil, "he had a really unique personality." This assertion is nothing new to anyone with experience living with other animals, but it undercuts the conventional, industrial massification of nonhuman animals as infinitely replaceable units of production for factory farms, experimental tools for laboratories, or indeed companionship through such entities as puppy mills. It is undoubtedly the case that nonhumans, predominantly dogs, are generally represented as endearing, loving companions to humans in *Year of the Dog*. This style of representation risks elision with what we have previously described as the "cutification" of nonhuman animals, primarily as mediatized representations (Cole and Stewart, *Our Children* 102; and see Malamud). Cutification facilitates the narcissistic construction of caring human identities, while distracting us from our responsibilities to nonhuman victims of human oppression. However, in *Year of the Dog*, canine personalities and behavior are more diverse and complex than the cute stereotype. The clearest example is Valentine, an Alsatian dog who Newt encourages Peggy to foster. Valentine's behavior is sometimes aggressive, including biting Peggy and later in the film, killing another dog, Buttons (the killing occurs off-screen). The killing leads an upset Newt to send Valentine to the city pound to be killed, but Peggy refuses to accept this decision, and rushes to (unsuccessfully) attempt to save him from execution—Valentine's "crime" does not make him irredeemable in Peggy's eyes. Another example that positions other animals as unique subjects, rather than as interchangeable objects, is that Pencil's death is partly a result of his own misadventure: Refusing Peggy's admonition to return to the house after being let out for night-time urination, Pencil prefers to follow his nose, which ultimately leads him to consume poisonous slug pellets in Al's garage. Here, Pencil is represented as an autonomous subject.

Fourthly then, while Pencil's death may be framed as resulting from "disobedience," such a victim-blaming reading overlooks the structural conditions that killed him: the existence of "slug pellets," designed to kill members of another nonhuman species, starkly illustrates the fundamentally speciesist character of human-dominated social structures. Within this context, nonhumans are enmeshed in environments littered with traps which are potentially lethal for nonhuman companions, free-living urban denizens, as well as target "pests." The aborted visit to the Poultry Queen slaughterhouse and Peggy's impulsive rescue of 15 dogs from the city pound directly expose the socio-structural conditions for the oppression of other animals. The Poultry Queen visit also briefly exposes the obfuscatory mediatization of exploitation: the slaughterhouse is signposted with a logo of a cartoon clucking hen's head in profile.

Fifthly, the representation of human and nonhuman characters facilitates inter-species empathy throughout the film. Early in the narrative, Pencil dies, apparently poisoned, and Peggy is shown as being distraught with grief. Pencil's death is unequivocally a significant tragedy in Peggy's life, and it is the foundation for her eventual vegan activism. The sincerity and significance of Peggy's grief is reinforced by a scene in which her friend Layla ineffectually attempts to console Peggy. In turn, Layla suggests that she try Xanax (a pharmaceutical treatment for anxiety), getting drunk, getting laid, or watching films together. Peggy's response is that she does not want to not feel sad. Peggy's empathy contrasts with Al's lack thereof. On an ill-fated date, Al tells Peggy about having shot his allegedly beloved dog, Tessie, "in a hunting accident," instead of his target "mooses." Later in the evening, Al shows an increasingly horrified Peggy his hunting weapons and trophies, referring to a decapitated deer's head with the degendering/objectifying, "isn't it a beauty?" Peggy begins to suspect that Al is responsible for Pencil's death by poisoning, brushing off his sexual advance while she investigates for evidence of his guilt. This date sequence pays off toward the end of the film, when Peggy hides in wait for Al with one of his hunting knives, and ineffectually attacks him when he returns home from a night out. Recalling the experience in the aftermath, Peggy reflects to her brother, "I wanted him to know what it felt like … to be hunted." This misguided lesson in empathy reflects Peggy's desperation at the apparent lack of empathy expressed by Al, and by extension, the empathic deficit of hegemonic masculinity.

The sixth principle, concerning intersectionality, therefore plays an important role through the construction of gender identities and relationships in the film. Newt represents an atypical masculine identity founded on empathy. By contrast, Peggy's relationships with Al, and to a lesser extent, Robin, dramatize facets of hegemonic masculinity that pivot on exploitation or indifference toward other animals: this dynamic plays out through Peggy's burgeoning inter-species compassion being contrasted with, respectively, Al's manipulative sexual advances toward her, and Robin's unreflexive assumption of the primacy of human interests and triviality of nonhuman animals' interests. The latter plays out, for instance, in Robin's rationalization for vivisection when instructing Peggy to stop gathering signatures for an anti-vivisection petition at work. It is also noteworthy that Peggy is not sexualized in the narrative. Her loneliness and grief play a role in attracting her to Newt, but Newt does not reciprocate. Peggy finds meaning through veganism, not through romance or through the heteronormative approbation of men.

The final principle is most clearly evident in the overall narrative, although this is somewhat undermined by some of its uses of real nonhuman animals. The film itself is clearly a sympathetic portrayal of vegans and veganism. Both Newt and Peggy are social misfits to some extent, out of joint with conventional mores. But it is precisely their misalignment which empowers them to wholeheartedly embrace veganism, as a *departure* from convention. By the same token, their misfit personas prevent vegans from being portrayed as heroic superhumans in *Year of the Dog*. Newt and Peggy are both flawed and complex characters, antitheses of the elitist, literally super-powered, vegan cipher in *Scott Pilgrim vs. the World*. Peggy over-reaches her capacities and burns out in her newly vegan zeal, until recovering her strength and renewing her activism as a permanent, integral facet of her life. At the end of the film she says, "How do I explain the person I've become? I believe life is magical […] this is my love […] and it compels me on." This internal monologue plays over the film's final scene, which shows Peggy on a bus with other activists *en route* to a protest. During the monologue, the bus is shown passing a "livestock" transporter, full of chickens implicitly *en route* to a slaughterhouse. The film thereby subverts its own "happy ending"—Peggy has found an identity through veganism that gives her life meaning, but it is an identity grounded in confronting the massive scale of exploitation that surrounds her. This short-circuiting of a fully cathartic ending once again recenters the meaning of veganism on our relationship with other animals, and particularly on actively opposing their exploitation. A vegan identity in this construction *compels* Peggy, but it is not a *comfortable* one; rather, it is a processual becoming with emotional and social costs.

At this point we could segue straight into a discussion of *Beatriz at Dinner*, which shares this characteristic of subverting its potentially cathartic ending. Instead we choose to subvert the cathartic ending of our own analysis of *Year of the Dog*, by focusing on some of the nonhuman animals in the film itself: the film gravitates toward a vegan ideal type, but does not fully realize it. The final of our vegan theses includes the imperative to "reveal and critique any exploitation of nonhuman animals involved in the production process." It is unclear as to the fate of the real chickens in the transporter in the final scene, though it is at least plausible to assume that some or all of them experienced some distress from the process. However, the DVD commentary track does reveal that the film used at least some dead animals in the production: Real furs were used in a scene in which Peggy ruins Bret's fur coats in the bath during the baby-sitting sequence. In a restaurant scene featuring Peggy, Layla, and Layla's errant boyfriend, he is shown eating real "ribs." The messy gusto with which he eats appears to be chosen to invoke some level of disgust; his enthusiasm for the consumption of flesh parallels his enthusiasm for infidelity; the selfish indulgence of sexual and carnivorous desires rounds out the character as a cipher for hegemonic masculinity. However, this gesture toward the sixth vegan thesis is undercut by the realness of the ribs. There is a tragic irony in using the flesh and bones of real dead cows to subtly critique the absent referent: real absent referents to highlight the conceptual absent referent.

Beatriz at Dinner: "all your pleasures are built on other's pain"

Beatriz at Dinner (2017), released ten years after *Year of the Dog*, is tonally and situationally very different, but thematically similar in important respects. It was markedly more commercially successful than *Year of the Dog*, with global box office takings of $7,425,391 though again 96 percent of these were comprised of U.S. receipts ("*Beatriz at*"). The film takes place over the course of one evening, in which Beatriz (Salma Hayek), a professional healer and immigrant to the United States from Mexico, attends a high society dinner party for the California business elite as an impromptu, misfit, guest after her car has broken down, leaving her stranded. Through the course of the evening, Beatriz becomes progressively more estranged from the hosts and other guests (but not their serving staff, some of whom implicitly share her migrant background). Her estrangement pivots on the gradual revelation of the exploitation and suffering that underpins "high society" and Beatriz's refusal to forego her experiential and empathic solidarity with its nonhuman and human victims, for the sake of playing along with the interactional norms established between the other guests. Her outsider status is emphasized by her polite but confident rejection of acceding to the social hierarchy of the gathering: while other guests defer ultimately to businessman Doug Strutt's (John Lithgow) centrality in the social encounter afforded due to his gender, economic status, and whiteness, Beatriz continues to offer relevant stories from her own perspective as equal and equally valid contributions. The social awkwardness prompted by her presence is emphasized through her persistence at seeking this conversational social equality. This estrangement and resistance culminate in Beatriz fantasizing about killing Doug. Instead of acting on this violent visualization, Beatriz chooses to leave the party and apparently commit suicide. As above, rather than retell the plot in detail, we proceed by considering some of the ways in which the seven vegan principles play out within it.

This time, we begin with the sixth principle: the highlighting of intersectionality and complexity, because it is arguably the central theme of the film itself. Unlike Peggy Spade, Beatriz is not clearly identified as a vegan, and does not refer to herself as such in the film. The party's hostess, Cathy (Connie Britton) identifies her as a vegetarian to a waiter, but she is later served sorbet (i.e. a dairy-free dessert) and does not partake in any animal products in the film. For similar reasons, Laura Wright interprets the character as inferred to be vegan in "Dinner with Beatriz" (261). Beatriz is repeatedly shown as caring for other animals throughout the film, which places her at odds with Doug's boastful after-dinner hunting tales and his and others' enjoyment of other animals' flesh at the dinner table. But Beatriz is also at odds with some or all of the party's hosts and guests through her ethnicity, gender, and class position. Rather than separate out distinct forms of oppression, the film skillfully weaves them together through Beatriz's recounted biographical experiences, such as her displacement by a hotel development in her native Mexico, and through her acts of resistance to casual sexism, racism, or speciesism through the course of the evening. Doug stands as the antithesis of Beatriz such that the characters themselves could be mapped onto the vegan–anti-vegan ideal types from Table 28.1. This opposition is baked into the character's names: Beatriz derives from Latin, its meaning approximating to, "she who makes happy." Conversely, Doug's belligerence and arrogance are summed up in his "Strutt" surname (with a double-t, as if to emphasize his supercharged hubris). This opposition crystallizes in an after-dinner scene, when Beatriz confronts Doug about the damage he causes to others, both personally as a hunter and through his business operations as a property developer, which displace indigenous peoples, destroy local employment opportunities, and wreck local environments: "You think killing is hard? Try healing something, that is hard, that requires patience. You can break something in two seconds, but it can take forever to fix it […] all your pleasures are built on other's pain."

The character of Doug comes to stand as an omni-perpetrator—all Others are potential victims of his unrestrained desire to control and consume. In one scene, Beatriz searches for Doug online and finds news footage suggesting that he has evaded punishment for corporate crimes. As Wright puts it, Strutt is an allegorical figure, who stands in for "any man driven by capitalist greed and imperialist desire to conquer" (Wright 265). Doug is therefore erased as an individual, and instead represents the grotesque outcome of intersecting structures of privilege in terms of ethnicity, gender, class, and species (connecting theses 2 and 6). Grotesque because unreflexive and unaccountable privilege continually manifests in systematic violence and exploitation, which reproduces those same structures of privilege. The erasure of Doug as an individual therefore also facilitates reading his character as a metaphor for the socio-structural conditions of oppression (fourth thesis). The interactional order of the party itself is shown to depend on intersecting structural inequalities of class and ethnicity between guests and serving staff, as well as on the elevated status of the male partygoers relative to their female partners, and on the routinized consumption of other animals.

The polarizing of Beatriz and Doug enables a quantum leap forward in the fictional representation of intersectionality and complexity from *Year of the Dog*. While the earlier film was able to critique the intersection of patriarchy and speciesism through Peggy's relationships with Al and her boss Robin, and Layla's relationship with her boyfriend, *Beatriz at Dinner* is able to go much further. This is because Beatriz is deprivileged relative to Peggy in terms of ethnicity and class, while Doug is maxed-out on privilege. For example, when first meeting Beatriz, Doug mistakes her for a waitress; expresses casual racism by making a joke out of being unable to pronounce her Mexican hometown; asks, "ever dance in Vegas?" simultaneously sexualizing Beatriz and unashamedly outing himself as a voyeuristic consumer of women; and questions her status as a legal immigrant. Beatriz is also implicitly a vegan of much longer standing than Peggy. Peggy's veganism looms so large partly because of its newness in her life; she is caught up in the whirl of alienation, grief, outrage, and zeal that will be a familiar experience for many viewers who have recently become vegan. For Beatriz, veganism is intrinsic to her being as a healer, with empathy for all who are oppressed; she does not discriminate on the basis of species or any other characteristic, and recognizes the common source of all forms of oppression. In the scene in which she imagines attacking Doug, she stabs him in the neck (perhaps an allusion to slaughterhouse methods of killing) and speaks to him as he lays bleeding to death: "All tears flow from the same source." The other female guests then rush in and cry at the sight of Doug's mortally wounded body, which snaps Beatriz from her reverie, as if to communicate that even the Dougs of this world cannot be opposed with violence, without perpetuating the flow of tears. Beatriz's wisdom in pulling back from enacting revenge, rooted in oceans of socio-biographical grief, contrasts with Peggy's well-intentioned, yet naïve enacted "attack" on Al borne from the raw grief of Pencil's death and her new encounter with veganism.

In terms of the sixth vegan thesis, *Beatriz at Dinner* is arguably closer to a vegan ideal-type than *Year of the Dog*, in spite of not explicitly foregrounding veganism. However, veganism remains implicitly central, sometimes through notable similarities in the two scripts. For instance, the fifth thesis, concerning empathy, is expressed through Beatriz memorializing Geronimo, a goat she refers to as having been murdered by her neighbor early in the film. Beatriz reminisces, "I could still feel his pain," after finding Geronimo already dead, and "he was such a fun personality." As Wright points out ("Dinner with Beatriz" 267), the individualized murderer—her neighbor—morphs into the generalized murderer—Doug—through the course of the narrative. The initial memorialization and personalization of Geronimo echoes Peggy's grief for Pencil. Geronimo, however, is a member of a less anthropomorphized (and less cutified) species than Pencil, amplifying his significance in terms of acknowledging the difference and unknowability of other animals, but still their capacity to suffer as victims of human oppression, and our capacity as humans to empathize with them in spite of their difference. This theme of empathy for less cutified Others recurs in a later scene, in which Beatriz reminisces about her father—a fisherman—at the dinner party. She recounts him catching and kicking an octopus. Beatriz recalls refusing her father's instruction to kill the octopus, explaining, "I could feel the pain of this octopus." The other guests are discomfited by Beatriz's tangential subjectification of, and empathy for, the absent referents on whom their dinner depends. In a flashback, Beatriz is shown with Geronimo as well as two dogs in her bedroom; the first thesis is also amplified here: the oppression of goats (typically constructed as "livestock") is challenged through their juxtaposition with dogs (typically constructed as "companions") in an intimate domestic space. By the same token, speciesist knowledge claims about other animals that legitimate their oppression are critiqued (third thesis). By discursively repositioning Geronimo from a setting that befits massified "livestock" to one that befits individualized "companions," *Beatriz at Dinner* reflexively highlights the constructed nature of categorizing other animals according to the uses we make of them.

Vegan themes are also explored in the pivotal after-dinner scene of Doug recounting his safari hunting exploits. Here, Doug holds court while describing killing a rhinoceros: "facing that creature down, and looking in its eyes and taking it—I don't consider it murder." Instead, for Doug it is an affirmation of human supremacy (second thesis) in "the struggle for survival." The imbrication of patriarchy with the domination of other animals is laid bare in this scene (again touching on the sixth thesis). Alex, a younger aspirant to Doug's status, admiringly intones, "that thing is massive" when looking at a photograph of Doug's dead victim. It is telling that Doug degenders and thereby deindividualizes the rhinoceros: "it," and Alex joins in with the objectifying epithet, "that thing." Doug further justifies his behavior by contending, "those animals would basically be gone if it wasn't for hunting." In this rhetorical maneuver, Doug erases the suffering of individual animals by massifying them as interchangeable units within a species. Beatriz, her politeness exhausted by the impermeable wall of privilege that the hosts and other guests unreflexively perpetuate, upsets the interactional order with an outraged interjection: "Are you for real? This is disgusting [...] I think it's fucking sick." With these few words, oppression is challenged (first thesis) and the rationalization of human species privilege is exposed (second thesis). Although in a different register, Beatriz's emotional response to Doug's rationalization echoes a contrast between Peggy's emotional condemnation of vivisection ('animal testing, it's evil') and Robin's rationalist defense of it in *Year of the Dog*. The female protagonists feel an empathic connection with the victims of oppression which is inaccessible to the privileged male rationalists.

As with *Year of the Dog*, questions remain about the use of real nonhuman animals in the film. As Randy Malamud argues, "the well-being of every animal counts" (155), including the relatively small numbers directly harmed in the film industry, relative to the scale of killing in "livestock" farming, commercial fishing, and so on. In the case of *Beatriz at Dinner*, the DVD we used to conduct our analysis did not include a commentary track or any additional material that documents how the nonhuman participants were procured, trained, treated on set, or what happened to them after shooting ended. Likewise, we are unclear as to whether real "animal products" were used in the costuming, as food in the dinner party scenes, or served to the film crew during production. We have no reason to assume that dead animals are used as props, nor that any of the living nonhumans suffered, nor even that the production was not vegan-catered. As Malamud points out, the American Humane Association's (AHA) reassurance that "No animals were harmed in the making of this movie" only extends to living animals on set. It does not cover harms suffered by deceased animals used as props, costumes, or to cater to the production. Moreover, it does not extend to the ideological content of a movie, and therefore does not refer to harms that may be perpetuated by speciesist ideologies. Even notwithstanding the limitations of the AHA guarantee, the absence of easily accessible information remains problematic, and indicative of a wider problem for film and television production when it comes to critically representing veganism. A fully vegan production is arguably unachievable without forgoing the exploitation of living or dead nonhuman animals, and without explicitly making those decisions known in the course of production, promotion, distribution, and physical media or online streaming releases. However successful *Beatriz at Dinner* is as a vegan film, certainly in relation to the first six theses from Table 28.1, this lacuna about the production process is a crucial component for contextualizing media and its ability to evade enmeshment with nonhuman animal exploitation.

At the end of our analysis of *Year of the Dog*, we subverted a cathartic ending along similar lines to the previous paragraph, but returning to the narrative itself, *Beatriz at Dinner* subverts its own gesture toward catharsis: Beatriz leaves the party with a tow truck driver who collects her broken down car. As he drives away, she tells him "that man [Doug] killed my goat." He then asks him to pull over, and climbs down a cliff onto the shore, despite the driver's protestations, and walks into the sea. The implied suicide suggests defeat. While Beatriz dies, a cut scene shows the party guests laughing as they release wishing lanterns into the night sky, the waters of their ocean of privilege closing over the disruption of Beatriz's forgotten intrusion, discursively drowning her as she drowns herself. This narrative defeat though, arguably translates through the movie screen into its opposite for the audience. The neatness of a cathartic revenge ending would risk satisfying the viewer with a vicarious victory, thereby ending the story with quiescence—Beatriz would have done our work for us. Instead, Beatriz's fictional suicide may awaken and empower the Beatriz within us all.

Conclusion

Taking a cue from *Beatriz at Dinner*, our decision in focusing on Mike White's two films for the bulk of this chapter has been guided by a combination of methodological and ethical reasons. Methodologically, it enabled us to test the ideal type constructs in relation to "vegan" and not just "anti-vegan" media. Given the gender of the writer (White) and directors (White and Arteta) the films demonstrate that male filmmakers can tell stories that subvert male privilege and the privileges that intersect with it. However, a limitation of this chapter is the absence from it of "vegan" films written and directed by women and written by people of color. Furthermore, the brief overview of our previous research placed our relatively optimistic analysis of *Year of the Dog* and *Beatriz at Dinner* in the context of the swathe of anti-vegan media production. Optimism is tempered by the sober commercial reality of the vastly greater cultural penetration of anti-vegan cultural output. *Scott Pilgrim vs. the World* took $47,664,559 at the global box office, 66 percent of which was in the United States (Box Office Mojo). In its own terms, *Scott Pilgrim* was a commercial failure, losing money against its $60 million budget. However, taking box office receipts as a crude measure of cultural impact, *Scott Pilgrim's* "vegan" elitist trope had thirty times the commercial reach of Peggy Spade's earnest, quirky vegan character, and over six times the commercial reach of Beatriz's witness to neo-colonial, macho, human supremacism. *Scott Pilgrim* also found a much wider international audience outside the United States than either of Mike White's films discussed here. *Scott Pilgrim* itself is dwarfed by the cultural behemoths of Disney, et al., which our earlier research has found to be fairly close approximations to negative, anti-vegan ideal types which serve to legitimate and perpetuate the exploitation and destruction of other animals.

Given that anti-vegan cultural context, ethically, we wanted to offer some hope and inspiration to readers (whether vegan or not-yet vegan). As Peggy's story reminds us, being vegan in a non-vegan world is sometimes exhausting and traumatizing. For us, this includes repeatedly analyzing anti-vegan media over the course of many years and thereby regularly imbibing the ideological poison that justifies unimaginable violence. Being able to laugh along with some of Peggy's trials and tribulations is restorative (the dubious faces of her co-workers in a scene where she offers them vegan cupcakes resonated very deeply). As vegan authors, we feel that we owe a personal debt of gratitude to Mike White for giving us some renewed hope, for the possibility of producing and enjoying vegan media in a non-vegan world. While *Year of the Dog* was restorative, *Beatriz at Dinner* was energizing. The film can be watched as a dystopian critique of the present, and as such, an articulation of the scope of the task that confronts us in overcoming it. The particular gift of the film was to sharpen the focus on the intersectional source of "all tears"; rather than fragmenting our efforts across all the diverse manifestations of suffering that flow from oppression, our efforts can coalesce around opposing the common wellspring of oppression. The suffering of one cannot be leavened on the basis of ignoring or perpetuating the suffering of another.

Works cited

Adams, Carol J. *The Sexual Politics of Meat: A Feminist-Vegetarian Critical Theory*. 20th Anniversary ed., Continuum, 2010.
Almiron, Nuria, Cole, Matthew and Freeman, Carrie Packwood. "Critical Animal and Media Studies: Expanding the Understanding of Oppression in Communication Research." *European Journal of Communication*, vol. 33, no. 4, 2018, pp. 367–380. https://doi.org/10.1177/0267323118763937
Babe. Directed by Chris Noonan, Kennedy Miller Productions, 1995.
Beatriz at Dinner. Directed by Miguel Arteta, Killer Films and Bron Studios, 2017.
Doctor Who: Praxeus. Directed by Jamie Magnus Stone, BBC, 2020.
Box Office Mojo, "Beatriz at Dinner." *IMDbPro*, 2020a, https://www.boxofficemojo.com/release/rl3128591873/. Accessed April 9 2020.
Box Office Mojo, "Scott Pilgrim vs. the World." *IMDbPro*, 2020b, https://www.boxofficemojo.com/title/tt0446029/?ref_=bo_se_r_1. Accessed April 9 2020.

Box Office Mojo, "Year of the Dog." *IMDbPro*, 2020c, https://www.boxofficemojo.com/release/rl3128591873/. Accessed April 9 2020.

Chicken Run. Directed by Peter Lord and Nick Park, Aardman Animations, 2000.

Cole, Matthew. "'The Greatest Cause on Earth': The Historical Formation of Veganism as an Ethical Practice." *The Rise of Critical Animal Studies—From the Margins to the Centre*, edited by Nik Taylor and Richard Twine, Routledge, 2014, pp. 203–224.

Cole, Matthew and Morgan, Karen. "Vegaphobia: Derogatory discourses of veganism and the reproduction of speciesism in UK national newspapers." *British Journal of Sociology*, vol. 61, no. 1, 2011, pp. 134–153. https://doi.org/10.1111/j.1468-4446.2010.01348.x

Cole, Matthew, and Stewart, Kate. *Our Children and Other Animals: The Cultural Construction of Human–Animal Relations in Childhood*. Ashgate, 2014.

Cole, Matthew and Stewart, Kate. "'I need fish fingers and custard': The irruption and suppression of vegan ethics in *Doctor Who*." *Meat Culture*, edited by Annie Potts, Brill Publishing, 2016, pp. 198–221. https://doi.org/10.1163/9789004325852_012

Cole, Matthew and Stewart, Kate. "Socializing Superiority: The Cultural Denaturalization of Children's Relations with Animals." *International Research Handbook on ChildhoodNature: Assemblages of Childhood and Nature Research*, edited by Amy Cutter-McKenzie, Karen Malone and Elisabeth Barratt Hacking, Springer, 2018a, pp. 1237–1261. https://doi.org/10.1007/978-3-319-51949-4_66-1

Cole, Matthew and Stewart, Kate. "Speciesism Party: An Intersectional Vegan Critique of *Sausage Party*." *International Studies in Literature & Environment*, vol. 24, no. 4, 2018b, pp. 767–786. https://doi.org/10.1093/isle/isx075

Fires of Pompeii, The. Directed by Colin Teague, BBC, 2008.

Lion King, The. Directed by Roger Allers and Rob Minkoff, Walt Disney Feature Animation, 1994.

Malamud, Randy. "Looking at Humans Looking at Animals." *Critical Animal and Media Studies: Communication for Nonhuman Animal Advocacy*, edited by Nuria Almiron, Matthew Cole, and Carrie Packwood Freeman, Routledge, 2015, pp. 154–168.

Molloy, Clare. *Popular Media and Animals*. Palgrave Macmillan, 2011.

Sausage Party. Directed by Conrad Vernon and Greg Tiernan, Annapurna Pictures, Point Grey Pictures, Nitrogen Studios and Columbia Pictures, 2016.

Scott Pilgrim vs. the World. Directed by Edgar Wright, Marc Platt Productions, Big Talk Films, Closed on Mondays Entertainment and Dentsu, 2010.

Secret Life of Pets, The. Directed by Chris Renaud, Illumination Entertainment, 2016.

Stewart, Kate, and Cole, Matthew. "The Conceptual Separation of Food and Animals in Childhood." *Food, Culture and Society*, vol. 12, no. 4, 2009, pp. 457–476.

Stewart, Kate and Cole, Matthew. "Reproducing the Speciesist Boundaries of the Social: Cultural rupture in representations of 'urban foxes' in UK newspapers." *Critical Animal and Media Studies: Communication for Nonhuman Animal Advocacy*, edited by Nuria Almiron, Matthew Cole, and Carrie Packwood Freeman, Routledge, 2015, pp. 124–137.

Voyage of the Damned. Directed by James Strong, BBC, 2007.

Wright, Laura. "Dinner with Beatriz: The Enmeshed Rhetoric of Vegan Studies." *Through a Vegan Studies Lens: Textual Ethics and Lived Activism*, edited by Laura Wright, University of Nevada Press, 2019, pp. 257–269.

———. *The Vegan Studies Project: Food, Animals and Gender in The Age of Terror*. The University of Georgia Press, 2015.

Year of the Dog. Directed by Mike White, Plan B Entertainment, 2007.

29

Merchandizing veganism[1]

Simon C. Estok

One of the many things that is missing from all of the news about the 2020 coronavirus pandemic is the centrality of meat in the origins and initial spread of the pathogen. As with the swine flu and the avian flu (and their lethal subtypes), meat is the core origin of the Covid-19 pandemic, the *sine qua non* of human vulnerability to the death and unprecedented changes that the pathogen offers.[2] And yet, somehow, mainstream media and its personalities do not register that the pathogen found its way to humans through merchants of live and dead animals in filthy "wet markets."[3] Worse yet, mainstream media seems to enjoy pretending that all of this was unpredictable, unimaginable, and inevitable. "Unimaginable." That's the word CNN's Nic Robertson used to describe the streets of London on the 23rd of March 2020, following British Prime Minister Boris Johnson's "stay at home" order. But it *was* imagined. Danny Boyle's 2002 post-virus-apocalypse horror film *28 Days Later* shot scenes of desolate streets and thoroughfares in London—one of them Piccadilly Circus, precisely the spot Nic Robertson was surveying when he said that the images of desolation were unimaginable. To say that the current circumstance is unimaginable is simply dishonest. Mainstream media treatments of veganism are indeed rife with lies and misrepresentations that undermine both the ethical history and the voices that made the movement possible in the first place. Media treatments of meat-eating and veganism need serious attention—now more than ever—because the implications of these representations are increasingly matters of life and death. Through an analysis of Louie Psihoyos's 2018 documentary *The Game Changers* and discussion of the recent popularity of the Beyond Burger, this chapter examines the paradox of veganism as marketable merchandise and the media's tendency to obscure and misrepresent the history of veganism and ignore the structural issues linking meat-eating with gender, race, and class issues.

Until recently, mainstream media has had little interest in marketing veganism and has been unwelcoming to vegans. Mere mention of alternatives to meat-eating, for instance, has long been fodder for comedy—from the vegetarian restaurant in the 1955 movie *The Seven Year Itch* that Carol J. Adams describes "as an environment for cranks" (*Burger* 89) to Arnold Schwarzenegger telling Sylvester Stallone "you hit like a vegetarian" in the 2013 movie *Escape Plan*. The deaths of billions of animals per year for human consumption (upward of 60 billion) is an inconvenient truth for people who like to eat meat, and it is a fact that rarely (relatively speaking) appears in mainstream media. Even among people concerned about the environment, it has been hard to shake the market-driven frameworks of understanding that consumerist commercial media rains down upon us.

At the banquet for the 1999 Association for the Study of Literature and the Environment (ASLE) conference (the first I attended), veganism was unfashionable, and I was directed to lettuce when I inquired about food for vegetarians. I was surprised by this and by the plenitude of meat on offer. Odd, I thought, for scholars who claim to be concerned about the environment. Years later in an interview with Kip Anderson for the film *Cowspiracy*, Howard Lyman would articulate perfectly the position I also held and had held since becoming vegetarian in 1983: "You can't be an environmentalist and eat animal products. Period. Kid yourself if you want, if you want to feed your addiction, so be it, but don't call yourself an environmentalist." It is a point that Jonathan Safran Foer also makes in *Eating Animals*: "most simply put, someone who regularly eats factory-farmed animal products cannot call him [or her]self an environmentalist without divorcing that word from its meaning" (59). But I didn't have these authoritative voices with me in 1999, and I felt a bit out of my depth; moreover, I was still five years out from being vegan and was already feeling the heat. Even so, I decided to begin each conference talk with an off-hand question about how many vegetarians might be in the audience—and my talks always included something about meat. The opening question and the challenging of meat did not go unnoticed. Often people responded only to the "vegetarian question" in my talks, riled and apparently unable to focus on anything else. Within a decade, Scott Slovic was explaining in the Editor's Note to the Fall 2009 edition of *ISLE* that "Ecocritics who've been treated to one of Simon Estok's provocative conference presentations know very well that he tends to fish for audience responses, looking at listeners as he asks, 'How many of you are vegetarians? Let me see a show of hands'" ("Editor's Note" 681). As I have pointed out elsewhere,[4] I've never fished (and it is an ugly image to be associated with me). Not only are vegetarian options two decades later now fashionable at these conferences: meat isn't! Nevertheless, mocked in print, I stopped asking, but the resistance to people who offer such challenges keeps up.

Harold Fromm—one of the editors of the field-initiating *Ecocriticism Reader*—offers one example of intense response to vegan ethical practice and theorizing and argues vigorously in *The Chronicle of Higher Education* against vegans. Laura Wright explains in "Vegan Studies as Ecofeminist Intervention" that Fromm wrote to her about how he "stumbled" upon a reference she had made to his article. He claimed that the editors of *The Chronicle of Higher Education* had over-edited and misrepresented his original intentions. The article, however, is still available, and the damage it does continues. In it, Fromm claims that "Veganism, while perhaps harmless enough, especially if you don't care about being part of society or alienating potential friends who may find you more trouble than you're worth, fails on both counts [theory and practice]" (Fromm). The implication is that one cannot be a part of society if one is vegan. The power of marketing to mold both social relationships on the one hand and what passes as knowledge and truth—even among academics—on the other is formidable.

In a compelling book about post-truth, Lee McIntyre argues that one of the things pushing us away from saying the things that need to be said is "a desire not to offend our friends" (60) and that this leads to the kind of post-truth world in which we currently live. Saying things about meat at an eco-conference with a majority of meat-eaters is offensive. For Fromm, fear of alienating potential friends trumps ethical eating. Some might view this silencing as cowardice. Moreover, the "abandonment of evidential standards" (1) about which McIntyre speaks is flagrant in Fromm's rant, which offers a particularly shocking example of how, "when we are emotionally invested in a subject … our ability to reason well will probably be affected" (McIntyre 55). Post-publication regrets notwithstanding, one can only wonder what Fromm's original intentions were in his anti-vegan rant. Anyway, all of his comments against ethical veganism are easily countered.

The health benefits of a vegan diet have only recently become marketable data, but these benefits have nevertheless long been well known.[5] The environmental benefits have also long been well known.[6] In the opening pages of his colossal *The Bloodless Revolution: A Cultural History of Vegetarianism from 1600 to Modern Times*, Tristram Stuart notes that "in the era preceding the Industrial Revolution, the question of meat-eating was one of the fiercest battle-fronts in the struggle to define humanity's proper relationship with nature" (xvii). So what happened? How did the topic about meat-eating and humanity's relationships with nature become so obscure at a time when, more than ever before, such relationships had become so important? How is it that

> Veganism, which had enjoyed a mild and even at times positive reception during the preceding two decades, became at the dawn of the 21st century suspect in its sudden associations with fundamentalism, radicalism, and anti-government protest; [how is it that] in its deviation from the Standard American Diet (SAD), it appeared alien and dangerously ethnic, influenced by the dietary and political ideologies of the non-Western world. (Wright, Vegan Studies Project 42)?

And how is it, moreover, that by 2018, veganism had become "the most popular nutrition topic on social media" (Dahm and Freunde)? A search of Google trends reveals a more than 400 percent increase in searches for "vegan" from 2004 to 2019 (Figure 29.1).

At least part of what is at play in the rise of veganism, I would venture to say, is that social media has, to an important degree, wrested "food" as a topic out of the hands of mainstream media. It is a thesis that seems to have support from consumer surveys showing that "the exponential growth in the number of vegan consumers is only likely to continue due to the diet's high visibility in social media and popular culture in general" (see GlobalData 2018). As more and more millennials[7] tell their stories, talk about their foods, and post their pictures, the lies of companies that have been peddling untruths for so long simply will become untenable. And as more and more reports come out, veganism will gain more and more traction. When, for instance, GlobalData (2017) noted that "six percent of U.S. consumers now claim to be vegan, up from just one percent in 2014" in a blandly entitled "Top Trends in Prepared Foods 2017," the data was quickly snapped up and repackaged in much flashier garb: Maria Chiorando's headline for a June 26, 2017 article for plantbasednews.org reads "Veganism Skyrockets by 600 Percent In America To Six Percent Of Population." There is no question about it" that, as Professor of Food and Nutrition Fabio Parasecoli explains, "food has invaded the internet," allowing users to take control of the production and distribution of knowledge about food, "to post information and pictures about their meals and the dishes they cook, exchange tips about restaurants and stores, and discuss food related issues" (15). Parasecoli summarizes so well how

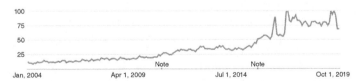

Figure 29.1 Google trends Vegan.

Source: *Google trends (10 April 2020).*

media also functions in producing confusion that his comments are worth quoting here at length: "Media organizations," he explains,

> often carry news about health, nutrition, and dieting as concerns about these topics intensify among their audiences. Always looking for exciting stories, writers, bloggers, and newscasters are quick to relay research results without providing any background information. Scientific studies are turned into simple, digestible tips that fit well into forms of communication that favor easy, well-defined explanations of complex topics. Readers are offered bits of unrelated news about this specific nutrient or that substance, without any systematic and thorough explanations. Journalists may opt for clear, simple, ready-to-apply pieces of advice and do-it-yourself recipes, avoiding complex issues and providing a mass of information that often stokes health-related fears. The deluge of piecemeal—at times even contradictory—suggestions from the media gives the impression that science cannot be trusted, with the consequence that consumers may end up heeding the opinions of friends, family, bloggers, influencers, and self-proclaimed experts (often co-opted and paid by special interests and the food industry itself). (67)

The snowballing of media is not to be underestimated, even when (perhaps particularly when) the merchandise is lies.

Admittedly, Millenials are the force behind the current move away from meat, but there is a history here that is getting short-shrift. A blog article boldly entitled "The Age of Veganism: Vegan Statistics for 2020" goes as far as to say that "all of this [the vegan movement] is thanks to, you guessed it, Millenials." In reality, however, "all of this" was made possible not by the Millenials but by the hard work of the vegetarians and vegans who preceded them. For James Wilks (former Mixed Martial Arts champ and narrator of the 2018 documentary film *The Game Changers*) to summon a host of professional athletes, actors, famous director, and doctors who claim to have discovered this "new" healthful diet and to state that "as groundbreaking as all of this nutritional science [is]," it is also "really confusing" is dishonest. To call it groundbreaking is dishonest as well. Perhaps the immediacy and the perceived ephemerality of social media valorizes the present at the expense of the past, but there is a history to arguments for being vegan, arguments that have only now become very marketable. Making similar arguments (but with a lot more dubious science behind them than the scholars and activists, feminists and ethicists, radicals and environmentalists before them), people such as Wilks have the money and means to do what many before them have struggled to do:[8] to get people to stop eating meat and animal products. But what is the cost of mainstreaming veganism? At the cost of consigning the very voices that made it all possible to the ephemerality of auditory debris, to muffling those voices out of history, and to silencing the women (and men) who set the stage for the changes now in play? And it is more than simple dishonesty at play here: there is also a creepy buttressing of some of the very things veganism stands against.

Part of what is involved in the merchandizing of veganism is an ethics of consumption and exploitation that plainly runs counter to the ethics of veganism itself. It's a bit of a Catch-22 here, and in a very real sense, the mainstreaming of veganism is incommensurable with vegan ideology itself. As Laura Wright has meticulously argued in reference to veganism, "as an ideology it is marked by conscious individual actions that nonetheless stand in stark opposition to the consumer mandate of U.S. capitalism, and for this reason, the actions of individual vegans pose a substantial—if symbolic—threat to such a paradigm" (22). Wright also indicates that one of the ways to resist co-optation of "vegan" by mainstream media is by having "a frame of reference from which to deconstruct the mainstream and media-based discourse that often depends upon and reinforces a singular yet constantly shifting conception of veganism" (23).

Greta Gaard argued almost a decade ago that "In the near future, ecofeminism and feminist ecocriticisms will need to articulate an interspecies focus within ecocriticism, bringing forward the vegetarian and vegan feminist threads that have been a developing part of feminist and ecological feminist theories since the nineteenth century" (651). That near future has come, as Wright and others are demonstrating. With the phenomenal recent growth of veganism in the United States and Canada, understanding what actually gets served up on the vegan plate has perhaps never been more important or timely. It is no secret that the remarkable recent merchandizing success of veggie burgers (such as the Impossible Whopper and Beyond Meat products) is owing in large part to the facts that "the packaging for these products don't include veggie or vegan anywhere on them" (Valinsky), and that the products are in the meat aisle rather than in the vegetable section. The distancing from vegetal realities is a clear marketing bonus, as *The Game Changers* makes plain: CNN's Daniel Gallan explains that "terms like veganism and vegetarianism are deliberately avoided" (Gallan).[9] What is fascinating about this film and the men who produced and star in it (as with the people who make and market the new meatless burgers that are currently in vogue) is not just that they all come across as having discovered (or re-discovered) something no one else knew about; they do something more disturbing: in actively asserting a muscular veganism dripping in machismo and testosterone, a film such as *The Game Changers* seems to re-write vegan histories as some sort of specifically *male* discovery dating back to the time of the gladiators (referenced at the outset of the film).[10] The combined disavowal of women in vegan and vegetarian histories, the disavowal of vegetal realities, and the notion that veganism is a new (or re-discovered) thing is deeply problematical for the ecophobia and sexism that it serves up.

Wright begins an important exploration of "the discourse surrounding perceptions of male veganism—particularly the ultramasculine category of 'heganism'—and the cultural backlash against a perceived crisis in masculinity that such an identity category has engendered" (108).[11] Wright contextualizes the various cultural resistances to narratives linking meat with masculinity—representations of "women who aspired to enter the hallowed all-male realm" (115) where meat consumption reigns supreme, the men who reject meat and maintain their strength, the growth of a classed vegan industry, and so on. It is important to note, in addition to these observations, that we've moved beyond men maintaining their sense of masculinity without meat to assertions that such an identity is, in fact, better fostered by an entirely plant-based diet. And this is where the problems begin. In the main, there have been three reasons to go vegan in the past (health, ethics, and environment), and arguments against any of these have been relatively easy to counter. The new marketing strategies (which are very successful in producing results) are much more dangerous than the deniers—the Fromms, the climate deniers, and the mockers. Marketing manliness and machismo via veganism is a great step backward and a disservice to the very anti-sexism that veganism stands for.

Certainly, meat and vegetables have long been gendered, but placing veggie patties in the meat section of supermarkets not only fails to address the problem: it accentuates and reifies the problem by re-gendering vegetables and, in the process, implicitly denying their very vegetality. If this assertion seems a stretch, then perhaps we need to look more closely at the target audience of *The Game Changers* along with the target consumers of the new veggie burgers (and I for one am not entirely comfortable with calling them meatless burgers, since, as I will show, this rhetorical strategy seems to play into a misogynist and ecophobic narrative). So while the CEO of Beyond Meat has said repeatedly that vegetarians are not the target (which makes sense, since we all—we vegans and vegetarians—want to see meat-eaters become vegetarian or vegan), putting the product into an aisle so loaded with misogyny seems to taint the food. Ethical vegans don't go down meat aisles. Meatless burgers implicitly target men who get their food from the meat aisle. But *The Game Changers* plays even more unmistakably to the defensive machismo.

The Game Changers

The Game Changers falls into the category of what Wright presciently describes as "attempts to reconceptualize veganism as an alternative ultramasculine choice" (*The Vegan Studies Project* 124). The film is all about high-performance athletes and the importance of a vegan diet. It uses (or at least gestures toward some) science. It undoes a lot of misinformation about how to get proteins. It refutes claims that vegetarians and vegans are weak. To be fair, so far, so good. At the same time, however, it is a documentary dripping muscular veganism, replete—as if in parody of itself—with a penis measuring scene! Three men consent to measuring their penises after eating meat and again after eating only vegetables, all under the supervision of Dr. Aaron Spitz of the American Urological Association. Result? Eat veggies and your penis will grow bigger and harder for longer periods of time. If you don't have a penis, then you are probably not the intended audience to whom this film is marketing its message about virile veganism and muscular heterosexuality.[12]

Like the veggie burgers in the meat section, a film such as *The Game Changers* can only leave a person with very mixed feelings. On the one hand, it is doing what so many of us have been failing to do for so many years: it is reaching those men who eat meat, and it is making them think long enough about the subject to possibly question and change their behaviors. On the other hand, it is making them do it for all of the wrong reasons—reasons that got us into factory farms and Covid-19 in the first place. Changing male meat-eaters into vegans through arguments and visions that continue a focus on the all-important penis will not, I suspect, change the structures that have caused the problems. If, as Wright has claimed, "veganism has gained a foothold as a means to masculine physical strength and prowess" (144), then it has done so with a vengeance in *The Game Changers*—a vengeance with implications.

I choose my words carefully here, since what is going on with the mainstreaming of veganism very often *does* seem to involve a kind of vengeance against the very things that so many vegans have also been fighting against. The reformulation of "vegetarian" and "vegan" as "meatless" and "plant-based" and the implied backlash against feminism, against environmentalism, and, indeed, against veganism itself here is clear. Nature is the absent referent here, and the hegan stands alone. Moreover, as Wright observes, "male veganism only seems acceptable if it is *not* linked to animal welfare" and that "we are left without many positive representations of male veganism as predicated upon an animal-liberation or animal-rights ethic" (129). Rather than confronting the misogyny implied in the equations between meat and masculinity, current trends reiterate it; rather than challenging the exploitative nature of the meat industry, current trends transfer it to veganism (and veggies are the resource to strengthen your dick); rather than addressing the core issues, current trends are addressing the symptoms. The "profound denunciation of vegetarian and vegan diets as indicators of weakness, ethnicity, and femininity" that Wright describes (114) in 2015 has by 2018 morphed into a *celebration* of vegetarian and vegan diets as indicators of *triumph* over weakness, ethnicity, and femininity; the structure and ultimate victims of the hegan are the same as they were with the old flesh-chomping he-men. Meet the new. Same as the old.[13] *The Game Changers*, like Burger King's 2006 "Manthem" commercial that Wright skillfully unpacks, "implies that women have actually oppressed men and that men need to be liberated" (119).

The heroic male works alone when not working *against* others, and the notion of interdependence and cooperation is the very antithesis of this model. In this sense, muscular veganism (of the sort embodied in films such as *The Game Changers* and in its executive producers Jackie Chan and Arnold Schwarzenegger, or vegans such as convicted rapist and former boxer Mike Tyson) is more part of the problem than solution, more part of a fight against anything that it is not than an attempt to work together toward solutions. It is a position that at core does not embrace but rejects ecological thinking. We call such a rejection ecophobia. Muscular male veganism, moreover, at its core rejects women[14] and feminist thinking. We call such a position sexism.

It is bizarre, surreal, and uncanny to hear Arnold Schwarzenegger, of all people, making some of the same arguments as Carol J. Adams pioneeringly made, and later that a long list of other people (including Deane Curtin, Laura Wright, Greta Gaard, Josephine Donovan, Lori Gruen, Marti Kheel, Deborah Slicer, myself, and others) have also made in reference to the work of Adams, work on which we have sometimes built and always benefited—arguments about "the sexual politics of meat" (the phrase comes from Adams) "selling the idea that real men eat meat." The second quote in the previous sentence is—startlingly—from Schwarzenegger, and of course, he does not reference Adams or the many other feminists who have made such observations. It is almost as if he (and the rest of the narrators in the film) thinks that this idea is new, a discovery of clearly nonfeminist men. The notions that veganism is new, that the health benefits of it are an original insight (and a clearly muscular male discovery), and that meatlessness is great (with the absent referent being vegetables and all of the nature that they imply)—these are not game changers. But the pandemic of sexism infecting veganism *is* new—and dangerous. Mazel tov that meat-eating men all over America (and maybe the world) might stop eating meat and start going vegan, but the reasons are important. While much of the discourse of heganism confirms Wright's claim that "these power males became vegan *after* establishing their prowess and power while they were eating meat" (126), *The Game Changers* is directly resisting this and arguing that men can only really be strong alpha males *if* they are vegan. It is the very point of the film.

The recent success of veggie burgers and the sudden growing acceptance of vegetable diets for men *may* have very good effects; however, it seems that to have such hope in the current trends—in what we might call the new veganism—is to fall victim to a deceptively sexist and ecophobic guiding narrative. As environmental issues exponentially worsen, it is increasingly difficult to believe our self-consolations that we are achieving very much in terms of actually slowing, halting, or reversing the global devastation we are causing, and it is more urgent than ever to understand that ecophobia and sexism may very well be at the core of what seems so good and right, so promising and progressive, so long overdue and so necessary. After all, the most immediate thing we can do (in addition to writing and talking to each other about the issues) is to stop participating in animal agriculture: if everyone became vegan today, the world would be better tomorrow—except that the core problems of sexism and ecophobia would remain. Among the lessons we must learn in the Trump era, Lee McIntyre explains, "is that one must always fight back against lies" (155). My worry is about how the absent referents, the omissions, the conceptual occlusions, the motives, and the ethics of the new veganism reiterate dangerous lies.

The value of "a vegan theoretical analysis," Wright argues in "Doing Vegan Studies" is that it helps us not get fooled: it "works to draw attention to absences and silencings—of animals and of humans—in texts that ostensibly may have nothing to do with veganism" (xvii). And let's face it: *The Game Changers* has nothing to do with veganism. Veganism is not only about what we eat. It is more than simply a dietary matter. Veganism, Carol J. Adams explains, also involves "resisting the regressive, anti-environmental, misogynistic, and anti-free speech" philosophies and legislation of people such as Mr. Trump ("Sexual Politics of Meat during the Trump Era" 66). It involves recognizing "the fallacies of an ahistorical teleology" (*ibid*). *The Game Changers* is not about veganism. Similarly, much of mainstream media coverage of veganism is just about the food rather than the ethics and lifestyle choices involved. Veganism and sexism are simply incommensurable. You can't be a vegan and not be a feminist: a vegan who is not a feminist is just a person who doesn't eat animal products. Vegan theoretical analyses of media representations of veganism are more urgent than ever *because* they draw attention to the "absences and silencings" and to how these are increasingly putting human lives (and all other lives) in mortal danger. To call things "unimaginable" that were imagined, and to pretend to discover things long known and silenced—these are mainstream media crimes that vegan theoretical analyses bring to light.

Notes

1 This chapter is a much-expanded version of my "Theorizing Ecophobia on a Vegan Plate" (forthcoming in *Ecozon@*, vol. 11, no. 2, Autumn 2020).
2 It is also important to remember that Covid-19, like the Black Death before it, is an environmental event. In his *Environmental History of Medieval Europe*, Richard Hoffmann explains that the Black Death was "the largest ecological and demographic event in pre-modern European history" (289). Citing Hoffmann, medievalist Shawn Normandin argues that the social effects of the pandemic—the disappearance of villages, the collapse of economies, changes in agricultural practices, and so on—had profound effects that we can, to some degree, chart in the literature of the time (see Normandin, esp. pp. 1–50). The Covid-19 pandemic is a meat-based environmental catastrophe.
3 Certainly, there has been *some* coverage of this in mainstream media, with articles recognizing "wet markets" as the source of Covid-19 (see Greenfield), understanding that zoonotic leaping of viruses from animals to humans will continue at such places (see Davies), and calling for bans on markets with wild animals (see Bosley).
4 See *The Ecophobia Hypothesis*, p. 19, note 25.
5 On the on reduced incidence of obesity in vegan diets, see Clarys et al.; on cardiovascular benefits and reduced risks of type 2 diabetes among people who live a vegan lifestyle, see Le & Sabaté, and Esselstyn et al.; on the overall health benefits of a vegan diet, see Johansson and Larsson; and on the reduced risks of cancers, see Dinu et al. There are, in reality, mountains of references on the benefits of a vegan diet—far too many to include here.
6 It is hard to argue against the idea eloquently summarized by Tony Weis in *The Ecological Hoofprint* that directly consuming the product of photosynthetic activity is a fundamental part of the radical new ecological efficiencies that will be needed to contain the magnitude of change in the Anthropocene and sustainably feed an increasingly urbanized world of 7 going on 9+ billion people. (153)
Again, there are thousands too many references to cite here that prove the ecological friendliness of a vegan diet.
7 According to an article in *Forbes* by Michael Rowland, "millennials are driving the worldwide shift away from meat" (see Rowland).
8 Executive producers of *The Game Changers* include James Cameron, Arnold Schwarzenegger, Jackie Chan, Pamela Anderson, and 20 others.
9 James Wilks, one of the film's producers (himself a former UFC fighter) explains that there is a stigma attached to being vegan and that he, like many other people, see the vegan as (in his words), a "skinny, long-haired hippie—[a] tree hugging [person who] lives in a commune."
10 In the film, Schwarzenegger even states outrageously that "fifty years ago, no one talked about hey maybe you should just get your protein from vegetables," but this is not true on any level. Fifty years ago, and many years before (as the film itself states in reference to the gladiators), there were such people saying that vegetables provide all that we need.
11 On the origins and definition of the term "hegan," see Wright (126).

12 Vegan sexuality has been the topic of study before, notably in Annie Potts and Jovian Parry's "Vegan Sexuality: Challenging Heteronormative Masculinity through Meat-Free Sex." In this article, Potts and Parry note that there are "powerful links between meat-eating, masculinity, and virility in western societies" (53) but that "the 'real' manliness (and sexuality) of vegetarian and vegan men typically comes under scrutiny by men who eat meat" (58). It seems that in *The Game Changers*, there is a shift in who is analyzing what, and it is vegan men (or supporters of vegan men) who scrutinize vegan male sexuality—but in the most crudely unnuanced of terms. For Spitz, it all boils down to erections, it seems. Not very delicate reasoning or discussion here.
13 My reference here with the old and the new is *The Who* song "Won't Get Fooled Again."
14 I do not mean to suggest that top ranking athletes are only men, but I am unaware of experiments correlating female sexuality with vegetables: the dick measuring of *The Game Changers* has no clitoral parallel to my knowledge.

Works cited

Adams, Carol J. *Burger*. Bloomsbury, 2018.
——. "The Sexual Politics of Meat in the Trump Era." *Through a Vegan Lens: Textual Ethics and Lived Activism*, edited by Laura Wright, University of Nevada Press, 2019, pp. 51–67.
Boseley, Sarah. "Calls for global ban on wild animal markets amid coronavirus outbreak." *The Guardian*, 24 January 2020. https://www.theguardian.com/science/2020/jan/24/calls-for-global-ban-wild-animal-markets-amid-coronavirus-outbreak
Chiorando, Maria. "Veganism Skyrockets by 600% In America to 6% of Population, Claims Report The lifestyle is gaining traction." *Plant Based News*, 26 June 2017. https://www.plantbasednews.org/culture/veganism-skyrockets-by-600-in-america-over-3-years-to-6-of-population
Clarys, Peter, Deliens, Tom, Huybrechts, Inge, Deriemaeker, Peter, Vanaelst, Barbara, De Keyzer, Willem, Hebbelinck, Marcel, and Mullie, Patrick. "Comparison of Nutritional Quality of the Vegan, Vegetarian, Semi-Vegetarian, Pesco-Vegetarian and Omnivorous Diet." *Nutrients*, vol. 6, no. 3, 2014, pp. 1318–1332.
Cowspiracy: The Sustainability Secret. Directed by Kip Andersen and Keegan Kuhn, Appian Way Productions, A.U.M. Films, First Spark Media, 2014.
Critical Reviews in Food Science and Nutrition, vol. 57, no. 17, 2017, pp. 3640–3649.
Dam and Freunde Blog. "Veganism is the Most Popular Nutrition Topic on Social Media." *Vegconomist: The Vegan Business Magazine*, 7 September 2018. https://vegconomist.com/society/veganism-is-the-most-popular-nutrition-topic-on-social-media/
Davies, Dave. "New Coronavirus 'Won't Be the Last' Outbreak to Move from Animal to Human." Goats and Soda: Stories of Life in a Changing World. *NPR (National Public Radio)*. 5 February 2020. https://www.npr.org/sections/goatsandsoda/2020/02/05/802938289/new-coronavirus-wont-be-the-last-outbreak-to-move-from-animal-to-human
Dinu, Monica, Abbate, Rosanna, Gensini, Gianfranco, and Casini, Alessandro. "Vegetarian, vegan diets and multiple health outcomes: A systematic review with meta-analysis of observational studies." *Critical Reviews in Food Science and Nutrition*, vol. 57, no. 17, 2017, pp. 3640–3649.
Esselstyn Jr, Caldwell B., Gendy, Gina, Doyle, Jonathan, Golubic, Mladen, and Roizen, Michael F. "A way to reverse CAD?" *Journal of Family Practice*, vol. 63, no. 7, 2014, pp. 356–364.
Estok, Simon C. *The Ecophobia Hypothesis*. Routledge, 2018.
Foer, Jonathan Safran. *Eating Animals*. Little and Brown, 2009.
Fromm, Harold. "Vegans and the Quest for Purity." *The Chronicle of Higher Education*, 4 July 2010. www.chronicle.com/article/Vegansthe-Quest-for/66090/? sid¼cr.
Gaard, Greta. "New Directions for Ecofeminism: Toward a More Feminist Ecocriticism." *ISLE: Interdisciplinary Studies in Literature and Environment*, vol. 17, no. 4, 2010, pp. 643–665.
Gallan, Daniel. "Macho vegans: The documentary that's changing the script on plant-based diets." *CNN*, 19 December 2019. https://edition.cnn.com/2019/12/18/sport/game-changers-documentary-james-wilks-spt-intl/index.html
GlobalData. "Top Trends in Prepared Foods 2017: Exploring trends in meat, fish and seafood; pasta, noodles and rice; prepared meals; savory deli food; soup; and meat substitutes." *Report Buyer*, June 2017. https://www.reportbuyer.com/product/4959853/top-trends-in-prepared-foods-2017-exploring-trends-in-meat-fish-and-seafood-pasta-noodles-and-rice-prepared-meals-savory-deli-food-soup-and-meat-substitutes.html

GlobalData. "Quorn's investments in vegan foods is further evidence that veganism successfully captures consumers' secondary dieting concerns." *GlobalData*, 25 July 2018. https://www.globaldata.com/quorns-investments-vegan-foods-evidence-veganism-successfully-captures-consumers-secondary-dieting-concerns/

Greenfield, Patrick. "Ban wildlife markets to avert pandemics, says UN biodiversity chief." *The Guardian*, 6 April 2020. ban-live-animal-markets-pandemics-un-biodiversity-chief-age-of-extinction

+Health Careers. "The Age of Veganism: Vegan Statistics for 2020." *+Health Careers*. 7 January 2020. https://healthcareers.co/vegan-statistics/

Hoffmann, Richard C. *An Environmental History of Medieval Europe*. Cambridge University Press, 2014.

Johansson, Gunnar K., and Larsson, Christel. "Dietary intake and nutritional status of young vegans and omnivores in Sweden." *The American Journal of Clinical Nutrition*, vol. 76, no. 1, 2002, pp. 100–106.

Le, Lap Tai and Sabaté, Joan. "Beyond Meatless, the Health Effects of Vegan Diets: Findings from the Adventist Cohorts." *Nutrients*, vol. 6, no. 6, 2014, pp. 2131–2147.

McIntyre, Lee. *Post-Truth*. The MIT Press, 2018.

Normandin, Shawn. *Chaucerian Ecopoetics: Deconstructing Anthropocentrism in the Canterbury Tales*. Palgrave Macmillan, 2018.

Parasecoli, Fabio. *Food*. MIT Press, 2019.

Potts, Annie, and Jovian Parry. "Vegan Sexuality: Challenging Heteronormative Masculinity through Meat-free Sex." *Feminism Psychology*, vol. 20, no. 1, February 2010, pp. 53–72.

Rowland, Michael Pellman. "Millennials are Driving the Worldwide Shift Away From Meat." *Forbes*, 23 March 2018. https://www.forbes.com/sites/michaelpellmanrowland/2018/03/23/millennials-move-away-from-meat/#3648d9dda4a4

Slovic, Scott. "Editor's Note." *ISLE*, vol. 16, no. 4, 2009, pp. 681–684.

Stuart, Tristram. *The Bloodless Revolution: A Cultural History of Vegetarianism from 1600 to Modern Times*. Norton, 2006.

The Game Changers. Directed by Louie Psihoyos, ReFuel Productions, 2018.

The Who. "Won't Get Fooled Again." By Pete Townshend, *Who's Next*, Decca, 1971.

Valinsky, Jordan. "Beyond Burgers are coming to Costco." *CNN*, 6 December 2019. https://edition.cnn.com/2019/12/05/business/beyond-meat-costco/index.html

Weis, Tony. *The Ecological Hoofprint: The Global Burden of Industrial Livestock*. Zed, 2013.

Wright, Laura. "Doing Vegan Studies: An Introduction." *Through a Vegan Lens: Textual Ethics and Lived Activism*, edited by Laura Wright. University of Nevada Press, 2019, pp. vii–xxiv.

———. *The Vegan Studies Project: Food, Animals, and Gender in the Age of Terror*. University of Georgia Press, 2015.

———. "Vegan Studies as Ecofeminist Intervention." *Ecozon@*, vol. 11, no. 2, 2020, pp. 101–108.

30
"Friends don't let friends eat tofu"
A rhetorical analysis of fast food corporation "anti-vegan-options" advertisements

Erin Trauth

Introduction

Vegan and vegetarian diets are on the rise worldwide, gaining mainstream acceptance among a wide range of demographics. While there are many ways to achieve optimum health, many experts posit that nutrition may be one of the most impactful ways to increase human health outcomes and reduce risk for disease. A 2017 *Critical Reviews in Food Science and Nutrition* study found that reducing or eliminating animal products through either a vegetarian or vegan diet could have a significant impact on reducing risks for two major disease groups, including heart disease and total cancer (Dinu et al. 3640).

As the number of vegans is growing worldwide, fast and fast-casual food corporations in the United States have reacted in a number of ways. Some have seemingly embraced the growing vegan market, offering expanded plant-based options and advertisements promoting them; in 2019 alone, Carl's Jr., Red Robin, Burger King, Qdoba, TGIFridays, and Del Taco, among other fast or fast-casual establishments, debuted their own meat-and-dairy-free options (Tyko). As part of its recent rebranding efforts, Olive Garden, long known for its meaty Italian menu, revealed its new vegan menu offerings. The choice of multinational food chains to move beyond a "vegan salad option" and offer a wider range of options for vegan eaters adds to the evidence that veganism might be on track to garner even more widespread accommodation by the corporations serving meals to at least one in three people in the United States every day (Centers for Disease Control). However, despite gains in vegetarian and vegan offerings, the majority of U.S. citizens are still primarily carnivorous or omnivorous; a 2016 Harris Poll found that 3.3 percent of U.S. citizens are vegetarian, and about half that number are vegan, meaning some 96 percent of the country still consumes meat and dairy products at least some of the time (Harris).

Understanding these numbers, and thus knowing the prevailing consumer base's preferences for animal products, some fast food corporations have ostensibly countered against the "vegan options" movement under a veil of humor; for example, in 2015, McDonald's aired commercials proclaiming: "All vegetarians…kindly avert your eyes. You can't get juiciness like this from soy or quinoa…" as a giant Big Mac hovered on the screen. In 2017, Arby's aired commercials asking: "Are you a vegetarian? Do you struggle with urges to find and devour this meat?" as an image of bacon simmering on a grill takes over the screen. The narrator encourages viewers to call the "Arby's Vegetarian Support Hotline" at 1-855-MEAT-HLP (which routes to a recorded message promoting brown sugar bacon products). And in 2018, Arby's revealed a print advertisement campaign centered on the message: "Friends don't let friends eat tofu. Just eat meat." In May 2019, Hardee's debuted a new video advertisement campaign, "Save the Veggies," which "jokes" about veggies in the vein of animal welfare campaigns. Advertisements such as the Arby's and Hardee's campaigns have varied impacts on vegan viewers, ranging from those that seem to take little offense, noting the "playful" and subsequently "harmless" nature of the ads, while others comment that they feel offended or even marginalized, resulting in some decreeing all-out bans of such establishments. Mocking people for their dietary choices is not a new phenomenon, and the technique has been used worldwide by a variety of food companies and restaurants to get more people in their doors—sometimes with major consequences. Polls have shown that consumers will choose not to buy from a brand if they find even one advertisement from the company to be distasteful: a 2010 Adweek Media/Harris Interactive poll found that more than one-third of Americans (35 percent) have refrained from purchasing from a certain brand if they found an advertisement distasteful; another 22 percent say they have not refrained from purchasing from said companies after seeing a distasteful ad but have considered it ("Hardee's Gets"). Often, people choose to commit to a vegan lifestyle for rather serious and deeply personal reasons: whether for preserving health, protecting against major disease, saving the planet's resources, or saving the lives of countless animals, the motives are typically not insignificant. It seems obvious that for so many, then, being prodded for a daily life decision—or even a daily necessity—would not be taken lightly. Further, the influences of media penetrate deeply into the choices and policies of our cultures; as such, every time a vegan or vegetarian diet is mocked in mainstream culture, it is important that we pay particular attention to how this could influence those who are most vulnerable and impressionable.

Food allergies are an example of how dietary restrictions have been subject to prodding in various streams of media (Abo et al. 803). Though those making the jokes often claim that they are "all in good fun," this rhetoric, over time, can take hold and impact real situations. Janis Goldie writes, "all artifacts of media culture, are simultaneously constructing and replicating meanings about people, events, and issues in our lives." When food allergies are mocked in popular culture, they are "represented as an insignificant, unimportant, self-induced, and individual problem or concern. In addition, those that have food allergies are portrayed as weak, ridiculous and incapable of coping with life's various, often every day, threats" (Goldie 4). Further, over time, "implied meanings from popular culture can have real-life effects on people, institutions, and policies" (Goldie 4). Extrapolating this idea to mocking vegans, then, particularly those who might opt for a vegan diet for health reasons, we can see how a simple "joke" can take hold in a negative way.

In *Rhetoric, Humor, and the Public Sphere: From Socrates to Stephen Colbert*, Elizabeth Benacka writes that "categorizing humor as a rhetorical discourse means that it has the potential to influence public opinion" (1). In communication theory-based humor research, three theories of humor typically emerge: relief, incongruity, and superiority (Meyer 310). Some public reactions to advertisements mocking plant-based eating seem to center on a feeling of "winning" or having "strength" that a vegan supposedly might not be able to achieve due to an alleged deficiency. Meyer writes that through the superiority theory of humor, "people laugh outwardly or inwardly at others because they feel some sort of triumph over them or feel superior in some way to them" (310). Through its transmission, the rhetorical functions of humor can serve to differentiate and divide groups, leading to feelings of harmony with those who agree and feelings of aggression against the "outsiders" (310). Humor, then, "also may conceal malice or allow the expression of aggression without the consequences possible from direct confrontation" (Meyer

317). Add to this situation the layer of protection offered by communication in digital spaces, and the stage is set for inflammatory conversations about vegans and vegan options in response to "joke" advertisements.

When we consider the pre-existing audiences for advertisements from corporations such as Arby's and Hardee's, particularly in social media settings where users self-select many of the messages and ads they might receive through their own profiles, we can also posit that many of these viewers might already have a predilection for carnivorous food options and perhaps hold a predisposed disagreement with those seeking primarily vegan options, since vegans would be the "outsider" in these instances. In these cases, "an audience in strong disagreement with a subject of humor, even with great familiarity with the issue, will experience differentiation through humor use" and, consequently, "the differentiation function of humor serves rhetors by making clear divisions and oppositions among opinions, people, and groups" (Meyer 323).

When multi-million-dollar, multinational restaurant corporations use humor and isolation (in the form of a public declaration that it will not cater to this group's dietary preferences and needs, as Arby's continues to convey) to sell products at the expense of one major and growing group of food consumers (vegans), the corporations are also, in a sense, making a public argument that that group is inferior to meat-eaters, thus permeating public discourse, opinion, and subsequent actions with potentially negative notions about vegans—no matter if the message is "harmless" or "just an ad" or "meant to be funny."

In this chapter, I provide a discussion of two "anti-vegan-options" campaigns presented through "humorous" advertisements from major U.S. fast-food chains Hardee's and Arby's. I examine the types of humor employed and discuss the rhetorical impacts of this humor, as foregrounded in communication studies. I also examine public responses to these communications, both from people defending the corporations and from those decreeing offense, focusing my discussion on the "veganism dichotomy" this rhetoric propagates and the subsequent implications for those who might be vegan-curious but hesitant for sociocultural reasons. In providing this discussion, I seek to capture a portion of the current rhetoric of "anti-vegan-options" discourses embodied by these ad campaigns, as well as an understanding of the tangible impacts this rhetoric might have on various stakeholders in the future.

Hardee's "Save the Veggies" campaign

Hardee's, part of CKE Restaurant Holdings, Inc., operates more than 1800 restaurants in 40 U.S. locations and ten international locations. The Hardee's brand contributes a significant portion of the fast-food market, holding strong as a continual staple in the Standard American Diet (SAD).

Interestingly, Hardee's officials claim the brand has been making moves to distance its branding from sister company Carl's Jr, which is known for raunchy advertisements, often with bikini-clad models eating cheeseburgers and the like. In a 2018 press release, Jason Marker, CEO of CKE Holdings, announced that Hardee's would make moves to further distance itself from provocative and potentially inflammatory advertising campaigns, instead moving in the direction of a wholesome, down-home image. Jeff Jenkins, Hardees' CMO, said "No fast food brand has 'comfort culture' more core to its DNA than Hardee's…we're going to use this new campaign to introduce customers to 'comfort culture' at Hardee's, placing a heavy emphasis on local pride and quality food."

In April 2019, Hardee's debuted a new advertising campaign to U.S. outlets, titled "Save the Veggies." In a video advertisement, a somber soundtrack plays as the camera pans in on a woman, dressed in what purportedly could be farmer's clothing, walking through a vegetable farm. "Every day," she says, "thousands of innocent vegetables are consumed each day across America."

On screen, a knife cuts through various vegetables. "But it doesn't have to be like this," the woman continues. "You can help save a veggie. Get two delicious Hardee's original roast beef sandwiches for just five dollars…not a slice of tomato or a leaf of lettuce in sight." The camera pans in on the woman biting into a beef sandwich, and she asks, "Won't you help save the veggies?"

The campaign is what many call a "tongue-in-cheek" play on the rhetorical techniques used by countless organizations over the past several decades to promote animal welfare, vegetarianism, and veganism, including organizations such as People for the Ethical Treatment of Animals (PETA) and the Society for the Prevention of Cruelty to Animals (SPCA), among others. Perhaps the most well known of all the campaigns, and the campaign that the Hardee's "Save the Veggies" campaign seeks to mimic in its choice of tone, audio, and even phrasing in some cases, is a well-known 2007 British Columbia (BC) SPCA campaign featuring singer-songwriter Sarah McLachlan. While her somber song, "Angel," plays in the background, several dogs and cats—some with obvious signs of neglect or abuse shown on their bodies—are featured in the video advertisement. McLachlan, while petting a yellow retriever, says:

> Will you be an angel for a helpless animal? Every day innocent animals are abused, beaten, and neglected. And they are crying out for help…join the BC SPCA with a monthly gift right now…You'll help rescue animals from their abusers… Right now there is an animal who needs you. Your call says I'm here to help. Please call right now.

While McLachlan pleads for our help, several other abused or neglected animals are shown. The commercial ends with a dog looking somberly into the camera.

The 2019 Hardee's commercial makes some obvious nods to the BC SPCA campaign, particularly in its script. The "tongue-in-cheek" rhetorical question by Hardee's—"Won't you help save the veggies?"—aligns directly with McLachlan's serious question in the BC SPCA campaign: "Will you be an angel for a helpless animal?"

The BC SPCA Sarah McLachlan campaign received national attention for its haunting images and provocative use of pathos to prompt action from viewers. Images of dirty and sad-looking animals, kittens missing eyes, and the subdued tone of McLachlan's background song as well as her impassioned tenor while reading the script made for a memorable—and, for many, an impactful—plea. Since its debut in 2007, this campaign proved the most successful fundraising campaign ever made by SPCA, bringing some $30 million back to the organization (Lefave).

The Hardee's campaign, however, did more to inflame audiences and help add to the differentiation between plant-based eaters and meat eaters. To help illustrate this fact, I turn to a brief sample of consumer responses to the ad on Hardee's social media sites (primarily Twitter for this campaign, as most of the consumer reactions happened on this platform):

> On April 29, 2019, Twitter user @user47 wrote: "Stop… alienating those who want an alternative to meat. You can and must do better."
>
> On May 5, 2019, Twitter user @WayfarerMarine1 wrote: "Noticed how you started your commercial like it was either regarding tortured and neglected animals or starving children… Damn."
>
> On May 5, 2019, Twitter user @lisaobrien111 wrote: "You sound ridiculous making a mockery of the poor innocent animals that suffer…Animals really do suffer."
>
> On May 7, 2019, Twitter user @dkh9353 wrote: "Your new ad campaign is immoral. To equate the slaughter of animals to vegetables sickens me…"

Some viewers, on the other hand, praised its creativity and "avoidance of being politically correct ("PC")." On May 2, 2019, Twitter user @ JohnWil66453546 wrote: "I think they are brilliant. More of this, because it will go viral. People are tired of the PC stuff." Then, on May 6, 2019, an additional video advertisement by "The Miz," a World Wrestling Entertainment character, debuted on Twitter, reiterating the "save the veggies" message, further fanning the flames.

Adding in phrasing that alludes to language frequently utilized by ethical vegans to argue against animal cruelty and butchery, The Miz writes that he "can't help but shed a tear when [he hears] about the *senseless slaughter* of thousands of vegetables every day." By referencing the "senseless slaughter" of vegetables, this tweet takes the Hardee's message a step further, playing on the ultimate end-of-life narrative ethical vegans often use to argue for vegan diets. Most of The Miz's Twitter audience showed delight and support, expressing that the ad was "hilarious" or celebrating the potentially "triggering" nature of the ad for actual vegans. Lorenz writes that "laughter forms a bond and simultaneously draws a line" (253), and the comments to this video illustrate this notion well. One user, the @The_Ghost_YT10, claimed superiority of "meat-gans"—another user, @Spardisjx, suggested followers commit "vegicide."

Others chimed in opposition to the video; for example, on May 13, 2019, Twitter user @benshelley1956 wrote: "…Some sick ad agency dreamed this up. They should be fired and Hardee's CEO should resign." On May 7, 2019, Twitter user @TheChrisShepard wrote: "Belittling the abuse and suffering of factory farmed animals for a stupid ad campaign for a company that actively profits from the exploitation of the abuse is not only backwards and moronic, but counterintuitive to a healthy and compassionate life."

The Miz, with a Twitter audience of 3.1 million, and the WWE, with a Twitter audience of 10.8 million, has substantial viewer power: between the two posts, the videos were viewed, as of February 2020, at least 23,700 and 10,800 times, respectively. Companies, of course, are going to continue to market to consumers based on current dietary trends, and they are likely to do whatever they can to sell to consumers. But the act of mocking a group of eaters, particularly in ways that could dig at the moral principles some vegan eaters have followed for years or perhaps a lifetime, can cause lasting damage to vegans, long after the ads have passed through viral explosions and an onslaught of social media shares and comments. For example, how many WWE viewers, who are 63 percent male, and with 66 percent holding a high school diploma or less ("Tracking Fan Avidity for the Fight Game"), might have been influenced to also "make fun" of animal welfare efforts as a result of this campaign? How many of these viewers might have been further entrenched in the stereotype of "strong men eat meat"? In the chapter "Men, Meat, and Hegan Identity: Veganism and the Discourse of Masculinity" in *The Vegan Studies Project*, Laura Wright explores the "male activity of eating meat," theorizing that the media, among other factors, has helped "engender not only a glorification of red meat and blue-collar work but also a profound denunciation of vegetarian and vegan diets as indicators of weakness, ethnicity, and femininity, all of which have been constructed as threats to a traditional 'American' way of life" (114). When we add together the layers of humor present in ads such as the Hardee's campaign, told through an initial ad mocking an SPCA animal rights campaign and then filtered through the ultra-masculine lens of a beefed-up professional WWE wrestler, we can easily see how such ads can lend themselves to further building an anti-vegan narrative via "humor." By poking fun at the ethical principles aligned with veganism, such a narrative leads ultimately to the rhetorical act of differentiation. The resulting consumer response, presented through a barrage of social media platform comments, helps illuminate just how polarizing such "humorous" messages can be.

Interestingly, and perhaps not so surprisingly, in October 2019, Hardees began to offer Beyond Meat (which is 100 percent vegan), available as a burger and in breakfast sausage form, and, by December 2019, Beyond Meat offerings became a regular feature in Hardee's social media advertising. There is no further mention, as of February 2020, of the "Save the Veggies" campaign. Some viewers took note of the "about face" Hardee's made when it began to promote vegan burgers. For example, on October 16, 2019, Twitter user @user47 wrote: "Remember the ridiculous #SaveTheVeggies ads @Hardees was running five months ago or so to mock #plantbased diets? Love to see such an abrupt about face!"

Hardees also began to show some greater awareness of other diets gaining popularity, including the keto diet, in January 2020. On January 5, 2020, Hardee's Tweeted to low-carb keto dieters, claiming that it would "keep offering low carb ways to enjoy your favorite foods." Remarkably enough, the keto image offered in tandem with this post shows a Hardee's burger smashed between layers of *vegetables*, including a fully lettuce bun.

As another example of an "anti-vegan-option" rhetorical technique employed recently by a major restaurant chain, I now turn to several Arby's advertising campaigns aimed at propelling the brand as a meat-centric establishment.

Arby's "friends don't let friends eat tofu"

Arby's, a fast-food restaurant with more than 3000 locations worldwide, specializes in roast beef, turkey, and Angus beef sandwiches. The company has a long history of focusing on its meat offerings, and, in the face of a growing vegetarian and vegan market, has thus far chosen to stick to its meat-centric menu. Further, Arby's has gone beyond simply keeping to its traditional menu option and has used its emphasis on meats as a marketing tool. The company has a history of meat-focused advertisements and even responses—and, according to some viewers, attacks—directed at vegetarian and vegan eaters.

In a 2015 "open letter to Vegetarians across America," Arby's responded to vegan and vegetarian offense with yet another "joke." The company wrote:

> Dear Vegetarians;
> …It is understandable that you disapprove of our meat-bravado. Your voices have been heard… We love our meats, but realize they're not for everyone.
> Then on Sunday, June 28, we launched a meat innovation that has likely tempted you: Brown Sugar Bacon…It may be hard to resist…even for you…
> We're giving you a number to call: 1-855-MEAT-HLP. This is a Vegetarian Support Hotline. When your nose betrays you and alerts the rest of your senses to find and devour this sweet meat, please call 1-855-MEAT-HLP. You will receive the support you need to resist this gateway meat and get tips on how to avoid temptation…
> Sincerely,
> Arby's

In an article posted to *Huffington Post* in 2015, "Thanks but No Thanks, Arby's: Vegetarians Don't Want Your Meat," author and founder of Mercy for Animals, Nathan Runkle, wrote directly back to Arby's:

> You may have chosen to target vegetarians in your latest advertising stunt because you're scared of us and our growing power as consumers. I don't blame you. The number of

vegetarians and vegans in America is skyrocketing while meat consumption has dropped significantly over the past several years…

The fast-food restaurants embracing this trend are flourishing. Those rejecting it are getting butchered in a market increasingly driven by eco-, ethics-, and health-conscious consumers.

So, Arby's, it's time to seek help. Meat is dead and dying, and your business will someday follow suit if you don't change your ways…

Beyond Runkle's response, vegan and vegetarian eaters from around the world responded with similar distaste, and many promised to ban the company altogether. As shown through this dialogue, Arby's has had a contentious relationship with vegan and vegetarian eaters in the past, especially when the company utilizes humor and satire in public spaces to respond to serious concerns from consumers.

In February 2018, Arby's launched a print campaign with a simple tagline: "Friends don't let friends eat tofu. *Just eat meat.*" The Arby's logo is emblazoned on the "just eat meat" portion of the ad, further perpetuating the brand's hold on what has become a long-running advertising scheme: essentially, the company, in what many defend as a "joke," wants to portray that it not only has the best meats, but that something is inherently wrong with tofu, a staple of many vegetarian and vegan diets. Arby's posted this ad to social media outlets, including its Twitter feed, and responses came through this space, as well as via Facebook and Reddit.

The "Friends Don't Let Friends Eat Tofu" campaign enraged many and caught the attention of many news outlets and vegan or vegetarian groups and publications. In early 2018, one Facebook user wrote: "It's obvious they are feeling threatened by the growing vegan movement, or else they wouldn't feel the need to make fun of people who eat tofu." On February 9, 2018, Twitter user @KatePow3ll wrote: "Ads like this wouldn't be commissioned if meat pushers weren't panicked by the growth of veganism. This type of ad wouldn't have been made 15 years ago. It only serves to make meat eaters/producers/sellers look more petty and desperate. Imagine being this rattled by TOFU."

> On February 9, 2018, Twitter user @miriame33 wrote: "OMG! I'm so disappointed @Arbys! I didn't think they would be so low to say something like that! We all know that meat causes cancer! If Arby's was smart they would include #Vegan options in their menu! #GoVegan"

On February 10, 2018, Reddit user RykrosDynasty wrote: "And this just shows the ignorance at Arby's to be honest. Tofu has been eaten by omnis (omnivores) for literally thousands of years. It was never intended to be a meat replacement, it just became a good alternative due to a high protein content."

Some users pointed out that Arby's misses an opportunity when they poke fun at vegan eaters instead of trying to cater to them: on February 10, 2019, Reddit user johnboyauto wrote: "They'd make more money if they diversified their customer base instead of being raging assholes." On February 10, 2018, Reddit user Double_X_Helix wrote:

> But vegans and vegetarians are growing at a great rate each year each increasing by the next…It's only a matter of time and when but by this ad we can see that Arby's is hella scared of us and eventually if they don't step up their game like other restaurants they are going to lose so many [customers].

Similar to Nathan Runkle's response to the Arby's "Helpline," plant-based food brands got in on the defense in response to the "Just Eat Meat" messaging. On its Facebook page, plant-based meat company No Evil Foods wrote in response to Arby's: "The threat is real and we're coming for you Arby's. When a leading fast-food chain stoops to promoting an anti-health, anti-plant campaign, it's clear that the resistance is strong, and we're not going down without a fight!"

As they did with Hardee's, consumers also chimed in to defend Arby's, citing the joking and thus "harmless" nature of the ads. On February 10, 2018, Reddit user Frannoham wrote:

> You are way over thinking this. Arby's style of branding is [for the] over the top meat lover, not health food. As offensive as this is to non meat eaters, it's really not about tofu. It's a joke. Unfortunately the response puts vegans in the crazy people of Facebook crowd, with all the "big meat is running scared." It's just silly and achieves nothing.

Other comments are illustrative of some of the aforementioned gendered stereotypes; for example, on Facebook, user Anthony López wrote: "As a man, I refuse to eat anything that gives me estrogen. I'll stick with rare/medium rare steaks with a glass pint of beer."

Another Facebook user, Jessica Sharma, wrote: "I just ate Arbys 2 days in a row. Meat good, tofu bad," illustrating a purported dichotomy between tofu and meat. Another Facebook user, Robert L. Lynch, wrote: "To all the vegans trying to shame Arby's for this, I don't think they're going to lose any customers. The Venn diagram of people who love tofu and people who love Arbys is two non-intersecting circles."

Sharma's and Lynch's comments seemingly separating tofu and people who love meat and/or people who love Arby's are of particular interest, as they project a dichotomous frame on the situation that could be rhetorically damaging. People who enjoy fast food and/or consider themselves omnivores are not excluded from enjoying tofu dishes. In fact, omnivorous people are dipping into plant-based options at unprecedented rates; a 2012 survey by the John Hopkins School of Public Health showed that at 245 food service sites in the United States, "more than 40 percent saw an increase in vegetable sales and 24 percent noted a decrease in consumer selection of meat options" (Sodexo). Many omnivorous and even primarily carnivorous consumers are also taking part in plant-based initiatives such as Meatless Mondays, which reserve one day of the week for vegetarian or vegan meals.

Additionally, one only needs to look to the surging popularity of "meat-like" plant-based burger options such as the Beyond Burger and the Impossible Burger, among others, to understand that meat and vegan options need not be mutually exclusive for those seeking to make incremental changes in an otherwise typically meat-heavy diet. If the numbers tell a story, these brands are succeeding: Beyond Burger sales were expected to hit $210 million in 2019, a doubling from 2018. Nivedita Balu and Tina Bellon of Reuters write, "The burgers, a hit with consumers switching to a 'flexitarian' diet, feel, smell and taste like real meat." The Impossible Burger is experiencing high demand, especially after launching its plant-based burger found in many mainstream fast- and fast-casual restaurants such as Qdoba, Red Robin, and Burger King: "Since the launch of the Impossible Burger 2.0 in January 2019, the company has seen a 50 percent jump in revenue," states Impossible Food's Vice President of Communications, Jessica Appelgren.

In short, consumers who enjoy fast food are also indeed eating—or at least trying—plant-based options in droves. Separating consumers into "those who eat at Arby's" and "those who eat tofu" creates an opposition that disallows diet experimentation and discourages people who might benefit from mixing up their diets to do so. While the nature of the Arby's advertisement is, of course, seemingly based in humor, susceptible, impressionable audiences could be impacted in ways that could potentially not serve them well in terms of dietary diversity.

Unlike Hardee's recent about-face move in offering Beyond Meat products, Arby's seems to be holding strong in its proudly meat-centric menu as of February 2020. As of the time of this chapter's writing, Arby's menus in the United States still do not offer—or publicly promote—a plant-based or vegetarian burger patty option of any kind. The brand continues to use its "We Have the Meats" tag line in its print and digital advertising campaigns. And the brand seems proud of its past campaigns—it even features the vegetarian helpline campaign on its timeline of major Arby's events, seen here under the guise of "Helping Vegetarians" on its website in February 2020. In many ways, this doubling down is a differentiating factor for the Arby's brand, as is the company's prerogative. However, the continued emphasis on mocking vegan or vegetarian diets can have tangible impacts on impressionable audiences, thus adding to the rhetoric of poking fun at plant-based eaters and perhaps dissuading certain groups of eaters from ever considering a change in dietary choices.

Discussion

"Humorous" advertisements are hardly a new phenomenon; print advertisements dating to the early 1900s feature "jokes" about everything from women's appearances and roles in the household to Santa's favorite brand of cigarettes. Humor, as a rhetorical technique to connect with projected consumers, is used frequently in advertising. However, the aforementioned advertisements from Hardee's and Arby's promote a slightly different form of humor—through a close alignment with non-profit style ads reminiscent of fundraising campaigns for causes fighting for animal welfare (Hardee's) or a position that discourages (even jokingly) vegan experimentation (Arby's) and seemingly alienates vegan customers. Such advertising strategies can easily cause offense for some viewers, and, further, can help create even more marked divides in consumer groups on a topic that could surely benefit from unification. As such, as the plant-based eating trend continues to grow in the United States, and as more omnivorous and even carnivorous consumers try plant-based options at other fast or fast-casual restaurants, restaurants poking fun at vegan options might, in particular, offend and/or lose a consumer base they might have otherwise captured.

With so many fast and fast-casual restaurants now starting to offer vegan and vegetarian options, perhaps Arby's and Hardee's sought to brand themselves as differentiated in what is becoming a saturated vegan market. And, judging from the consumer support often exuded on the companies' social media platforms, these advertising choices might humor a group of eaters who wish to see the brands they know stick to long-running traditions and classic meat-centric options. Further, through certain gendered stereotypes, as seen in Hardee's collaboration with The Miz, some followers will feel a sense of strength or superiority as a result of the rhetoric employed. These types of advertisements might also speak to a group of consumers who appreciate the lack of "political correctness" found in the ads, as illustrated in some of the customer social media responses to the ads discussed in this chapter. In the current political climate, we are living in times of ever-widening dichotomies; choosing a side and fighting unflinchingly seems to be a matter of principle for so many, especially when veiled by the anonymity and physical protection offered by typing comments to arguments from a distance via social media platforms and profiles. These issues become even more complicated when we evaluate how such ads in the mainstream might help dissuade some consumers from trying vegan options even elsewhere or propagating ideas that plant-based dietary choices are mutually exclusive from meat-eating.

Does the technique of mocking vegans actually dissuade some in these groups from trying or adopting plant-based options or diets? Research on the rhetorical functions of humor would tell us that the potential for such a response is great. Add to this the impact of social psychological dynamics in the form of values and beliefs and their influence on consumer food demand and choices: as explained by Gossard and York "values and beliefs have a greater influence on the choice of a vegetarian diet than do demographic factors" (2). Research in sociology has found that "social psychological factors have a greater influence on consumer demand than do demographic and economic factors" (2). There is a continued pattern of heavy meat consumption in the United States—despite an explosion in the availability and variety of plant-based options to many consumers, meat is still often tied to beliefs—whether attached to gender, geographical location, family, or other reasons. We still attach much of our human identity and social structure to meat: research has shown that "meat consumption is clearly not the outcome of biological necessity, but a practice embedded within a complex of social forces" (Gossard and York 8). Add in the continued gendered pressures to eat meat for males—so as not to be "penalized, to be considered weak and/or effeminate" (Wright 128), particularly when considering the long-range impacts of the Hardee's campaigns—and we can see how the multiple layers add up to show emphasize the superiority of meat eaters and to ultimately differentiate and divide.

As vegan diets and offerings continue to grow in popularity across demographics, genders, and political lines, perhaps the issue of making fun of vegan food by major food corporations will diminish or become less consequential as the social constructs of meat-eating continue to break down. Until then, we must continue to problematize the real rhetorical impacts of these advertisements and continue to discuss how humor used in advertisements to mock or alienate certain groups of eaters—especially when many of these eaters adhere to such diets by health necessity or by ethical principle—is perhaps not so "harmless" after all.

Works cited

Abo, Melissa M., Michael D. Slater, and Paul Jain. 2017. "Using Health Conditions for Laughs and Health Policy Support: The Case of Food Allergies." *Health Communication*, 32 (7): 803–811. https://doi.org/10.1080/10410236.2016.1172292.

"An Open Letter from Arby's to Vegetarians Across America." *PR Newswire*, 7 July 2015. https://www.prnewswire.com/news-releases/an-open-letter-from-arbys-to-vegetarians-across-america-300109374.html. Accessed February 15 2020.

Balu, Niedita, and Bellon, Tina. "Beyond Meat sees sales more than doubling in 2019, shares jump 21%." *Reuters*, 6 June 2019. https://www.reuters.com/article/us-beyond-meat-results/beyond-meat-sees-sales-more-than-doubling-in-2019-shares-jump-21-idUSKCN1T72Q7. Accessed February 1 2020.

Benacka, Elizabeth. *Rhetoric, Humor, and the Public Sphere: From Socrates to Stephen Colbert*. Lexington Books, 2016.

Capritto, Amanda. "The Impossible Burger shortage: Why it's hard to find this meat-free burger." *CNET*, 26 June 2019. https://www.cnet.com/news/the-impossible-burger-is-demand-outrunning-supply/. Accessed February 1 2020.

Davidson, Nathan. "The Greatest Anti-Vegan Signs of All Time." *Ranker*. https://www.ranker.com/list/funny-anti-vegan-signs/nathandavidson. Accessed February 15 2020.

Dinu, Monica, Abbate, Rosanna, Gensini, Gian Franco, Casini, Alessandro, and Sofi, Francesco. "Vegetarian, vegan diets and multiple health outcomes: A systematic review with meta-analysis of observational studies." *Critical Reviews in Food Science and Nutrition*, vol. 57, no. 17, 2017, pp. 3640–3649. doi:10.1080/10408398.2016.1138447

Fryar, Cheryl D., Hughes, Jeffery P., Herrick, Kirsten A., and Ahluwalia, Namanjeet, "Fast Food Consumption Among Adults in the United States, 2013–2016." Centers for Disease Control and Prevention. https://www.cdc.gov/nchs/products/databriefs/db322.htm. Accessed 15 February 2020.

Goldie, Janis. "The 'Funny' Thing about Food Allergies…in Canadian Media Culture." *The Spaces and Places of Canadian Popular Culture*, edited by V. Kannen and N. Shyminsky, Canadian Scholars Press, 2019.

Gossard, M.H., and York, R. "Social Structural Influences on Meat Consumption." *Human Ecology Review*, vol. 10, no. 1, 2003. https://www.researchgate.net/publication/229051259_Social_Structural_Influences_on_Meat_Consumption. Accessed February 15 2020.

"Hardee's Gets a Brand Makeover under New Advertising Campaign: Tastes Like America." *Business Wire*, 10 April 2018. https://www.businesswire.com/news/home/20180410005399/en/Hardee%E2%80%99s-Brand-Makeover-New-Advertising-Campaign-%E2%80%9CTastes. Accessed February 15 2020.

"Hardee's makes impassioned plea to 'Save the Veggies' with roast beef LTO." *QSRWeb*, 30 April 2019. https://www.qsrweb.com/news/amid-plant-based-eating-popularity-hardees-makes-impassioned-plea-to-save-the-veggies/.

"How Many Adults in the U.S. are Vegetarian and Vegan? How many Adults eat Vegetarian and Vegan Meals when eating out?" *The Vegetarian Resource Group*. Accessed 15 February 2020. Centers for Disease Control and Prevention. 2018. Fast Food Consumption among Adults in the United States, 2013–2016.

Kalof, L. E., T. Dietz, P. C. Stern, and G. A. Guagnano. 1999. Social psychological and structural influences on vegetarian beliefs. *Rural Sociology*, vol. 64, no. 3, pp. 500–511.

Lefave, Samantha. "Sarah McLachlan Reveals the Truth About Those Sad ASPCA Ads." *Redbook*, 4 January 2016. https://www.redbookmag.com/life/pets/news/a41805/sarah-mclachlan-aspca-commercial/. Accessed February 1 2020.

Lorenz, Konrad. *On Aggression*. New York: Harcourt, Brace and World, 1963.

Meyer, John C. "Humor as a Double-Edged Sword: Four Functions of Humor in Communication." *Communication Theory*, vol. 10, no. 3, 2000. https://doi.org/10.1111/j.1468-2885.2000.tb00194.x

Mourdoukoutas, Panos. "Veganism and Vegetarianism Are Changing Fast Food." *Forbes*, 31 August 2019. https://www.forbes.com/sites/panosmourdoukoutas/2019/08/31/veganism-and-vegetarianism-are-changing-fast-food/#329f085a29a5. Accessed February 1 2020.

"Over One-Third of Americans Will Not Purchase a Brand Because of a Distasteful Advertisement." *Business Wire*, 26 March 2010. https://www.businesswire.com/news/home/20100326005057/en/One-Third-Americans-Purchase-Brand-Distasteful-Advertisement. Accessed February 1 2020.

Runkle, Nathan. "Thanks But No Thanks, Arby's: Vegetarians Don't Want Your Meat." *HuffPost*. 15 July 2015. https://www.huffpost.com/entry/thanks-but-no-thanks-arby_b_7772676. Accessed February 1 2020.

Street and Smith's Sports Business Journal. Tracking Fan Avidity for the Fight Game. 2 April 2013. https://www.sportsbusinessdaily.com/Journal/Issues/2013/04/22/In-Depth/Fight-fan-avidity.aspx

Strom, Stephanie. "Ad Featuring Singer Proves Bonanza for the A.S.P.C.A." *The New York Times*, 25 December 2008. https://www.nytimes.com/2008/12/26/us/26charity.html?_r=1&mtrref=undefined&gwh=6A59FA90A528C54B352953B501A30C57&gwt=pay&assetType=REGIWALL. Accessed February 1 2020.

"The Beyond Burger is Officially Joining TGIFridays Menus Nationwide." *Beyond Meat*, 2 January 2018, https://www.beyondmeat.com/whats-new/the-beyond-burger-is-officially-joining-tgi-fridays-menus-nationwide/.

Tran, Karen K. "My vegetarian diet is none of your business." *The Ontarion*, 22 March 2018. https://theontarion.com/2018/03/22/my-vegetarian-diet-is-none-of-your-business/. Accessed February 15 2020.

Tyko, K. "Vegan and meat-free fast-food options are growing. Here's where to find them." *USA Today*, 15 April 2019. https://www.usatoday.com/story/money/2019/04/15/vegan-menu-items-now-more-fast-food-chains-del-taco-blaze-beyond-carls-jr-burger-king/3432412002/. Accessed February 15 2020.

Vegetarian Resource Group. How Many Adults in the U.S. are Vegetarian and Vegan? 2016 https://www.vrg.org/nutshell/Polls/2016_adults_veg.htm

Williams, Lara. "Why Even Vegans Crave Burgers That 'bleed.'" *Vice*, 15 November 2018. https://www.vice.com/en_uk/article/nepbad/why-even-vegans-crave-burgers-that-bleed

Wright, Laura. *The Vegan Studies Project: Food, Animals, and Gender in the Age of Terror*. Athens, University of Georgia Press, 2015.

@Arbys. "Friends Don't Let Friends Eat Tofu." *Twitter*, 2018. https://twitter.com/Arbys

@Hardees. "Hardees Save the Veggies Campaign." *Twitter*, 2019. https://twitter.com/Hardees

@mikethemiz. "Hardees Save the Veggies Campaign." *Twitter*, 2019. https://twitter.com/mikethemiz; https://www.cdc.gov/nchs/products/databriefs/db322.htm

31
The vegan myth
The rhetoric of online anti-veganism

Carmen Aguilera-Carnerero and Margarita Carretero-González

In October 2018, food journalist Selene Nelson emailed William Sitwell, the editor of *Waitrose & Partners Food*, proposing a series of plant-based recipes for the magazine. Sitwell replied by suggesting "a series on killing vegans, one by one. Ways to trap them? How to interrogate them properly? Expose their hypocrisy? Force-feed them meat? Make them eat steak and drink red wine?" (Di Stefano; Higgins). The editor's dismissive response went viral and he eventually decided to tender his resignation. Even if Sitwell's reply could simply be taken as just another instance of sardonic – and definitely tasteless – humor, very much in line with the tone displayed in a piece he wrote for *The Telegraph* in January 2020, in which he reflected on the event while taking the challenge to go vegan for a week, the editor's email unquestionably evinced pervasive hostility against veganism and vegans, an antipathy for which a term has been coined: vegaphobia.

The hypocrisy Sitwell accused vegans of is possibly one of the most frequent charges faced by people who abstain from eating or wearing animals or animal products on ethical grounds, a view expressed in attacks predating even the use of the word "vegetarian." In 1803, Henry Broughan wrote a vitriolic review of Joseph Ritson's *An Essay on Abstinence from Animal Food, as a Moral Duty* (1802), in which he accused Ritson of "starving calves by drinking milk, aborting chickens by eating eggs, and murdering whole ecologies of microscopic organisms every time he washed his armpits," while stressing the hypocrisy of "using a quill plucked from a goose, ink made from crushed insects" and "lighting his desk with a 'whale-tallow' candle'" (qtd. in Stuart 368) in order to write his tract. The association of vegetarianism with radicalism and dissenting groups seems to go back to the very coinage of the term (Thomas 295–296), when being a vegetarian became "a fixed identity – indelibly associated with crankiness" (Stuart 423) and the language used to refer to vegetarianism or vegetarians was almost invariably disparaging. At the time, in fact, the arguments used by Brougham, in which he ridiculed "the vegetarian language that traces occulted paths of commodity production," according to Morton (26), "played dangerously between serious and comic registers," with Ritson himself becoming the subject of a now famous caricature (Figure 31.1).

It should be evident that, when attacking the hypocrisy he perceived in Ritson, Brougham was not precisely ditching him for not going all the way and embracing veganism (a term which had not even been coined at the time, and a concept that would most likely have elicited an even

Figure 31.1 Joseph Ritson ("Impiger iracundus inexorabilis acer"), by James Sayers, published by Hannah Humphrey etching and aquatint, published 22 March 1803.

Source: *National Portrait Gallery.*

harsher response from Brougham), but rather stressing the absurdity of Ritson's proposal by pointing out what he perceived to be the author's moral flaws, which, for Brougham, rendered him a hypocrite.

Whether vegan-based discrimination is or is not an issue now or will be in the future, empirical studies have shown the reality of vegaphobia, not just in anti-vegan discourse but also in general attitudes. Cole and Morgan (2011) observed the tendency of U.K. newspapers to discredit veganism often, in Brougham's line, through ridicule or stressing the impossibility to maintain it in practice, while tending to stereotype vegans as "ascetics, faddists, sentimentalists, or in some cases, hostile extremists" (134). This stereotyping results in "a derogatory portrayal of vegans and veganism" which the authors termed "vegaphobia." A study published by MacInnis and Hodson in 2015 revealed that vegetarians and vegans were equivalently or more negatively evaluated than several common prejudice target groups, more negatively evaluated than several nutritional outgroups (particularly if vegetarianism or veganism was embraced on ethical grounds), and vegan and vegetarians reported experiencing negativity due to their ethical choice. More recently, a survey from Lifesum, a weight-loss app of U.K.- and U.S.-based vegans, revealed that "92 percent of respondents experienced vegaphobia from family and friends, 59 percent experienced it while dining out, 55 percent in the workplace, and 21 percent while grocery shopping" (Krishnan).

In view of this data and taking into account the fertile ground online social media provides for the propagation of fake news and hate speech, it should come as no surprise that vegaphobia is also rampant on the Internet. Behind the apparent ephemerality of posts, memes, and hashtags that go viral one day only to be forgotten the next, is the reality that they still leave a mark on their recipients, who unquestioningly assume the validity of the post they like and/or share. Similarly to what Cole and Morgan observed in the British press, anti-vegan posts contribute to the reproduction of cultural speciesism spreading generalizations based most of the time on misinformation, but some others on intentional misrepresentation by replicating "simplified versions of veganism" that associate it derogatorily with "ascetic restriction, middle-class lifestyle fads, or Western ethical imperialism [which] have steadily ossified within dominant cultural narratives" (Quinn and Westwood 3). Irrespective of whether some of the crudest anti-vegan posts are mere instances of bad taste or risk being taken as cases of extreme speech, discourse analysis offers a very useful tool to look at them via the lens provided by vegan studies' critical examination of "the social and cultural discourses that imagine the vegan body and vegan identity" (Wright 23). Such an analysis is what we will undertake in the pages that follow.

Our analysis of the selected corpus will reveal that anti-vegan discourse on social media (Facebook in our study) contributes to the delegitimization of veganism and vegans by making use of the same strategies that allow for the perpetuation of carnistic ideology, which Joy and Tuider (2016) refer to as "Carnistic Defense Mechanisms," defined as "the set of social and psychological defense mechanisms that distort reality and dissociate people, psychologically and emotionally, from their actual experience" (vii). Of the two said defense mechanisms they identify – denial and justification – they rightly argue that the first is no longer an option, given the overwhelming evidence of the atrocities of animal agriculture; therefore, justification has taken now a predominant position, in a triad that transforms myths into fact and which they term "the *Three Ns of Justification*: eating animals is *normal, natural, and necessary*" (vii). It is not the purpose of this essay to study how these myths have been used – and are still used – to justify many other instances of violence against human and more-than-human nature; suffice it to say for now that, even if some of the posts that we have analyzed are presented as mere instances of playful banter, they effectively contribute to the perpetuation of the carnistic status quo. Indeed, although humor very often challenges the social status quo, on occasions it does precisely the opposite; by mocking the ideology that threatens to destabilize the status quo, it actually reinforces it. Therefore, we add a third carnistic defense mechanism to Joy and Tuider's classification: ridicule.

Corpus of data

Our corpus of data consists of a series of posts from three Facebook pages written in Spanish: *Reich Animalista* (Animal Activist Reich), *El Mito del Veganismo* (The Vegan Myth), and *Vida Naturopatética* (Naturopathetic Life) collected from January 2019 to August 2019.

As a social social networking website where users can post comments, show photographs and videos, post links to news or other interesting content on the web, chat live, and watch short-form videos, Facebook offers different possibilities to share information either through a personal profile, a public page or a group. While the latter is reserved for a closed community, and the administrator(s) of the page has either to accept users' requests to join or invite them to be part of it directly, public pages are accessible to everybody without needing any kind of permission by the administrators. The selected pages belong to the latter group.

The great majority of the posts from our corpus are written in Spanish although some photos and, above all, the videos, are in English (probably shared from similar English-speaking pages); these are, most of the time, captioned with a Spanish translation or explanation by the administrators. Although the three pages are written in Spanish, the lexicon used reveals dialectal differences. Thus, the page *El Mito del veganismo* is written in Peninsular Spanish whereas the administrators of the other two pages *Vida Naturopatética* and *Animal Reich* use South American Spanish. The latter also contain more satirical and informal content than the content posted in *El mito del Veganismo* (The Vegan Myth), which tries to offer a more rational critique of veganism and vegans.

The names of the pages themselves are quite meaningful and anticipate the type of material they contain. Animal Reich attempts to make a pun on the Third Reich, highlighting the fascist character of vegans who always try to impose their life choices on others; Naturopathetic Life is a portmanteau between "natural" and "pathetic," which unveils a non-neutral stance on natural alternatives of life; and finally The Vegan Myth makes reference to the fact that veganism is a myth, i.e. "a commonly believed but false idea."[1] The selection of these three pages was based on their popularity, since all of them have more than 10,000 supporters each and, in the case of *Vida Naturopatética*, the number surpassed 80,000, which means their arguments are widely spread and reach a broad audience.

Characteristics of online anti-vegan discourse

Online anti-vegan discourse is extreme and polarized, sharing many of the features of populism through different linguistic realizations both textual and visual.

Legitimation strategies and topoi

The posts on the chosen pages follow a pattern that alternates written texts, images and videos, since Internet communication is multimodal in nature. The role of images is essential to shape and support the anti-vegan arguments in a more clear and diret way, their source of power relying on their emotional appeal (La Grandeur 120).

One of the most distinctive features of anti-vegan discourse is the polarization of its narratives, arising from the incompatibility of goals between two social participants (Bar-Tal et al.): vegans and non-vegans. As Richardson and Wodak state, the construction of in-and-out groups necessarily implies the use of strategies of positive self-representation and the negative presentation of others (247).

As is usually the case in other types of discourse, mainly populist, in the construction of the "other" (the vegans) the creation of fear (the imposition of an unhealthy future) becomes a dominant public perspective and part of the social daily landscape: "In such crisis situations, both politics and media tend to reduce complex historical processes to snap-shots which allow constructing and triggering Manichean dichotomies-friends and foes, perpetrators and victims, and so forth" (Engel and Wodak 5). Wodak points out that the discursive strategies of "victim-perpetrator reversal," "scapegoating," and the "construction of conspiracy theories" are the backbone of the rhetoric of conflict (*The Politics of Fear*). By discursive strategies we refer to the plan of practices adopted to achieve a particular goal whether it is social, political, psychological, or linguistic. Three main groups of strategies can be distinguished:

a. referential or nomination strategies deal with the discursive *construction*[2] of social actors, objects, phenomenon, events, processes, and actions.
b. predicational strategies focus on the discursive *characterization* of social actors, objects, phenomena, events, processes, and actions (e.g., positively and negatively), and
c. argumentation strategies *persuade* addressees of the validity of specific claims of truth and normative rightness. (Reisigl 52)

One of the most recurrent and effective strategies within this last group is the use of *topoi*, "parts of argumentation which belong to the required premises. They are formal or content-related warrants or 'conclusion rules' which connect the argument(s) with the conclusion, the claim" (Žagar 5). Although the methodological formulation of *topoi* has been thoroughly criticized by authors such as Žagar, it is undeniable that the analysis of *topoi* has proven to be very useful to unveil the way vegans are perceived online. To give an example from the corpus, let us focus on the so-called "*topos* of disadvantage," which could be paraphrased as follows:

a. Person X is aging badly/feeling sick
b. Person X is vegan
c. Veganism makes you age badly and feel sick (= veganism is not good for health)

Different kinds of *topoi*, which we will see below, can be found within the strategies of legitimation in the corpus. These strategies encompass four major categories (van Leeuwen and Wodak 104–111): authorization, moral evaluation, rationalization, and mythopoesis. Most of the posts on the Facebook pages analyzed fall into at least one of these four classes:

1. **Authorization** is legitimation by referring to the authority, be that a person, tradition, custom, or law. In the selected corpus, this type of legitimation is achieved through two types of opinions in the corpus: ex-vegans and public figures. These ex-vegans have become implacable anti-vegan activists who display a wide array of Youtube videos in which they explain their experiences. Most of them allude to the health problems they had while they were vegan, almost taking them to the verge of death in the most extreme cases. In the case of public figures, we found testimonies in our corpus of popular people in the Spanish-speaking world, ranging from Sociology Professor Amando de Miguel to Argentinian singer Andrés Calamaro or TV presenter Frank de la Jungla (Frank of the Jungle). Their opinions are very straightforward and somehow coincidental, underlying the idea that animal activism is the illness of the century while simultaneously vindicating human rights activism above animal rights activism.
2. **Moral evaluation** implies legitimation by reference to value systems. These are the main ideas that refer to vegans as objects of moral evaluation:

   a. Vegans are not better human beings than non-vegans

This kind of argument is based on the so-called "red herring fallacy" (*ignoratio elenchi*) in which the arguer tries to divert attention from the argument by employing an unrelated sentimental argument. Veganism is, indeed, for many of its detractors, the evidence of misanthropy, a mere excuse to camouflage the hate vegans feel for their own species. One of the post reproduces a text in which a woman states how scary is to hear sentences such as "dogs are better than humans," since a lot of people love their pets instead of respecting their fellow human beings. Therefore, such a claim actually hides a master–slave relationship and a tyrannical love since a dog cannot complain.

The whole argument is based on the false antagonism that presents humans and animals as mutually exclusive options that apparently cannot be embraced simultaneously. That rhetoric is built upon disjunction - "EITHER humans OR animals" - rather than on coordination - "both humans AND animals." The vegan and animal liberationist hierarchy status in which humans are not actually below animals but both are presented at the same level is the most recurrent argument anti-vegans provide to justify their depiction of vegans' misanthropy. The cover page picture of the page *Reich Animalista* (Animal Activist Reich) dwells on that idea since it is a photo of starving African children and the caption "Humans First" appeals directly to this emotional populist narrative.

This kind of argument goes a step further in anti-vegan manipulation of vegan ethics, implying that vegans actually demote humans and position them below nonhuman animals, rather than looking at the decentralization process that places both groups at the same level. In fact, extreme anti-vegan arguments claim that animal rights activists give nonhuman animals the respect that should be afforded only to human beings, while mistreating their fellow humans:

b. Veganism is a radical, intolerant cult

Vegans are depicted in these Facebook groups as a cult both in a literal and a metaphorical way. Metaphorically, their association with religious sects that are often considered to be cults – such as the Mormons or the Jehovah's Witnesses – is constant, mainly based upon the analogy of their insistence on preaching about their lifestyle, a fact that is interpreted as the repetition of arguments strategy to brainwash the listener. Literally, commenters of the pages make reference to some cults such as the "People's Temple," which induced in 1978 the mass suicide of 918 members who followed a vegetarian diet with high carbohydrate ingestion. These posters argue that a vegetarian diet that was low in protein and high in carbohydrates was imposed to easily control the minds of members of the People's Temple. Moreover, the high correlation between cults and the practice of vegetarianism was also enumerated by anti-vegan speakers on Facebook as one of the causes of mental illnesses.

The vegan cult perception can also be extended to the family context. Veganism is blamed for the mistreatment of children by parents who feed their babies or toddlers vegan diets or vegan-based milks during the lactation period.

c. Vegans are elitist and arrogant

In online anti-vegan discourse, veganism is claimed to be elitist and arrogant, practiced by people who feel superior by virtue of not eating animals. Indeed, online anti-vegans think it is a matter of privilege to criticize someone else's diet neglecting aspects such as the means and resources available to (some) non-vegans. One of the pictures on the page illustrates this idea. A White middle-aged man accuses a poor African farmer of speciesism suggesting alternative sources of protein, which are clearly unattainable to him.

Veganism is thus described as the new inquisition, and vegans depicted as the new inquisitors looking down on non-vegans from their arguably judgmental, self-proclaimed morally superior position.

3. **Rationalization** tries to achieve legitimation through appeals to knowledge claims or arguments. Within this group of strategies we can find a general claim that rules over the rest: veganism is unhealthy. The argument is always presented following the same pattern: there is a display of "before and after" pictures or videos of recent or former vegans. The anti-vegan discourse emphasizes the visible process of aging or getting sick after becoming vegan or, conversely, the much healthier and younger aspect after abandoning vegan practices. A picture in the page shows two pictures of actress, former model, and environmentalist vegan activist Suzy Amis Cameron when she was 48 years old and not a vegan (left) and

at 56, after she had become vegan (right). The comparison is based on the fallacy that her veganism is the main reason for her visible aging without any mention to the obvious effects of the passage of time, apart from the fact that the image has obviously been doctored to make her appear older than she is. This strategy clearly falls within the group of carnistic defense mechanisms that justifies eating animals by arguing that it is necessary, the third N of justification identified by Joy and Tuider (viii–ix).

4. **Mythopoesis** is legitimation achieved by narratives, *i.e.*, small stories of fragments of narrative structures about the past or future. This strategy is based on the dichotomy vegan fantasy vs. non-vegan reality and can be summarized visually in the following meme "What some imagine nature to be like vs. what nature actually is like," or, in other words, vegans live in a completely fictitious world, radically different from the actual one. The meme consists of a top image taken from the 1942 Disney animated film *Bambi* in which plenty of beautiful animals cohabit in nature in love and perfect harmony, and an image below in which a lion is eating a zebra. Disney's movies are blamed for the idyllic mental image that has been in the minds of hardcore vegans since they construct a vegan paradise in which all animals respect each other.

The *topos* present in this legitimation strategy can be defined as the *topos* of human nature and be paraphrased as follows:

a. All predators kill and eat animals.
b. Humans are predators.
c. Humans have the same right as animals to kill and eat meat.

This legitimation strategy tries to justify meat consumption as part of the cycle of nature so that contravening it would be completely unnatural, in line with Joy and Tuider's second N of Justification (viii–ix).

Extreme speech

As Gagliardone contends, the so-called "globalization of hate" allows for the emergence of online aggressive behavior for which a wide range of labels exist, from fear speech to dangerous speech through violent extremist speech, cyberhate or microaggression, just to name some of the most popular. A new proposal in the field is the one made by Udupa and Pohjonen who suggest the term "extreme speech" as an alternative to the broad concept of "hate speech" to point out "a spectrum of cultural practices" (Hervik 3107), which is not exclusively limited to online spaces. In the pages analyzed, hate speech takes two directions: one is aimed at vegans (they are the objects of extreme speech) and the other presents vegans as constant producers of extreme speech.

The argument of presenting animal rights activists as creators of extreme speech is in line (the side of the extreme indeed) with the characterization of vegans as arrogant, radical, and cruel to non-vegan citizens. In the Spanish context, there was a popular social debate built aroundthree animal rights netizens that wished for the death of Adrian, a three-year-old boy with cancer who stated his wish to become a bullfighter. The Hate Crime Division requested a sentence of one year in prison for the three animal rights activists who expressed their feelings online. Vegans, perceived as arrogant, extreme animal liberationists, are represented in the same way. Even though Charles Patterson had already elaborated on the analogy almost 20 years before, in 2019 philosophy professor Ernest Castro was sued by the Movimiento contra la Intolerancia

(Movement Against Intolerance) for comparing pig slaughter to the Nazi Holocaust. Another popular case frequently cited by anti-vegans is that of Mel Capitán, a young hunter who committed suicide, arguably after two years of continuous harassment by vegans and animal rights activists. These cases are mentioned particularly to point out the intolerant and aggressive forms of speech of vegans and animal rights activists.

On the other hand, vegans are also the objects of extreme speech as the page Animal Activist Reich of our corpus reveals. In their hashtags and posts, vegans are qualified as "descerebrados" (brainless), "fanáticos" (fanatics), "ignorantes" (ignorant), "ridículos" (ridiculous), "locos" (crazy), "basura" (rubbish), "inhumanos" (inhuman), or even "psicópatas" (psychopaths).

Animal rights activists lack a basic logic argumentation as a result of following a contradictory doctrine. They ignore that one can only have rights when, alternatively, there is a minimum capacity to have duties. This argument is complemented by several hasthags, thus #AnimalRightsActivism is described as #irrational or lacking any common sense or logic hence its qualification as #MentalIllness or, even, as the #Illnessofthecentury.

The first post of the year of one of the pages studied wished for a 2019 free of vegans as if the targeted group constituted a plague to be eradicated.

The immediate and participatory nature of social media communication has made the cybersphere a breeding ground for the expression and dissemination of a range of exclusionary, intolerant, and extremist discourses, practices and beliefs, as Kopytowska argues. The loss of individuality paired with the loss of personal responsibility (and somehow accountability) typical of Internet discourse are related to the concepts of group salience and polarization that favor the birth and consolidation of "cyber mobs" (Citron 87) who compete to spread hate and attack individuals online.

Internet discourse subgenres: memes and hashtags

One of the most frequent elements of popular culture born from the Internet are memes. The term "meme" was coined by biologist Richard Dawkins (1976, 1982) to describe the flow and flux of culture. For Milner memes, as networks of mediated cultural participation, are *multimodal artifacts*, where image and text are integrated to tell a joke, make an observation or advance an argument with two basic characteristics:

a. A cultural element (with a communicative intention),
b. Almost always a joke (or a remark intended to be funny) (11)

According to Dawkins (1976), memes are used to represent discourses and identities, the latter being ultimately perspectives of self and society mediated through texts and discourses (22). Moreover, memes are discursive constructions used to articulate argumentations so that humor is added to successfully convey certain ideas and being argumentation units in themselves (26).

Humor is a very controversial concept, and the notion of linking extreme hatred and humor is disturbing, for it is easier to assume that bigotry is essentially humorless. Indeed, humor is often used to draw boundaries between social groups (Fine; Speier), which is the reason why the jokes that one group enjoys might not be shared by another group.

Udupa highlights four aspects of fun to delineate fun as a metapractice: (a) being "funny" as tactical ways to enter and rise to prominence within the online sphere; (b) deriving fun from the sheer freshness of colloquialism in political debates that stands in contrast to the serious tone of political deliberation; (c) fun as satisfaction of achieving a goal by working with one's own resources; (d) and fun as a group identification and collective (if anonymous) celebration of aggression (3107).

Anti-vegan memes fall into the fourth group of aspects. Some of the memes actually are examples of non-offensive humor, making fun of the "lighter" stereotypes usually attributed to vegans, such as their imperious need to inform everybody of their veganism, but on other occasions, criticism can be harsher, usually ascribing qualities to vegans as individuals (for instance, being hypocritical, judgmental, and arrogant) to demonize the whole movement.

Although a minority, one can find memes full of hate making fun of animals' deaths or of the preference to eat vegetables.

Hashtags (#)—a common typographical convention created on the social platform Twitter to mark the topic of the tweet and later export it to other social media platforms such as Instagram or Facebook—are one of the linguistic creations born out of the Internet. As Zappavigna contends, the presence of hashtags—which convey interpersonal and ideational meanings—eases the function of "ambient affiliation" among microbloggers: "The kind of evaluative language ... suggests that the tweet may be forming a more interpersonal social function in which users are affiliating around values" ("Ambient Affiliation" 801). The way in which social media facilitates the expression of interpersonal meaning enables users to form virtual communities that are defined as "social aggregations that emerge from the [Internet] when enough people carry on those public discussions long enough, with sufficient human feeling, to form webs of personal relationships in cyberspace" (Rheingold 5) and helps them create social bonds within a network of values (Knight). Hashtags do not frequently make linguistic utterances per se but they are written at the end of a sentence to express the speaker's stance about the content of what s/he has written. Except in the very general case of #animallovers, the rest of hashtags in the corpus either disqualify the animalist and vegan movement or its practitioners. According to their content, the hashtags found on the three Facebook pages studied can be classified in several subgroups:

a. Disqualification of vegans or animalists:

    #NoalRadicalismo (#notoradicalism)
    #BastadeAnimalloversRadicales (#stopradicalanimallovers)
    #DinoalRadicalismo (#saynotoradicalism)
    #Animalloversdescerebrados (#brainlessanimallovers)
    #AnimalistasInhumanos (#Inhumananimalactivists)
    #Humanismoperdido (#losthumanism)
    #animalocos (#animalcrazypeople)
    #Basuranimallover (#rubbishanimallover)
    #animalovershipocritas (#hypocriteanimallovers)
    #animalloversridiculos (#ridiculeanimallovers)

b. Ascription of negative qualities to the movement:

    #Enfermedadmental (#mentalillness)
    #Ignorancia (#ignorance)
    #fanatismo (#fanaticism)
    #antinatalismo (#antinatalism)
    #enfermedadmental (#mentalillness)
    #laenfermedaddelsiglo (#illnessofthecentury)

#ReichAnimalista (#AnimalRightsReich)

c. Concern and worry about a future in which animal rights activists or vegans may get more power:

#Adondevamosaparar (#wherearewegoingto)
#cuidandonosdelalocuranimalista (#protectingourselvesfromtheanimalrightscraziness)

d. Disney's unreal depiction of the animal world:

#Disneymeoprime (#Disneyoppressesme)
#Disneyteengaña (#Disneydeceivesyou)

e. A miscellaneous group in which the speakers express their philosophy on the animal question ranging from their preference for humankind the omnivorous nature of humans, and the pseudoscientific essence of veganism:

#primeroloshumanos (#humansfirst)
#Todosecome (#everythingisedible)
#somosomnivoros (#weareommivores)
#stopPseudociencias (#stoppseudosciences)

Conclusions

The analysis of the content of our corpus data has shown that online anti-vegan discourse in the Spanish-speaking context contributes to reproduce cultural speciesism, in a similar way to that of the British press in the study by Cole and Morgan but with an interesting difference, possibly due to the different nature of social media. The Facebook pages studied did not dissociate veganism from debates concerning nonhuman animal rights or liberation (as was the case in the British newspapers) but rather elaborated on that connection to make absurd claims and spread generalizations based on ignorance or distortion of the core principles underlying the movement, hence blaming it and its followers for reasons totally unrelated to its philosophy. As a result, online anti-vegan discourse is polarized, exclusionary and built upon stereotypes. Since online discourse is not rigid but can be considered as a continuum upon which vegans are portrayed as elitist, snobbish, and pretentious, and alternately as as manipulators and abusers. Similarly veganism can be depicted as unnatural in the mildest approaches or as dangerous in the most radical versions. Reality is built upon fake premises and presented in binary terms dependent upon an unavoidable choice (humans vs. animals) with the impossibility of selecting both alternatives; hence vegans are automatically labeled as inhuman misanthropists. This misrepresentation of veganism ridicules vegans and perpetuates "a moral injury to omnivorous readers who are not presented with the opportunity to understand veganism and the challenge to speciesism that it contains," while obscuring and reproducing "exploitative and violent reactions between human and nonhuman animals" (Cole and Morgan 134).

The peculiar features of online communication favor hostility because of a perceived anonymity in the speakers that leads them to disinhibition and the false belief of lack of accountability. Both the sense of de-individuation together with the need of group belonging foster the spread of hate toward the other.

Notes

1 https://dictionary.cambridge.org/dictionary/english/myth.
2 The italics are ours.

Works cited

Bar-Tal, Daniel, Ariel W. Kruglanski, and Yechiel Klar. "Conflict Termination: An Epistemological Analysis of International Cases." *Political Psychology*, vol. 10, no. 2, 1989, pp. 233–255. doi:https://doi.org/10.2307/3791646
Citron, Keats Danielle. "Cyber civil rights." *Boston University Law Review*, vol. 89, 2009, pp. 61–125.
Cole, Matthew and Karen Morgan, "Vegaphobia: Derogatory Discourses of Veganism and the Reproduction of Speciesism in UK National Newspapers." *The British Journal of Sociology*, vol. 62, no. 1, 2011, pp. 134–153.
Dawkins, Richard. *The Extended Phenotype*. Oxford University Press, 1982.
———. *The Selfish Gene*. Oxford: Oxford University Press, 1976.
Di Stefano, Mark. "This Vegan Journalist Pitched to Waitrose Food Magazine, and the Editor Replied Proposing a Series about Killing Vegans." *Buzzfeed*, 29 October 2018. https://www.buzzfeed.com/markdistefano/waitrose-food-killing-vegans-freelance-journalist. Accessed January 8 2020.
Engel, Jakob, and Ruth Wodak. "'Calculated ambivalence' and Holocaust Denial in Austria." *Analysing Fascist Discourse: European Fascism in Talk and Text*, edited by Ruth Wodak and John E. Richardson, Routledge, 2013, pp. 73–96, https://www.researchgate.net/publication/290297413_Calculated_ambivalence_and_holocaust_denial_in_Austria. Accessed July 12 2019.
Fine, Gary Alan. "Sociological Approaches to the Study of Humor." *Handbook of Humor Research*, edited by Paul McGhee and Jeffrey Goldstein, Springer-Verlag, 1983, pp. 159–182.
Gagliardone, Iginio. "Defining Online Hate and Its 'Public Lives': What is the Place for Extreme Speech?" *International Journal of Communication*, no. 13, 2019, pp. 3068–3087.
Hervik, Peter. "Ritualized opposition in Danish practices of Extremist Language and Thought." *International Journal of Communication*, no. 13, 2019, pp. 3104–3121.
Higgins, Abigail. "Why do People Hate Vegans so much?" 10 November 2018. https://www.vox.com/future-perfect/2018/11/2/18055532/vegans-vegetarian-research-uk. Accessed January 8 2020.
Joy, Melanie, and Jens Tuider. "Foreword." *Critical Perspectives on Veganism*, edited by Jodey Castricano and Rasmus R. Simonsen, E-book, Palgrave Macmillan, 2016, pp. v–xv.
Knight, Naomi. "'Still Cool ... and American Too': An SFL Analysis of Deferred Bonds in Internet Message Humour." *Systemic Functional Linguistics in Use*, edited by Nina Norgaard, Odense Working Papers in Language and Communication no. 29, 2008, pp. 481–502.
Kopytowska, Monika, "Introduction: Discourses of Hate and Radicalism in Action." *Contemporary Discourses of Hate and Radicalism across Spaces and Genres*, edited by Monika Kopytowska, John Benjamins, 2017, pp. 1–12.
Krishnan, Manika. "There's a Term for Hating on Vegans and It's Vegaphobia." 26 November 2018. https://www.vice.com/en_au/article/vbabp9/theres-a-term-for-hating-on-vegans-and-its-vegaphobia. Accessed January 8 2020.
LaGrandeur, Kevin, "Digital images and classical persuasion." *Eloquent Images*, edited by Mary Hocks and Michelle Kendrick, MIT Press, 2003, pp. 117–136.
McInnis, Cara C., and Gordon Hodson. "It Ain't Easy Eating Greens: Evidence of Bias toward Vegetarians and Vegans from both Source and Target." *Group Processes & Intergroup Relations*, vol. 20, no. 6, 2015, pp. 721–744.
Milner, Ryan M. *The World Made Meme: Discourse and Identity in Participatory Media*. 2012. University of Kansas, PhD Dissertation, https://kuscholarworks.ku.edu/handle/1808/10256. Accessed July 17 2019.
Morton, Timothy. *Shelley and the Revolution in Taste: The Body and the Natural World*. Cambridge University Press, 1994.
Pohjonen, Mati. "A Comparative Approach to Social Media Extreme Speech: Online Hate Speech as Media Commentary." *International Journal of Communication*, no. 13, 2019, pp. 3088–3103.
Quinn, Emelia, and Benjamin Westwood. "Introduction: Thinking through Veganism." *Thinking Veganism in Literature and Culture*, edited by Emelia Quinn and Benjamin Westwood, E-book, Palgrave Macmillan, 2018, pp. 1–24.
Reinghold, Howard. *The Virtual Community: Homesteading on the Electronic Frontier*. Addison-Wesley, 1993.

Reisigl, Martin. "The Discourse-Historical Approach (DHA)." *The Routledge Handbook of Critical Discourse Studies*, edited by John Flowerdew and John E. Richardson, Routledge, 2017, pp. 44–59.

Reisigl, Martin, and Ruth Wodak. "The Discourse-Historical Approach (DHA)." *Methods for Critical Discourse Analysis*, edited by Ruth Wodak and Michael Meyer, Sage, 2009, pp. 87–121.

Richardson, John, and Ruth Wodak. "The impact of visual racism: Visual arguments in political leaflets of Austrian and British far-right parties." *Critical Discourse Analysis. Vol. IV. Applications, Interdisciplinary Perspectives and New Trends*, edited by Ruth Wodak, Sage, 2013, pp. 245–274.

Sitwell, William. "Carnivore William Sitwell is Challenged to Go Vegan... Will He Last the Week?" *The Telegraph*, 3 January 2020, https://www.telegraph.co.uk/food-and-drink/in-depth/carnivore-william-sitwell-challenged-go-vegan-will-last-week/. Accessed January 8 2020.

Stuart, Tristram. *The Bloodless Revolution: Radical Vegetarians and the Discovery of India*. HarperPress, 2006.

Speier, Hans. "Wit and Politics: An Essay on Laughter and Power." *American Journal of Sociology*, vol. 103, no. 5, 1998, pp. 1352–1401.

Thomas, Keith. *Man and the Natural World. Changing Attitudes in England 1500–1800*. Penguin Books, 1984.

Toffler, Alvin. *The Third Wave*. Bantam, 1980.

Udupa, Sahana. "Nationalism in the Digital Age: Fun as a Metapractice of Extreme Speech." *International Journal of Communication*, no. 13, 2019, pp. 3143–3163.

Udupa, Sahana, and Matti Pohjonen. "Extreme Speech and Global Digital Cultures." *International Journal of Communication*, no. 13, 2019, pp. 3049–3067.

Van Leeuwen, Theodore, and Ruth Wodak. "Legitimizing Immigration Control: A Discourse-Historical Analysis." *Discourse Studies*, vol. 1, no. 1, 1999, pp. 83–119.

Wodak, Ruth. *The Politics of Fear: What Right-Wing Populist Discourses Mean*. Sage, 2015.

Wright, Laura. *The Vegan Studies Project: Food, Animals, and Gender in the Age of Terror*. Kindle ed., University of Georgia Press, 2015.

Žagar, Igor. "*Topoi* in Critical Discourse Analysis." *Lodz Papers in Pragmatics*, vol. 6, no. 1, 2010, pp. 3–27.

Zappavigna, Michelle. "Ambient Affiliation: A Linguistic Perspective on Twitter." *New Media and Society*, vol. 13, no. 5, 2011, pp. 788–806.

———. *Discourse of Twitter and Social Media: How We Use Language to Create Affiliation on the Web*. Continuum, 2012.

Part 6
Vegan geographies

32
Vegan food tourism
Experiences and implications

Francesc Fusté-Forné

Introduction and objective

Food tourism refers to the discovery of cultural and natural heritages through food (Berno and Fusté-Forné; Long). While food-based tourism includes a wide range of activities and experiences, eating out is one of the most relevant practices when traveling (Björk and Kauppinen-Räisänen; Levitt et al.). Previous research acknowledged that one third of tourist expenditure is devoted to food and gastronomy, restaurants taking the most significant portion (Graziani; Telfer and Wall). In the context of food tourism, this chapter aims to analyze food tourism consumption from a vegan perspective—considering the different stages of the travel experience.

Veganism is a phenomenon which is rapidly growing (see Ruby). Previous research highlighted "ethics" and "health" as the two principal motivations for being vegan (see, e.g., Phua, Jin and Kim). According to The Vegan Society, cited by Greenebaum, a vegan is

> someone who tries to live without exploiting animals, for the benefit of animals, people and the planet. Vegans eat a plant-based diet, with nothing coming from animals-no meat, milk, eggs or honey, for example. A vegan lifestyle also avoids leather, wool, silk and other animal products for clothing or any other purpose. (129)

In this sense, to be vegan refers to a lifestyle and a philosophy which includes what people "eat, consume and purchase" (132). The current chapter focuses on veganism, and vegan tourists, in relation to their food tourism experiences.

Negotiating food tourism within the context of vegan studies

According to the Vegan Society,

> to be vegan is to ascribe to a philosophy and way of living which seeks to exclude all forms of exploitation of, and cruelty to, animals for food, clothing or any other purpose; and by extension, promotes the development and use of animal-free alternatives for the benefit of humans, animals and the environment. In dietary terms it denotes the practice of dispensing with all products derived wholly or partly from animals. (qtd. in Wright 727)

Veganism is an identity lifestyle where, as Alekova reports, consumption choices are responsible and are concerned with health, animals, and the environment. Added to this, Ciocchetti affirms that "vegans don't eat animal products of any sort because of the morally objectionable practices of current animal agriculture and they argue that we should move towards a food production system that doesn't depend on animal agriculture" (406). According to Phua et al., vegan diet refers not only to the consumption of animal-free products and dishes but also to the exclusion of unethical and unsustainable food production practices.

In this sense, "vegans represent a new form of social movement that is not based on legislation or identity politics, but instead is based on everyday practices in one's lifestyle" (Cherry 156). Within the rise of veganism, celebrities have largely contributed to the visibility of vegan culture by adopting vegan diets (Doyle; Smith; Wright). When considering the vegan movement as a dietary style, veganism is featured by "eating only plant-based foods and abstaining from all animal products" (Sneijder and Molder 622), as reported above. Here, veganism goes beyond vegetarianism's mandate to avoid meat consumption: "in addition to not eating meat, fish, or fowl, [vegans] also do not consume any animal products such as dairy and eggs. Since veganism focuses on eliminating animal products from people's diets and lifestyles" (Cherry 155). Previous research acknowledged an increase in plant-based eating (Huang et al.) and the subsequent impact of food consumption on the environment (Rosi et al.). Given veganism's increasingly visible status, people are becoming more aware of the impact of what they eat, consume, and purchase. In this context, "with the amount of vegan consumers expected to continue to rise, it will be important to understand how vegans relate to the products and services around them through their consumer choices" (Alekova 28). This chapter contributes to this discussion by analyzing food consumption from a vegan tourist perspective, which also represents a growing business opportunity (Huang et al.).

An approach to the evolution of veganism in the context of food tourism

According to Batt, the first Vegan Society was founded in England in 1944. The second half of the 20th century has witnessed the creation of vegan associations, businesses, and publications, led by *The Vegan Magazine*. Vegan population has progressively grown, and World Vegan Day was launched in 1994 (Forgrieve). The interest in veganism and the number of vegans are continuously rising ("The Economist"). This growth largely influences destinations' portfolios and tourism stakeholders, which increasingly rely on gastronomy as part of their planning and marketing strategies (Henderson; Du Rand and Heath; Rachão et al.). Within this context, vegan consumption is expected to be at the core of the sustainable development of food tourism futures (Fusté-Forné and Jamal).

Long is one of the first authors to focus on the relationship between gastronomy and tourism, understanding culinary tourism as the exploration of a culture through food. Food tourism is defined as the journey to gastronomic regions, with entertainment and recreational motivations, which includes visits to food producers, gastronomic festivals and food fairs, events, farmers' markets, cooking shows, and demonstrations, tasting food products, or other food-based tourist activities (Hall and Sharples). Consequently, vegan food tourism can be defined as a journey to culinary destinations in order to experience animal-free products and activities. Previous research scarcely examined the relationships between food tourism and veganism—only few examples have focused on the study of the vegan travel experience (see, e.g., Bertella).

Bordelon highlighted that

> for most people who would like to take a trip, traveling is as simple as selecting a destination, making air and hotel reservations, boarding an airplane, and enjoying the experience. Once at the destination, travellers can leisurely select restaurants and visit attractions. (1)

However, people with specific food "preferences," such as vegans, need to accurately plan their travel, especially in terms of food consumption and eating out. Authors such as Kansanen have previously investigated that "vegan tourists often come across difficulties during their travels. [...] Meat, milk and eggs are products that vegans avoid. These can be difficult to replace in cultures where they are acting a big role in the cooking" (1). In this sense, it is important to further scrutinize to what extent vegan people are influenced by their vegan lifestyle when choosing a destination – i.e., accessibility to vegan food (Hoek et al.; Lee, Scott and Packer). Drawing from a demand perspective, this chapter analyses the food tourist experience of vegan travelers.

The spread of vegan food experiences

Paralleling the growing significance of food tourism as a crucial attraction and motivating travel factor, both public and private destination management organizations have gradually incorporated veganism as part of their gastronomic offerings, and vegan food tourism is experiencing continuous growth. This growth results in an increasing number of vegan restaurants, vegan tours, and vegan festivals, to cite some examples. Data shows that "there were 11,655 vegan food and drink businesses launched in Europe in 2019, an increase of 93 percent from 2016 which was 6,041" ("The Vegan Society"). From the perspective of the tourism industry, specialist travel agencies are organizing vegan journeys (e.g., "Tarannà"), which do not only include the gastronomic ingredient but also vegan accommodation options (Slate; "Vegan Hotels"). Furthermore, Lonely Planet released *The Vegan Travel Handbook* in December 2019, and welcomed the year 2020 with a vegan tour across Europe (Martin).

As Peltier reports, "there's no question that vegan travellers appreciate the attention and effort to design food tours that are just as delicious as any other." Accordingly, "plant-based tours are springing up in cities where meaty cuisine traditionally rules – and these choices also explore some of Europe's coolest urban districts" (Wilson) – such as Amsterdam, London, Prague, or Warsaw. Others include Barcelona and Madrid ("Vegan Experiences"). For example, in Barcelona, vegan gastronomic tourism practices include a combination of cultural and culinary visits to restaurants that offer a taste of the Mediterranean diet, which was acknowledged by the UNESCO as a World Intangible Cultural Heritage expression in 2013. Travelers can also experience vegan food activities offered by the sharing economy platforms ("Airbnb"). Moreover, in Madrid there is also a wide range of vegan experiences for *conscious* travelers. As observed in the website of Madrid Vegan Travel, vegan food proposals include tapas food tours and cooking classes, together with special tours that combine gastronomy with culture and shopping from a vegan perspective.

In this context, media plays a critical role in the democratization of the vegan movement. Social media and food influencers have contributed to the propagation of veganism during recent years (Joyce; Pevreall). Examples are found on YouTube cooking channels, with series such as *The Whole Food Plant Based Cooking Show*. Added to social media networks, both newspapers and television have also integrated veganism in their schedules—culinary television shows have extended the social influence of veganism, with recent productions such as *Living On The Veg* (Chiorando) arriving to mainstream television. Previous research analyzed the presence of food in media, reporting the progressive importance of "vegan food" (Fusté-Forné).

Methodology

The objective of this chapter is to understand the tourist experience from a vegan perspective. In particular, the aim of the research is to analyze the expectations, perceptions, and experiences of vegan tourists by focusing on their food tourism consumption. To achieve it, the study

Table 32.1 Profile of the participants

N	Name	Gender	Age	Education	Profession	Vegan for
1	Gala	Female	34	High school	Make-up artist	6 years
2	Lucia	Female	53	Bachelor	Journalist	8 years
3	Maria	Female	33	Master	Floral designer	2 years
4	Marina	Female	29	Bachelor	Cook	6 years
5	Nuria	Female	30	Bachelor	Cook	6 years
6	Regina	Female	30	Bachelor	Event planner	1 year

method relies on a non-probability convenience sampling technique. The sample was composed by six self-defined vegans, all based in Spain. Recent studies show that veganism in Spain is rapidly growing. While only 0.5 percent of Spanish inhabitants are vegan (approximately 200,000 people), vegans in Spain doubled in the last three years, between 2017 and 2019 ("Lantern"). According to The Green Revolution report, vegan consumers in Spain are predominantly millennial women, who live in urban environments, and with a vocational or academic degree. They are concerned about their health, are sensitive to animal suffering, and are respectful of the environment ("Asociación de Fabricantes y Distribuidores"). With regard to the study sample, the first participant is an interviewee that the author knew was vegan. After a conversation with her, the author reached out to a social group of vegan female entrepreneurs, to recruit other participants for the project. Six in-depth interviews with vegan tourists were conducted during the months of December 2019 and January 2020. Each of the interviews lasted between 60 and 90 minutes. Table 32.1 shows the participants' profile.

The interviews were divided into two parts. In the first part, the interviewees were questioned about when and why they became vegans, and their individual understanding of vegan lifestyle. The second part of the interviews specifically focused on food tourism consumption of the participants, including the different stages of the travel experience.

Results

All participants stated that they understand and apply veganism to their daily habits as the non-use of animal products in all aspects of their lives. In this sense, for example, Gala and Lucia are vegans because of animal ethics and animal rights. The former affirmed that "I don't want to eat anything from animal origin. I totally disagree that animals serve for human consumption, and there are alternatives to do so." For these participants, the vegan lifestyle, in addition to food and eating habits based on products without animal origin, means living in a respectful way with everything around them, with attitudes like recycling, zero waste, reducing the use of plastic and using sustainable transport (on foot, by bicycle, or by electric vehicle). According to Marina and Nuria (who are in a relationship), veganism decreases their negative impact on the planet negative impact on the planet, starting with animal respect. Regina and Maria shared the same idea. The latter emphasized that the vegan lifestyle is

> everything, it is not only a diet. It is what you wear when you get up in the morning, it is to use less with plastics, it is to have an ethical awareness of everything you buy and that this is local. We need to gain awareness and values not only with our personal life but also by being generous with the planet.

Following, the next subsections describe the vegan food tourism experience from a demand perspective.

Planning before the travel experience

Prior to the tourist experience, most interviewees emphasized that being vegan often influences the planning of their dining experiences. For example, Gala stated that

> being vegan restricts a little… but it is not decisive. For example, when I travel, before booking, I look for food options. If there are not many, I ask myself if I sacrifice or if I change the destination. Also, sometimes I book the trip and then look for what's there, knowing that I won't be able to eat as balanced, complete, and varied as at home.

In general, interviewees agreed that there is a wide range of vegan offerings in European capitals – more than in Spanish cities. Also, while most of them revealed that there is a lot of vegan food available everywhere, sometimes the concept "vegan" is not apparent in restaurant marketing and as part of destination promotion; therefore vegan options lose visibility. Vegan options are wide, without being categorized. "It's relatively easy to eat vegan in some places in Asia where the base of the diet and the typical dishes are already vegetarian, for example in Thailand," emphasized Lucia. Maria also reported the same:

> You can eat anywhere in the world food that is not of animal origin. In all cultures, vegetarianism has already existed, and increasingly, veganism, plant-based or raw diets. Fruit, vegetables, rice, legumes, chocolate, nuts are everywhere. You need to put a label on it?

Participants usually plan the places they want to eat out during their trips. Marina and Nuria said that "we almost never go without knowing where we are going [to eat]. We don't walk around the streets to find vegan places." In this case, they believe that veganism affects destination choice from a positive perspective, because they have to search and therefore discover more to find vegan options. Similarly, Lucia stated that

> now I prepare myself much more than before. As I prepare better, I am more demanding and I only go to places where I know I can eat, I am stricter in the choice of the restaurant. Fortunately, the offer now is much larger. A decade ago, they didn't know what it was to be vegan, but now it has changed. And it gives you more security, less fear.

As a consequence, when they are planning the trip, most of them use an online site called "Happy Cow," a website that allows user to search for vegan options in both vegan and vegetarian restaurants, as well as non-vegan venues, and they also search through the Internet and their social networks.

However, vegan offerings are difficult to find in some destinations, especially if they are not urban areas. Gala revealed that when traveling, "I know some places I want to go, to enjoy quality and balanced vegan food at least once a day. But I know that all other meals I have to eat whatever wherever, or to buy foods at supermarket." In particular, Maria emphasized the vegan tourism experience is very different depending with whom she travels. In this sense, Gala reported that her partner is omnivorous, which is a challenge when planning the gastronomic part of the trip. Restaurants need to work more on the identification of vegan dishes on their menus. "Now they are starting to know the vegan concept and they make traveling easy for you. Also, now I prepare less because I know more about what I can eat and what I can't. I relax more. I know it will not be the best meal of my life. I try to enjoy more the rest of the journey than food itself. I am not stressed. If I have to eat bread all day, nothing happens. I assume that," mentioned Gala.

Regina also pointed out that

if it is a very touristy and vegan-friendly city there is more to offer. Now you can eat healthier. Also, there is a growing offer of vegan places and even in destinations where you think it is difficult to find. For example, in [the Spanish region of] Castile-and-León they have a meat-based culinary tradition, but you can also eat vegan.

This ability to find vegan options confirms the growing availability of vegan food. On the other hand, Lucia stated that "since I am vegan, I travel much less, both to respect animals and the environment. The traditional mass tourism is a disaster for destinations from an environmental perspective." The vegan lifestyle therefore applies not only to what one eats when traveling, but also to how one travels. Marina and Nuria highlighted that "it is important to take care of the planet, not just from a gastronomy perspective."

Dining during the travel experience

When vegan tourists are already at a destination, often expectations they have with regard to the vegan dining experience may not be very favorable – although it largely depends on the destination. Gala expressed that "I hope to find options so I can eat, and I wish I don't find much violent and awkward situations in relation to animals' disrespect." Regina emphasized that she hopes

> that there will be a wide range of vegan gastronomic offer. At least two or three places to go on different days. And I hope that they are not only vegan, but also healthy, in a cosy place and environmentally friendly.

Furthermore, all the interviewees agreed they miss vegan gourmet experiences. They also stated that many times restaurants seem to have difficulties on thinking about vegan dishes. For example, if they offer a rice dish with lobster, why not can it be substituted for a rice dish with vegetables? Similarly, it is not that difficult to offer a pizza without cheese, or with vegan cheese.

The interviewees highly appreciate that vegan alternatives beyond salad or grilled vegetables are available at omnivorous restaurants. It's not just about designing a "simple" vegan dish, Maria said, but also that the plate is nutritionally complete. Positive experiences are remembered very kindly by vegan tourists. Regina stated that "Amsterdam has a lot of restaurants with 'fake' dishes that look like meat and fish and are very well made." For example, this is the case of a burger bar

with vegan burgers. The interviewees also highlighted Barcelona and Madrid as cities with a wide range of vegan options. However, as Nuria pointed out, it is easier to find vegan burgers than fine dining vegan option. Maria also said that while there are many examples of "fast good" like vegan burgers, traditional vegan restaurants still represent a market opportunity.

Step by step many different establishments are also opening up to veganism, albeit at different scales. While restaurant offerings are growing and diverse, other types of food venues are slower in terms of adding vegan options. For example, hotel breakfast buffets, Gala said, "are pretty poor for vegans. You can't eat pastries, eggs, bacon, cold cuts, cheese… and you can only take juice, fruit, coffee with vegetable milk, and toast with jam. They are not much adapted to vegan options." However, in some countries, hotels are incorporating a specific vegan option as part of their breakfast buffets. The same difficulties are encountered with tapas bars. "In *pintxo* bars there is nothing, you can't eat even a Gilda. I go for *pintxos* in the Basque Country and I can't eat anything. It's awful," declared Lucia.

In addition, coffee shops and bakeries follow the same pattern, with oatmeal and soy milk being the only vegan offering in a generalized way. There are often no vegan sandwiches or vegan pastries when, as Regina noted, it is not so difficult to provide a margarine-based croissant instead of a butter-based croissant. "You can go to a non-vegan restaurant and at least they will offer one dish, because they just prepare it. But cafes and bakeries don't do it right away and there aren't vegan options." Maria also thinks that bakeries "have a problem because everything includes the use of eggs and milk of animal origin. They aren't working enough with either residents or tourists to allow us [vegans] to go for a sweet breakfast as a routine." The solution is to make food at home: "we eat healthier, without additives, handmade and on the go," concluded Maria. In this sense, the participants also underlined some negative experiences, which are less and less common. For example, "once in a burger shop, I could only eat onion rings," said Lucia. As Gala stated, sometimes vegans are abused by negative comments such as "you only eat grass," or only offered a "simple" salad of lettuce and tomato. "When I go to an omnivore restaurant, I try to avoid the 'vegan' concept. I change ingredients without saying I am vegan. By being vegan you are sometimes discriminated [against] and you may feel mistreated, and misled," expressed Gala. A growing vegan-based cuisine and the increasing awareness of non-vegan restaurants contribute to the reduction of those attitudes.

Francesc Fusté-Forné

Assessing after the travel experience

The participants manifested that there is still much room to improve the vegan offerings, not only when traveling. Many times, the problem with non-vegan establishments is that they "make a vegan dish just like an omnivore dish but without animal protein. If they remove it and not replace it…," declared Gala. All interviewees agreed that vegan dishes must be made from scratch, not just without the animal protein, and restaurants are expected to include complete vegan menus, including desserts, as part of a vegan gourmet experience. Lucia thinks that sometimes one of the worst enemies of veganism is the poor quality of vegan food. She expressed that

> there are places that offer vegan burgers, but it's not that good. I mean the other restaurant food is better. They [restaurants] don't put as much love to vegan food. They [omnivores] eat a "big" dish and they [restaurants] bring you Brussels sprouts. Do not remove the ham from the plate, put something in return … some mushrooms. Vegan is understood as "removing," and this reduces the overall food quality.

Here, "fake" foods can help travelers to face these perceptions—both appearance and, especially, nutritional value of foods, contribute to the creation of an attractive and healthy vegan gastronomic offer. Restaurants are expected to design alternatives to non-vegan food—such as meat—without losing flavors and by securing a complete dish, as discussed above. For example, a salad with salmon and cheese can be changed for a salad with plant-based chicken and lentils, or a dish of macaroni *alla* Bolognese can be substituted for macaroni *alla* Bolognese of tofu, which would achieve the culinary sensation of a Bolognese, reported Lucia.

"Fake" foods generate a diversity of opinions in the interviewees. For example, Gala told that

> I love "fake" things. No one consumes them daily. We don't need them but at the beginning when you become vegan, they help. I didn't become vegan because I didn't like meat or fish. I love the sausage taste. "Fake" foods are also a motivation for non-vegans to eat a product without animal origin. They serve to satisfy caprices.

Maria, on the other hand, thinks that

a meat-hamburger does not catch my attention. I do not want to replace the taste of meat. I don't want to feel the taste of ham, chicken again... I don't like it, it would remind me of the original taste, and the animal. I don't need it, and I don't want it. But I understand the nostalgia for foods you liked.

Can a "fake" burger that looks like a burger contribute to relevant food experiences of vegan travelers?

Finally, the participants also highlighted that they often share their vegan tourist experiences through social networks (e.g., personal and professional Instagram accounts), and also privately with friends and family. However, Marina affirmed that more vegan networks need to be created to communicate and engage with vegan (food) tourism experiences.

Discussion and conclusion

This chapter analyzed the food experience of vegan travelers. Previous research acknowledged vegans

> as a quickly growing consumer segment that merits consideration from both producers and researchers alike, followed by an evaluation of the implications of ethical purchasing for societal change and the significance of veganism as an ethical consumer movement for the global market. (Alekova 25)

Results of this research showcase that destinations need to improve their vegan experiences in order to identify and publicize vegan dishes that are already offered by non-vegan restaurants and to increase the offerings of vegan food venues, not only in terms of restaurants but also with regard to pastry shops or cafes. Previous studies confirmed that "vegan tourism limits one's travel choices" (Huang et al. 3). At the same time, the interviewees reported the limited offer of gourmet experiences. However, they also highlighted examples of unique vegan meals, which can result in an aesthetic experience (see Ciocchetti)—where vegan meat can play a critical role (Hopkins and Dacey). According to Ciocchetti,

> this kind of new aesthetic experience helps us live better by modifying a particular identity, offering new aesthetic experience, and bringing us in touch with the world in a different way. Likewise, the synthetic meat-substitutes might be seen as a less-bold transformation, allowing some continuity with previous traditions. (416)

The word "vegan" is, according to some of the interviewees, still not understood by some people. Here, a change in marketing and advertising management can also have an influence on non-vegan people and encourage them to go to vegan restaurants—by performing aesthetic, varied, and healthy menus, with locally sourced origin, and without the use of animal products. In this sense, it is essential to understand the seasonality of the products, as well as their contextualized offer as part of the culinary tourism activities and practices of a region (Fusté-Forné). As reported by Ciocchetti,

> growing tomatoes can highlight the transitoriness of life. Eating seasonally is feasible in many places, and one only need to do it occasionally to engage with the world. Perhaps meat has an advantage here, but it seems unlikely. Plants have life cycles too. Identity might be the most important one here, since the previous objection left it untouched. (414)

Practical implications of this chapter are derived from the analysis of the expectations, perceptions, and experiences of vegan tourists. Results demonstrated a generalized necessity to accurately plan the gastronomic part of the travel experience. While vegan offerings are growing worldwide to parallel an increasing number of vegans, there is still much room for improvement. Specifically, being vegan is a challenge when traveling to destinations where a language barrier exists. One of the participants mentioned the case of Japan—as part of the travel planning, she prepares a card on which she writes in both English and Japanese that she cannot eat food of animal origin. Furthermore, the vegan travel experience is not only about "food" but also how we travel —considering sustainable accommodation and transportation options because recent evidences already debated the contribution of unsustainable traveling to climate change (Peeters et al.). For example, sustainability of accommodation alternatives is also increasingly important for tourists (Khatter et al.). However, there are still few vegan-friendly hotels which understand veganism not only as part of their food offer but also as a philosophy of travel.

This research contributes to the theoretical understanding of the role of veganism within tourism, and particularly, with regard to food-based tourism experiences. The research sample was composed of six female vegans, which limits the generalization of the results and represents an opportunity for further research. Forthcoming studies could analyze the vegan tourist experience from both quantitative and qualitative perspectives – focused on different genders and sociocultural backgrounds. What undoubtedly emerged from this research is that, nowadays, vegan lifestyles applied to tourism experiences are founded on values such as respect (Bertella). Here, vegan diets are rising (Jones) and vegan people "may well represent the vanguard of a form of ethical consumerism to which food producers, processors and retailers will need to be increasingly responsive in the near future" (Beardsworth and Keil 24). In the United Kingdom, ethical veganism has recently been recognized as an ideology and a philosophical belief ("BBC"). Veganism does not only refer to a diet free of animal-based products, but also includes health, environmental, and ethical concerns. This is also transferred to the tourist experience—vegan food as part of a vegan lifestyle and of vegan tourism.

Acknowledgments

The author wants to acknowledge the enthusiasm and friendliness of the interviewees.

Works cited

Alekova, Gergana. *A Vegan Perspective on Animal-based Tourism Services: Thematic Analysis of Blogs*. University of Lapland, 2019.
Batt, Eva. *Here's Harmlessness: An Anthology of Ahimsa*. American Vegan Society, 1964.
Beardsworth, Alan D., and E. Teresa Keil. "Vegetarianism, veganism, and meat avoidance: Recent trends and findings." *British Food Journal*, vol. 93, no. 4, 1991, pp. 19–24.
Berno, Tracy, and Francesc Fusté-Forné. "Imaginaries of cheese: Revisiting narratives of local produce in the contemporary world." *Annals of Leisure Research*, ahead-of-print, 2019, pp. 1–19.
Bertella, Giovanna. "Animals off the menu: How animals enter the vegan food experience." *Animals, Food, and Tourism*, edited by Carol Kline, Routledge, 2018, pp. 67–81.
Björk, Peter, and Hannele Kauppinen-Räisänen. "Interested in eating and drinking? How food affects travel satisfaction and the overall holiday experience." *Scandinavian Journal of Hospitality and Tourism*, vol. 17, no. 1, 2017, pp. 9–26.
Bordelon, Bridget M. "To travel or not to travel: exploring food allergy policy in the tourism and hospitality industry." *Travel and Tourism Research Association: Advancing Tourism Research Globally*, no. 12, 2016, pp. 1–8.

Cherry, Elizabeth. "Veganism as a cultural movement: A relational approach." *Social Movement Studies*, vol. 5, no. 2, 2006, pp. 155–170.
Chiorando, Maria. "Plant-Based Cookery Show Coming To UK Mainstream TV - Starring BOSH!" *Plant Based News*, 20 November 2019, https://www.plantbasednews.org/culture/-vegan-cookery-show-uk-mainstream-tv-bosh. Accessed December 1 2019.
Ciocchetti, Christopher. "Veganism and living well." *Journal of Agricultural and Environmental Ethics*, vol. 25, no. 3, 2012, pp. 405–417.
Doyle, Julie. "Celebrity Vegans and the Lifestyling of Ethical Consumption." *Environmental Communication*, vol. 10, no. 6, 2016, pp. 777–790.
Du Rand, Gerrie E., and Ernie Heath. "Towards a framework for food tourism as an element of destination marketing." *Current Issues in Tourism*, vol. 9, no. 3, 2006, pp. 206–234.
"Ethical veganism is philosophical belief, tribunal rules." *BBC*, 3 January 2020, https://www.bbc.com/news/uk-50981359. Accessed January 10 2020.
Forgrieve, Janet. "The Growing Acceptance of Veganism." *Forbes*, 2 November 2018, https://www.forbes.com/sites/janetforgrieve/2018/11/02/picturing-a-kindler-gentler-world-vegan-month/#342f0fc12f2b. Accessed April 1 2020.
Fusté-Forné, Francesc, and Tazim Jamal. "Slow food tourism: An ethical microtrend for the Anthropocene." *Journal of Tourism Futures*, ahead-of-print, 2020, pp. 1–6.
Fusté-Forné, Francesc. "Seasonality in food tourism: wild foods in peripheral areas." *Tourism Geographies*, ahead-of-print, 2019, pp. 1–21.
Fusté-Forné, Francesc. *Food Journalism: Building the Discourse on the Popularization of Gastronomy in the twenty-first century*. Universitat Ramon Llull, 2017.
Graziani, Janie. "Travel spending leads to 5,000 more restaurants in AAA Tourbook Guides." *Business Wire*, 17 December 2003, https://www.businesswire.com/news/home/20031217005635/en/Travel-Spending-Leads-5000-Restaurants-AAA-TourBook. Accessed October 1 2019.
Greenebaum, Jessica. "Veganism, identity and the quest for authenticity." *Food, Culture and Society*, vol. 15, no. 1, 2012, pp. 129–144.
Hall, C. Michael, and Liz Sharples. "The consumption of experiences or the experience of consumption? An introduction to the tourism of taste." *Food Tourism around the World: Development, Management and Markets*, Butterworth Heinemann, edited by C. Michael Hall, Liz Sharples, Richard Mitchell, Niki Macionis, and Brock Cambourne, 2003, pp. 13–36.
Henderson, Joan C. "Food tourism reviewed." *British Food Journal*, vol. 111, no. 4, 2009, pp. 317–326.
Hoek, Annet C., Pieternel A. Luning, Annette Stafleu, and Cees de Graaf. "Food-related Lifestyle and Health Attitudes of Dutch Vegetarians, Non-vegetarian Consumers of Meat Substitutes, and Meat Consumers." *Appetite*, vol. 42, no. 3, 2004, pp. 265–272.
Hopkins, Patrick D., and Austin Dacey. "Vegetarian meat: Could technology save animals and satisfy meat eaters?" *Journal of Agricultural and Environmental Ethics*, vol. 21, 2008, pp. 579–596.
Huang, Yu-Chin, Li-Hsin Chen, Cih-Wei Lu, and Jui-Lin Shen. "Being a vegetarian traveller is not easy." *British Food Journal*, ahead-of-print, 2019, pp. 1–16.
"Interest in veganism is surging." *The Economist*, 29 January 2020. https://www.economist.com/graphic-detail/2020/01/29/interest-in-veganism-is-surging. Accessed March 12 2020.
Jones, Lora. "Veganism: Why are vegan diets on the rise?" *BBC*, 2 January 2020. https://www.bbc.com/news/business-44488051. Accessed March 10 2020.
Joyce, Gemma. "Food Influencers: The Biggest Food Trends of 2018." *Brandwatch*, 21 August 2018, https://www.brandwatch.com/blog/react-food-trends-2018. Accessed December 1 2019.
Kansanen, Iiris. *Vegan travel- The ways how vegan diet influences travel experience*. Haaga-Helia University of Applied Sciences, 2013.
Khatter, Ajay, Michael McGrath, Joanne Pyke, Leanne White, and Leonie Lockstone-Binney. "Analysis of hotels' environmentally sustainable policies and practices: Sustainability and corporate social responsibility in hospitality and tourism." *International Journal of Contemporary Hospitality Management*, vol. 31, no. 6, 2019, pp. 2394–2410.
Lee, Kuan-Huei, Noel Scott, and Jan Packer. "Where does food fit in tourism?" *Tourism Recreation Research*, vol. 39, no. 2, 2014, pp. 269–274.
Levitt, Jamie A., Pei Zhang, Robin B. DiPietro, and Fang Meng. "Food tourist segmentation: Attitude, behavioral intentions and travel planning behavior based on food involvement and motivation." *International Journal of Hospitality and Tourism Administration*, vol. 20, no. 2, 2019, pp. 129–155.
Long, Lucy M. "Culinary tourism: A folkloristic perspective on eating and otherness." *Southern Folklore*, vol. 55, no. 3, 1998, pp. 181–204.

Long, Lucy M. *Culinary tourism: Exploring the other through food*. University of Kentucky Press, 2004.
Martin, James Gabriel. "Kick off 2020 with a vegan tour across Europe." *Lonely Planet*, 2 January 2020. https://www.lonelyplanet.com/articles/2020-vegan-food-europe. Accessed March 10 2020.
"Mediterranean diet." *UNESCO*, 16 November 2013, https://ich.unesco.org/en/RL/mediterranean-diet-00884. Accessed January 10 2020.
"Statistics." *The Vegan Society*, https://www.vegansociety.com/news/media/statistics. Accessed 21 March 2020.
Peeters, Paul, James Higham, Scott Cohen, Eke Eijgelaar, and Stefan Gössling. "Desirable tourism transport futures." *Journal of Sustainable Tourism*, vol. 27, no. 2, 2019, pp. 173–188.
Peltier, Dan. "Vegans Find New Options as Part of Next Wave of Food Tourism." *Skift*, 20 November 2018. https://skift.com/2018/11/20/vegans-find-new-options-as-part-of-next-wave-of-food-tourism. Accessed October 1 2019.
Pevreall, Katie. "How Digital Media Has Transformed the Vegan Movement." *Live Kindly*, 9 January 2018. https://www.livekindly.co/digital-media-vegan-movement. Accessed February 1 2020.
Phua, Joe, S. Venus Jin, and Jihoon (Jay) Kim. "The roles of celebrity endorsers' and consumers' vegan identity in marketing communication about veganism." *Journal of Marketing Communications*, ahead-of-print, 2019, pp. 1–23.
Rachão, Susana, Zélia Breda, Carlos Fernandes, and Veronique Joukes. "Food tourism and regional development: A systematic literature review." *European Journal of Tourism Research*, vol. 21, 2019, pp. 33–49.
Rosi, Alice, Pedro Mena, Nicoletta Pellegrini, Silvia Turroni, Erasmo Neviani, Ilario Ferrocino, Raffaella Di Cagno, Luca Ruini, Roberto Ciati, Donato Angelino, Jane Maddock, Marco Gobbetti, Furio Brighenti, Daniele Del Rio, and Francesca Scazzina. "Environmental Impact of Omnivorous, Ovo-lacto-Vegetarian, and Vegan Diet." *Scientific Reports*, vol. 7, no. 1, 2017, p. 6105.
Ruby, Matthew B. "Vegetarianism: A blossoming field of study." *Appetite*, vol. 58, no. 1, 2012, pp. 141–150.
Slate, Theodore. "Vegan Tourism Offers Vegan Meals and Vegan Hotels." *Tourism Review News*, 14 January 2019. https://www.tourism-review.com/vegan-tourism-businesses-grow-in-numbers-news10898. Accessed February 1 2020.
Smith, Josh. "Vegan Celebrities Who are Inspiring Us to Adopt a Plant-based Diet for 2020." *Glamour Magazine*, 17 April 2020. https://www.glamourmagazine.co.uk/gallery/celebrities-who-are-vegan. Accessed June 20 2020.
Sneijder, Petra, and Hedwig te Molder. "Normalizing Ideological Food Choice and Eating Practices. Identity Work in Online Discussions on Veganism." *Appetite*, vol. 52, no. 3, 2009, pp. 621–630.
Telfer, David J., and Geoffrey Wall. "Linkages between Tourism and Food Production." *Annals of Tourism Research*, vol. 23, no. 3, 1996, pp. 635–653.
"The Green Revolution 2019." *Lantern*, http://www.lantern.es/papers/the-green-revolution-2019. Accessed 1 April 2020.
"The Green Revolution." *Asociación de Fabricantes y Distribuidores*, https://www.aecoc.es/articulos/c84-the-green-revolution. Accessed 12 March 2020.
"Travel Vegan, Travel Happy!". *Vegan Hotels*, https://veganhotels.com. Accessed 6 April 2020.
"Vegan Food Tours." *Vegan Experiences*, https://www.veganfoodtours.com. Accessed 3 April 2020.
"Vegan Gastronomy Food Tour." *Airbnb*, 1 January 2017, https://www.airbnb.es/experiences/1165885. Accessed 1 April 2020.
"Viajes veganos." *Tarannà*, https://viajesveganos.com. Accessed 3 April 2020.
Wilson, Antonia. "Best Vegan and Vegetarian Food Tours in European Cities." *The Guardian*, 8 September 2019. https://www.theguardian.com/travel/2019/sep/08/best-vegan-vegetarian-food-tours-europe-cities-london-berlin-amsterdam. Accessed January 10 2020.
Wright, Laura. "Introducing Vegan Studies." *ISLE: Interdisciplinary Studies in Literature and Environment*, vol. 24, no. 4, 2017, pp. 727–736.
———. *The Vegan Studies Project: Food, Animals, and Gender in the Age of Terror*. University of Georgia Press, 2015.
"Your Amazing Experiences." *Madrid Vegan Travel*, https://madridvegantravel.com. Accessed 3 April 2020.

33
Toward a new humanity
Animal cruelty in China in light of COVID-19

Ruth Y.Y. Hung

Introduction

This essay considers the way that human dietary choices have imposed and sustained centuries of tyranny over all species in the world and, in the process, alienated homo sapiens from its humanity and species at large from the right not to be instrumentalized. Looking at a set of quintessentially, though not exclusively, Chinese ways of living—historical and cultural, ancient and contemporary—that have founded and sustained the Chinese meat provisioning system, I explore the following issues. First, I will discuss the historical, cultural, and contemporary relations of Chinese eating practices to global infectious disease emergencies. Specifically, coronavirus disease 2019 (COVID-19), the third reported case of viral interspecies transmission in less than 20 years, calls for a critical review not only of Chinese live-animal markets but also of the defensive nationalist cultural discourses around them. Second, the evolution of certain Chinese practices and concepts of the human that are incorporated into corporeal politics trivialize, neutralize, and moralize the way humans slaughter their fellow animals. Finally, COVID-19 opens the possibility that Chinese culinary practices and culture might one day adapt to and advocate veganism on moral grounds, that is, for ethical reasons rather than health, or novelty, or variety.

Nationalists would no doubt reject my "Chinese characteristic" focus in the discussion of what is, in fact, a speciesist problem—what Melanie Joy has called "human carnism" (Joy 109), dismissing it as nothing more than a racialist ploy to wreak anti-Chinese vengeance. In reality, I would argue that rather than acting on a primarily cultural and national conception of humanity, a significant number of individuals in the People's Republic of China (PRC) and beyond, no matter their filiations and affiliations, are guilty of indefensible moral failures. Even before COVID-19, it is impossible not to judge those who, for generations, have woven their humanity into the standing of such a monument of shame as the "Huanan Seafood Wholesale Market"—arguably the breeding ground for the latest coronavirus. The Market, essentially a 50,000 m^2, multi-story slaughter yard situated in the most populated capital city in 21st-century central China, houses and expedites the daily butchering and killing of an unscrupulous amount of animal lives.[1] *South China Morning Post* reported on January 29, 2020 that the market had a section selling around "120 wildlife animals across 75 species" (Li).

Still, a meaningful evaluation of the practical embodiment of a concept of the human as Chinese and subsequently that of its potential to engage in the moral baseline and impetus of veganism is best achieved by investigating, rather than dismissing altogether, the possibility of such a concept. This chapter aims to trace the development of some elements in the discourse of Chinese food culture and its industry. As the discussion seeks to weigh their representativeness in the history and future of human–nonhuman animal relations, it will consider some of their coalescence with practices beyond the PRC. Finally, this chapter proposes putting forward the value of a "lived life" and "lived politics" as a point of engagement with vegan studies in an age of globalizing viruses.

From crisis to opportunity: veganism in China

Human food production, transportation, and consumption, both wild and "farmed," periodically lead to zoonotic outbreaks (Belay et al.). This knowledge became well established at the beginning of the 19th century, with the first cholera pandemic in India in 1817. Our expertise has grown through the continuous and lurking threat of E. coli and such prion diseases as Variant Creutzfeldt-Jakob Disease (vCJD) to the present age's ever-growing list of food-borne diseases, topped by several coronaviruses: COVID-19, Middle East Respiratory Syndrome-related Coronavirus (MERS-CoV), and Severe Acute Respiratory Syndrome Coronavirus (SARS-CoV). The International Committee on Taxonomy of Viruses (ICTV), staying within the confines of the physics and designations of viruses and working strictly under guidelines of nomenclature, declared on March 2, 2020 that COVID-19 was "the third documented spillover of an animal coronavirus to humans in only two decades" (Coronaviridae Study Group of the ICTV). It went on to name it "SARS-CoV-2" in acknowledgment of its identity as a member of the coronavirus family and its genetic similarities with the deadly respiratory virus responsible for the SARS epidemic 17 years ago.

There is thus nothing "new" about "Wuhan pneumonia 武汉肺炎," or what has now come to be called COVID-19, even if on December 31, 2019, when China first reported a spike in illness, health officials described the infection as caused by a "previously unknown," "novel" pathogen (Wuhan Municipal Health Commission). In the wake of China's alert, the World Health Organization (WHO) likewise identified the virus as the "2019 novel coronavirus," new but similar to the one that caused the former epidemic. The WHO's hopeful approach to the pandemic was to name the subject under study by de-historicizing it so that it might be engaged and contained by the combined efforts of all susceptible countries. Hope aside, the WHO must acknowledge its feebleness and recognize the need to consider the situation of animals as it relates to the role played by the (Chinese) food culture in the global meat industry. Our industry of animal-for-food consumption—cruel, exploitative, noxious, and unethical—often results in moral shocks. Yet these shocks have led and bound us, disappointingly, not to corrective actions but to a collective pathological reaction and backlash that substitutes might for ethics, wanting for thinking.

Meanwhile, contrary to existing reports on the dire conditions of wildlife in contemporary China, analyses of some emerging lifestyles and dietary habits, contextualized within the realities of certain lines of ethical and religious practices in the PRC, have indicated that the current crisis might be an opportunity. It will lead to potentially new and renewed commitments to narrowing the gap between decisive moral actions and the social complexities that accompany them.

A critical tradition speaks of "animal liberation." In diverse ways, we see this representatively in the work of animal welfarists and activists such as Peter Singer and Temple Grandin. In general, the tradition has its base in thinking about humanity's place in nature as much as it is devoted to the exposition of an anthropocentric sense of justice and rights. It deduces, tautologically, our species' superiority over nonhuman animals from within the framework of evolutionary ethics, which places animals lower on the ladder of advancement leading toward the all-too-human definition of moral life. Singer has discussed such thinking as it coincides with discourses of racism and sexism in Europe during an era of critical theory and postmodernism, while Grandin has explicitly restricted her focus to the practice of animal welfare. Meanwhile, in China that emerged from Buddhism and Confucian tradition of worldly ascetic ethics emphasizes the struggle for identity within battles for greater individual freedom—identities based on the (Western) concept of the modern self as much as, if not more than, those founded on religion under the circumstances of the PRC's one-party authoritarianism. Thus, until recently, even this tradition has been uniquely national and political, if not ideological, in its starting point.

Efforts to connect Chinese religious beliefs and ethics to veganism's moral baseline and the absolutists' animal rights position (Gruen) have not enjoyed unqualified success, although they are immensely important. I will thus suggest one line of thinking for the development of veganism in the PRC, especially as it integrates Confucius's teachings (ideology) and a rapidly developing "green" lifestyle (consciousness) in conjunction with Buddhist dietary doctrines (practice). Differently put, what is sometimes referred to as "secular Buddhism" in contemporary China plays a role in the formation of vegan consciousness by virtue of its being at once worldly and spiritual, as well as backed by a popular, easily accessible, and well-developed culinary and dietary choice. Chinese Buddhist practices can be traced back to ancient times, and thus they have an active history of over 2,000 years. Currently, China has the largest Buddhist population in the world, around 254 million, or 18.3 percent of the country's population. These Buddhists, along with ascetic Confucius followers, safely make up at least one-fifth of China's 1.4 billion population (Goossaert and Palmer). Were these 254 million people to step up from regular to full vegetarianism, and from such a base and within a reasonable time advance logically to veganism, which "involves" living without "the exploitation of sentient life" (Cross 14), the vegan community would represent half of the current 600 million mix of vegetarians and vegans worldwide. It would also cease being "a minority within a minority" (Parker).

Indeed, despite "the problem of China"—"avarice," "callousness," and "cowardice"—which has remained relevant since Bertrand Russell coined the term in 1922 (Russell 112), certain social groups in contemporary China have emerged to embrace dietary change and have sometimes expressed such change in political statements. These groups, consisting mainly of urban dwellers and the middle class—a derogatory label in "socialist" China—seek to promote "food safety" and "dietary health" (Klein) revealing the strengths and weaknesses, the breadth and limits, of Singer's utilitarian argument for animal liberation (Singer). I hold at bay one aspect of the contemporary Chinese formation of a vegan trend of practice, that which leads and appropriates veganism as a lifestyle within the parameter of human well-being and health benefits. At the same time, I would like to preserve and redirect a critical element of such an emerging practice, namely, that which has to do with what I will call the "mindfulness" of the vegan. Veganism, if cast in the light of the effects of radical politics motivated by the impulse for conscious and conscientious living, might imagine its task as sustaining a counterpart to the effects of Chinese statist capitalism in the sphere of food culture. In this sense, Chinese veganism should provide the global movement with a firm basis to think through several threats. These threats include specifically the proliferation of certain discourses of cultural narcissism across and within Chinese social groups (Thomson), as well as the brutal realities of our globalized meat industry.

In the domain of Vegan Studies, I follow the critical ethics and imagination of Laura Wright, J.M. Coetzee, and others in insisting on "the lived politics of listening, care, emotion, and the empathetic imagination" (Wright viii). I rely on the dual nature of theoretical work, particularly critical, intellectual work, as ideally intended to engage responsibly in day-to-day ontological and anthropocentric struggles while conducting critical humanist scholarship with the most intense rigor. In seeking to write for Vegan Studies in the time and in light of COVID-19 from "the China angle," not only is it necessary to focus on the question of individual life choices as demonstrated in contemporary relations to "Chinese characteristics" but also to understand the historical and genealogical formations of these relations.

The witch hunt

On February 11, 2020, Tedros Adhanom Ghebreyesus, the director-general of the WHO, renamed the "2019 novel coronavirus" COVID-19 ("CO" for corona; "VI" for virus; "D" for disease; and "19" for 2019, the year the first cases were detected). Redundantly, hence, COVID-19 stands for the coronavirus disease found in 2019. As noted, the new name excludes references to the location of its first detection, unlike MERS-CoV and Ebola (named after a river in the Congo), both of which refer to their location of discovery despite the WHO's statement against naming viruses after a place (World Health Organization). This time, the WHO rejected such convenient options as "Wuhan pneumonia" and "SARS-CoV-2" as candidates for naming the new disease.

The blandness of the name does not matter most; there is nothing new in discussing the WHO's public pressure to ensure a global power's statism and coercion. The central challenge to an international organization naming the virus, in this case, is bringing together the largest number of resources to fight against a highly contagious, deadly virus that has returned in less than two decades in a much more "deceptive" manner and with a vengeance. In so doing, it must mitigate fear and discrimination by being ethnically sensitive, politically inclusive, and diplomatically delicate when providing specific information about the virus, including its history, its origin, its cause, and the social memory that will come to envelop and circulate it. The WHO, as it has claimed, works "from a risk communications perspective," and the organization was worried that the name SARS could "have unintended consequences in terms of creating an unnecessary fear for some populations, especially in Asia" (World Health Organization). Ultimately, the WHO's rationale was to avoid references to a specific geographic location, a specific animal, or a specific group of people when naming the disease so that a "discussion on […] prevention, spread, transmissibility, severity, and treatment" could be facilitated (World Health Organization).

While concerns about "risk communications" might alleviate racialized remarks and assumptions, for example, counterpoising nationalists' ambition to shore up fascist sentiments and militaristic thoughts, there is something amiss about the WHO's caution. The PRC today, itself a neo-colonial state operating through its "Belt and Road Initiative," is incomparable to the late-Qing of the 19th century when it was the victim of Anglo-European colonialism and imperialism. Caution against a racialization process that would *not* amount to oppression because the supposed oppressed group is a system powerful enough to defend itself is an admonition overstretched (BBC; Lam, Zhu, and Guan). Hence, when the local French paper *Le Courrier Picard* ran a frontpage story on January 26, headlined "Alerte jaune (yellow alert)," evoking "yellow peril"—the phrase that was popular among 19th-century Europeans seeking to warn against a supposed health threat from Asian immigrants—the paper "apologized" soon after (*Le Courrier Picard*). Even Donald Trump came around quickly and set aside his xenophobia when he pulled back from using the term "China virus" (Vazquez). However, being consistently himself, Trump threatened to "put a very powerful hold on money [...] to the WHO," which he accused of "calling the virus wrong" and being "very China centric" (Smith). Political correctness at a time most susceptible to the threat of "the China Model" neither effectively addresses the issue of racism in global capitalism nor adequately confronts the imminent danger of a SARS reemergence in and after 2020, as our scientists years before COVID-19 anticipated and now continue to issue warnings (He, Ge, and Wang; see also Lung and Yuen).

Embedded in the power of naming is the ability to frame an issue for people, to supply a beginning point so that facts, beliefs, and assumptions find a pattern and an ending. When rightly placed, a "beginning," argued Edward W. Said, is a meaningful first step in the intentional making of meaning and the production of difference from preexisting conditions (5). As a strain of a virus, COVID-19 is "novel" only because there is no record of its emergence in a human population. The virus, as was its forerunner, is yet another zoonosis that originated in a live-animal market. It is from a family of viruses that has frequented humans and has become a stigma in the 21st century. In the last two decades alone, zoonotic disease outbreaks have led, and threaten to lead, to pandemics every four years on average. They are, namely, SARS (an epidemic in 2003, it mutated to become a pandemic in 2020), H1N1/Swine Flu (pandemic, 2009), H7N9/Bird Flu (an endemic since 2013), Ebola (an epidemic in 2014 to 2016, it resurged into a new outbreak, unconnected to the previous one, in 2018[2]), and, of course, COVID-19 (pandemic, 2019). In this particular case of COVID-19, as in that of the coronavirus found in civets during SARS (Guan et al.), research worldwide has substantial evidence to contend the likelihood that "Wuhan pneumonia" began with a bat-borne coronavirus, which was transmitted to humans, with pangolins as the intermediate medium.[3]

The concern about stigmatization aside, COVID-19, as a name, downplays the more important fact that the disease is the result of a lesson in the past neither learned nor remembered, and as such, the current war-like global pandemic is history repeating itself on a draconian scale, a farce long doomed. Inseparable from the name "SARS-CoV-2" is the acknowledgment that the new human coronavirus is not a product of difference but a pattern and a replication borne out of a set of "preexisting conditions" that have matured fast. This acknowledgment needs to be entered clearly into contemporary history, historical knowledge, and popular memory so that when discussed and circulated, it is interwoven with the global history of human pathogens as this has to do with the role that SARS, along with its history and legacy, has played in 21st-century science and humanity. Recall a 2013 article that introduced a series of papers in *Antiviral Research* marking the 10th anniversary of SARS. The authors concluded that "[i]n the absence of a re-emergence of SARS, there was little incentive to pursue these initiatives, and recent years have not seen progress towards a credible SARS vaccine" (Hilgenfeld and Peiris 292). COVID-19, instead of SARS-CoV-2, has transposed the old-new coronavirus from a domain of evolution to a domain of emergence. In the pseudo novelty that it has constructed, it bars both the dispersed points centering on the Chinese bushmeat trade's continuous threat to the world and the arrival of a "beginning" having the potential to call for interpretation, evaluation, and judgment. In short, the invalid name stripped of all narrative potential and association with China constrains the memory and intention society will need.

Animal trade: "an inferior cultural product of the Chinese People"

All careful research discoveries wither when confronted by the silent permission of statist power and the proliferation of populism, especially in this era of the new media. On March 18, 2020, Yuen Kwok-yung, a microbiologist and infectious disease expert at the University of Hong Kong (HKU), and David Lung, Yuen's colleague and microbiologist, published in the local

Hong Kong paper *Ming Pao* an opinion piece, titled, "This Pandemic Originated in Wuhan; Lessons from Seventeen Years Ago Utterly Forgotten 大流行緣起武漢 十七年教訓盡忘" (Lung and Yuen, see also Jim). Appearing against the background of the Chinese Communist Party's (CCP) continuing attempt to deflate Wuhan's role in the pandemic, the piece touched the Chinese state's most sensitive nerve as it put forward the name "Wuhan coronavirus" for popular use. According to Lung and Yuen, while research and communication within the medical field must stick to COVID-19 and SARS-CoV-2, laymen terms like "Wuhan coronavirus" and "Wuhan pneumonia," as consensus and convention, are also "acceptable" given the currency already gained in the general public, including the PRC Chinese during the early stage of the outbreak. These "simple" and "straightforward" terms are "jargon-free" and hence "effective for communication" (Lung and Yuen). The microbiologists also called on people to respect facts and stop spreading groundless allegations. Given the many controversies stirred up by the article, including the one by Jon Solomon of the Université Jean Moulin in Lyon, who risked threatening academic freedom by pressuring HKU to dismiss Yuen (Solomon; see also Carrico; Wong), it is worthwhile to quote the article at length:

> What the internet circulates—that the virus comes from the U.S.—is unsubstantiated. To avoid becoming a laughingstock, stop deceiving yourself, stop flowing fake news. As a rule of thumb, transparent communication and disinterested, rational analysis are forefront conditions in the fight against a pandemic. [...] The failure to swiftly and firmly close down all bushmeat markets after SARS was a grave mistake. We need to learn from this pandemic, face facts, and not repeat the same errors and shift blame on to others. *Wuhan coronavirus is an inferior cultural product of the Chinese people's reckless consumption of wildlife animals. It is some of the deep-rooted bad habits of the Chinese people—lack of respect for animals and lives, as well as the continuous consumption of bushmeat for the satisfaction of various desires—that are the root cause of the virus.* If we continue in this attitude [of self-deception], SARS 3.0 will emerge. (Lung and Yuen, my italics and translation)

Lung and Yuen tried to prove, from within their field of knowledge, that there is a deep cultural connection between food, attitudes toward life, and the disruption of society by the virus. Their conclusion is at once a warning and a formal accusation aimed at a people and a power that have not learned and cannot adapt their interests, let alone the interests of others—both human and nonhuman. Notwithstanding Yuen's standing as a leading authority on SARS in the world, the opinion piece, notable for its intellectual honesty and forthrightness about the Chinese wildlife trade, was immediately set on fire by populist nationalism and no doubt censorship attacks. On the same day of its publication, the authors publicly retracted the piece, regretting the "misunderstanding" caused inadvertently by some of their "wrongly-worded" and "inappropriate" expressions.[4]

Partisan scholars immediately rebuked the Yuen and Long. Bai Tongdong, the Chair Professor of Philosophy at Fudan University, for example, published in *Ming Pao* a two-part essay on March 27 and March 30, respectively (Bai). Bai's articles expressed a typical air of cultural imperialism that should concern us. In his opinion, Lung and Yuen's critique of the Chinese bushmeat trade was motivated by internal racism, for the Chinese practice does not amount to an exceptional case, is not representative of contemporary Chinese life, and remains extrinsic to the study of Chinese culture and dietary habits. Bai's article, clear, familiar, and authoritative, typifies the aggressive-defensive approach of a CCP ideologue. As the articles contextualized the Chinese wildlife animal trade in arbitrarily comparative terms, they sought to generalize and make banal the Chineseness of the practice so that it could be externalized into and in the world. In today's language, we need to "flatten the curve"—not only of the coronavirus but also China's engagement in the global bushmeat business. Contrary to the coronavirus, reducing the degree to which the world perceives the scale and state of animal cruelty in China would, overall, increase public receptiveness for the "China Model" in this regard. Ultimately, encouraging the development of a blasé attitude toward animal suffering and extinction is nothing more than a defense mechanism to counteract or diminish whatever ethics and efficacy of moral shocks that vegans and animal abolitionists so rely on in motivating reform (Wrenn).

In the ideals of criticism in socialist China, as I have demonstrated at length in my study of Chinese Marxist intellectuals (Hung), both partisan and imperial impulses have shepherded the discussion's direction toward engaging static power interests rather than processes of knowledge, thinking, judgment, and truth. With Bai's cultural conservatism, absolutism, and fundamentalism combined, the Chinese "wet market" and its varied forms survived SARS in 2003 and will continue to thrive. For Bai, animal consumption and trade continue not because they are morally permissible but because they are no more and no less than being Chinese. This almost religious air of self-assuredness is the basis on which the Chinese state creates in the international arena an interpretative room for anything Chinese, no matter ancient or contemporary, exotic or mainstream, inherited or acquired, wherein by being Chinese one is simultaneously a supreme interpreter of the value of all life forms *and* the supreme and final judge of the interpreter itself. The defense of the Chinese food culture industry, one must remember, has one of the longest histories, and given its deep archaic roots, it is one of the most anthropocentric, nationalistic, and self-defensive. The top two on "The List of the 6 Most Sadistic Dishes from Around the World" are both Chinese: "wind-dried chicken 風乾雞" and "live-fresh donkey 活叫驢" (Strusiewicz). The utmost viciousness involved in the cooking of these dishes, along with that in the many other unspeakably brutish dishes in China's classical cuisine (Strittmatter: *Ye wei*), present to the task of criticism a particular dilemma. I feel a moral agony and duty to write about these acute human crimes. Yet, I lack the terms to do so, unless I risk reproducing them through representation or making those involved in the making of these specialties and these specialties as a culture too easily human.

One might counter-argue, as Bai and his likes indeed have, that the same kind of brutalities holds true in other national dishes like the French foie gras or the Japanese ikizukuri. It is mostly true. Yet, humanity moves indeterminately, even if all the time it remains vested in megalomaniacal states and economies. Given the expansion of the world system of capital into new markets and cultures, and the emergence of new consuming classes and new patterns of desire, taste, and imagination, there is an increasingly felt need for new ways of thinking about humanity. These new ways of thinking should depend on neither the universalizing effort of modern Western anthropocentric ambitions nor the particularistic concepts persistent in the inherited forms of some global-capitalist latecomers.

In meat-eating cultures, much cruelty is committed following their creeds and in the function of their rituals. Each culture finds its own "edible" animals and does so by counting on the degree to which it effectively blocks a people's moral imagination. Jean Anthelme Brillat-Savarin's classical study of gastronomy has long since made the point about the action of taste—how we came to putting into practice the ideology that some flesh is food—which paved the way for the interdisciplinary field of Food Studies (Brillat-Savarin). For human carnivores, the difference between one dead body and another is whether socialization is effective enough to allow one to bring it into one's mouth. Edible equates not to the ability to consume but to the ideas that bring about consumption. Given the same method of "cooking," how a duck claw has come to being considered delicious while a roasted human offender disgusting is a matter of moral inconsistency and the effect of cultural disconnect.

Regarding the dish "Roast Duck Claws," the Chinese invented the cooking method of "*paoluo* (炮烙 staking)," which was also a torture device in ancient China. The culinary process involves placing a live duck on a slightly heated and seasoned iron plate. As the fire below continues to give heat, the duck keeps walking and then jumping until finally its claws are cooked, slashed, and served. In a recent TV adaptation of the classical Chinese novel *The Investiture of the Gods* 封神演义, a character named Bigan, who likes to develop some fresh ways of eating, performs this specialty at a court banquet. After a formal, almost priestly process of preparing the dish, one of his guests asks him to change the subject of the dish and finds the technical know-how to extend the cooking method to grilling political dissidents. By the end of the episode, the "cooking-cum-torture" method, which all the guests conclude to be "too cruel," is endorsed by Emperor Zhao, the last Emperor of the ancient Shang Dynasty, whom classical Chinese literature hails as the prototype of savage tyrants (Woo-chul). According to the *Records of the Great Historian*—the Basic Annals of Zhou—Emperor Zhao resided in a pleasure palace featuring a "wine lake" and a "meat garden." Encaged in an exuberant mass of liqor and flesh, he and his queen, Daji, enjoyed the spectacle of the infamous "cannon burning punishment"—prisoners, strapped to a hollow bronze cylinder stuffed with burning charcoal, being slowly grilled until death.

Something is revolting and unappetizing about the food culture that Bai defends, and to the same degree, about the unabashed way his defense assails the notion of culture. In *The New Science* of 1744, Giambattista Vico gives an account of the state of human violence strongly reminiscent of Machiavelli, if not also Hobbes: "[W]henever a people has grown savage […] so that […] laws have no longer any place amongst it, the only powerful means of reducing it is religion" (Vico, Bergin and Fisch 70). This axiom, as Vico immediately explained, demonstrated the process through which "divine providence" imposed upon "the fierce and violent" a "confused idea of divinity" so that these inherently violent people, now terrified, moved "from an outlaw state to humanity and entered upon national life" (Vico, Bergin and Fisch 70). It might be worthwhile to mention that Bai's 2019 book titled *Against Political Equality: The Confucian Case* sought to export the Confucian model of meritocracy as a viable political alternative to liberal democracy.[5] The struggle for global acceptance exists even for Bai; despite nationalism and cultural pride, he sought to reinstate Confucianism as not only a state ideology in a rising China but also one having relevance to contemporary global politics. Confucianism, as a form of statist power conceived culturally and a marker for Chineseness, has reemerged out of the ashes of the May Fourth Movement of 1919 and Mao Zedong's Cultural Revolution (1966–76). In the event of Bai's attack of the HKU scientists, it is to become a cultural alibi to the Chinese bushmeat trade more religiously indoctrinated and propagated than many religions. Wherever there are religion and its extensions—foremost among them concerning the discussion here, inferior cultural products and practices, populism, statist capitalism, and carnism—there is also a specter of banal cruelty as if the former is a sponsor of the latter, and the latter the core of the former.

The beginning of an end

William Empson has taught us the importance of historical knowledge: "the only means of moral progress" is "to become morally independent of one's formative society" (Empson 72). In speaking of progress in food culture, we do not look elsewhere or awry but at our formative society. Instead of sinking into a systematic pattern of defensive attacking or offending in the face of criticism, our task is to look squarely at what we already know—the culture of our own and how it is a manifestation of the way we cultivate perceptions, feelings, and wants. When we begin with our formation, we focus on the humanity that springs forth whenever we transform "impulses" to conscious responses based firmly on an awareness of *the* cultural conditioning that disconnects humility from humanity and, in so doing, forms a people.

Here it is, one hopes, the beginning of an end. Shenzhen, the coastal city closest to Hong Kong and one of the PRC's "special administrative regions," will be the first Mainland Chinese city to ban eating cats and dogs, effective May 1. The animal legislation is a step-up measure of an action by the National People's Congress (NPC) to prohibit all wildlife trade and consumption permanently.[6] In this legislation, the authorities have been *un*characteristically Chinese in two regards. First, they acknowledge that the prohibition of wild animal consumption is "a common practice in developed countries and a general condition for modern civil society" and that "the harmonious coexistence of man and nature," which the new law promotes, is "foundational to the creation of an urban civilization model" (Shenzhen Daily A04). Second, the new law stipulates a "white list" of edible animals and their products, instead of a "blacklist" of prohibited animals.[7] Here, we might say that the Chinese authorities have initiated a public consciousness of animal cruelty from the end. They start from what they take to be a firm and clear legal—as opposed to cultural—definition of what is "edible," the execution problem, if any, lies only in clarifying posterior queries for an already accomplished fact, the fact of wildlife trade prohibition and cessation. Should the legislation succeed and sustain, the PRC would be one step closer to the goal of putting into place a stringent animal welfare law, after more than a decade since its last failure in 2009 to pass the "animal protection law" (Sima and O'Sullivan).

With the PRC being the largest producer of meat and fur in the contemporary world, this legislation, no doubt a much-belated response to the repeated appeal against China's animal cruelty by international organizations (PETA) and scholars from Hong Kong and beyond (C. J. Kim, see also May Pokfulam), will be the first of what I hope will be a series of institutionalizing procedures to bridle the Chinese tongue both literally and literarily. Worthy of note, especially considering the level and official nature of the legislation, is that the authorities use dietary culture as a measure to evaluate a people's standard of (economic) development and civility. In identifying "developmental" differences, they show that national and cultural preferences reflected in dietary habits are codes to convey messages about a people's global worth. This logic establishes the goal of a "developed" and "modern civil" China as a reformed "civilization" using a non-Chinese standard, which orients much closer to the ethics of veganism—a radical humanism from the point of view, we might say, of the end of anthropocentrism.

The case of Shenzhen notes, for one, that some consciousness and standards have begun to recognize the ecological havoc of our profligate consumption, pushing back the boundaries we have overstepped. In practice, the new animal legislation will be one crucial move to maintain a minimum standard of care for animals without resorting to other such measures as property right laws. Ideologically, this act of self-inspection and transformation—from denial to authenticity, apathy to empathy, complacency to compassion, and ignorance to awareness—is precisely the kind of shift necessary to achieve veganism's vision of species commensurability, not merely survival when it comes to how we relate to each other and to nonhuman animals. If the legislation starts as a law that protects animals from humans' felonious consumption, its spirit mirrors what we see in the best animal laws around the world, which not only protect animals from positive cruelty but also humans' vacuous assertion of sovereign capacity over all species—the kinds of behavior and attitude that are at the root of most animal problems. For PETA, this Chinese turn is a milestone in the history of global animal protection: "If China can reexamine its relationship with dogs, then the West can reexamine its relationship with chickens, cows, pigs, and turkeys" (PETA).

Living in the time of coronavirus, one must embrace the Chinese ban on wildlife trade and Shenzhen's reclassification of dog and cat as "pets" rather than "livestock" as indicators of fresh starts; as the beginning point for possible interspecies cohabitation and justice. Meanwhile, as J.M. Coetzee has reminded us, "fresh starts" are the lesser choices best imagined by the "new men" coming out of an "obscure chapter in the history of the world" (Coetzee). The man of conscience would, instead, "struggle on with the old story, hoping that before it is finished, it will reveal to [him] why it was that [he] thought it was worth the trouble" (Coetzee). Were we to measure the species' debt in the wake of the COVID-19 pandemic, let us not forget about the lives of the animals abandoned, disposed of, and murdered by us because we contaminated them with our viruses. In Wuhan (Kim; see also World Journal), in Pakistan (Agence France-Presse), and in Lebanon (Lewis), hundreds and thousands of domesticated animals died in cages waiting for food, water, light, and ventilation that did not come. Those who survived "sat among the dead, trembling" (Agence France-Presse). Our coronaviruses and our fellow animals are everywhere intertwined. By the time we do away with COVID-19, one hopes that we will also be a step closer to doing away with violence and cruelty against our fellow animals—the myriad life forms that are our animality and humanity in the first place.

Notes

1 Less than two months before the coronavirus outbreak, in an article dated October 7, 2019, Trip.com, "one of the world's leading providers of travel services," was still promoting the allure of the "Huanan Seafood Wholesale Market" as a place that, according to the recommendation, "at once appalls and attracts" people (Huanyou anlijun 環遊安利君).
2 In August 2018, the Ministry of Health of the Democratic Republic of Congo notified the world of a new outbreak of Ebola. This new outbreak, unconnected to the one that ended in 2016, was to go on to become the second-worst epidemic of Ebola on record (World Health Organization).
3 The hunt for the animal source of COVID-19 is still ongoing, although virologists at the Wuhan Institute for Virology contended in a paper published in *Nature* that the genetic makeup of the 2019 coronavirus is 96% identical to that of a coronavirus found in bats (Zhou, Yang and Wang; see also Ge, Wang and Zhang). In another more recent paper, also published in *Nature*, the findings suggest an 88.5% to 92.4% similarity between COVID-19 and a coronavirus found in Malayan pangolins in terms of metagenomic sequencing (Lam, Zhu, and Guan).
4 In the statement, they expressed regret about any misunderstanding that the article may have generated. They also said that the article may have been wrongly worded, and they may have expressed their thoughts in an inappropriate way that deviated from their intentions. They also wished to be given space to do research and be left outside of politics.
5 Rana Mitter, a Professor of Modern Chinese History and Politics at the University of Oxford, referred to it as "an insightful guide to a mode of thinking becoming ever stronger in a China that has turned strongly against liberalism" (Mitter).
6 On February 24, at a session of its 13th Standing Committee Meeting, the NPC passed the decision on "Comprehensively Prohibiting the Illegal Trade of Wild Animals, Eliminating the Bad Habits of Wild Animal Consumption." For details of the National Congress's decision to permanently ban wildlife trade and consumption and Shenzhen's subsequent ban of eating cats and dogs, see, respectively, the *Xinhua News* of February 24, 2020 (The 16th Session of the 13th National People's Congress Standing Committee) and the *Shenzhen News* of April 2, 2020 (Shenzhen Daily).
7 According to the authorities, given the numerous kinds of wild animals in nature, and more than 2,000 species of them are under protection in China alone, the list of wild animals banned by local governments will be too long to answer the question of "what animals can eat." Formulating a "white list" of edible animals can better achieve a clear and operable list management effect. Specifically, the white list contains two types: one is pigs, cattle, sheep, donkeys, rabbits, chickens, ducks, geese, pigeons, nine kinds of poultry, and livestock; the other is aquatic animals legal for eating according to laws and regulations. At the same time, to further meet the people's daily needs, the Shenzhen Municipal People's Government supplements and formulates a catalog of other edible poultry and livestock in accordance with national regulations and Shenzhen's actual conditions.

Works cited

Agence France-Presse. "Coronavirus Lockdown: Hundreds of Abandoned Animals Die at Pakistan Markets." 8 April 2020. https://www.scmp.com/news/asia/south-asia/article/3078864/coronavirus-lockdown-hundreds-abandoned-animals-die-pakistan.

Bai, Tondong. "Examining Inferior Culture and Inferior System in the Light of the Coronavirus Outbreak (Part 1 of 2) 在新冠疫情下看劣質　文化與劣質制度(上)." 27 March 2020a. https://news.mingpao.com/ins/%E6%96%87%E6%91%98/article/20200327/s00022/1585230577432. Accessed April 2020.

Bai, Tongdong. "Examining Inferior Culture and Inferior System in the Light of the Coronavirus Outbreak (Part 2 of 2) 在新冠疫情下看劣質文化與劣質制度(下)." 30 March 2020b. https://news.mingpao.com/ins/%E6%96%87%E6%91%98/article/20200330/s00022/1585479855344. Accessed April 2020.

BBC. "Coronavirus: French Asians Hit Back at Racism with 'I'm Not a Virus.'" 29 January 2020. February 2020. https://www.bbc.com/news/world-europe-51294305

Belay, Ermias D., Ryan A. Maddox, Elizabeth S. Williams, Michael W. Miller, Pierluigi Gambetti, and Lawrence B. Schonberger. "Chronic Wasting Disease and Potential Transmission to Humans." *Perspective* 10 (Number 6-June 2004).

Brillat-Savarin, Jean Anthelme. *The Physiology of Taste*. New York: Counterpoint, 1949.

Carrico, Kevin. "Ming Pao Row: If We Learn Anything from the Virus Outbreak, It Should Be the Importance of Free Speech." 25 March 2020. https://hongkongfp.com/2020/03/25/ming-pao-row-learn-anything-virus-outbreak-importance-free-speech/. Accessed March 2020.

CNN. *CNN World+*. 15 April 2011. http://edition.cnn.com/2011/WORLD/asiapcf/04/14/china.animal.keyring/index.html. January 2020.

Coetzee, J.M. *Waiting for the Barbarians*. New York: Penguin Books, 2010.

Coronaviridae Study Group of the International Committee on Taxonomy of Viruses. "The Species Severe Acute Respiratory Syndrome-Related Coronavirus: Classifying 2019-nCoV and Naming it SARS-CoV-2." *Nature Microbiology*, vol. 5, 2020, pp. 536–544.

Courrier Picard. *À propos de Notre une du 26 janvier (About our January 26 front page)*. 26 January 2020. https://www.courrier-picard.fr/id64729/article/2020-01-26/propos-de-notre-une-du-26-janvier. Accessed March 2020.

Cow, Mini. "Living Animal Keychains from China." 11 December 2016. https://www.playbuzz.com/kiyaethridge10/living-animal-keychains-from-china. Accessed January 2020.

Cross, Leslie J. "In Search of Veganism." *The Vegan: Advocating Living Without Exploitation*, vol. IX, no. 8, 1949, pp. 13–15. https://www.vegansociety.com/go-vegan/definition-veganism.

Empson, William. "Volpone." *Essays on Renaissance Literature*, Vol. 2, edited by John Haffenden, Cambridge: Cambridge University Press, 1994.

Ge, X., N. Wang, and W. Zhang. "Coexistence of Multiple Coronaviruses in Several Bat Colonies in an Abandoned Mineshaft." *Virologica Sinica*, vol. 31, 2016, pp. 31–40.

Goossaert, Vincent and David A. Palmer. "Chapter 11: The Evolution of Modern Religiosities." *The Religious Question in Modern China*, edited by Vincent Goossaert and David A. Palmer, Chicago and London: University of Chicago Press, 2011, pp. 271–314.

Guan, Y. et al. "Isolation and Characterization of Viruses Related to the SARS Coronavirus from Animals in Southern China." *Science*, vol. 302, no. 5643, 2003, pp. 276–278.

He, B., X. Ge, and L. Wang. "Bat Origin of Human Coronaviruses." *Virology Journal*, vol. 12, no. 221, 2015. https://doi.org/10.1186/s12985-015-0422-1.

Hilgenfeld, Rolf, and Malik Peiris. "From SARS to MERS: 10 Years of Research on Highly Pathogenic Human Coronaviruses." *Antiviral Research*, vol. 100, no. 1, 2013, pp. 286–295.

Huanyou anlijun 環遊安利君. *Trip.com*. 9 October 2019. https://hk.trip.com/blog/wuhan-things-to-do-1044182/. Accessed February 2020.

Hung, Ruth Y.Y. "'Time Has Begun': Hu Feng's Poiesis in Socialist China, 1937–1950." *Canadian Review of Comparative Literature*, vol. 44, no. 3, 2017, pp. 579–593.

Jim, Clare. "Adviser to Hong Kong on Coronavirus Pulls Controversial Column, Apologizes." 19 March 2020. https://www.reuters.com/article/us-health-coronavirus-hongkong/adviser-to-hong-kong-on-coronavirus-pulls-controversial-column-apologizes-idUSKBN2160Z9. Accessed March 2020.

Joy, Melanie. *Why We Love Dogs, Eat Pigs, and Wear Cows: An Introduction to Carnism*. San Francisco, CA: Conari Press, 2009.

Kim, Allen. "Cats and Dogs Abandoned at the Start of the Coronavirus Outbreak are Now Starving or Being Killed." 15 March 2020. https://edition.cnn.com/2020/03/15/asia/coronavirus-animals-pets-trnd/index.html. Accessed March 2020.

Kim, Claire Jean. "The Optic of Cruelty: Challenging Chinatown's Live Animal Markets." *Dangerous Crossings: Race, Species, and Nature in a Multicultural Age*, edited by Kim, Claire Jean. New York: Cambridge University Press, 2015, pp. 63–100.

Klein, Jakob A. "Buddhist Vegetarian Restaurants and the Changing Meanings of Meat in Urban China." *Ethnos: Journal of Anthropology*, vol. 82, no. 2, 2016, pp. 252–276.

Lam, T.Y. Tommy, H.C. Zhu, and Yi Guan. "Identifying SARS-CoV-2 Related Coronaviruses in Malayan Pangolins." *Nature*, vol. 583, 2020, pp. 282–285.

Le Courrier Picard. "À propos de Notre une du 26 janvier (About Our January 26 FrontPage)." 26 January 2020. https://www.courrier-picard.fr/id64729/article/2020-01-26/propos-de-notre-une-du-26-janvier. Accessed March 2020.

Lewis, Emily. "Pets Killed, Abandoned in Lebanon Due to False Link to Coronavirus." 31 March 2020. https://english.alarabiya.net/en/features/2020/03/31/Pets-killed-abandoned-in-Lebanon-due-to-false-link-to-coronavirus. Accessed March 2020.

Li, Peter J. "First SARS, Now the Wuhan Coronavirus. Here's Why China Should Ban Its Wildlife Trade Forever." 29 January 2020. https://www.scmp.com/comment/opinion/article/3047828/first-sars-now-wuhan-coronavirus-heres-why-china-should-ban-its. Accessed April 2020.

Lung, David, and Kwok-yong Yuen. "This Pandemic Originated in Wuhan; Lessons from Seventeen Years Ago Utterly Forgotten 大流行緣起武漢 十七年教訓盡忘." 18 March 2020. https://news.mingpao.com/ins/文摘/article/20200318/s00022/1584457829823/大流行緣起武漢-十七年教訓盡忘(文-龍振邦-袁國勇). Accessed March 2020.

May Pokfulam (blogger). "On 'Dog Meat Festival.'" Hong Kong: Weibo, 11 June 2014. Blog.

Mitter, Rana. "Do Hierarchies Lead to a Stronger Society?" 23 January 2020. https://www.ft.com/content/5eabce22-3c4b-11ea-b84f-a62c46f39bc2?shareType=nongift. Accessed January 2020.

Parker, John. "The Year of the Vegan Where Millennials Lead, Businesses, and Governments Will Follow." *The Economist*, December 2019.

PeTA (People for the Ethical Treatment of Animals). "The Chinese Fur Industry." [Year not indicated]. April 2020a. https://www.peta.org/issues/animals-used-for-clothing/fur/chinese-fur-industry/.

PeTA (People for the Ethical Treatment of Animals). "PETA Statement re China Reclassifying Dogs as 'Pets.'" 9 April 2020b. https://www.peta.org/media/news-releases/peta-statement-re-china-reclassifying-dogs-as-pets/. Accessed April 2020.

Russell, Bertrand. *The Problem of China*. New York: The Century Co., 1922.

Said, Edward. *Beginnings: Intention and Method*. New York: Columbia University Press, 1985.

Shenzhen Daily. "Complete Prohibition of Wild Animals Consumption and Severely Punishes Related Illegal Acts 深圳全面禁止食用野生動物 嚴厲處罰相關違法行為." 2 April 2020. http://sztqb.sznews.com/PC/content/202004/02/content_840754.html.

Sima, Yangzi, and Siobhan O'Sullivan. "Chinese Animal Protection Laws and the Globalisation of Welfare Norms." *International Journal of Law in Context*, vol. 12, no. 1, 2016, pp. 1–23.

Singer, Peter. *Animal Liberation: A New Ethics for Our Treatment of Animals*. New York: HarperCollins, 1975.

Smith, David. "Trump Threatens to Hold WHO Funding, Then Backtracks, Amid Search for Scapegoat." 8 April 2020. https://www.theguardian.com/us-news/2020/apr/07/trump-coronavirus-who-funding-deaths-briefing. Accessed April 2020.

Solomon, Jon. "Call for HKU to Investigate and Condemn Colonial Racism." March 2020. http://chng.it/7gC2ZLYNgC. March 2020.

Strittmatter, Kai. *China: An Introduction to the Culture and People*. London: Haus Publishing, 2012.

Strusiewicz, Cezary Jan. "The 6 Most Sadistic Dishes From Around The World." 12 January 2009. https://www.cracked.com/article_16951_the-6-most-sadistic-dishes-from-around-world.html. Accessed December 2019.

The 16th Session of the 13th National People's Congress Standing Committee. "Nationwide Banning of Wildlife Animal Trade; Extermination of the Bad Practice of Excessive Bushmeat Consumption 我国全面禁止非法野生动物交易、革除滥食野生动物陋习." 24 February 2020. http://www.xinhuanet.com/2020-02/24/c_1125620750.htm. Accessed March 2020.

The Gods 封神演义. Dir. Shin Woo-chul. Perf. Likun Wang, et al. Hunan Television. 2019. TV Drama.

The Shenzhen Municipal People's Congress Standing Committee. "Shenzhen Special Economic Zone Prohibits the Consumption of Wildlife Animals 深圳經濟特區全面禁止食用野生動物條例." 2 April 2020. *people.cn*. http://sz.people.com.cn/BIG5/n2/2020/0402/c202846-33921287.html. Accessed April 2020.

Thomson, Billie. *MailOnline*. 11 March 2020. https://www.dailymail.co.uk/news/article-8099995/Chinese-company-claims-eating-dogs-way-cultural-confidence.html. April 2020.

Vazquez, Maegan. "Trump Says He's Pulling Back from Calling Novel Coronavirus the 'China Virus.'" 24 March 2020. https://edition.cnn.com/2020/03/24/politics/donald-trump-pull-back-coronavirus-chinese-virus/index.html. Accessed March 2020.

Vico, Giambattista, Thomas Goddard Bergin, and Max Harold Fisch. *The New Science of Giambattista Vico*. Ithaca and London: Cornell University Press, 1984.

Wong, Ka Ho Kenneth. "Stop Repressing Hong Kong's Freedom of Speech in the Name of Political Correctness." April 2020. https://www.change.org/p/jon-solomon-stop-repressing-hong-kong-s-freedom-of-speech-in-the-name-of-political-correctness. Accessed April 2020.

World Health Organization. "Ebola Situation Reports: Democratic Republic of the Congo (Archive)." August 2018. https://www.who.int/ebola/situation-reports/drc-2018/en/. Accessed April 2020.

World Health Organization. "Naming the Coronavirus Disease (COVID-19) and the Virus that Causes It." 11 February 2020. https://www.who.int/emergencies/diseases/novel-coronavirus-2019/technical-guidance/naming-the-coronavirus-disease-(covid-2019)-and-the-virus-that-causes-it. Accessed March 2020.

World Health Organization. "Naming of the Novel Coronavirus." 28 May 2013.

World Journal (China News Group). "Coronavirus Outbreak in Wenzhou Village: Authorities Not Only Lockdown Village but also Massacre Dogs 溫州小村爆疫情 當局不僅封村還屠殺. ..." 15 February 2020. https://www.worldjournal.com/6787077/article-溫州小村爆疫情-當局不僅封村還屠殺/. Accessed February 2020.

Wrenn, Corey Lee. "Resonance of Moral Shocks in Abolitionist Animal Rights Advocacy: Overcoming Contextual Constraints." *Society & Animals*, vol. 21, 2013, pp. 379–394.

Wright, Laura. "Doing Vegan Studies: An Introduction." *Through a Vegan Studies Lens: Textual Ethics and Lived Activism*, edited by Laura Wright, Reno, NV: University of Nevada Press, 2019, pp. vii–xxiv.

Wuhan Municipal Health Commission. *Wuhan Municipal Health Commission*. 5 January 2020. http://wjw.wuhan.gov.cn/front/web/showDetail/2020010509020. Accessed February 2020.

Zhou, P., X. Yang, and X. Wang. "A Pneumonia Outbreak Associated with a New Coronavirus of Probable Bat Origin." *Nature*, vol. 579, 2020, pp. 270–273.

34
Vegan geographies in Ireland

Corey Wrenn

Introduction

Ireland is stereotyped as a land of "meat"[1] and potatoes given its traditional reliance on animal-based production, but plant-based dietary practices and anti-speciesist mobilization in Gaelic, colonial, and free Ireland suggests another narrative. Celtic culture, which established in approximately 400BC, was highly animist, positioning Nonhuman Animals[2] as agential persons and often heralding them as superior and admirable members of the community (Green 249). This strong relationship with other animals was rooted in early Ireland's "cattle" economy in which wealth and power was embodied by cows (more valuable alive than dead) and the precious breastmilk they produced. The very landscape of Ireland has been directly shaped by human relationships with these cows and other animals as evidenced in mass deforestation and the construction of thousands of stone "livestock" enclosures. So, too, have Irish bodies been shaped as humans have evolved to maintain lactose tolerance well beyond the natural age of weaning.

Medieval colonization under the Vikings and the Normans would extend this co-development as new dominant classes brought advancements in animal-based agriculture which coincided with shifts in Irish social life. British colonization, furthermore, the longest lasting and most influential foreign domination of Ireland, would amplify this speciesist economy to the extreme, dramatically increasing the production and exploitation of Nonhuman Animals, and, in doing so, increasing the suffering of Irish humans. While speciesism expanded, the diet of the average Irish person (now likely to be living in considerable poverty and vulnerability) paradoxically shrunk. "Meat" and dairy made their way to Britain and its other colonies while Irish persons, many of whom were rendered landless tenants to make way for a growing population of cows and sheeps,[3] subsisted primarily on potatoes, cabbages, and forage. Gaelic semi-vegetarianism rooted in communal living with domesticated animals (McCormick 35) would be replaced by a vegetarianism enforced by the structural violence of colonialism, a diet one Irish nationalist, himself a teetotaling vegetarian and advocate of whole foods, referred to as "dead food for half dead bodies" (Russell 375).

Both Ireland's indigenous Gaelic culture and the pressures of colonialism would lay the foundations for a modern Ireland that, in spite of its persistent speciesist agricultural economy, is relatively conducive to vegan ethics. The production, consumption, and culture of Irish food have undergirded its historical progression, shaping national values related to freedom and fairness. The British mandated industrial exploitation of Nonhuman Animals fueled colonial oppression (Nibert 126), but vegetarian consumption which predominated in this era at the same time sustained the Irish peasantry (Kellogg 264–5, 289). Some Irish activists, furthermore, explicitly recognized the relevance of Nonhuman Animals and plant-based consumption to Irish nation-building (famed author James Joyce featured a Dublin vegetarian restaurant in his *Ulysses*[4] given its status as a rebel rendezvous) (Adkins 2). Nationalist hero James Connolly cast a critical eye on animal agriculture, identifying it as a considerable point of vulnerability for a truly independent Ireland given its heavy dependency on foreign markets:

> It has been felt – and rightly – that the land so given up to cattle would be better occupied by human beings. That it were better to see thriving men and women and children, and happy homes than to see sheep and cows. ("Capitalism and the Irish Small Farmers")

The same consciousness to human–nonhuman entanglement persists today. Modern Irish society is increasingly multicultural, amenable to climate change, and concerned with the many injustices imposed on other animals. Development in sustainable and regional food production is positioned as essential to Irish self-sufficiency and successful competition in an international market beyond the harbors of Great Britain. Although many Irish "farmers" have celebrated "meat" and dairy production as crucial to this independence, others are now exploring veganism as an alternative, more sustainable and ethical pathway to a thriving society. Ireland's emerging vegan ethic, therefore, cannot be divorced from its rich history of animism, vegetarianism, and nationalist crusading.

Human–nonhuman relationships in Gaelic Ireland

Ancient Ireland and Animism

The relationship between Irish society and flesh consumption has fluctuated considerably across history as related to various political and economic shifts. While this culture has admittedly always been animal-based, it has not always been animal-intensive. Early Irish peoples relied on Nonhuman Animal "meat" and milk as a major source of calories for thousands of years, but this consumption (especially that of "meat") was comparatively low (Green 11; Lucas 8). Human communities of this region were uniquely lactose tolerant, a recent evolutionary adaptation to the colder climate of Northern Europe which limits growing seasons. Cows were exploited primarily for dairy production and plowing and sheeps for their hair and breastmilk. It was primarily older, unproductive animals who would be killed to procure their flesh (Green 11; Hickey, "The History of Irish Cuisine") or their male children who could not produce prized breastmilk. The bodies of those who were killed for this purpose were largely reserved for higher classed individuals.

Humans treated various species differently based on their socially constructed purpose in Irish society, a trend consistent with sociological observations of contemporary human relationships with other animals (Cole and Stewart 22). As mentioned above, domesticated animals were most often targeted as food, but free-living animals were less frequently so as Neolithic human relationships with the natural world were profoundly meaningful and often sacred. This animism was particularly marked with the arrival of Celtic culture. The exaltation of human relationships with free-living animals and the symbolic importance of the "hunt" surfaces regularly in Irish mythology. "Hunting" was primarily utilized for maintaining social hierarchies, such as male dominance, elite rule, and human supremacy. Archaeological evidence suggests that Iron Age communities before the arrival of the Celts engaged in "hunting" more infrequently. Wild flora, especially hazelnuts, constituted the bulk of their diet (MacLean 5–6). Fishes, eels, and mollusks were likely eaten as well (although very few of their fragile skeletons have survived to the present in Ireland's acidic soil), but "hunting" of mammals such as pigs and hares primarily took place only in the winter season. As one researcher summarizes, the early Irish diet was "rich in plant foods" (MacLean 8).

Animism provided some cultural protections in early Irish society, but it clearly had its limitations given the degree of anthropocentrism it entertained. Domesticated animals such as horses, sheeps, pigs, oxen, and cows ultimately represented wealth, and this economic function would more dramatically aggravate their vulnerability to human violence and exploitation. Animals were given as tribute to early clan leaders in pre-colonial Ireland, as is fabled of the famous Brian Boru (otherwise known as Brian of the Cattle Tributes) (Newman 200). Furthermore, kingships were defined by exploits in "cattle" raiding and the robustness of their herds. That said, although this economy was both patriarchal and anthroparchal, the value placed on cows as living commodities ensured that they were less vulnerable to being killed for human consumption as would later become the norm.

Traditional Gaelic foodways

Despite these decidedly speciesist practices, it would probably be most accurate to describe ancient Ireland as agrarian, with "meat" consumption reserved for the wealthy. In addition to cows' breastmilk, the early Irish diet was cereal-based and heavy in barley, flax, oats, and sometimes wheat (Salaman 247, 253, 317). Bread and porridge, rather than "meat" constituted the bulk of Gaelic cuisine (Lucas 8). Indeed, the bounteousness of fruit and vegetables is highlighted in Celtic legends as evidence of a kingdom's success, similar to that of exalted "cattle" herds. Early Irish humans also collected (or, beginning in the medieval era, also cultivated) a wide variety of herbs, seaweeds, nuts, berries, and mushrooms (Hickey, "The History of Irish Cuisine"). With the coming of Christianity and its monasteries and, later, the Normans, the diversity of plant agriculture increased to include beans, peas, and cabbage. Plant-based eating, in other words, was conventional to Gaelic Ireland and informed Irish culture as much as its "cattle" economy.

The impact of Christianity on Irish human–nonhuman relationships

Ireland may have avoided colonization by the Romans, but it did interact with Roman Britain, and Christianity would dramatically alter its medieval culture. New "husbandry" practices intensified animal-based agriculture, and, although Catholicism could often be critical of speciesism, new Christian ideologies would worsen Nonhuman Animals' welfare overall. Many monks and saints practiced vegetarianism and even veganism (Bitel 207), but many others promoted speciesist consumption or encouraged the ritual killing of other animals for holy days. While animist Celts respected other animals as sacred, Roman thought would shift the Irish relationship with other animals to one of robust anthropocentrism such that Nonhuman Animals in early Christian Ireland were increasingly subordinated as divinely sanctioned resources (Bitel 32–5; Green 239). Nonetheless, some concern for other animals does emerge from the new faith. The church penalized hippophagy, for instance, a pagan holdover which had sustained destitute humans in times of hunger (Simoons 187). To this day, the Catholic faith encourages believers to abstain from animal flesh on Fridays, particularly during Lent.

The adoption of Christianity did entrench speciesism and fan anthropocentrism, but many of these changes in human relationships with other animals represented a blending of continental Christian practices with pagan Irish ideas and practices, such that many Gaelic values remained relatively intact. Ireland's incorporation into the modern world system via colonialism would arguably have a far more dramatic impact on Ireland's Nonhuman Animals. Under British rule, Ireland's meadows, farms, and pastures were increasingly subsumed under the jurisdiction of absentee British landlords and allied Irish elites who were especially interested in producing "beef," "butter," "wool," and living animals for export. The indigenous Irish population would soon find itself without political representation, land rights, or food security. Subsequently, "meat" and dairy would become items of luxury, privilege, and status. In a time of increased agricultural sophistication in Ireland, animal products would ironically become less accessible to the overwhelming majority of its populace.

Post-1500 tenant farming, famine, and British colonialism

Following the British monarchy's split from the Catholic Church and its commitment to creating a Protestant kingdom inclusive of Ireland, European trade expanded considerably into what would become a world system (Halley 34). England's renewed interest in subduing the Irish in tandem with Ireland's now vulnerable position on the periphery of a new global economy would significantly transform traditional ways of life; it was a troublesome transition to say the least. The majority of the Irish population experienced intense impoverishment well into the 19th century due to land privatization and heavy taxation (Salaman 283, 520). Most lacked the same rights and privileges afforded to the people of England, including those related to food accessibility. One's relationship within the hierarchical colonial system determined life quality and access to resources, such that, for most subjugated Irish persons, the using and killing of other animals for consumption was simply too expensive. Land clearances made it difficult to care for Nonhuman Animals for the purposes of individual consumption. Instead, landlords utilized confiscated lands for large scale "cattle," dairy, and "wool" production. For the most part, the only non-vegan consumption available to the Irish peasantry came in the form of hens' eggs, sometimes cows' breastmilk, and the occasional flesh of pigs who could be fed cheaply on scraps and potatoes (Sexton "Food and Drink at Irish Weddings and Wakes" 186). Indeed, without land on which to independently farm, tenants came to rely on these potatoes as well since they could be grown in poor and rocky soil inappropriate for large-scale farming of interest to colonialists.

Non-vegan consumption was further encumbered by laws designed to protect class boundaries through the regulation of food and human relationships with other animals. "Hunting," for instance was prohibited by both the Normans and the British with regard to their Irish subjects. The Irish peasantry would have little opportunity for hunting, in any case, as it would entail trespassing on land no longer at their legal disposal. Even the keeping of dogs (who might aid in "hunting" expeditions) was closely regulated by colonialists (Finlay 55). For political and economic reasons, then, most Irish subjects subsisted on plant-based diets. With no hint of irony, many colonialists justified the subjugation of their conquests by pointing to this vegetarianism as a marker of inferiority, backwardness, and need for rule and development (Adams 9; Nally 727), a phenomenon historians have described as "dietary determinism" (Eagleton 16). Famed British historian Thomas Carlyle, for instance, visited Ireland at the height of famine, reporting back on the "Irish physiognomy" as slovenly and dimwitted, regularly juxtaposing this characterization with the population's overreliance on lackluster stirabout (Irish porridge), limited supplies of "meat" and dairy, and its overall "potato culture" (12). Colonial administrator Charles Trevelyan was more explicit in the connection between Irish subhuman animality, need for British rule, and the potato diet:

> The Irish small holder lives in a state of isolation [...] rather than in the great civilized communities of the ancient world. A fortnight for planting, a week or ten days for digging, and another fortnight for turf-cutting, suffice for his [sic] subsistence; and during the rest of the year, he [sic] is at leisure to follow his own inclinations, without even the safeguard of those intellectual tastes and legitimate objects of ambition which only imperfectly obviate the viles of leisure in the higher ranks of society. [...] The excessive competition for land maintained rents at a level which left the Irish peasant the bare means of subsistence; and poverty, discontent, and idleness, acting on his excitable nature, produced that state of popular feeling which furnishes the material for every description of illegal association and misdirected political agitation. [...] The domestic habits arising out of this mode of subsistence were of the lowest and most degrading kind. The pigs and poultry, which share the food of the peasant's family, became, in course, inmates of the cabin also. (5–7)

Subsequently, vegetarianism was no longer associated with the legacy of an animist Gaelic culture; rather, it became a marker of inferior class position. By way of another example, the 1830 *Good Housekeeper* sings the praise of the "beef-eating" British colonialists, equating power and masculinity with "meat" consumption:

> In every nation on earth the rulers, the men of power whether princes or priests, almost invariably use a portion of animal food. The people are often compelled, either from poverty or policy, to abstain.—Whenever the time shall arrive, that every *peasant* in Europe is able to "put his pullet in the pot," even of a Sunday, a great improvement will have taken place in his character and condition; when he can have a portion of animal food, properly cooked, once each day, he will soon become *a man*. (Hale 12)

The working classes of Britain were also experiencing extreme poverty and malnourishment in this era of colonial conquest, but, on the whole, the English population's diet would become much more varied as a result of its speciesist and classist domination of Ireland (Clarkson and Crawford 60). In fact, as this exploitation intensified, the diets of Ireland's poor became increasingly vegan. Workhouse records from the early 19th century, for instance, document meals based in potatoes and sometimes cow's breastmilk or fishes' flesh. Cows' milk became increasingly scarce, however, as the industrialization of Britain increasingly usurped this product for factory workers and urban dwellers which inflated its price (Wiley, *Re-imagining Milk* 45). The toiling of Ireland's poor made these products possible, but most were too beggared to purchase any for themselves (this is not to invisibilize the Nonhuman Animals whose labor went completely unrecognized, compensated only with enough food, water, and shelter as was necessary to keep them alive). Animal products were considered precious and generally reserved for special occasions such as holidays, weddings, and to a lesser extent wakes (Sexton "Food and Drink at Irish Weddings and Wakes" 115). Aside from those of the dominant class, most Irish persons could only access animal flesh in the form of organs and entrails, which were too perishable to be exported (Sexton, "I'd ate it" 172). "Meat" and dairy were simply too luxurious for colonial subjects. By the 19th century, approximately 90 percent of the Irish population was relying on potatoes as their primary source of calories (Salaman 317).

The Great Famine of 1845–1849 (what some have deemed a euphemism for genocidal colonial practices) was the infamous result of this tenuous foodway (Coogan 230). The plant-based practices of traditional Ireland, which had sustained its human population for thousands of years before the comforts of modern agriculture, had now been replaced by a vegetarian diet of subsistence. Indigenous agricultural practices had long been forgotten under so many years of colonialist control over food production, and this loss only intensified their vulnerability (Lucas 8). Potatoes sustained millions of Irish peasants under a system of extreme colonial oppression, but this strategy of vegetarian precariousness entailed considerable risk. A number of food shortages and blights plagued Ireland, culminating in several episodes of mass starvation which claimed over a million human lives (as well as countless nonhuman lives who arguably had even less access to resources in such times of dearth).

The nature of relief efforts

Precarious vegetarianism that had manifested as a response to colonial oppression was thus a major contributor to one of Ireland's greatest tragedies, but indigenous Gaelic vegetarianism and emerging vegan politics provided new strategies for resistance. Famine victims looked to the fields and forests for sustenance as their ancestors once did. Parsley, nettles, sorrel, charlock, leeks, and other native herbs and wild-growing plants were gathered and eaten. Cabbage was heavily depended upon, particularly so in the early summer months when other vegetables were not yet harvestable (Cowan and Sexton 80). Both Irish and non-Irish charities provided plant-based relief as well. For instance, The Quakers provided a number of grains and staple goods, especially oatmeal. Soup kitchens regularly provided vegetarian fare, though sometimes they contained animal flesh. In these cases, even starving famine victims were reported to have abstained in accordance with their religious convictions as Catholics (Hatton 149).

The legacy of famine

The post-Famine diet appears to have remained plant-based as Ireland continued to export expensive animal products (Clarkson and Crawford 36). It was a vegetarianism of necessity and subsistence, rather than a diet rooted in indigenous values or healthfulness. The increasing availability of processed foods, black tea, and sugar made possible by Britain's wider empire, would have a deleterious effect on the population and worried food reformers and policy-makers alike (Clarkson and Crawford 234–238; Friel and Nolan i; Russell 376). As such, food remained highly political with regard to the nutritional inadequacy of Ireland's precarious vegetarianism in tandem with its traumatic history with mass starvation. To be clear, animal-based agriculture was foundational to the oppressive relationship between Britain and Ireland: it maintained Ireland's dependency upon British markets, discouraged the production of nutritious and diverse vegetables, grains, and other crops for human consumption, and necessitated an overall disconnect between the Irish and their own land. As previously discussed, many nationalists, not surprisingly, considered the role of agriculture and diet in the Irish struggle for independence.

Indeed, vegan politics are greatly entwined with nation-building efforts (Wright 30-42). In the British Isles, speciesism and non-vegan food production provided the impetus for Britain's colonial expansion and global imperialism, and because of this, Nonhuman Animals were at the heart of Ireland's bid for freedom and new Republican identity in the world system. The exploitation of vulnerable peripheries like Ireland provided the wealth and resources necessary to increase "meat" and dairy production, as animal-based agriculture is extremely resource intensive and difficult to sustain without regular expansion to secure new resources and markets (Nibert 126). By the late 19th century, more than half of the island and two-thirds of its wealth were tied up in the "cattle" industry (Ross 30).

The modern Irish food system

The suffering of the Irish people, therefore, cannot be fully appreciated or understood without also acknowledging the suffering of the Irish cows, pigs, sheeps, fishes, and other animals and the oppressive ideologies that accommodated it. Identity and status associated with consumption patterns further supported this oppressive system. Britons portrayed Irish persons, on one hand, as brutish in their consumption of blood and raw flesh (Fitzpatrick 41), while, on the other, as weak and in need of rule due to their vegetarianism and reliance on potatoes (Noonan 154). Irish nationalists thus faced a conundrum: they could emphasize their Celtic and Gaelic indigenousness by celebrating vegetarianism and rejecting animal-based agriculture as a colonial system of oppression, or, they could embrace the colonial animal-based system and assimilate into the world system as equals as exemplified by their production and consumption of other animals. As with other postcolonial nations such as China (Gambert and Linné 137) and India (Wiley "Growing a Nation (Wiley, "Growing a Nation" 41)" 41), Ireland ultimately adopted the latter approach.

Ireland's gradual progression toward independence would eventually improve the status of its subjects and, subsequently, their privilege to oppress and consume Nonhuman Animals for their own benefit. Yet, it would not be until relatively recently that Ireland's foodscape would begin to witness any significant change, thanks in part to the influx of economic security and prosperity. A millennial food consumption survey suggests that "increasing affluence and changing lifestyles" had resulted in a dramatic change in Irish dietary habits (Higgins iii). Certainly, the industrialization of animal-based agriculture was partly responsible. Irish "meat" consumption increased by an extraordinary 74 percent, while the consumption of fishes tripled (Friel and Nolan 26). The Irish food industry experienced significant restructuring in the mid-1980s, and "meat" and dairy production would see even greater growth as a result of product diversification and rationalization of production techniques (Harte 32). Although entry into the European Union would expand Ireland's previously agriculturally dominant economy into other areas of production, such as technology services and pharmaceuticals, "meat" and dairy remain high priority businesses (Friel and Nolan 42; McDonagh and Commins 349; Tovey 333). Indeed, animal-based agriculture dominates the modern Irish economy, much as it did under British rule, accounting for 69 percent of food and drink exports. In 2014, the country exported approximately 6.6 billion euros worth of living and nonliving Nonhuman Animals and products made from their breastmilk (Bord Biá "Export Performance & Prospects 2013–2014" 4). If nation-states are defined by their economic activity, it would seem that modern Ireland is now characterized by its domination over Nonhuman Animals. This structural arrangement is unfortunate given its roots in colonial oppression and continued reliance on the exploitation of workers, Nonhuman Animals, consumers, and any and all impacted by the environmental consequences of animal-based agriculture. Yet, it was this same history with structural violence that would urge Irish nation-builders to embrace a speciesist economy, concerned as they were with building wealth and self-sufficiency in a country where a long-entrenched animal-based system of agriculture appeared to be one of few available assets.

The Republic of Ireland emerged from revolution with an explicit celebration of equality as a principle that was extended to "all its citizens," "the whole of the nation and all its parts" and "all the children of the nation equally."[5] And, although the early years of the Republic were characterized by deep-rooted Catholicism, a protective economy, and a general conservatism, values of freedom and justice have persisted with prominence in Irish culture, particularly as Ireland entered the late 20th century. For Nonhuman Animals, this Irish ethic has been a mixed bag. Today's Irish agriculture has transitioned from subsistence to surplus, and the meaning of food is imbrued with a sense of abundance and national pride. In addition to reinvigorating domestic consumption, international consumption has been greatly bolstered by depictions of nonhuman victims as happy and consenting in lush Irish fields (Henchion and McIntyre 634). Despite the remarkable growth the food sector has already experienced, the Irish state at the time of this writing plans to further increase exports, primarily "meat," dairy, and "seafood," to at least 19 *billion* euros by 2025 under its "Food Wise" ten-year initiative (Department of Agriculture, Food and the Marine 3). Because expected growth in export will also necessitate growth in the Nonhuman Animal population (and the environmental impacts of increased flesh and dairy production are likely to be significant), this strategy will surely be disastrous with regard to climate change (Burke-Kennedy, "Analysis: Agri-food Roadmap Fails"). Many Irish Nonhuman Animal rights activists, indeed, have pressed this concern with regard to speciesism and its environmental consequences.[6]

The Irish Nonhuman Animal rights movement

As previously alluded to, a vegan imagination (distinct from both traditional Gaelic vegetarianism and precarious colonial vegetarianism) did manifest in Ireland in response to its colonial experience and transition into a republic. Although activists were not always vegan, many did position their diet as an explicitly *political* rejection of exploitation (for both humans and other animals). Rebel leaders such as AE (George Russell) critiqued Ireland's animal-based production and consumption as threats to Ireland's ability to achieve full independence: "There is no doubt that the vitality of Irish people has seriously diminished and that the change has come about with a change in the character of the food consumed. When people lived with porridge, brown bread and milk, as main ingredients in their diet, the vitality and energy of our people were noticeable, though they were much poorer than they are now. With increasing prosperity, in the financial sense, we have grown much poorer, if our standards are biological and not financial" (375). The Vegetarian Society in Dublin, furthermore, insisted that Ireland's suffering was directly tied to the speciesist economy Britain had constructed there. At The Vegetarian Society's fourteenth anniversary soiree in 1861, the organization's secretary Reverend James Clark exclaimed:

> in the North-west of Ireland whole town-lands have been left desolate; many families have been thrust out of their dear homes, and the land of their birth, in order that the land which supplied food for human beings might be used for the multiplication of cattle. And this must be increasingly the case unless the consumption of animal food be diminished. Vegetarianism provides a remedy for this conflict, and would, not be a cause of it. There would certainly be no use for the enormous number of animals now in the country if we were all Vegetarians […] (14)

Vegetarian restaurants sprouted up Dublin and in the North of Ireland, providing much needed sites for radical praxis in consumption behaviors as well as meeting sites for radical visions for a future republic. A number of nationalists (some of whom were also feminists and socialists) convened in these sanctuaries (O'Connor 18), and, perhaps as a testament to the political threat this intersection represented, they were regularly surveilled by police. The 1916 *Proclamation of the Republic of Ireland* was even signed on the premise of one such establishment (McNally "From a Vegetarian Restaurant").

Nonhuman Animals were not always absent referents or political objects in the larger narrative of Irish independence. A number of Irish politicians, elites, celebrities, and activists contributed to major advancements in Nonhuman Animal rights in the West. Some of the first books published on Nonhuman Animal rights can be attributed to Irish authors, such as William Drummond (1838) and James Haughton (1877), the likes of whom greatly influenced the Irish intelligentsia, important activists in the United States (such as William Lloyd Garrison) (Merrill 13), and institutions emerging to cater to Nonhuman Animal interests. Playwright George Barnard Shaw incorporated Nonhuman Animal rights in his work as well, with his vegetarianism comprising a major part of his public persona.

Beyond the realm of ideas, some Irish persons succeeded in manifesting real policy change and lasting charities. Richard Martin, an MP from Galway, succeeded, after many years of struggle, in passing the 1822 Cruel Treatment of Cattle Act which attempted to reduce the suffering of cows and other animals destined for slaughter (many of these animals were beaten, starved, and dehydrated as they were marched to their deaths). The legislative success inspired Martin and his ilk to attempt further campaigns against various forms of speciesist violence, such as bull "baiting." It also hastened the creation of the Society for the Prevention of Cruelty to Animals in Great Britain as Martin's law originally depended upon the public to uphold its aims (Phelps 100); Martin was especially active in its early years offering leadership and funding. The SPCA, which would later become the Royal SPCA with Queen Victoria's patronage, spread elsewhere in the West, including the United States in the 1860s and Australia in the 1880s. Irish vegetarian societies established in the mid-19th century, while vegan collective action began to emerge in the early 20th century (Vegetarian Society of Ireland 1).

Other leading charities and campaigns were founded by Irish women, such as the notorious Frances Power Cobbe who founded the National Anti-Vivisection Society (NAVS) and later the British Union for the Abolition of Vivisection (BUAV) following the disappointing results of the Cruelty to Animals Act of 1876 (Phelps 144). Cobbe had taken a leading role in designing the act, but its passage had the unintended consequence of streamlining and legitimizing vivisection. Undeterred by such setbacks, she was a tireless and prolific author, regularly producing essays, magazines, and legislation on behalf of Nonhuman Animals throughout her life. In the preface to her exposé on vivisection, *The Modern Rack*, she remarks on thirty years of dedication to the antivivisection cause:

> such has been the guidance of my life under pressure of claims from which I could not turn away; and, sickening as is the retrospect which the reprinting of these papers has cost me of years filled with helpless indignation and pity, I do not regret that so it has been. It will be enough if I can close my work with the conviction that, sooner or later, the God-given consciences of men [sic] will surely revolt against this deadly practice, and make an end of it for ever [sic]. (Cobbe vi)

Numerous other women in Ireland committed themselves to anti-speciesism. Anglo-Irish nationalist Charlotte Despard, for instance, advanced vegetarianism alongside her socialist and feminist activism. She is perhaps most famously known for her involvement in the Brown Dog Affair, whereby a memorial statue to vivisection victims was erected in Battersea which led to considerable agitation between the established medical community and the statue's defenders (Lansbury 15). When laying out her principles for the women's movement, she included vegetarianism. As fellow "sub-humans," women were expected to be the "voice of the voiceless" and demand both food reform and an end to vivisection (Despard 44). Co-founder of the Irish Vegetarian Society, Margaret Cousins, meanwhile, frequented the aforementioned vegetarian restaurant in Dublin featured in *Ulysses* which was operated by fellow leader of the Irish Women's Franchise League, Jenny Wyse Power (Power was also a founder of the nationalist party Sinn Féin). Cousins would later move to India to join fellow Irish vegetarian socialist Annie Besant to combat the ills of colonialism and sexism there (Rappaport 166). For Cousins, vegetarianism was not only a matter of morality, but a strategic means to advance her feminism as plant-based cooking gave women "more time to think" (296). Power, on the other hand, promoted the consumption of Irish produce as a means of Irish independence (O'Neill 54).

Although some decades of conservative rule in Ireland stifled vegan expansion, veganism would reemerge as a viable alternative by the late 20th century. Following the weakening of the Catholic Church, Ireland's incorporation into the European Union, and an increasing interest in embracing a new multicultural identity, Irish veganism was coming into its own. Britain's Vegan Society made inroads as early as the 1940s, primarily in the North of Ireland. Irish vegans were trailblazers in their own right, however. One of the world's first vegan celebrities, Jack McClelland, a long-distance swimmer, retailer of natural food shops, and leader in Britain's Vegan Society, hailed from Belfast. He astonished the Irish (and international) public in the 1950s and 1960s with several record-breaking (and plant-based) athletic stunts (Gunn-King, 1996).

McClelland and his contemporaries advanced veganism as a catchall solution to many social ills in an Ireland struggling against postcolonial dependencies, a claimsmaking strategy that would lay the groundwork for subsequent activists campaigning in a millennial society more conducive to veganism. They would be shocked, undoubtedly, by the popularization of veganism in such a short amount of time. Bord Biá[7] ("Dietary Lifestyles Report" 53) reports that over four percent of Irish persons now identify as vegan, one in four Irish persons claim to be reducing their intake of dairy, and one in four are reducing their consumption of "red meat." A survey of Tripadvisor results in 2019 even determined Dublin to be the world's top destination with regard to vegan options (McCarthy, 2019). Guinness, perhaps the most infamous of all Irish consumables, went vegan in 2017, citing its desire to appeal to vegans (Stack, 2015) (Bailey's soon followed suit with a vegan version of its cream liqueur). Consider also Cornucopia, Dublin's most prominent vegetarian restaurant in successful operation since 1986, which is now almost exclusively vegan in an effort to meet demand. Even Cork's historic English Market, once a hub of animal trade and slaughter and now distinguished by its commitment to Ireland's speciesist "sustainability" campaigning, now includes vegan vendors. Vegan festivals, too, are now commonplace since the 2010s, as is vegan discourse in the public sphere. Go Vegan World, a small nonprofit based on County Meath, has for several years now blanketed bus stations, buildings, billboards, newspapers, and other mediums with appeals to veganism, a campaign that has exacted considerable media attention (as well as industry pushback).

Conclusion

Irish culture is often stereotyped as inherently incompatible with veganism, but centuries of cultural interactions, be they forced or friendly, have nurtured a seedbed that is conducive to plant-based living and respectful relations with other animals. This transferal of values and capital through Celticism, Catholicism, colonialism, and globalization may have entrenched speciesism, but it has also created awareness to alternatives. Ireland, in fact, has played an important role in the formation of the 19th-century Nonhuman Animal rights movement, and it continues to participate with its own indigenous contributions to vegan and anti-speciesist activism today. Given the tendency for Britain and the United States to dominate in the historical narratives of anti-speciesism and veganism, it is important to recognize that Ireland's veganism is not simply a small-scale replica of its neighbors, but rather a manifestation of something distinctly Gaelic, global, and postcolonial. It is part of a larger Irish tradition of freedom and resistance to injustice.

The persistence of Ireland's "meat" culture today stems from that very oppression. It is a legacy of British colonization, one that has strengthened over many years and economic developments encouraging an assimilation with human supremacy at the expense of transspecies solidarity. Colonization ensured that millions of Ireland's humans would starve or flee while Nonhuman Animals were "raised" on British-owned Irish land would be exported, both living and dead, to feed the privileged. Perhaps, then, it would be accurate to understand Ireland as a "land of meat and potatoes" insofar as Irish suffering and resilience will always be bound to the killing of animals for absentee elites, the meager consolation potatoes would bring, and the struggles of the marginalized in a speciesist, postcolonial society. The state today has embraced "meat" and dairy production with ambitious plans of expansion in international markets by drawing on the world's romantic fascination with the Irish rural idyll despite serious concerns that the strategy will have negative consequences for human, nonhuman, and environmental well-being. Now more than ever, it behooves Irish activists and their allies to underscore veganism as a politic of resistance that is more familiar than foreign to Ireland both past and present.

Notes

1 Euphemistic or otherizing language that objectifies Nonhuman Animals is placed in quotation marks to denote its contested nature.
2 This is capitalized as a political measure to emphasize its status as a marginalized group in human society.
3 Mass terms such as "sheep" are disrupted here as a measure of recognizing their individuality and personhood.
4 Considered a classic in modern literature, *Ulysses* offers a contemporary critique of Anglo-Irish politics in the years of independence.
5 From the *Proclamation of the Irish Republic*, 1916.
6 See the aims and objectives of Vegan Ireland (http://www.vegan.ie) as well as Go Vegan World's 2018 *Vegan Guide*.
7 Translates to "Food Board."

Works cited

Adams, Carol. *The Sexual Politics of Meat*. Continuum, 2000.
Adkins, Peter. "The Eyes of That Cow: Eating Animals and Theorizing Vegetarianism in James Joyce's Ulysses." *Humanities*, vol. 6, no. 46, 2017, pp. 1–15.
Bitel, Lisa. *Isle of the Saints: Monastic Settlement and Christian Community in Early Ireland*. Cornell University Press, 1990.
Bord Biá. *Export Performance & Prospects 2013–2014*. Irish Food Board, 2014, https://www.bordbiaperformanceandprospects.com/contentFiles/reports/Export-Performance-and-Prospects-2013-2014.pdf. Accessed March 16 2020.
Bord Biá. *Dietary Lifestyles Report*, https://www.bordbia.ie/globalassets/bordbia.ie/industry/marketing-reports/consumer-reports/dietary-lifestyles-report-november2018.pdf. Accessed March 7 2020.

Burke-Kennedy, Eoin. "Analysis: Agri-food Roadmap Fails to Assess Environmental Impact." *The Irish Times*, 3 July 2015. http://www.irishtimes.com/business/agribusiness-and-food/analysis-agri-food-roadmap-fails-to-assess-environmental-impact-1.2271717. Accessed 7 March 2020.
Carlyle, Thomas. *Reminiscences of My Irish Journey in 1849*. Harper & Brothers, 1882.
Clark, J. "The Fourteenth Annual Meeting of The Vegetarian Society." *The Dietetic Reformer and Vegetarian Messenger*, vol. 5, 1862, pp. 1–15.
Clarkson, Leslie, and Margaret Crawford. *Feast and Famine: A History of Food and Nutrition in Ireland 1500–1920*. Oxford University Press, 2001.
Cobbe, Frances. *The Modern Rack: Papers on Vivisection*. The Aberdeen University Press, 1889.
Cole, Matthew, and Kate Stewart. *Our Children and Other Animals*. Ashgate, 2014.
Connolly, James. "Capitalism and the Irish Small Farmers." *The Harp*, November, 1909.
Coogan, Tim. *The Famine Plot*. Palgrave Macmillan, 2012.
Cowan, Cathal and Regina Sexton. *Ireland's Traditional Foods*. Teagasc, The National Food Centre, 1997.
Cousins, Margaret. *Vegetarian Messenger and Health Review*, vol. 4, 1907, p. 296.
Department of Agriculture, Food and the Marine. (2015). "Local Roots, Global Reach: Food Wise 2025: A 10-year Vision for the Irish Agri-food Industry." *DAFM*, http://www.agriculture.gov.ie/media/migration/agri-foodindustry/foodwise2025/report/FoodWise2025.pdf. Accessed July 1 2015.
Despard, Charlotte. *Theosophy and the Woman's Movement*. Theosophical Publishing Society, 1913.
Drummond, William. *The Rights of Animals, and Man's Obligation to Treat them with Humanity*. J. Mardon, 1838.
Eagleton, Terry. *Heathcliff and the Great Hunger: Studies in Irish Culture*. Verso, 1995.
Finlay, John. *A Treatise on the Laws of Game and Inland Fisheries in Ireland*. John Cumming, 1827.
Fitzpatrick, Joan. "Food and Foreignness in Sir Thomas More." *Early Theatre*, vol. 7, no. 2, 2004, pp. 33–47.
Friel, Sharon and Geraldine Nolan. *Changes in the Food Chain since the Time of the Great Irish Famine*. National Nutrition Surveillance Centre, 1996.
Gambert, Iselin and Tobias Linné. "From Rice Eaters to Soy Boys: Race, Gender, and Tropes of 'Plant-food Masculinity.'" *Animal Studies Journal*, vol. 7, no. 2, 2018, pp. 129–179.
Green, Miranda. *Animals in Celtic Life and Myth*. Routledge, 1992.
Gunn-King, Brian. Jack McClelland. *The Vegan*, vol. 7, Spring, 1996.
Hale, Sarah. *The Good Housekeeper, or The Way to Live Well and To Be Well while We Live*. Weeks, Jordan and Company, 1830.
Halley, Jean. *The Parallel Lives of Women and Cows: Meat Markets*. Palgrave Macmillan, 2012.
Harte, Laurence. "Creeping Privatization of Irish Co-operatives: A Transaction Cost Explanation." *Strategies and Structures in the Agro-food Industries*, edited by Jerker Nilsson and Gert van Dijk, Van Gorcum & Comp, 1997, pp. 32–54.
Hatton, Helen. *The Largest Amount of Good: Quaker Relief in Ireland, 1654–1921*. McGill-Queen's University Press, 1993.
Haughton, Samuel. *Memoir of James Haughton*. E. Ponsonby, 1877.
Henchion, Maeve, and Bridín McIntyre. "Regional Imagery and Quality Products: The Irish Experience." *British Food Journal*, vol. 102, no. 8, 2000, pp. 630–644.
Hickey, Kate. "The History of Irish Cuisine – Over 8,000 Years Old and Hardly Any Potatoes." *Irish Central*, 17 July 2015, http://www.irishcentral.com/culture/food-drink/The-history-of-Irish-cuisine---over-8000-years-old-and-hardly-any-potatoes.html. Accessed April 8 2020.
Higgins, M. "Forward." *North/South Ireland Food Consumption Survey*, edited by Mairead Kiely, Food Safety Promotion Board, 2001, p. iii.
Kellogg, John. *The Natural Diet of Man*. Coastalfields Press, 2006.
Lansbury, Coral. *The Old Brown Dog: Women, Workers, and Vivisection in Edwardian England*. University of Wisconsin Press, 1985.
Lucas, A. "Irish Food before the Potato." *Folk Life*, vol. 3, no. 2, 1960, pp. 8–43.
MacLean, Rachel. "Eat Your Greens: An Examination of the Potential Diet Available in Ireland during the Mesolithic." *Ulster Journal of Archaeology*, vol. 56, 1993, pp. 1–8.
McCarthy, Niall. "The Most Vegan-friendly Cities Worldwide." *Forbes*, 10 October 2019. https://www.forbes.com/sites/niallmccarthy/2019/10/10/the-most-vegan-friendly-cities-worldwide-infographic. Accessed 7 March 2020.
McCormick, Finbar. "Cows, Ringforts and the Origins of Early Christian Ireland." *Emania*, vol. 13, 1995, pp. 33–37.

McDonagh, Perpetua and Patrick Commins. "Food Chains, Small-scale Food Enterprises and Rural Development: Illustrations from Ireland." *International Planning Studies*, vol. 4, no. 3, 1999, pp. 349–371.

McNally, Frank. "From a Vegetarian Restaurant in Dublin to the Presidency of India." *The Irish Times*, 19 April 2019. http://www.irishtimes.com/opinion/from-a-vegetarian-restaurant-in-dublin-to-the-presidency-of-india-1.3865990. Accessed 7 March 2020.

Merrill, Walter. *The Letters of William Lloyd Garrison, Volume IV*. The Belknap Press, 1979.

Nally, David. "'That Coming Storm': The Irish Poor Law, Colonial Biopolitics, and the Great Famine." *Annals of the Association of American Geographers*, vol. 98, no. 3, 2008, pp. 714–741.

Nibert, David. *Animal Oppression & Human Violence*. Columbia University Press, 2013.

Newman, Roger. *Brian Boru: King of Ireland*. Mercier Press, 2011.

Noonan, Kathleen. "'The Cruell Pressure of an Enraged, Barbarous People': Irish and English Identity in Seventeenth-century Policy and Propaganda." *The Historical Journal*, vol. 41, no. 1, 1998, pp. 151–177.

O'Connor, Maureen. *The Female and the Species*. Peter Lang AG, International Academic Publishers, 2010.

O'Niell, Marie. *From Parnell to De Valera: A Biography of Jennie Wyse Power, 1858–1941*. Blackwater Press, 1991.

Phelps, Norm. *The Longest Struggle*. Lantern Books, 2007.

Rappaport, Helen. *Encyclopedia of Women Social Reformers, Volume 1*. ABC CLIO, 2001, pp. 166–168.

Ross, Eric. "An Overview of Trends in Dietary Variation from Hunter-gatherer to Modern Capitalist Societies." *Food and Evolution: Toward a Theory of Human Food Habits*, edited by Marvin Harris and Eric Ross, Temple University Press, 1987, pp. 7–56.

Russell, George. "Food Values." *Selections from the Contributions to* The Irish Homestead, edited by Henry Summerfield, Colin Smythe Ltd., 1978 (1913), pp. 374–377.

Salaman, Redcliffe. *The History and Social Influence of the Potato*. Cambridge University Press, 1985.

Sexton, Regina. "'I'd Ate It Like Chocolate!': The Disappearing Offal Food Traditions of Cork City." *Disappearing Foods: Studies in Foods and Dishes at Risk. Proceedings of the Oxford Symposium on Food and Cookery 1994*, edited by Harlan Walker, Prospect Books, 1995, pp. 172–188.

Sexton, Regina. "Food and Drink at Irish Weddings and Wakes." *Food and the Rites of Passage: Leeds Symposium on Food History*, edited by Laura Mason, Prospect Books, 2002, pp. 115–142.

Simoons, Frederick. *Eat Not this Flesh: Food Avoidances from Prehistory to the Present*. The University of Wisconsin Press, 1994.

Stack, Liam. "Guinness Going Vegan." *The New York Times*, 4 November 2015, http://www.nytimes.com/2015/11/05/business/guinness-is-going-vegan.html. Accessed March 7 2020.

Tovey, Hilary. "'Of Cabbages and Kings': Restructuring in the Irish Food Industry." *The Economic and Social Review*, vol. 22, no. 4, 1991, pp. 333–350.

Vegetarian Society of Ireland. *Irish Vegetarian News*, vol. 1, October/November, 1978.

Wiley, Andrea. *Re-imagining Milk*. Routledge, 2011.

Wiley, Andrea. "Growing a Nation: Milk Consumption in India Since the Raj." *Making Milk*, edited by Mathilde Cohen and Yoriko Otomo, Bloomsbury Academic, 2017, pp. 41–60.

Wright, Laura. *The Vegan Studies Project*. University of Georgia Press, 2015.

Wrenn, Corey. *Animals in Irish Society*. SUNY Press, 2021.

Index

Aaronson, Trevor 135, 145
ableism 239, 244, 246, 249n28
Abramson, Julia 177, 179
absent referent 11, 12, 71, 81, 82, 86, 174, 212, 226, 263, 319, 322, 327, 329, 338, 339, 402
Acaranga Sutra 218, 225
Achebe, Chinua 273, 281
activism 45, 57, 125, 153, 178n4
Adams, Carol J. 11, 12, 13n7, 32, 34, 36, 79, 81, 102–105, 174, 177, 195, 201, 212, 213, 229, 231, 247n6, 248n16–248n17, 258, 273, 276, 277–279, 301, 303, 333, 339–340; rhetorical devices 125, 126; *Sexual Politics of Meat* (1990, 2000) 12, 53, 57, 59, 208–209, 226, 263, 264
Adorno, T. 253
advertisements 343–353
advertising 124, 139, 153, 264, 286, 377
Adweek Media Poll 344
Animal Enterprise Protection Act (AEPA) of 1992 144
Aesop 89, 98; picaresque tradition 90–91
affect 176–178
African Americans 6, 28–29, 200, 314; anti-racism (radical recipe) 282–294
Afua, Queen 7
agency 55, 72, 73, 107, 275, 290, 322, 394
ag-gag laws 135–136, 139
agribusiness 131, 191, 269, 288
Aguilera-Carnerero, Carmen xi, 354–365
ahimsa (Sanskrit, non-violence) 205, 206, 208, 209, 211, 212, 217, 218, 222
Ahimsa (AVS journal, 1960–2000) 212
Ahmed, Sara 265
Ajwar, Abram 200
Alaimo, Stacy: *Exposed* (2016) 51, 59
Albala, Ken (Ed.): *Routledge International Handbook of Food Studies* (2014) 173, 178n2, 179
Albert Schweitzer Foundation 45
Alekova, Gergana 370, 377
Alexander, Jonathan 123, 124, 132
Ali, Abdullah Yusuf 229, 233
Allen and Myers 34
Alston, Ashanti 141, 145

Alvarez, Linda 131–132
Amazon 208, 237n1, 248n13
American Academy of Religion (AAR): Animals and Religion consultation (2003–) 190–191
American Cancer Society 310
American Diabetes Association 310
American Humane Association (AHA) 330
American Legislative Exchange Council 143
American Society for Environmental History 247n7
American Sociological Association 155
American Urological Association 338
American Vegan (AVS journal since 2000) 212
American Vegan Society 212
American Wild Horse Campaign 137
Amstell, Simon: *Carnage* (2017) 315–316, 317
anachronism 187–188
analytic philosophy 39–49, 251–253
Andersen, Kip 309–315, 317n7, 317, 334
Andersen, Pamela 311
Anderson, Pamela 340n8
Androcydes 25n25
Anima International 45
animal agriculture, animal farming 41, 58, 69, 111–112, 118, 121n2, 127, 206, 212, 253, 254–255, 258, 339, 356, 370, 378, 395, 399–400; harmful impact 216
Animal Attitudes Scale 164, 169
animal consumption 174, 178n3
animal-consumption ethics 258n1
animal cruelty 167, 171, 202, 209, 216; China 381–393; legislation and ballot initiatives (USA) 138–139
Animal Enterprise Terrorism Act (USA, 2006) 143; chilling effect 144
animal ethicists 47–48
animal ethics 40, 48, 91, 250–260, 372; definition 39; introduction for VS scholar 39–49; political turn 46–47; and vegan studies 47–48
animal exploitation 29, 36, 51, 174, 175
animal interests 120n1; avoidance of suffering 41–42
animalized protein (Adams) 209

407

Index

Animal Legal Defense Fund (ALDF) 134, 137, 138, 139, 142, 143
animal liberation 40–43, 45–46, 54, 382
animal liberation movement 241, 254
animal *logos* 25n16
animal parchment 200, *200*, 202
animal products 77, 111, 114, 116, 118, 119, 202, 216
animal rationality 21–22, 25n26–25n34
animal rights 5–6, 24, 43–44, 46–47, 48, 54, 56, 86, 87, 98, 127, 176–178, 190, 201, 202, 206, 241, 296, 314, 372, 383; definition 8; ~ discourses 55; vegan advocacy films 312
animal rights activism 177, 302, 313, 361
animal rights movement 127, 177, 251, 258, 303, 401–403
animals: already dead (ethics of eating) 41; annual death toll for meat consumption 333; annual slaughter rate 172; communicative abilities 22, 25n33; endowed with both *phronesis* and *pronoia* (Aristotle) 25n26; moral importance 111, 120n1; "possess inherent moral rights" 177; problem of pain (Christianity) 184–186; relegation to non-rational status 16–17, 20, 21
animal sacrifice 16, 23, 24n3, 25–26n35–38, 202, 205, 210–211, 229–231
Animals and Society Institute 9
animal sentiency 16–17, 19–22, 24, 25n18, 25n26–25n34, 41, 42, 44, 46, 47, 69, 185–186, 216, 222
Animals, Men, and *Morals* (Godlovitch, Godlovitch, and Harris, Eds., 1971) 40, 48
animals talk 95
animal studies 9, 11, 12, 50–51, 55, 242, 243; posthumanist 52; prongs 7–10, 58
animal suffering 68, 113, 212, 251–252, 256, 312, 387; affront to divine justice 185, 186; *versus* animal death 43
animal testing 152
animal theology (Christian) 190–191
animal "training" 223
animal use 46
animal welfare 166, 177, 201, 232, 344, 347, 351, 383, 389; vegan advocacy films 312
animism 394, 395–396
anorexia 274–275, 280, 281
anthroparchy 68, 69
Anthropocene 54, 71, 72, 74, 76, 80, 90, 243, 246, 248n19, 249n27, 340n6
anthropocentrism 10, 51–52, 54, 55, 58, 68, 98, 109, 151, 157, 183, 185, 187, 190, 191, 242, 253, 265, 383, 384, 387, 396
anthropomorphism 55, 242, 266, 322
anti-capitalism 101–110
anti-racism 282–294
anti-veganism 321–323
Antiviral Research (2013) 385

apocalyptic thinking 80–84
Appelgren, Jessica 350
Arby's 343–344, 345, 348–351; open letter to vegetarians 348
argument of marginal cases 91, 98n2
Aristotle 25n26, 125; definition of rhetoric 122; *Eudemean Ethics* 21, 24n9; *Nicomachean Ethics* 24n9; *On Soul* 21; *Rhetoric* 122–123
Arkansas 136, 140
Armstrong, Franny: *Age of Stupid* (DVD, 2009) 314, 315, 317n5, 317
Arora, Alka 104, 109
Arteta, Miguel (director): *Beatriz at Dinner* (2017) 320, 324, 331
Asad, Talal: *Formations of the Secular* (2003) 231, 233
asastriya vratas 210, 213; definition 211
aspirational veganism 215, 257, 268–269
Association for Study of Literature and Environment (ASLE, 1992–) 238, 247n7, 334
Association of Vegan Society 77
athletes 21, 156, 338, 341n14, 403
Atlantic (2015) 173
attitudes (non-cognitive factor) 162–164, 167
Atwood, Margaret 76–88; *MaddAddam* (2013) 76, 87 (veganism and survival 84–86); *Oryx and Crake* (2003) 76, 78, 87, 88 (speciesism and apocalyptic thinking 80–84); "Writing Oryx and Crake" (2005) 78, 87; *Year of Flood* (2009) 76, 78, 87, 126 (veganism and survival 84–86)
Augustine, St. 185
Auschwitz 114–115
Australia 35, 237, 402
autism 242
Autoboulus 19

B12 deficiency myth 79
Babe (film, 1995) 86, 88
Baboumian, Patrik 313
Badatz Machzikei HaDat *199*
Bahri, Deepika 274–275, 281
Bailey's (vegan cream liqueur) 403
Bai Tongdong 386–388, 391; *Against Political Equality: Confucian Case* (2019) 388, 390n5
Baldwin, Alec 127, 132
Balu, Niedita 350, 352
Bambi (Disney, 1942) 360
Barad, Karen 55, 59
Barcallet Pérez, María Luisa 94–95, 98
Barcalow, Julia 69
Barcelona 371
Barcino (shepherds' name for Berganza) 96, 93
Barkas, Janet: *Vegetable Passion* (1975) 30, 36
Barnard, Tanya 28, 36
Basque Country 375
Bate, Jonathan: *Song of the Earth* (2000) 239, 240–241, 248n13–248n14
Batt, Eva 370, 378

Baur, Gene 70
beans 15, 207, 283, 396
Beard, George 273
bears 241, 313
Bedborough, George: *Stories from Children's Realm* (1914) 67, 74
beef 36, 37, 45, 79, 273, 348, 397, 398; supply chain waste 112
bees 71, 72, 120, 151, 246
Belafonte, Harry 289
Belasco, Warren 173
beliefs and justifications (cognitive factor) 165
Bellon, Tina 350, 352
Belt and Road Initiative 384
Benacka, Elizabeth: *Rhetoric, Humor, and Public Sphere* (2016) 344, 352
Bentham, Jeremy 251, 252
Berganza (talking dog) 89, 92–99
Berger, John: *Pig Earth* 242
Berkeley City Council 143
Berkman, John 184, 192
Berman, Louis A: *Vegetarianism and Jewish Tradition* (1980) 195, 203
Berry, Wendell 242
Berson, Josh 36
Bertuzzi, Niccolò 157, 158
Besant, Annie 403
bête-machine (Descartes) 185–186
Beyond Burger 350
Beyond Meat 311, 337–338, 348, 351
bhikkhu (ordained member of *Sangha*) 218–219, 221, 224n7
Bible Christian Church 4, 186–187
Big Five Factor model 164
binding foundations 163–164
biodiversity 216, 290, 342
bioengineering 82, 83
biomedical experimentation 143, 144, 186
birds 184, 196, 213, 227, 241, 246
Bishua *vrata* 211
Bishul Akum 197
Bishul Yisroel 196, 197, 198
Black Death 340n2
black female vegans 6, 14
Black Panthers 261, 270n5, 290
Black, Rachel 172–173, 179
Blatte, David 219, 224
blogosphere 29, 118–119, 336; vegan rhetoric 128–130
BlyssPluss pill 80
Bodenstein, Dan: *Steven the Vegan* 71
bodhichitta (enlightened mind) 220
Bodhisattva 220–223, 224n1, 224
Bollywood 207, 214
Bord Biá (Food Board) 403, 404n7
Bordelon, Bridget M. 370, 378
Bordo, Susan 274

Bosco, S. J. Mark 84, 87
Boston University 173
Boult, Frances L. 66–67
Boyle, Danny: *28 Days Later* (film, 2002) 333
Bradley, Katharine 175, 179
Brahmadatta, King (Benares) 222
Brahmajala Sutra 219, 224n8
Brang, Peter: *Ein Unbekanntes Russland* (2002) 35, 36
Braunstein, Mark 178n3
bread 279, 396, 401
Brian Boru 396
Brillat-Savarin, Jean Anthelme 387, 391; *Physiologie du Goût* (1825) 173
British Columbia 346
British Library 65–66
British Union for Abolition of Vivisection 402
Brougham, Henry 4, 354–355
Brown Dog Affair 402
Brown, Wendy: *Edgework* (2005) 126, 127, 132
Brueck, Julia Feliz 34, 36, 69, 131, 132
Bryant, Christopher J. 303, 304
Bryant, Clifton 152
Buddha 4, 205, 211, 216, 218–222
Buddhism 35, 195, 205, 206, 210–211, 383; animal rights 221–223; interface between "identity" and "aspiration" 215–225; prohibition on killing 217–221; traditions and geographical spread 224n1
Buddhist scriptures 215–216
Budolfson, Mark 111–112, 121n3, 121
Buell, Lawrence 12, 238; *Future of Environmental Criticism* (2005) 239–240, 241, 247–248n9–12, 249
buffaloes 209, 212
bulimia 274–275
Bundt Cake 289, 290, 291
Burger King 338, 350
Burke, Kenneth 122, 123, 125, 128, 129–130, 132
Bush, George W. 143
bushmeat 385–388, 392
butchers 96, 97–98, 111, 117, 142, 230, 252, 313
Butler, Judith 39, 253, 266, 269, 270
butter 140, 208, 209, 210, 214, 221, 375, 397
Buzhu, Anissa 228, 230
Byron, Lord 241

cabbage 208, 394, 396, 399, 406
Calamaro, Andrés 358
Calarco, Matthew 109, 110, 256–257, 259, 263
California 139, 144, 327; animal cruelty legislation 138; ballot initiatives 138; Department of Food and Agriculture 140; farm workers 290–291; Milk and Dairy Food Safety Branch 140; Modoc National Forest 137
Calvert, Amy 104, 110

Index

Calvo, Luz 282–292; chef, educator, healer 284
camels 227, 229
Cameron, James 311, 340n8
Cameron, Suzy Amis 359–360
Campbell, T. Colin 312, 318
Campbell II, Thomas M. 318
Canada 196, 337
cancer 286, 295, 309, 312, 343, 349, 360
Canis Africanis (Swart and van Sitter, Eds.) 9
capitalism 32, 33, 76, 77, 80, 87, 90, 173, 175, 176, 242, 289, 290, 298, 299, 303, 319, 328, 336, 387, 399; gender and vegan studies 297–299
Capitán, Mel 361
cardiovascular disease 300, 309, 312, 340n5; heart disease 127, 284, 285, 286, 291, 300, 343
Carl's Jr 345
Carlassare, Elizabeth 13n5, 13
Carlyle, Thomas 397
Carmichael, Stokely 289
carnistic defense mechanisms 364; definition 356; three Ns (normal, natural, necessary) 356, 360
carnophallogocentrism (Derrida) 53, 57, 255, 256, 258, 263–264
Carretero-González, Margarita xi, 107, 110, 354–365
Caruth, Cathy 103, 109, 110
Castany Prado, Bernat 98n8, 99
Castro, Ernest 360–361
Catholicism 24n10, 396–397, 399, 401, 403, 404
cats 44, 46, 47, 138, 231, 246, 346, 389, 390n6; kittens 237–238
cattle 24n13, 130, 152, 184, 227, 229, 276, 280, 394, 401, 402
Catton, William R. 151, 158
causal impotence problem 111–121; complicity 113–115; individual consumer 111–113; overturned 113, 117–119; respect 115–117
Cavalieri, Paola 251, 256, 259; *Animal Question* (2001) 8, 13
Cavero, Jorge Bergua 90
celebrities 311, 370
Center for Consumer Freedom 143
Cera, Michael 319
Cervantes, Miguel de: *Dialogue of Dogs* 89–100; *Don Quijote* 92, 93–94, 98n6, 99; education 91; imprisonment 98, 98n9
Chaiken, Shelly 300, 304
Chakrabarti, Kunal 210, 213
Chan, Jackie 311, 339, 340n8
Chappell, Bill 136, 146
Chapple, Christopher 221–222, 224
Charlton, Anna 46, 48
Chavez, Cesar 290
cheese 161, 175, 206, 207, 220, 310, 374
Chen, Mel Y. 266, 271
Cherry, Elizabeth xi, 103, 110, 150–160

Cherry, Lynn 72
Chicago Rabbinical Council 198
Chicken Run (film, Dreamworks, 2000) 322, 332
chickens 42, 44, 45, 47, 71, 81–82, 112, 113, 117–118, 127, 135, 233, 246, 277, 300, 325–327, 387, 389
Child as emblem of futurity 266–268, 270n10
children 16, 22, 24n9, 42, 241, 277, 280, 359; socialization 300; vegan literature 65–75
children's books 237, 238, 247n4
children's films 321
Children's Garden: Magazine of Juvenile Vegetarian Movement (1900) 66
Children's Realm (1906–1914) 66–67, 74
children's rights 70
chimpanzee 141–142
China 400; animal cruelty 381–393; animal trade 385–388; beginning of an end 388–390; largest producer of meat and fur 389; National People's Congress 389, 390n6; one-party authoritarianism 383; veganism 382–384; white list of edible animals 389, 390n7; witch hunt 384–385
China Study (Campbell and Campbell, 2005) 312, 318
Chinese Communist Party (CCP) 386
Chiorando, Maria 335, 341
Chittilapally, Joslyn 206, 213
chocolate 300
Christian asceticism 187–188
Christian ecotheology 184
Christianity 183–193; animal theology 190–191; animal turn 183, 192n1; animals and problem of pain 184–186; antivivisection movement 186–187; fasting and abstinence 187–188; *Imago Dei* and human uniqueness 183–184, 190; impact on Irish human-nonhuman relationships 396–397; note on anachronism 187–189; NT and vegan anachronism 188–189
Christian veganism (biblical case) 189–190
Christian vegetarian saints 187, 191, 192n2, 193
Chronicle of Higher Education 334
Chrysippus 17, 22
Chu, Shanti 175–176, 179n5, 179
Ciocchetti, Christopher 370, 377, 379
Cipión (dog) 91–94, 97, 99
CKE Restaurant Holdings, Inc. 345
Clare, John 241
Clark, Gillian 25n15, 25n26, 26
Clark, Reverend James 401
Clark, Katie: *I'm a Supervegan* (2019) 72, 73, 74
Clark, Timothy: *Ecocriticism on Edge* (2015) 239, 243–246, 248–249n19–28
classism 239, 246, 398
classroom: transformational potential 240
climate change xv, 76, 77–80, 86, 87, 88, 138, 176, 238, 243, 245, 273, 314, 378, 401

Clough, David 191, 192
Clubb, Henry S. 36n1
CNN 333, 337, 341
Cobbe, Frances Power 402; *Modern Rack* (1889) 402, 405
Cochrane, Alasdair 46–47, 48
Cockrell, Marian 67
cockroaches 268
Coetzee, J.M. 39, 90, 217, 384, 390; Elizabeth Costello protagonist 39, 257; *Lives of Animals* (1999) 257, 259
cognitive factors 161, 164–165, 167; beliefs and justifications 165, 167; definition 164; perceptions 165, 167
cognitive skills 161, 165–166, 167, 168; definition 165
Cohen's d 162
Cohoon, Christopher 297, 304
Cole, Matthew xi, 66, 74, 79, 84, 178, 179, 319–332, 355, 356, 364
Coleridge, S.T. 215
colonialism 7, 58, 173, 175, 230–232, 246, 281, 282, 287, 289, 290, 314, 394–395, 403, 404
common-sense morality 42
companion animals 45, 46, 231, 237, 242, 322
companion species (Haraway) 10, 51, 54–55, 56, 60, 256
compassion 69, 221, 222, 302, 389
Compassion Over Killing 134
complexity 9, 51, 52, 53, 56, 58, 81, 112, 127, 253, 258, 266, 267, 304, **321**, 328
complicity 113–115; not sufficient for "wrongdoing" 115
concentrated animal feeding operations (CAFOs) 135
Confucianism 383, 388
Congo 13n4, 384, 390n2, 393
Connell, Raewyn W. 300, 304
Connolly, James 395, 405
Conrad, Joseph 13n4, 273
consumerism 35, 93, 101, 102, 239, 287, 334, 378
consumption 243; causally efficacious 117–119
contextual moral vegetarianism (Curtin) 11
continental philosophy 253–258
Contois, Emily 172, 174, 177, 179
cookbooks 206–207, 282–294
Cooke, Steve 48
coronavirus pandemic (2020) 333, 338, 340n2–340n3; animal cruelty (China) 381–393
cosmetics 207–208, 221; ban on animal testing 138
Costa Rica 237–249; no army 247n2; pineapple production 248n23
Costello, Elizabeth (fictional) 39, 257
cotton 200, 211
Counihan, Carole 173

Cousins, Margaret 403
Covey, Allison xi, 183–193
covo (kale) 275–276
Cowell, Edward B. 223, 224
Cowherd, William 186
cows 45, 46, 71, 111, 135, 209–210, 212, 246, 276–277, 317, 327, 389, 394, 396, 400, 402
Cowspiracy (Andersen and Kuhn, 2014) 310–311, 314, 315, 317, 334
Crab, Roger 4
Crakers 80
criminal legal system: vegan activists (USA) 143–144
critical animal studies (CAS) 7–8, 9, 13n2, 51, 53, 58, 59, 150, 153, 159, 250–260; critical task 253; definition 8; humanist veganism (perspectives from analytic philosophy) 251–253, 257–258; towards intersectional veganism 257–258; political stance 250; post-humanist veganism (perspectives from continental philosophy) 254–258
Critical Inquiry (2012) 12–13, 14
Critical Reviews in Food Science and Nutrition (2017) 343
critical theory 28, 74n1, 125, 383
Crook, Edgar 35, 36
Cross, Joe 312, 318
Cross, Leslie J. 187
crowdfunding 310–311
Cruel Treatment of Cattle Act (1822) 402
Cruelty to Animals Act (UK, 1876) 186, 402
Cudworth, Erika 58, 59
cultural studies 34, 126, 195; micro- and macro-scale ~ 35–36
culture 27, 153, 154–155, 156, 157, 200–202, 246, 247n9, 283, 361
Curtin, Deane 11, 13
cutification 266, 325, 329
Cynic School 90, 94, 98, 98n8

Dahl, R. 67
Dahlan, Magfirah xi, 226–233
dairy industry 33, 210, 231, 310, 312, 313, 314
dairy products 29, 77, 175, 194, 196, 209, 216, 310, 319, 343, 395, 400, 401, 404
Daisy Basket (VS magazine, 1893–1904) 66
Dalai Lama 217, 224n6
Dandelion, Dave (blogger) 130
Dangarembga, Tsitsi: *Nervous Conditions* (2004) 272–281
Darwin, Charles 4, 9
Davies, Shelley Lee 312, 318
Dawkins, Richard 361, 364
Dead Sea Scrolls 188, 193
Dean, Tim 268
Deane-Drummond, Celia 184, 192
d'Eaubonne, Françoise 247n5

Index

Deckha, Maneesha 273, 281
Decolonize Your Diet (Calvo and Esquibel, 2015) 282–292
Decolonizing Foodways Conference (2015) 282
"De Colores" (folk song) 290–291
deep ecology 90, 99, 106, 241
deer 222, 326
de Fontenay, Elisabeth 98n7, 99
Deleuze, G. 257
Delforce, Chris: *Dominion* (film, 2017) 312, 318
Delos: Altar of Pious 23, 26n37
DeMello, Margo: *Animals and Society* (2012) 8, 13
Dennis, Brady 137, 146
derere (vegetables) 275–276
Derrida, Jacques 8, 11, 13, 14, 39, 50, 52, 53, 58, 242, 248n16, 254–259, 260, 263, 271; *Animal That Therefore I Am* (2008 translation) 254, 259
Descartes, René 90, 242; Cartesian dualism 7–8, 9, 184–185; *Discours de la Méthode* (1637; 2003 translation) 95, 184–185, 192
Despard, Charlotte 403
Despret, Vinciane 56, 60
Devries, Mark (director): *Speciesism* (2013) 312, 318
Dexter, Brandon 302–303, 304
Dhammapada 215, 217–218, 223, 224n5, 224
dharma 212, 213, 215
Dharma Voices for Animals 219
diabetes 7, 284, 285, 286, 288, 291, 309, 310, 312, 340n5
Dialogue of Dogs (Cervantes) 89–100; Aesop and picaresque tradition 90–91; animals talk 95; dogs are faithful and remember 95; dogs contribute to social welfare 97; dogs do their job well 96–97; dogs have feelings 96; dogs learn 96; dogs make decisions based on experience 96; gossip dogs 91–94; meat consumption, greed, social corruption 97–98; Plutarch's *Moralia* 94–95
Diamond, Cora 40, 48, 257, 259
Dicaearchus 18, 25n15, 26
DiCaprio, Leonardo 311
diet 31–33
dietary choices (casual impact) 45
dietary colonialism 179n5
dietary decolonization 289
différance (Derrida) 254
Dinshah, H. Jay 212, 213, 217
Diogenes (slave) 98
Dionysus 20
Direct Action Everywhere (DxE) 143
discourse analysis 356
disgust 79, 82, 162, 327, 330, 387
Disney 242, 322, 331, 360, 363
disordered eating 278–281
divine justice 185–186
divine king myth (Slotkin) 106
Doctor Who (BBC) 322, 323, 332
documentary films 123–124, 131, 313, 317n2

dogs 9, 41, 46, 47, 51, 55, 103, 105, 138, 151, 242, 246, 323–331, 346, 358, 389, 390n6, 397; Cervantes 89–100; contribute to social welfare 97; do job well 96–97; faithful and remember 95; have feelings 96; learn 96; make decisions based on experience 96
dolphins 141, 242
Dombrowski, Daniel A. 22, 24, 25n34, 26, 42, 48
Donaldson, Sue 47, 48, 231, 233
donkeys 17, 387, 390n7
Donovan, Josephine 297
Dooren, Thom van 50, 61
Dorfeld, Natalie M. 314, 318
Douglas, Mary 155, 158
Doyle, Julie 36, 37, 311
Drewett, Zoe 66, 74
Dreyer, Stephanie 70
Drummond, William 402, 405
Dublin 401; vegetarian restaurants 401, 403
Duchsher, Towani 131
ducks 387–388
dumpster diving 111–112
Dunlap, Riley E. 151, 158

e-commerce 207–208
Earthlings (documentary, 2005) 131
eating well 255–256, 259
Ebola 384, 385
Ebrahim, Shaazia 228, 230, 233
ecocriticism 12; challenges 243; Clark 239, 243–246, 248–249n19–28; coined by Ruekert (1978) 247n5; Costa Rican view 237–249; definition 238; divide from ecofeminism 238; emphasis on emotion missing 246; first-wave and second-wave ~ 239, 247n9; "glaring omission" of Vegan Studies 245; main weakness of field 240; vegan ecofeminist queer ecological view 237–249
Ecocriticism Reader (Glotfelty and Fromm, Eds., 1996) 238, 249, 334
ecoethics 76, 84, 86
ecofeminism 7, 10–13, 40, 52, 53, 56, 58, 150, 172, 177, 190, 297, 304; Costa Rican view 237–249; definition 12, 239, 248n10; divide from ecocriticism 238; origin of term (1974) 247n5; primary tenet 12
ecofeminist revolt 101–110
Ecological Indian figure 241
ecological masculinities (Hultman and Pulé) 302, 304
economies of scale 118
ecopedagogy 72–73, 74
ecophobia xii, 245, 337, 339, 341
ecopoesis 241
Edelman, Lee 267, 271
Edwards, G. Fay 25n34, 26
Edwards, Jason 270n3
effective-altruism movement 45

eggs 4, 11, 29, 47, 68, 71, 77, 101, 139, 131, 140, 175, 187, 196, 206, 208, 209, 277, 397
Egypt 231, 233
Eid al-Adha 229–230
Eilperin, Juliet 137, 146
ekphrasis (evocative writing) 124, 127
elephants 138, 141, 222–223, 224n10
Eleventh of September terrorist attacks (2011) 78, 175, 300–301
elitism 77, 176, 201, 220, 258, 273, 274, 287, 359, 363
Eliyahu, Mordechai (Chief Sephardic Rabbi) 197
Eller, Donnelle 136, 146
El Mito del Veganismo (Vegan Myth) 356–357
embodied ideology (Hertweck) 177, 179
emergent human rights concept 89, 90
Emmerman, Karen S. 78, 87
emotion 6, 12, 16, 22, 24, 44, 56, 68, 69, 71, 77, 91, 106, 107, 122–132 *passim*, 152, 153, 161, 167, 176, 227, 237, 241, 242, 269, 287, 295, 304, 327, 334, 356, 357, 359; missing from ecocriticism 246–247; non-cognitive factor 162, 167
empathy xvi, 20, 56, 65, 109, 162, 165, 177, 247, 258, 267, 277, 298, 310, 312, 318, 320, **321**, 322, 326, 329, 330, 384, 389
empirical data 150–160
Empson, William 388, 391
Endangered Species Act (USA) 137
energy 43, 67, 76, 90, 144, 207, 285–286, 401
Engfehr, Kurt 312, 318
Enlightenment 231, 253, 266
entangled empathy (Gruen) 267
environment 5, 137–138, 217, 247n9, 248n23
Environmental History (journal) 247n7
Escape Plan (film, 2013) 333
Esquibel, Catriona Rueda 282–292; chef, educator, healer 284
Essenes 188
Esterik, Penny Van 173
Estok, Simon C. xii, 13n6, 14, 333–342
ethical responsibility 54–57
ethical veganism 5, 6, 10, 48, 67, 141, 174–175, 187–191, 195, 208, 215, 239, 246, 335, 378, 379
ethics of care 50, 298
ethics education 166, 171
Ethics Position Questionnaire 164, 169
ethos (ethics) 122, 124, 125, 126, 128, 129, 130
Eurocentrism 176
extreme speech 360–363, 365

Facebook 349–350, 356; rhetoric of online anti-veganism 354–365
factory farming 69, 71, 119, 136, 139, 143, 242, 252, 313, 322, 325, 334, 338, 347
Fahey, Judge 141–142
failure 268–270
Fairlife dairies 139

Falkowitz, Max 233
famine 275, 397–400, 404; malnutrition 284; starvation 18, 19, 23, 41, 359
Fanon, Frantz: *Wretched of Earth* (1961) 272, 274, 281
Farm Sanctuary 70, 200
farming profession: Jain prohibition 208
farmworkers 290–291
fascism 357
fast food 124, 174, 179n5, 285, 343–353
fat-shaming 154
Feltz, Adam xii, 161–171
Feltz, Silke xii, 161–171
feminism 10–12, 132, 201, 265, 290, 339, 403
Feminist Care scholars 258
feminist ethics 229
feminized protein (Adams) 209
film 319–332; possibility of representing veganism 323–324; vegan and anti-vegan representations 320, **321**
Finland 68, 162
First Amendment (USA) 136, 140, 143, 144
Fischer, Bob 112, 119, 121n2
fish 41, 42, 45, 84, 97, 153, 178n1, 184, 188, 196, 208, 248n22, 300, 334, 396, 398, 400; seafood 207, 341, 381, 390n1, 401; shellfish 194; ~ without scales 194
Florida 142; greyhound racing ban (2018) 138
Foer, Jonathan Safran 178n3, 267; *Eating Animals* (2009) 310, 311, 318, 334; *We are the Weather* (2019) 72, 74
foie gras 139, 387
Foltz, Richard (2006) 229–230, 233
food 258n1; terminology 125, 172, 174, 177, 335, 377
food allergies 344
Food and Foodways 173
food disparities 286
food ethics 45, 48
food justice movement 284
food labelling 139–140
food practices 299–301
food studies 172–179, 387; content 172–174; morality, animal rights, and affect 176–178; relationship with vegan studies 174–176
Food Studies (2012–) 173
Forbes 77
Foreman, Michael 72
Forsyth, Donelson R. 164, 169
Forward, Charles Walter: *Fifty Years of Food Reform* (1898) 31, 37
Foster, Kate 68–69, 74
Foucault, M. 253–254, 259, 260
Fraiman, Susan 12–13, 14, 50–51, 53, 60, 248n16
France 68, 129, 156–157, 230
Francione, Gary L. 46, 48, 109, 110
Francis, Pope: *Laudato Si'* (2015) 184, 192
Frank de la Jungla 358

Index

Franklin, Sarah 57, 60
Freedom of Information Act (USA) 134–135, 140, 142
freeganism 44; definition 41
Freetown (Virginia) 289
Freud, S. 9
Frey, R.G. 121n4, 121
Friends don't let friends eat tofu (Arby's advertising slogan) 348–351
Fromm, Harold 217, 221, 224, 246, 334–335, 337
fruits 208, 276, 277, 286, 288, 290, 300, 396
Fuentes, Agustín 266, 268, 271
Fulkerson, Lee: *Forks Over Knives* (2011) 312, 318
fun 361–362
fungi 9, 196
fur 138, 221, 268, 327
Fusté-Forné, Francesc xii, 369–380

Gaard, Greta 12, 13, 72, 74, 177, 247n6, 248n16, 258, 262, 297, 337
Gaarder, Emily 102, 110
Gadia, Madhu: *Indian Vegan Kitchen* (2009) 206, 213
Gagliardone, Iginio 360, 364
Gallan, Daniel 337, 341
Galloway, Katie 135, 145
Gandhi, Leela: *Affective Communities* 273
Gandhi, M.K. 273, 275; debt to West 32–33; *My Experiments with Truth* (1927, 1929) 206, 209, 213; vegetarianism 208–209
Garland, Christopher xii, 122–133
Garlick, Steve 298, 299, 204
Garner, Eric 131
Garrard, Greg: *Ecocriticism* (2004, 2011, 2012) 12, 13n6–13n7, 14, 238, 239, 241–243, 248n15–248n18, 249
Garrison, William Lloyd 402
Gastronomica 173
Gay Male Vegetarians (GMV) 261, 262, 263, 270n1–270n2, 270n5
geese 47, 196, 390
Gehl, Dudley 178n3
gender 12–13, 77, 79, 104, 153, 155–156, 176, 199, 200, 229, 240, 248n16, 290, 326, 328, 331, 351, 352; food practices as constant validation 299–301; hybrid identities 302–303; plural masculinities 302–303; vegan feminisms 302–303; vegan studies under capitalism 297–299; veganism and ~ 263–264
gender pay gap 296
gender studies 173, 295–305
genital mutilation 296
geo-culture 205–214
geography 50, 54, 153
Gera, Deborah Levine 25n16, 26
Ghazzala, Anwar 190–191

Ghebreyesus, Tedros Adhanom 384
Ghosh, Joyjit xii, 215–225
Giraud, Eva xii–xiii, 50–61, 267; *What Comes After Entanglement* (2019) 57, 60
GlobalData 335, 341–342
globalization 240, 360, 382, 383, 392, 404
Global South xii, 244, 246
Glotfelty, Cheryll 238, 249
goats 200, 209, 212, 233, 329, 330, 341
Godlovitch, Ros 40, 48
Godlovitch, Stanley 40, 48
God's Gardeners 83, 85
Goldie, Janis 344, 352
Gomez, Manel I. 275–276, 281
Good Food Institute 45
Good Housekeeper (1830) 398
Goodison, Lorna: *To Us, All Flowers are Roses: Poems* (1995) 289, 293
Google 128–129, *335*
Gosine, Andil 244
Gossard, M.H. 352, 353
gourmands 20, 25n19
Go Vegan World 403, 404n6
Graduate Journal of Food Studies 172, 174
Graham, Sylvester 32, 37
grains 207, 277, 288, 399
Grandin, Temple 56, 382–383
greed 97–98
Greenebaum, Jessica 156, 158, 288, 293, 302–303, 304
Green, Joshua 188, 192
green moralism 244–245
Greenpeace 245, 311
Green, Veronica: *Veggie Vero* (2017) 70, 74
Gregory, Dick 7
Gregory, James 186, 192
Gruen, Lori 10, 13, 128, 132, 215–216, 220, 221, 248n16, 267, 268, 303, 304, 383; *Entangled Empathy* (2015) 56, 60; "What Motivates Us to Change What We Eat?" (2020) 56, 60
Guardian 194
Guggenheim, Davis 317n2
guilt 162

habeas corpus 141–142
Haenfler, Ross 156, 159
halal slaughterhouses 233
Halberstam, J. Jack: *Queer Art of Failure* (2011) 268, 269, 271
Hale, Sarah 398, 405
Hall, Stuart 28, 37
Halpern, Nancy 143, 147
Halteman, Matthew C. 118, 121
hamartiology 185
Hamilton, Carrie 270, 270n7, 271
Han Kang: *Vegetarian* (2015 translation) 101–110

Haraway, Donna 43, 52, 242, 256, 266; argument against veganism 266–267; from ethical responsibility to response-ability 54–57, 59; rejects posthumanist label 50, 54, 58

Haraway, Donna (works): *Companion Species Manifesto* (2003) 51, 56, 60; "Promises of Monsters" (1992) 55; "Species Matters, Humane Advocacy" (2011) 55, 60; "Staying with Manifesto" (2017) 57, 60; *Staying with Trouble* (2016) 54, 60; *When Species Meet* (2008) 9–10, 14, 51, 54–57, 59, 60, 87

Hardee's 350, 351, 352; Save the Veggies campaign (2019) 344, 345–348

Hardy, Thomas: *Tess of d'Urbervilles* (1991 edition) 216–217, 224

hares 217, 396

Harmonial Vegetarian Society (Arkansas) 34

harm reduction 45–46, 47

Harper, A. Breeze 53, 176, 240, 270n50, 279, 281; blog 6; *Sistah Vegan* (2010) 6–7, 14, 34, 314

Harris, John 40, 48

Harris Poll 343, 344

Harvard University 114

Hashgacha Pratit 199

hashtags 362–363

Haubrich, William S. 31, 37

Haughton, James 402

Hausen, Julie 69

Haussleitner, Johannes 24n4, 26

Hays, Sharon 154, 159

health disparities 279, 282, 285, 287

healthism 154

Hebrew Bible 194, 196, 197, 198–199, 232; Abraham, Isaac, Jacob, Rachel 201; Flood 189, 196; Garden of Eden diet (originally plant-based) 189; Genesis 4–5, 24n10, 183, 184; Isaiah (11:9) 189; Leviticus 196; Moses, Amos, King David 201; Noah 196; Proverbs 202; Psalm twenty-three 202

hechshers (kosher symbols) 197, 198

Hediger, Ryan: *Animals and War* 9

hedonistic utilitarians 42–43

hegans 300, 304, 337, 340n11

Heidegger, Martin 253

Heine, Steven J. 296, 305

Helstosky, Carol 175, 176, 179

hens 68, 131, 138, 139, 209, 212, 286, 397

Hereth, Blake 115–117, 121

Herrera, Hank 175, 179

Hertweck, Tom xiii, 27–38, 177, 179

Herzog, Harold A. 164, 169

Hesford, Wendy 123, 132

Hesiod: *Works and Days* 15

heteronormativity 237, 239, 258, 261, 262, 267, 271, 326, 342

hiddur mitzvah 202

Hills, Arnold Frank 67, 74

himsa (Sanskrit, violence) 205

Hinduism 30, 195, 205, 206, 273; cow milk and vegan feminism 209–210; food categories 206; *vratas* as vegan rite 210–212

historiography 27–28, 32

history and foundational texts 3–61; analytic philosophers (Singer, Regan) 39–49; framing vegan studies 3–14; posthumanists (Wolfe and Haraway) 50–61; Pythagoras, Plutarch, Porphyry 15–26; vegetarian and vegan history 27–38

history beyond food 200–202

HIV-AIDS 268, 269

Hobbes, Thomas 30, 388

Hobgood-Oster, Laura 191

Hodson, Gordon 355, 364

Hoffman, Martin 312, 318

Hoffmann, Richard C.: *Environmental History of Medieval Europe* 340n2, 342

Holmes, Jessica xiii, 172–179

homa (sacrifice) 210; *homa* (sacrifice) 211

homophobia 244, 245, 264, 265, 270, 297

honey 71, 77, 151, 119–120, 175, 188, 196, 206, 208, 210, 369

Hong Kong University 385–386

horses 46, 96, 137, 142, 146, 148, 396

Horsthemke, Kai 73, 74

Huanan Seafood Wholesale Market 381, 390n1

Hudgins, Lisa 212, 213

Hudson, D. Dennis: *Body of God* (2008) 210, 213

Hudson Valley Foie Gras 139

Huerta, Dolores 290

Huffington Post 348

Huggan, Graham 266–267, 271

Hultman, Martin 102, 302, 304

human (category) 51, 79, 262, 266, 297, 301

human–animal kinship and affiliation 266–268

human–animal studies (HAS) 7, 8–9, 150; definition 8

human carnism (Joy) 381

Humane League 45

human exceptionalism 9, 10, 54, 266, 323; illusionary nature 55

Human Exemptionalist Paradigm (HEP) 151

human genome 9

Humanistic Judaism 195

humanist posthumanism 54

humanist veganism 254; perspectives from analytic philosophy 251–253, 257–258

humanities 65–178; Atwood's MaddAddam trilogy (veganism, ecoethics, climate change) 76–88; causal impotence 111–121; Cervantes *Dialogue of Dogs* 89–100; food studies 172–179; Han Kang's *Vegetarian* (ecofeminist revolt) 101–110; rhetoric of veganism 122–133; psychology 161–171; sociology 150–160; US legal system 134–149; vegan literature for children 65–75

human nature 20, 24n11, 231, 260, 356, 360

Index

human rights 7, 28, 137–138, 273
humans: non-rationality 22, 25n29
humans in fur suits 55, 56
human species privilege **321**, 324, 329–330
human supremacism 163, 319, 320, 331, 396, 404
human uniqueness (Christianity) 183–184
human values 164, 171
humor 83, 129, 310, 315, 316, 323, 343–364
Hung, Ruth Y.Y. xiii, 381–393
hunger strikes 274–275
hunter-gatherers 201, 406
hunting 19, 41, 44, 49, 222, 274, 299, 326, 328, 329–330, 396, 397
Huntingdon Life Sciences (HLS) 144
hybrid identities 302–303
Hypatia 10, 14, 303, 304
hypertension 284, 285, 291

Iacobbo, Karen 4, 7, 14, 33
Iacobbo, Michael 4, 7, 14, 33
Idaho 136
ideal types 319, 323, 327, 328, 329, 331; polarity (vegan and anti-vegan representations) 320, **321**
identity veganism 257, 266, 268
ikizukuri 387
Illinois 138
Imago Dei 183–184, 190
immigrants 244, 287, 394, 327, 328, 384
Impact Partners 310
Impossible Burger 350
Impossible Whopper 337
incarcerated vegans 140–141
India 4, 30–34, 202n2, 400, 403; vegan culture 206–208
Indiana University 173
Indiegogo (crowdfunding website) 310–311
individual choice 243–244, 245
individual consumer: benefiting from wrongdoing 113–114; causal impotence problem 111–113
individualizing foundations 163–164
industrial farming 11, 228, 233, 276, 286, 313, 315, 400
industrialization 29, 76, 101, 107, 230, 284, 398, 400
industrialized culture 216–217
inequality 155–156
inherent value 44; definition 43
injustice 18–22, 114, 172, 257, 265, 268, 289–292, 395, 404
insects 4, 194, 196–197, 208, 213, 354
institutional racism 284
intellect 20–21, 22, 25n29
intelligence 21, 165, 167
interdisciplinary inquiry 9, 36, 50, 124, 126, 150, 157, 172, 173, 177, 247
interests 40–41, 252; definition problem 40
International Committee on Taxonomy of Viruses (ICTV) 382

International Vegetarian Union (Davis) 29
internet 373, 386; memes 361–362
intersectional disgust (Twine) 262, 271
intersectionality xv, xvi, 10, 11, 35, 56, 58, 69, 123, 124, 125, 128, 131, 172, 175, 177, 238, 241, 244, 246, 272, 283, 284, 288, 303, **321**, 326, 327–329, 331, 402; vegan studies and queer theory 261–271
intersectional veganism 257–258
interventions 166
intra-action (Barad) 55, 56
inventio (method used for discovery of argument) 127
Investiture of Gods 封神演义 (classical Chinese novel) 388
Invisible Vegan (Leyva, Kenny and Jasmine, directors, 2019) 314, 318
Iowa 136
Ireland: animal rights movement 401–403; British colonialism 397–401, 404; famine 397–399, 404; famine legacy 399–400; famine relief efforts 399; genocidal colonialism 399, 404; human-nonhuman relationships 395–400; modern food system 400–401; tenant farming 397; vegan geographies 394–406
Irish Vegetarian Society 403
Irish Women's Franchise League 403
Islam 226–233; dietary laws 227
ISLE 12, 238, 246n6–246n7, 334
Israel 198, 199; most vegans per capita 199, 202n2
Isserles, Rabbi Moshe 201
Italy 128

Jainism 205, 206, 210–211, 217; and veganism 208
Jamaica 289
Jameson, Fredric 73, 74
Japan 378
Jarrett, Susan A. 124
Jataka Tales 215, 221–223, 224n9–10, 224
Jauss, Hans Robert 90, 99
Jay, Alison 72
Jenkins, Jeff 345
Jenkins, Stephanie 256, 259
Jerusalem *199–200*, 201; Village Green vegan restaurant (1992–) *199*
Jesus 188, 190, 191, 192
Jewish Studies 194; intersection with vegan studies (literature review) 195
Jewish Vegetarianism and Veganism (Labendz and Yanklowitz, Eds., 2019) 195, 203
Jewish Vegetarians of North America 202
Jiménez Rodríguez, Adriana xv, 237–249
jiva (immortal soul) 208
Jivaka Sutta 218–219; *Jivaka Sutta* 219, 224
Johannine epistles 189
Johnson, Boris 333
Johnson, Justine A. 303, 304
John the Baptist, St. 188

Jones, Michael Owen 36, 37
jones, pattrice 298, 304
Jones, Robert C. 69, 74, 128, 132, 215–216, 220, 221, 268
Jorgensen, Beth 123, 127, 132
Joseph, John: *Meat is for Pussies* 303
Josephus 188, 192
Joy, Melanie 216, 224, 356, 360, 364, 381, 391
Joyce, James: *Ulysses* 395, 404, 404n4
Judaism 183, 188, 194–204; agrarian origins 201; Conservative movement 199; kashrut industry 198–200; kosher diet 195–196; messianic redemption and rebuilding of Holy Temple in Jerusalem 201; religion, culture, and history beyond food 200–202
Juitiya fast 211
justice 44, 46–47

Kagan, Shelly 117, 121
kairos (timeliness) 125
Kansanen, I. 371, 379
Kansas 136, 142
Kant, I. 252
Karma *vrata* 211
kashrut (Jewish religious dietary laws) 194–201, 202n1
Kashruth Council of Canada (COR) 196
Katz, B. 71, 74
Kearney, Jackie: *Vegan Street Foods* (2015) 207, 214
Kellman, Steven G. 104, 110
Kellogg, John Harvey 36, 38
Kennamer, Paul David: *Eating You Alive* (2018) 312, 318
keto diet 348
Keys, Ancel, *et al.*: *Seven Countries* (1980) 127
Khan, Ya'eesh 228
Kheel, Marti 13, 190–191, 248n16
kidney damage (healing) 288
killing: animal and human (association) 18–19
Killoren, David xiii, 111–121
Kim, Claire Jean 250, 259–260
Kim, Won-Chung 109, 110
Kimmel, Michael 296, 298–299, 305
kinship 266, 271
Knight, John: *Herding Monkeys to Paradise* 9
knowledge 165, 167, *168*, 262, 283, 334
Ko, Aph 106, 110, 176, 240, 270n5
Ko, Syl 106, 110, 240, 270n5
koala 237, 246
Koljonen, M. 66, 74
Kolkata: Ubuntu Community Café 207
Komorowska, Joanna xiii, 15–26
Kopytowska, Monika 361, 364
Korean War 105, 114
Korsgaard, Christine 252, 260
kosher 194–204; meat-dairy cross contamination 196, 197; slaughter rules 196; *versus* treif 194; vegan restaurants and certified foods 196–198

kosher diet 195–196
kosher meat 195, 202
Kramer, Sarah 28, 36
Krishna 209–210, 214
kshirasagara (ocean of milk) 210
Kubisz, Marzena xiii-xiv, 65–75
Kuhn, Keegan 309–315, 317
Kumar, Saurav xiv, 205–214
Kymlicka, Will 47, 48, 231, 233

Labendz, Jacob A. 195, 203
labor union activity 120
Lady Chatterley's Lover 280
Lamberti, Adrienne P. 127, 132
language 129
language barrier 377
Lankavatara Sutra 215, 218, 220, 225
Lappé, Frances Moore: *Diet for Small Planet* (1971, 1982) 127, 132
Latour, Bruno 244, 249; *We Have Never Been Modern* (1993) 55, 60
Lavin, Chad 231, 233
Lawlor, Leonard 256, 260
leather 77, 83, 96, 101, 111, 154, 188, 200, 221, 257, 268, 270, 369
Le Courrier Picard 384
Lee, Young-Hyun 107, 110
leftover beef sandwich ethics 112
Lempel, Jesse 198, 203
Lent 187–188
lentils 207, 210, 376
Lesbian Reader (1975) 13
lesbianism 261, 264–265, 266, 296, 304
Lévi-Strauss, Claude 154–155, 159
Lewis, Edna 289–290, 293
LGBTQ+ 195, 237, 247n1, 265; transgender 65
Li, Chien-hui 186, 192
Lifesum 356
Linzey, Andrew 7, 14; *Animal Rights* (1976) 190, 192; *Animal Theology* (1994) 190, 192
Lion King (Disney, 1994) 322
lions 183, 212, 322, 360
literary-environmental studyland 237–249
livestock 56, 96, 206, 214, 242, 276, 280, 314, 315, 323, 324, 326, 329, 330, 389, 390n7, 394
livestock industry: harmful impact 216
local criticism (Brown) 126, 127
Lockwood, Alex xiv, 295–305; *Pig in Thin Air* (2017) 296, 305
locusts 183, 188, 196
logos (logic) 122, 124, 127, 130, 131
London Vegetarian Society 66
Lonely Planet: *Vegan Travel Handbook* (2019) 371
Long, Lucy M. 370, 379
Losh, Elizabeth M. 123, 133
loss in translation 240, 248n12
lost innocence 17–19, 23, 24, 24–25n12–17
Louisiana 142

Index

Luciano, Dana 266, 271
Luke, Brian 299–300, 305
Lund, Thomas B. 164, 170
Lung, David 385–386, 390n4, 392
luxury 18, 19, 20
Lyman, Howard 334

Macfarlane, Robert 72, 74
Machiavelli, N. 388
machismo 337–338, 341
Madrid Vegan Travel website 371
Mahabharata 210, 212
Mahamati 218
Mahaparinirvana Sutra 215, 218, 219
Mahavira, Vardhamana 205, 208
mainstream media 174, 175, 319, 333, 335, 336–337, 340, 340n3
Maiti, Krishanu xiv, 215–225
maize 275, 279
Malamud, Randy 330, 332
Malebranche, Nicolas 185–186
Malthus, T.R. 30
mammals 44, 154, 196, 197, 396
Manchester (Iowa): Cricket Hollow Zoo 137, 143, 147
Mann, Clare: *Vystopia* (2018) 73, 74
Marcus, Erik 29, 37, 130
marginal cases argument 41–42
Marker, Jason 345
market freeganism 119, 120
market threshold view 118
marketing 139, 146, 286, 287, 303, 313, 315, 333, 334, 337, 338, 348, 370, 373, 377
Marrero Henríquez, J.M. 89–100
Marshall, Liz: *Meat the Future* (2020) 314, 318
Martin, Richard 402
Marx, Karl 151, 159
masculinity(ies) 156, 246, 249n27, 258, 262, 263, 264, 265, 266, 269, 295, 297–299, 300–303, 326, 327, 337, 398
mashgiach (inspection assistants) 198
mashgichot 199
Masri, A.B.A: *Animal Welfare in Islam* (2014) 227, 230, 233
Matthew, Saint 188
Mayo, Liz xiv, 101–110
McCance, Dawne, *Critical Animal Studies* (2013) 7, 13n2, 14
McCarthy, Cormac 127
McCarthy, Mary: *Birds of America* 104–105
McCartney, Lady (Linda) 152
McCartney, Sir Paul 152, 159
McDavid, Eric 135, 145
McDonald's 45, 343
McDonald, Barbara 5–6, 14, 104, 110
McInnis, Cara C. 355, 364
McIntyre, Lee 334, 339, 342

McKay, Robert 40, 49, 57, 60, 264, 266, 268, 271
McLachlan, Sarah 346
McMullen, Steven 118, 121
McPherson, Tristram 113–115, 117, 121
Mead, George Herbert 151
mealies 275, 279
means of persuasion 122–133
meat 102–105, 107, 131, 156, 196, 198, 207, 208, 278–281, 288, 395, 396, 398–399, 400, 401, 404; carcinogen 309; unhealthfulness and unsuitability 20–21, 25n22–25n25
meat and dairy industry 310, 312, 313, 314
meat consumption 97–98, 152, 153, 162, 166; and social degradation 89–100
meat-eaters: categories (Pick) 300, 305
meat-eating 262, 276, 278, 295; Buddhist doctrine 218–221; men *versus* women (global statistic) 299; unhealthy diet 216
Meat-Eating Justification scale (Rothgerber) 165, 170
meat industry 33, 243, 245
media 3, 36, 77, 79, 87, 126, 155, 158, 175, 237, 309, 313, 319, 342
media organizations 336
Medium (online platform, 2012–) 129
Meet Your Meat (PETA, 2002) 123, 127, 132, 317n7, 318
Meijer, Eva: *When Animals Speak* (2019) 47, 49
Meir of Rothenberg, Rabbi 201
mental health system 107–109
merchandizing veganism 333–342
Mercy for Animals 134, 136, 348
metempsychosis (transmigration of souls) 15, 17, 22, 24, 25n30
metta (loving-kindness) 221
Mexican Americans: anti-racism 282–294
Mexico 282, 327, 328
Meyer, John C. 344–345, 353
Midgley, Mary 40, 49
Miguel, Amando de 358
Miguel Beriain, Íñigo de 98n2, 99
Mikhail, Alan: *Animal in Ottoman Egypt* 231, 233
Milburn, Josh xiv, 39–49
milk 4, 11, 19, 32, 69, 71, 118, 129, 140, 169, 187, 196, 206, 207, 209–210, 221, 276–277, 280, 395, 397, 398, 401
millennials 335, 336, 340n7, 372
Miller, Ian 31, 37
Miller Wolfson, Marisa: *Vegucated* (film, 2011) 313–314, 315, 318
millet 285–286
Mills, Brett 315, 318
Milner, Ryan M. 361, 364
Ming Pao 386
Mintz, Sidney 173
Miriam Makeba in Concert 289
misanthropy 130, 358–359, 363

misogyny 80, 81, 110, 244, 265, 270, 301, 338, 338, 340
Missouri 139
Mittal, Abhishek 207
Mitter, Rana 390n5, 392
mitzvot (commandments) 202
Miyoko's Kitchen 140, 147
The Miz 347, 351
Mohanty, Chandra Talpade 274
monkeys 241
monoculture 10, 246, 248n23
Monsanto 10, 288
Monson, Shaun (director): *Earthlings* (2005) 310, 312, 317n3, 318
Monstrous Thesis 185–186
Moor, Robert 102, 110
Moore, Michael 309, 317n2
moral elitism 220–221
moral evaluation 358–359
morality 176–178
moral puritanism 268
moral purity 255
Moran, Victoria 217, 224
More, Thomas 32
Moreau, Jean Baptiste 129
Morgan, Karen 79, 84, 355, 356, 364
Morris, Robert: *Reasonable Plea for Animal Creation* (1746) 34, 36
Morton, Timothy 86, 88, 354, 364
Moskowitz, Isa Chandra 28, 37
motivation (non-cognitive factor) 162
Movimiento contra la Intolerancia 360–361
Moylan, Tom 315–316, 318
Muhammad 227
Mullen, Ginger 68, 74
multidisciplinarity 13n2, 177
multimodal artifacts 361
Muñoz Gallarte, Israel 98n3
Muñoz, José Esteban: *Cruising Utopia* (2009) 269, 271
Mwangi, Evan Maina: *Postcolonial Animal* 274
myth: definition 357, 364n1
mythopoesis 360

naming 4, 126, 127, 129, 256, 384–385, 391
Nancy, Jean-Luc 253, 260
Narayanan, Yamini 209–210, 214
National Anti-Vivisection Society (NAVS) 402
National Conference of Catholic Bishops (NCCB, USA) 188, 192
National Conference on Rhetoric (1970) 122
National Environmental Policy Act (USA) 137
nationalism 78, 314, 365, 381, 384, 386, 387, 388, 394, 395, 399, 400, 402, 403
natural affinity argument 17
natural world 106, 107, 109, 183
nature 101–102, 104, 108, 205, 211, 238, 239, 240, 247n9, 249n28, 335, 338

Nature 390n3
Navarro, Marilisa C. xiv, 282–294
Nazi period 114–115, 195, 198
Negrín de la Peña, José Antonio 98n5, 99
Nelson, Selene 354
Netflix 309, 311
Netherlands 228
Neubecker, Robert 70
Nevada 139
New Ecological Paradigm (NEP) 151
new rhetoric 122–124
newspapers 122, 158, 166, 355, 356, 363, 371
New Testament 187; and vegan anachronism 188–189
New York 233; Hostos Community College 173
New York Court of Appeals 141–142
New York State 138; Kosher Food Law (1915) 198, 199
New York Times 124
New York University 173
New Zealand 264–265
Ngai, Sianne 266, 271
Nietzsche, F. 257
Nixon, Rob 273, 281
Nobis, Nathan 86, 88
no harm (or failure to benefit), no foul principle 115, 116–117, 121n8
non-cognitive factors 161–164; attitudes 162–164, 167; emotions 162, 167; motivation 162; values 164
nonhuman animals (NHAs) xi, 8, 13, 27–30, 51, 52, 55, 58, 69, 95, 109, 132, 137–157 *passim*, 165, 172, 174–178, 183, 185, 186, 190, 191, 222, 224n10, 229, 232, 237, 239, 240, 242, 246, 247n4, 248n16, 249n28, 261–269 *passim*, 277, 298, 301, 304, 314, 319–332, 359, 383, 389, 394–404 *passim*
Nonhuman Rights Project (NhRP) 134, 141–142, 147, 148
Noonan, Chris: *Babe* (film, 1995) 86, 322, 323, 325, 331
normal, necessary, natural, nice (4Ns) 163, 166
Normandin, Shawn 340n2, 342
North Carolina 136
Norwich 66
numeracy 166, 167, *168*
nursery rhymes 68–69, 70
Nussbaum, Martha 251, 252, 260
nutrition 285–286, 287, 288, 343, 375
nuts 197, 211, 216, 285, 373, 396

O'Brien, Abigail 128, 133
oikeiosis 22, 25n32, 26
Oliver, Kelly 256, 260
onions 208, 275, 286, 288, 375
online anti-veganism 354–365; research data 356–357

419

Index

online anti veganism (characteristics of anti-vegan discourse) 357–363; extreme speech 360–363; hashtags 362–363; images 357; legitimation strategies and *topoi* 357–360; memes 361–362; polarization technique 357
ontology 51
Oregon 138, 142
orientation: definition 6
Orphics 16
Orr, David W.: *Ecological Literacy: Education* (1992) 72, 74
Orthodox Judaism 194, 198, 199, 201, 202
othering 53, 78, **321**, 365
Our Children and Other Animals (Cole and Stewart, 2014) 66, 74
Ovadia, Rabbi Haim 197, 198, 204
overpopulation 80, 237, 244
Ovid 15
oxen 211, 396
Oxford University 216
Oxford Vegetarians 40, 48
Ozeki, Ruth: *My Year of Meats* 245, 249

Padilla, Gilbert 290
Page, Tony: *Buddhism and Animals* (1999) 220–221, 225
pain 163, 184–186
Pallotta, Nicole 142, 148
Parasecoli, Fabio 335–336, 342
Parry, Jovian 83, 88, 264–265, 271, 301, 305, 341n12
parve (neutral) food 196, 197, 198
pathos (emotion) 122, 124, 125, 127, 128, 129, 131
Patiño, Carlos 73, 74
patriarchal dividend 300
patriarchy 11, 58, 81, 86, 101, 103, 107, 176, 226, 239, 243, 245, 248n23, 258, 263, 274–278, 280–281, 295–305, 329, 396
Patterson, Charles 360
Paul, St. 185
peanuts 197, 211
Pedersen, Helena 51, 54, 60
Peltier, Dan 371, 380
People for Ethical Treatment of Animals (PETA) 123, 127, 132, 134, 153, 154, 178n4, 188, 245, 264, 303, 317n7, 346, 389
People's Temple 359
perception 22, 25n27, 25n29
perceptions (cognitive factor) 165
Pérez Jiménez, Aurelio 92, 98n4, 99
Peripatetics 19, 21
person: definition 42
personality traits 164
personhood 42
pesticides 290, 293
Peterson, Jan 291
pets 80, 138, 171, 223, 241, 268, 312, 322, 358, 389, 392

Phelps, Norm: *Great Compassion* (2004) 220, 225
Philadelphia Bible Christians 31, 32
Phillips, Ryan. J. 127–128, 133
Phillips, Tim xiv, 134–149
philosophical animal ethics: definition 39
philosophy 21, 25n23
Phoenix, Joaquin 249n24, 311
Phua, Joe 370, 380
Piazza, Jared 300, 305
Pick, Anat 267, 300, 305
Pico della Mirandola, Giovanni: *On Human Dignity* (1486) 95
Pierschel, Marc: *End of Meat* (film, 2017) 314; *Live and Let Live* (documentary, 2013) 313
pigs 41, 67, 85–86, 97, 127, 131, 135, 138, 246, 322, 361, 389, 396, 397, 398, 400
pineapples 245, 248n23
PlanEat (Shlomi and Davies, 2010) 312, 318
plant-based diet 6, 15, 17, 18, 47, 153, 174, 175, 187, 188, 194, 206, 211, 272, 273, 279, 281, 283–284, 285, 287, 300, 303, 310, 312–313, 337, 351, 369, 394, 397
plastics 323, 372, 373
Plato, 15, 24n1, 26
Pliner, Patricia 300, 304
Plotinus 15
Plum, Violet 68, 74
Plumwood, Val 108, 110, 248n17, 249n28, 257
Plutarch 89, 90; *On Animal Cleverness (De Sollertia Animalium)* 16–23, 25n17, 25n20; *On Eating of Flesh (De Esu Carnium)* 15–21, 24–25; *Gryllus* 15, 16, 92, 95, 97; *Moralia* 91–99; *Parallel Lives* 91, 93
PMLA 34
Pohjonen, Matti 360, 365
Poisson, Nicolas-Joseph 185–186
Poland 68, 195
political conservatism 163–164
political correctness (PC) 347, 351, 385
political turn (animal ethics) 46–47
Pollan, Michael 173–174, 217
pollution 72, 80, 165, 184, 216, 323
popular culture xv, 126, 131, 174, 287, 297, 335, 361; definition 28
pork 78, 104, 105, 125, 194, 218
pornography 80, 81, 101, 107
Porphyry: *On Abstinence* 16–26
porridge 275, 285–286, 396, 398, 401
Porter, Natalie 266, 268, 271
Portman, Natalie 311
postcolonial studies 258, 272–274; definition 272; questions examined 272–273
posthumanism 7, 9–10, 222; animal studies 51; criticized 51; definition 52; definition problem 50; messy category 51, 58; perspectives from continental philosophy 253–258; tensions 51–52; universalist tendencies 59; usage of term 51

posthumanists 43, 50–61
poststructuralism 50–51, 58
post-truth 334, 342
potato 208, 273, 278, 279, 285, 286, 394, 397–400, 404, 406
Potts, Annie 57, 60, 264–265, 271, 301, 305, 341n12
poverty 241, 244, 273, 278, 284, 398
power 6, 11, 19, 28, 51, 55, 79–80, 83, 93, 101–104, 120, 129, 135, 143, 164, 253, 272, 273, 278, 285, 287, 295, 300, 323, 385, 388, 394, 398; disempowerment 102, 201; empowerment 68, 72–73, 123, 154, 268, 289–291, 326, 330; powerlessness 113, 254, 266, 298
Power, Jenny Wyse 403
practice theory 155
Prasadam-Halls, Smriti 70
predators 20, 45, 97, 231, 360
Preece, Rod: *Sins of Flesh* (2008) 30, 37
preference utilitarians 42–43
prefiguration 156–157
Prince and Knight 237, 247n2
prison diets 140–141
processed foods 285, 286, 399
Proclamation of Republic of Ireland (1916) 402
Prorokova-Konrad, Tatiana 76–88
protein 82, 207, 209, 228, 285, 298, 310, 338, 340n10, 349, 376
Psihoyos, Louie: *Game Changers* (2018) 311, 313–314, 318, 333, 336–340, 340n8–10, 341n12
psychology 161–171; clarifications and caveats 161; cognitive factors 161, 164–165; cognitive skills 161, 165–166, 167; interventions 166; non-cognitive factors 161–164; opportunities and future directions 166–168
public nuisance lawsuits 142–143
public records (USA) 134–135, 140, 142
Puig de la Bellacasa, Maria 50, 51, 60
Pulé, Paul 302, 304
Puranic vratas 210–212, 213; definition 211
Puskar-Pasewicz, Margaret 31, 37
Pythagoras 4, 15, 16, 17, 22, 24, 188; how to profit without injustice 19–20
Pythagoreans 16, 23

queer animals 242, 248n18
queer theory 57, 261–271; failure and utopianism 268–270; kinship and affiliation 266–268; queer vegans 264–265; veganism and gender 263–264
quelites (lamb's quarters) 288
Quinn, Christopher Dillon, director: *Eating Animals* (DVD, 2018) 311, 318
Quinn, Emelia xv, 57, 60, 79, 213, 220, 261–271
Qur'an 226–229, 232–233

Rabbanit 199
rabbis 196–199
rabbit 85, 138, 217, 222, 390n7

Rabkin, Richard 196–197, 204
race 5, 10, 11, 12, 51, 73, 131–132, 155–156, 176, 200, 240, 244, 270n5, 314; health disparities 6–7
racial difference 287–289
racialized food inequities 284
racism 8, 36, 175, 176, 244, 245, 246, 258, 282, 297, 328, 383; definition 278, 285
Radhakrishnan, S. 218, 223, 224
Radical Lesbians 261
radical recipe 282–294; cookbooks 282; cookbooks as case studies 283–292; cultivating anti-racist vegan praxis 291–292; decolonizing diets 284–287; dismantling whiteness in veganism 287–289; reframing vegan food politics 282–283; resistance and empowerment 289–291; spices, song, struggle, survival 289–291; subjugated knowledges and racial difference 287–289
Rahman, Muzna 275, 281
rape 81, 101, 105, 107, 108, 109, 296, 339; sexual violence 209, 258; violence against women 229
rationalization 359–360
Ray, John 186
real world 8, 117, 118, 125, 273, 322
Reason 251, 253, 254
reciprocal relationship (animal and human) 19–20, 25n18–25n21
reciprocity principle 21, 23
Reddit 349, 350
red herring fallacy (*ignoratio elenchi*) 358
red meat 36, 248n22, 300, 309, 347, 403
reflexivity **321**, 326, 330
reformed humanism (Steiner) 251, 253
Regal Vegan (Brooklyn) 139
Regan, Tom 7, 11, 14, 90, 231, 252–253, 258; *Case for Animal Rights* 43–44, 47, 49; Kantian 252; legacy (abolitionism and political turn in animal ethics) 46–47; moral importance of animals 120n1; philosophical father of animal rights 43
Reich Animalista (Animal Activist Reich) 356–357, 359, 361, 363
religion 183–233; Christianity 183–193; Hinduism and Jainism 205–214; Islam 226–233; Judaism 194–204
Religious Land Use and Institutionalized Persons Act (USA) 140
Renaud, Chris (director) *Secret Life of Pets* (film, 2016) 322, 332
replaceability argument 41, 42–43; rejected by Regan 44
reproductive futurism (Edelman) 267
respect 44, 47, 48, 115–117
response-ability 56, 59
Revolutionary People's Constitutional Convention 261
rhetoric 122–133; definition (Aristotle) 122; fast-food advertisements 343–353; online anti-veganism 354–365; usage 123

Index

rhetorical analysis 123, 124, 127, 132, 343–353
rhinoceros 329
Rhu, Sarah xv, 272–281
Ribero Martins, Pedro 24n7, 26
Richardson, John 357, 365
ridicule 33, 77, 154, 228–229, 354, 355, 356, 362, 363
Rig Veda 210
Rise of Critical Animal Studies (Taylor and Twine, Eds., 2014) 153, 159
risk communications 384
Ritson, Joseph: *Essay on Abstinence from Animal Food* (1802) 4, 354–355, *355*
Robbins, John 178n3
Roberts, Holly H. 192n2, 193
Robertson, Nic 333
Rodrigo Terronez Memorial Clinic 290
Roth, Ruby 66, 67, 69, 74–75; *That is Why We Don't Eat Animals* (2009) 67, 69, 74; *V is for Vegan* (2013) 69–70, 71, 73, 75; *Vegan is Love* (2012) 69, 72, 73, 74
Rothgerber, Hank 162, 165, 170
Rousseau, J.-J. 30, 95
Routh, Brandon 319
Rozenberg, Guillaume 35, 37
Ruby, Matthew B. 165, 171, 296, 305
Ruekert, William 247n5
rukweza (millet) 275
Rundell, Katherine 65, 68, 75
Runkle, Nathan 348–349
Russell, Bertrand: *Problem of China* (1922) 383, 392
Russell, George 401
Russia 30, 68, 195
Rutz, Jim 79
Ryan, Derek 221, 224

sadza (porridge) 275, 277–278
Sáez, Adrián J. 93, 98n3, 99
Safeway and Guimarra Vineyard Corporation 290
Said, Edward W. 385, 392; *Orientalism* (1978) 273, 281
salad 286, 290, 291, 300, 302
Salih, Sara 267, 271
Salt, Henry: *Plea for Vegetarianism* 208–209
Samsara: definition 221
samudramanthana 210
San Francisco Bay Area 282, 284
San José (Costa Rica) 247n1
Sandis, Constantine 129–130, 133
Santa Claus (reindeer-oppressor) 70
sarkophagia (consumption of meat) 16, 18, 19, 21, 22
Sarsgaard, Peter 320
Sartre, Jean-Paul 274
satire 5, 83, 261–262, 264, 349, 357
Satter, Linda 136, 148
sattvik (sacred) food 206, 210, 219

Saunders, Trevor J. 25n15, 26
sausage: etymology 129
Sausage Party (Vernon and Tiernan, 2016) 322–323, 332
Sawhney, Anuradha: *Vegan Kitchen* (2012) 207, 214
Sayer, John William 143, 148
Sayers, James *355*
Scala Naturae 16–17, 24n9–11
Schlosser, Eric 174
Schopenhauer, A. 32
Schowalter, Elaine 79
Schuster, Joshua 269–270, 271
Schwartz, Richard H. 195, 202, 204
Schwartz Value Survey 164, 171
Schwarzenegger, Arnold 311, 313, 333, 339, 340n8, 340n10
Schwitzgebel, Eric 166, 171
Science 183, 193
science and technology studies (STS) 50, 52
security (basic human value) 164
Sedgwick, Eve Kosofsky 262, 265, 271
Seglin, Vicky 221, 225
Selam, Ophelia 109, 110
Seneca 15, 20, 25n19, 32
Seong-kon, Kim 102, 110
Seventh Day Adventism 31, 195
Seven Year Itch (film, 1955) 333
Severe Acute Respiratory Syndrome Coronavirus (SARS-CoV) 382, 384–387
Severin, Sybil: *Lena of Vegitopia* (2014) 72, 75
Seville 97
sex 80–81, 106–107
sexism 81, 125, 176, 177, 238, 239, 245, 246, 248n23, 258, 289, 297, 328, 337, 339–340, 383, 403
sexuality 240, 244, 249n28, 268, 280, 341n14
Seymour, Nicole 315, 316, 318
Shannon, Molly 324
Shantz, J. 106, 110
Shapiro, Ryan 140
Shaw, George Bernard 30, 402
sheep 200, 394, 395, 396, 400, 404n3
Shelley, Percy 36, 37
Shenzhen 389–390, 390n6–390n7
shepherds and shepherdesses 201–202
Shiva, Vandana 177
Shlomi, Or 312, 318
shofar 200, *200*, 201, 202
Shona foodways 274–278; plant-based diet 272–281
Shove, Elizabeth 155, 159
Shprintzen, Adam 31, 32, 36n1, 37
Sick, Fat, and Nearly Dead (Cross and Engfehr, 2010) 312, 318
Sierra Club 311
Sikhism 206
Siliguri: Vegan Nation (restaurant) 207
silk 221, 369

Silverstone, Alicia 28
Simonetti, Luca 128, 133
Simonsen, Rasmus Rahbek 260, 265, 268–269, 271
Simpsons: "Lisa Vegetarian" episode 5, 13n1
Sinclair, Upton 30
Sindelarova, Petra 70–71
Singer, Peter 11, 90, 111, 114, 120n1, 121n8, 132, 217, 231, 251–252, 258, 382–383; *Animal Liberation* (1975) 7–8, 13, 14, 28, 40–43, 47; fortieth anniversary preface 130–131; legacy (harm reduction) 45–46; not a vegan theory 43, 47; rhetorical appeals 124–125
Singla, Anupy: *Vegan Indian Cooking* (2012) 206–207, 214
Sinhababu, Neil 118–119
Sitwell, William 354
Skilled Decision Theory 166, 167–168, *168*, 169
Skinny Bitch (Freedman and Barnouin) stereotype 154, 158
slaughterhouses 56, 90, 92, 93, 97, 111, 112, 114, 135–136, 143, 246, 299, 322, 325, 326, 329; lack of glass walls 152, 159
slavery 31, 114, 116, 176, 241, 248n14, 258, 289, 314
Slotkin, Richard 106, 110
Slovic, Scott 334
slow food movement 128, 133
slow violence 273, 281
Smilansky, Saul 114, 121
snakes 210, 212, 217, 268
Snyder, G. 241
Sobal, Jeffery 299, 300, 302, 305
social class 155, 240, 314, 328, 397, 398
social constructionist epistemology **321**, 325
social corruption 97–98
social dominance orientation 163
socialization 387
social justice 29, 54, 178n4, 288
social justice movements 175, 177, 178
social media 123, 128, 216, 335, 336, 345, 346–347, 348, 349, 351, 371; anti-vegan rhetoric 354–365
social movements 31, 156–157, 248n14
social sciences: differentiated from natural sciences 151
Society of Ethical and Religious Vegetarians 202
Society for Prevention of Cruelty to Animals (later RSPCA) 346, 347, 402
sociology 58, 150–160; adjacent work and institutions 152–153; animal studies 152; cultural turn 154–155, 157; empirical data 150–160; environmental turn 151–153, 157; future directions 157; identity (gender and race) 155–156; precursors to vegan studies 151–152; social movements 156–157; symbolic interactionism 153–154
socio-structural context **321**, 325, 328
Soclarus 19

Solomon, Jon 386
soma (sacred drink) 210
song 289–291
souls 20, 21, 24n9, 184–186, 196, 202, 205, 211; transmigration 15, 17, 22, 24, 25n30, 26, 212–213, 221
South Africa 228, 289, 290
South China Morning Post 381
sovereign subject (deconstruction) 253–260
soy 10, 79, 83, 197, 207, 208, 246, 286, 343, 375, 405
Spain 68, 360, 372
Sparks-Franklin, Jonathan xv, 250–260
Specht, Joshua 36, 37
species consciousness **321**, 328
species dissidence (McKay) 266
species-humility 319, 320
speciesism 80–84, 85, 86, 104, 124–125, 131, 157, 163, 166, 175, 239, 241, 244, 245, 246, 247n4, 248n16, 248n23, 249n28, 251, 297, 304, 319–332, 356, 359, 363, 394, 396, 397, 398, 399, 400, 401, 403, 404; definition 41
species overlap argument 42, 48
species role programming 261
Spencer, Colin: *Vegetarianism: A History* (1993, 2000) 4–5, 14, 29, 30, 37
spices 289–291
Spurlock, Morgan 309
Stallone, Sylvester 333
Standard American Diet (SAD) 284, 286, 287, 335, 345
Stanescu, James 268, 271
Star-K (kashrut agency) 199
Stein, Rachel 80, 88
Steiner, Gary 13n3, 251, 255, 260, 263–264, 271
Stengers, Isabelle 56
stereotypes 53, 58, 106, 155, 156, 265, 283, 301, 347, 351, 355, 363, 403
Stewart, James J. 219, 225
Stewart, Kate xv, 66, 74, 319–332
Stiefel, Barry L. xv–xvi, 194–204
stigma 154, 158, 287, 288, 340n9, 385
Stockton, Kathryn Bond 270n10
Stoics 17, 19, 21, 22, 24n11, 25n31, 25n34
Stop Huntingdon Animal Cruelty (SHAC) 144
Strato 21
Strickland, Lloyd 185–186, 193
structural racism 282, 285, 287, 291–292
structure and agency 154–155, 159
Stuart, Tristam 79; *Bloodless Revolution* (2006) 3–4, 14, 30–31, 32–33, 335
studies: definition (Wright) 126
Subaltern Studies Group 273
Subercaseaux, Bernardo 90, 100
subjectivity 250, 251
subject-of-a-life 44, 46
subjugated knowledges 287–289; definition 288
subsistence 179n5, 275, 279, 398, 399, 401

Index

subsistence hunting 41, 44, 49, 274
sugar 29, 173, 211, 285–286, 288, 290, 344, 348, 399
suicide 104, 295, 305, 327, 330, 359, 361
Sullivan, Heather I. 80, 88
supply and demand 118–119, 121n17
supply chains 112, 118
Support Vegans in Prison System (USA) 141
Surangama Sutra 215, 219, 221, 225
survival 289–291; veganism and ~ 84–86
sustainability 239
Sutra Piṭaka 221
Suzuki, Daisetz Teitaro 218, 220, 225
Swart, Sandra 9
sweet potato 285–286
symbolic interactionism 153–154
synthetic materials 200
systemic racism 282, 283, 292

tallit (ritual prayer shawls) 200, 201
Talmud 196, 197, 198–199
taste 18, 20, 85, 173, 176, 177, 211, 218, 255, 277, 278, 290, 350, 371, 376, 387
Tavuyanago, Baxter 275, 281
Taylor, Chloe 253–254, 260
Taylor, Joan E. 188, 193
Taylor, Nik 153, 159; *Animals at Work* 9
Teej *vrata* 211
tefillah (prayer) 200
tefillin 200, 201, 202, 203
television 310, 319–332, 371; possibility of representing veganism 323–331; vegan and anti-vegan representations 320, **321**
Tellai, Baya 228
Terry, Bryant 28, 37; *Afro-Vegan* (2014) 282–294; chef, educator, healer 284
Theophrastus 15, 23, 24n2
theoretical engagements 237–305; anti-racism 282–294; critical animal studies 250–260; Dangarembga's *Nervous Conditions* (2004) 272–281; ecocriticism (ecofeminist queer view) 237–249; gender studies 295–305; queer theory 261–271; radical recipe 282–294
Theory of Planned Behavior 167, 168
Thinking Veganism (Quinn and Westwood, Eds., 2018) 57, 60, 220, 262–263
Thomas, Margaret A. 303, 305
threshold model 117–118
Thunberg, Greta 65, 73, 75
Tibet 218
Tiffin, Helen 266–267, 271
Times of Israel 198
Tiplady, Catherine M. 167, 171
Tlili, Sarra 232, 233
tofu 118, 344, 348–351, 353, 376
Tofurky 140
Tolstoy, Leo 30
tomato 104, 208, 275, 346, 375, 377

Tommy Thumb's Song Book 68
topoi 358–360, 365
Torah 200, *200*, 201, 202
torture 95, 103, 105, 117, 132, 216, 220, 223, 246, 314, 315, 346, 388
Trader Joe's 139
trauma 105, 107, 109, 288, 331
Trauth, Erin xvi, 343–353
travel agencies 371
treif 196, 197, 198
Trevelyan, Charles 398
Trice, Linda 72
triggering purchase 117–118
Trump, Donald 137–138, 146, 339–340, 384–385
Tuider, Jens 216, 224, 356, 360, 364
turkeys 67, 135, 348, 389
Tutton, Phil 70
Twigg, Julia 31
Twine, Richard 153, 159, 175, 179, 253, 260, 262, 265, 271
Twitter 129, 346–347, 348, 349, 362–363, 365
Tyler, Tom 57–58, 61, 267
Tyron, Thomas 4
Tyson, Mike 339

Udupa, Sahana 360, 361–362, 365
UNESCO: World Intangible Cultural Heritage 371
United Farm Workers (UFW) 290–291
United Kingdom 4, 29, 30–31, 32, 33, 35, 39–40, 141, 186, 196, 324, 377, 404; suicide 295
United Nations: Food and Agriculture Organization (FAO) 172, 179
United States 6, 10, 11, 30, 31, 32, 33, 35, 36, 126, 131, 132, 172, 178n2, 198, 313–314, 324, 327, 331, 337, 402, 404; Animal and Plant Health Inspection Service (APHIS) 135; animal rights activists 157; anti-racism (radical recipe) 282–294; Court of Appeals for Eighth Circuit 137, 147; Court of Appeals for Ninth Circuit 135, 136, 138, 142; Department of Agriculture (USDA) 134–135, 142; Farm Service Agency 135; fast-food advertisements 343–353; FDA 33; individualism 155; percentage of vegans 343; Supreme Court 138
United States (legal system) 134–149; animal cruelty (legislation and ballot initiatives) 138–139; animals' legal status 141–142; border wall with Mexico 137–138; challenging ag-gag laws 135–136; efforts to protect human rights and environment 137–138; environmental laws (used to protect animals) 137; food labeling 139–140; incarcerated vegans 140–141; public nuisance lawsuits 142–143; requesting public records 134–135; vegan activists in criminal legal system 143–144

universalism (basic human value) 164
University of Massachusetts 273
University Purchase Card receipts 166
Utah 136, 146
utilitarianism 7, 11, 40, 41, 121n8, 164, 251–252; definition 42
utopia 73, 74, 268–270

Valenze, Deborah: *Milk: Local and Global History* 210
values: definition 164; non-cognitive factor 164
Vandello, Joseph. A. 296, 305
van Sittert, Lance 9
Vata Savitri vrata 211–212
veal calves 131, 138
Vedas 205, 209
vegan: definition 3, 126; reasons to become ~ 3, 118–119, 220, 337
vegan activists: criminal legal system (USA) 143–144
vegan advocacy films 309–318; animal other to self and back 312–315; editorial control 310, 317n5; finance 310–311; humor 315–316; narrative strategies and visual tactics 312–315; style and affect 315–316; vision of future 314–315
vegan and anti-vegan representations 320, **321**
vegan camp (Quinn) 270n4, 271
Vegan Children's Stories (website) 68
vegan.com 130
vegan culture 119
vegan diet: environmental benefits 216, 335, 340n5, 340n6
vegan ecofeminism (Yilmaz) 297–298
vegan ethics 51, 53, 57
vegan feminism 209–210, 302–303
vegan food: kosher status 196–198, 204; spatial geography of cities 265, 270n9
vegan food tourism 369–380; assessment after travel experience 375–376; definition 370; dining during travel experience 374–375; evolution of veganism 370–371; "fake" dishes 374, 376–377; further research 377; methodology (non-probability convenience sampling technique) 372, **372**; planning before travel experience 373–374, 377; results 372, 377; VS context 369–372
vegan geographies 369–406; China (animal cruelty) 381–393; Ireland 394–406; vegan food tourism 369–380
vegan history 27–38; internationalization 35; locating usable past 28–33; race and gender issues 34–35; recovery of little-known sources 34; translation 35
vegan identity 175, 266, 269; psychological factors 161–171
vegan imperative (Steiner) 251
Vegan Ireland 404n6

veganism: advantages 79–80; as anti-capitalism 101–110; causal impotence (possible ways forward) 111–121; climate change era 77–80; definition 77, 119; dismantling whiteness 287–289; distinctions from "vegan studies" 175; dual perception (Wright) 87; ecoethics and climate change 76–88; identity and practice 5–7; legal status (philosophical belief) 66, 74; lifestyle preference 6; misinterpretations 79; "new inquisition" 359; preponderance of women (UK, USA) 299; primary motivation 187; "radical, intolerant cult" 359; religion 183–233; separate identity from vegetarianism 4; and survival 84–86; terminology 258n2; "vision for humanity, not just for food" 178; white-centric discourse 131–132
veganism in media 309–365; fast-food advertisements 343–353; film and television 319–332; merchandizing veganism 333–342; online anti-veganism (rhetoric) 354–365; vegan advocacy films 309–318; vegan myth 354–365
veganism in world of causally efficacious consumption 117–119; threshold model 117–118; why-be-vegan question 118–119
vegan "killjoy" 175, 176, 179, 265
vegan literature for children 65–75
Vegan Magazine 370
vegan methodological principles 320, **321**
vegan myth: rhetoric of online anti-veganism 354–365
vegan praxis 50–53, 57–59, 250
Vegan Prisoners Suppport Group (1994–) 141
Vegan Publishers 69, 74, 75
Vegan Renaissance (1994–) 67–68
vegan restaurants 196–198, 204, 207; *see also* vegan food tourism
vegan rhetoric 122–133; academy instances 127–128; blogosphere example 128–130; canon 124–127; future 130–132
vegan rules 119–120
vegan sexuality 264–265, 301, 338, 341n12
Vegan Society (1944–) 3, 29–30, 33, 37, 57, 119, 126, 174–175, 178, 187, 315, 403; definition of veganism (1951) 319
vegan studies (VS) 27–28; and animal ethics 47–48; essential distinction from animal studies 28; frame 3–14; gender under capitalism 297–299; origins in literary and cultural studies 39; philosophical issues 39; sociology 150–160; tensions with posthumanism 52, 53, 57–58, 59
vegan theory xv, 40, 43, 46, 47, 205, 258, 263, 267, 269
Veganuary 46, 299
vegan unconscious 243, 248n11, 274, 281
vegaphobia 155, 158, 354–356, 364

Index

vegetables 5, 82, 106, 208, 275–276, 277, 279, 280, 286, 289, 290, 314, 337, 340n10, 341n14, 374, 396, 399
Vegetarian (Han Kang): ecofeminist revolt 101–110; veganism as anti-capitalism 101–110
Vegetarian America (Iacobbo and Iacobbo, 2004) 7, 14, 33
Vegetarian Archives 34
vegetarian argument: sources 16, 24n5–24n8
vegetarian choice: Pythagoras, Plutarch, Porphyry 15–26
Vegetarian Federal Union 67, 74
vegetarian history 27–38
Vegetarian International Congress (London, 1897) 66–67
vegetarianism: future 33–36; history of paradoxical ideology 3–5; reverberation with feminist meaning (Adams) 125; terminology 258n2
Vegetarian Resource Group 29, 37
Vegetarian Society (UK, 1847–) 4, 29, 66, 186
Vegetarian Society of America 36n1
Vegetarian Society of Ireland 402, 406; Vegetarian Society in Dublin 401
verdolagas (purslane) 288–289
Vico, G.: *New Science* (1744) 388, 393
Vida Naturopatética (Naturopathetic Life) 356–357
Vietnam War 105
visual rhetoric 123–124, 127
vitamins 216, 279, 285, 286, 288
vivisection 99, 185, 273, 326, 330, 402–403, 405; Christian perspective 186–187, 192
Volkswagen 114
vrata: definition 210; as vegan rite 210–212
vulnerability 232–233, 257

Waitrose & Partners Food 354
Waldau, Paul 191
Wallace, David Foster 178n3
war and aggression 18
Warkentin, Traci 10–11, 13n3, 14
War on Terror 300
Washadi, Shlomo *200*
Washington State 138
Watson-Crick Institute 81
Watson, Donald 29, 178, 187
Watson, Dorothy 187
Weik von Mossner, Alexa xvi, 309–318
Weil, Kari 10, 303, 304
Weis, Tony: *Ecological Hoofprint:* (2013) 340n6, 342
welfare reform 45, 46
welfarist vegans 43
Western Plains Animal Rescue (WPAR) 142
Westwood, Benjamin 57, 60, 79, 213, 220, 262–263, 268, 271
wet markets 333, 340n3
whale 4, 141, 154

What the Health (Andersen and Kuhn film, 2017) 309–313, 315, 317
Whatmore, Sarah 50, 61
Wheeler, Mortimer 30
White, E.B. 67
White, Lynn, Jr. 183–184, 190, 193
White, Mike: *Year of Dog* (2007) 320, 323–331; *Beatriz at Dinner* (2017) 323–324, 327–330, 331
Whittaker, J. 323
Who: Won't Get Fooled Again 341n13
why-be-vegan question 118–119
wild animals 45, 142, 184, 227, 231, 246, 340n3, 341, 389, 390n6–390n7, 392
wildlife xi, 137–138, 143, 152, 216, 273, 317n2, 342, 381, 382, 386, 389, 390n6–390n7, 392
Wilks, James 336, 340n9
Williams, Evan 129
Williams, Howard: *Ethics of Diet* (1883, 1896, 2003) 31–33, 38
Wilson, Brian C. 36, 38
wine 25n22, 25n25, 196, 204, 354, 388
Wittgenstein, Ludwig 40, 257, 259
Wodak, Ruth 357, 365
Wolfe, Cary 9–10, 14, 50, 51, 55, 59, 60, 257, 260; *Animal Rites* (2003) 11, 52–54, 61; *What is Posthumanism?* (2010) 52–54, 61
women 28, 32, 35, 40–41, 156, 176, 178n4, 199, 201, 203, 241, 274–281, 283, 290, 328, 331, 337, 372, 403; gender studies 295–305; veganism as anti-capitalism 101–110; *vratas* 211–212
women's studies 13
Wood, David 255–256, 260, 263–264, 271
wool 19, 68, 77, 111, 200, 221, 369, 397
World Bank 206, 214
World Health Organization (WHO) 309, 382
World Vegan Day (1994–) 370
World Wrestling Entertainment (WWE) 347
Wrenn, Corey xvi, 33, 38, 106, 110, 153, 157, 160, 298–299, 303, 305, 394–406
Wright, Edgar (director): *Scott Pilgrim vs. World* (2010) 319, 326, 331, 332
Wright, Laura xvi, 38, 48, 49, 52, 58, 61, 66, 71, 75, 77, 86, 90, 100, 229, 245, 248n14, 248n16, 328, 329, 332, 334, 336, 337, 338, 339, 384; Dangarembga's *Nervous Conditions* (2004) 272–281; definition of veganism 265; instantiation of coherent field of vegan studies (2015) 33, 35; personal narrative 249n26; pro-environmental potential of veganism 77–78; rhetoric 125–127; *Through Vegan Studies Lens* (2019) 177, 178n2, 179, 195, 298; vegan body as "contested" 101–102; vegan studies "creates conversation about oppression" 109; *Vegan Studies Project* (2015) 3–14, 78–79, 84, 87, 88, 150, 174–175, 195, 226, 297, 300–301, 311, 335; veganism "gendered as female undertaking" 313

Wuhan 386, 390
Wuhan Institute for Virology 390n3

xenophobia 78, 245, 384

Yanklowitz,
    Shmuly 195, 203
Yilmaz, Ayce F. 297, 305
yoni (womb) 212–213
York, R. 352, 353
Young, Richard Alan 188, 193

YouTube cooking channels 371
Yuen Kwok-yung 385–386, 390n4, 392

Žagar, Igor 358, 365
Zappavigna, Michelle 362, 365
Zephaniah, Benjamin 67, 71, 75
Zhao, Emperor 388
Zimbabwe 272–281
Zoopolis (Donaldson and Kymlicka, 2011) 47, 48
zoopolitics 47

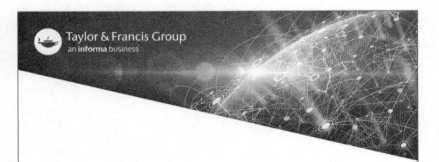